The Psychological & Social Impact of Illness and Disability

5th Edition

Arthur E. Dell Orto, PhD, CRC, is Professor and Program Director of Rehabilitation Counseling in the Department of Occupational Therapy and Rehabilitation Counseling, Sargent College of Health and Rehabilitation Sciences at Boston University and is the Associate Executive Director of Boston University's Center for Psychiatric Rehabilitation.

He received a PhD in Counseling and Rehabilitation from Michigan State University in 1970. Dr. Dell Orto is a licensed psychologist and a Certified Rehabilitation Counselor whose academic and clinical interests relate to the role of the family in the treatment and rehabilitation process. Dr. Dell Orto has given many presentations and workshops focusing on the needs of families living with illness and disability.

He has co-authored and co-edited with Paul Power: *Families Living With Chronic Illness and Disability* (2004); *The Resilient Family* (2003); *Brain Injury and the Family: A Life and Living Perspective* (2000); *Head Injury and the Family: A Life and Living Approach* (1994): Awarded Pyramid of Distinction and an Award of Excellence by the New England Association of the American Medical Writers; *Illness and Disability: Family Interventions Throughout the Life Span* (Springer, 1988); *Role of the Family in the Rehabilitation of the Physically Disabled* (1980). He has also co-edited the following books: *The Encyclopedia of Disability and Rehabilitation* (1995): Awarded an "Excellence in Media Award" by The National Rehabilitation Association; *The Psychological and Social Impact of Disability* (Springer, 1999 & 1991); *The Psychological and Social Impact of Disability* (Springer, 1984 and 1977); and *Group Counseling and Physical Disability* (1979).

Paul W. Power, ScD, CRC, is an Emeritus Professor of Counseling, University of Maryland, and Adjunct Professor at the College of William and Mary, Williamsburg, Virginia. Dr. Power received a ScD from Boston University and he is the author of numerous articles, books, and book chapters on the topic of the family and disability, and vocation/career assessment. His speeches and workshops, on both national and international levels, have also focused on the roles of the family on the treatment and rehabilitation process. Specifically, he has co-authored and co-edited with Arthur Dell Orto: *Families Living With Chronic Illness and Disability* (2004), *The Resilient Family* (2003), *Brain Injury and the Family: A Life and Living Perspective* (2000), *The Role of the Family in the Rehabilitation of the Physically Disabled* (1980), and *Family Interventions Throughout Chronic Illness and Disability* (Springer, 1988).

The Psychological & Social Impact of Illness and Disability

5th Edition

Arthur E. Dell Orto, PhD, CRC

and

Paul W. Power, ScD, CRC

SPRINGER PUBLISHING COMPANY

New York

Springer Publishing Company, LLC
11 West 42nd Street, 15th Floor
New York, NY 10036-8002

Acquisitions Editor: Sheri W. Sussman
Production Editor: Peggy M. Rote
Cover designer: Mimi Flow
Composition: Aptara, Inc.

08   09   10/   5   4   3   2

ISBN-13: 978-0-8261-0244-7

Library of Congress Cataloging-in-Publication Data

The psychological & social impact of illness and disability / [edited by]
Arthur E. Dell Orto, Paul W. Power,. – 5th ed.
   p.   cm.
   Rev. ed. of: The psychological and social impact of disability. 4th ed. 1999.
   Includes bibliographical references and index.
   ISBN 0-8261-0244-1 (hardback)
   1. People with disabilities–United States–Psychology.   2. People with
disabilities–Rehabilitation–United States.   3. People with
disabilities–Family relationships–United States.   4. People with
disabilities–Sexual behavior–United States.   5. People with
disabilities–United States–Public opinion.   6. Public opinion–United
States.   I. Dell Orto, Arthur E., 1943-   II. Power, Paul W.   III. Title:
Psychological and social impact of illness and disability.   IV. Title:
Psychological and social impact of disability.

HV1553.P75   2007
155.9'16–dc22

2007005548

Printed in the United States of America by Bang Printing.

This book is dedicated to all of our friends, mentors, and role models who have lived or are living with the challenges, insights, gifts, and opportunities that are part of the complete human experience that is often enriched by illness and disability.

ADO
PWP
Hardwick, MA
2007

Contents

Appendix A: Perspective Exercises

Appendix B: Personal Perspectives

Contributors

Richard Antonak, PhD
University of Massachusetts
Boston, MA

Tosca Appel, MS
Newton, MA

Richard Beaulaurier, PhD, MSW
Florida International University School of Social Work
Miami, FL

Joan Beder, DSW, LMSW
Yeshiva University
New York, NY

Bernadette
Atlanta, GA

Malachy Bishop, PhD, CRC
University of Kentucky
Lexington, KY

Barbara J. Bowers, PhD, RN, FAAN
University of Wisconsin
Madison, WI

Ruth W. Brannon, MSPh, MA
National Institute on Disability & Rehabilitation Research
Washington, DC

Martin G. Brodwin, PhD, CRC
California State University, Los Angeles (CSULA)
Los Angeles, CA

Lydia P. Buki, PhD
University of Illinois, Urbana-Champaign
Champaign, IL

Elizabeth Cardoso, PhD, CRC
Hunter College-City University of New York
New York, NY

Jane Case-Smith, EdD
Ohio State University
Columbus, OH

Mitka Chacon, LPCI
San Benito, TX

Wendy Coduti, MA, PhD
Michigan State University
East Lansing, MI

David Collins, MED
Montgomery College
Rockville, MD

Amy B. Collins, PhD
Texas A&M University
College Station, TX

Nancy M. Crewe, PhD
Michigan State University
East Lansing, MI

Albert H. DeGraff, EdD
Fort Collins, CO

Paul Egan, MS
Dracut, MA

Susan C. Eggman, MSW
Portland State University, Regional Research Institute
Portland, OR

Albert Ellis, PhD
Albert Ellis Institute
New York

Pamela Fadem, MPH
University of California
Berkeley, CA

Cheryl J. Gagne, ScD
Boston University
Boston, MA

Carol J. Gill, PhD
University of Illinois at Chicago
Chicago, IL

James T. Herbert, PhD, CRC
The Pennsylvania State University
University Park, PA

Rosemary B. Hughes, PhD
Baylor College of Medicine
Houston, TX

Mary R. Hulnick, PhD
University of Santa Monica
Santa Monica, CA

H. Ronald Hulnick, PhD
University of Santa Monica
Santa Monica, CA

Judy Kaye, PhD
USC College of Nursing
Los Angeles, CA

Bethanne Keen, MD
Arizona Department of Corrections
Phoenix, AZ

Donald G. Kewman, PhD
University of Michigan
Ann Arbor, MI

Lori Kogan, PhD
Colorado State University
Fort Collins, CO

Marvin D. Kuehn, EdD, CRC
Emporia State University
Emporia, KS

Janet Lingerman, MS, CRC
Ipswich, MA

Hanoch Livneh, PhD, CRC
Portland State University
Portland, OR

Barbara J. Lutz, PhD, RN, CRRN
University of Florida
Gainesville, FL

Irmo Marini, PhD, CRC
University of Texas, Pan American
Edinburg, TX

Eva Miller, PhD
University of Texas, Pan American
Edinburg, TX

Meredith Minkler, DPH
University of California
Berkeley, CA

Chris Moy, MS
Scranton, PA

Christine A. Nelson, MS, RN
Oregon Health Services University
Portland, OR

Patricia B. Nemec, PsyD, CRC
Boston University
Boston, MA

Robert J. Neumann
Chicago, IL

Carol S. North, MD, MPE
Washington University School of Medicine
St. Louis, MO

Margaret A. Nosek, PhD
Baylor College of Medicine
Houston, TX

Randall M. Parker, PhD
University of Texas
Austin, Texas

Sara Pedersen, PhD
University of Montreal
Montreal, Canada

David Pfeiffer, PhD
Center on Disability Studies, University of Hawaii at Manoa
Honolulu, HI

Andrew Phemister, PhD
Minnesota State University
Mankato, MN

Constance Pledger, EdD
National Institute on Disability & Rehabilitation Research
Washington, DC

Ora Prilleltensky, PhD
Vanderbilt University
Nashville, TN

Senthil Kumar Raghavan, MD
University of South Carolina
Columbia, SC

Tracey A. Revenson, PhD
The Graduate Center of the City University of New York
New York, NY

Franklin C. Shontz, PhD
University of Kansas
Lawrence, KS

Julie F. Smart, PhD, CRC
Utah State University
Logan, UT

David W. Smart, PhD
Brigham Young University
Provo, UT

Tristen Star, MS
California State University, Los Angeles (CSULA)
Los Angeles, CA

Linda Stacey
Framingham, MA

Mark A. Stebnicki, RhD, CRC, LPC, CCM
East Carolina University
Greenville, NC

Denise Tate, PhD
University of Michigan
Ann Arbor, MI

Samuel H. Taylor, DSW
University of Southern California
Los Angeles, CA

Judy Teplow, MSW
Canton, MA

Maye Thompson, PhD, RN
Oregon Health Services University
Portland, OR

Virginia P. Tilden, DNSc, RN, FAAN
Oregon Health Services University
Portland, OR

Susan W. Tolle, MD, FACP
Oregon Health Services University
Portland, OR

Patti Uman, BS
Colorado State University
Fort Collins, CO

Jean Vanier, PhD
L'Arche Movement
Trosly-Breuil, France

Dale Walsh, ScD
Cambridge, MA

Jon R. Webb, PhD
University of Michigan
Ann Arbor, MI

Robert P. Winske
Medford, MA

Beatrice A. Wright, PhD
University of Kansas
Lawrence, KS

Steve Zanskas, MS, PhD
Michigan State University
East Lansing, MI

Irving Kenneth Zola, PhD
Brandeis University
Waltham, MA

Foreword

In the mid-1970s I discussed with my colleague, Art Dell Orto, the notion of a textbook compiling the important literature related to the psychological and social impact of disability. Neither of us expected that 30+ years later and with four editions complete, we would still be working on the "book." I am pleased that I continue to be part of the journey. However, in this edition, it is as a passenger rather than a driver—that role has been taken up by my friends and colleagues.

In these 30 years, changes in the field of rehabilitation and the view of disability have been dramatic. These have been chronicled through the previous four editions and reflected throughout this current work.

A most significant change for people with disability and our society is that disability has come out of the closet. The rapid increase in the number of persons with disability, the changing social policy toward more equal access and the rise of the independent living and other consumer movements have resulted in increased visibility of persons with disability in our schools, workplaces, malls, and other public venues. The media, whether print or visual, highlight the successes and tragedies of those with disability—not always in the manner of which we approve.

Consumer involvement of persons with disability has evolved into increased self determination and empowerment. The control of life is not simply given to others but embraced by oneself for better or worse.

The view of disability has expanded to include personal, family, environment, and social/cultural perspectives. New paradigms that encompass the role of the total environment as a significant physical, psychological, and social barrier has allowed for a broadened view of the interventions available to improve the lives of persons with disability. Those with disability and their families are not expected to cope in solitude with disability. The isolated view of disability as the "cross" to bear is largely cast off.

Disability is increasingly viewed as an enabling experience. This has allowed for the development of personal growth in life domains and contributions to the lives of others that were previously unavailable.

The editors of this fifth edition have been masterful in their collection of articles, both classic and contemporary, that elucidates these themes. The personal perspectives, experiential exercises, and discussion questions allow the reader to incorporate the themes more deeply. Let us hope that this book is one contribution of many that will improve the lives of persons with disabilities and those who live, love, and work with them.

Robert P. Marinelli, EdD, CRC
Morgantown, WV

Preface

Today, an increasing focus in the delivery of rehabilitation services is on uniquely improving the quality of life of persons with illness and/or disabilities. Both distinctive technology advances and policy developments are facilitating this improvement. What also fuels the engines of life and living progress for those with illness and/or disabilities is evolving philosophical beliefs that, in turn, become foundational to rehabilitation research and practice. One of those beliefs, which has now become thematic to rehabilitation intervention efforts is the necessity for emphasizing consumer empowerment. Such a belief includes consumer self-determination and the encouragement of self-expression.

The exploration and understanding of illness and/or disability in light of its psychological and social impact continues as the main direction of this book. But this fifth edition also highlights the personal perspectives or stories of those faced with the many demands of living with an illness or disability. These perspectives reflect an opportunity to speak out and express one's needs and expectations. The personal journeys and perspectives included in this volume add to the book's uniqueness. They also create perspectives that build a bridge between the documented research results or varying models of understanding illness and disability and the realities that are ever-present when coping with severe handicaps. Further, an additional orientation of this book is to help the reader become aware that making this connection between relevant theory and insightful practice results eventually in a more enhanced quality of life for all individuals living with the illness and/or disability experience.

The benchmarks for the selection of articles in this edition are how these readings capture and then cogently explain the many developing concepts, theories, and intervention approaches related to illness and/or disability. Since the publication of the first edition in 1977, literature in our field has broadened due to the establishment of many new and innovative illness and disability-related journals. Each of the five parts in this new edition includes articles representing journals published by professionals from many different rehabilitation related fields. They bring a diversity of viewpoints that only enrich the reader's understanding of what is important when engaging in rehabilitation practice. In addition, we have included "classic" articles selected from the previous four editions of "Psychological and Social Aspects of Disability." The context of this material is viewed as timeless and the principles and reflections can have a continued influence on generating important insights for rehabilitation interventions.

The many personal perspectives were selected from people for whom a serious illness and/or disability has affected different facets of their life and who then chose to become a victor rather than a victim. The assumption that guided the earlier editions, that illness and disability affect people in very different ways, is reflected in the personal perspectives of this fifth edition. These stories of personal beliefs and journeys provide us with a deeper understanding of what it means to strive for a better quality of life regardless of a significant illness and/or disability.

We would like to thank Alana Stein and Sheri Sussman of Springer Publishing Company, LLC, and Peggy Rote of Aptara, Inc., for their continued support during the project. Our deepest gratitude goes to Robert Marinelli, whose vision 30 years ago was the inspiration for the first edition. A special acknowledgment is made to Barbara Power for her clerical assistance and organizational skills that made this edition possible. We also gratefully acknowledge all those who have shared their personal stories, been our mentors, friends, and role models. This book is dedicated to them.

PART I

Historical and Current Perspective on Illness and Disability

Introduction to Part I

Since the publication in 1977 of the first edition of this book, *Psychological and Social Impact of Physical Disability*, exciting, demanding, and challenging times have characterized and hallmarked the field of rehabilitation. Disability policy has evolved at a dramatic pace. The life and living experience of people living with, and often in spite of and beyond, illness and disability is being redefined, so much so that this experience is now being construed as embracing not only personal characteristics but also social and environmental factors. Disability policy models are also emerging that shift the delivery of rehabilitation services from an exclusive focus on the individual with a disability to include societal influences. All of these realities establish a thematic foundation for the articles and personal perspective presented in Part I.

The dominant themes evident in all of these articles are that policies concerning people living with illnesses or disabilities should not be developed nor implemented without their participation, and professional rehabilitation providers should encourage such participation and recognize and embrace the need for self-determination. Disability, consequently, is both a contextual variable and an opportunity to view this experience as an invitation for one's personal involvement and to make decisions on how such services are delivered. These themes generate within the articles of Part I conceptual frameworks that promote practices that maximize the consumer's participation in exploring an expanded range of options and choices. The reader will also discover from these articles a chance to decide, when choosing what should be a dominant focus in the delivery of rehabilitation services, whether disability is fundamentally a personal tragedy, an opportunity, a form of social oppression, or an integral part of life; or is it all of these factors?

Pfeiffer, in his article "The Disability Paradigm," posed the question: "Does disability have a reality and a fixed existence, or in many circumstances is it transitory?" He provokes the consideration that those with a

3

disability may not be an oppressed minority because many consumers are not oppressed. Yet he elaborates both on the positions that professionals and even family members must change in the way people with disabilities are understood, and on how their participation in policy development is absolutely necessary.

Lutz and Bowers emphasize two perspectives identified previously in the literature. In their article, "Understanding How Disability Is Defined and Conceptualized in the Literature," they discuss both the conceptualization of disability and how to advocate that consumers should be independent and have the same rights and responsibilities as people without disabilities. These authors then suggest an integrated model, which includes one's health condition as a defining construct. They also extend a call to expand research to include the input of those with a disability.

Tate and Pledger in their article "An Integrative Conceptual Framework of Disability: New Directions for Research" also suggest a new paradigm for understanding the disability experience. Their distinctive contribution addresses the "multifactorial" aspects of this experience, highlighting that living with a disability is unique and demands persistent efforts for adaptation and coping. These authors further emphasize that the current knowledge about various facets of disability needs to be reevaluated. They provide readers with information about this reevaluation. This article also challenges the reader to explore the "dynamic intersect" of the person with a disability and the environment, and how this challenge is encouraged by advances in technology and medicine.

The article, "Transforming Psychological Practice and Society" by Gill, Kewman, and Brannon, offers an understanding of disability through a social paradigm, with a focus on reframing the way health professionals define problems related to disability. Their discussion also emphasizes the need for a growing appreciation of the "importance of including the disability cultural perspective in the planning and delivery of services." An interesting item of their article is the discussion of the evolving controversy prompted by new disability frameworks.

Designing a conceptual framework that maximizes consumer involvement in one's rehabilitation process can be quite additive when planning relevant intervention efforts. Beaulaurier and Taylor develop such a framework in their article, "Social Work Practice With People With Disabilities." A unique feature of this article is their discussion of how, on an organizational level, groups of people with disabilities can be empowered. They also elaborate on the mandate that health professionals must be keenly aware of the consumer's need for self-determination.

Smart and Smart, in "Models of Disability: Implications for the Counseling Profession," reiterate what has been often written in the disability literature, namely, that the paradigm for understanding disability is changing. But their article provides a distinctive, needed, historical perspective and a clear elaboration of the four models of disability currently recognized by health professionals. This article's uniqueness is further underlined by an important discussion of the implications of those models for the counseling profession. These models, for example, influence the type and quality of professional services offered by rehabilitation practitioners.

Is there a historical voice that portends the changing disability paradigm? Vanier, in his classic article "The Contributions of the Physically and Mentally Handicapped to Development," reprinted from the third edition urged readers over 30 years ago to listen carefully to the viewpoints of those with a disability. Listening is a beginning step to promoting consumer respect and then advocating consumer self-determination. He then discussed the provocative dictum: "We will be healed through listening." Vanier's article also suggests the implication that listening to consumer choices not only can stimulate healing but also eventually engenders consumer responsibility.

CHAPTER ONE

The Disability Paradigm

David Pfeiffer

People in the fields of rehabilitation and disability studies are familiar with the medical model of disability in which the professional decides what needs to be done to overcome a supposed "deficit" or "problem" and the person with a disability must follow the doctor's orders or suffer dire consequences, some of which are not related to the condition. These consequences can include the stopping of financial and even medical assistance, the creation of family estrangement, and the declaration that the person with a disability has not "accepted" the disability.

As a person with a disability, I never quite knew how I was to "accept" my disability. Celebrate it in song? Drink toasts to it in the bar? Talk endlessly about tragedy? Decry a poor quality of life? Limp bravely into the sunset giving inspiration to all other people? I never did any of these things. Instead, when I had polio at the age of 9, I acknowledged the disability and went on with my life.

In a more general sense, the medical model is found lacking because the person with a disability must occupy the "sick" role. In this role, the person must follow the doctor's orders in order to get well. He or she is exempt from social obligations but is also denied social rights because only the professional can make important decisions. Even unimportant decisions are reserved to the professional. The medical model of disability is woefully inadequate for policy formation and for understanding what disability is all about.

From "The disability paradigm," by D. Pfeiffer, 2000, *Journal of Disability Policy Studies,* *11,* 98–99. Copyright 2000 by PRO-ED, Inc. Reprinted with permission.

Some persons may argue that this approach sets up a "straw man" by describing the medical model in this manner and that the helping professionals no longer hold this view. Quite the contrary: if you are in a helping profession, or if you are a provider carrying out helping professionals' orders, probe beneath the statements of colleagues and listen to what is said in times of stress. There will be that straw man. It is alive and well.

As is known and acknowledged, in some fields, alternative paradigms did emerge to replace the medical model. The social constructionist view of disability says that it is a judgment about a person made (constructed) by other people in society. Being unable to fulfill "normal" functional roles in society, people with disabilities are viewed by others as abnormal and therefore lacking, dependent, and tragic.

Because the social constructionist paradigm offered on a small possibility of change, other individuals set forth the view that people with disabilities are an oppressed minority. They are oppressed by nondisabled people, are denied the share of common resources, and are consigned to a second class citizenship. Once that oppression is recognized and dealt with (usually through demonstrations and protests) there is hope of a better life in the sense of a larger share of the resources.

As with the medical model, neither of these paradigms (social constructionist or oppressed minority) accurately and sufficiently describes disability (all types) and people with disabilities. The social constructionist view is rejected for two reasons, although most people do not agree with the first one (that first reason is that the social constructionist view of disability relies on the notion that groups and society are real.). The number of policymakers, however, holds the position (elaborated in social choice theory) that only individuals are to be perceived. Some individuals are speaking for groups, but groups (aside from an individual or a collection of individuals) are never perceived. Social roles and groups, it is said, are a friction for the convenience of the people who prescribe what they should be. They do not exist independently of an individual.

The second reason the social constructionist view is rejected is that it gives disability a reality and a fixed existence. If there are normal functions or roles in society, not functioning in a normal manner is objective proof of disability. However, disability is a transitory, fluid thing that exists some times but not at other times. It is often described as being a continuum of varying degrees. Or a person is described as having a disability in some circumstances and not in other contexts. In other words, disability does not have a fixed reality. The social constructionist paradigm is not sufficient and is even dangerous for people with disabilities. It certainly is not an adequate basis for the formation of public policy or for understanding disability.

The oppressed minority perspective is rejected simply because many people with disabilities are not oppressed. For example, I have a high quality of life, better than that of most people in the United States. I live in Hawaii, where the temperature averages 85 degrees during the day and 75 degrees during the night, and where there are superb beaches, mountains, and everything people might want. I have a dream job where I do research and write, and I occasionally come to the mainland to talk about disability. However, I will be the first to admit that I have a high quality of life because I am a rich white man. And there are many rich white men who also have a disability. There are also some rich white women and some rich non-white men and women who have disabilities.

Most population surveys do not count any of them as having a disability either because the definition is lacking (being based on a functional or an unemployment definition) or they do not identify themselves as having a disability. Granted, many persons with disabilities are oppressed, but many are not. Therefore, the oppressed minority group paradigm is lacking in explanatory power and as a basis for creating public policy.

We must adopt another disability paradigm, one that says that disability exists when discrimination is encountered. When a person is treated in an unfair or in an unequal manner due to the existence of an artificial condition (like the use of a wheelchair), then that person experiences disability. *Handicapism* (the preferred term in this case) exists in a parallel manner to racism, sexism, ageism, and homophobia. When a person is treated in a fair and equal manner, there is no disability and the person does not feel disabled. Equal protection and due process (treating all people in the same way and in a fair manner) is a remedy for discrimination.

Obviously, this paradigm needs more elaboration, but the purpose for presenting it is to point out its implications for consumers (a terrible word), families, professionals, providers (another terrible word), and policymakers. The implications can be summed up in one phrase: nothing about us without us. Policy regarding people with disabilities cannot be made, implemented, or evaluated without the participation of people with disabilities. Granted, many people do not want to participate, but their involvement must be sought and not excluded, as it is today.

A professional or a provider would never decide if a "normal" person (whatever that means) should reside in an institution, be limited in educational opportunities, be prohibited from entering buildings, be unable to receive information, be passed over for job opportunities, be allowed to die, or any of the many terrible things that happen to people with disabilities each day.

People with mental health problems (whatever that means) or with developmental disabilities (which are only legally defined) have what are called "inappropriate behaviors": On what basis are these behaviors defined as inappropriate? If it is believed that a person is being harmful to him or herself or to others and if a person is exhibiting disgusting behavior that can be changed (there are a lot of celebrities who behave in a disgusting manner but almost nothing can be done about it), intervention might be called for. Otherwise, there is no right to intervene unless asked to do so by that person.

Families of persons with disabilities are among the worst rights violators. When a child is treated as dependent from infancy, he or she will probably remain dependent forever. When an adult with a new disability is treated as dependent, harsh alienation is the most likely result. In other cases, tragedy is the result. The real catastrophe is that usually the family is urged by professionals to view the person with the disability as a dependent. The family would like another outcome, but tragedy is the self-fulfilling prophecy.

What about the professionals and the providers? They are not going to agree with what was just written because their salaries depend on interventions or supervising others who intervene to change these so-called "inappropriate" behaviors. And most of the schemes (incorrectly called programs) to intervene in the lives of people with disabilities are failures. The only ones that actually work (but not in the intended way) are the ones that so anger people with disabilities that they develop means for keeping professionals out of their lives. Other people do not have to spend time and resources keeping professionals out of their lives. Why should people with disabilities have to do so?

Maybe professionals stopped institutionalizing people for the sole reason of getting them out of sight, but professionals and providers still make it very clear that what their "clients" are doing, what they are saying, and how they are acting is not acceptable behavior. The clients are being forced to change and behave in a normal way, when actually the change must be in the way professionals, providers, and even family members view people with disabilities. The change must occur in the accepted paradigm of disability.

Disability policy today is largely a failure. If not a failure, it is seen as terribly expensive and not always the morally correct thing to do. Until professionals, providers, family members, and policymakers recognize that people with disabilities have the right to equal protection, to due process, and to be a part of the process, disability policy will remain a failure. Nothing about us without us.

CHAPTER TWO

Understanding How Disability is Defined and Conceptualized in the Literature

Barbara J. Lutz and Barbara J. Bowers

A primary goal of rehabilitation nursing research is to enhance the care of the person with disabilities (PWD) by minimizing the effects of disability. Rehabilitation nursing practice is based philosophically and theoretically on both the rehabilitation model of disability and the conceptual models and theories of nursing (Derstine & Hargrove, 2001; Secrest, 2000). While nursing theories and models for practice conceptualize how to provide care to PWDs, the rehabilitation model of disability provides the framework for conceptualizing disability. The rehabilitation model, and therefore rehabilitation nursing, is based on a functionalist perspective of illness and conceptualizes disability as a problem of individual functioning.

The social model, an alternative model of disability, is based on the civil rights and social justice perspectives. The social model conceptualizes disability as a problem of the social and physical environments constructed by society. Recognizing the discrepancies between the two perspectives and the resulting models, rehabilitation researchers and practitioners have developed new models that are designed to integrate the two perspectives (Brandt & Pope, 1997; Peters, 1996; World Health Organization, 2001). This chapter explores how disability is conceptualized from the rehabilitation, social, and integrated perspectives; highlights some of the differences; and discusses implications for rehabilitation nursing policy, practice, and research.

THE REHABILITATION PERSPECTIVE

The rehabilitation perspective evolved from the social institution of medical care and is rooted in Parsons' (1951) sociological paradigm of functionalism. In this paradigm, the social world "exists as a whole unit or system which is comprised of interrelated functioning parts" (Bowers, 1988, p. 33). For the system to function effectively, all of the parts (in this case, human beings) must be able to fulfill their expected roles. That is, it is the responsibility of human beings to function in socially expected roles that promote optimal operation of the larger system. According to this paradigm, when individuals deviate from their expected roles, the larger system cannot operate properly. Therefore, to promote optimal function of society, social institutions have the power and authority to ensure that people are able to perform their socially defined roles (Parsons).

For example, in health care, professionals have the social power to control, modify, or eliminate the "deviant" behavior of illness (Weiss & Lonnquist, 1997). From this perspective, healthcare providers have a responsibility to cure "sick" people and return them to full function by eliminating their disease. Conversely, it is the responsibility of "sick" people to seek help from, and comply with, the instructions or "orders" of healthcare professionals (Edge & Groves, 1994; Roberts & Krouse, 1988). The tenets of this paradigm are pervasive and implicit, not only in rehabilitation definitions and models of disability (Myers, 1965; Nagi, 1965), but also in many of the nursing theories that guide rehabilitation nursing practice (Fawcett, 1993; Meleis, 1997). In a functionalist paradigm, PWDs are "obligated to try to become rehabilitated if possible" (Myers, 1965, p. 38). One of the consequences of this paradigm is that as long as a person is not "fully functional," he or she is "exempted from [his or her] normal social responsibilities" (p. 38) and is expected to be dependent on others for care. Therefore, for PWDs who cannot regain full function, the assumptions inherent in this perspective place the PWD in a chronic role of dependency.

Past and present definitions and models of disability in the rehabilitation literature reflect these functionalist assumptions. Myers in 1965

(p. 35) described a person with a disability as "one who, because of his physical or mental handicap, cannot or is not permitted by community members to function in his social roles." A second definition, written 30 years later in a study commissioned by the Institute of Medicine, has the same focus on function and performance of expected roles as its predecessor:

> Disability is defined as a limitation in performing certain roles and tasks that society expects an individual to perform. Disability is the expression of the gap between a person's capabilities and the demands of the environment—the interaction of a person's limitations with social and physical environmental factors. (Brandt & Pope, 1997, p. 25)

While this later definition includes a statement about the interaction of the person with the environment, its focus remains on a person's ability to function in socially expected roles, and it carries with it the assumptions of the previous definitions that were developed from a functionalist perspective.

The rehabilitation models of disability, on which rehabilitation nursing research and practice is based, were developed from this perspective and carry with them the same assumptions. The first draft of the rehabilitation model was developed by Nagi (1965) as an extension of the medical model.

The medical model is conceptualized as a linear model beginning with the etiology of the disease, followed by its pathology, and the resulting manifestations (Minaire, 1992). The medical model focuses on the disease process itself, with the goal of curing the disease and returning the patient to normal functioning. While the medical model was useful for research and practice in the diagnosis and initial treatment stages of a disease, rehabilitation professionals recognized that there were other factors to be considered when studying the effect of a chronic disease or disability on a person's long-term ability to function in society (Nagi, 1965).

Nagi (1965) adapted the medical model and developed a more comprehensive model of disability. Several other researchers have revised this framework in the past 35 years. In the late 1970s, the World Health Organization (WHO) developed the International Classification of Impairments, Disabilities, and Handicaps (WHO ICIDH) (WHO, 1980). While the WHO ICIDH model does not acknowledge the influence of the Nagi scheme, there are many similarities in these models. These two models are the most commonly referenced models in the rehabilitation literature and are the philosophical and theoretical frameworks of disability that guide rehabilitation nursing practice (Derstine & Hargrove, 2001; Secrest, 2000). While both the Nagi scheme and the WHO ICIDH provide a more comprehensive schema of disability than does the medical model, they are based in the functionalist paradigm and their central (and defining) construct is the disease or pathology and its resulting effect on functioning.

In the past 10 years, rehabilitation health services researchers have revised the Nagi (1991) and ICI DH models. The revisions included the addition of societal limitations (Jette, 1994); environmental and individual factors, and risk factors (Verhrugge & Jette, 1994); and quality of life and health status (Ebrahim, 1995; Pope & Tarlov, 1991). Yet, even with these revisions, it is the rehabilitation model and all of its variations that locates disability in the person; its central focus is on the disease process and the patient's resulting functional limitations. This model is also known as the individual model of disability in sonic literature.

THE SOCIAL PERSPECTIVE

The second perspective has its roots in the historical and political tradition of the civil rights movement, social justice, and consumerism (DeJong, 1979; Hahn, 1993). This perspective began to emerge in the late 1960s, and was in partial response to the prevailing emphasis on functioning and the focus of the rehabilitation perspective that disability was a form of deviance to be eliminated or reversed (DeJong; Hahn). These sociopolitical movements evolved from the belief that certain groups or classes of individuals, such as PWDs, are oppressed by the more powerful classes in society—for instance, healthcare professionals. The main purpose of these movements was to make visible the imbalances in power and to secure the rights of the less powerful people in this society. The goal was to shift the emphasis and the burden of disability from the PWD to society.

This perspective presumes that people with disabilities are discriminated against, marginalized, and oppressed (Hahn, 1993). Resulting definitions and social models of disability focused on minimizing disability and improving quality of life by affording PWDs the same rights and opportunities afforded to other members of society. A major assumption of the social perspective is that PWDs should be independent and should have the same rights and responsibilities as people without disabilities. This is accomplished through empowerment, self-determination, and activism (DeJong, 1979).

This perspective defines disability as a product of the social and physical environment. Disability results from restrictions created and imposed by society, which, in turn, causes restricted opportunities for the PWD. The approach to ameliorating disability centers on changing social attitudes, institutions, and policies. This perspective is evident in the following definitions:

> Disability is not a condition of the individual. The experiences of disabled people are of social restrictions in the world around them, not being a person with a 'disabling condition.' This is not to deny that individuals experience 'disability'; rather it is to assert that the individual's experience of 'disability' is created in interactions with a physical and social world. (Swain, Finkelstein, French, & Oliver, 1993, p. 2)

DISABILITY DEFINED

> Disability is manufactured by attitudinal and environmental barriers rather than functional limitations. (Finkelstein, 1993, p. 39)

The models coming from the social perspective "locate disability not in an impaired or malfunctioning body, but in an excluding and oppressive social environment" (Marks, 1997, p. 88). Disability is perceived as the result of the discrimination, prejudice, and stigmatization (Hahn, 1993), and forced dependence on relatives and healthcare and other professionals (DeJong, 1979).

The most widely referenced of the social models in the United States is the independent living (IL) model. From its perspective, the rehabilitation process, because of its "dependency-inducing features" (DeJong, 1979, p. 443), is viewed as part of the problem of disability. The IL model identifies the problem of disability as "not only the rehabilitation process but also the physical environment and the social control mechanisms in society-at-large" (DeJong). Advocates of this model propose that PWDs trade the dependent role of patient or client, for the independent role of consumer and activist (DeJong; DeJong & Brannon, 1998; Marks, 1997).

In the IL model, proposed solutions to the problem of disability include empowerment, self-determination, advocacy, consumer control, removal of environmental barriers, and political activism (DeJong, 1979; DeJong & Brannon, 1998). A primary tenet of the IL model is that PWDs have expertise about disability and that programs and services should be determined, designed, and directed by PWDs. For example, according to the model, personal care assistant services in particular should be individually controlled and directed by the PWD, rather than by formal systems of care. In other words, personal care workers should be recruited, hired, trained, managed, paid, disciplined, and fired (if necessary) by, and be accountable to, the PWD rather than to an organization. This model also advocates flexible policies and benefits systems whereby PWDs determine the

best use of funds that have been allocated for their well-being (DeJong &
Brannon).

INTEGRATING THE MODELS

Recognizing that the rehabilitation and social models were oppositional
in nature, but that there were strengths in each, several researchers in the
past 5 years have attempted to integrate them by placing more emphasis
on the interaction of the person with the environment (Brandt & Pope,
1997; Peters, 1996; WHO, 2001). However, these integrated models were
derived primarily from the earlier rehabilitation models and the assumptions inherent in those earlier models still held. Most importantly, in the
integrated models the health condition (i.e., the disease or disorder) and
resulting functional limitations of the patient remain the central focus.

For example, the WHO International Classification of Functioning,
Disability, and Health (ICF) (2001), which evolved from the International
Classification of Diseases and the first WHO ICIDH model (described
earlier), was designed to integrate the components of the medical and the
social models of disability (Gray & Hendershot, 2000; WHO, 2001). According to its authors, this integrated model provides unifying dimensions
and domains of health conditions for researchers and providers when
classifying or mapping the impact of a disease or disorder on individual
functioning (Gray & Hendershot; WHO).

While the goal of the ICF is to integrate the perspectives of the social
and medical models, as in previous rehabilitation models, the defining
construct is the health condition (i.e., the disease or disorder) and its
resulting effect on individual function. Disabling barriers of society are
considered as context; however, functionalist assumptions prevail in the
1CF by continuing to direct our attention (as researchers and practitioners) to the health condition and its effect on a person's ability to function
in social roles.

DISCUSSION AND IMPLICATIONS

The conceptual models of disability found in the literature reflect two
very different perspectives. The rehabilitation perspective locates physical
disability within the person and presumes that he or she is dependent on
society until he or she can function in socially expected roles. If this is not
possible, then the person remains permanently in a dependent role.

This perspective tends to reduce disability to a problem of individual
functioning resulting from a disease or disorder that requires professional

intervention. The unit of analysis is the patient and outcomes are determined by that person's level of functional improvement. In this model, practice patterns and policies tend to be provider-driven and focus on eliminating (to the extent possible) the condition that is causing the physical disability. Rehabilitation nursing practice is guided by this perspective and definition of disability. For example, the Functional Independence Measure (FIMTM) (Keith, Granger, Hamilton, & Sherwin, 1987), a tool that is widely used in rehabilitation nursing, is based on this model.

Disability also has been defined from a civil rights and social justice perspective, which is commonly described as the social model of disability. This model identifies disability in society and presumes that it is society's responsibility to change to provide equal opportunities for PWDs. This perspective tends to discount (or even ignore) the problem of the disabling condition at the individual level and focuses on changing society. The unit of analysis in the social model is society, and outcomes are measured by the degree of social equality that is achieved. This perspective assumes that the PWD should be independent and self-determining, that all PWDs have the expertise and desire to have total control over decisions affecting their lives (including healthcare decisions), and that they have a responsibility to be activists to change society. It also assumes that PWDs should accept their disabling condition as part of who they are and that they must embrace the ideals of this perspective.

Both the rehabilitation and social perspectives and the resulting models described in the preceding paragraphs provide some insight into important attributes of the concept of disability. However, each perspective also imposes assumptions about how PWDs should be. The WHO's attempt to integrate the models is a step forward. However, concern remains that when endorsing and implementing the new model of disability, approaches to research and practice will continue to carry the implicit assumptions of the previous perspectives, in particular the functionalist assumptions.

In addition to being directed by the rehabilitation model of disability, rehabilitation nursing texts and curricula also incorporate conceptual models and theories of nursing practice, such as those proposed by Orem, Roy, Henderson, and King (Derstine & Hargrove, 2001; Secrest, 2000). While these nursing theories and models are patient-focused and help define how to care for PWDs, they are, like the rehabilitation model of disability, either firmly rooted in, or carry undertones of, a functionalist perspective (Fawcett, 1993; Meleis, 1997). While more recent nursing theories, such as those of Parse and Newman (Fawcett, 1993), broaden our definitions of nursing from a functionalist perspective to integrating the perspectives of people and populations, these broader definitions are not yet reflected in our teaching and practice. Therefore, the implicit assumptions of a functionalist perspective often guide both our definitions of disability and our approaches to the care of PWDs.

Services, practice, and research for PWDs designed from either of the perspectives described in this chapter will continue to be fragmented, incomplete, and inherently too narrowly focused, centering on one perspective while virtually eclipsing the other. For example, services designed solely from a functionalist perspective focus on the physically disabling condition and the resulting effect on functioning, often eclipsing other important aspects of a person's life. Conversely, services designed from the disability rights perspective focus on changing society and promoting self-determination for PWDs, placing them in an often unchosen and unwanted role of care manager, advocate, activist, and expert.

Zola (1989) argues for "real" integration of the two perspectives to form a "universal" approach to disability. He contends that both the social and rehabilitation models tend to segregate PWDs, focusing on their differentness and special needs. He calls for a "universal policy toward disability" (p. 421), in which the uniqueness and interdependence of people in society are recognized by designing a flexible social world for all. However, the fact that PWDs do have special issues and needs cannot be discounted. Research into the unique needs of the PWD is limited, but several authors have identified issues specific to them that include more vulnerable health status, secondary limitations, accelerated aging, complex service needs, problems with insurance, and limited opportunities for gainful employment (Brandt & Pope, 1997; DeJong & Brannon, 1998; DeJong, et al., 2002; Nosek, 1993).

CONCLUSION

People with disability experience it within the larger context of living their lives. When the disease process or societal barriers are central in our research, policies, and practice, the effect of disability is considered out of the larger context of living a life. This narrow focus results in programs and policies that often eclipse other important aspects of a person's life.

Rehabilitation nursing can help expand this focus by recognizing that disability is often conceptualized from a provider-defined, functionalist perspective within our practice environments. Recently, rehabilitation nurse researchers have begun to explore how people who are living with disabilities perceive disability and its influence on their lives (Paterson & Stewart, 2002; Pilkington, 1999; Secrest & Thomas, 1999; Treloar, 1999). To enhance our understanding of disability, we must continue to expand research to include the perspectives of people living with disability. Research questions and practice must focus on what is important in their lives, how disability influences their abilities to live their lives, and what policies and services will help them meet their needs. This approach is supported by other rehabilitation researchers (Brown & Heinemann, 1999; Crow, 1996; Marks, 1997; Treloar, 1999).

Gaining a better understanding from PWDs about how they experience disability will continue to provide rehabilitation nursing researchers, policy makers, and practitioners new insights into the dimensions of disability that are most salient, and the strategies that PWDs employ to mediate the effects of their disability on their abilities to live the lives they want to live. This heightened understanding will help to bridge the gaps that have been identified among the perspectives discussed here.

ACKNOWLEDGMENTS

The authors gratefully acknowledge the National Institute of Nursing Research (Grant numbers: F31 NR07229-0 I and T32 NR07102-02) and the Rehabilitation Nursing Foundation and Sigma Theta Tau International for their support of this work.

REFERENCES

Bowers, B. (1988). Grounded theory. In B. Sarter (Ed.), *Paths to knowledge: Innovative research methods for nursing* (pp. 33–59). Washington, DC: National League for Nursing.

Brandt, E.N., & Pope, A.M. (Eds.). (1997). *Enabling America: Assessing the role of rehabilitation science and engineering.* Washington, DC: National Academy Press.

Brown, M., & Heinemann, A.W. (1999). DRR's new paradigm: Opportunities and caveats. *Rehabilitation Outlook, 4*(4), 1, 6–7, 9.

Crow, I. (1996). Including all of our lives: Renewing the social model of disability. In C. Barnes & G. Mercer (Eds.), *Exploring the divide: Illness and disability* (pp. 55–73). Leeds: The Disability Press.

DeJong, G. (1979). Independent living: From social movement to analytic paradigm. *Archives of Physical Medicine and Rehabilitation, 60,* 435–446.

DeJong, G., & Brannon, R. (1998). Trends in services directed to working-age people with physical disabilities. In S.M. Allen & V. Mor (Eds.), *Living in the community with disability: Services needs, uses, and systems* (pp. 168–194). New York: Springer Publishing Co., Inc.

DeJong, G., Palsbo, S.E., Beatty, P.W., Jones, G.C., Kroll, T., & Neri, M.T. (2002). The organization and financing of health services for persons with disabilities. *The Milbank Quarterly, 80,* 261–301.

Derstinc, L.B., & Hargrove, S.D. (2001). *Comprehensive rehabilitation nursing.* Philadelphia: W.B. Saunders.

Ebrahim, S. (1995). Clinical and public health perspectives and applications of health-related quality of life measurement. *Social Science and Medicine, 41,* 1383–1394.

Edge, R.S., & Groves, J.R. (1994). *The ethics of health care: A guide for clinical practice.* Albany, NY: Delmar.

Fawcett, J. (1993). *Analysis and evaluation of nursing theories.* Philadelphia: F.A. Davis, Co.

Finkelstein, V. (1993). Disability: A social challenge or an administrative responsibility? In J. Swain, V. Finkelstein, S. French, & M. Oliver (Eds.), *Disabling barriers—Enabling environments* (pp. 34–43). London: Sage Publications.

Gray, D.B. & Hendershot, G.E. (2000). The ICIDH-2: Developments for a new era of outcomes research. *Archives of Physical Medicine, 81*(Suppl. 2), S10–S14.

Hahn, H. (1993). The political implications of disability definitions and data. *Journal of Disability Policy Studies, 4*(2), 41–51.

Jette, A.M. (1994). Physical disablement concepts for physical therapy research and practice. *Physical Therapy, 74,* 380–386.

Keith, R.A., Granger, C.V., Hamilton, B.B., & Sherwin, F.S. (1987). The Functional Independence Measure: A new tool for rehabilitation. In M. G. Eisenberg & R.C. Grzesiak (Eds.), *Advances in Clinical Rehabilitation* (pp. 6–18). New York: Springer.

Marks, D. (1997). Models of disability. *Disability and Rehabilitation, 19,* 85–91.

Meleis, A.I. (1997). *Theoretical nursing: Development and progress.* (3rd ed.). Philadelphia: Lippincott.

Minaire, P. (1992). Disease, illness and health: Theoretical models of the disablement process. *Bulletin of the World Health Organization, 70,* 373–379.

Myers, J.K. (1965). Consequences and prognoses of disability. In M.B. Sussman (Ed.), *Sociology and rehabilitation* (pp. 35–51). Washington, DC: American Sociological Association.

Nagi, S.Z. (1965). Some conceptual issues in disability and rehabilitation. In M.B. Sussman (Ed.), *Sociology and rehabilitation* (pp. 100–113). Washington, DC: American Sociological Association.

Nagi, S.Z. (1991). Disability concepts revisited: Implications for prevention. In A.M. Pope & A.R. Tarlov (Eds.), *Disability in America: Toward a national agenda for prevention* (pp. 309–327). Washington, DC: National Academy Press.

Nosek, M.A. (1993). Personal assistance: Its effect on long-term health of a rehabilitation hospital program. *Archives of Physical Medicine and Rehabilitation, 74,* 127–132.

Parsons, T. (1951). *The social system.* Glencoe, IL: The Free Press.

Paterson, J. & Stewart, J. (2002). Adults with acquired brain injury: Perceptions of their social world. *Rehabilitation Nursing, 27,* 13–18.

Peters, D.J. (1996). Disablement observed, addressed, and experienced: Integrating subjective experience into disablement models. *Disability and Rehabilitation, 18,* 593–603.

Pilkington, F.B. (1999). A qualitative study of life after stroke. *Journal of Neuroscience Nursing, 31,* 336–347.

Pope, A.N., & Tarlov, A.R. (Eds.). (1991). *Disability in America: Toward a national agenda for prevention.* Washington, DC: National Academy Press.

Roberts, S.J., & Krouse, H.J. (1988). Enhancing self-care through active negotiation. *Nurse Practitioner, 13*(8), 44–52.

Secrest, J.A. (2000). Rehabilitation and rehabilitation nursing. In P.A. Edwards (Ed.), *The specialty practice of rehabilitation nursing* (4th ed., pp. 2–16). Glenview, IL: Association of Rehabilitation Nurses.

Secrest, J.A., & Thomas, S.P. (1999). Continuity and discontinuity: The quality of life following stroke. *Rehabilitation Nursing, 24*, 240–246.

Swain, J., Finkelstein, V., French, S., & Oliver, M. (Eds.). (1993). *Disabling barriers - Enabling environments.* London: Sage Publications.

Treloar, L.L. (1999). People with disabilities—The same, but different: Implications for health care practice. *Journal of Transcultural Nursing, 10*, 358–364.

Verhrugge, L.M., & Jette, A.M. (1994). The disablement process. *Social Science and Medicine, 38*, 1–14.

Weiss, G.L., & Lonnquist, L.E. (1997). *The sociology of health, healing, and illness* (2nd ed.). Upper Saddle River, NJ: Prentice Hall.

World Health Organization (1980). International classification of impairments, disabilities, and handicaps. Geneva, Switzerland: World Health Organization.

World Health Organization (2001). *ICF: International classification of functioning, disability, and health.* [On-line]. World Health Organization. Retrieved, 2002, from http://www.who.int/classification/icf/intros/ICF-Eng-Intro.pdf.

Zola, I.K. (1989). Toward the necessary universalizing of a disability policy. *The Milbank Quarterly, 67*(Suppl. 2, Part 2), 401–430.

CHAPTER THREE

An Integrative Conceptual Framework of Disability[1]

New Directions for Research

Denise G. Tate and Constance Pledger

Kerlinger (1979) has stated that the purpose of research is to develop and test theories and thereby advance knowledge, stimulate product development, and promote technological advances that contribute in the long term to economic development and competitiveness in a market-based economy. Although a pragmatic approach, his assumption is based on the idea that fostering excellence in research will have long-lasting effects in society. As a societal goal, improving the quality of life for persons with disabilities (i.e., physical, emotional, mental, sensorial) rests on the development of science knowledge that goes beyond discoveries in basic science but also addresses disability within a broader socioecological context.

Researchers, policymakers, health care providers (including psychologists), and, most important, persons with disabilities and their families recognize that translating the many remarkable scientific breakthroughs

From "An integrative conceptual framework of disability: new directions for research," by D. Tate and C. Pledger, 2003, *American Psychologist, 58,* 289–295. Copyright 2003 by the American Psychological Association. Reprinted with permission.

[1] *Editor's note.* This article is intended to promote the exchange of ideas among researchers and policymakers. The views expressed in it do not necessarily reflect the position of the U.S. Department of Education.

into practices and policies of everyday life is an urgent and essential task. Failure to do so has profound implications for the lives of those with disabilities. As a field of knowledge, rehabilitation has produced research contributing to the quality and the breadth of clinical interventions. Scientific, technological, and clinical advances in the treatment of neuromuscular diseases, mental illnesses, blindness, and deafness, for example, have resulted from such efforts and have helped the public to understand disability resulting from injuries and chronic illnesses. Many of these advancements have been generated within a socioecological context.

The disability and rehabilitation community is celebrating a renewed focus on a socioecological framework for understanding disability. The new paradigm of disability emphasizes the importance of integrating participatory action research methods and the person—environment conceptualization of disability and is having an increasing impact on how health care providers practice and conduct research. Within this holistic framework, researchers are encouraged to acknowledge the dynamic interaction between the person and the environment, to be aware of the importance of consumer participation in the planning, implementation, and evaluation of research activities and interventions strategies, and to recognize the limitations of traditional, more medically oriented, definitions and measures of disability.

GUIDING PARADIGMS IN RESEARCH ON DISABILITY AND REHABILITATION[2]

Recognition of the new paradigm of disability is an important conceptual advancement in the rehabilitation research and health-related disciplines. The new paradigm of disability distinguishes between the medical model and the socioecological model of disability. Research efforts examining and comparing these models have helped to identify ways that the environment influences the disabling process and the adverse impact of a strictly medical orientation.

Many advances have been made during the past decade; however, much of the knowledge about the role of the environment was contributed by early researchers. For example, Moos (1979) described four types of variables as making up a new integrative socioecological conceptual framework of disability: (a) the environmental system, including physical setting, organizational factors, human aggregate, and social climate;

---

[2] This section was developed by Constance Pledger. Melissa G. Warren served as action editor of this section.

(b) the personal system; (c) mediating factors such as appraisal, activation, and adaptation; and (d) health status and health-related behavior. Both the environmental system and the personal system can affect health and disability outcomes with or without mediating factors. For example, cognitive and emotional appraisal is an important mediating factor in determining the issues affecting the quality of life of persons with disabilities.

Engel (1977) illustrated the importance of the environmental context with the introduction of the biopsychosocial model. This model presents a holistic, systems approach and identifies the influence of various dimensions of the social and cultural environment on the individual. Engel eloquently argued for a more balanced approach between the use of scientific medical knowledge and personal and social issues in treatment environments. Essentially, Engel advocated for an approach that integrates the micro (interactional), meso (community or organizational), and macro (structural) social levels approach that emphasizes the role of social structural factors as determinants and influences on outcomes.

Trieschmann (1987) put it best by describing four factors that influence functioning and health: behavior (B), a function of the interaction of psychosocial (P), biological—organic (O), and environmental (E) forces, expressed as $B = f(P, O, E)$. In a discussion about medicine, aging, and disability, Trieschmann suggested that fractionating the whole robs researchers of a true understanding of individual functioning:

> We have ignored the concepts of wholeness and system in our western medical treatment and deceive ourselves that true understanding comes from analyzing the body into component parts in order to understand how it works. On the contrary, you can never understand a system by fragmentation and analysis alone. Unless you put the parts back into the context of the system, there is no understanding, no true knowledge, only collection of facts without coherence or unity. (Trieschmann, 1987, p. 49)

The disability experience is multifactorial, including personal characteristics, as well as environmental, societal (Fine & Asch, 1988; Meyerson, 1988), and psychological factors that may play a role. The relative degree of disability and the disability experience fluctuate depending on condition, time, and setting. Thus, disability is a contextual variable, dynamic over time and circumstance. Verbrugge and Jette (1994) and Fine and Asch (1988) have suggested that disability is situational and is expressed within a social context. Functional limitations can be exacerbated by social and environmental factors (Verbrugge & Jette, 1994), and the extent of constraints imposed by the physical and social environments mediates the disability experience (Scotch, 1988). The disability experience is a unique, individualized experience involving multiple factors, including individual characteristics and behaviors, culture, social stigmas, attitudes, and other factors that have the potential to enable or disable.

The revised *International Classification of Impairments, Disabilities, and Handicaps* (*ICIDH;* World Health Organization, 1980) also supports this emerging conceptualization of disability as a social phenomenon. The revised version includes an expanded focus that emphasizes the personal, social, and physical context of disability. The terminology and definitions for disability reflect the need for more neutral, less medically biased terminology: *disability* has become *activity,* and *handicap* has become *participation* (Wade & DeJong, 2000, p. 1387).

This integrative conceptual framework outlines the importance of efforts for adaptation and coping with illness and disability, which may in turn change the environmental or the personal system and may therefore influence health behaviors and outcomes (Hahn, 1991). Recent research on wellness programs for persons with disabilities, for example, focuses on well-being from a holistic and integrative perspective. In designing methods to study fitness for persons with disabilities, researchers take into account not only how to change health beliefs and behaviors that promote fitness, but also personal resources, social support, and community access to specialized exercise equipment and devices needed for those with disabilities who wish to become physically active (Rimmer, 1999).

Despite research efforts that identify the benefits of a holistic, integrative approach, the significance of this conceptualization of disability has not been widely adopted in broader research or clinical communities or across relevant disciplines. Although empirical studies are undertaken at each systems level, research findings often are not satisfactorily translated through clinical/treatment interventions or community and training environments. For example, training programs still have not adequately incorporated the new paradigm framework into the training curriculum in most disciplines responsible for the delivery of health care, psychological, and other rehabilitation services. However, the research and practice communities are in a period of transition in which the socioecological model is increasingly informing research, training, policy, and practice. Advancements over the past 30 years have contributed to current knowledge, policies, procedures, practices, and understanding of the disability phenomenon.

CONCEPTUAL CONTRIBUTIONS

During the late 1970s and early 1980s, with the advent of independent living as a social—political movement in rehabilitation, a new paradigm of disability was described in the literature (DeJong, 1983). As DeJong and Hughes (1982) explained, in rehabilitation, often the problem is not the individual but the environment, including its physical and social characteristics. This paradigm of disability differs from the traditional medical rehabilitation paradigm.

The U.S. Department of Education (2000) has provided one way of emphasizing the differences between the new and the traditional paradigms:

> The old paradigm which was reductive to medical condition has presented disability as the result of a deficit in an individual that precludes him/her from performing functions and activities.... The new paradigm is integrative and holistic and focuses on the whole person functioning in an environmental context. (p. 9)

This is perhaps one of the best summary statements regarding the delicate yet complex conceptual changes underlying research on disability and rehabilitation.

Methodologically, this theoretical viewpoint is included in what is known in the fields of sociology and anthropology as participatory action research (PAR). PAR provides researchers in the field of rehabilitation and disability science with a new way of studying social issues. In her discussion of the paths to useful knowledge, Dembo (1974) emphasized the need to make rehabilitation research useful to persons with disabilities. Similarly, in more recent literature on the social model of disability, Olkin (1999) discussed the relevance of rehabilitation research, the responsibilities of the researcher, the impact of policy, and the role of individuals with disabilities in shaping the research agenda. Olkin emphasized the need for increased participation of individuals with disabilities in research activities to improve services and decision making and to enhance prevention efforts. In essence, research and the knowledge and products generated from research bear little importance if they do not involve and benefit or have meaning for consumers.

PAR models have been used successfully to demonstrate the importance of defining and thus researching disability issues from a consumer's perspective. By involving consumers of rehabilitation services in the research process, professionals can ensure the relevance of their own work and its value to the lives of persons with disabilities. This is particularly true for rehabilitation engineers who design technological products that fit the needs of persons with disabilities. Thus, in designing a motorized wheelchair for someone with a high level paralysis, for example, engineers will need to follow certain technical specifications for height, weight, and posture, while at the same time addressing the expectations of the consumer for functionality, price, durability, and cosmetic appearance.

Likewise, psychologists have advanced PAR as a method of investigation by framing it within the context of ecological psychology. Psychologists have used PAR to deal with naturalistic studies of a person's everyday behavior and psychological situation. Willems (1977) provided researchers with an illustration of this approach to problems of health status and health care by focusing on naturalistic studies of the process of rehabilitation from spinal cord injuries. He found that the degree of independence shown by patients with spinal cord injuries varied dramatically among hospital settings; that, contrary to expectations, patients showed more independence and active initiation of behavior in the cafeteria and hallways of the rehabilitation unit than in physical and occupational therapy treatment rooms; and that patients' behavioral changes varied substantially among hospital settings. These behavioral inconsistencies often lead to disagreements among professionals and persons with disabilities about the goal of treatment and the amount of progress achieved. Willems's work represents an excellent example of key intervening variables affecting rehabilitation treatment outcomes, variables that often operate in the context of the larger social environment. These changes in behavior that influence outcomes may not be fully understood, depending on the research paradigm adopted.

REFLECTING ON THE CURRENT STATE
OF THE SCIENCES

Although research studies provide valuable information, current knowledge about the various facets of disability and researchers' understanding of the disabling process need to be re-evaluated, particularly in the context of scientific advancements. Relatively little has been written about the dynamic intersect of person and environment, disability trajectories, and the challenges presented by advances in technology and medicine, such as innovations in biomedicine and biotechnology. What is not clear is the extent to which disability is mediated by aspects of the built social and cultural environments and the potential impact of advancements that alter the natural life course and disabling process.

For example, little is known about the ethical challenges presented by advancements in the area of stem cell research or biotechnology. Scientific advancements examining the role of stem cells could help further the understanding of human development, illness, and disability. In addition, a better understanding of cell division and specialization will help to advance cell therapies that have the potential for development of new treatments for diseases, conditions, and disabilities, such as Parkinson's and Alzheimer's diseases, spinal cord injury, stroke, burns, heart disease, diabetes, osteoarthritis, and rheumatoid arthritis (see the National Institutes of Health Web site http://www.nih.gov/news/stemcell/primer.htm). Although the benefits of stem cell research are discussed, the research is controversial and challenges the research community to answer questions about ethical issues and the impact of life-altering interventions.

Advancements in scientific knowledge of stem cells will potentially expand the role of psychologists in the research community. For example, psychologists may play a crucial role in examining issues of quality of life and providing psychological assessments of readiness and adjustment for cell and organ transplantation. Key research topics might include the ethical issues and decision making involved in the extension and termination of life. The examination of psychological factors will likely emerge as a primary issue for better understanding of the consequences and outcomes for individuals with disabilities and chronic illnesses and for others taking advantage of advancements in stem cell research. Although scientific knowledge is improving the quality of life for individuals with disabilities, questions about the methods used to achieve this goal continue to challenge the research and clinical communities to examine the role of consumers in the decision-making process.

Applied and basic research relating to rehabilitation and disability should reflect the most critical needs of persons with disabilities. Furthermore, the determination of what is relevant to study should not be the sole province of practitioners and researchers. Limiting the determination of relevance to these two groups disenfranchises the ultimate beneficiaries of such research: persons with disabilities (Tate, 2000).

Aside from the intriguing controversy surrounding the ethics of research advancements, research has introduced new approaches and interventions that improve understanding of disability and chronic illness. However, in addition to ethical issues, research often raises questions about methodological and theoretical considerations, particularly the impact of including individuals with disabilities in the planning, conduct, and evaluation of research activities, as proposed by the PAR model. For example, biomedical research activities such as deep-brain stimulation, another controversial area, challenge psychology and the larger research community to explore scientific activities within the context of a biopsychosocial approach. Psychologists can help to explore the biopsychology of implantation of electrodes into the human brain to reduce or alleviate tremors or to improve mobility. What are the implications for treatment intervention strategies, policy, decision making, and rehabilitation outcomes in an environment already concerned with prejudicial attitudes toward chronic illness and disability and uncertain about the extent to which technology should be used to alter the life course?

Researchers working on the development of ultrasensitive diagnostics also face challenges. This nanobiotechnology will assist with detecting disease by means of electrical signaling. Future developments include plans for a home-testing version of nanobiotechnology for consumers. Although this technology has the potential for enormous benefit, the inherent risk for misuse and abuse of information has not been adequately explored. Researchers can play a crucial role by examining the implications of nanobiotechnology, including the benefits, risks, and psychosocial factors. Although nanobiotechnology may be unfamiliar territory for some psychologists, it is the wave of the future and will potentially involve consumers who are seeking the assistance of psychologists. Therefore, knowledge about this newly emerging field of study is important to the practice of psychology. By taking a broader view of uses of technology from a socioecological and psychological perspective, researchers may be better informed about the influences and impact of technology on outcomes.

Research is also advancing the use of virtual technology for rehabilitation and assessment of individual functioning. Telemedicine, telerehabilitation, virtual learning laboratories, and telework activities raise questions about the lack of human contact and the potential for individuals with disabilities to be socially isolated. In addition, limited information about the cost-effectiveness and limited evidence of the effectiveness and efficacy of some technologies with particular disabilities compound this problem. On the other hand, technology is often viewed as a solution to access barriers that prevent the integration and participation of individuals with disabilities in society.

The rapid proliferation of technology and technology transfer challenge researchers and clinicians to quickly understand and master new technologies. The psychologist's perspective on the impact of rapidly changing technology used in clinical settings and the community could contribute to the understanding of the effects of technological change on clinical staff and consumers. The socioecological perspective for investigating this concern should explore uses of technology within an environmental conceptualization of disability by including cultural, individual, and social factors that affect rehabilitation outcomes. For example, research might examine access to technology from a cultural psychology approach by exploring the *digital divide* in relation to use and abandonment of technology by traditionally underserved racial and ethnic populations.

These examples of the state of the science suggest the need for psychologists to collaborate with other disciplines to ensure expertise on issues that are not often studied by psychologists. Azar (1998a) examined the value of melding expertise to further research and described the value of collaboration. Azar suggested that increasing numbers of psychologists are engaging in research with scientists from other domains, resulting in new discoveries. Similarly, Azar (1998b) described the value of sharing data with researchers in other fields. Collaboration and pooling of resources provide the opportunity to examine issues and analyze data from a variety of unique perspectives; this, according to Azar, helps to expand the overall knowledge base.

Coordination across disciplines also has important implications for generating evidence-based intervention strategies. Wade and DeJong (2000) suggested that the importance of organized rehabilitation services and coordination is increasingly recognized. In their description of important advancements in rehabilitation, they discussed the transition from a medical model to a model that recognizes psychological and sociocultural aspects as an important development in establishing a more holistic and coordinated approach to providing rehabilitation services.

Current evidence strongly supports the provision of well-organized, coordinated, multidisciplinary rehabilitation services based on a problem-oriented approach. In the future, specific interventions will be more evidence based, leading to more appropriate use of interventions and more appropriate referrals to specialist services (Wade & DeJong, 2000, p. 1385).

In many ways, the revised *ICIDH* (World Health Organization, 1980) has contributed to better understanding among disciplines and has fostered more consistent communication among professionals from different disciplines by encouraging a more systematic analysis of rehabilitation interventions. It also brings structure and order to research. Most important, it has facilitated the change of emphasis within rehabilitation from a mechanistic, medically driven process of physical medicine to a comprehensive, more socially driven form of rehabilitation (Wade & DeJong, 2000, p. 1388). Development of this more socially oriented classification system provides the structure and standardization necessary for interdisciplinary coordinated efforts, while also acknowledging the importance of the multifactorial nature of disability.

NEW DIRECTIONS FOR USEFUL RESEARCH

Several assumptions have guided the authors' thinking when describing new directions for research on disability and rehabilitation. First, useful research requires the input of consumers, especially people with disabilities, in research. Second, the best explanatory paradigm for rehabilitation research as described earlier is based on a socioecological model of disability. Third, inherent to this integrative model is the need for interdisciplinary collaboration to promote a holistic approach to useful research and practices. Fourth, more emphasis must be devoted to translating the yield of basic and clinical research into effective treatments and products for persons with disabilities. On the basis of these assumptions, the following directions for research are summarized.

Advancements and Uses of Technology

Advances in technology present serious ethical dilemmas. For example, prenatal testing can help to identify the probability that a newborn will have a disability. Consumers and health professionals have the option of making decisions based on identifiable risks, as demonstrated by prenatal testing. The availability of this information is the genesis of controversies about who should have the authority to determine which individuals are allowed to live or die. This is one example of biomedical technology and scientific advancements that can potentially alter the life course. Psychologists can contribute to a better understanding of the social and psychological impact of advanced scientific and innovative intervention strategies.

Consumer Input in Research

Persons with disabilities, their families, and their significant others should have opportunities to participate with researchers and practitioners in the process of generating meaningful research questions. Including consumers in the research process promotes empowerment and social acceptance. It is through empowerment that persons with disabilities can gain mastery over their own affairs (Zimmerman & Warschausky, 1998). Research that is developed to promote and facilitate empowerment will in turn become more meaningful to its users. However, the inclusion of consumers as researchers and evaluators of research is continually challenged and raises questions about their competencies and qualifications to play a key role in the planning, development, and evaluation of the merits of research. Consumer—researcher collaboration will be better understood when researchers further examine the impact of consumer involvement and identify the skills researchers need to effectively work with individuals with disabilities in research.

Methodological and Design Issues for a Socioecological Perspective on Disability

Studying environmental and social variables at higher levels of integration poses unique methodological challenges. We believe that these challenges discourage many researchers from pursuing investigations based on socioecological models of disability. Perhaps the most basic challenge is that many ecological variables are less subject to experimental control and manipulation than intrapersonal ones. Creativity, persistence, advocacy, and interdisciplinary teamwork are likely to be required by professionals and researchers working with persons with disabilities to achieve the types of environmental changes that warrant study. When studying the effects of changes in behavior settings on health and rehabilitation-related choices and actions, it is no longer possible to randomly assign individuals to experimental conditions. Larger units of analysis, or behavior settings, such as hospitals, clinics, work sites, community agencies, or health care systems may require random assignment. Such studies (often multicenter trials) are complex and costly, and only a few can be conducted when sufficient funds are made available by the sponsoring agencies. Research focusing on broader topics, such as employment, health and function, and community integration are good examples of this socioecological model of disability. Successfully addressing the many methodological challenges inherent to this conceptual approach is vital to the scientific progress of rehabilitation and disability studies as a discipline of study.

ETHNOCULTURAL INFLUENCES ON REHABILITATION OUTCOMES

By the year 2050, approximately 47% of the U.S. population will be underserved populations, particularly individuals from racial and ethnic populations (Day, 1996). The predicted demographic shift suggests a need to examine the specific needs of underserved racial and ethnic populations. Researchers have found that these populations' experiences in the rehabilitation system are distinctly different from those of their Caucasian counterparts (Capella, 2002; Wilson, Alston, Harley, & Mitchell, 2002). However, research exploring the relationships among race, ethnicity, and rehabilitation outcomes is inconclusive regarding the influence of race and ethnicity. It is unclear whether these factors are determinants of outcomes or whether differential outcomes continue to persist following the institution of policy and legislative mandates to alleviate inequitable treatment of underserved populations, especially in publicly funded rehabilitation programs.

NEED FOR INTERDISCIPLINARY COLLABORATION

Work being conducted in various fields of knowledge, including cell and molecular biology, neuroscience, general rehabilitation, cognitive rehabilitation, bioengineering, biomechanics, gerontology, psychology, nursing, public health, and others, must be integrated to best address the needs of persons with disabilities. Although specific needs may vary according to disability-specific diagnosis (e.g., spinal cord injury, traumatic brain injury, stroke), many common issues exist (e.g., aging, secondary conditions) that can benefit from past and current collaborations across disciplines. Cross-fertilization of ideas among the various disciplines interested in common problems from different perspectives can certainly facilitate the generation of common knowledge. The process can be further enhanced by expanding collaborations beyond national lines. Research that takes advantage of learning from other environments, for example, in countries whose populations are aging at a faster rate than in the United States, can prove very helpful. Multiple geographical and cultural settings may need to be studied to achieve sufficient variation in environmental and policy variables for investigators to study their associations with behavior.

Rapid changes across health care, juxtaposed against continuous scientific advances in neurosciences, bioengineering, and genetics, raise urgent questions about the efficacy and effectiveness of current interventions for persons with disabilities. What interventions are best? How can health care providers be sure that a specific intervention is both appropriate and of high quality? How can those in need afford to pay for these interventions? This line of questions suggests the need for efficacy research examining whether a particular intervention has a specific measurable effect and also addressing questions concerning safety, feasibility, and appropriateness. These questions also emphasize the importance of effectiveness research to identify whether efficacious interventions can have a measurable, beneficial effect when used by those with different disabling conditions. Consistent with the socioecological model, research on disability and rehabilitation needs to focus on service systems. This includes the cost of various care options to an entire system; the use of incentives to promote optimal access to care; and the effect of legislation, regulation, and other public policies on organizations and on the delivery of services. In this respect, a service system must have a strong method for understanding the clinical nature of an individual's impairment and its functional limitations and barriers to full participation. Study designs for research on service systems should incorporate elements of intervention efficacy as described above.

CONCLUSION

Professionals generally agree that the ultimate goal of research on disability and rehabilitation is to improve the lives of persons with disabilities. Depending on the selected paradigm, professionals are less likely to agree on what groups determine how to define improvement and what is, thus, a relevant and viable researchable question. It is clear that the new socioe-cological paradigm first requires the input of consumers and their families and that this should be followed by the input of practitioners and other professionals working with them.

Over the past 50 years, the choice of priorities for research on reha-bilitation and disability has gone in waves, with the impetus coming more from legislative activities and funding sources than from serious reflection on the state of knowledge or from solid theoretical or conceptual under-pinnings (Olkin, 1999). An important role for research on disability and rehabilitation in addressing this limitation is, thus, to offer the method-ological means to develop, evaluate, and refine safe and efficacious inter-ventions designed to improve the lives of persons with disabilities. How-ever, this effort is in many ways contingent on development of improved methodologies for measuring disability, which is another important role for research. Unlike basic research, research on relevant interventions and services demands the broadest possible levels of interest and participation on the part of psychologists, nurses, physicians, occupational therapists, physical therapists, rehabilitation engineers, policymakers, and especially those who will consume these services.

However, interdisciplinary research efforts to illuminate the trans-actions between people and their environments, as well as the impacts of these transactions on human functioning, are somewhat thwarted by the paucity of standard measures that adequately capture the dynamic intersection of the individual and contextual environments. Although the conceptual framework of the new paradigm has helped to advance disabil-ity and rehabilitation research, the reliability of measures of disability are complicated by the person—environment conceptual framework. Inter-disciplinary research can help improve the methodologies for measuring disability by addressing the basic requirement of identifying and separat-ing measures of the impact of the environment from measures of ability and by "disentangling true change in individual functioning and the so-cial and environmental contexts" (Mathiowetz & Gooloo, 2000, p. 30). Currently, the lack of experience with collecting survey data that separate these factors is a potential source of error in research. "Little is known about how ability (capacity) is measured independent of environmental context (participation) in research" (Mathiowetz & Gooloo, 2000, p. 39).

As the new paradigm of disability postulates, a socioecological per-spective provides a distinctive framework by which the transactions be-tween people and their environments, and the impacts of these transac-tions on human functioning, can be best conceptualized. As such, this approach is extremely valuable in addressing the many concerns of con-sumers and psychologists (with and without disabilities) working in the health and rehabilitation fields.

Advances in research can help to strengthen the thesis that disability is a social phenomenon largely shaped by the environment and can downplay the characterization of disability as individual deficit. The socioecological framework contests the perspective of the medical model and raises issues about the implications of the socioecological model for future training, research, and interventions. By revisiting the many issues associated with the medical model and addressing critical problems associated with the lack of understanding of the disability phenomenon within the context of a socioecological—biopsycological framework, psychologists can play a critical role in improving rehabilitation outcomes.

However, the current mainstream of psychology has tended to relegate disability and chronic illness to a peripheral area of concern and to subspecialties such as rehabilitation psychology. This practice has posed a significant challenge for psychology because they are in an environment where the consumer is increasingly challenging policymakers, demanding that providers be knowledgeable about disability, and questioning systems that deny access and prevent full integration of individuals with disabilities into the community.

REFERENCES

Azar, B. (1998a, May). Melding expertise, furthering research. *APA Monitor, 29*(5), 1, 16.

Azar, B. (1998b, May). Sharing data with other fields yields important discoveries. *APA Monitor, 29*(5), 14–15.

Capella, M. E. (2002). Inequities in the VR system: Do they still exist? *Rehabilitation Counseling Bulletin, 45*, 143–153.

Day, J. C. (1996). *Population projections of the United States by age, sex, race, and Hispanic origin: 1995–2050* (U.S. Bureau of the Census Current Population Rep. No. P25-1130). Washington, DC: U.S. Government Printing Office.

DeJong, G. (1983). Defining and implementing the independent living concept. In N. Crewe & I. Zola (Eds.), *Independent living for physically disabled people* (pp. 4–27). San Francisco: Jossey-Bass.

DeJong, G., & Hughes, J. (1982). Independent living: Methodology for measuring long-term outcomes. *Archives of Physical Medicine and Rehabilitation, 63*(1), 68–73.

Dembo, T. (1974). The paths to useful knowledge. *Rehabilitation Psychology, 21*, 124–128.

Engel, G. (1977, April 8). The need for a new medical model: A challenge to biomedicine. *Science, 196*, 129–136.

Fine, M., & Asch, A. (1988). Disability beyond stigma: Social, interaction, discrimination, and activism. *Journal of Social Issues, 44*, 3–21.

Hahn, H. (1991). Alternative views of empowerment: Social services and civil rights. *Journal of Rehabilitation, 57*, 17–19.

Kerlinger, F. N. (1979). *Behavioral research: A conceptual approach.* New York: Holt, Rinehart, & Winston.

Mathiowetz, N., & Gooloo, S. W. (2000). *Survey measurement of work disability.* Washington, DC: National Academy Press.

Meyerson, L. (1988). The social psychology of physical disability: 1948 and 1988. *Journal of Social Issues, 44,* 173–188

Moos, R. H. (1979). Social—ecological perspectives on health. In G. C. Stone, F. Cohen, & N. E. Adler (Eds.), *Health psychology: A handbook* (pp. 259–275). San Francisco: Jossey-Bass.

Olkin, R. (1999). *What psychotherapists should know about disability.* New York: Guilford Press.

Rimmer, J. H. (1999). Health promotion for people with disabilities: The emerging paradigm shift from disability prevention to prevention of secondary conditions. *Physical Therapy, 70,* 495–502.

Scotch, R. K. (1988). Disability as the basis for a social movement: Advocacy and the politics of definition. *Journal of Social Issues, 44,* 159–172.

Tate, D. G. (2000, November). *Participatory action research: Including consumers on your team.* presented at the Assistive Technology Research and Development: NIH/Whitaker Workshop, Chicago, Illinois.

Trieschmann, R. (1987). *Aging with a disability.* New York: Demos.

U.S. Department of Education, Office of Special Education and Rehabilitative Services, National Institute on Disability and Rehabilitation Research. (2000). *Long range plan: 1999–2003.* Washington, DC: Author.

Verbrugge, L. M., & Jette, A. M. (1994). The disablement process. *Social Science Medicine, 38,* 1–14.

Wade, D. T., & DeJong, B. A. (2000). Recent advances in rehabilitation. *British Medical Journal, 320,* 1385–1388.

Willems, E. (1977). Behavioral ecology. In D. Stokols (Ed.), *Perspectives on environment and behavior* (pp. 259–275). New York: Plenum Press.

Wilson, K. B., Alston, R. J., Harley, D. A., & Mitchell, N. A. (2002). Predicting VR acceptance based on race, gender, education, work status at application, and primary source of support at application. *Rehabilitation Counseling Bulletin, 45,* 132–142.

World Health Organization. (1980). *International Classification of Impairments, Disabilities, and Handicaps* (Rev. ed.). Geneva, Switzerland: Author.

Zimmerman, M. A., & Warschausky, S. (1998). Empowerment theory for rehabilitation research: Conceptual and methodological issues. *Rehabilitation Psychology, 43,* 3–16.

CHAPTER FOUR

Transforming Psychological Practice and Society

Policies That Reflect the New Paradigm

Carol J. Gill, Donald G. Kewman, and Ruth W. Brannon

In the last three decades, women, African Americans, gay, lesbian, and bisexual people, and others from socially marginalized communities have urged psychologists to attend to the social determinants of human inequality, thus challenging and sometimes unseating historically dominant theories of biological difference (Jenkins & Ramsey, 1991; Sleek, 1999; Trickett, Watts, & Birman, 1994; Vasquez & Eldridge, 1994). This shift in emphasis from biological to sociopolitical explanations of group disadvantage has generated critical changes in psychology's policy orientation toward minority groups. For example, diagnostic classification has been revised to depathologize homosexuality and to eliminate gender stereotypes. In addition, the American Psychological Association (APA) has initiated a variety of policy advocacy efforts on behalf of women and other minority groups to address social issues such as abuse, hate crimes, access to AIDS treatment, educational equity, and minority discrimination in American institutions.

As people with disabilities mobilize to oppose discriminatory practices and social exclusion, they, too, challenge psychology to consider the sociopolitical foundations of their disadvantaged status (Asch, 1998; Olkin, 1999). Many call for adoption of the new paradigm of disability, that is, the shift from viewing disability as a medical problem located completely in the individual to viewing disability as a limitation produced by the complex interaction between individual difference and the social environment (DePoy, 2002; Hahn, 1996). Congress's recognition of people with disabilities as a "discrete and insular minority" group in the Americans With Disabilities Act ([ADA] § 2(a)(7)) in 1990 provided legal affirmation of the social basis of disability and inspired a heuristic change in psychology's approach to research, practice, and advocacy for persons with disabilities and their families. Implications for research and clinical practice are addressed in other chapters in this special section. This chapter focuses primarily on policy implications of the new paradigm, including recent public policy developments that invite the involvement of psychologists in new or expanded roles and potential policy changes within the discipline that guide its orientation to the disability community.

For purposes of this discussion, policy can be defined as "a definite course or method of action selected from among alternatives and in light of given conditions to guide and determine present and future decisions" (*Merriam-Webster's Collegiate Dictionary*, 1998, p. 901, definition 2a). Policies are influenced by sociopolitical events and changing cultural norms. In the sections below, we examine how psychologists can help implement national policy agendas such as those expressed in the ADA. We also explore the potential impact of the new paradigm on policies within psychology that guide training, consulting, and advocacy, as well as formal organizational and disciplinary policies (see Rhoda Olkin & Constance Pledger's [2003] chapter in this issue for a discussion of the impact of the new paradigm on assessment and treatment). Finally, we discuss how national policy decisions such as those associated with reimbursement may affect the ability of psychologists to practice and receive training within a new-paradigm framework. Throughout these sections, we highlight some of the points of controversy prompted by the new paradigm of disability that remain open to illumination from the field.

BACKGROUND

The intersection of psychology, disability, and policy is not completely new subject matter for this journal. The May 1984 issue of the *American Psychologist* featured several chapters addressing psychology's orientation to disability issues (see, e.g., Asch, 1984; Task Force on Psychology and the Handicapped, 1984). Among major themes presented in that issue were recommendations urging psychologists to focus greater attention on the handicapping impact of social arrangements and practices in their research, training, and service activities. Several policy issues regarding psychology as a discipline were highlighted, including the importance of improving access for disabled participants at professional meetings and in training programs, educating psychologists about their own disability biases, ensuring inclusion of psychologists with disabilities in APA governance, supporting the advancement of psychologists with disabilities in professional careers, and rejecting terminology or measures that unnecessarily categorize or stereotype people with disabilities. Psychology's contribution to policy issues extending beyond the borders of the discipline also was discussed, including the importance of supporting "freer access to education" (Task Force on Psychology and the Handicapped, 1984, p. 550) for persons with disabilities and the need to oppose social practices that unfairly discriminate against and segregate disabled citizens.

In June of 1990, the year that the ADA became law, the *American Psychologist* published another set of chapters, this time examining, in a rather broad sense, the ways in which policies associated with disability and rehabilitation research could be converted into action in the clinical setting, in training mechanisms, and in the public arena (see, e.g., Elliott & Gramling, 1990; Solarz, 1990). Other topics included the potential impact of reimbursement on rehabilitation psychologists and the need to improve psychologist training by providing more information on disability. The section concluded with a call for psychologists to develop a legislative agenda to track and influence legislation ranging from reimbursement for rehabilitation psychologists to distribution of assistive technology.

Today—almost two decades after the publication of the first set of these historically significant chapters and a decade after publication of the second set—most of the recommendations remain relevant. Arguably, they are more compelling than ever given the new paradigm's emphasis on the interaction between individual and environment and the importance of self-determination for people with disabilities as a social group. Viewing disability in social context suggests significant opportunities to reframe the way psychologists define problems related to disability, the emerging relationships between psychologists and people with disabilities, and psychologists' professional responsibilities with respect to people with disabilities. All of these changes convey important policy implications.

REFRAMING DISABILITY AND DISABILITY PROBLEMS

Historically, psychology has approached disability as the study of the so-called atypical individual. Accordingly, research and intervention traditionally focused on individual adaptation to functional loss or limitation, with the goal of containing the negative impact of impairment so that persons with disabilities could function as normally as possible (Wright, 1960). In the 1970s, disability scholars and activists began to reframe disability as a socially constructed disadvantage predicated on, but not inevitably caused by, physical and mental differences (Linton, 1998). Drawing parallels to race and gender, these advocates called for a relocation of disability from the narrow domain of individual biology to the broader realm of society and its practices and beliefs. The resulting conceptual framework in all its variants—such as the social model in the United Kingdom (Oliver, 1996) and the minority group model in the United States (Hahn, 1985; Longmore, 1985)—is often referred to as the new paradigm of disability. These new models of disability bear some resemblance to ecological frameworks that have posited a person-versus-environment interaction (Nagi, 1991). However, although ecological frameworks indicate that the environment mediates the consequences of an individual's functional differences (through barriers or accommodations), those differences still are deemed aberrant or abnormal at the level of individual functioning. In contrast, the new models treat both disability and normality ontologically as socially constructed statuses. New-paradigm proponents acknowledge physical or mental impairment as a common aspect of human experience and view persons with disabilities as hindered primarily not by their intrinsic differences but by society's response to those differences. In a sense, then, the new paradigm is compatible with viewing disability as a policy-linked phenomenon in that disability is determined significantly by social practices and underlying values.

The opportunities afforded by the disability paradigm shift may include new problems to address, innovative approaches to intervention, and more venues for practice. The new paradigm beckons psychologists to examine dynamic interactions between individuals with disabilities and their families, immediate environments, systems, public policies, culture, and society. Furthermore, as the understanding of disability increasingly highlights the importance of social, cultural, political, and economic determinants, disability ceases to be primarily the concern of rehabilitation or clinical psychologists and becomes a widely relevant dimension of human experience. Psychology's adoption of the new disability paradigm would further expand the discipline's focus on problems beyond the clinic to encompass social intervention, including issues of access, empowerment, and inclusion.

REFRAMING RELATIONSHIPS WITH CONSUMERS

A significant impact of the new disability paradigm—one that has been challenging to many professionals—is the increasing participation of consumers in decision making and policy setting affecting their lives. This change reflects several recent developments in the status of citizens with disabilities and patients' rights in health care settings. First, the contemporary disability rights movement and the anti-discrimination legislation it has fostered have increased the public presence of people with disabilities and their agency in their own affairs, including the services they seek from professionals (Boyce, 1998). Second, as they become more sophisticated about the sociopolitical dynamics of disability, advocates with disabilities and their professional allies are increasingly dissatisfied with service models that reinforce client passivity or power inequities between provider and recipient (Boyce, 1998; Krogh, 1998). Third, as people with disabilities are increasingly recognized as a social minority community, there is growing appreciation of the importance of including the disability cultural perspective in the planning and delivery of services (Kosciulek, 1999; Longmore, 1995).

Increased consumer participation has the potential to affect long-standing practices and policies regarding psychological services. Some of these changes acknowledge the importance of the consumer in decision making, some reflect a redistribution of power between the consumer and the professional, and some raise important ethical issues about the role of psychologists in determining an individual's need for treatment or protection.

For instance, peer advocacy is an important form of consumer involvement in service settings. It has been institutionalized since the 1970s in the network of hundreds of disability resource centers, referred to as centers for independent living (CILs), throughout the country run by and for people with disabilities. To the extent that rehabilitation psychologists have recognized that some of the most effective strategies for improving quality of life are those that promote participation and environmental accommodation, they have developed collaborations between such community agencies and medical systems (Tate & Forchheimer, 1998). Peer counselors trained by the CILs regularly co-teach rehabilitation patient and family education classes on independent living topics in the hospital setting with medical center professional staff. They also make individual contacts with rehabilitation outpatients and their families or significant friends to provide support and guidance as individuals with recent disabilities reestablish themselves in the community following discharge from the hospital.

Another important form of consumer involvement is the participation of people with disabilities in the formal development and implementation of service programs. For example, the Health Resource Center for Women With Disabilities at the Rehabilitation Institute of Chicago, Illinois, is a genuine professional–consumer partnership that evolved from a series of meetings between women with disabilities seeking accessible women's health services and a group of health and mental health professionals who wished to improve services to their disabled women clients (Gill, Kirschner, & Panko Reis, 1994). Today, the center is codirected by a rehabilitation physician and by an administrative executive who is an advocate from the disabled women's community. A community board of women with disabilities provides substantive direction and support for the center's programs, which include gynecological services, counseling, research, education, peer support, and peer mentoring. This center and efforts like it serve as templates for integrating consumer direction in clinical services.

A final example of a consumer advocacy initiative that has been controversial and that may have a profound impact on practice policies is the psychiatric survivors movement. On March 25, 2000, a collective of individuals with psychiatric disabilities issued a public statement calling for a mental health system that is founded on "self-determination, respect, ethical behavior, and humane voluntary services and supports" ("Highlander Statement of Concern and Call to Action," 2000, ¶ 4). This group, like other disability advocates, endorsed better utilization of peer support and equitable professional–consumer partnerships in the delivery of professional services. They asked psychologists and other health professionals to acknowledge the history that has often thwarted self-determination for persons with disabilities and mental health needs and to help establish policies favoring voluntary collaborative service models that centralize consumer choice over more restrictive expert-centered models.

The key to the success of delivery systems that promote participation is joint consumer–professional development of these systems. This collaboration is likely not only to lead to systems of care that are more responsive to consumer needs but also to increase consumer empowerment. As Iscoe (1974) pointed out more than 25 years ago, this kind of collaboration can lead to power realignment between professionals and consumers. Furthermore, successful programs can lead to reduced reliance on professional assistance. Indeed, the new paradigm of disability invites psychologists to expand opportunities for consumer participation in the planning, development, implementation, and evaluation of psychology practice programs. This approach promotes the inclusion of people with disabilities and improves access to those sociopolitical decision-making activities that influence quality of life. This approach may also expand concepts of practice venues to include not only health care settings but also home, school, workplace, and settings where public policy is made.

REFRAMING THE RESPONSIBILITIES OF PSYCHOLOGISTS REGARDING DISABILITY ISSUES

In addition to influencing the way psychologists frame disability problems and approach relationships with consumers, the new paradigm implies new responsibilities for psychologists that can be incorporated in policies guiding professional activities. Because people with disabilities represent almost 20% of the U.S. population (LaPlante & Carlson, 1996), psychologists may need to reconsider the tradition of viewing the disability community as a special population and, instead, consciously include persons with disabilities in all aspects of their work with the general population. For example, research investigators could provide access to their procedures and materials, including recruitment announcements and consent forms, to persons with physical, sensory, intellectual, and other disabilities. Services that welcome individuals with disabilities as clients, family members, and professional consultants are likely to be most highly sought after by consumers. The new disability paradigm also affects psychologists' roles and responsibilities as advocates, teachers, and consultants.

Role of Psychologists in Implementing Disability Policy Agendas

To examine further the relationship between the new paradigm and policy issues for psychologists, it is critical to look at important public policy initiatives in the disability arena and to think about how these provide opportunities and challenges to psychologists in many settings. The disability rights activism that undergirds these policy developments beckons community psychologists interested in empowerment, social psychologists interested in public attitudes toward marginalized groups, and political psychologists interested in the development of political movements. New laws for individuals with disabilities have expanded the potential role of psychologists in the public sector. For example, consulting and advocacy efforts will be vitalized by advances in disability policy and law mandating inclusive education and nondiscriminatory employment practices.

Policies on school inclusion require sophisticated psychological assessments and consultations to negotiate the best and least restrictive fit between a student's needs and the school system's resources. The Individuals With Disabilities Education Act (IDEA) amendments of 1997 focused on raising academic expectations for children with disabilities while increasing the involvement of regular education teachers, parents, and disabled students themselves in the academic assessment and goal-setting process. These advances challenge school psychologists to keep abreast of governmental inclusion mandates and their implications for special education assessment and instruction. More specifically, the current movement for reform in special education has focused on such goals as (a) promoting instructionally valid assessment techniques, (b) providing access to service without labels, (c) addressing child and family assets rather than deficits, and (d) fostering the achievement of quality outcomes through high expectations and empirically validated instructional techniques (Telzrow, 1999). Children with disabilities are living in an exciting era in which inclusion mandates and technology access can allow them to join their siblings and neighborhood friends in their local schools rather than being placed in separate settings. Psychologists who provide assessment of educational disabilities enter a challenging and often controversial arena of shifting diagnostic constructs and classification criteria (Reschly, 1999). This is important work that offers professionals the opportunity to help define and validate concepts and techniques in a practice area that affects the futures of a significant portion of the student population.

Laws banning discrimination against persons with disabilities in work settings and public services open up new areas for research and consulting in organizational psychology. For instance, the ADA not only mandated access to public accommodations but also offered protections from employment discrimination to persons with disabilities. Psychologists may find opportunities to consult in the determination of reasonable workplace accommodation for persons with psychiatric, learning, and intellectual disabilities (Foote, 2000) and to provide expert testimony in employment discrimination cases (Goodman-Delahunty, 2000). Psychologists also have an essential role in evaluating neurological, learning, and psychological impairments and function as part of the process of determining reasonable accommodation for both students and employees with disabilities.

Laudably, the APA has a long history of taking strong public positions in opposition to discrimination and in support of programs serving minority interests. Sometimes, as in APA's (1998) position paper on hate crimes, disabled people are included among the affected groups; however, there are opportunities for psychology to offer more support for just and beneficial public policies affecting people with disabilities. For example, psychologists could participate in providing amicus briefs, congressional testimony, APA board resolutions, position papers, and fact sheets regarding the psychological and social importance of school inclusion, workplace accommodation, and funding for assistive technology to promote the dignity and self-determination of disabled citizens. Legislative efforts to fund affordable in-home personal assistance services as a dignified alternative to nursing home placement have been advocated vigorously over the past decade by such national disability rights groups as American

Disabled for Attendant Programs Today (ADAPT). These efforts would be strengthened by the increased public support of psychologists who can attest to the benefits of community living versus institutional confinement. In addition to these particular advocacy responsibilities, all psychologists would benefit from learning more about the social experience of disability consistent with APA's policies on promoting cultural competency in activities within the discipline. Psychologists can be instrumental in facilitating the incorporation of new-paradigm concepts and language in guidelines and policies established within the discipline and beyond its borders.

Impact of the New Paradigm on Training Policies

Many disabled advocates and scholars have been calling attention to a deficit in professional training regarding disability, particularly with respect to the voices and culture of the disability community. Addressing this deficiency requires policy decisions on several levels, including decisions about curricula, accommodation needs of psychologists with disabilities, and the impact of national funding policies on training for psychologists.

The idea that life with a disability can be a distinct cultural experience or the basis of a positive minority identity is rarely represented in psychology training. Yet, in the "Ethical Principles of Psychologists and Code of Conduct" published by APA in 2002, disability is listed along with race, gender, age, sexual orientation, and other dimensions of human diversity that may require specialized training and experience to ensure professional competence. Consideration of individual differences, social factors, cultural influences, and ethical values is implicitly and explicitly part of psychology training of all types and levels. There has been recognition by rehabilitation psychologists that having a disability has a number of social and psychological effects. The challenge of how this information can be incorporated more universally into psychology training programs and curriculum remains.

Meeting this challenge requires examination of training policies at the university and professional level. It is important to develop policies and methods that provide the perspective of persons with a disability through readings, videos, and opportunities for instruction and discussion with individuals who have disabilities. Psychology departments can adopt policies to promote the recruitment and retention of faculty with disabilities, incorporating such goals within broader diversity initiatives. Some universities have disability studies programs with readily available coursework that can be included in psychology training programs (Kasnitz, Bonney, Aftandelian, & Bromfield, 2000). Other relevant curriculum sources are courses in sociology (including the sociology of minority groups) and anthropology.

Increasingly, undergraduate programs offer community service opportunities. These can involve working in disability advocacy organizations and CILs or assisting persons who have a disability with daily activities. Visits to the homes of persons with a disability allow the trainee to appreciate better the daily life of and the effect of a home environment on individuals with disabilities and their families. Training experiences in school settings with the special education population are sometimes overlooked as possible clerkship placements in clinical training programs. These training experiences provide an important general exposure to social and environmental aspects of disability experience. Recognizing the importance of these experiences in training programs may require changes in existing policies about what constitutes appropriate curricula for psychologists.

Another policy concern is the extent to which training programs are accessible to disabled students. ADA requirements provide equal access to training programs for students with disabilities. Responsibilities of training programs extend beyond the need for ramps and other components of structural access and include student recruitment, ongoing programmatic supports, and the provision of training materials and assignments in formats accessible to blind, hearing-impaired, and learning-disabled students. A particularly entrenched problem is that few textbooks and journal chapters are readily available to blind or learning-disabled students who rely on alternative formats such as Braille or online text formats that can be translated by specialized software. In view of the pervasiveness of digital technology in publishing today, this access barrier could be ameliorated through the establishment of policies, such as those adopted by the state of California, requiring publishers to provide their materials in electronic format in addition to conventional hard-copy or inaccessible online formats. Understandably, it is disconcerting to psychology students with disabilities to know that the solution to text access is readily achievable yet rarely provided. The APA and state psychology organizations can adopt resolutions supporting the rights of disabled students and professionals to alternate formats and urging publishers to cooperate with that goal. Such organizations also can encourage academic psychologists and training program administrators to include access as an essential consideration in developing reading assignments. Until such standards are established, it will be difficult to ensure consistent answers to such questions as "If this individual receives reasonable accommodation for disability-related limitations, is she/he otherwise qualified to serve as a psychologist?" The issue of accessibility standards is an important policy consideration at both the university and the professional levels.

The training of psychologists with disabilities confronts the discipline with major internal policy issues. Instances of overt discrimination against psychology students with physical disabilities seeking positions in training programs have been reported (Hauser, Maxwell-McCaw, Leigh, & Gutman, 2000). Discrimination against individuals with mental disabilities (cognitive, emotional, or behavioral) provides another set of challenges, including questions about what constitutes a reasonable accommodation and how to gauge the effect of the disability on professional functioning (Hadley, 1998). For instance, for a trainee with dyslexia or an expressive writing disorder, it may be difficult to decide whether the capacity to read or produce written communications constitutes an essential skill necessary for clinical practice or whether allowing someone to read to her or him or take dictation is a reasonable accommodation. Another example may be a trainee with attention-deficit/hyperactivity disorder that, although treated with medication, still interferes with listening comprehension and the organization of written expression. What is the role of the program in altering expectations of the trainee's performance, suggesting assistive devices, or helping the trainee to develop compensatory strategies to reduce the effect of the impairment on functioning? Laws such as IDEA, mandating nondiscriminatory public education for students with disabilities, and ADA have focused attention on this issue (Crewe, 1994).

There are some examples of programs that affirmatively recruit trainees with a disability. One example is the APA-approved predoctoral internship training in Psychology and the Deaf Population that is part of the Deaf Wellness Center at the University of Rochester's Department of Psychiatry (Pollard, 1996). The APA Committee on Disability Issues in Psychology (CDIP) is piloting a mentoring program for psychology graduate students and professionals with disabilities. In addition, CDIP and APA's committee on psychological tests and assessments have identified issues that relate to the use of testing materials by psychologists with disabilities as well as their applications to clients with disabilities (APA CDIP, personal communication, April 6, 1999). For many psychologists, interns, and students with disabilities, the new paradigm validates their conviction that their productivity and competence are limited not by individual differences but by narrowly constructed standards and environmental obstacles. It is this set of humanly constructed impediments that most urgently calls for redress through policy development.

Effect of External Policies on Integration of New-Paradigm Approaches

Reimbursement policies of both private and public sector payers may affect the rate at which new-paradigm principles become incorporated into practice and training activities of psychologists. Until recently, there was steady growth in clinical training opportunities for health psychologists, neuropsychologists, and rehabilitation psychologists at the internship and postdoctoral level. With ever-tightening health care budgets, limited federal funding for psychology training, and Medicare regulations that restrict billing by trainees, a decline in training opportunities for rehabilitation psychologists is beginning to occur. This decline may likely have a serious impact on the field's ability to expand curricula to reflect disability perspectives and disability culture and to move outside traditional clinical settings for training activities. Fortunately, there may be two new sources of training funds. First, the Graduate Psychology Education program was approved by Congress in December 2001. It will support programs that train psychologists to work with underserved populations, such as older persons, children, rural communities, victims of terror and abuse, and people with disabilities or chronic illnesses (Murray, 2002). Second, the APA is working with Congress and the Department of Health and Human Services (HHS) to promulgate regulations that will extend graduate medical education funding to psychology internship programs. HHS has interpreted existing rules to allow hospital-based postdoctoral programs that are APA approved to apply for funding from Medicare's Graduate Medical Education program, the main source of federal government funding for training health professionals (Daw, 2002). Advocacy efforts by psychologists are needed to refine and expand the use of these funds for different training venues.

Similarly, reimbursement affects practice. The ability to extend the application of psychological services to promote social participation and environmental accommodation depends on funding policies that encourage these efforts. Reimbursement for psychological services is almost exclusively funded by third-party payment for services that are oriented toward reducing psychopathology in individuals. This medical-model-driven reimbursement system requires psychologists to record a reimbursable diagnosis to be paid for and to focus therapeutic efforts on ameliorating psychopathology. Consequently, psychologists sometimes feel compelled to downplay their appreciation of the importance of broader strategies that they use to promote individual adaptation, as well as environmental and social accommodations.

It remains an ongoing challenge for psychology to justify the overall social and individual benefits of environmental and social interventions to payers. Efforts to work in an integrated fashion with physical health providers are sometimes further hampered by carve-outs that separately manage mental health services and by a lack of parity for payment for such services. The future suggests that a reverse trend is beginning to occur with carve-ins and efforts to seek mental health parity through legislation (Kiesler, 2000). However, these forces may be further battered by the effects of the prospective payment system for inpatient rehabilitation facilities that was implemented January 1, 2002, for Medicare beneficiaries. Facilities are now paid a lump sum for each Medicare patient, similar to the way hospitals are reimbursed for other acute inpatient medical patients. Because a large portion of individuals with physical disabilities and chronic medical problems are Medicare beneficiaries, this change may have a negative impact on access to rehabilitation services and could result in poorer rehabilitation outcomes in terms of functional independence (Hagglund, Kewman, & Ashkanazi, 2000). On the positive side, these changes could facilitate the growth of community-based programs emphasizing prevention and health promotion that are integral to patients' long-term success and to cost control (DeJong, 1997). Psychologists have an important role to play in advocating for a seamless continuum of care for persons with disabilities.

CONCLUDING THOUGHTS

Psychologists, as well as others who are viewed as mental health professionals, have sometimes been seen as serving an ancillary or peripheral role in the health care system. In recent years, psychologists have striven to broaden the field's identity by conducting research and providing services in more medically related arenas via health, pediatric, and rehabilitation psychology, and neuropsychology. A potential drawback of this expanded identity as a health care profession is the possibility of becoming too closely aligned with a biomedical model that emphasizes an impairment- or pathology-oriented perspective of disability. Fortunately, the continued infusion of multiple conceptual models in the training of psychologists is an important buffer to this tendency.

Indeed, adherents of the new paradigm of disability call on psychology to further strengthen training that provides sociological, anthropological, humanistic, and social policy perspectives related to disability. With this broader perspective, psychologists can collaborate with consumers to construct policies and services that bridge the gap between policymakers and persons with disabilities. However, the more immediate and realistic challenge of the new paradigm is to create opportunities for greater consumer involvement in the design and delivery of a broader continuum of services that makes possible full social participation of persons with a disability. To accomplish this task will require the building of stronger coalitions between organized psychology and consumer groups to promote disability policy enlightened by the knowledge and perspectives of the groups involved. Mutual suspicions, prejudices, and biases of these groups will necessarily result in a bumpy relationship that can only be sustained by perseverance and the understanding that such broad-based efforts are more likely to bring about significant advances in disability policy. Coalitions that have included organized psychology have successfully advocated for major social policy initiatives such as IDEA, ADA, and Ticket to Work and Work Incentives Improvement Act (1999). Similar broad-based coalitions are needed to advance other pressing policy initiatives such as in-home personal care assistance and Medicare prescription benefits.

REFERENCES

American Psychological Association. (1998). *Hate crimes today: An age-old foe in modern dress.* Washington, DC: Author.

American Psychological Association. (2002). Ethical principles of psychologists and code of conduct. *American Psychologist, 57,* 1060–1073.

Americans With Disabilities Act, 42 U.S.C. § 12101 et seq. (1990).

Asch, A. (1984). The experience of disability: a challenge for psychology. *American Psychologist, 39,* 529–536.

Asch, A. (1998). Distracted by disability. *Cambridge Quarterly of Health-care Ethics, 7,* 77–87.

Boyce, W. (1998). Participation of disability advocates in research partnerships with health professionals. *Canadian Journal of Rehabilitation, 12,* 85–93.

Crewe, N. M. (1994). Implications of the Americans with Disabilities Act for the training of psychologists. *Rehabilitation Education, 8,* 9–16.

Daw, J. (2002, January). Some psychology postdoc programs now qualify for federal financial support. *Monitor on Psychology, 33*(1), 19.

DeJong, G. (1997). Primary care for persons with disabilities: An overview of the problem. *American Journal of Physical Medicine and Rehabilitation,* 76(Suppl.), S2–S8.

DePoy, E. (2002). Will the real definition of disability please stand up. *Psychosocial Process, 15,* 50–53.

Elliott, T. R., & Gramling, S. E. (1990). Psychologists and rehabilitation: New roles and old training models. *American Psychologist, 45,* 762–765.

Foote, W. E. (2000). A model for psychological consultation in cases involving the Americans With Disabilities Act. *Professional Psychology: Research and Practice, 31,* 190–196.

Gill, C. J., Kirschner, K., & Panko Reis, J. (1994). Health services for women with disabilities: Barriers and portals. In A. J. Dan (Ed.), *Reframing women's health: Multidisciplinary research and practice* (pp. 357–366). Thousand Oaks, CA: Sage.

Goodman-Delahunty, J. (2000). Psychological impairment under the Americans With Disabilities Act: Legal guidelines. *Professional Psychology: Research and Practice, 31,* 197–205.

Hadley, R. L. (1998). The Americans With Disabilities Act of 1990: Faculty and student perceptions of reasonable accommodations versus competency in graduate psychology programs. *Dissertation Abstracts International: Section B. The Sciences & Engineering, 58*(11-B), 6235.

Hagglund, K. J., Kewman, D. G., & Ashkanazi, G. S. (2000). Medicare and prospective payment systems. In R. G. Frank & T. R. Elliott (Eds.), *Handbook of rehabilitation psychology* (pp. 603–614). Washington, DC: American Psychological Association.

Hahn, H. (1985). Toward a politics of disability: Definitions, disciplines, and policies. *Social Science Journal, 22,* 87–105.

Hahn, H. (1996). Antidiscrimination laws and social research on disability: The minority group perspective. *Behavioral Sciences and the Law, 14,* 41–59.

Hauser, P. C., Maxwell-McCaw, D. L., Leigh, I. W., & Gutman, V. A. (2000). Internship accessibility issues for deaf and hard-of-hearing applications: No cause for complacency. *Professional Psychology: Research and Practice, 31,* 569–574.

Highlander statement of concern and call to action. (2000). Retrieved March 25, 2003, from http://www.narpa.org/highlander.htm

Individuals With Disabilities Education Act Amendments of 1997, 20 U.S.C. ch. 33 (1997).

Iscoe, I. (1974). Community psychology and the competent community. *American Psychologist, 29,* 607–613.

Jenkins, J. O., & Ramsey, G. A. (1991). Minorities. In M. Hersen, A. E. Kazdin, & A. S. Bellack (Eds.), *Clinical psychology handbook* (2nd ed., pp. 724–740). Elmsford, NY: Pergamon Press.

Kasnitz, D., Bonney, S., Aftandelian, R., & Bromfield, I. (2000). *A survey of disability studies programs at colleges and universities.* Oakland, CA: Rehabilitation Research and Training Center on Independent Living and Disability Policy, World Institute on Disability.

Kiesler, C. A. (2000). The next wave of change for psychology and mental health services in the health care revolution. *American Psychologist, 55,* 481–487.

Kosciulek, J. F. (1999). The consumer-directed theory of empowerment. *Rehabilitation Counseling Bulletin, 42,* 196–213.

Krogh, K. (1998). A conceptual framework of community partnerships: Perspectives of people with disabilities on power, beliefs and values. *Canadian Journal of Rehabilitation, 12,* 123–134.

LaPlante, M. P., & Carlson, D. (1996). *Disability in the United States: Prevalence and causes, 1992* (Disability Statistics Rep. No. 7). Washington, DC: U.S. Department of Education, National Institute on Disability and Rehabilitation Research.

Linton, S. (1998). *Claiming disability: Knowledge and identity.* New York: New York University Press.

Longmore, P. K. (1985). A note on language and the social identity of disabled people. *American Behavioral Scientist, 28,* 419–423.

Longmore, P. K. (1995). Medical decision making and people with disabilities: A clash of cultures. *Journal of Law, Medicine and Ethics, 23,* 82–87.

Merriam-Webster's collegiate dictionary. (1998). Springfield, MA: Merriam-Webster.

Murray, B. (2002, March). Psychology training gets major recognition. *Monitor on Psychology, 33*(3), 22–23.

Nagi, S. Z. (1991). Disability concepts revisited: Implications for prevention. In A. M. Pope & A. R. Tarlov (Eds.), *Disability in America: Toward a national agenda for prevention* (pp. 309–327). Washington, DC: National Academy Press.

Oliver, M. (1996). *Understanding disability: From theory to practice.* New York: St. Martin's Press.

Olkin, R. (1999). *What psychotherapists should know about disability.* New York: Guilford Press.

Olkin, R., & Pledger, C. (2003). Can disability studies and psychology join hands? *American Psychologist, 58*, 296–304.

Pollard, R. Q., Jr. (1996). Professional psychology and deaf people: The emergence of a discipline. *American Psychologist, 51*, 389– 396.

Reschly, D. J. (1999). Assessing educational disabilities. In A. K. Hess & I. B. Weiner (Eds.), *Handbook of forensic psychology* (2nd ed., pp. 127–150). New York: Wiley.

Sleek, S. (1999, January). Three decades after King, a report card. *American Psychological Association Monitor, 30*(1), 24–25.

Solarz, A. L. (1990). Rehabilitation psychologists: A place in the policy process? *American Psychologist, 45*, 766–770.

Task Force on Psychology and the Handicapped. (1984). Final report of the Task Force on Psychology and the Handicapped. *American Psychologist, 39*, 545– 550.

Tate, D. G. & Forchheimer, M. (1998). Enhancing community reintegration following inpatient rehabilitation for persons with spinal cord injury. *Topics in SCI Rehab: Part I, 4*, 42–55.

Telzrow, C. F. (1999). IDEA amendments of 1997: Promise or pitfall for special education reform? *Journal of School Psychology, 37*, 7–28.

Ticket to Work and Work Incentives Improvement Act, Pub. L. No. 106-170, 113 Stat. 1860 (1999).

Trickett, E. J., Watts, R. J., & Birman, D. (Eds.). (1994). *Human diversity: Perspectives on people in context.* San Francisco: Jossey-Bass.

Vasquez, M. J. T., & Eldridge, N. S. (1994). Bringing ethics alive: Training practitioners about gender, ethnicity, and sexual orientation issues. *Women and Therapy, 15*, 1–16.

Wright, B. A. (1960). *Physical disability: A psychological approach.* New York: Harper & Row.

CHAPTER FIVE

Social Work Practice With People With Disabilities in the Era of Disability Rights

Richard L. Beaulaurier and Samuel H. Taylor

Over the years, social work practice in health care has managed to innovate and adapt many of its essential functions. Traditionally these functions have included information and referral, counseling, resource acquisition (brokerage) and case advocacy. Such elements of practice are congruent with the norms, procedures and interdisciplinary arrangements encountered in health and rehabilitation organizations. Increasingly, however, some people with disabilities are questioning the efficacy and assumptions inherent in social work's traditional helping role. Many individuals with disabilities are becoming increasingly interested in empowerment. In the process, some have come to distrust social workers and other professionals whom they believe often do things *to* rather than *with* people with disabilities (Kailes, 1988, p. 4; Mackelprang & Salsgiver, 1996, p. 11; Zola, 1983b, pp. 355–356).

As these attitudes emerged and gathered strength during the 1970s and 1980s, alternatives to various social work activities took shape, influenced in large measure by the disability rights movement (Frieden, 1983; Lachat, 1988; Roberts, 1989). This movement sought to gain some of the services necessary for people with disabilities to be able to live in communities outside institutions and they pressed for more formal acknowledgements of their right to do so. New associations and organizations were formed to meet the needs of people with disabilities and raise their levels of awareness about their basic civil rights as well as the possibility of achieving new levels of integration into community life. Included among these were groups that focused solely on policy, legislative change and community organizing such as American Disabled for Assistance Programs Today (ADAPT[1]) the World Institute on Disability (WID), the American Coalition of Citizens with Disabilities (ACCD), Disabled in Action (DIA), and others. In part because of grass roots support from these and other groups of people with disabilities, new laws, such as the Americans with Disabilities Act (ADA) were drafted to protect the rights of individuals with disabilities and to remove structural barriers hindering their integration into society.[2]

THE DISABILITY RIGHTS MOVEMENT

While intellectual and academic support for advancing the civil rights of people with disabilities began as early as the 1940s (Berkowitz, 1980, chap. 6; Meyerson, 1990), it was during the 1970s and 1980s that people with disabilities began to organize for political action. A principal purpose was to be able to gain increased opportunities for independent and self-determined lifestyles in the wider community. They founded organizations that advocated the integration of people with disabilities into mainstream communities to the maximum extent possible. Such advocacy groups were formed by consumers to benefit consumers (DeJong, 1981, chap. 2; Frieden, 1983; Lachat, 1988). With help from others, these groups were successful enough to have their conceptualizations of self-determination, consumer control and non-discrimination codified in a variety of laws, the most important of which are the Rehabilitation Act of 1973, its amendments (1978), the Individuals with Disabilities Education Act (1997) and the Americans with Disabilities Act of 1990. The Acts contain mandates for the inclusion of people with disabilities into mainstream American life to the maximum extent possible.

These laws are symbolic of a dramatic shift in legislative thinking about the concept of disability. Hahn (1984) has called this change in perspective a transition from a "medical" to a "minority group" perspective. Legislation has increasingly recognized people with disabilities as a minority group subject to and, or, at risk of exclusion and discrimination. Since 1973, disability laws, especially at the federal level have increasingly emphasized the need for the protection of their rights to inclusion in mainstream American life.

The emphasis on civil rights exhibited by many disabilities interest groups is partly due to a growing recognition that historically people with disabilities have been systematically persecuted, neglected and forced into isolation. In the early part of this century in the United States many people with disabilities were incarcerated and even sterilized against their wills. At one point virtually every state had laws that supported the segregation or sterilization of various categories of people with physical, mental and developmental disabilities often rationalizing this on social Darwinist or similarly eugenic grounds (Berkowitz, 1980; Johnson, 1903; Reilly, 1991; Varela, 1983; Wolfensberger, 1969). By the late 20th Century laws in support of eugenic policies had been virtually eliminated. Even so, authors such as Goffman (1963) and Wright (1960, chap. 2) recognized the prevalent stigma and biased treatment accorded to people with disabilities. There is little doubt that all too often people with disabilities remain isolated and effectively segregated from mainstream society today, in part because of a lack of physical access, but also because of stereotypical attitudes about their capabilities. While laws no longer actively prevent people with disabilities from participating in society, a range of physical barriers and disability related discrimination has continued to result in a lack of opportunities for disabled people to become integrated into American society.

This is not so much the product of a will to discriminate on the part of the general public, but rather a failure to take the needs of people with disabilities into account. We design buildings with steps, doors that are too narrow and floors that are too slick for many of our citizens. Educational systems continue to use timed tests in ways that bias against intelligent students who process or write what they know comparatively slowly. We forget that people of all abilities need to use public washrooms. This prompted an early pioneer of the movement to observe that decades after Rosa Parks moved to the front of the bus, many people with disabilities still could not even get on one (Roberts, 1989).

The crux of the new thinking about disability is that it is not so much a person's impairment that is disabling, but rather the *lack of accommodation* for them that creates problems. Discrimination is less likely to result from open hostility than from omitting them from consideration altogether. We do not put stairs in buildings because we hate disabled people. We simply fail to take the needs of people who use wheelchairs into account. This failure to be responsive to the needs of people with disabilities has resulted in social and physical conditions that effectively bar many people with disabilities from full participation in society.

Social attitudes that have made people with disabilities the quintes-sentially "worthy poor" have ironically also had the reverse effect of making them the objects of pity and charity (Adler, Wright, & Ulicny, 1991). This orientation to disability emphasizes the *in*abilities (literally characterizing them as pitiful) of people with disabilities rather than their capabilities, particularly with regard to their ability to lead full and pro-ductive lives that include working, studying, maintaining social relation-ships and consuming in the marketplace in much the same way as everyone else.

The main purpose of the Americans with Disabilities Act (ADA), passed in 1990, was to help eliminate impediments, whether they be physical barriers or related to stereotypical attitudes. This law does not so much overturn past legislation which served to prevent inclusion (as did prior civil rights law) but rather promotes accommodation. Physical and social accommodations of people with disabilities that had heretofore been merely hypothetically possible are now mandated by law. Failure to accommodate the needs for social and physical inclusion of people with disabilities is now considered a violation of their civil rights.

Traditional Approaches to Disability in Health and Rehabilitation Settings

Efforts to provide medical rehabilitation, particularly as it gained effec-tiveness and prominence following World War II, brought social workers into more frequent contact with people with disabilities. Medical reha-bilitation efforts generally utilized a team approach that relied heavily on the contributions of social workers (Berkowitz, 1980, chap. 4). The professional role of preparing the family and the individual with a new disability for life outside the hospital milieu was highly compatible with social casework approaches already in use (Bartlett, 1957, p. 87; Burling, Lentz, & Wilson, 1956, p. 128; Cannon, 1930 pp. 90–96).

Historically medical rehabilitation efforts have sought to "restore" patients to their fullest levels of physical functioning (Cannon, 1952, 205; Wright, 1960, pp. 18–19) Originally this was undertaken for the express purpose of encouraging patients to enter or return to remunerative oc-cupations by *altering* patients in ways that made them more physically capable of dealing with an unaltered world (Berkowitz, 1980, pp. 109–112). This has remained an important part of the rehabilitative process, particularly in the acute stages, when it is still unknown what level of physical functioning people with new disabilities will be able to regain. However, the goal of maximizing physical functioning can also have un-intended psychological consequences for the patient, particularly when carried to extreme levels. Decades ago Wright (1960, chap. 2) observed that more narrowly focused efforts to help people maximize their physical functioning can lead to feelings of shame about their disability by emphasizing the notion that their limitations were unacceptable and needed to be removed. She noted that this stood in contrast with attitudes toward persons of various racial and ethnic groups. When people of color embraced characteristics particular to the cultural norms of their group, they were thought to have appropriate pride in their heritage. People who accepted their impairments and were ready to build lives that included them (particularly if this meant not accepting heroic or invasive corrective procedures) have often been labeled as persons with neurotic adjustment problems.

Partisans in the independent living and disability rights movements take a different approach. They accept the impairment in the person and emphasize organizing and working for environmental accommodations to physical limitations. Rather than altering the patient, they favor altering the norms and structures that limit full participation in society. Barriers, whether they be physical or attitudinal, are being challenged as discriminatory and unnecessary (Hahn, 1984; Kailes, 1988).

Advocates point out that there may be some good reasons for embracing a disability. Some are obvious. For example, a person might choose an artificial prosthetic foot made of light composite materials because of the greater range of motion it offers when engaging in sports, making it preferable to a less functional prosthesis that looks more "normal."[3]

Another example involves arranging for assistance from others. An individual with a disability may well be inclined to seek assistance from another person, such as a personal care attendant, even for things they are physically capable of doing by themselves. An acquaintance of the author uses a personal care attendant to help with getting dressed in the morning although he is physically able to dress himself without such help. The reason is that dressing by himself takes about two hours and leaves him physically exhausted. By contrast, the attendant enables him to get dressed him in about ten minutes. He is then able to use the time gained for more rewarding activities related to his career as a university history professor. This is not so much an argument against achieving gains in physical functioning, but rather is an effort to call attention to alternative factors that can promote social independence.[4]

ORIENTATION TOWARD THE ROLE OF THE PATIENT: THE PATIENT-CONSUMER CONUNDRUM

Many disability rights authors maintain that many, if not most, medical and rehabilitation professionals have tended to view people with disabilities as relatively passive beneficiaries of their treatment regimes (DeJong,

1981; DeJong, 1983, pp. 15–20; Kailes, 1988; Mackelprang & Salsgiver, 1996, p. 9; Nosek, Dart, & Dart, 1981, p. 1; Zola, 1983a). As medical and rehabilitative treatment strives to return the person with a disability to the most "normal" state of physical functioning possible, control of the process tends to be maintained by the technical experts (DeJong, 1981, pp. 28–31; Zola, 1979, 453–454). However, since the actual functioning levels of people with disabilities cannot always fully reach "normal" standards, success is often thought of in terms of completion of the treatment regime. The goal of working to achieve actual social integration and a normalization of social relations is not emphasized and may not even be one of the principal objectives of rehabilitation (DeJong, 1983, pp. 15–20).

Dejong (1981) suggests that this makes for a rather sharp philosophical difference between the goals of *traditional* medical and rehabilitation institutions and disability rights groups. The former tend to define disability as the inability of a person to perform certain *activities of daily living* (ADLs) as the working problem. In this view problems are located within the individual, since they are seen to be *caused* by a *person's inabilities* and impairments. It is, therefore, the individual who needs changing. It follows that changing individuals to improve their performance on ADLs requires that they follow a treatment plan laid out by experts in rehabilitation medicine and technology (e.g., the rehabilitation team). The exclusive focus on the impairment is often reflected in the language that professionals use to describe patients, who are often referred to by their condition (e.g., "paraplegics") rather than as *people with* a disabling condition.[5]

Conversely, disability rights groups tend to define and perceive the "disabler" as outside the person. This emerging perspective considers that some of the most important problems of people with disabilities reside in inflexible and insensitive health organizations that are more interested in maximizing profits and maintaining the status quo than in assisting them with what they believe to be their actual needs (DeJong, 1981).[6] In an era of cost cutting and cost consciousness, health administrators usually seek to set up a menu of standardized treatment options designed to maximize achievement of ADLs at the lowest possible cost. The emphasis is on medical aspects of the impairment rather than social advocacy aimed at bringing about important alterations in living and work environments.

The disability rights perspective departs radically from such viewpoints. Advocates tend to view people with disabilities (a) as experts on their particular condition, and (b) the most appropriate persons to make decisions about the kind and the course of treatments they are to receive. Client self determination is operationalized by the disability rights movement as being active and informed involvement with the key decision making processes that are central to the medical and rehabilitative treatment of the person being treated. One of the most important roles of the social worker may be to help both the team and the person with a disability to move toward this type of complementary role arrangement. During the course of medical and, or, rehabilitation treatment, social workers need to be able to help the person take control of the process to the fullest extent possible. One of the ways that social workers can do this is by educating and advocating on behalf of the importance and the rights of patients to control of these decisions. Another is by helping patients to advocate on their own behalf in order to realize their wishes and goals. While some patients, due to an inability to articulate their desires or the acute nature of their condition, may not have much control over treatment processes in the beginning, social workers should be expected to work to help them achieve maximal decision making control as soon as practicable and certainly before they are discharged. This process involves helping patients with the critical change as they move from being passive recipients of care in the medical system to active *consumers:* persons with basic rights and the capacity to understand and even control the course of their treatment.

Orientation Toward Independence

The key to comprehending how disability has been reconceptualized is to understand the term *independence* as it is used by disability advocates. Traditionally, both rehabilitation professionals and members of the disability rights movement have favored the maximization of independence as an important and desirable goal of rehabilitation. As noted earlier, many rehabilitation specialists believe the term has a very particular meaning: the ability to do things with minimal assistance either from other people or from machines. This creates a hierarchy of desirable treatment outcomes. Best is when the patient becomes able to approximate the activities of an unimpaired, robust individual without human or mechanical assistance. Next best is when the person can perform such tasks with the use of the latest assistive devices. The least desirable outcome is when, at the end of the rehabilitative process, the individual still requires human assistance to perform the activities of a robust, unimpaired individual (Zola, 1983b).

The meaning of the term "independence" is more complex and less obvious when defined and used by members of the disability rights movement. Their usage tends to emphasize *social* independence and has a meaning closer to self-determination and the ability to "call one's own shots." This meaning is clearer in some other languages. In German, for example, independent living is referred to as "*selbstbestimmtes Leben,*" literally, "self-determined living." For people in the disability rights movement, the most important determinant of independence is not whether one relies on others or devices for assistance, but the degree to which decisions about assistance and other aspects of life are determined by the individual with a disability. Zola (1983b) contended that the emphasis of medical and rehabilitation professionals was almost exclusively in relation to *physical independence* rather than *social independence*. The former is independence from devices or attendants while the latter is the ability to be fully involved in planning the course of one's own treatment and care. He contends that when these two values are at odds, gains in physical independence are almost never worth the losses in social independence (pp. 345–347).

To be sure, this does not always create a dilemma, particularly in the acute stages of the rehabilitation process when major gains can be expected in physical functioning. It becomes more of a dilemma when the expectation is for small gains in physical functioning or where "solutions" are intrusive, highly time-consuming, very fatiguing, experimental or do not really contribute to psycho-social reintegration into mainstream life. In the earlier example of the former rehabilitation patient who has given up dressing himself and now allows an attendant help him with this activity, it is notable that he initially spent many months in rehabilitation learning to dress himself, only to give up the activity when he decided on a more efficient alternative approach. Most often social workers are the only members of rehabilitation teams who have the knowledge and responsibility to focus on the *social* life and needs of patients. Therefore it is incumbent on social workers to help the teams recognize this "new" definition of social independence and client self-determination.

It may also be necessary for social workers to more fully emphasize their role as educators in their work with patients and the teams. Social workers need to be attuned to the new realities of life with a disability, which make it far less restrictive and offer consumers more life options than were available in the past. Overemphasis on dealing with fears about life with a disability, and "heroic" efforts to restore "normal" functioning are often perceived by the disability rights community as misguided. They contend that such forms of practice are based on stereotypes, on overly gloomy visions about what life with a disability will be like, or visions of life in institutionalized settings. Most of the general public are probably unaware of the many people with disabilities who are now able to live, work and shop in mainstream communities, while also forming meaningful social relationships, in spite of severe disabilities. Social workers need to become familiar with case examples and be able to communicate this perspective (or even connect patients with such individuals) so that newly impaired individuals and their families may become aware of how life can be full and rich even with the acquisition of a severe impairment. Such an awareness may also lead them to reconsider the effort and attention they are asked to expend in order to achieve relatively minor gains in physical ability that may be less than worth the effort.[7]

Another important role for social workers is helping both the rehabilitation team and the patient with the process associated with transitioning decision making power from the professionals to the patient. By the time of discharge, and ideally even before that, people with disabilities should be able to weigh and articulate their desires and preferences with regard to the various treatment options.

On a seemingly more mundane level it is important to remember that a sense of consumer control tends to be maximized to the extent that assistance personnel are hired and fired by the person with the disability (Haggstrom, 1995). For this reason many people in the disability movement tend to eschew professional helpers who are not under their control, but rather answer directly to a third party health system or payer. Disability rights advocates tend to favor the use of low cost, paraprofessional aides that they themselves are able to hire and fire rather than more skilled aides such as home health nurses (DeJong, Batavia, & McKnew, 1992). In recent years disability activist groups have been working to create payment schemes that make personal care attendants more widely available and bring them under greater consumer control (DeJong et al., 1992). Zola (1983b) noted that such aides often contribute to the sense of "independence" of people with disabilities by helping them to perform basic tasks quickly, easily and reliably. In many cases, these are everyday activities that more professionalized helpers do not perform since the tasks are not medical in nature. However, these are the very services that are often vital to an individual's ability to remain socially independent. One of the major priorities of the disability rights movement today is to develop political and legislative support for funding such paraprofessional helpers. To this end, the largest and most important disability activist organization, ADAPT, has shifted its activities from an emphasis on public transportation to attendant care services.[8]

Orientation Toward Technology

The development of technologies such as portable respirators, powerful but cheap computing devices, longer lasting batteries and light weight materials have helped make it possible for many people with disabilities to live independently. In light of these innovations and their contributions to people with disabilities it is somewhat ironic that the disability rights community tends to favor the use of "low technology" assistive devices whenever possible. Their reasoning is rather straightforward: The simpler the technology, the easier and cheaper it is likely to be to repair and maintain assistive devices. Space age technologies are often high cost, and are accompanied by hordes of professionals who are needed for training, servicing and repairs. This can lead to an ironic situation in which disabled people feel controlled and limited by the devices that held promise for offering independence.[9]

However, Zola (1983b) concluded that an intervention that is profitable to build, requires periodic attention by health professionals, and is "technologically fascinating" will often be promoted as the next best thing to a "cure" when it is presented in the rehabilitation literature. "Thus does high-technology medicine pursued in a questionable manner contribute to greater dependence of those who seek its help" (Zola, 1983b, p. 346).

Disability rights advocates, more often than not, favor reliable, low-technology solutions that also allow for greater social integration. Examples of such arrangements include the construction of ramps, hiring and training of attendants and sign-interpreters, negotiated accommodations with employers, accessible housing and other *environmental* changes that promote the person's ability to participate in mainstream life. A friend of the authors, for example, who has a mobility impairment traded in his van with an electronic lift for a car into which he could comfortably place and store his wheelchair. While this arrangement required a little more effort, it did not break down the way his electric lift often did, leaving him stranded until a technician-specialist could arrive to repair it.

Many in the deaf community would argue that the debate over cochlear implants for children is another case in point. Members of the medical community, as well as some of the more traditionally oriented deaf services organizations have advocated for the use of cochlear implants even when the level of improvement in auditory functioning is only marginal. More radically militant members of the deaf community view this as surgical "maiming" of innocent deaf children, potentially ostracizing them from their *birthright of deafness* and inclusion in the deaf community, as well as segregating them from the hearing community that will never accept them as "normal" (Barringer, 1993; D'Antonio, 1993). A part of this debate is a basic philosophical difference with regard to the nature of deafness. For most professionals in the medical community, deafness is a crippling medical condition to be conquered. For many in the deaf community, deafness is not so much a limiting handicap as a difference, one with its own culture and benefits. Deaf advocates argue that the *option* of deafness is worthy of consideration; one that may well be chosen over the alleged benefits of invasive procedures that all too often produce no more than marginal improvements in hearing ability. They favor informing potential recipients about all of the various consequences these procedures may have, as well as presenting information about other options. In the case of cochlear implants, medical professionals often prefer to perform surgery in order to gain even a marginal improvement in hearing, though this often creates social difficulties for the patient. Dependency on technical experts is fostered, not just around the technologies of the procedure and treatment, but also for its prescribed goals and criteria of success. This requires that people with disabilities: (1) view the rehabilitation professional as an expert; (2) view themselves as in an undesirable state; and (3) work toward a prognosis and recovery that has been predefined for them (DeJong, 1981, p. 31). As this example suggests, the goals may be defined too narrowly in terms of function and not in terms of social costs. The former holds that *some* hearing is better than none. Activist elements of the deaf community would argue that it may well be better to be part of *their* community than not to be fully integrated into *any* community. Often a person with a cochlear implant, they reason, does not gain *enough* hearing to be seen as "normal," but may have just enough so that they no longer fit into the deaf community.[10]

Relatively low tech, non-medical services may even be sufficient to help many individuals with severe disabilities remain in their homes. At one time such persons would have required institutionalized care. For patients to remain at home, social workers need to become aware of some different community based resources. Volunteer or moderate cost carpentry, plumbing, house cleaning, paraprofessional attendant care, etc., are available in many communities but they do not tend to advertise and must be sought out. Independent living centers are often well versed in these necessary services, have resource locators and in some cases have developed independent living educational materials for both consumers and providers (Shreve & Access Living, 1993). Independent living centers can be found in most urban areas due in large part to the support they receive from federal funding as well as local resources (U. S. Congress, 1978).[11]

OPERATING OUT OF A DISABILITY RIGHTS PERSPECTIVE

Social workers may need to initiate ongoing liaisons with independent living centers and other alternative sources of information if they are to expand their knowledge to include options, resources, and services that go beyond what is currently available (Zola, 1983b, pp. 346–347). This suggests that there may be a role for social workers to engage in client and systems advocacy within their organizations, with third party payers and with legislators, to ensure that funding and services are available for people with disabilities.

Moreover active partnerships with social workers to achieve services that promote independent living should go a long way toward ameliorating some of the resentment felt by many people with disabilities. In light of the failure of the medical and rehabilitation establishment to even recognize these relatively new perspectives that are now embraced by the disability rights movement, some activists openly question whether professionals can be counted on for help in working toward the empowerment of people with disabilities. In their view, over the years all too many rehabilitation professionals have tended to promote dependence rather than independence (Berrol, 1979; Zola, 1979). A recent study suggests, however, that social workers may be moving somewhat closer to the aspirations and goals of disabled people (Beaulaurier & Taylor, 2000). The authors conclude based on their findings, that there may be an important role for social workers to perform as intermediaries between health services professionals and organizations and the people they seek to serve.

Before social workers can do that, however, they must become educated themselves, and have their consciousness raised. Health and rehabilitation professionals may have the best of intentions and might be "dismayed" to be told that they are helping to foster "technological dependence" and that this is not supportive of disability rights movements' goals for empowerment, self-determination and social integration at the community level.

It is important to recognize that up to now the disability rights movement has largely been a self-help movement, and sometimes it has taken on an adversarial role toward professionals whom they have not seen to be particularly supportive. It may be incumbent, therefore, for social workers to demonstrate to such groups that they have valuable skills and knowledge that can be beneficial to their purposes. Berrol suggests that professionals seeking to promote independent living and foster the empowerment of people with disabilities must...

> ...provide leadership in their areas of expertise without dominance, they must provide services, they must be active advocates, they must share their unique skills, and they must provide training. They must assure that there are the same opportunities to develop positive role models as are available to the able-bodied population. (Berrol, 1979, p. 457)

As social workers begin to reach out to the disability rights community the roles that may be most valuable to and appreciated are those of educator and advocate (Zola, 1983b, p. 57). These are not new roles for social workers. However, this does suggest that community organizing, organizational practice, case management and advocacy skills may take on heightened importance in working effectively with this population.

Empowering People with Disabilities

Managed care settings may well create even greater needs for social work mezzo and macro skills. Tower (1994, p. 191) has suggested that given increasing caseloads and service demands, and decreasing social service budgets in the health services sector, client self determination may be "the first thing to go" as social workers struggle to balance their workloads. In light of the increasing activism and assertiveness of many people with disabilities this could put social workers at odds with clients and client groups. Effective social work practice with people with disabilities requires a refocused conceptual framework that will support and promote self-determination. This framework must be designed to enable people with disabilities to:

1. Expand their range of options and choices.
2. Prepare them to be more effective in dealings with professionals, bureaucrats and agencies that often do not understand nor appreciate their heightened need for self-determination.
3. Mobilize and help groups of people with disabilities to consider policy and program alternatives that can improve their situation.

Direct practice with clients with disabilities will certainly remain a primary activity of health and rehabilitation social workers (with perhaps greater secondary emphasis on mezzo and macro skills). However, this practice must increasingly emphasize empowerment objectives rather than mere compliance with medically prescribed treatment plans and, or, our traditional psycho-social clinical interventions. Fostering the independence and empowerment of people with disabilities requires enabling them to become motivated and skilled at helping themselves. Independent living services, inspired by the disability rights movement, emphasize concepts that rely on preparing consumers to help themselves:

The staff's role is to provide only what relevant training and problem solving is needed in acquiring and using services until the consumer becomes self-reliant. The move from dependence on staff to self-direction marks the shift from "client/patient mentality" to "consumer mentality" (Kailes, 1988, p. 5).

Social workers can approach practice in a similar way in order to help negotiate the transitions that will enable people to move from the passive role of patient to the active role of informed and empowered consumers. Several authors have discussed and outlined approaches to advocacy practice that seem particularly useful for health social workers in their work with people with disabilities. These authors include: Hardcastle, Wenocur and Powers (Hardcastle, Wenocur, & Powers, 1997, chap. 12), Herbert and Levin (1996), Herbert and Mould (1992), McGowan (1987), Mickelson (1995), Sosin and Caulum (1983) and Tesolowski, Rosenberg, and Stein (1983).

Gutiérrez (1990) has identified four psychological changes that are particularly important in empowering clients: (1) self efficacy—the belief that one's actions can produce desired changes, (2) group consciousness—identification as a member of a class and recognition of how political, social and physical structures effect the class, (3) reduction of self-blame for negative consequences of being a member of the class, (4) assuming personal responsibility for change—preparing to take action to improve one's own situation. As social workers assess their practice with people with disabilities they need to focus more on helping them accomplish these person-in-context changes.[12]

The lack of control that many people with disabilities experience while they are in the treatment process is, however, not simply a psychological phenomenon. Social workers in health and rehabilitation settings must develop and demonstrate skills that will facilitate helping their clients to press for inclusion in the planning and decisions that will be made about the their treatment. Social workers will also need to consider more emphasis on their practice role as educators in order to help clients become effective advocates and negotiators for their own interests. This will require that practitioners modify customary approaches to include more emphasis on dealing with organizations and systems enabling...

> ...people to identify issues, to partialize the sources of their problem, and to speculate about possible solutions. The worker converses about power and conflict, encourages people to challenge preconceived notions, and works to unleash [their] potential. (Grosser & Mondros, 1985, p. 162)

Emphasis on such practice includes familiarity and skill with the advocacy and negotiation modalities that focus on dealing effectively with bureaucracies, administrative structures and centers of power that make decisions and allocate resources. In order to accomplish this, social workers may need to interact more deliberately and purposefully with practitioners engaged in both the independent living and disability rights movements. This suggests a need for more inter-organizational dialogues and agency agreements for working together to identify issues and concerns, formulate agendas and develop reciprocal understandings.

Finally, health social workers must gain increased levels of knowledge about the particular issues that are of concern to the disability community. Direct services social workers need to be responsive to issues such as the isolation and lack of group consciousness that many people with disabilities experience. These feelings often derive from limited contacts with other people with disabilities. People with recently acquired disabilities need to interact with *empowered* people with disabilities. Pinderhughes, writing from an ethnic minority perspective, encourages creating linkages with natural support systems such as family, church groups, fraternal and social organizations (1994, p. 23). Such natural gatherings of networks of individuals who share similar characteristics and a desire for empowerment simply did not exist among people with disabilities until relatively recently. In the past quarter century however, much progress has been made by people with disabilities who are working to develop and create more functional community supports. In some communities independent living centers have been organized, developed and administered by and for people with disabilities and they often collaborate with more advocacy oriented organizations such as ADAPT, ACCD, DIA and others previously mentioned. They sponsor and produce newsletters and newspapers, electronic bulletin board services and internet newsgroups.[13] Social workers need to have first hand familiarity with such functional communities in order to be able to link their clients to them. This requires more than a general awareness that such sources exist. Social workers also need to have the community liaison skills to create and maintain linkages and networks between such groups, services and their own health services organizations (Taylor, 1985; Weil & Gamble, 1995).

CONCLUSIONS

ADA marked a turning point for people with disabilities. With its passage in 1990, the law began to favor the notion of societal integration of people with disabilities whenever practicable and to offer recourse at those times when they were excluded or the victims of discrimination. It also marked a turning point for disability activism in that some of the most important battles, such as for accessible public transportation, accessible public spaces and protection from discrimination, were waged and won. This has not, however, resulted in complacency or a diminution of the movement's of militancy.[14] In part this is a recognition that exercising and campaigning for *rights* is only a part of what is necessary to achieve independence and self-determination. What is also required are a range of essential community based services. In particular this means developing and increasing access to personal attendant care as well as related services and programs that support and complement clients' abilities to engage in remunerative work (DeJong et al., 1992; DeJong & Brannont, 1998). In fact, people with disabilities are increasingly seen as leaders in the push for consumer oriented and consumer directed services (Beaulaurier & Taylor, 2001).

This trend is especially observable when reviewing the literature on aging, developmental disability and mental health (Ansello & Eustis, 1992; Tower, 1994; Wehmeyer, 1997; Wilk, 1994). For many, "person with a disability" has gone from meaning "person with severe limitations" to "person with rights to accommodation and inclusion" (Beaulaurier & Taylor, 2001). An interesting consequence is that the notion and concept of disability is increasingly being used as a unifying theme in the literature about developmental disabilities, mental illness and aging. There seems to be a recognition that "disability" has a more universal meaning for many different kinds of problems that vulnerable and at-risk groups experience (Racino & Heumann, 1992; Wehmeyer, 1997; Wilk, 1994).

In spite of this activity there have been only a few exploratory studies on social work practice with people with disabilities that were guided by the assumptions, issues and concerns of the disability rights movement (Renz-Beaulaurier, 1996) At present the authors are not aware of any systematic research that has described or assessed practice modalities that incorporate such perspectives. Clearly research in this area is needed.[15]

Even without the benefit of extensive empirical research it is clear that people with disabilities are becoming increasingly militant about their right to be involved in planning and making decisions regarding their treatment. They are no longer content to accept the "wisdom" of experts. They are challenging predominant medical and rehabilitation treatment philosophies that tend to emphasize restoring them to relative physical "normality" all too often at the expense of their social integration. These considerations, in addition to the newly imposed budgetary constraints associated with managed health care, have and will create turbulence in the health and rehabilitation task environment.

It is incumbent upon all social workers to reconsider how they view their practice with people who have disabilities. In the coming years we need to learn to emphasize...

...strengths rather than pathology, solution seeking rather than problem detecting, competence promotion rather than deficit reduction, and collaborative partnerships rather than professional expertise. (O'Melia, DuBois, & Miley, 1994, p. 164)

> It is equally important for social workers in health settings to augment their practice capabilities with regard to organizational and community work, negotiating skills and advocacy. This practice knowledge and skill must be combined with efforts to acquire clearer understandings of the administrative structures and priorities that operate in health settings and their task environments, so that this knowledge may be used to help people with disabilities develop increased self-determination in their dealings with health systems and professionals.

NOTES

1. The organization has remained one of the most important disability advocacy groups, however the acronym has changed over time to reflect current legislative and lobbying efforts. Originally it stood for "American Disabled for Accessible Public Transportation," and for a short time "American Disabled for Access Power Today" before adopting its current name. Insiders typically refer to the organization simply as "ADAPT."

2. Other laws include sections of the *Rehabilitation Act* of 1973, the *Education for All Handicapped Children Act* of 1975, The *Individuals with Disabilities Education Act* of 1997, etc.

3. Less obvious is when the advantage is social rather than physical. A person might want to use a wheelchair instead of crutches, since wheelchairs are often more comfortable and less tiring to use even though the wheelchair makes the individual "look" relatively more disabled. The advantages of a wheelchair's speed and mobility may outweigh the advantages of appearing to be less disabled and more "normal."

4. Zola has stated (1982, p. 346) "... there is literally no physical circumstance in which increased physical independence is worth Decreased social and psychological independence."

5. For an excellent discussion about the subtle bias that language and attitudes of professionals often convey see the discussion by Wright (1980; 1988; 1989). Moreover, activist people with disabilities have expressed a strong preference that the word "people" always appear when describing them, as in "diabetic person," or "person with a disability." This chapter also follows the "person first" rule, as in "person with a disability" which emphasizes the humanity of a person before referring to the person's condition. This symbolically highlights the fact that the person has a condition rather than suggesting that the condition characterizes the person. Perhaps the best reference on how to talk to and about people with disabilities is available from the Eastern Paralyzed Veterans Association at www.epva.org (Cohen, 1998).

6. As an example, the Southern California Chapter of ADAPT—a militant disability rights organization, chose a prominent health organization as the target of its annual social action in 1994.

7. Akin to overly bleak fantasies about life with a disability are overly rosy imaginings about the benefits of new or experimental treatments. Such prognostications about treatment approaches have made Christopher Reeve and the team working with him something of a lightning rod for criticism by the disability rights movement. Many advocates feel that (a) the chances for a "cure" for spinal chord injury are minimal, and (b) what gains from experimental approaches are actually on the horizon are minimal and expensive. Many people in the disability rights movement feel that the cause of people with disabilities would be far better served by efforts to adapt environments to people with disabilities than to seek rather minimal gains in functioning at enormous expense. Media treatments of the actor generally note how this vital and healthy man in his prime was "struck down," and is now heroically working to overcome

his "terrible affliction." Rarely do media reports note that he continues to have a full life, maintains a career as an actor, is still relatively healthy, has a warm and supportive family, lives in a non institutionalized setting, heads major charitable enterprises. Some might argue that he has gained far more fame and prominence as a person with a disability than he ever had prior to his injury. In short, he continues to have a life that in some ways may be more full and meaningful by virtue of his impairments. There are many more mundane cases where this is so, and many individuals now appear to be more conscious of how their lives have continued to be full and rewarding after the onset of disability.

 8. The most comprehensive list of such centers is available at <www.ilru.org>.
 9. Again, the controversy appears to center around differing notions of "independence." Rehabilitation professionals tend to view independence as the ability of persons with disabilities to function with minimal assistance from other people.
10. This is particularly the case when there is just enough hearing so that patients (and families) focus on normal speech (which they may well *not* master) and do not learn sign language.
11. See the list maintained at <www.ilru.org>.
12. Such client change and development is critical in that it helps people with disabilities begin to constructively deal with their own feelings of powerlessness and their all too frequent exclusion from treatment planning and decision making.
13. These include such electronic media such as "Dimenet" and other resources with links at <www.ilru.org>. The SERIES electronic bulletin board dates back to the late 1980s and allowed disability advocates to communicate about progress on the ADA well before the internet made computerized communication ubiquitous. Many individual ILCs also have publications and newsletters in conventional print form.
14. Hahn and Beaulaurier have recently reported on current militant activities of ADAPT, for example (2001).
15. This may require advocacy targeted toward organizations and institutes that fund research. June Kailes, a prominent independent living consultant, contends that "... the Rehabilitation Services Administration would still rather fund a program to teach paraplegics to walk on their hands than to fund programs that promote real independent living options for people with disabilities" (personal communication, Los Angeles, 1990).

REFERENCES

Adler, A. B., Wright, B. A., & Ulicny, G. R. (1991). Fundraising portrayals of people with disabilities: Donations and attitudes. *Rehabilitation Psychology, 36* (4), 231–240.

Ansello, E. F., & Eustis, N. N. (1992). [Eds.]. Special Issue: Aging and Disability. *Gerontologist, 16* (1), entire issue.

Barringer, F. (1993). *Pride in a Soundless World: Deaf Oppose a Hearing Aid:* New York Times.

Bartlett, H. M. (1957). Influence of the Medical Setting on Social Case Work Services. In D. Goldstine (Ed.), *Readings in the Theory and Practice of medical social work* (pp. 85–96). Chicago, IL: University of Chicago Press.

Beaulaurier, R. L., & Taylor, S. H. (2000). Challenges and inconsistencies in providing effective advocacy for disabled people in today's health services environment: An exploratory descriptive study. *SCI Psychosocial Process, 13* (3).

Beaulaurier, R. L., & Taylor, S. H. (2001). Dispelling fears about aging with a disability: Lessons from the disability rights community. *Journal of Gerontological Social Work, 35* (2).

Berkowitz, E. D. (1980). *Rehabilitation: The Federal Government's Response to Disability 1935–1954.* New York: Arno Press.

Berrol, S. (1979). Independent Living Programs: The Role of the Able-Bodied Professional. *Archives of Physical Medicine and Rehabilitation, 60,* 456–457.

Burling, T., Lentz, E. M., & Wilson, R. N. (1956). *The Give and Take in Hospitals.* New York: G. P. Putnam's Sons.

Cannon, I. M. (1930). *Social work in hospitals: A contribution to progressive medicine.* (Revised Ed. ed.). New York: Russel Sage Foundation.

Cannon, I. M. (1952). *On the social frontier of medicine: Pioneering in medical social service.* Cambridge, MA: Harvard University Press.

Cohen, J. (1998). *Disability etiquette: Tips on interacting with people with disabilities.* New York: Eastern Paralyzed Veterans Association.

D'Antonio, M. (1993). *Sound and Fury:* Los Angeles Times Magazine.

DeJong, G. (1981). *EnvironmentalAccessibility and Independent Living Outcomes: Directions for Disability Policy and Research.* East Lancing, MI: University Center for International Rehabilitation, Michigan State University.

DeJong, G. (1983). Defining and Implementing the Independent Living Concept. In N. M. Crewe & I. K. Zola (Eds.), *Independent Living for Physically Disabled People* (pp. 4–27). San Francisco, CA: Jossey-Bass.

DeJong, G., Batavia, A. I., & McKnew, L. B. (1992). The Independent Living Model of Personal Assistance in National Long Term-Care Policy. *Generations, 16* (1), 43–47.

DeJong, G., & Brannont, R. (1998). Trends in services to working-age people with disabilities. In S. M. Allen & V. Mor (Eds.), *Living in the community with disability* (pp. 168–196). New York: Springer.

Frieden, L. (1983). Understanding Alternative Program Models. In N. M. Crewe & I. K. Zola (Eds.), *Independent Living for Physically Disabled People* (pp. 62–72). San Francisco, CA: Jossey-Bass.

Goffman, E. (1963). *Stigma: Notes on the Management of Spoiled Identity.* Englewood Cliffs, NJ: Prentice-Hall.

Grosser, C. F., & Mondros, J. (1985). Pluralism and participation: The political action approach. In S. H. Taylor & R. W. Roberts (Eds.), *Theory and Practice* of *Community Social Work* (pp. 154–178). New York: Columbia University Press.

Gutiérrez, L. M. (1990). Working with women of color: An empowerment perspective. *Social Work, 35* (2), 149–161.

Haggstrom, W. C. (1995). For a democratic revolution: The grassroots perspective. In J. E. Tropman, J. L. Erlich, & J. Rothman (Eds.), *Tactics and techniques of community intervention* (3rd ed., pp. 134–142). Itasca, IL: F. E. Peacock.

Hahn, H. (1984). Reconceptualizing disability: A political science perspective. *Rehabilitation Literature, 45* (11–12), 362–374.

Hahn, H., & Beaulaurier, R. L. (2001). Attitudes toward disabilities: A research note on "adapters" and "consumers" with disabilities. *Journal of Disability Policy Studies, 12* (1).

Hardcastle, D. A., Wenocur, S., & Powers, P. (1997). *Community practice: Theories and skills for social workers.* New York: Oxford University Press.

Herbert, M., & Levin, R. (1996). The advocacy role in hospital social work. *Social Work in Health Care, 22* (3), 71–83.

Herbert, M. D., & Mould, J. W. (1992). The advocacy role in public child welfare. *Child Welfare, 71,* 114–130.

Johnson, A. (1903). Report of committee on colonies for segregation of defectives, *Proceedings of the National Conference of Charities and Correction at the Thirtieth Annual Session Held in the City of Atlanta, May 6–12, 1903* (pp. 245–252): Fred J. Heer.

Kailes, J. I. (1988). *Putting Advocacy Rhetoric into Practice: The Role of the Independent Living Center.* Houston, TX: Independent Living Research Utilization.

Lachat, M. A. (1988). *The IndependentLiving Service Model: Historical Roots, Core Elements, and Current Practice. Hampton,* NH: Center for Resource Management.

Mackelprang, R. W., & Salsgiver, R. O. (1996). People with disabilities and social work: Historical and contemporary issues. *Social Work, 41* (1), 7–14.

McGowan, B. G. (1987). Advocacy, *Encyclopedia of Social Work* (18th ed., Vol. 1, pp. 89–95). Silver Spring, MD: National Association of Social Workers.

Meyerson, L. (1990). The Social Psychology of Physical Disability: 1948 and 1988. In M. Nagler (Ed.), *Perspectives on Disability* (pp. 13–23). Palo Alto, CA: Health Markets Research.

Mickelson, J. S. (1995). Advocacy, *Encyclopedia of Social Work* (19th ed., Vol. 1, pp. 95–100). Silver Spring, MD: National Association of Social Workers.

Nosek, P., Dart, J., Jr., & Dart, Y. (1981). *Independent Living Programs: A Management Perspective.* Washington, DC: Unpublished document.

O'Melia, M., DuBois, B., & Miley, K. (1994). The role of choice in empowering people with disabilities: Reconceptualizing the role of social work practice in health and rehabilitation settings. In L. Gutiérrez & P. Nurius (Eds.), *Education and Research for Empowerment Practice* (pp. 161–170). Seattle, WA: Center for Policy and Practice Research.

Pinderhughes, E. (1994). Empowerment as an intervention goal: Early ideas. In L. Gutiérrez & P. Nurius (Eds.), *Education and Research for Empowerment Practice* (pp. 17–30). Seattle, WA: Center for Policy and Practice Research.

Racino, J. A., & Heumann, J. E. (1992). Independent Living and Community Life: Building Coalitions Among Elders, People with Disabilities, and Our Allies. *Generations, 16* (1), 43–47.

Reilly, M. D., Philip R. (1991). *The surgical solution: A history of involuntary sterilization in the United States.* Baltimore, MD: Johns Hopkins University Press.

Renz-Beaulaurier, R. L. (1996). *Health social workers' perspectives on practice with people with disabilities in the era of the Americans with Disabilities Act: An exploratory-descriptive study.* Unpublished Doctoral Dissertation, University of Southern California, Los Angeles, CA.

Roberts, E. V. (1989). A History of the Independent Living Movement: A Founder's Perspective. In B. W. F. Heller, Louis M., Zegens, Leonard S. (Ed.), *Psychosocial Interventions with Physically Disabled Persons* (pp. 231–244). New Brunswick, NJ: Rutgers University Press.

Shreve, M., & Access Living. (1993). *Access Living's independent living skills training curricula.* (2nd ed.). Chicago, IL: Access Living.

Sosin, M., & Caulum, S. (1983). Advocacy: A Conceptualization for Social Work Practice. *Social Work, 28,* 12–17.

Taylor, S. H. (1985). Community Work and Social Work: The Community Liaison Approach. In S. H. Taylor & R. W. Roberts (Eds.), *Theory and Practice of Community Social Work* (pp. 179–214). New York: Columbia University Press.

Tesolowski, D. G., Rosenberg, H., & Stein, R. J. (1983). Advocacy Intervention: A responsibility of Human Service Professionals. *Journal of Rehabilitation, 49,* 35–38.

Tower, K. D. (1994). Consumer-centered social work practice: Restoring client self-determination. *Social Work, 39* (2), 191–196.

U. S. Congress. (1973). *Rehabilitation Act of 1973, PL 93-112.* Washington DC: U.S. Government Printing Office.

U. S. Congress. (1978). *Rehabilitation, Comprehensive Services and Developmental Disabilities Amendments of 1978, PL 95-602.* Washington DC: Government Printing Office.

U. S. Congress. (1990). *Americans with Disabilities Act of 1990, PL 101-336.* Washington, DC: Government Publishing Office.

Varela, R. A. (1983). Changing social attitudes and legislation regarding disability. In N. M. Crewe & I. K. Zola (Eds.), *Independent living for physically disabled people* (pp. 28–48). San Francisco, CA: Jossey-Bass.

Wehmeyer, M. (1997). Self-determination as an educational outcome: A definitional framework and implications for intervention. *Journal of developmental and physical disabilities, 9* (3), 175–209.

Weil, M. O., & Gamble, D. N. (1995). Community Practice Models, *Encyclopedia of Social Work* (19th ed., Vol. 1, pp. 577–594). Silver Spring, MD: National Association of Social Workers.

Wilk, R. J. (1994). Are the rights of people with mental illness still important? *Social Work, 39* (2), 167–175.

Wolfensberger, W. (1969). The origin and nature of our institutional models. In R. B. Kugel & W. Wolfensberger. (Eds.), *Changing Patterns in Residential Services for the Mentally Retarded* (pp. 59–172). Washington DC: President's Committee on Mental Retardation.

Wright, B. A. (1960). *Physical disability: A psychological approach.* New York: Harper and Row.

Wright, B. A. (1980). Developing constructive views of life with a disability. *Rehabilitation literature, 41* (11–12), 274–279.

Wright, B. A. (1988). Attitudes and the fundamental negative bias: Conditions and corrections. In H. E. Yuker (Ed.), *Attitudes Toward Persons with Disabilities.* New York: Springer.

Wright, B. A. (1989). Extension of Heider's ideas to rehabilitation psychology. *Rehabilitation literature, 44* (3), 525–528.

Zola, I. K. (1979). Helping one another: A speculative history of the self help movement. *Archives of Physical Medicine and Rehabilitation, 60,* 452–456.

Zola, I. K. (1982). Social and Cultural Disincentives to Independent Living. *Archives of Physical Medicine and Rehabilitation, 63,* 394–397.

Zola, I. K. (1983a). Developing New Self-Images and Interdependence. In N. M. Crewe & I. K. Zola (Eds.), *Independent Living for Physically Disabled People* (pp. 49–59). San Francisco, CA: Jossey-Bass.

Zola, I. K. (1983b). Toward independent living: Goals and dilemmas. In N. M. Crewe & I. K. Zola (Eds.), *Independent Living for Physically Disabled People* (pp. 344–356). San Francisco, CA: Jossey-Bass.

CHAPTER SIX

Models of Disability

Implications for the Counseling Profession

Julie F. Smart and David W. Smart

Disability is a natural part of human existence and is growing more common as a larger proportion of the U.S. population experiences some type of disability (Americans With Disabilities Act [ADA], 1990; Bowe, 1980; Employment and Disability Institute, 1996; Pope & Tarlov, 1991; Trieschmann, 1987; U.S. Department of Education, Special Education and Rehabilitation Services, National Institute on Disability and Rehabilitation Research, 2000). Due to medical advances and technology, wider availability of health insurance, and a generally higher standard of living that provides more services and support, people who would have died in the past now survive with a disability. In the same way that the viewpoints, experiences, and history of various ethnic/linguistic/cultural groups have been incorporated into the broader American culture, people with disabilities wish to have their social context and experiences become a valued and acknowledged part of American life. These contributions will strengthen and enrich the lives of those who do not experience disability (Akabas, 2000). In the past, clients with disabilities were served primarily by rehabilitation counselors, probably because of the misconception that the client's disability was the sole or, at minimum, the

From "Models of disability: Implications for the counseling profession," by J. F. Smart and D. W. Smart, 2006, *Journal of Counseling & Development, 84,* 29–40. ACA. Reprinted with permission. No further reproduction authorized without written permission from the American Counseling Association.

most important concern. However, because disability is both a common and a natural fact of life and because all individuals, including people with disabilities, have multiple identities, roles, functions, and environments, clients with disabilities require the services of counselors in all specialty areas: aging and adult development; gay, lesbian, bisexual, and transsexual issues; multicultural concerns; community mental health; school counseling; group counseling; marriage and family counseling; career counseling; and spiritual, ethical, and religious values.

To meet minimum standards of practice, therefore, counselors will be required to become proficient in disability issues (Hayes, 2001; Hulnick & Hulnick, 1989). Indeed, Humes, Szymanski, and Hohenshil (1989) suggested that counselors have not facilitated the personal growth and development of their clients with disabilities: "The literature includes many testimonies of persons with disabilities...who have achieved successful careers despite roadblocks they perceived to have been imposed by counselors" (p. 145). However, in spite of this need, which continues to grow, very few university counseling programs provide adequate training about disability issues (Kemp & Mallinckrodt, 1996; Olkin, 1999; Pledger, 2003).

This lack of training and the resulting failure to provide services may be due to the powerful influence of models of disability, because these models determine in which academic disciplines the experience of disability is studied and taught. Thomas (2004) made the point that only rehabilitation counselors are trained in disability issues. A growing interest in models of disability has emerged in recent years, led by a variety of counseling practitioners, educators, and policy makers (Bickenbach, Somnath, Badley, & Ustun, 1999; Humes et al., 1989; Melia, Pledger, & Wilson, 2003; Olkin & Pledger, 2003; J. F. Smart, 2001, 2004; Tate & Pledger, 2003). Examining these changing models can assist the counseling profession, and individual practitioners, to reorient service provision. Counselor educators and counseling practitioners, regardless of specialty, theoretical orientation, or professional setting, should recognize that disability is never entirely a personal, subjective, and idiosyncratic experience, nor is disability a completely objective, standardized, and universal experience.

The conceptualization of disability as an attribute located solely within an individual is changing to a paradigm in which disability is thought to be an interaction among the individual, the disability, and the environment (both social and physical; Dembo, 1982; Higgins, 1992). Typically, the disability is not the single defining characteristic of the individual; rather the disability is one of several important parts of the individual's self-identity. When counselors dismiss or ignore the disability, a critical part of the client's self-identity must remain unexplored. On the other hand, counselors may tend to overemphasize the salience of the disability and automatically assume that the disability is the "presenting problem" or the cause and source of all the client's concerns. Indeed, the "roadblocks" referred to by Humes et al. (1989) may be due to a lack of understanding, training, and experience with disability issues. Many individuals with disabilities view their disability as a valued part of their self-identity, see positive aspects in the disability, and would choose not to eliminate the disability if they had this option. In contrast, few counselors conceptualize the client's disability as a source of self-actualization.

In this chapter, we draw both theoretical and practice implications, which may assist practitioners and educators in gaining a clearer understanding of counseling clients who have disabilities, from four broad models of disability. Intended as a broad overview of the major models and an introductory discussion of ways in which these models can affect the profession of counseling, we present several different ways of conceptualizing the experience of disability. The four broad models discussed here are (a) the Biomedical Model, (b) the Functional Model, (c) the Environmental Model, and (d) the Sociopolitical Model. In this chapter, the Functional Model and the Environmental Model are presented together because both are interactive models, or stated differently, these two models define disability as an interaction between the individual and his or her environment and functions. Furthermore, it is these two models, the Functional and Environmental models, that are most closely related to the practice of counseling. The Sociopolitical Model is considered separately because it is the newest of the models, and more important, this model conceptualizes people with disabilities as belonging to a minority group of individuals who have not yet received their full civil rights.

THE BIOMEDICAL MODEL

The Biomedical Model of disability has a long history, is the most well-known to the general public, and carries with it the power and prestige of the well-established medical profession. This model, rooted in the scientific method and the benefactor of a long tradition, has had dominance in shaping the understanding of disability. The strength of the Biomedical Model lies in its strong explanatory power, which far exceeds the explanatory power of other models. Moreover, this model defines disability in the language of medicine, lending scientific credibility to the idea that disabilities are wholly an individual experience. Due to this "individualization," "privatization," and "medicalization" of disability, the Biomedical Model has remained silent on issues of social justice. Indeed, this model is not considered to be an interactional model because the definition, the "problem," and the treatment of the disability are all considered to lie within the individual with the disability. In addition, interprofessional collaboration is rarely implemented when the disability is medicalized.

Underlying the Biomedical Model is the assumption that pathology is present, and, in addition, disabilities are objective conditions that exist in and of themselves. This "objectification" process opens the door to the possibility of dehumanizing the person because attention is focused on the supposed pathology (Albrecht, 1992; Longmore, 1995). Bickenbach (1993) described this definition of disability as deviance:

> The most commonly held belief about [this model of] disablement is that it involves a defect, deficiency, dysfunction, abnormality, failing, or medical "problem" that is located in an individual. We think it is so obvious as to be beyond serious dispute that disablement is a characteristic of a *defective person,* someone who is functionally limited or anatomically abnormal, diseased, or pathoanatomical, someone who is neither whole nor healthy, fit nor flourishing, someone who is biologically inferior or subnormal. The essence of disablement, in this view, is that there are things *wrong* with people with disabilities. (p. 61)

It is interesting that Bickenbach considered the Biomedical Model to have roots in the religious model of disability, in which biological wholeness was viewed as virtue and righteousness. The combination of religion and science in the Biomedical Model has had a formidable influence.

Furthermore, there is a clear-cut normative aspect to the Biomedical Model in that the disability is considered to be biological inferiority, malfunction, pathology, and deviance when compared with (or normed on) individuals without disabilities (McCarthy, 1993). Thus, the individual with a disability, regardless of personal qualities and assets, understands that he or she belongs to a devalued group. Frequently when clients with an identified disability seek professional services, such as counseling, they understand that, in the view of others, a life with a disability is worth less investment (McCarthy, 2003). Joanne Wilson, the commissioner for the Rehabilitation Services Administration from 2002 to 2005, is blind. She summarized the devaluation and the normative aspect of having a disability when she stated, "It's not quite respectable to have a disability" (Wilson, 2003). Furthermore, many individuals with disabilities may see no value in trying to integrate into a society that automatically discounts and pathologizes them. Taken to its extreme, the normative aspect of this model views a perfect world as a world without disabilities, and the possibility exists of providing the medical profession the mandate with which to eliminate disabilities and the people who experience them (Singer, 2000).

The Biomedical Model places people with disabilities in stigmatizing categories, therefore allowing the "general public" to view them as their category—"the blind," "quads" (individuals with quadriplegia), or "the mentally ill" (Nagi, 1969). Regardless of the category, categorized people are viewed as their category and not as individuals. Schur (1971) described the effects of categorization:

> Others respond to devalued persons in terms of their membership in the stigma-laden category. Individual qualities and actions become secondary.... Individuals of devalued categories are treated as being... substitutable for each other.... Stigmatized persons, then, are little valued as persons. Classificatory status tends to displace alternative criteria of personal worth.... Others may claim license—implicitly, if not explicitly—to treat stigmatized individuals in exploitative and degrading ways. (pp. 30–31)

This categorization according to disability type has had many pervasive, institutional, and systematic consequences, some of which have resulted in inferior services or a lack of services from the counseling professions. In addition, this categorization has fragmented people with disabilities from their own community and robbed them of a collective history (Hahn, 1985, 1988, 1993). Categorization has also successfully taught society to focus on the disability category rather than the universal problems and challenges faced by people with all types of disabilities. Because of the strength and prestige of the Biomedical Model, both the general public and individuals with disabilities have come to see people with disabilities as categories.

In the Biomedical Model, the disability exists totally within the individual, and, accordingly, the individual responsible for the "problem" should also be totally responsible for the solution (Kiesler, 1999). This view, therefore, has the authority to relieve society of any responsibility to accord civil rights to individuals with disabilities. After all, the disability is the individual's flaw and tragedy. A disability is thought to be bad luck, but it is the individual's bad luck. Society often communicates to people with disabilities: "This is how the world is. Take it or leave it." Not only does the Biomedical Model legitimatize prejudice and discrimination, but to the general public, its treatment of people with disabilities often does not appear to be prejudicial and stigmatizing. For example, when individuals with disabilities are not integrated into the workplace, schools, and other social institutions, their absence is usually not noticed. After all, according to this attribution theory, individuals with disabilities are thought to be responsible for their stigmatization. Clinicians have attempted to include environmental issues in their classification/diagnostic systems; however, the degree of prejudice and discrimination experienced or the lack of accommodations is typically not considered when medical professionals determine the level of severity of the disability or render a percentage of impairment.

In the traditional view of the Biomedical Model, both the cause of the disability and the solution and treatment rest with the individual. Liachowitz (1988) described an additional responsibility placed on individuals with disabilities: "Recent medical textbooks go further and construe disability as a variable dependent upon characteristics of motivation and adaptability as well as the limiting residue of disease and injury" (p. 12). Individuals concerned with the rights of people with disabilities derisively refer to this as the "Try Harder" syndrome. One hundred years ago, people with disabilities were often given moral and religious education in an attempt to "rehabilitate" them (Byrom, 2004).

These aspects of the Biomedical Model—the pathologizing, the objectification, the categorization, and the individualization of a disability—are dependent on the diagnosis and classification systems used by the medical professions. Certainly, the diagnostic systems of the medical professions are the most objective, standardized, reliable, and morally neutral assessments compared with those of the other models (American Psychiatric Association, 2000; Peterson, 2002; World Health Organization, 1980, 2001). Medical diagnoses are, however, only as valid as the classification systems used, and further, medical diagnoses can be subjective, impressionistic, value-laden judgments of individuals (Clendinen & Nagourney, 1999; Kirk & Kutchins, 1992; D. W. Smart & Smart, 1 997a). L. Eisenberg (1996) stated, "Diagnostic categories and classification schemes are acts of the imagination rather than real things in the world. . . . We must not mistake this for reality itself" (p. xv), whereas Stone (1984), in a chapter titled "Disability as a Clinical Concept," referred to these systems as "false precision" and stated that medical diagnoses are not the product of "a scientific procedure of unquestionable validity, free from error" (p. 111). Stone concluded by pronouncing the determination of a diagnosis as "an unattainable quest for neutrality" (p. 111). Disability scholars (Albrecht, 1992; Reno, Mashaw, & Gradison, 1997) have posited that all diagnoses are based on the dual concepts of clinical neutrality and clear-cut measures of "normality" and that neither complete clinical neutrality nor absolutely clear-cut measures exist.

The Biomedical Model of disability does not provide a strong basis for the treatment and policy considerations of chronic conditions, which include most disabilities (J. F. Smart, 2005a, 2005b). Because of the long history of the two-outcome paradigm of medicine—total cure or the death of the individual—medical professionals work best with acute injuries rather than chronic, long-term disabilities. Vestiges of this two-outcome paradigm remain in insurance payment policies, which dictate that payments for services—such as counseling—are withdrawn once medical stabilization has been achieved and progress toward a full recovery has terminated. This has a kind of reasonableness, because the business of medical insurance was originally based on the Biomedical Model, with physicians acting as gatekeepers and policy makers.

Furthermore, due to the Biomedical Model's lack of attention to the individual's environment and its focus on the individual, this model is less useful for mental and psychiatric disabilities, which are episodic and very responsive to context and environment (Stefan, 2001). In short, the Biomedical Model is much stronger, in both diagnosis and treatment, when dealing with physical disabilities. This narrow emphasis presents difficulties because the definition of disability is enlarging and evolving beyond that of only physical disabilities to include such impairments as learning disabilities, mental illness, and other disorders.

The Biomedical Model is often conceived to be a model of experts in control (J. F. Smart, 2001, 2004), therefore reducing individuals with disabilities to the role of passive and compliant patients. Because most individuals with disabilities do not possess the expertise, knowledge, education, and experience of physicians, they may not be accorded respect as decision makers. For example, many individuals with disabilities have consistently reported that "doctors always underestimate the quality of my life." Thus, the subordinate, dependent, and inferior status of people with disabilities is reinforced by the power differential inherent in the Biomedical Model. Conrad (2004) described another result of the use of medical experts:

> Because of the way the medical profession is organized and the mandate it receives from society, decisions related to medical diagnoses and treatment are virtually controlled by the medical professions. . . . By defining a problem as medical, it is removed from the public realm where there can be discussion by ordinary people and put on a plane where only medical people can discuss it. (p. 22)

As would be expected, much of the current conceptualization of disability is a reaction against the Biomedical Model (Brant & Pope, 1997; Gill, Kewman, & Brannon, 2003; Pope & Tarlov, 1991; Scotch, 1988). In spite of its shortcomings, no one, including proponents of the other models, suggests totally abandoning the Biomedical Model, nor is any intentional harm on the part of the medical profession implied. Indeed, the medical profession itself is moving away from many of the assumptions of this model. Furthermore, in the final analysis, it is the broader society that has endowed the medical professions and the Biomedical Model of disability with the appearance of reality, science, and objectivity.

FUNCTIONAL AND ENVIRONMENTAL MODELS

The Functional and Environmental models are considered together in this article because both are interactional models. In these two models, it makes no sense to discuss the definition of disability, or the ways in which to intervene, without first considering the functions of both the individual and the individual's environment. Therefore, biology becomes less important. Disability is defined in relation to the skills, abilities, and achievements of the individual in addition to biological/organic factors. Thus, these models do recognize the biological factors of a disability. Disadvantages or limitations such as poverty or a lack of education, although social ills, are not considered to be disabilities. Also, although everyone is required to successfully negotiate difficult environments, to undertake demanding functions, and to experience disadvantages, not everyone has a disability.

These two models are considered to be interactive models because the disability (of the individual) interacts with functions and environment (Dembo, 1982; Tanenbaum, 1986; Thomason, Burton, & Hyatt, 1998). Therefore, the definition of disability, the causal attribution, and the solution attribution are not found wholly within the individual (or his or her disability). Instead, adherents of these models of disability recognize the importance of biology but also posit that the environment can cause, contribute to, and exaggerate disability. Furthermore, these models do not view the "problem" of disability as located totally within the individual, suggesting that many of the difficulties of disability are also located outside the individual, specifically within the environment and its functional requirements (Wolfensberger, 1972). If the location of the problem shifts, the onus for the solution of the problem also shifts. By viewing the definition, the cause, and the difficulties of disability as interactional, helping professionals can aim interventions at adapting the environment and functional demands to the needs of the individual with a disability in addition to "rehabilitating" the individual.

Causal attribution differs also, but it is safe to state that for most individuals, the Biomedical Model's conception of causation is much easier to understand. As we have pointed out, in the Biomedical Model the causes and solutions to the disability are found in the individual, and generally the social solution and the built environment are ignored. In contrast, the Environmental and Functional models of disability posit that society can cause disabilities, exaggerate disabilities, and, in the words of some disability scholars, "make disabilities" (Higgins, 1992). Two examples illustrate these models. Itzak Perlman, the world-famous violinist and a survivor of polio, stated that people with disabilities experience two problems: (a) the physical inaccessibility of the environment and (b) the attitudes of the people without disabilities toward disability and people with disabilities (J. F. Smart, 2004). As difficult as these problems are, it can be seen that neither problem concerns the disability itself (or the individual with the disability). Indeed, one of the results of the ADA has been the increased public awareness that many of the problems and obstacles experienced by people with disabilities are due to their environments. Also, it can be seen that for Perlman's major professional function, playing the violin, his difficulty in walking is not a functional disability. The definition of disability varies with the roles expected of the individual. In addition, it can be seen that both of Perlman's difficulties can be ameliorated.

World War II and the resulting demands for a large number of military personnel changed both the functional and environmental definitions of disability. During World War I and World War II, many men who had been residents of institutions for the long-term care of individuals with mental retardation entered the U.S. military and fought in the wars' battles. Sobsey (1994) told of 13 men from such an institution in Connecticut who, in spite of being labeled as having mental retardation, enlisted to fight in World War II. Four of these men were promoted to higher ranks, and 7 were wounded in action. In spite of their war records, most of these men returned to the institution after the war. Sobsey concluded, "wars and labor shortages have repeatedly redefined who has mental retardation" (p. 132). It can be seen that nothing in the disability or the individual changed, but rather changes in the environment occurred.

These two examples also illustrate the disabling effects of prejudice and discrimination, and therefore in both the Environmental and Functional models, the potential exists for incorporating some degree of societal prejudice and discrimination when attempting to render a rating of the severity of a disability. For example, a young African American man with schizophrenia would probably experience more prejudice and discrimination than a Euro-American man who is blind. Medical ratings of the level of severity of these two disabilities might be relatively equal, but the difficulties experienced are probably much greater for the man with schizophrenia, mostly because of societal attitudes. Schizophrenia is a disability that is considered highly stigmatizing, and blindness is not. Furthermore, other perceived characteristics of the individual who "carries" the disability label (such as racial/cultural/ethnic identification, gender, sexual orientation, or age) intersect with the public perception of the disability.

There is a tendency to think that each individual's environment and functions are exclusively unique to that individual. However, broad, general changes in both environment and function can affect the daily life of an individual with a disability. For example, in a society based on physical labor such as farming or mining, a physical disability presents more difficulties than a cognitive disability, but in a service-, information-, and technology-based economy, a physical disability does not cause as many difficulties as does a cognitive disability. Liachowitz (1988) in her book, *Disability as a Social Construct: Legislative Roots,* made a compelling argument that literally overnight, the federal government has the capability to define disability and, therefore, to determine who has a disability. Nazi Germany is an extreme but clear-cut illustration of the Environmental Model and its power to shape the response to disability. Because of the political-social environment (Nazism), "Aryan" Germans with disabilities were systematically mass murdered by their government (Friedlander, 1995; Gallagher, 1990).

The causal attributions of these two models are not as sharply defined and as easily understandable as those of the Biomedical Model; certainly one of the strengths of the Biomedical Model is its strong explanatory power. Nonetheless, both the Functional Model and the Environmental Model possess strengths that the Biomedical Model does not. In addition, the bases of the Functional and Environmental models are more closely related to the theoretical assumption and practice orientations of most counselors.

Viewing the client as a complete person with skills, abilities, and demands and conceptualizing the client within a context allow the counselor to see the client as more than a disability. If the disability is not the only factor in the equation of disability, then the diagnoses and labels attached to the individual will not acquire as much power to define the individual to himself or herself and to others. It will be more difficult to dehumanize people with disabilities and to think of the person with a disability as "not one of us." Labels and diagnoses, and the professionals who render them, will not be as powerful as they once were.

In contrast to the Biomedical Model, the Environmental and Functional models deal more flexibly with psychiatric disabilities that are

> episodic, highly responsive to context and environment, and exist along a spectrum, which theoretically could be cause for hope—people with mental disabilities are frequently strong, talented, competent, and capable, and their environments can be structured in a way to support and increase their strengths, talents, competence, and capabilities. (Stefan, 2001, p. 10)

Because an individual's cultural identification defines his or her functions, roles, and environment to a great extent, the Functional and Environmental models provide a better basis from which to understand and respond to the disabilities experienced by individuals who are not White, middle-class, heterosexual, male, or Euro-American (D. W. Smart & Smart, 1 997b; J. F. Smart & Smart, 1997). The Functional and Environmental models are also more appropriate for chronic conditions, which most disabilities are. With chronic conditions, after medical stabilization, the treatment focus is on maintaining the highest quality of life, avoiding secondary disabilities and complications, supporting independence, acquiring the appropriate assistive technology, and assisting the individual in negotiating developmental tasks. It can be seen that most of these interventions require functional and environmental adaptations—rather than focusing solely on "rehabilitating" the individual.

In the Functional and Environmental models, it is more difficult to dehumanize individuals with disabilities because of the following factors: (a) Categorization by disability type is less likely; (b) the power differential is reduced when the individual is viewed as a total person and not as a stigmatized, medicalized category; and (c) partial responsibility for the response to the disability devolves upon "society" to provide a physically accessible and nonprejudiced environment.

Perhaps most important, the discomfort, anxiety, defensiveness, and existential angst experienced because of the fear of acquiring a disability are decreased when individuals without disabilities take the opportunity to associate with friends, colleagues, and clients with disabilities. Thus, by viewing the individual as more than the disability and conceptualizing the environment and the functional requirements as major determinants of the difficulties experienced by people with disabilities, the fear of acquiring a disability will be greatly reduced.

THE SOCIOPOLITICAL MODEL

The Sociopolitical Model, also referred to as the Minority Model of Disability (Hahn, 1985, 1988, 1991, 1996, 1997; Kleinfield, 1979), is the most recently developed model and, more important, is a fundamental and radical change from the previous models. The Sociopolitical Model (in contrast to the Biomedical Model and the Environmental and Functional models) has the capability to explain and describe more of the day-to-day life of people with disabilities. Certainly, for most people with disabilities, the prejudice and discrimination found in the broader society are more of an obstacle than are medical impairments or functional limitations.

Madeline Will (cited in Weisgerber, 1991), former assistant secretary for education and head of the Office of Special Education and Rehabilitation Services underscored this:

> Most disabled people [sic] ... will tell you that despite what everyone thinks, the disability itself if not what makes everything different. What causes the difficulties are the attitudes society has about being disabled,

attitudes that make a disabled person embarrassed, insecure, uncomfortable, dependent. Of course, disabled people *[sic]* rarely talk about the quality of life. But it has precious little to do with deformity and a great deal to do with society's own defects. (p. 6)

In this model, people with disabilities view themselves as members of a U.S. minority group. Indeed, some disability rights advocates have described Americans with disabilities as "foreigners in their own country" (Higgins, 1992). The hallmarks of this model include self-definition, self-determination, the elimination (or reduction) of the prejudice and discrimination (sometimes referred to as "handicapism"), rejection of medical diagnoses and categories, and the drive to achieve full equality and civil rights under U.S. law.

The Sociopolitical Model refuses to accept the inferior, dependent, and stigmatizing definition of disability; furthermore, in this model, disability is defined as a social construction in that the limitations and disadvantages experienced by people with disabilities have nothing to do with the disability but are only social constructions and therefore unwarranted. If society constructs disability, society can also deconstruct disability. Stigmatization, prejudice, discrimination, inferiority, and handicapism are not inevitable, natural, or unavoidable consequences of disabilities. Inherent in this definition of disability are three aspects: (a) People with disabilities must define disability; (b) people with disabilities must refuse to allow "experts" or "professionals" to define the disability, determine the outcomes of their lives, or judge the quality of their lives; and (c) people with disabilities refuse the "disabled role" of deviance and pathology. Whereas in the past, professionals defined disabilities and the experiences available to individuals with disabilities, disability rights advocates assert their rights to self-definition and self-determination. It can be seen that much of the Sociopolitical Model seeks to displace the "expert in control" basis of the Biomedical Model.

In the past, the disabled role was determined by people who did not have disabilities and therefore had no experience in managing a disability on a day-to-day basis. Individuals with disabilities were expected to learn the rules of this role; to live the rules; and, most important, to believe in the rules. The rules and expectations of this role, although unwritten, were strongly enforced, and individuals who did not comply with these expectations often experienced severe consequences, including lack of services and social isolation. These rules included the following: always be cheerful; face the disability with courage, optimism, and motivations; manage the disability as well as possible (in the view of others); adhere to medical and rehabilitation regimens; request only those accommodations and assistance that others feel are necessary; make others comfortable with the disability; and keep all aspirations at a reasonable level, or stated differently, do not ask for much. Often, a person with a disability who is perceived to have adopted the disabled role is considered to be a "Tiny Tim" by disability rights advocates.

Adherents of the Sociopolitical Model resist medical categorization by diagnosis and, indeed, view this categorization to be a source of prejudice and discrimination (although they acknowledge that prejudice and discrimination were not the intention of the medical profession). According to the Sociopolitical Model, categorization has resulted in (a) teaching individuals who bear the diagnoses to accept the meanings of these labels as their self-identity, (b) allowing the general public to avoid focusing on the universal problems of people with all types of disabilities, (c) fragmenting the disability community so that it cannot form broad coalitions with which to effect sociopolitical changes, and (d) leading "society" to believe that disability is inferiority and that, therefore, the prejudice and discrimination toward people with disabilities are inevitable consequences of the inferiority.

Thus, the Sociopolitical Model minimizes dependence on an academic discipline or professional area of expertise, and it does not consider causal attribution to be a relevant concern. This model is considered to be an interactional model. Disability, in this model, is not viewed as a personal tragedy but as a public concern.

Many scholars and researchers state that the prejudice and discrimination directed toward people with disabilities have been more pervasive than the prejudice and discrimination directed toward any other group of people, and, further, much of this has been due to the Biomedical Model. In their book, Fleischer and Zames (as cited in McCarthy, 2003) pointed out the tendency to overlook prejudice against persons with disabilities:

> In *The Anatomy of Prejudice* (1996), Elisabeth Young-Bruehl analyzes what she believes to be "the four prejudices that have dominated American life and reflection in the past half-century—anti-Semitism, racism, sexism, and homophobia." No reference is made to disability discrimination. Misrepresented as a health, economic, technical, or safety issue rather than discrimination, prejudice based on disability frequently remains unrecognized. (p. 210)

Albrecht (1992) summarized,

> More recent studies suggest that prejudice against impaired persons is more intense than that against other minorities. Bowe (1978) concludes that employer attitudes toward impaired workers are "less favorable than those toward elderly individuals, minority group members,

ex-convicts, and student radicals," and Hahn (1983) finds that handicapped persons are victims of great animosity and rejection than many other groups in society. (p. 245)

Proponents of the Sociopolitical Model assert that this prejudice and discrimination against individuals with disabilities is long-standing, systematic, and institutionalized in American life. The ADA (1990) states,

> Individuals with disabilities are a discrete and insular minority who have been faced with restrictions and limitations, subjected to a history of purposeful unequal treatment, and relegated to a position of political powerlessness in our society, based on characteristics that are beyond the control of such individuals and resulting from stereotypical assumptions not truly indicative of the individual ability of such individuals to participate in and contribute to society. (Seventh Finding)

The ADA (1990) further asserts, "unlike individuals who have experienced discrimination on the basis of race, color, sex, national origin, religion, or age, individuals who have experienced discrimination on the basis of disability have often had no legal recourse to redress such discrimination" (Fourth Finding). Moreover, it is the prejudices, stereotypes, and stigma, and not the disability itself, that are the true handicap and obstacle.

Much like other civil rights movements in the United States and, indeed, building on the history and the methods of the successes of African Americans and the women's movement, the disability rights advocates view the only commonality among people with disabilities as being the prejudice and discrimination they experience. If the occurrence of the disability appears to be unfair and unpredictable, then society's response to disability can nevertheless be equitable, moral, and predictable. A perfect world is not a world without disabilities but a world in which accommodations and services are provided to people with disabilities, and, more important, disability is not viewed as inferiority.

THE POWER OF MODELS

Lack of Interagency Collaboration

All four broad models answer the question, "What is a disability?" (Berkowitz, 1987). Because each model provides a different answer to this question, the needs of the individual with a disability are also determined differently in each of the models (Bickenbach, 1993). All four models contain a definition of disability that reduces it to a single dimension, thus ignoring and excluding other important aspects. Therefore, all of these models are considered to be reductionistic, unidimensional, and somewhat time bound and culture bound. As a result, these incomplete definitions of disability may impede the type of interagency collaboration that has the potential to provide a range of services to individuals with disabilities. In addition, funding policies (which pay for services) are often based on these unidimensional definitions. Occasionally, the meanings ascribed to the disability experience by professional service providers and funding agencies may remain invisible simply because these meanings are not questioned or challenged.

Despite these basic differences, three of the models of disability lump individuals into categories such as "the blind," "the mentally ill" or "quads" (M. G. Eisenberg, Griggins, & Duval, 1982; Wright, 1991). Furthermore, the simple act of "placing" or "assigning" people to categories robs them of their individuality; to counteract this, counselors can assist clients with disabilities in dealing with the effects of automatic categorization.

These definitions of disability vary with the purposes, values, and needs of the definers. Zola's (1993) chapter, "Disability Statistics, What We Count and What It Tells Us," provides an excellent introduction to the varying definitions of disability. Zola's title clearly communicates that definitions (and statistics) of disability are a reflection of the values and needs of the defining group, and because of this, none of the models can be entirely value free or morally neutral.

Blaming the Victim

Models ask the questions, "Who is responsible for the disability" and "Who is responsible for the solution?" (Berkowitz & Hill, 1986; Yelin, 1992) Again, each model answers these questions differently. Determining the onset or acquisition of the disability attempts to understand *how* the disability occurred, or more precisely stated, the etiology of the disability. Often, the search for the etiology or cause of the disability becomes distorted, resulting in implicit or explicit blame, fault, and moral accountability placed on the individual or his or her parents. Nonetheless, for purposes of calculating financial benefits and allocation of services, many disability programs require a clear-cut causal attribution. It is true that regardless of etiology or causal attribution, the treatment of a particular type and severity of disability is almost identical. However, the response of the general population, and hence the personal experience of the person with the disability, is a result of the public's assumptions of causal attribution. For example, an individual who is born with spina bifida is often considered a victim, whereas a person who acquires a spinal cord injury in combat is thought to be a hero, and a person who acquires a spinal cord injury while intoxicated and speeding on a motorcycle, without a helmet, is viewed as a culprit. The attribution of responsibility also determines which professions serve people with disabilities (Albrecht, 1981; Davis, 1997; Reno et al., 1997).

The history of these models can be easily traced simply by looking at the attributions of cause and responsibility in each model and the resulting formulation and implementation of policies and services. Furthermore, these attributions have had a profound effect on the lack of counseling services provided to people with disabilities, simply because the Biomedical Model of disability has dominated. Most important, attribution theory (Heider, 1958) has the power to individualize and privatize the experience of disability by looking for (and seemingly finding) both the cause and the solution for the disability wholly within the individual rather than within the social system. Attribution theories that privatize disability (rather than viewing disability as a public concern) often view the individual as a "patient" or as a "victim," or both.

The models described in this article place varying emphasis on the medical, functional, environmental, and sociopolitical needs and rights of the person with a disability. Three of the models emphasize definitions of disability rather than determining ways in which to intervene. In order for needs to be met, they must be clearly defined (Zola, 1989). For example, in the Biomedical Model, needs are considered to be solely medical; in the Environmental and Functional models, the needs are thought to be those of adapting the environment and functional requirements to fit the requirements of the individual with the disability; and in the Sociopolitical Model, the needs are considered to be full social integration and civil rights. The counseling interventions that flow from each model dictate different responses from the counselor. In order to be even minimally effective, counselors should understand the implications of each model for their manner of practice.

Shaping Self-Identities and Daily Lives

One model, the Biomedical Model, provides labels, diagnoses, categories, and theories of causation and responsibility that are derived from seemingly authoritative and prestigious sources. Diagnostic categories, however, can often be distorted to become stereotypes and uninformed assumptions (Clendinen & Nagourney, 1999). Moreover, these stereotypes are continually socially reinforced in the media and in the educational system, eventually becoming an accepted part of the social environment and, consequently, often remain unidentified and unquestioned (Stone, 1984). The individual with a disability may come to accept these diagnoses, and occasionally the stereotypes, as self-identifiers (Goffman, 1963). Often the individual with a disability is required to label himself or herself with a negative diagnosis or other label to be declared eligible for services and benefits. If disability is thought to be an unbearable personal tragedy, the individual (with a disability) is often effectively taught to be both inferior and dependent.

Despite the fact that these models are only representations of reality, and not reality itself, the assumptions, definitions, and history of each model are so persuasive and long-standing that they are often mistaken for fact (Hannah & Midlarsky, 1987). In addition, the personal daily functioning of the individual with a disability is determined, in large part, by assumptions derived from these models. Where the individual lives, how (and if) the individual is educated, the type and quality of professional services offered, and the degree of social integration afforded the individual are all influenced by the model of disability that is implemented.

Determining Which Academic Disciplines Teach About the Disability Experience

The disability experience, despite the large number of individuals with disabilities, remains invisible in most university curricula (Bauman & Drake, 1997; Hogben & Waterman, 1997). Students in counseling training programs, with the exception of rehabilitation counseling (Thomas, 2004), are typically not required to learn about people with disabilities. Simply because disability has been considered solely a biological and medical concern, only medical schools and the allied health professions have offered course work in disability issues. The "medicalization" of the disability experience has effectively kept the history and viewpoints of people with disabilities outside the realm of counseling education and professional training. Models of disability have provided the explanatory rationale for academic disciplines, and therefore most graduates of counseling programs do not possess competencies to provide services to clients with disabilities. Olkin and Pledger (2003) reported that students are trained *not* to notice the absence of disability issues. In their view, the lack of disability information "in curricula, and among peers and professors—is a powerful statement about the marginalization of people with disabilities" (p. 297). Furthermore, research on disability and people with disabilities, including rigorously designed and executed studies, is often of questionable value because of negative and biased assumptions toward disability. Certainly, any disability-related research study is only as valid as the model of disability upon which it is based. Myerson (1988) provided the following summary:

> The number of investigations that are flawed from inception by prejudicial commonsense assumptions, by theoretical bias, or by methodological error remains high. . . . These errors are functions, in great part, not of [the researchers'] incompetence in the mechanics of research, but

of asking the wrong questions, of incorrect notions of the meaning of disability to those who live with it, and of lack of understanding.... A particular source of error is the narrowly trained clinician who believes that clinical criteria are appropriate measures of problems that arise from systematic social injustice. (pp. 182–1 83)

Myerson concluded that "like others, to the extent that their thinking incorporates cultural myths, [researchers] become prisoners of plausible but erroneous hypotheses" (p. 183).

IMPLICATIONS FOR THE COUNSELING PROFESSION

Biology is still a factor in the equation of disability; however, biology does not matter as much as has been previously thought (J. F. Smart, 2005c). For counselors, this assumption has important implications because for the client with a disability, self-identity and the conceptualization of his or her life situation are derived from these basic concepts. In contrast, many professionals may, consciously or unconsciously, ascribe more importance to the biological and physical aspects of the disability than the client does. The individual with a disability certainly does not conceive of his or her life in these four neatly (and artificially) explained models. However, counselors can, albeit unintentionally, reinforce the status quo by unquestioningly accepting the assumptions, including expectations for the client's self-actualization, of these models and their labels and diagnoses. Clients with disabilities, on the other hand, may enter the counseling relationship with the expectation of receiving inaccurate (and often negative) diagnoses and inadequate services, often provided in offices that are inaccessible. Nevertheless, counselors are in a unique position to recognize the interplay of personal characteristics and environmental factors in a developmental context. Furthermore, counselors have long recognized the value of empowerment for all clients. The following is a listing of some implications for the counseling profession.

1. Counselors should engage in an ongoing examination of clients' feelings about the experience of disability and the resulting interaction of the counselor's own identity with that of the client. Taken to the extreme, the counselor may focus more on himself or herself if the disability of the client arouses feelings of existential angst, anxiety, and defensiveness, much of which is a result of the widely held view of the Biomedical Model of disability. If the counselor views disability as a tragic inferiority, then he or she will more likely experience a negative, emotional response to the client with a disability. Countertransference, and other emotional reactions to the disability of the client, may prevent the counselor from

fully understanding the client and therefore negatively affect the counseling relationship.

2. Counselors should recognize that most individuals with disabilities do not accept the basic tenets of the Biomedical Model of disability. Rather, they may view the disability as a valued part of their identity; see positive aspects in having the disability; not view the disability as tragic or limiting or being an inferiority; and would not choose to eliminate the disability if they could. At times, it may be necessary to ask the client about his or her identity as a person with a disability. Counselors must recognize that clients with disabilities want respect and not sympathy (Harris, 1992). Indeed, sympathy and lowered expectations may be considered to be stigmatizing and prejudicial; sympathy and lowered expectations toward people with disabilities often result in withholding helpful and honest feedback, reduce the range of opportunities open to the individual, foster dependence, and subtly communicate the message to clients with a disability that standards will be lowered for them because they are not perceived (by the counselor) to be capable.

3. Counselors should recognize that the disability is simply one part of the individual's identity. As does everyone, the client with a disability has multiple identities and multiple roles. Disability is not the "master status." Furthermore, a deeper and more complete understanding of the client's varied identities, functions, and environments will facilitate the implementation of the Environmental and Functional models of disability in the counseling process. Disability identity also constantly shifts and develops, as do all identities.

4. Counselors know that empowerment refers to the processes and outcomes relating to issues of control, critical awareness, and participation (Perkins & Zimmerman, 1995). For clients with disabilities,

> empowerment values provide a belief system that governs how our clients and we as professionals can work together. Based on this paradigm shift, there are substantial changes to be made to our practice.... Empowerment values include attention toward health, adaptation, and competence, and the enabling environment. As professionals, our goal is to promote our clients' full participation and integration into their communities. The collaboration ... is itself an empowering process. (Tate, 2001, p. 133)

5. As with any other client, the counselor may occasionally need to guard against imposing his or her values on the client with a disability (Norcross, 2002). Clients with disabilities have, at times, interpreted their counselors' guidance as a type of the "Try Harder Syndrome," or some individuals with disabilities have felt themselves to have been given the

negative label by counselors of denying their disability. Often, clients with disabilities are not denying the presence, implications, or permanence of the disability, but rather they are denying the "disabled role" of pathology, inferiority, and deviance. Therefore, these clients may terminate counseling prematurely because they have felt misjudged.

6. The power differential between counselor and client with a disability should be addressed. Often, the power differential is increased when the client has a disability and the counselor does not. If the counselor subscribes to the Biomedical Model, with its strong normative emphasis, this increased power differential may impede the establishment of rapport and trust. Furthermore, this power imbalance in the therapeutic setting may simply reflect the broader world in which the client functions.

7. Counselors should listen to their clients and be willing to hear about experiences of prejudice and discrimination experienced by their clients with disabilities. Learning the basic tenets of the Sociopolitical Model of disability will provide counselors with some introductory understanding of this stigmatization and discrimination, and, accordingly, counselors will be able to set aside some of their preconceived notions concerning the experiences of their clients with disabilities. Counselors should recognize that many clients with disabilities may not seek services at counseling agencies because they understand that often the counselors at these agencies may reinforce the prejudice and discrimination of the broader culture. On the other hand, counselors need to avoid attributing all the client's issues and problems to prejudice and discrimination. Nonetheless, for most people with disabilities, self-identification as a person with a disability does not automatically translate into group consciousness or political action (Scotch, 1988).

8. Counselors should recognize that, for many of them, their professional training may be inadequate to prepare them with the skills and competencies to work with clients with disabilities. Also, some theoretical approaches and counseling practices have their basis in the Biomedical Model and therefore, simply "adapting" these approaches and orientations for clients with disabilities may be at best ineffective and at worst harmful. Stated differently, the little professional training counselors have received may be faulty and ill conceived. Counselors who do not have adequate training must seek opportunities for additional education.

9. Counselors should examine their willingness to broaden their vision about the experience of disability. On one hand, counselors may have strong needs to be knowledgeable, skilled, and helpful, but on the other hand, counselors may view disability as ambiguous and inferior. Students in counseling programs should seek out course work (such as is available in Rehabilitation Counseling programs) and other workshops that focus on disability issues. Certainly, information about a client's identity and

feelings about his or her disability must come from that individual, but obtaining a broad knowledge of the topic of disability is imperative. It is not ethical or appropriate to expect clients with disabilities to teach counselors about the world of disability.

10. Both outreach efforts and collaborative learning among counseling professions can be achieved by learning which agencies people with disabilities typically go to for assistance (such as state Vocational Rehabilitation offices) and then establishing professional relationships with these agencies.

11. Professionals, in all aspects of counseling, should intervene at institutional and political levels when appropriate and possible. Although individual counseling and support for clients with disabilities can make a contribution to the larger society, advocating for changes in systems and policies, alerting the public to manifestations of prejudice and discrimination in the media, and advocating for environmental accessibility can also be valuable contributions. Counselors, both as individuals and as part of statewide, regional, or national professional organizations, can create change.

12. Counselors should recognize that it is necessary to clearly articulate the assumptions about models of disability that underlie research studies. Research can be more sharply focused if the basic assumptions and values about people with disabilities are made clear. Articulating these values as they relate to one or more of the four models of disability would help both researchers and consumers of research evaluate the research findings.

In order to provide ethical and effective services to clients with disabilities, counseling professionals in all aspects of the field will be required to examine the ways in which they conceptualize the experience of disability. For some counseling professionals, many of these ideas, derived from the models of disability, may be new and different ways of responding to people with disabilities. For others, these ideas will provide a useful adjunct to the counseling services or the counseling training and education they provide.

REFERENCES

Akabas, S. H. (2000). Practice in the world of work. In P. Allen-Meares & C. Garvin (Eds.), *The handbook of social work: Direct practice* (pp. 449–517). Thousand Oaks, CA: Sage.

Albrecht, G. L. (Ed.). (1981). *Cross national rehabilitation policies: A sociological perspective*. Beverly Hills, CA: Sage.

Albrecht, G. L. (1992). *The disability business: Rehabilitation in America*. Newbury Park, CA: Sage.

American Psychiatric Association. (2000). *Diagnostic and statistical manual of mental disorders* (4th ed., text rev.). Washington, DC: Author.

Americans With Disabilities Act of 1990, 42 U.S.C.A. § 12101.

Bauman, H. D. L., & Drake, J. (1997). Silence is not without voice: Including deaf culture within the multicultural curricula. In L. J. Davis (Ed.), *Disability studies reader* (pp. 307–314). New York: Routledge.

Berkowitz, M. (1987). *Disabled policy: America's programs for the handicapped.* London, England: Cambridge University Press.

Berkowitz, M., & Hill, M. A. (Eds.). (1986). *Disability and the labor market: Economic problems, policies, and programs.* Ithaca, NY: Cornell University Press.

Bickenbach, J. E. (1993). *Physical disability and social policy.* Toronto, Ontario, Canada: University of Toronto.

Bickenbach, J. E., Somnath, C., Badley, E. M., & Ustun, T. B. (1999). Models of disablement, universalism and the International Classification of Impairments, Disabilities and Handicaps. *Social Science & Medicine, 48,* 1173–1187.

Bowe, F. (1980). *Rehabilitation America: Toward independence for disabled and elderly people.* New York: Harper & Row.

Brant, E. N., & Pope, A. M. (Eds.). (1997). *Enabling America: Assessing the role of rehabilitation science and engineering.* Washington, DC: National Academy Press.

Byrom, B. (2004). A pupil and a patient: Hospital schools in progressive America. In S. Danforth & S. D. Taff (Eds.), *Crucial readings in special education* (pp. 25–3 7). Upper Saddle River, NJ: Pearson-Merrill, Prentice Hall.

Clendinen, D., & Nagourney, A. (1999). *Out for good: The struggle to build a gay rights movement in America.* NewYork: Simon & Schuster.

Conrad, P. (2004). The discovery of hyperkinesis: Notes on the medicalization of deviant behavior. In S. Danforth & S. D. Taff (Eds.), *Crucial readings in special education* (pp. 18–24). Upper Saddle River, NJ: Pearson-Merrill, Prentice Hall.

Davis, L. J. (1997). Constructing normalcy: The bell curve, the novel, and the invention of the disabled body in the nineteenth century. In L. J. Davis (Ed.), *Disability studies reader* (pp. 307–314). New York: Routledge.

Dembo, T. (1982). Some problems in rehabilitation as seen by a Lewinian. *Journal of Social Issues, 38,* 131–139.

Eisenberg, L. (1996). Foreword. In J. E. Mezzich, A. Kleinman, H. Fabrega Jr., & D. L. Parron (Eds.), *Culture and psychiatric diagnosis: A DSM-IV perspective* (pp. xiii–xv). Washington, DC: American Psychiatric Association.

Eisenberg, M. G., Griggins, C., & Duval, R. J. (Eds.). (1982). *Disabled people as second-class citizens.* New York: Springer.

Employment and Disability Institute. (1996). National health interview survey. Retrieved August 10, 2003, from www.disabilitystatistics.org

Friedlander, H. (1995). *The origins of Nazi genocide: From euthanasia to the final solution.* Chapel Hill: University of North Carolina Press.

Gallagher, H. G. (1990). *By trust betrayed: Patients, physicians, and the license to kill in the Third Reich.* New York: Holt.

Gill, C. J., Kewman, D. G., & Brannon, R. W. (2003). Transforming psychological practice and society: Policies that reflect the new paradigm. *American Psychologist, 58,* 305–312.

Goffman, E. (1963). *Stigma: Notes on the management of spoiled identity.* Englewood Cliffs, NJ: Prentice Hall.

Hahn, H. (1985). Toward a politics of disability: Definitions, disciplines, and policies. *Social Science Journal, 22,* 87–105.

Hahn, H. (1988). The politics of physical differences: Disability and discrimination. *Journal of Social Issues, 44,* 39–47.

Hahn, H. (1991). Alternative views of empowerment: Social services and civil rights. *Journal of Rehabilitation, 57,* 17–19.

Hahn, H. (1993). The political implications of disability definitions and data. *Journal of Disability Policy Studies, 4,* 41–52.

Hahn, H. (1996). Antidiscrimination laws and social research on disability: The minority group perspectives. *Behavioral Sciences and the Law, 14,* 41–59.

Hahn, H. (1997). Advertising the acceptable employment image: Disability and capitalism. In L. J. Davis (Ed.), *The disability studies reader* (pp. 172–186). New York: Routledge.

Hannah, M. E., & Midlarsky, E. (1987). Differential impact of labels and behavioral descriptions on attitudes toward people with disabilities. *Rehabilitation Psychology, 32,* 227–238.

Harris, R. (1992). Musing from 20 years of hard earned experience. *Rehabilitation Education, 6,* 207–212.

Hayes, P. A. (2001). *Addressing cultural complexities in practice: A framework for clinicians and counselors.* Washington, DC: American Psychological Association.

Heider, F. (1958). *The psychology of interpersonal relations.* New York: Wiley.

Higgins, P. C. (1992). *Making disability: Exploring the social transformation of human variation.* Springfield, IL: Thomas.

Hogben, M., & Waterman, C. K. (1997). Are all of your students represented in their textbooks? A content analysis of coverage of diversity issues in introductory psychology textbooks. *Teaching of Psychology, 24,* 95–100.

Hulnick, M. R., & Hulnick, H. R. (1989). Life's challenges: Curse or opportunity? Counseling families of persons with disabilities. *Journal of Counseling & Development, 68,* 166–170.

Humes, C. W., Szymanski, E. M., & Hohenshil, T. H. (1989). Roles of counseling in enabling persons with disabilities. *Journal of Counseling & Development, 68,* 145–150.

Kemp, N. T., & Mallinckrodt, B. (1996). Impact of professional training on case conceptualization of clients with a disability. *Professional Psychology: Research and Practice, 27,* 378–385.

Kiesler, D. J. (1999). *Beyond the disease model of mental disorders.* Westport. CT: Praeger.

Kirk, S. A., & Kutchins, H. (1992). *The selling of the DSM: The rhetoric of science in psychiatry.* New York: Aldine Degruyter.

Kleinfield, S. (1979). *The hidden minority: A profile of handicapped Americans.* Boston: Atlantic Monthly Press.

Liachowitz, C. H. (1988). *Disability as a social construct: Legislative roots.* Philadelphia: University of Pennsylvania Press.

Longmore, P. K. (1995). Medical decision making and people with disabilities: A clash of cultures. *Journal of Law, Medicine and Ethics, 23,* 82–87.

McCarthy, H. (1993). Learning with Beatrice A. Wright: A breath of fresh air that uncovers the unique virtues and human flaws in us all. *Rehabilitation Education, 10,* 149–166.

McCarthy, H. (2003). The disability rights movement: Experiences and perspectives of selected leaders in the disability community. *Rehabilitation Counseling Bulletin, 46,* 209–223.

Melia, R. P., Pledger, C., & Wilson, R. (2003). Disability and rehabilitation research. *American Psychologist, 58,* 289–295.

Myerson, L. (1988). The social psychology of physical disability. *Journal of Social Issues, 44,* 173–188.

Nagi, S. Z. (1969). *Disability and rehabilitation: Legal, clinical, and self-concepts and measurements.* Columbus: Ohio State University Press.

Norcross, J. C. (Ed.). (2002). *Psychotherapy relationships that work: Therapist contributions and responsiveness to patient needs.* New York: Oxford University Press.

Olkin, R. (1999). *What psychotherapists should know about disability.* New York: Guilford.

Olkin, R., & Pledger, C. (2003). Can disability studies and psychology join hands? *American Psychologist, 58,* 296–298.

Perkins, D. D., & Zimmerman, M. A. (1995). Empowerment theory: Research and applications. *American Journal of Community Psychology, 23,* 569–579.

Peterson, D. B. (2002). *International Classification of Functioning, Disability, and Health (ICF): A primer for rehabilitation psychologists.* Unpublished manuscript, New York University.

Pledger, C. (2003). Discourse on disability and rehabilitation issues. *American Psychologist, 58,* 279–284.

Pope, A. M., & Tarlov, A. R. (1991). *Disability in America: Toward a national agenda for prevention.* Washington, DC: National Academies Press.

Reno, V. P., Mashaw, J. L., & Gradison, B. (Eds.). (1997). *Disability: Challenges for social insurance, health care financing, and labor market policy.* Washington, DC: National Academy of Social Insurance.

Schur, E. M. (1971). *Labeling deviant behavior: Its sociological implications.* New York: Harper & Row.

Scotch, R. K. (1988). Disability as a basis for a social movement: Advocacy and the politics of definition. *Journal of Social Issues, 44,* 159–172.

Singer, P. (2000). *Writings on an ethical life.* New York: Ecco.

Smart, D. W., & Smart, J. F. (1997a). *DSM-IV* and culturally sensitive diagnosis: Some observations for counselors. *Journal of Counseling & Development, 75,* 392–398.

Smart, D. W., & Smart, J. F. (1997b). The racial/ethnic demography of disability. *Journal of Rehabilitation, 63,* 9–15.

Smart, J. F. (2001). *Disability, society and the individual.* Austin, TX: Pro-Ed.

Smart, J. F. (2004). Models of disability: The juxtaposition of biology and social construction. In T. F. Riggar & D. R. Maki (Eds.), *Handbook of rehabilitation counseling* (pp. 25–49). New York: Springer.

Smart, J. F. (2005a). Challenges to the Biomedical Model of disability: Changes to the practice of rehabilitation counseling. *Directions in Rehabilitation Counseling, 16*(4), 33–43.

Smart, J. F. (2005b). The promise of the International Classification of Functioning, Disability, and Health (ICF). *Rehabilitation Education, 19*, 191–199.

Smart, J. F. (2000c). *Tracing the ascendant trajectory of models of disability: Confounding competition or a cross-model approach?* Unpublished manuscript, Utah State University, Logan.

Smart, J. F., & Smart, D. W. (1997). Culturally sensitive informed choice in rehabilitation counseling. *Journal of Applied Rehabilitation Counseling, 28*, 32–37.

Sobsey, D. (1994). *Violence and abuse in the lives of people with disabilities: The end of silent acceptance.* Baltimore: Brookes.

Stefan, S. (2001). *Unequal rights: Discrimination against people with mental disabilities and the Americans with Disabilities Act.* Washington, DC: American Psychiatric Association.

Stone, D. A. (1984). *The disabled state.* Philadelphia: Temple University Press.

Tanenbaum, S. J. (1986). *Engineering disability: Public policy and compensatory technology.* Philadelphia: Temple University Press.

Tate, D. G. (2001). Hospital to community: Changes in practice and outcomes. *Rehabilitation Psychology, 46*, 125–138.

Tate, D. G., & Pledger, C. (2003). An integrative conceptual framework of disability. *American Psychologist, 58*, 289–295.

Thomas, K. R. (2004). Old wine in a slightly cracked new bottle. *American Psychologist, 59*, 274–275.

Thomason, T., Burton, J. F., Jr., & Hyatt, D. R. (Eds.). (1998). *New approaches to disability in the workplace.* Madison: University of Wisconsin Press.

Trieschmann, R. (1987). *Aging with a disability.* New York: Demos.

U.S. Department of Education, Office of Special Education and Rehabilitative Services, National Institute on Disability and Rehabilitation Research. (2000). *Long-range plan 1999–2003.* Washington, DC: Author.

Weisgerber, R. S. (1991). *Quality of life for persons with disabilities.* Gaithersburg, MD: Aspen.

Wilson, J. (2003, October). *Johnny Lingo: Helping clients to fulfill their potential.* Speech given at the national training conference of the National Council on Rehabilitation Education/Rehabilitation Services Administration/Council of State Administrators of Vocational Rehabilitation, Arlington, VA.

Wolfensberger, W. (1972). *The principle of normalization in human services.* Toronto, Ontario, Canada: National Institute on Mental Retardation.

World Health Organization. (1980). *International Classification of Impairments, Disabilities, and Handicaps: A manual of classification relating to the consequences of disease.* Geneva, Switzerland: Author.

World Health Organization. (2001). *International Classification of Impairments, Disabilities, and Handicaps: A manual of classification relating to the consequences of disease.* Geneva, Switzerland: Author.

Wright, B. A. (1991). Labeling: The need for greater person-environment individuation. In C. R. Snyder & D. R. Forsythe (Eds.), *Handbook of social and clinical psychology* (pp. 469–487). Elmsford, NY: Pergamon.

Yelin, E. H. (1992). *Disability and the displaced worker.* New Brunswick, NJ: Rutgers University Press.

Zola, I. K. (1989). Toward a necessary universalizing of a disability policy. *Milbank Quarterly, 67,* 401–428.

Zola, I. K. (1993). Disability statistics, what we count and what it tells us. *Journal of Disability Policy Studies, 4,* 9–39.

CHAPTER SEVEN

The Contributions of the Physically and Mentally Handicapped to Development

Jean Vanier

Those who live close to wounded people become rather accustomed to hearing talks about how so-called "normal" people should help their unfortunate brothers and sisters. We rarely ask what handicapped people can bring to others. The very thought rarely comes to mind; it seems so remote and farfetched.

And yet I feel deeply that handicapped people have an important part to play in the development of the world, in helping it to find its equilibrium. They can ensure that development is not just a development of mind and matter, but a development of the total human person, who is certainly intelligence and creativity, activity and productivity, but who is also a heart, capable of love, a seeker of peace, hope, light, and trust, striving to assume the reality of suffering and of death.

From "The contributions of the physically and mentally handicapped to development," by J. Vanier, 1975, Development and Participation—Operational Implications for Social Welfare. Proceedings of the XVIIth International Conference on Social Welfare, Nairobi, Kenya, 290–297. Published in 1975 for the International Council on Social Welfare by Columbia University Press, New York & London. Also published in The Psychological and Social Impact of Illness and Disability, 1st Edition. NY: Springer, 1977. Reprinted by permission.

I have had the grace and joy to live with mentally handicapped adults over the last ten years. With friends, we have been able to create some forty-five small homes for men and women who were either roaming the streets, locked up in asylums, or just living idly—though frequently in a state of aggression or depression—with families who did not know how to cope with them. These homes of l'Arche are in France, Canada, the United States, England, Scotland, Belgium, and Denmark, as well as in Calcutta and Bangalore in India; our first home in West Africa is just beginning in the Ivory Coast. Each of these homes welcomes and finds work for eight to ten handicapped men and women and for their helpers or assistants. They try to be communities of reconciliation where everyone can grow in activity, creativity, love, and hope. Some of the handicapped people leave us and find total autonomy; others, who are more severely handicapped, will stay with us always.

It is this experience of daily living, working, and sharing with my handicapped brothers and sisters that has made me so sensitive to the question of their contribution to the development of our world. A man or woman can only find peace of heart and grow in motivation and creativity if he or she finds a meaning to life. If they are there only to be helped and can bring nothing to others, then they are condemned to a life of simply receiving, of being the last, the most inferior. This will necessarily bring them to depression and a lack of confidence in themselves. This in turn will push them into anguish and make them aggressive towards themselves and others. For them to find real meaning in life, they must find people who sense their utility, their capacity for growth, and their place in the community and in the world.

The tragedy of humanity is not primarily the lack of development of peoples, or even poverty. It is the oppression, the despisal, and the rejection of those who are weak and in want. It is the horrible and disastrous inequality of wealth and opportunity and lack of sharing. The tragedy of man is his hardness of heart, which makes individuals and nations endowed with the riches of this world despise and consider as inferior those who are poor and handicapped. They not only refuse to help them, they tend also to reject and exploit them.

The tragedy of mankind is the collective national or religious prejudices and pride that close nations and peoples upon themselves, making them think and act as if they were the elected ones and the others enemies to be rejected and hurt, whose development and expansion should be checked. Our world today, with its terrible divisions and hatred, with its continual sounds of war, with its vast budgets being poured into armaments instead of into works for love and justice, is the result of these prejudices and fears.

The tragedy of our world today is that man is still afraid of man. Far from seeing other individuals and peoples as collaborators in the mystery of universal human growth, we see them as enemies of our own growth and development.

It is of course terribly important that misery and starvation be erased from our earth. It is of course terribly important that everyone has access to social and medical benefits. But it is even more important that the hearts of all men open up to universal love and to the understanding of others, to gentle service to mankind and especially to its weaker members. For if we do not work together to create a world of fraternity and of peace, we will sink in wars, economic crises, and national disasters.

There is a continual struggle in all our countries between traditional religious and moral values, lived through family ties, and economic and industrial development. Highly industrialized countries offer a certain financial prosperity, but so frequently this prosperity has been achieved at the cost of the values of community. Competition and the desire for wealth, individual leisure, and liberty have tended to crush compassion and understanding. So it is that we find old people lingering in homes for the aged, handicapped people in large institutions, and a mass of marginal and suffering people unable to work because of alcoholism, drugs, and social ills. We find thousands of children abandoned and given over to social agencies, a frightening rise in delinquency, and prisons that offer only punishment instead of reeducation and so cause the high rise in recidivism. We find mental disease rampant, because in our search for efficiency we have lost our acceptance of "the other" and prefer to label people "mad" rather than to understand them. We condemn more and more people to live like strangers, in terrible loneliness, in our large urban conglomerations. The growing population of our cities, our disastrous housing, and inhuman working conditions bring a real disequilibrium of the human heart in its quest for love, peace, and truth.

In the small villages of Africa and India, or in rural areas of North America and Europe, there are still sturdy people living simply off the land and artisans bound closely to the matter with which they work. There is deep love and commitment among families. There is a spirit of gentleness and openness, sharing and welcome for the stranger, which has often been lost in the big cities. Certainly this is a generalization, for there are also tribal warfares and social injustices and individual anguishes. But we must not forget the values of fraternity and community held by simple people, which are so often crushed with the coming of economic development. We can see the gradual breakdown of these values as the desire for material possessions is stimulated, as the attractions of big-city leisure activities become stronger, and the older generation and its ways are rejected.

Of course, it is essential that people should develop and find the benefits of greater wealth and security. But it is even more essential that this development take place in a human context that safeguards and strengthens the forces of sharing, participation, and responsibility. Where economic development coincides with the breakdown of cultural and ethnic ties, where villages are destroyed; where children are displaced and men obliged to leave their homes for far-off lands, the situation is extremely serious: It can gradually cause the destruction of what makes a human a person.

In each of us there is a mixture of weakness and strength. Each of us is born in weakness, unable to fend for ourselves, to find nourishment, to clothe ourselves, or to walk. The growth to autonomy is long and slow, and demands many years of loving education. The period of strength and capacity, during adolescence and manhood, the period during which we are able to act efficaciously and to defend ourselves, to struggle against the forces of nature and environment, is in fact short. After it, we all enter a period of weakness, when our bodies become tired and sick, when we are hurt by the trials and sufferings inherent in human life. And all of us are then called to the last and final poverty of death.

The child in his weakness has all the potential of activity that must grow in him. The strongest of men is inherently weak, because he has a mortal body, and also because he is called to love and is vulnerable to the sufferings of love and of infidelity in friendship; he is weak because he is capable of depression and sadness, drowning in the vicissitudes of life.

The society that encourages only the strong and the intelligent tends to forget that man is essentially weak. We are all potentially handicapped, and we are all created to suffer and to die. So often the search for riches, or hyperactivity in work, is a flight from these essential realities which we must all face one day. What is the meaning of our life, and of suffering, and of death? Are we called simply to be active and to gather wealth, or does man find peace of heart, interior liberty, and happiness in the growth of love? Is it not in service to others, sharing, and mutual understanding—which is not mere sentimentality—that we find this inner peace and human fulfillment?

If people do not refind this energy of love and acceptance of their own intrinsic poverty, if they do not discover that joy comes more in giving then in taking, we are heading for more conflict. If we do not grow in the desire to give our lives rather than to exploit and take the lives of others, than we are all doomed to destruction.

In all societies there are vast numbers of weaker brothers and sisters: those who are aged or depressed, those who have been struck by sickness while young and cannot take on a working life. Are these people just misfits who must be gradually eliminated? Are they just people we must try to reeducate so that they become active members of society? Or have they a special place and role in the development of our society? This is the question we must ask ourselves.

My experience of living with the wounded, the weak, is that they have very precious values that must be conserved for the full development of society. Their experience of rejection, their experience of suffering, which is a taste of death, has brought them closer to certain realities that others who have not suffered flee and pretend do not exist.

Handicapped people have all the rights of other men: the right to life, to medical and social help, and to work. They are able, when this is recognized, to develop in so many ways. With the right educational and work techniques, many can find their place in the world of work and become totally integrated in that world. I have seen men who at the age of six were judged incapable of any growth, working in a factory at the age of twenty and living quite autonomously. Others who were condemned to asylums, to beggary, or to total inactivity are now finding fulfillment as artisans and enjoying life in the community. With care, loving attention, and the right kind of technical help, many can find their place in society.

Handicapped people, and particularly those who are less "able," are frequently endowed with qualities of heart that serve to remind so-called "normal" people that their own hearts are closed. Their simplicity frequently serves to reveal our own duplicity, untruthfulness, and hypocrisy. Their acceptance of their own situation and their humility frequently reveal our pride and our refusal to accept others as they are.

I had occasion once to appear on television with Helen and some others. Helen has cerebral palsy. She cannot talk, she cannot walk, she cannot eat by herself. She is condemned to a wheelchair for the rest of her life. Her only means of communication is through a typewriter, on which she laboriously expresses her thoughts with two fingers. But Helen has the most beautiful smile. She gives herself through her smile. At one moment in the program, someone asked her if she was happy. She broke out into a big smile and typed: "I wouldn't change my life for anything in the world." Her smile got even bigger, and as the program closed, the camera picked up the last word she was writing: "Alleluia!"

Helen, who has nothing except her joy and her love, revealed to me, and to so many who possess the goods of this earth, that fulfillment does not come from material riches but from some inner strength and liberty. Through her acceptance of herself and her condition, she showed how poor we are, in all our petty quarrels, pride, and desires.

At a weekly meeting with some two hundred people, there was a handicapped man called Glen. He could not use his legs, and he lay on the floor. During the last day, there was a period when each person could express what he felt about the week's activity. Glen propped himself up and just said: "I have only one thing to tell you: I love you all so much." His simple words broke down the barriers of convention and of fear in many of us. He wasn't afraid to talk of love.

So often "normal" people have interior barriers that prevent them from relating with others in a simple way. All of us have deep needs to love and to be loved. All of us are in the conflict of our fear of death and of our own poverty. We so quickly pretend we are more clever, more intelligent, and more powerful than we actually are. So often we flee reality by throwing ourselves into activity, culture, and the struggle for power and prestige. We lose contact with our deep inner selves. Handicapped people do not always have these barriers. In their poverty, they are more simple and loving, and thus they reveal to us the poverty of our riches.

The weaker members of society are total human persons, children of God. They are not misfits or objects of charity. Their weaknesses and special needs demand deep attention, real concern, and continuing support. If we listen to their call and to their needs, they will flourish and grow. If we do not, they will sink into depression, sadness, inward revolt, and a form of spiritual suicide. And we who carry responsibilities will have closed our beings to love and to a strength that comes from God and which is hidden in the smallest and the weakest.

Those who take time to listen to them, who have the inner peace and patience to respond to their silent call, will hear crying in them the great dry of all humanity for love and for peace. A great Dutch psychiatrist has written of the schizophrenic that he is not insane, not made of wood, but is "the loudspeaker from whom the sufferings of our time ring perhaps most clearly" (Foundraine, 1974). The same can be said for all weak and handicapped people who cannot fend for themselves.

If we listen to them, then we, the so-called "normal" people, will be healed of our unconscious egoisms, our hardness of heart, our search for power and for dissipating leisure. We will discover that love, communion, presence, community, and deep interior liberty and peace are realities to be found and lived. We will discover that these can become the inspiration for all men. We will realize more fully that men are not machines or objects to be used, exploited, tyrannized, and manipulated by law and by organizations, but that each one is beautiful and precious, that each one in his uniqueness is like a flower that should find its place in, the garden of humanity for the fulfillment and beauty of all mankind.

If each one of us who holds a responsible place in society pays attention to the heartbeats of the smallest, the weakest, and the companionless, then gradually we will make of our countries not lands of competition, which favor the strong and powerful, but lands of justice, peace, and fraternity where all men unite and cooperate for the good of every man.

Then nations will no longer rival each other in their search for power, prestige, and wealth, but will work together. They will turn from fear and from group prejudices and from the creation of large and horribly expensive armies. They will use their intelligence, strength, wealth, and natural resources for the growth of all men throughout the world, and especially for the smallest, the weakest, and the companionless. Mankind will then, through the heart of the poor and those crucified in their flesh, refind the road to unity and universal love, where all can be themselves without fear, growing together in love and in the peace of God, our beloved Father.

REFERENCE

Foundraine, J. (1974). *Not made of wood*. London: Quartet Books.

PART I

Discussion Questions

1. What prevents a professional service provider from assisting those with disabilities to express self-determination or to voice their own needs?
2. What do you believe is more important for the personal adjustment of someone with a disability: to address the barriers of a disabling environment or to focus on the consumer's personal characteristics impeding adjustment?
3. Compare the benefits and deficits of persons who have disabilities when they are viewed from the perspective of the "minority group" versus the "functional limits model."
4. Why is the "minority group" model challenging the "functional limitations" model?
5. What are the differences between a sociopolitical perspective and the medical and/or economic definition of disability?
6. Do you believe that the sociopolitical perspective of disability has been empowering to people with disabilities?
7. Why is it important for the concept of disability to be re-evaluated in this 21st century?
8. Do you believe that there is something unique about disability that requires special policies and programs?
9. What is your personal experience about any change in our understanding of the concept of disability?
10. If people with disabilities are to actively participate in the development and implementation of their rehabilitation plans, would such participation undermine the role of the professional as the "expert"?

PART I

Personal Perspective

Dale Walsh

The meaning of these articles in Part I take on an engaging implication with the Personal Statement of Dale Walsh, which is reprinted from the fourth edition. Personal statements show graphically and poignantly how the concepts presented in the literature assume a forceful meaning when they are "lived out" in daily life. Dr. Walsh, both a professional of mental health services and a consumer of these same services, discusses her own difficult recovery journey. She echoes the truth identified in several of the articles that consumer empowerment is more than a vital component of recovery; it promotes an environment that really fosters recovery. In her statement of what stimulates the coping with stigma and discrimination associated with a severe mental health condition, she emphasizes the consumer's initiating behavior emerging from a participatory role in one's rehabilitation. This behavior of involvement is just one of many positive outcomes from the conceptual models of disability proposed in the articles of Part I.

Note: This chapter is based on a presentation at the Alliance for the Mentally Ill/Department of Mental Health Curriculum and Training Committee Annual Conference in Boston, MA April 19, 1996.

From *Psychiatric Rehabilitation Journal*, Fall 1996, 20(2), pp. 859. Reprinted with permission. Reprinted from 4th Edition of *The Psychological and Social Impact of Disability*, 1999, Springer.

COPING WITH A JOURNEY TOWARD RECOVERY: FROM THE INSIDE OUT

Dale Walsh

I have worked in the field of mental health for about 30 years. I can talk about this part of my life easily. I have also been a survivor of a long-term psychiatric disability for most of my childhood and adult life, and I am a survivor of the mental health system, both public and private. This is the harder part of my life to talk about. I have walked on both sides of the fence, so to speak. I want to share with you my own personal path toward recovery and what I see as a consumer practitioner to be necessary to support the recovery process of people who use the mental health system.

First, a word about language. There is no clear consensus within either the professional mental health community or among the people who have actually experienced psychiatric treatment as to what we are to be called. In the 1970s, when people who were former "patients" started to come together and share their experiences, they called themselves just that—ex-patients or former patients. Later, as the movement developed and grew and people collectively began to express their anger, some people used the name "psychiatric inmate" to make clear their dissatisfaction with the prevailing power inequities of the medical model and with the way they were treated. In California, the term "client" came to be used, because it met the dual goals of neutrality and descriptiveness. And in the 1980s the term "consumer" began to be used, mostly by the mental health system and by family groups (usually groups of parents who had an adult child with a severe psychiatric disability) in an attempt to find a label that was nonstigmatizing, yet acceptable to them. Other people who have been through the mental health system and consider themselves in recovery may use the phrase "psychiatric survivors." This debate over language is more than semantics. What people choose to call themselves is a key element in forming a group identity. It is also an indication of people's felt sense of empowerment and the place they feel they occupy within the hierarchy of the system of mental health care or services. It is important for the mental health system to be respectful and to take careful note of the names or phrases used to describe the people who use their services. Since I knew I was one, I have called myself a "survivor" or "person with a psychiatric disability." Recently I have been with some colleagues who prefer the phrase "person with a psychiatric label." I like that because the phrase speaks to the stigma carried and experienced by those of us who have been through psychiatric "treatment."

I have been dealing with the aftereffects, the stigma, and the shame of having a psychiatric disability for most of my life. As a child I was overly good. I was very anxious. I had multiple physical problems, nightmares, and trouble sleeping. As an adult, I have always been restricted in performing many of life's everyday functions—going to a shopping mall or to the bank, taking vacations or doing other leisure activities, going to social events like weddings, and working full time. Many times just leaving my house has been too anxiety provoking for me to handle. I have had many episodes of depression so severe that basic functioning has been difficult. Most of the time I live with some level of anxiety and a sense of terror and foreboding that come not from the present but from my past history of abuse. Feeling safe in the world is something I work on a daily basis.

For many years I believed in a traditional medical model. I had a disease. I was sick. I was told I was mentally ill, that I should learn to cope with my anxiety, my depression, my pain, and my panic. I never told anyone about the voices, but they were there, too. I was told I should change my expectations of myself and realize I would always have to live a very restricted life.

After I was diagnosed, I was put in a box up on a shelf. Occasionally I was taken down and my medication was changed. But no one really talked to me. No one helped me figure out why I should be content to take my medication and be grateful things were not worse. After all, at least I did not have to live my life in the back wards of a state hospital.

Because of my history and because of the society in which I lived, I easily turned the notion of illness into thinking there was something wrong with me. I was the problem. I felt deformed, everything I did was wrong. I had no place in the world. I was a freak. I was deeply ashamed of who I was and I tried my best to cover up my abnormality. I learned from those around me that psychiatric disability and its aftereffects were something to hide. As a result I lived marginally. I worked in a constant state of terror and tried to look normal. For the most part I succeeded— but at a tremendous cost to myself in terms of my energy, my self-image, my fear, and my inferiority. There were times when the stresses got to be too much and I ended up hospitalized, defeated, and feeling a failure because I couldn't tolerate even the day-to-day problems of what seemed to be a fairly simple life.

I worked in the field of mental health and I was very careful not to let anyone know my shameful secret. I was constantly terrified someone would find me out. I kept myself in entry-level positions because I was having a hard enough time without the added stresses of climbing up the ladder in my field. I went to therapy. I took my medication and waited to feel better. I waited and waited. . . .

I sometimes felt angry at my caregivers, but mostly I felt angry at myself. At times my symptoms were better but I wasn't. I felt powerless. I felt empty. I looked outside myself to the doctors and professionals to cure me, or at least take away some of my pain. But they didn't. Maybe I was one of those hopeless cases. I felt despair and deep loneliness.

This old patriarchal system of treatment and culture of disease is characterized by a hierarchical arrangement of power, a mechanistic view of the mind, causality due to organic forces outside the person's self, an emphasis on a person's deficits, and treatment administered by an expert— always at a professional distance. Did they think they might catch it? Why were they all so careful to maintain that professional distance? For years I felt trapped because I knew no other way to look at myself and my process.

Then about 8 years ago I read *The Courage to Heal*. I started talking to people—professionals and survivors who knew about the effects of trauma and psychiatric disability. I was lucky enough to stumble on 12-Step and other self-help groups. Finally my symptoms, my dreams, and my fears started making sense. I discovered the principles and the practices of recovery. I discovered hope. I had lived for years in despair because the pills and the therapy did not make me better. I began to see that if my life was to become better, I would have to do it myself. I saw that other people with histories similar to mine had been able to move beyond their symptoms. I started working with a therapist who was able to communicate to me that she trusted and believed in my own capacity to grow and move forward. She was willing to assist me but she respected my own pacing. I began to believe I could actually participate in a healing process. As I looked within myself I discovered over the following years, slowly and sometimes painfully, that healing, making positive changes in my life, and feeling better, were all possible. Especially helpful to this process were several self-help groups where I didn't have to hide, where people understood and were engaged in struggles similar to mine. I saw people who were further along in their recovery who served as role models. I also got to know people who were not so far along as I was—whom I could mentor. Giving back and learning how to get out of myself and into someone else's frame of reference has been, and continues to be, an important step in my recovery.

What I found through my own experience is that in order to travel the path of true recovery I could not rely on externals, wait, hope to be rescued, or be made better because of someone or something outside me. Instead, I learned that both the power and the possibility of change reside within me. I could make decisions that would affect my life. But I found I could not do this alone. I needed a supportive community around me. Slowly and gradually I found people who understood. I found friends and support people who could help me hold the hope when I was going through tough times and when I reached what felt like an insurmountable obstacle. These people believed in my capacity, to heal. As I learned to take risks, I found that I could actually set and accomplish goals very much like people who were chronically normal.

Recovery is not a return to a former level of functioning. I have heard so many people—professionals and survivors alike—say that mental illness is not curable. I agree that we can never go back to our "premorbid" selves. The experience of the disability, and the stigma attached to it, changes us forever. Instead, recovery is a deeply personal and unique process of changing one's attitudes, values, self-concept, and goals. It is finding ways to live a hopeful, satisfying, active, and contributing life. Everyone is changed by major happenings in their lives. We cannot return to the past. Recovery involves the development of a new meaning and purpose in one's life. It is looking realistically at both the limitations and the possibilities. It is much more than mere symptom relief.

As I continued on my path of recovery, I found I could handle responsible jobs. I am now slowly expanding my social network as I feel safer in the world and more comfortable with who I am. And, very importantly, I have come out of the closet and announced publicly, as a representative of those with psychiatric labels, who I am, where I have been, and where we as a community of oppressed people can go if we can find our voices, recapture our power, and exercise it to take charge of our lives and our journey toward wholeness. I am still in recovery, for it is a process—not a sudden landing.

Discovering and participating in this culture of healing has given me the hope and courage to travel the path of recovery. This is a culture of inclusion, hope, caring, and cooperation; of empowerment, equality, and humor; of dignity, respect, and trust. Forming relationships and creating systems of mental health care based on these principles are vital to supporting the growth of people who are users of the system. Traditionally, people who have been labeled as mentally ill have been considered to have poor judgment. They need to be taken care of. They do not know what is best for them. They are told what is wrong with them, what they need, what their future is to be like, and what is in their best interest. The stigma and discrimination that those of us who are labeled as mentally ill have suffered steals our hope, isolates us, and is a barrier to our healing.

Part of healing and recovery is the ability to participate as full citizens in the life of the community. As psychiatric survivors begin to break their silence and advocate for their humanity, the call and demand for basic civil rights becomes increasingly stronger. People want to be able to make their own choices about their own lives. They want to be seen, heard, and taken seriously. They want to be part of the decision making that so deeply affects their everyday experiences. This taking back of power and being taken seriously are both necessary components of recovery.

The notion that there is a recovery process that goes on internally within each person with a psychiatric label, often very separate from the treatment the person receives, is a new and somewhat threatening concept of the psychiatric treatment community. As recovery begins to be talked about and recognized by psychiatric survivors, it offers a way of taking back dignity, self-responsibility, and a sense of hope for the future.

By taking back power from the system of care, a consumer/survivor acknowledges that the ability to cope and heal comes from within. No one else, including the best of service providers, can do anything but facilitate the healing process. However, this facilitation—if it takes the form of good attention, respect, validation, and genuine connection—is an essential part of recovery.

Empowerment is a vital component of our recovery. Allowing and supporting a change within a program, agency, or system requires trust among administrators, staff members, and the people served. This change requires a shift from power being retained exclusively by administrators to it being shared among all constituencies. It requires a willingness to take risks in not only allowing—but actively encouraging—people to work toward their own goals. It means that choice and self-determination are to be considered foremost when consumer/survivors and staff members are developing treatment and rehabilitation plans. When treatment or rehabilitation is seen as more than prescribing the right formula, and when the emphasis is placed on maintaining the functioning and identity of the person, an atmosphere that promotes recovery is created. We who use the mental health system need to play a significant role in the shaping of the services, policies, and research that affect us. We need to have a place at the table and become participants in a shared dialog.

When people assert control over their own lives and make their own decisions, they also take on responsibility for the consequences of their decisions. Often, as service providers, we want to protect people from failure. We know, or at least think we know, what is best. We do not like to see people fail—both because of the pain it may cause to the person, but also because of the pain and feelings of failure we may experience. Sometimes when psychiatric survivors decide to make changes in their lives, they may not succeed. And, like other people, they may or may not learn from their failures. Like other people, they have a right to take risks. And sometimes they succeed, surpassing all expectations.

How many of you have tried something new and found it did not work? An investment perhaps? Or maybe a new relationship, or a marriage? You were allowed to take these risks even if the money you put into the investment was money you could not afford to lose, even if the relationship was the same kind of destructive relationship you had been through in the past. Maybe you learned from these situations, but maybe you didn't. People with psychiatric labels have these same rights. Part of sharing power is nurturing, encouraging, and fostering these rights.

Decision making in an environment that fosters recovery involves more people and more time. It is much easier for an administrator to make a decision alone than to bring it to the community for discussion and input. Often, decision making has to be taught to people who have grown accustomed to having their decisions made for them, who have been told so many times that, because of their "illness," they are unable to make responsible choices, and that any preferences they do express should be discounted because they are sick and unstable.

It takes time, patience, and a lot of listening to teach people to take the major risk of making their own choices again. But this type of power sharing through conversation can provide for a climate of equality, which can insure that all people can be free to express and reach for their own hopes and aspirations. Power sharing allows both staff members and clients alike to become much more involved in, and invested in, their own growth. In an environment that fosters recovery, the barriers of discrimination and stigma, which destroy self-esteem, perpetuate learned helplessness, and convince people they are incapable of self-determination, are broken down.

Many people who have been diagnosed as mentally ill hate labels and object strongly when people are called schizophrenic, bipolar, or borderline. After people are diagnosed, everything that happens to them is seen through the filter of their labels. A couple of years ago I was admitted to a hospital on an emergency basis. The next morning I called my office to say I wouldn't be in because I was in the hospital. At the time I worked in a very progressive agency with several people who themselves had psychiatric disabilities. My colleagues assumed I was in a psychiatric unit. These same colleagues called every psychiatric unit in the Boston area trying to find me. In reality, I had been admitted to the hospital because of a respiratory infection. They had assumed that if I was in the hospital on an emergency basis of course I was having a psychiatric emergency.

An environment that fosters recovery must be one in which hope is an essential component of each activity. Often people with psychiatric labels have lost hope. They see their disability as a death sentence. They think they can never get any better. When you are in the midst of despair it is almost impossible to see the other side. Too often providers echo these feelings and cement them into reality for those with whom they work. Have you ever found yourself angry at a person who has given up hope? I have.

During difficult times it can be easier to give up. Do we blame ourselves? Sometimes. This can serve to fuel our own despair. More often, though, I think professionals blame the people who are in despair. Despairing clients are seen as lazy, noncompliant, and manipulative, and they don't want to get better. They don't want help. They should be discharged from the program so they can hit bottom—then maybe they will appreciate how good they had it.

In a system where this continually happens, people within the system and the system itself can get caught up in the despair and become rigid, distancing, and lifeless. As an administrator, I try to use these times to take an honest look at the services my agency is providing: are they relevant to what people need and want? Are staff members burning out and in need of support from me or from each other?

In these days of more work and fewer resources I often find that the issues, the traumas, and the life experiences of the people who use the mental health center trigger myself and my staff. We can only be with people in their pain to the extent we are willing to be with our own pain within our own life experiences. I model this with my staff by talking about the feelings the work evokes in me. And I invite others to share also. I have found that creating an environment of safety for staff members as well as for clients is necessary for this open sharing to go on. Safety to reveal one's own vulnerabilities without fear of sanctions is vital for an environment that fosters recovery. Confidentiality, respect, and sincere attempts to empathize and demonstrate understanding to others are components of such an environment. Well-developed interpersonal skills, on the part of both staff members and administrators, can serve to support the atmosphere of safety and compassion.

When I decided to return to school to get my doctorate, I did so for several reasons. First of all I wanted to learn more. Second, I thought that the title "doctor" before my name would help me feel validated, and that I had a place in the world. And third, because I wanted to give back some of what had been given to me by those who supported my recovery. As I looked at various programs I was disappointed at the values and the sterility of the various programs. Then I talked to someone at Boston University, where I had gotten my master's many years before. I liked the idea of rehabilitation with its emphasis on functioning rather than illness and limitations. It was suggested to me that I read some of Bill Anthony's work to see if the principles expressed resonated with my own. As I did, I found that both the principles and practices gave a context and a structure as well as a guide for helpers to foster recovery instead of encouraging passivity and compliance. In psychiatric rehabilitation the person and his or her preferences and thoughts are essential to the process. When I learned of the values of involvement, choice, comprehensiveness, support, and growth potential, I saw these were the same values that helped free me from feeling trapped in traditional treatment. I was excited at the possibility of learning how to put these values into practice with other survivors of the psychiatric system. I learned in the very best way possible—by teaching. I taught courses in rehabilitation counseling for 4 years. Over the past several years I have been using these principles to help mental health systems put a recovery paradigm into practice. I have seen, in myself and in the people with whom I work, that when these values form the basis of the structure and programming within a system, people learn to take responsibility for themselves and their actions. These principles provide the soil for people to choose to grow and change. I have come to think of psychiatric rehabilitation as providing an external structure, while recovery is the internal process.

Through recovery I have found myself capable of making changes toward more satisfaction and success in my life. The quality of my life has greatly improved. I still have my limitations—I am not a finished product. And from an acceptance of my limitations has become a belief in my own unique possibilities. I have the power to move toward wholeness.

PART I

Perspective Exercise 1

Reflections on Jean Vanier

HOW FAR HAVE WE COME? HOW FAR MUST WE GO?

Read over the points made in the article by Jean Vanier, "The Contributions of the Physically and Mentally Handicapped to Development."

1. Do you agree with the points made by Vanier?
2. What was of concern to you?
3. Has much changed in the past 32 years?
4. What are the areas that need particular attention and further discussion?
5. Discuss the current world issues related to illness and disability.

PART II

The Personal Impact of Disability

Introduction to Part II

A disability or chronic illness, which has its origin either in birth or in an event occurring during teenage, adult, or later-life years, has a profound impact on one's life adjustment, opportunities, and quality of life. An almost seesaw process of adaptation begins with the advent of a disability or other major life and living changes. The dynamics of this adaptation, and also the factors that may hinder this adjustment, are cogently discussed in the articles of Part II. A review of these articles indicates several themes: (a) The multidimensional response to disability or chronic illness involves a contribution and confluence of many different psychosocial factors; (b) cultural and genders issues must be considered when exploring a person's coping and adjustment to a disabling or challenging condition; (c) the models of psychosocial adjustment to disability which have been developed from research, as explained in the following articles, all suggest distinctive interventions; and (d) precipitating events causing a mental or physical disability are quite varied. Importantly, each article offers a somewhat different perspective and dynamic on the disabled-related, adaptive process.

Livneh and Antonak, in their article "Psychosocial Adaptation to Chronic Illness and Disability: A Primer for Counselors," identify and insightfully discuss three broad domains of psychosocial adaptation. From this discussion emerges an explanation of assessment measures that, in turn, suggests appropriate interventions. Such theory-driven intervention strategies are then carefully explained, following a three-step sequence. The authors also state "these eclectic interventions aim at offering a logical match between specific psychotherapeutic strategies and those reactions evoked during the process of adaptation ... "

Psychosocial adaptation to disability often includes the personal management of stigma. Phemister and Crewe, in their article "Objective Self-Awareness and Stigma: Implications for Persons With Visible Disabilities," provide specific insights into how these factors play a particular role in one's adaptation to a disability. They identify new findings on the theory of objective self-awareness and then illustrate how this theory suggests that the experience of stigma, added to the experience of self-awareness, has a decided effect on those with a disability. Stigma is a psychosocial reality, impacting the individual's adjustment process, and resulting in a devaluation of the person who may be considered different because of disability. In their article they discuss how the implications of stigma are often integrated with objective self-awareness, and this awareness should receive attention when planning appropriate interventions.

Gender issues are often neglected in the psychosocial literature relevant to mental and physical disability. Nosek and Hughes make a singular contribution to the literature in their article: "Psychosocial Issues of Women With Physical Disabilities: The Continuing Gender Debate." They discuss a new and promising body of research and identify major psychosocial factors affecting the life situation of women with disabilities. Their life situation is complex and saturated with social, economic, and attitudinal barriers. But recommendations are suggested for helping professionals to alleviate these barriers. The authors also address the relevant psychosocial factors for developing appropriate interventions.

A more specific aspect of women with a disability, especially for those coping with a spinal cord injury, is sexuality-related issues. Miller and Marini, in their article "Female Sexuality and Spinal Cord Injury: Counseling Implications," explore the sexuality-related barriers and myths associated with women with a spinal cord injury as well as discuss other common psychosocial aspects of this injury. They explain many interventions to manage sexuality issues, but stimulate the reader's attention with an explanation of a five-component framework to delineate specific sexuality concerns of these women. Such information can be a most useful guide for helping professionals when assisting women with spinal cord injury to a more enhanced life adjustment.

The factor of one's cultural background must be considered when exploring the psychosocial dynamics of adaptation to a disability. Marini, in his article "Cross-Cultural Counseling Issues of Males Who Sustain a Disability," discusses different cultural values and emphasizes that the perceptions of disability and masculinity are different in different cultures. He also pinpoints selected counseling interventions when assisting males with disabilities to appropriate personal adjustment. Of particular interest is his explanation of the two major schools of thought concerning how a persons adjusts to a traumatic severe disability.

A timely article written by North, "Psychiatric and Psychological Issues in Survivors of Major Disasters," expands the causal factors of disability. She makes an important contribution to the psychosocial literature on disability by affirming that natural disasters, technological accidents, and terrorism produce severe mental health effects in its victims. One effect that needs attention by health professionals is Post Traumatic Stress Syndrome (PTSD). The author discusses its risk factors, symptoms, the incidence and course of the disorder, and effective interventions. A further, brief discussion on bioterrorism arouses the attention of the reader as to how two recognized models of human behavior are quite relevant to understanding psychological responses to this form of terror.

Psychosocial adaptation and quality of life are two concepts that are often understood as related when exploring the process of personal adjustment to a disability. M. Bishop, in his article "Quality of Life and Psychosocial Adaptation to Chronic Illness and Acquired Disability: A Conceptual and Theoretical Synthesis," explains how these concepts can be linked. He defines psychosocial adaptation and quality of life and emphasizes that adaptation and quality of life are both multidimensional constructs and subjective processes. The author further explains that the determinants of quality of life can be associated with the process of adaptation to a disability. A "Disability Centrality Model" is proposed to show the connection, and the advantages for using this model for assisting those with disabilities in the adaptation process are explained.

A "classic" article by Shontz, "Six Principles Relating Disability and Psychological Adjustment," reprinted from the third edition of this book, is included in this Part II because the six general propositions are as relevant today as they were 30 years ago. They pinpoint those psychosocial markers that are guidelines for developing effective interventions. They become even more relevant over time as the truth is reaffirmed that psychosocial adaptation to a disability is a multifactor concept.

CHAPTER EIGHT

Psychological Adaptation to Chronic Illness and Disability

A Primer for Counselors

Hanoch Livneh and Richard F. Antonak

Chronic illnesses and disabling conditions are common occurrences in the lives of many individuals. It has been estimated that approximately 54 million Americans (about 1 in 5) have physical, sensory, psychiatric, or cognitive disabilities that interfere with daily living (Bowe, 2000). Furthermore (a) more than 9 million Americans with disabilities are unable to work or attend school; (b) costs of annual income support (e.g., supplemental security income, social security disability insurance) and medical care provided by the U.S. government to assist people with disabilities is about $60 billion; (c) disabilities are higher among older people, minorities, and lower socioeconomic groups; and (d) 8 of the 10 most common causes of death in the U.S. are associated with chronic illness (Eisenberg, Glueckauf, & Zaretsky, 1999; Stachnik, Stoffelmayr, & Hoppe, 1983).

Many disability- and nondisability-related factors interact to create a profound effect on the lives of individuals with chronic illness and

From "Psychological adaptation to chronic illness and disability: A primer for counselors," by H. Livneh and R. Antonak, 2005, *Journal of Counseling & Development, 83,* 12–20. ACA. Reprinted with permission. No further reproduction authorized with out written permission from the American Counseling Association.

disabilities (CID). Among these, the most commonly recognized factors include the degree of functional limitations, interference with the ability to perform daily activities and life roles, uncertain prognosis, the prolonged course of medical treatment and rehabilitation interventions, the psychosocial stress associated with the incurred trauma or disease process itself, the impact on family and friends, and the sustained financial losses (e.g., reduced income, increased medical bills).

The intent of this article is to provide the reader with an overview of (a) the dynamics (i.e., process) of psychosocial adaptation to CID, (b) methods commonly used to assess psychosocial adaptation to CID, and (c) intervention strategies applied to people with CID.

THE DYNAMICS OF PSYCHOSOCIAL ADAPTATION TO CID

The onset of CID is typically associated with a disease process (e.g., multiple sclerosis [MS], cancer) or a traumatic injury (spinal cord injury, traumatic brain injury). CID is also dichotomized into congenital, or evident at birth (e.g., spina bifida, cerebral palsy), and adventitious, or acquired later in life (Parkinson's disease, amputation). In this chapter, we focus on psychosocial adaptation to acquired disabling conditions.

This overview of the literature on psychosocial adaptation to CID is grouped under three headings: basic concepts, CID-triggered reactions, and CID-related coping strategies.

BASIC CONCEPTS

Included here are the concepts of stress, crisis, loss and grief, body image, self-concept, stigma, uncertainty and unpredictability, and quality of life.

Stress

Individuals with CID normally face an increase in both the frequency and severity of stressful situations (Falvo, 1999; Horowitz, 1986). Increased stress is experienced because of the need to cope with daily threats that include, among others, threats to (a) one's life and well-being; (b) body integrity; (c) independence and autonomy; (d) fulfillment of familial, social, and vocational roles; (e) future goals and plans; and (f) economic stability (Falvo, 1999).

Crisis

The sudden onset of many medical impairments and disabilities (e.g., myocardial infarction, spinal cord injury, traumatic brain injury, amputation) and that of life-threatening diagnoses or loss of valued functions (e.g., cancer, vision impairment) is highly traumatic. As such, these conditions constitute a psychosocial crisis in the life of the affected person (Livneh & Antonak, 1997; Moos & Schaefer, 1984). Although crisis, by definition, is time-limited (e.g., Janosik, 1984), during its presence life is affected by disturbed psychological, behavioral, and social equilibrium. The psychological consequences of crisis are, in contrast, long lasting and may even evolve into pathological conditions such as posttraumatic stress disorder (PTSD).

Loss and Grief

The crisis experienced following the onset of a traumatic or progressive CID triggers a mourning process for the lost body part or function. In a manner parallel to that evidenced following the loss of a loved one, the individual exhibits feelings of grief, bereavement, and despair (Parkes, 1975; B. A. Wright, 1983). The term *chronic sorrow* has often been used to depict the grief experienced by persons with CID (Burke, Hainsworth, Eakes, & Lindgren, 1992; Davis, 1987). Unlike grief associated with non-bodily losses, CID serves as a constant reminder of the permanency of the condition. Furthermore, daily triggering events act to remind the affected person of the permanent disparity between past and present or future situations (e.g., Teel, 1991).

Body Image

Body image has parsimoniously been defined as the unconscious mental representation or schema of one's own body (Schilder, 1950). It evolves gradually and reflects interactive forces exerted by sensory (e.g., visual, auditory, kinesthetic), interpersonal (e.g., attitudinal), environmental (e.g., physical conditions) and temporal factors. CID, with its impact on physical appearance, functional capabilities, experience of pain, and social roles, is believed to alter, even distort, one's body image and self-concept (Bramble & Cukr, 1998; Falvo, 1999). Successful psychosocial adaptation to CID is said to reflect the integration of physical and sensory changes into a transformed body image and self-perception. Unsuccessful adaptation, in contrast, is evidenced by experiences of physical and psychiatric symptoms such as unmitigated feelings of anxiety and depression, psychogenic pain, chronic fatigue, social withdrawal, and cognitive distortions (Livneh & Antonak, 1997).

Self-concept

One's self-concept and self-identity are linked to body image and are often seen as conscious, social derivatives of it (Bramble & Cukr, 1998; McDaniel, 1976). However, self-concept and self-identity may be discordant for many individuals with visible disabilities. The sense of self (i.e., self-identity), which is privately owned and outwardly presented, may be denied in social interactions with others who respond to the person as "disabled" first (i.e., focusing on appearance rather than identity), thereby losing sense of the person's real self (Kelly, 2001).The person's self-esteem, representing the evaluative component of the self-concept, gradually shows signs of erosion and negative self-perceptions following such encounters.

Stigma

The impact of stereotypes and prejudice acts to increase stigma toward people with CID (Corrigan, 2000; Falvo, 1999). Restrictions imposed by CID lead to deviations from several societal norms and expectations (e.g., utilization of health care services, occupational stability). They are, therefore, viewed negatively by society and result in stigmatizing perceptions and discriminatory practices. Moreover, when internalized by people with CID, these stigmatizing encounters with others result in increased life stress, reduced self-esteem, and withdrawal from social encounters, including treatment and rehabilitation environments (Falvo, 1999; B. A. Wright, 1983).

Uncertainty and Unpredictability

Although the course of some CIDs is rather stable or predictable (e.g., amputation, cerebral palsy) most conditions may be regarded as neither stable nor predictable (e.g., epilepsy, cancer, diabetes mellitus, MS). Put differently, the insidious and variable course of these conditions is fraught with intermittent periods of exacerbation and remissions, unpredictable complications, experiences of pain and loss of consciousness, and alternating pace of gradual deterioration. Indeed the concept of "perceived uncertainty in illness" (Mishel, 1981, p. 258) was coined by Mishel to depict how uncertainty, or the inability to structure personal meaning, results if the individual is unable to form a cognitive schema of illness-associated events. Medical conditions, such as cancer and MS, that are marked by heightened levels of perceived uncertainty regarding disease symptoms, diagnosis, treatment, prognosis, and relationships with family members were found to be associated with decreased psychosocial adaptation (Mishel, 1981; Wineman, 1990).

Quality of Life

The ultimate psychosocial outcome in rehabilitation practice is believed to be that of post-CID quality of life (QOL; Crewe, 1980; Roessler, 1990). As a global and multifaceted construct, QOL includes the following functional domains (Flanagan, 1982, Frisch, 1999): (a) intrapersonal (e.g., health, perceptions of life satisfaction, feelings of well-being), (b) interpersonal (e.g., family life, social activities), and (c) extrapersonal (e.g., work activities, housing). In the context of adaptation to CID, for QOL there are typically assumptions in two primary domains: successful restructuring of previously disrupted psychosocial homeostasis and attainment of an adaptive person–environment (reality) congruence. Furthermore, QOL is considered to be linked to a more positive self-concept and body image, as well as to an increased sense of control over CID, and QOL is negatively associated with perceived stress and feelings of loss and grief (Dijkers, 1997; Falvo, 1999).

CID-TRIGGERED RESPONSES

Clinical observations and empirical research on the psycho-social process of adaptation to CID have been marred by conflicting findings and heated debate. In this section, we focus on the most frequently experienced psychosocial reactions to CID as cited in the rehabilitation research and disability studies literatures.

Shock

This short-lived reaction marks the initial experience following the onset of a traumatic and sudden injury or the diagnosis of a life-threatening or chronic and debilitating disease. The reaction is characterized by psychic numbness, cognitive disorganization, and dramatically decreased or disrupted mobility and speech.

Anxiety

This reaction is characterized by a panic-like feature on initial sensing of the nature and magnitude of the traumatic event. Reflecting a state-like (i.e., situationally determined) response, it is accompanied by confused thinking, cognitive flooding, and a multitude of physiological symptoms including rapid heart rate, hyperventilation, excess perspiration, and irritable stomach.

Denial

This reaction, also regarded as a defense mechanism mobilized to ward off anxiety and other threatening emotions, involves the minimization and even complete negation of the chronicity, extent, and future implications associated with the condition. Denial involves selective attention to one's physical and psychological environments. It includes wishful thinking, unrealistic expectations of (full or immediate) recovery, and at times, blatant neglect of medical advice and therapeutic or rehabilitation recommendations. Although denial may successfully mitigate anxiety and depression when used selectively and during initial phases of adaptation, its long-term impact is often considered maladaptive and life threatening (Krantz & Deckel, 1983; Meyerowitz, 1983).

Depression

This reaction, commonly observed among people with CID, is considered to reflect the realization of the permanency, magnitude, and future implications associated with the loss of body integrity, chronicity of condition, or impending death. Feelings of despair, helplessness, hopelessness, isolation, and distress are frequently reported during this time. Although depression has been found to be a wide-spread reaction among persons with CID (e.g., Rodin, Craven, & Littlefield, 1991; Turner & Noh, 1988), it is still unclear if it is (as some theoreticians and clinicians argue) a prerequisite to ultimate acceptance of the condition or attaining successful psychosocial adaptation (Wortman & Silver, 1989).

Anger/Hostility

The reaction of anger/hostility is frequently divided into internalized anger (i.e., self-directed feelings and behaviors of resentment, bitterness, guilt, and self-blame) and externalized hostility (i.e., other- or environment-directed retaliatory feelings and behaviors; Livneh & Antonak, 1997). When internally directed, self-attributions of responsibility for the condition onset or failure to achieve successful outcomes are evident. In contrast, externally oriented attributions of responsibility tend to place blame for the CID onset or unsuccessful treatment efforts on other people (e.g., medical staff, family members) or aspects of the external environment (e.g., inaccessible facilities, attitudinal barriers). Behaviors commonly observed during this time include aggressive acts, abusive accusations, antagonism, and passive-aggressive modes of obstructing treatment.

Adjustment

This reaction, also referred to in the literature as reorganization, reintegration, or reorientation, comprises several components: (a) an earlier cognitive reconciliation of the condition, its impact, and its chronic or permanent nature; (b) an affective acceptance, or internalization, of oneself as a person with CID, including a new or restored sense of self-concept, renewed life values, and a continued search for new meanings; and (c) an active (i.e., behavioral) pursuit of personal, social, and/or vocational goals, including successful negotiation of obstacles encountered during the pursuit of these goals.

CID-ASSOCIATED COPING STRATEGIES

The literature on CID-related coping strategies is vast (e.g., Moos, 1984; Zeidner & Endler, 1996). In this section, only a cursory overview of the most commonly reported strategies, directly related to coping with CID, is undertaken. First, however, the concept of coping is briefly discussed and its relevance to CID is illustrated.

Coping has been viewed as a psychological strategy mobilized to decrease, modify, or diffuse the impact of stress-generating life events (Billings & Moos, 1981; Lazarus & Folkman, 1984). Foremost among the defining characteristics of coping are those of (a) including both stable (i.e., trait-like) and situationally determined (i.e., state-like) elements; (b) accessibility to conscious manipulation and control; (c) hierarchical organization that spans the range from macroanalytic, global styles of coping (e.g., locus of control, optimism) to microanalytic, specific behavioral acts; and (d) being structurally multifaceted, including affective, cognitive, and behavioral aspects (Krohne, 1993; Zeidner & Endler, 1996). In addition, clinical and empirical studies of coping emphasize its (a) amenability to assessment by psychometric measures (there are currently over 20 psychological measures that purport to assess from 2 to almost 30 coping styles and strategies) and (b) divergent theoretical underpinnings (the nature of coping has been viewed differently by clinicians from various theoretical persuasions including psychodynamic, interpersonal, and cognitive-behavioral).

Research on coping with CID has spanned a wide range of conditions such as cancer, heart disease, spinal cord injury, epilepsy, MS, amputation, rheumatoid arthritis, and diabetes, as well as the experience of pain. Commonly assumed in these research endeavors is the existence of two broad categories of coping strategies, namely, disengagement and engagement coping strategies.

Disengagement Coping Strategies

These strategies refer to coping efforts that seek to deal with stressful events through passive, indirect, even avoidance-oriented activities such as denial, wish-fulfilling fantasy, self- and other-blame, and resorting to substance abuse (Tobin, Holroyd, Reynolds, & Wigal, 1989). This group of coping strategies is often associated with higher levels of psychological distress (i.e., increased negative affectivity), difficulties in accepting one's condition, and generally poor adaptation to CID.

Engagement Coping Strategies

These strategies refer to coping efforts that defuse stressful situations through active, direct, and goal-oriented activities such as information seeking, problem solving, planning, and seeking social support (Tobin et al., 1989). This group of coping strategies is commonly linked to higher levels of well-being, acceptance of condition, and successful adaptation to CID.

During the chronic, but often remitting and exacerbating, course of medical conditions and physical disabilities, coping strategies are differentially adopted to meet the fluctuating demands necessitated by the changing physical, psychosocial, spiritual, economic, and environmental needs of the person. The rehabilitation and disability studies literature suggests that coping strategies could occupy several roles in their relationship to psychosocial adaptation to CID. These include (a) direct or causal, such that their use might differentially determine or influence psychosocial adaptation; (b) indirect or mediating, such that their use acts to mediate between certain demographic (e.g., age), disability-related (e.g., severity or duration of condition), or personality (e.g., level of perceived uncertainty) variables, and outcomes of adaptation to CID; and (c) outcome variables, such that the type and valence of coping strategies are an indicator of how successful psychosocial adaptation is.

ASSESSMENT OF PSYCHOSOCIAL ADAPTATION TO CID

Over the past half century, a large number of measures of psychosocial adaptation to and coping with CID have been reported in the literature. In this section, only those psychometrically sound measures most frequently reported in the literature are reviewed. Readers may refer to Livneh and Antonak (1997) for a comprehensive discussion of these and other measures.

GENERAL MEASURES OF ADAPTATION TO CID

Millon Behavioral Health Inventory (MBHI; Millon, Green, & Meagher, 1979)

The MBHI is a 150-item self-report questionnaire, organized into 20 clinical scales. The scales are classified into four domains that include (a) coping styles, (b) psychogenic attitudes, (c) psychosomatic complaints, and (d) a prognostic index. The MBHI seeks to (a) describe the psychological styles of medical service recipients, (b) examine the impact of emotional and motivational needs and coping strategies on disease course, and (c) suggest a comprehensive treatment plan to decrease the impact of deleterious psychological reactions. The strengths of the MBHI include its sound psychometric (i.e., reliability and validity) properties, clinical usefulness, and applicability to a wide range of medical and rehabilitation settings. Weaknesses include empirically unconfirmed domain structure and potential reactivity influences and response bias.

Psychosocial Adjustment to Illness Scale (PAIS; Derogatis, 1977; Derogatis & Lopez, 1983)

The PAIS is a 46-item instrument designed to measure psychosocial adaptation to medical illnesses and chronic diseases. The scale can be administered both as a semistructured psychiatric interview by a trained clinician and as a self-report measure (PAIS-SR). In addition to an overall adjustment score, seven subscales are provided. These include Health Care Orientation, Vocational Environment, Domestic Environment, Sexual Relationships, Extended Family Relationships, Social Environment, and Psychological Distress (i.e., indicating reactions of anxiety, depression, guilt, and hostility, as well as levels of self-esteem and body image). The strengths of the PAIS include the psychometric robustness of its scales, having both self-report and clinician interview forms, and the availability of norm scores for several medical conditions (e.g., cancer, MS, renal failure). Weaknesses include lack of data on possible response bias influences.

Acceptance of Disability Scale (AD; Linkowski, 1971)

The AD Scale is a 50-item, 6-point, summated rating scale developed to measure the degree of acceptance of disability as theorized by Dembo,

Leviton, and Wright (1956). Items are summed to yield a single score representing changes in one's value system following the onset of physical disability.

Major strengths inherent in the AD Scale include its theory-driven rationale, reliability, and use in a large number of English-speaking and non-English-speaking countries. Weaknesses are suggested by the lack of investigation of its factorial structure, its unidimensional approach to a complex construct, and lack of data on response bias influences.

Sickness Impact Profile (SIP; Bergner et al., 1976; Gilson et al., 1975)

The SIP comprises 136 items that yield, in addition to scores on 12 subscales, a global scale score; 3 scales can be combined to create a physical dimension score (i.e., Ambulation, Mobility, and Body Care and Movement), 4 scales can be combined and yield a psychosocial dimension score (i.e., Social Interaction, Alertness Behavior, Emotional Behavior, and Communication), and the 5 remaining scales are viewed as independent categories and are typically scored separately (i.e., Sleep and Rest, Eating, Work, Home Management, and Recreation and Pastimes). Respondent-perceived impact of sickness is measured by directing the respondent to choose descriptors of currently experienced, sickness-related behavioral dysfunction.

The strengths of the SIP include its comprehensive and rigorous psychometric development and properties, extensive use with patients diagnosed with a variety of physical and health conditions, and the availability of a Spanish language version. Weaknesses may be related to its yet-to-be tested factorial structure and susceptibility to defensiveness and response set.

Reactions to Impairment and Disability Inventory (RIDI; Livneh & Antonak, 1990)

The RIDI is a 60-item, multidimensional, self-report summated rating scale. Its intended use is to investigate eight clinically reported classes of psycho social reactions to the onset of CID. The eight psychosocial reaction scales include Shock, Anxiety, Denial, Depression, Internalized Anger, Externalized Hostility, Acknowledgment, and Adjustment. The strengths of the RIDI include its comprehensive psychometric development, scale reliability, and multidimensional perspective on adaptation to CID. Weaknesses are suggested by scant concurrent validity data, lack of normative data across disabling conditions, and potential confounding effects of response bias influences.

Handicap Problems Inventory (HPI; G. N. Wright & Remmers, 1960)

The HPI is a 280-item checklist of problems believed to be attributed to the presence of physical disability. Respondents are asked to mark those problems that are caused or exacerbated by the existence of the condition. Items on the inventory are grouped into four life domains that include Personal, Family, Social, and Vocational subscales. The strengths of the HPI include domain comprehensiveness, its documented internal reliability estimates, and available normative data. Weaknesses include lack of supportive data on its validity, possible response bias, and its inordinate length.

SPECIFIC MEASURES OF ADAPTATION TO CID

A sizeable number of measures related to psychosocial adaptation to specific CIDs have been reported in the rehabilitation and disability studies literatures. Because of space constraints, these measures will not be reviewed here. Interested readers may refer to Livneh and Antonak (1997) for a comprehensive review of these scales. Readers may also wish to directly consult the following:

1. Measures of adaptation to cancer that include the Mental Adjustment to Cancer Scale (Watson et al., 1988)
2. Measures of adaptation to diabetes that include the Diabetic Adjustment Scale (Sullivan, 1979)
3. Measures on adaptation to epilepsy and seizure disorders that include the Washington Psychosocial Seizure Inventory (Dodrill, Batzel, Queisser, & Temkin, 1980)
4. Measures of adaptation to traumatic brain injury that include the Portland Adaptability Inventory (Lezak, 1987)
5. Measures of adaptation to rheumatoid arthritis that include the Arthritis Impact Measurement Scale (Meenan, 1982, 1986)
6. Measures of adaptation to spinal cord injuries that include the Psychosocial Questionnaire for Spinal Cord Injured Persons (Bodenhamer et al., 1983)
7. Measures of adaptation to visual impairments that include the Nottingham Adjustment Scale (Dodds, Bailey, Pearson, & Yates, 1991)
8. Measures of adaptation to hearing impairments that include the Social-Emotional Assessment Inventory for Deaf and Hearing-Impaired Students (Meadow, Karchmer, Peterson, & Rudner, 1980)

Counselors and clinicians who consider adopting traditional psychological measures (e.g., the Minnesota Multiphasic Personality Inventory, Beck Depression Inventory, Spielberger's State-Trait Anxiety Inventory) to address psychosocial adaptation to CID must be cognizant of the following two issues:

1. Physical and physiological symptoms (e.g., fatigue, weakness, sleep problems) directly associated with a number of CIDs (e.g., spinal cord injury, MS, Parkinson's disease) often mimic indicators of depression and anxiety among members of these populations. Counselors who work with people with CID should therefore (a) pay careful attention and differentiate, whenever possible, the more authentic indicators of depression and anxiety (typically cognitive and affective correlates) from those associated with the condition's physiological concomitants and (b) gain understanding of the literature that has examined the confounding effects of CID-triggered physiological symptoms on the scoring and interpretation of traditional psychological measures (e.g., Morrison, 1997; Pollak, Levy, & Breitholtz, 1999; Skuster, Digre, & Corbett, 1992).

2. Most traditional psychological and psychiatric measures lack scoring norms based on responses from populations of people with CID. This lack of normative data for people with CID renders these measures suspicious, even misleading, when their findings are interpreted indiscriminately. Counselors who adopt, or contemplate modifying, psychological tests for use with people with CID should carefully review the *Standards for Educational and Psychological Testing* (American Psychological Association, 1999) and Bolton (2001) for specific suggestions on this matter.

INTERVENTION STRATEGIES FOR PEOPLE WITH CID

Numerous theory-driven, reaction-specific, and clinically documented intervention strategies to assist people with CID successfully adapt to their conditions have been reported in the literature. In the following section, we review the major approaches to psychosocial interventions applied to people with CID.

Theory-Driven Interventions

These interventions focus on the clinical applications of widely recognized personality theories and therapeutic models to persons with CID and the perceived merits of their use with this population. Among the more commonly applied theories are psychoanalytic, individual (Adlerian), Gestalt (Perls), rational-emotive-behavioral (Ellis), cognitive (Beck), and behaviorist (Riggar, Maki, & Wolf, 1986; Thomas, Butler, & Parker, 1987).

When adopting theory-driven interventions, clinicians typically follow a three-step sequence. First, core concepts from a particular theory (e.g., defense mechanisms, feelings of inferiority, unfinished life situations, irrational beliefs) are identified and examined. Second, the usefulness of these concepts, within the context of psychosocial adaptation to CID (e.g., understanding the process of grieving for loss of body parts or functions) is scrutinized. Third, the benefits derived from these concepts, for practical counseling interventions, for people with CID are assessed and, if deemed appropriate, are applied to their life situations. Readers may wish to refer to Chan, Thomas, and Berven (2002), English (1971), Livneh and Antonak (1997), Livneh and Sherwood (1991), and Shontz (1978) for detailed reviews of these interventions.

Psychosocial Reaction-Specific Interventions

These eclectic interventions aim at offering a logical match between specific psychotherapeutic strategies and those reactions (or experiences) evoked during the process of adaptation to CID (e.g., anxiety, depression, denial, anger). Worded differently, the counselor seeks to link specific counseling strategies with clinically observed, or client-reported, psychosocial reactions (Dunn, 1975; Livneh & Antonak, 1997; Livneh & Sherwood, 1991). It is generally argued that strategies regarded as supportive, affective-insightful, or psychodynamic in nature (e.g., person-centered therapy, Gestalt therapy, Jungian therapy) may be more useful during earlier phases of the adaptation process. In contrast, strategies viewed as more active-directive, goal-oriented, or cognitive-behavioral in nature (e.g., cognitive therapy, behavioral therapy, coping skills training) may be more beneficial during the later stages (Dunn, 1975; Livneh & Antonak, 1997; Marshak & Seligman, 1993). To illustrate the above rationale, two examples are provided. First, disability- or loss-triggered depression can be approached by encouraging the client to vent feelings associated with grief, isolation, guilt, shame, and mourning for the lost function (e.g., mobility, vision, health). Protracted depression can be further managed by reinforcing social contacts and activities and by practicing self-assertiveness, self-determination, and independent living skills. Second, reactions (feelings and behaviors) of self-directed or other-directed anger may be dealt with by teaching and practicing anger expression in socially sanctioned forms, such as the pursuit of artistic endeavors and, if feasible, sports-related activities. Other strategies could include practicing behavior modification techniques to reduce physically and verbally aggressive acts.

Global Clinical Interventions

These comprehensive clinical interventions are geared toward assisting people with specific CIDs (e.g., cancer, heart disease, spinal cord injury) in successfully adapting to their condition and its impact on their lives. More specifically, these interventions provide the client and his or her family and significant others with emotional, cognitive, and behavioral support. In addition, these interventions equip the client with adaptive coping skills that could be successfully adopted when facing stressful life events and crisis situations. Among the most commonly encountered global clinical interventions are the following.

1. *Assisting clients to explore the personal meaning of the CID.* These strategies rest heavily on psychodynamic principles and focus on issues of loss, grief, mourning, and suffering. Emphasis is also placed on encouraging clients to vent feelings leading to acceptance of condition permanency, altered body image, and realization of decreased functional capacity. Rodin et al.'s (1991) three-phase approach to treating depression in medically impaired individuals best illustrates this strategy (i.e., assisting clients in expressing grief and mourning, providing clients with opportunities to seek personal meaning of their CID, and training clients to attain a sense of mastery over their emotional experiences).

2. *Providing clients with relevant medical information.* These strategies emphasize imparting accurate information to clients on their medical condition, including its present status, prognosis, anticipated future functional limitations, and when applicable, vocational implications. These approaches are best suited for decreasing initial levels of heightened anxiety and depression, as well as the potentially damaging effects of unremitting denial (Ganz, 1988; Razin, 1982).

3. *Providing clients with supportive family and group experiences.* These strategies permit clients (usually with similar disabilities or common life experiences) and, if applicable, their family members or significant others to share common fears, concerns, needs, and wishes. These experiences also allow clients to acquire greater insight and to gain social support and approval from other group participants, family members, and professional helpers. Common group modalities include educational groups, psychotherapeutic groups, coping-skills training groups, and social support groups (Roback, 1984; Seligman, 1982; Telch & Telch, 1985). Subramanian and Ell's (1989) group model for heart patients best exemplifies this approach because it incorporates (a) information on heart conditions and disability management, (b) coping-skills training to manage stressful life situations, and (c) cognitive skills teaching to manage maladaptive emotions.

4. *Teaching clients adaptive coping skills for successful community functioning.* These strategies, in a similar vein to those of group-based coping-skills training, focus on instilling in clients coping skills that will allow them to face a wide range of stressful conditions typically encountered by people with CID in physical, social, educational, and vocational settings. These skills include assertiveness, interpersonal relations, decision making, problem solving, stigma management, and time management skills. Craig and coauthors (Craig, Hancock, Chang, & Dickson, 1998; Craig, Hancock, Dickson, & Chang, 1997) have used a cognitive-behavioral therapy coping program to train clients who have sustained spinal cord injury. The authors' multifaceted approach uses relaxation techniques, visualization techniques, cognitive restructuring, and social and self-assertiveness skills training to help participants cope with psychosocial difficulties encountered on release into the community.

SUMMARY

Approximately 1 in 5 Americans is currently diagnosed with CID. People with CID often encounter physical, psychological, social, educational, financial, and vocational barriers that greatly interfere with their quality of life. In this chapter, we have attempted to provide counselors with the most useful and pragmatic concepts, processes, assessment tools, and intervention strategies related to psychosocial adaptation to CID.

When working with individuals who have sustained CID, counselors are commonly called to draw on their expertise in the areas of (a) stress, crisis, and coping with loss and grief; (b) the impact of traumatic events on self-concept, body image, and quality of life; and (c) the effects of disability-linked factors (e.g., uncertainty, unpredictability) and societal reactions (e.g., stigma, prejudice) on psychosocial adaptation to CID.

Counselors must also be cognizant of, and demonstrate clinical acumen when observing, clients' psychosocial reactions to their conditions and the external environment. Several CID-triggered responses (at times described as phases) have been discussed. These include (a) reactions of shorter duration that are more commonly experienced earlier in the adaptation process (e.g., shock, anxiety); (b) reactions of longer duration that normally suggest distressed and unsuccessful coping efforts (e.g., depression, anger); and (c) reactions that signal successful adaptation to the condition and renewed life homeostasis (adjustment).

Of the many measures available for assessing psychosocial adaptation to CID, six have been reviewed in this chapter. They were selected because of their (a) applicability to a wide range of CIDs, (b) sound psychometric development and structure, (c) frequent citations in the rehabilitation and disability studies literatures, and (d) clinical and research potential.

Assessment of clients' levels of psychosocial adaptation to their condition should pave the way to appropriate selection of intervention strategies. To this end, the chapter concludes with an overview of four psychosocial strategies most commonly applied to counseling people with CID. Reviewed were interventions based on innovative applications of traditional personality and psychotherapeutic interventions. Next, interventions that seek to address reactions linked to the onset of CID (e.g., anxiety, depression, anger) were highlighted. Finally, global, eclectic, clinical approaches that were typically developed for specific disabilities (e.g., cancer, heart conditions, spinal cord injury) were illustrated. The last group of interventions offers the counselor fertile ground for applying comprehensive, multifaceted approaches geared to meet the wide range of psychological, social, and vocational needs of clients with CID.

REFERENCES

American Psychological Association. (1999). *Standards for educational and psychological testing* (4th ed.). Washington, DC: Author.

Bergner, M., Bobbitt, R. A., Kressel, S., Pollard, W. E., Gilson, B. S., & Morris, J. R. (1976). The Sickness Impact Profile: Conceptual formulation and methodology for the development of a health status measure. *International Journal of Health Services, 6,* 393–415.

Billings, A. G., & Moos, R. H. (1981). The role of coping responses and social resources in attenuating the stress of life events. *Journal of Behavioral Medicine, 4,* 139–157.

Bodenhamer, E., Achterberg-Lawlis, J., Kevorkian, G., Belanus, A., & Cofer, J. (1983). Staff and patient perceptions of the psycho-social concerns of spinal cord injured persons. *American Journal of Physical Medicine, 62,* 182–193.

Bolton, B. (Ed.). (2001). *Handbook of measurement and evaluation in rehabilitation* (3rd ed.). Gaithersburg, MD: Aspen.

Bowe, F. (2000). *Physical, sensory, and health disabilities: An introduction.* Upper Saddle River, NJ: Merrill.

Bramble, K., & Cukr, P. (1998). Body image. In I. M. Lubkin (Ed.), *Chronic illness: Impact and interventions* (4th ed., pp. 283–298). Boston: Jones and Bartlett.

Burke, M. L., Hainsworth, M. A., Eakes, G. G., & Lindgren, C. L. (1992). Current knowledge and research on chronic sorrow: A foundation for inquiry. *Death Studies, 16,* 231–245.

Chan, F., Thomas, K. R., & Berven, N. L. (Eds.). (2002). *Counseling theories and techniques for rehabilitation health professionals.* New York: Springer.

Corrigan, P. W. (2000). Mental health stigma as social attribution: Implications for research methods and attitude change. *Clinical Psychology: Science and Practice, 7*, 48–67.

Craig, A., Hancock, K., Chang, E., & Dickson, H. (1998). The effectiveness of group psychological intervention in enhancing perceptions of control following spinal cord injury. *Australian and New Zealand Journal of Psychiatry, 32*, 112–118.

Craig, A., Hancock, K., Dickson, H., & Chang, E. (1997). Long-term psychological outcomes in spinal cord injured persons: Results of a controlled trial using cognitive behavior therapy. *Archives of Physical Medicine and Rehabilitation, 78*, 33–38.

Crewe, N. M. (1980). Quality of life: The ultimate goal in rehabilitation. *Minnesota Medicine, 63*, 586–589.

Davis, B. H. (1987). Disability and grief. *Social Casework, 68*, 352–357.

Dembo, T., Leviton, G. L., & Wright, B. A. (1956). Adjustment to misfortune—A problem of social-psychological rehabilitation. *Artificial Limbs, 3*(2), 4–62.

Derogatis, L. R. (1977). *Psychological Adjustment to Illness Scale.* Baltimore: Clinical Psychometric Research.

Derogatis, L. R., & Lopez, M. (1983). *Psychosocial Adjustment to Illness Scale (PAIS & PAIS-SR): Scoring, procedures and administration manual.* Baltimore: Clinical Psychometric Research.

Dijkers, M. (1997). Quality of life after spinal cord injury: A meta analysis of the effects of disablement components. *Spinal Cord, 35*, 829–840.

Dodds, A. G., Bailey, P., Pearson, A., & Yates, L. (1991). Psychological factors in acquired visual impairment: The development of a scale of adjustment. *Journal of Visual Impairment and Blindness, 85*, 306–310.

Dodrill, C. B., Batzel, L. W., Queisser, H. R., & Temkin, N. R. (1980). An objective method for the assessment of psychological and social problems among epileptics. *Epilepsia, 21*, 123–135.

Dunn, M. E. (1975). Psychological intervention in a spinal cord injury center: An introduction. *Rehabilitation Psychology, 22*, 165–178.

Eisenberg, M. G., Glueckauf, R. L., & Zaretsky, H. H. (Eds.). (1999). *Medical aspects of disability: A handbook for the rehabilitation professional.* New York: Springer.

English, R. W. (1971). The application of personality theory to explain psychological reactions to physical disability. *Rehabilitation Research and Practice Review, 3*, 35–47.

Falvo, D. (1999). *Medical and psychosocial aspects of chronic illness and disability* (2nd ed.). Gaithersburg, MD: Aspen.

Flanagan, J. C. (1982). Measurement of quality of life: Current state of the art. *Archives of Physical Medicine and Rehabilitation, 63*, 56–59.

Frisch, M. B. (1999). Quality of life assessment/intervention and the Quality of Life Inventory. In M. E. Maruish (Ed.), *The use of psychological testing for treatment planning and outcome assessment* (pp. 1277–1331). Mahwah, NJ: Erlbaum.

Ganz, P. A. (1988). Patient education as a moderator of psychological distress. *Journal of Psychosocial Oncology, 6*, 181–197.

Gilson, B. S., Gilson, J. S., Bergner, M., Bobbitt, R. A., Kressel, S., Pollard, W. E., et al. (1975). The Sickness Impact Profile: Development of an outcome measure of health care. *American Journal of Public Health, 65*, 1304–1310.

Horowitz, M. J. (1986). *Stress response syndromes* (2nd ed.). Northvale, NJ: Aronson.

Janosik, E. H. (1984). *Crisis counseling: A contemporary approach*. Belmont, CA: Wadsworth.

Kelly, M. P. (2001). Disability and community: A sociological approach. In G. L. Albrecht, K. D. Seelman, & M. Bury (Eds.), *Handbook of disability studies* (pp. 396–411). Thousand Oaks, CA: Sage.

Krantz, D. S., & Deckel, A. W. (1983). Coping with coronary heart disease and stroke. In T. G. Burish & L. A. Bradley (Eds.), *Coping with chronic disease: Research and applications* (pp. 85–112). New York: Academic Press.

Krohne, H. W. (Ed.). (1993). *Attention and avoidance*. Seattle, WA: Hugrefe & Huber.

Lazarus, R. S., & Folkman, S. (1984). *Stress, appraisal, and coping*. New York: Springer.

Lezak, M. D. (1987). Relationship between personality disorders, social disturbance, and physical disability following traumatic brain injury. *Journal of Head Trauma and Rehabilitation, 2*(1), 57–59.

Linkowski, D. C. (1971). A scale to measure acceptance of disability. *Rehabilitation Counseling Bulletin, 14*, 23 6–244.

Livneh, H., & Antonak, R. F. (1990). Reactions to disability: An empirical investigation of their nature and structure. *Journal of Applied Rehabilitation Counseling, 21*(4), 13–21.

Livneh, H., & Antonak, R. F. (1997). *Psychosocial adaptation to chronic illness and disability*. Gaithersburg, MD: Aspen.

Livneh, H., & Sherwood, A. (1991). Application of personality theories and counseling strategies to clients with physical disabilities. *Journal of Counseling & Development, 69*, 525–538.

Marshak, L. E., & Seligman, M. (1993). *Counseling persons with physical disabilities: Theoretical and clinical perspectives*. Austin, TX: Pro-Ed.

McDaniel, J. W. (1976). *Physical disability and human behavior* (2nd ed.). New York: Pergamon Press.

Meadow, K. P., Karchmer, M. A., Peterson, L. M., & Rudner, L. (1980). *Meadows/Kendall Social-Emotive Assessment Inventory for Deaf Students: Manual*. Washington, DC: Gallaudet College, Pre-College Programs.

Meenan, R. F. (1982). The AIMS approach to health status measurement: Conceptual background and measurement properties. *Journal of Rheumatology, 9*, 785–788.

Meenan, R. F. (1986). New approach to outcome assessment: The AIMS questionnaire for arthritis. *Advances in Internal Medicine, 31*, 167–185.

Meyerowitz, B. E. (1983). Postmastectomy coping strategies and quality of life. *Health Psychology, 2*, 117–132.

Millon, T., Green, C. J., & Meagher, R. B. (1979). The MBHI: A new inventory for the psycho-diagnostician in medical settings. *Professional Psychology, 10*, 529–539.

Mishel, M. (1981). The measurement of uncertainty in illness. *Nursing Research, 30,* 25 8–263.

Moos, R. H. (Ed.). (1984). *Coping with physical illness: New perspectives* (Vol. 2). New York: Plenum.

Moos, R. H., & Schaefer, J. A. (1984). The crisis of physical illness. In R. H. Moos (Ed.), *Coping with physical illness: New perspectives* (Vol. 2, pp. 3–31). New York: Plenum.

Morrison, J. (1997). *When psychological problems mask medical disorders: A guide for psychotherapists.* New York: Guilford.

Parkes, C. M. (1975). Psychosocial transitions: Comparison between reactions to loss of a limb and loss of a spouse. *British Journal of Psychiatry, 127,* 204–210.

Pollak, J., Levy, S., & Breitholtz, T. (1999). Screening for medical and neurodevelopmental disorders for the professional counselor. *Journal of Counseling & Development, 77,* 350–358.

Razin, A. M. (1982). Psychosocial intervention in coronary artery disease: A review. *Psychosomatic Medicine, 44,* 363–387.

Riggar, T. F., Maki, D. R., & Wolf, A. W. (Eds.). (1986). *Applied rehabilitation counseling.* New York: Springer.

Roback, H. B. (Ed.). (1984). *Helping patients and their families cope with medical problems.* San Francisco: Jossey-Bass.

Rodin, G., Craven, J., & Littlefield, C. (1991). *Depression in the medically ill: An integrated approach.* New York: Brunner/Mazel.

Roessler, R. T. (1990). A quality of life perspective on rehabilitation counseling. *Rehabilitation Counseling Bulletin, 34,* 82–91.

Schilder, P. (1950). *The image and appearance of the human body.* New York: Wiley.

Seligman, M. (1982). Introduction. In M. Seligman (Ed.), *Group psychotherapy and counseling with special populations* (pp. 1– 26). Baltimore: University Park Press.

Shontz, F. C. (1978). Psychological adjustment to physical disability: Trends in theories. *Archives of Physical Medicine and Rehabilitation, 59,* 251–254.

Skuster, D. Z., Digre, K. B., & Corbett, J. J. (1992). Neurologic conditions presenting as psychiatric disorders. *Psychiatric Clinics of North America, 15,* 3 11–333.

Stachnik, T., Stoffelmayr, B., & Hoppe, R. B. (1983). Prevention, behavior change, and chronic disease. In T. G. Burish & L. A. Bradley (Eds.), *Coping with chronic disease: Research and applications* (pp. 447–473). New York: Academic Press.

Subramanian, K., & Ell, K. O. (1989). Coping with a first heart attack: A group treatment model for low-income Anglo, Black, and Hispanic patients. *Social Work in Groups, 11,* 99–117.

Sullivan, B. J. (1979). Adjustment in diabetic adolescent girls: I. Development of the Diabetic Adjustment Scale. *Psychosomatic Medicine, 41,* 119–126.

Teel, C. S. (1991). Chronic sorrow: Analysis of the concept. *Journal of Advanced Nursing, 16,* 1311–1319.

Telch, C. F., & Telch, M. J. (1985). Psychological approaches for enhancing coping among cancer patients: A review. *Clinical Psychology Review, 5*, 325–344.

Thomas, K., Butler, A., & Parker, R. M. (1987). Psychosocial counseling. In R. M. Parker (Ed.), *Rehabilitation counseling: Basics and beyond* (pp. 65–95). Austin, TX: Pro-Ed.

Tobin, D. L., Holroyd, K. A., Reynolds, R. V., & Wigal, J. K. (1989). The hierarchical factor structure of the Coping Strategies Inventory. *Cognitive Therapy and Research, 13*, 343–361.

Turner, R. J., & Noh, S. (1988). Physical disability and depression: A longitudinal analysis. *Journal of Health and Social Behavior, 29*, 23–37.

Watson, M., Greer, S., Young, J., Inayat, Q., Burgess, C., & Robertson, B. (1988). Development of a questionnaire measure of adjustment to cancer: The MAC scale. *Psychological Medicine, 18*, 203–209.

Wineman, N. M. (1990). Adaptation to multiple sclerosis: The role of social support, functional disability, and perceived uncertainty. *Nursing Research, 39*, 294–299.

Wortman, C. B., & Silver, R. C. (1989). The myth of coping with loss. *Journal of Consulting and Clinical Psychology, 57*, 349–357.

Wright, B. A. (1983). *Physical disability—A psychosocial approach*. New York: Harper & Row.

Wright, G. N., & Remmers, H. H. (1960). *Manual for the Handicap Problems Inventory*. Lafayette, IN: Purdue Research Foundation.

Zeidner, M., & Endler, N. S. (Eds.). (1996). *Handbook of coping: Theory, research, applications*. New York: Wiley.

CHAPTER NINE

Objective Self-Awareness and Stigma

Implications for Persons With Visible Disabilities

Andrew A. Phemister and Nancy M. Crewe

Does self-consciousness affect how a person thinks or behaves in different situations? Social scientists and psychologists have studied this question for over a century and many have said, "yes, it does" (Cooley, 1902; James, 1890; Mead, 1934). For instance, giving a presentation, interviewing for a job, and inviting someone on a date are all common situations that will likely cause a person to feel more self-aware and sometimes self-critical (cf. Silvia & Duval, 2001; Duval & Wicklund, 1972). After such an event, the person may feel quite negatively about his or her appearance and performance. "I was terrible!" "Now they will never hire me!" "I looked foolish!"

It has been exhaustively discussed among scholars that inherent to such self-conscious events lies a "fulcrum" of awareness that balances a

From "Objective self-awareness and stigma: Implications for persons with visible disabilities," by A. Phemister and N. Crewe, 2004, *Journal of Rehabilitation 70*, 33–37. Reprinted with permission of the National Rehabilitation Association.

person directly between the anxiety-provoking experience of self as *both* object and subject. Rollo May (1967) fittingly referred to this experience as the "human dilemma," and asserted that such dual-awareness [of self as object and subject] is a necessary element to gratification in life. Perception of approval from others can lead to increased confidence and self-esteem, while perception of disdain or negative evaluation can produce the opposite results. People in general receive varying degrees of positive and negative appraisal, but does this dilemma of self-awareness impact a person differently when others can see that the person has a disability? From past experiences many people can probably relate to the above self-critical statements (e.g., "I looked foolish!"). However, on closer inspection such statements imply a deeper issue regarding the proposed dilemma of self-awareness, especially when visible disability is a factor. It is well observed that persons with disabilities experience social stigma much more than the general population, and the enduring presence of stigma in our society suggests that the answer to the above question might also be "yes,"— that because of stigma, it is conceivable that the acute experience of self-awareness may affect persons with visible disabilities differently than able-bodied persons. Stigma affects people who are in some way different from majority expectations (Coleman, 1997) and, in fact, even *perceived* stigma was found to be an independent predictor of depression in persons with leg amputations (Rybarczyk, Nyenhuis, Nicholas, Cash, & Kaiser, 1995).

Stigma has been around for a long time and social scientists have been studying it closely for perhaps just as long (e.g., Allport, 1954, Cooley, 1902; Fine & Asch, 1995; Heatherton, Kleck, Hebl, & Hull, 2000). In the early 1960s Erving Goffman posed the question, "how does the stigmatized individual respond to his (sic) situation?" (1963, p.9). In response to his own question, Goffman asserted that for some stigmatized individuals "it will be possible for him to make a direct attempt to correct what he sees as the *objective* basis of his failing," for instance plastic surgery for certain deformities (emphasis added, see below).

In keeping with these observations, this paper is concerned with the large number of persons with disabilities who may always be at risk of experiencing social stigma. The goal of this chapter is to employ a critical theory of self-awareness that offers much to the phenomenology of disability in a conceptual examination of the impact of stigma on persons with visible disabilities. Below is an introduction to the *theory of objective self-awareness* (OSA; Duval & Wicklund, 1972) and some recent developments. This is followed by a discussion of research on stigma, and the integration and implications of both OSA and stigma to disability studies and individual adjustment to disability.

OBJECTIVE SELF-AWARENESS AND VISIBLE DISABILITY

In its original form, the *theory of objective self-awareness* was a comprehensive theory intended to explain why individuals conform their behaviors, appearance, and beliefs to those of others (Duval & Wicklund, 1972). Duval and Wicklund formulated their theory on the basis of a distinction between two forms of conscious attention. They postulated that individuals have one innate consciousness with directional properties; attention can be dually focused either *outward* toward the environment or *inward* toward oneself. However, it was emphasized that attention cannot be simultaneously focused outward and inward; that a person can only attend to one thing at a time. For instance, a person is unable to focus attention on a personal characteristic while driving a nail into wood. Duval and Wicklund identified outward attention as the state of *subjective* self-awareness, and defined it as attention that is focused upon environmental characteristics. In subjective self-awareness the person is the "subject" who is observing and perceiving the various aspects of their environment. However, given this, it may seem more accurate to say that a subjectively self-aware individual is actually *environment*-aware rather than *self*-aware, and, as Duval and Wicklund explained, this is indeed accurate—at least in the "usual sense of the term" (refer to p. 2). But, the person is self-aware in that he or she receives and perceives feedback from the environment regarding his or her behaviors, attitudes, etc. Subjective self-awareness arises directly from the experience of oneself as the source of perception and action.

On the other hand, the theory asserted that when a person is *objectively* self-aware, then he or she has become *acutely* aware of those personal characteristics that most distinguish him or her from the majority. The occurrence of OSA can be understood in three ways. First, as indicated, the term *"objective"* specifies where attention is directed. That is, in a state of OSA, the person's attention is focused exclusively on the self; the person is the "object" of his or her own attention, and is now seeing himself (sic) as he thinks others are seeing him. It is this self-focused attention that induces an acute state of objective self-awareness. Second, induced OSA was theorized to automatically elicit comparisons between the self and perceived standards for social correctness in terms of specific behaviors, attitudes, traits, etc. Such standards of correctness were said to determine who or what a "correct" person is. For instance, a t-shirt and cutoffs typically are not considered appropriate attire for a job interview, and the person wearing them will draw much attention. Finally, if discrepancies are detected between a person and one or more standards, then negative affect was theorized to surface and, in order to reduce the negative affect, the person would either conform as best he or she could or avoid the situation altogether. Another consequence of this is that the person may also avoid other similar situations in which they feel objectively self-aware (e.g., formal gatherings).

Additionally, whether a person is objectively or subjectively self-aware, OSA theory contends that whatever is the focus of attention in any given situation will draw causal attributions (i.e., responsibility). It has been demonstrated that objectively self-aware persons are more likely to attribute the source of an event to themselves (Duval & Lalwani, 1999; Lalwani & Duval, 2000; Duval, 1971). According to the theory, attributing cause to oneself will occur because the objectively self-aware person is experiencing him or herself as somehow different and exhibiting salient characteristics that distinguish them from the majority. What this implies is that when a person with a visible disability (e.g., using a wheelchair or a having facial deformity) enters into a situation where he or she is the only one with such a characteristic then they will likely become objectively self-aware and focus attention on that characteristic. They will perceive themselves as they think others perceive them.

More recently however, new research has initiated fundamental changes to Duval and Wicklund's theory. One major change relevant to persons with visible disabilities emerged from controlled experiments on an individual's perceived rate of progress relative to the perceived discrepancy size. Duval, Duval, & Mulilis (1992) conducted three experiments using male Introduction to Psychology students. At one point, the participants were asked to meet an experimental standard by determining which of five two-dimensional figures when folded would match a three-dimensional figure previously displayed. It was discovered that when the participants were high in OSA and perceived sufficient progress toward reducing the discrepancy (i.e., meeting the experimental standard), they maintained involvement and effort. However, when participants high in OSA perceived insufficient progress to reduce the discrepancy then they would relax their efforts and avoid involvement.

This new finding for the *theory of objective self-awareness* is significant to an examination of stigma and visible disability because, generally, our society values good health, a particular physique, and the concept of "body beautiful" (Hahn, 1993; Wright, B. A., 1983). This is a social standard that, for many people with disabilities, simply cannot be met—a discrepancy that cannot be reduced—and, if that is the case, then what happens? Coleman (1997) stated that human differences are the basis for stigma and those individuals who have differences may feel *permanently* stigmatized in situations where their differences are pronounced (emphasis added). More importantly, Coleman further asserted that stigmas mirror our social and cultural beliefs, which, if so, and unless social attitudes change, could mean that the stigmatized individual will continually be struggling against the grain.

"NOTES ON STIGMA," OBJECTIVE SELF-AWARENESS, AND VISIBLE DISABILITY

In his classic work, *Stigma: Notes on the Management of Spoiled Identity*, Erving Goffman stated that stigma represents a special discrepancy between a person's "virtual social identity," which refers to what society assumes about a person, and their "actual social identity," which refers to those attributes that a person could in fact be proved to possess (1963). Goffman went on to define stigma as a term that highlights a deeply discrediting personal attribute that leads to assumptions about the person's character and abilities and often results in various forms of discrimination.

In general however, stigma is considered a social construction that is essentially based on individual or group differences and results in the devaluation of the persons who possess those differences (see Coleman, 1997; Dovidio, Major, & Crocker, 2000). Stigma dehumanizes and lessens the social value of an individual because he or she is appraised as being "marked," flawed, or otherwise less than average (Dovidio, Major, & Crocker, 2000; cf. Goffman, 1963). Several researchers have categorized stigma in various ways that make it easier to comprehend. For instance, Goffman (1963) identified three types of stigma: "abominations of the body" (e.g., physical deformities), "blemishes of individual character" (e.g., mental disorders, unemployment), and "tribal stigma" or "tribal identities" (e.g., race, religion, etc.). Similarly, Jones, Farina, Hastorf, Markus, Miller, & Scott (1984) defined six dimensions of stigma: 1) concealability (i.e., visibility), 2) course (i.e., salience and prognosis), 3) disruptiveness (i.e., during interpersonal interactions), 4) aesthetics (i.e., attractiveness), 5) origin (i.e., congenital vs. acquired conditions and personal responsibility), and 6) peril (i.e., threat of contagion).

Recently however it was argued that one of the most important issues to consider about stigma is its *visibility* (Crocker, Major, & Steele, 1998). Crocker et al asserted that the visibility of a particular stigmatizing attribute determines the schema through which an individual is understood or perhaps "defined" by society. This is significant to consider for persons with visible disabilities because, if we apply this to a situation in which a person feels objectively self-aware then, according to Duval and Wicklund's theory, it is plausible that the person may also feel highly self-critical as a direct result of OSA interacting with the stigmatizing attribute.

To elaborate, it has been argued that during any given situation where too much or too little attention is directed at one person (e.g., staring at or ignoring the person altogether), then that person's comfort and anxiety levels could be dramatically affected causing embarrassment and even shame (Buss, A. H., 1980; cf. Goffman, 1963). For a person with a visible disability, such attention may be a daily experience and a constant reminder that he or she "is" different (e.g., uses a wheelchair). Social Darwinism (Spencer, 1872) is implied in social appraisals like these because, invariably, when one person feels that he or she does not "fit in" (or must work harder in order to do so) then a social hierarchy is imposed. Social Darwinism is characterized by the phrase "survival of the fittest" and promotes the ideology that inferior races exist relative to superior races. For instance, in their controversial book, *The Bell Curve*, Herrnstein and Murray argued that social inferiority is a direct consequence of genetic inferiority (1994). In other words, for whatever reason, some people are "naturally" meant to be inferior. Social Darwinism has received little support but is still reflected in the attitudes and behaviors of our society today (i.e., stigma, prejudice, and discrimination).

Several experiments have revealed that feeling self-focused and self-aware in the presence of others can greatly impact a person's sense of physical attractiveness and self-evaluations (Thornton & Moore, 1993), the expression of their personal beliefs (Chang, Tai Hau, & Mei Gou 2001; Scheier, 1980; Wicklund & Duval, 1971), their level of shyness and social dysfunction (Bruch, Hamer, & Heimberg, 1995), and their individuation and feeling uncomfortably distinct from others (Ickes, Layden, & Barnes, 1978). It is therefore conceivable that the social appraisals of a person's difference, vis-a-vis stigma and causal attributions, could impact the adjustment process of an individual with a visible disability in ways we are not yet sure of, but are very important to understand.

In contrast, Buss (1980) argued that most people who experience increased self-awareness during social situations generally would not experience any ill effects (e.g., increased anxiety levels), presumably because they have not experienced the stigma that is often associated with having a visible disability (cf. Bruch, Hamer, & Heimberg, 1995). Yet, what seems pivotal is the extent to which the inducement of OSA may lead the individual to interpret the negative appraisals as being *realistically* based. In other words, can one's personal beliefs about oneself stand up against the perception that others believe differently—and for how long?

IMPLICATIONS FOR OBJECTIVE SELF-AWARENESS AND STIGMA

In a discussion on stigma effects and self-esteem, Crocker and Quinn (2000) argued that feelings of self-worth, self-regard, and self-respect are not stable characteristics. Instead, they are constructed in-situ as a function of the connotative meanings that a person attributes to a particular situation (cf. Heatherton & Polivy, 1991; Phemister, 2002; Sommers & Crocker, 1999). Crocker and Quinn asserted that what people bring to different situations are their sets of beliefs, attitudes, and values, and, when something negative (or positive) occurs, then self-esteem is subsequently affected by the meaning that they attribute to those events. The presumption here is that objective self-awareness and personal meanings may be phenomenologically linked. To illustrate, being turned down for both a date and a job will likely hold different implications for a person depending on which meant more to them. That is, the more something is desired by a person (e.g., getting a job), then the more meaningful it may be. Likewise, the more meaningful something is, the more he or she may feel objectively self-aware about appearing and performing in such a way that the event has a satisfactory outcome (e.g., being nicely dressed and trying to conceal an attribute that is believed will hinder the chances of being hired). But, if the person is rejected, then corresponding with the greater meaning ascribed to the situation, he or she could also experience a more heartfelt disappointment. Thus, for example, the individual may find it easier to invite another person on a date than to interview for another job and, as a result, perhaps avoid further interviews.

Symbolic interactionists such as Charles Horton Cooley (1902) compared the phenomenon of social appraisals to a "looking glass" and argued that we are continually affected by what we see reflected in another's eye (cf. Hewitt, 2000). Using Duval and Wicklund's (1972) theory as a backdrop, how likely is it that a person with a visible disability would indeed avoid situations where they feel objectively self-aware and stigmatized? Moreover, what if these situations were vital to one's quality of life such as in the case of interviewing for a job? For adults who have already established and maintained a lasting identity (e.g., vocational, familial, educational, and financial stability) this may not pose such a problem. However, for younger individuals who are likely to still be forming their identities, it is reasonable to assume that a prolonged state of objective self-awareness may negatively affect the beliefs they have regarding their competencies, abilities, and self-esteem (cf. Duval, Duval, & Mulilis, 1992), especially it seems if the person also attributes responsibility to their stigmatizing differences.

It has long been argued that society's attitudes and behaviors can and do dramatically impact individuals well after any actual interaction has occurred (Goffman, 1963; Laing, 1965; Szasz, 1961). Ronald Laing and Thomas Szasz in particular are well known for their theories that mental illness emerges from untenable social interactions, such as in the family, or as a socially imposed "myth" that justifies the mistreatment of certain individuals. Likewise, the self-identification literature stresses that groups of people cue relevant information in a person's memory about him or herself, the group, and the relationship between the person and the group (see Neisser & Jopling, 1997; Schlenker, 1986). Social appraisals can activate social roles, memories, present images, and conceivable goals for an individual in the present moment. Underscoring all of this is the minority group paradigm, which holds as a standard maxim that handicaps emerge from societally imposed barriers (Hahn, 1985). It is therefore conceivable that, if a person were to continually encounter stigmatizing situations, then he or she may begin to feel utterly unable to meet the standards set for those situations and, over time, form a new resolution about those situations and his or her assets in them (e.g., "Based on my experiences, I can see that I am not employable"). This resolution can be seen as reflecting the stigma and perhaps causal attributions that the person perceived others to have about him or her. Such a resolution may likely be a determining factor for the future choices a person makes regarding particular situations ("I will give up interviewing for jobs.") (cf. Magnusson, 1981; Pervin, 1981; Rommetveit, 1981). As a result, an individual may decide to engage primarily in situations that promote a desired identity and avoid situations that demote a desired identity. In effect, the person will "settle for less," which is clearly a significant barrier to the successful adaptation to life with a disability. This is significant because adaptation to disability connotes the restoration of a personal sense of wholeness, of bodily experience and integrity, and harmony, or *balance*, in life (see Charmaz, 1995; Trieschmann, 1988, Vash, 1980; Wright, B. A., 1983; Zola, 1991). That is, a person's life may feel "lopsided" if there are desired situations (e.g., finding employment) hat are avoided because of the erroneous introjection of other's stigmatizing attitudes.

In conclusion, what we can glean from Duval and Wicklund's theory is that when a person with a visible disability is perpetually at risk of being objectively self-aware and stigmatized, then he or she could perhaps become more susceptible to such erroneous introjection—a "hypothesis" that appears reinforced by the continuing existence of social Darwinism and discrimination against persons with disabilities.

REFERENCES

Allport, G. (1954). *The nature of prejudice*. Reading, MA: Addison-Wesley.

Bruch, M., Hamer, R., & Heimber, R. (1995). Shyness and public self-consciousness: Additive or interactive relation with social interaction. *Journal of Personality, 63*, 47–63.

Buss, A. (1980). *Self-consciousness and social anxiety*. San Francisco: W. H. Freeman and Company.

Charmaz, K. (1995). The body, identity, and self: Adapting to impairment. *The Sociological Quarterly, 36,* 657–680.

Coleman, L. (1997). Stigma: An enigma demystified. In L. Davis (Ed.). *The disability studies reader.* New York: Rutledge.

Cooley, C. H. (1902). *Human nature and the social order.* New York: Charles Scribner's Sons.

Crocker, J., Major, B., & Steele, C. (1998). Social stigma. In D. Gilbert, T. S. Fiske, & G., Lindzey (Eds.), *Handbook of social psychology* (4th ed., Vol. 2, pp. 504–553). Boston: McGraw-Hill.

Crocker, J., & Quinn, D. (2000). Social stigma and self: Meanings, situations, and self-esteem. In T. Heatherton, R. Kleck, M. Hebl, & J. Hull (Eds.). *The social psychology of stigma* (pp. 153–183). New York: The Guilord Press.

Dovidio, J., Major, B., & Crocker, J. (2000). Stigma: Introduction and overview. In T. Heatherton, R. Kleck, M. Hebl, & J. Hull (Eds.). *The social psychology of stigma* (pp. 1–32). New York: The Guilord Press.

Duval, S. (1971). *Causal attribution as a function of focus of attention.* Unpublished manuscript. University of Texas.

Duval, T. S., Duval, V. H., & Mulilis, J. P. (1992). Effects of selffocus, discrepancy between self and standard, and outcome expectancy favorability on the tendency to match self to standard or to withdraw. *Journal of Personality and Social Psychology, 62,* 340–348.

Duval, T. S., & Lalwani, N. (1999). Objective self-awareness and causal attributions for self-standard discrepancies: Changing self or changing standards of correctness. *Society for Personality and Social Psychology, 25,* 1220–1229.

Duval, S., & Wicklund, R. (1972). *A theory of objective self-awareness.* New York: Academic Press.

Fine, M., & Asch, A. (1995). Disability beyond stigma: Social interaction, discrimination, and activism. In N. G. Rule & J. B. Veroff (Eds.). *The culture and psychology reader* (pp. 536–558). New York: New York University Press.

Goffman, E. (1963). *Stigma: Notes on the management of spoiled identity.* New York: Simon and Schuster, Inc.

Hahn, H. (1985). Changing perception of disability and thr future of rehabilitation. In L. G. Perlman & G. F. Austin (Eds.). *Social influences in rehabilitation planning: A blueprint for the future.* A Report of the Ninth Mary Switzer Memorial Seminiar, Alexandria, VA: National Rehabilitation Association.

Hahn, H. (1993). The politics of physical difference: Disability and discrimination. In M. Nagler (Ed.). *Perspectives on disability* (pp. 39–47). Palo Alto, CA: Health Markets Research.

Heatherton, T., Kleck, R., Hebl, M., & Hull, J. (2000). *The social psychology of stigma.* New York: Guilford Press.

Heatherton, T., & Polivy, J. (1991). Development and validation of a scale for measuring state self-esteem. *Journal of Personality and Social Psychology, 60,* 895–910.

Herrnstein, R., & Murray, C. (1994). *The bell curve: Intelligence and class structure in American life.* New York: Free Press.

Hewitt, J. P. (2000). *Self and society: A symbolic interactionist social psychology.* (8th ed). Boston: Allyn and Bacon.

Ickes, W. Layden, M., & Barnes, R. (1978). Objective self-awareness and individuation: An empirical link. *Journal of Personality, 46*, 146–161.

James, W. (1890). *The principles of psychology*. New York: Henry Holt and Company.

Jones, E., Farina, A., Hastorf, A., Markus, H., Miller, D., & Scott, R. (1984). *Social stigma: The psychology of marked relationships*. New York: Freeman.

Laing, R. D. (1965). *The divided self: An existential study in sanity and madness*. New York: Penguin Books.

Lalwani, N., & Duval, T. S. (2000). The moderating effects of cognitive appraisal processes on self-attribution of responsibility. *Journal of Applied Social Psychology, 30*, 2233–2245.

Magnusson, D. (Ed.). (1981). *Toward a psychology of situations*. Hillsdale, NJ: Lawrence Erlbaum Associates, Inc.

May, R. (1967). *Psychology and the human dilemma*. New York: W.W. Norton and Company.

Mead, G. H. (1934). *Mind, self, and society*. Chicago: University of Chicago Press.

Neisser, U., & Jopling, A. (Eds.). (1997). *The conceptual self in context: Culture, Experiences, and self-understanding*. Cambridge: Cambridge University Press.

Pervin, L. (1981). The relation of situations to behavior. In D. Magnusson (Ed.). *Toward a psychology of situations* (pp. 157–169). Hillsdale, NJ: Lawrence Erlbaum Associates, Inc.

Phemister, A. A. (2002). Investigating the effects of objective self-awareness on the meaning attributions and job-hunting behaviors of persons with visible disabilities (Doctoral dissertation, Michigan State University, 2002). *Dissertation Abstracts International, 63*, 4421.

Rommetveit, R. (1981). On meanings of situations and social control of such meaning in human communication. In D. Magnusson (Ed.). *Toward a psychology of situations* (pp. 99–128). Hillsdale, NJ: Lawrence Erlbaum Associates, Inc.

Rybarczyk, B., Nyenhuis, D., Nicholas, J., Cash, S., & Kaiser, J. (1995). Body image, perceived social stigma, and the prediction of psychosocial adjustment to leg amputation. *Rehabilitation Psychology, 40*, 95–109.

Scheier, M. (1980). Effects of public and private self-consciousness on the public expression of personal beliefs. *Journal of Personality and Social Psychology, 39*, 514–521.

Schlenker, B. (1986). Self-identification: Toward an integration of the public and private self. In R. Baumeister (Ed.), *Public and private self* (pp. 212–230). New York: Springer-Verlag.

Silvia, P., & Duval, T. S. (2001). Objective self-awareness theory: Recent progress and enduring problems. *Personality and Social Psychology Review, 5*, 230–241.

Simon, R. W. (1997). The meanings individuals attach to role identities and their implications for mental health. *Journal of Health and Social Behavior, 38*, 256–274.

Spencer, H. (1872). *Social statics; or, the conditions essential to human happiness specified, and the first of them developed*. New York: Appleton.

Sommers, S., & Crocker, J. (1999). *Hopes dashed and dreams fulfilled: Contingencies and stability of self-esteem among graduate school applicants.* Chapter presented at the annual meeting of the Midwestern Psychological Association, Chicago.

Szasz, T. (1961). *The myth of mental illness.* New York: Dell.

Thornton, B., & Moore, S. (1993). Physical attractiveness contrast effects: Implications for self-esteem and evaluations of the social self. *Personality and Social Psychology Bulletin, 19,* 474–480.

Trieschmann, R. (1988). *Spinal cord injuries: Psychological, social and vocational rehabilitation.* (2nd ed.). New York: Demos.

Vash, C. L. (1981). *The psychology of disability.* New York: Springer Publishing Company.

Wicklund, R., & Duval, S. (1971). Opinion change and performance facilitation as a result of objective self-awareness. *Journal of Experimental Social Psychology, 7,* 319–342.

Wright, B. A. (1983). *Physical disability: A psychosocial approach* (2nd ed.). New York: Harper Collins.

Zola, I. (1991). Bringing our bodies and ourselves back in: Reflections on a past, present, and future "medical sociology." *Journal of Health and Social Behavior, 32,* 1–16.

CHAPTER TEN

Psychosocial Issues of Women With Physical Disabilities

The Continuing Gender Debate

Margaret A. Nosek and Rosemary B. Hughes

Women with disabilities constitute one of the largest and most disadvantaged populations in the United States. In the 10 years of research conducted by the Center for Research on Women with Disabilities, we have repeatedly been asked, "Why study only women?" In response to this challenge, we acknowledge the importance of studying the health of women with disabilities while contributing to a relatively new body of literature, that of gender-specific research and practice in the field of disability and rehabilitation. Dr. Marianne Legato (2002), a pioneer in gender-based medicine, stated, "It's not that the profession is overrun with poorly educated sexist practitioners.... It's the way we have been educated, as though women were simply small men and data we have about the male body were the standard for both sexes" (p. 1). We have little empirically based evidence suggesting that clinical practice is different in the psychosocial rehabilitation and community reintegration of women and men with disabilities. Like most of society, researchers and interventionists are not sufficiently responsive to the unique aspects of psychosocial health in women and men with disabilities. It is time to think and respond differently to femaleness and maleness in rehabilitation and research. It is time for this response to occur at every level and dimension of the rehabilitation research and practice community.

The gender debate is alive and well. Just a few years ago, the federal government issued a report stating that of 50 grant applications to the National Institutes of Health (NIH), only one fifth provided information about the gender of the population and, moreover, several proposed to study only men with no justification for a single-sex research design (Legato, 2002, summarizing a 1990 report from the General Accounting Office). Since that time, the NIH Office of Research on Women's Health has been established, and women are now being included in types of investigations that excluded them in the recent past. Within the past decade, positive change has come about as a result of women with and without disabilities advocating for equity, but much more change is necessary to bring about gender-related justice, especially in the context of disability.

In this article, we will explain why research on issues of concern to women with physical disabilities has been neglected for so long. We will further present information on how demographic and health statistics differ by gender and how women face different and, in some cases, more extreme psychosocial problems than men with disabilities or women in general. Finally, we will offer recommendations related to what rehabilitation researchers and practitioners can do to take gender into account in their examination of individual and program outcomes.

HISTORY OF RESEARCH ON WOMEN WITH DISABILITIES

The study of disability and rehabilitation has made its most significant advances during and after periods of war and, therefore, has been primarily concerned with the health and vocational problems of men. Guidelines for clinical treatment and interventions for reintegration into society have been developed for the most part based on the needs of men with spinal cord injury (SCI), amputation, and other adventitious musculoskeletal problems (Fine & Asch, 1988). Any services rendered to women used male norms and approached the needs of women according to traditional social roles. For issues related to congenital disabling conditions, such as cerebral palsy, spina bifida, or neuromuscular disorders, and adult-onset chronic disabling conditions, such as joint and connective tissue disorders (e.g., arthritis, lupus) and multiple sclerosis, gender has rarely been considered important in research or intervention development.

From the mid-1970s to the mid-1990s, interest in examining the needs of women with disabilities focused primarily on sexuality in response to the overwhelming preponderance of literature on the fertility and erectile dysfunction of men with SCI (Becker, 1979; Berard, 1989; Charlifue, Gerhart, Menter, Whiteneck, & Manley, 1992; Griffith & Trieschmann, 1975; Thornton, 1979). When the sexuality of women with disabilities was studied, it was often narrowly defined as fertility, pregnancy, labor, and delivery (Charlifue et al., 1992; Dechesne, Pons, & Schellen, 1986; Griffith & Trieschmann, 1975), as demonstrated by the number of studies on menstruation, fertility, pregnancy, and childbirth (Axel, 1982; Carty & Conine, 1988; D. I. Craig, 1990; Greenspoon & Paul, 1986; Jackson & Varner, 1989; Leavesley & Porter, 1982; Verduyn, 1986) and women's self-reports that if their fertility was not compromised, they were made to feel as if no other aspects of sexuality should matter (Cole, 1975).

In the late 1980s to early 1990s, researchers began to identify gaps in the study of sexuality in women with disabilities. In one of the few early studies dealing specifically with sexual issues of women with SCI, Charlifue and colleagues (1992) discovered that although 69% of 231 women surveyed were satisfied with their postinjury sexual experiences, they were not content with sexual information provided during rehabilitation. Women participating in the study identified a need for more literature, counseling, and peer support. In another investigation of gynecologic health care of women with disabilities, 91% had received breast and pelvic examinations and Papanicolaou (Pap) smears, but only 19% had received counseling about sexuality; women with paralysis, impaired motor function, or obvious physical deformity were rarely offered contraceptive information or methods (Beckmann, Gittler, Barzansky, & Beckmann, 1989). Only one third believed their health care provider knew enough about their disability to provide adequate sexual information.

The study of health and wellness in the context of disability for women is a relatively new avenue of investigation, opened only after researchers began to challenge entrenched stereotypes that disability is the polar opposite of health and that gender is far less important than the characteristics of the disability itself. Interest in research on women with disabilities emerged in the 1980s, about one decade after the rise of interest in women's health and interest in wellness and the prevention of secondary conditions in people with disabilities. Several researchers and feminist disability rights activists noted the lack of literature on women with disabilities and guided others to attend to this problem (Altman, 1982, 1985; Barnartt, 1982; Deegan & Brooks, 1985; Fine & Asch, 1985).

According to Altman (1996), before 1990, there was only one publication on demographics about women with disabilities using national population-based data (Bowe, 1984) and a few on access to benefits by women with disabilities (Johnson, 1979; Kutza, 1981; Mudrick, 1988). Although information about women with disabilities could be found in publications about people with disabilities in general (McNeil, 1993, 1997; Collins, 1993; LaPlante, 1988, 1991), Altman (1996) was the first to examine statistical information about risks, causes, and consequences of disability among women at the national level. Jans and Stoddard (1999) have made the only other similar effort to date. They compiled data from multiple national statistical data sources and individual research studies on the demographics, education, employment, and health status of girls and women with disabilities.

DEMOGRAPHIC AND HEALTH STATISTICS

Demographic and health statistics differ substantially between women and men with disabilities, as they do between women and men in the general population. Women and men differ in terms of types and prevalence of disabling conditions. The most prevalent disabling condition in women is back disorder (15.3%), followed by arthritis (13.3%), cardiovascular disease (9.7%), asthma (5.3%), orthopedic impairment of lower extremity (4.2%), mental disorders (3.3%), diabetes (3.3%), and learning disability and mental retardation (2.5%). Men are also most often disabled by back disorders (15.9%), but the list varies from there, with cardiovascular disease next (11.4%), followed by orthopedic impairment of lower extremity (6.1%), arthritis (5.8%), asthma (5.4%), learning disability and mental retardation (5.0%), mental disorders (4.6%), and diabetes (2.9%; LaPlante & Carlson, 1996). For disabilities resulting from trauma, such as SCI and brain injury, men outnumber women four to one. Women, however, have a greater prevalence of many physically disabling health conditions than do men, such as fibromyalgia (nine times more likely in women than in men), systemic lupus erythematosus (also nine times more likely), osteoporosis (four times), autoimmune disorders (three times), multiple sclerosis (two–three times), and rheumatoid arthritis (two–three times; National Women's Health Information Center, 2002). The prevalence of disability is highly correlated with age, with 40% of women 65 years and older having at least one functional limitation.

According to the 1994 and 1995 National Health Interview Survey (National Center for Health Statistics, 2002; Nosek, 2000), women with three or more functional limitations, compared to women in general, were less likely to be married (40% vs. 63%); more likely to be living alone (35% vs. 13%); more likely to have only a high school education or less (78% vs. 54%); less likely to be employed (14% vs. 63%); more likely to be living in households below the poverty level (23% vs. 10%), particularly in the 18-to-44 age group; and less likely to have private health insurance (55% vs. 74%).

Using data from the 1994–1995 *Survey of Income and Program Participation* (McNeil, 1997), Jans and Stoddard (1999) reported that women with disabilities constitute 21% of the population of women in the U.S. and outnumber men with disabilities (28.6 million vs. 25.3 million). Men earn substantially higher monthly incomes than do women, whether or not they have a disability ($2,190 vs. $1,470 for men and women without disabilities; $1,262 vs. $1,000 for men and women with severe disabilities). Men with work disabilities are more likely to receive benefits from Social Security (30.6% vs. 25.6%), but women with work disabilities are more likely to receive food stamps, Medicaid, and housing assistance (Jans & Stoddard, 1999; U.S. Bureau of the Census, 1992).

In her study of the health care needs and concerns of women with disabilities, Nosek (2000) found that women with functional limitations, especially younger women, are more likely to see a specialist; delay getting care due to cost; and be unable to get care for general medical conditions or surgery, mental health needs, dental needs, prescription medicine, or eyeglasses. Although hypertension, depression, stress, smoking, and being overweight are concerns for women in general, these problems are significantly greater among women with functional limitations. Nearly 33% of women with three or more functional limitations rated their overall health as poor, compared to less than 1% of women with no limitations.

In order to understand this finding, it is important to understand the impact of psychosocial factors and how these factors figure into the disability-related needs of women. To illustrate this point more specifically, we will now present evidence from the literature and our own studies about five major psychosocial problems that are disproportionately severe for women with disabilities, compared to men with disabilities and women in general. These problems involve depression, stress, self-esteem, social connectedness, and abuse.

MAJOR PSYCHOSOCIAL FACTORS

Depression

Gender disparities are prominent in depression. Women are at least twice as likely as men to experience depression (McGrath, Keita, Strickland, & Russo, 1990), and differences of race or ethnicity do little to change this disparity (Russo & Sobel, 1981). The American Psychological Association National Task Force on Women and Depression attributed this gender difference to biopsychosocial factors (McGrath et al., 1990). Women face biological, social, economic, and psychological factors increasing their vulnerability to depression (McGrath et al., 1990). Feminist theorists (Jordan, Kaplan, Miller, Stiver, & Surrey, 1991) have suggested that gender-based roles and socialization experiences contribute to depression in women. Women's depression has been associated with lower levels of perceived control, lack of social support, less income (Warren & McEachren, 1983), poverty, and experiences with abuse (McGrath et al., 1990).

Depression may be difficult to discern in the context of disability because the somatic criteria for depression are also common disability-related symptoms. Moreover, depression has been associated with conditions that often accompany disability, such as cerebral involvement and medications for the underlying disease (Cameron, 1987), pain (Tate, Forchheimer, Kirsch, Maynard, & Roller, 1993), and environmental factors (e.g., social isolation; Turner & Noh, 1988). In some cases, these confounding factors may lead to overestimating depression (Aikens et al., 1999). In most cases, however, those same somatic symptoms (e.g., reduced sexual interest, sleep disturbance) mask psychological distress (Franklin, 2000), leaving depression in persons with disabilities underdetected and undertreated.

The association of aging, depression, and disability is somewhat complex. First of all, aging with disability in both men and women usually entails the development of secondary conditions, such as fatigue and eating problems, which are common symptoms of depression. The development of secondary conditions could lead to an expectation that older women with disabilities are more likely to be depressed than younger women; however, this is not necessarily congruent with data gathered on women with disabilities (National Center for Health Statistics, 2002). This apparent contradiction is at least partially due to the way depression is measured. Using standard diagnostic criteria to identify clinical depression has been shown to lead to decreased levels of depression with age; however, symptom scales have yielded a greater prevalence of depression with age (Singh, 2000). Only highly rigorous research using diagnostic criteria will clarify the association between aging and depression in women with disabilities. It is likely that older women with disabilities, similar to people in general (Singh, 2000), experience a greater prevalence of subclinical depression but less clinical or major depression. Only well-designed research studies will contribute to an understanding of this issue. Like other health care professionals (Franklin, 2000), rehabilitation specialists may be more likely to attribute the somatic symptoms of depression to the physical disability rather than rule out depression and other psychological diagnoses.

The complexity of biopsychosocial risk factors for depression pervades the lives of women with disabilities (Nosek, 2000), who face the double jeopardy and marginalization of being female and disabled (Fine & Asch, 1988). Depression in persons with disabilities may be at least three times more common than in the general population (Turner & Beiser, 1990; U.S. Department of Health and Human Services, 2000). Again, according to *Healthy People 2010* (U.S. Department of Health and Human Services, 2000), the population of women with disabilities appears to be at an elevated risk for depression (30%), compared to men with disabilities (26%), women without disabilities (8%), and people in general (7%).

Several other studies have reported a greater prevalence of depression in women with disabilities, compared to their male counterparts (Coyle & Roberge, 1992; Fuhrer, Rintala, Hart, Clearman, & Young, 1993; Rintala, Hart, & Fuhrer, 1996). An assessment of depressive symptomatology in a community-based sample of 100 men and 40 women with SCI by Rintala, Hart, and Fuhrer (1996) revealed higher levels of depressive symptoms in women (47.5%) than men (25%).

Depression comprised the most prevalent self-reported secondary condition (44% lifetime; 40.7% within the past year) in an analysis of the health and health-promoting behaviors of 386 women with disabilities (Nosek et al., 2003). Hughes, Swedlund, Petersen, and Nosek (2001) found that there was a 59% rate of clinically depressive symptomatology among a sample of 64 women with SCI. This rate of depression is many times higher than the expected rate in the general population of U.S. women, of which approximately 4.5% to 9.3% experience symptoms of a major depressive disorder at any given time (Munoz, Hollon, McGrath, Rehm, & Vanden-Bos, 1994). According to the 1994–1995 *National Health Interview Survey* (National Center for Health Statistics, 2002), younger women with three or more functional limitations are more frequently depressed (30%) than women without disabilities (4%) and are eight times more likely to report having experienced major depression in the past year.

Stress

As reflected by the gender differences in stress levels found in the general population (Cohen & Williamson, 1988), women with disabilities report higher levels of stress than do men with disabilities (Rintala et al., 1996; Turner & Noh, 1988). As a result of being female and having a disability, women with physical disabilities may be more likely than their male counterparts to experience stress because of higher rates of poverty, social isolation, violence and other forms of victimization, and chronic health problems (McGrath et al., 1990). Their economic disadvantage is fueled by many stress-inducing factors reported earlier, such as earning lower income, having less education, being less likely to be married or employed, and having less access to disability benefits from public programs, compared to men with disabilities.

A study by Rintala and colleagues (1996) found that persons with SCI have higher levels of perceived stress than the general population. Stress in this population was associated with greater depressive symptomatology, less satisfaction with life, lower levels of self-assessed health, poorer social integration, and less satisfaction with social support. Women in the sample reported higher levels of perceived stress than did men.

According to preliminary findings from an analysis of the *National Health Interview Survey,* 21% of women with three or more functional limitations experience difficulty with day-to-day stress, compared to 2% of women with no limitations. For women with physical disabilities, perceived stress appears to be a significant problem associated with negative health consequences, including depressive symptomatology (Rintala et al., 1996), increased functional disability (Da Costa et al., 1999), and underlying disease progression (Schwartz, Foley, Rao, Bernardin, Lee, & Genderson, 1999). Hughes, Taylor, Robinson-Whelen, and Nosek (2003) conducted a study on perceived stress among 415 women with physical disabilities. Their preliminary findings suggest that after controlling for demographics and disability characteristics, perceived stress is greater for women with physical disabilities who have less social support, greater pain, and experience with abuse in the past year.

Self-Esteem

Self-esteem in women has been linked with employment status (Baruch & Barnett, 1986). Employment status, in turn, is commonly linked with economic resources. It logically follows that women with disabilities may experience problems with low self-esteem related to the loss of economic resources, especially women who are disadvantaged because of a lack of other opportunities. Women with disabilities have been called the "poorest of the poor" (Mulder et al., 2000, p. 24). In the context of disability, striking gender disparities exist at the poverty level. According to Jans and Stoddard (1999, p. 24) one out of three adult women with work disabilities lives in poverty, compared to one out of four men with work disabilities.

One of the most serious outcomes among women with physical disabilities is that of low economic status, which is associated with the lack of medical insurance and, consequently, the loss of access to medical care and health services. A woman's health and well-being may be unnecessarily compromised by lack of access to services, inaccessible medical equipment, inadequate public transportation, and lack of disability-related training among health care and other service providers (Nosek, 2000). As noted previously, women with disabilities share the economic-related problems of women in general, including low wages and occupational segregation (Schaller & DeLaGarza, 1995). They may, however, also experience restricted career opportunities associated with the nature of their disabilities, gender plus disability socialization experiences, and a lack of role models or mentors (Patterson, DeLaGarza, & Schaller, 1998).

Although a few studies have examined self-esteem among women with specific disabilities, only a couple of published studies have addressed self-esteem among cross-disability samples of women with physical disabilities (Hughes et al., 2003; Nosek et al., in press). It is interesting that investigations that evaluate self-esteem in the context of disability suggest that it is not disability per se but the contextual, physical, social, and emotional dimensions of disability that affect the sense of self (Barnwell & Kavanagh, 1997; Brooks & Matson, 1982; A. R. Craig, Hancock, & Chang, 1994; Walsh & Walsh, 1989).

Self-esteem and its related constructs appear to play a central role in the psychological well-being of persons with functional limitations (O'Leary, Shoor, Lorig, & Holman, 1988), including women with physical disabilities (Abraido-Lanza, Guier, & Colon, 1998). This psychological resource can be threatened at times of declining health and increased functional limitation associated with the development of secondary health conditions such as pain, fatigue, and other new symptoms (Burckhardt, 1985; Mahat, 1997; Schlesinger, 1996; Taal, Rasker, & Timmers, 1997). In the context of disability, self-worth may be compromised by internalizing the devaluation that society tends to assign physical impairment (Wright, 1960).

Disability is a stigmatizing phenomenon. When combined with women's social devaluation, its effects on sense of self can be profound. Yet, clinical experience suggests that many women who acquire disability at birth or later develop and maintain positive self-worth. The literature on self-esteem in the context of disability fails to explain these differences and the connections between self-esteem and health outcomes, particularly as related to men with disabilities and women in general. One 1997 survey of 946 women, half of whom had physical disabilities, revealed that the majority of women with disabilities reported high or moderately high self-esteem. On average, however, they reported lower levels of self-esteem and higher levels of problems associated with low self-esteem, including depression; unemployment; social isolation; limited opportunities to establish satisfying relationships; and emotional, physical, and sexual abuse, than did the women without disabilities (Nosek, Howland, Rintala, Young, & Chanpong, 2001).

It has been widely held for years that people's identities are developed based, in part, on their perceptions of how others evaluate them. This common understanding is similar to the phenomenon that Cooley (1902) called the "looking glass self." In other words, we look into the eyes of the other to assess our self-worth. This self dynamic has been linked to self-esteem (Adler, 1979; Bednar & Peterson, 1995; Mead, 1934). A qualitative study of women with physical disabilities suggested that negative messages, such as being a burden to the family, and positive expectations regarding a woman's potential profoundly influenced the woman's self-esteem (Nosek, 1996). Women with disabilities often must confront assaults on their self-esteem engendered by negative attitudes that they are "ill, ignorant, without emotion, asexual, pitiful, and incapable of employment" (Perduta-Fulginiti, 1996, p. 298).

We conducted a correlational analysis of self-esteem from the data gathered in our national study of women with and without disabilities described previously (Nosek et al., in press). In this study, we found that women with disabilities had significantly lower self-cognition and self-esteem and greater social isolation than the women without disabilities. They also had significantly less education, more overprotection during childhood, poorer quality of intimate relationships, and lower rates of remunerative employment.

Social Connectedness

Intimate relationships and other sources of connectedness and support may offer persons with disabilities an important validation of self-worth (Crisp, 1996). On the other hand, social isolation has been strongly associated with health problems and mortality (Berkman & Syme, 1979). Social isolation is regarded by some as a common secondary condition associated with any primary disability (Coyle, Santiago, Shank, Ma, & Boyd, 2000; Ravesloot, Seekins, & Walsh, 1997). Physical restrictions, such as mobility limitations and pain, may discourage people from making contact and connecting with others. Common knowledge and clinical experience suggest that the combination of multiple environmental barriers, negative societal messages, and diminished social opportunities may lead women with disabilities to become disconnected and isolated from sources of support and intimacy, employment opportunities, and health-promoting opportunities. Social isolation has also been linked with depression (Pope & Tarlov, 1991). In a study of women with SCI (Hughes et al., 2001), depression was associated primarily with stress and social isolation.

Part of the theoretical foundation for the intervention research at our center is the importance of social connectedness and self-efficacy in relation to self-esteem and other outcomes. First, social connectedness serves as a foundation for self-esteem in women (Jordan et al., 1991). Feminist theory (Jordan et al., 1991) postulates that women's groups may reduce social isolation by offering participants an opportunity to share common life experiences in order to connect with one another (Burden & Gottlieb, 1987; McManus, Redford, & Hughes, 1997) and address topics difficult to discuss in mixed gender groups (Enns, 1992). In the context of disability, greater self-esteem has been associated with better integration in social networks (Crisp, 1996). Women with physical disabilities appear to benefit from having mutually supportive relationships with one another (Crigger, 1996; Fine & Asch, 1988). In our group intervention studies, we have drawn successfully on the use of peer leaders, a practice grounded in the independent living movement, with its emphasis on role modeling, consumer participation, and empowerment (Hughes, Nosek, Howland, Groff, & Mullen, in press).

Abuse

Women are frequently victimized by domestic violence, sexual assault and abuse, rape, incest, and dating violence (National Women's Health Information Center, 2002). Women are five to eight times more likely than men to be victimized by an intimate partner. Women with disabilities experience the same risks for abuse as do other women; however, they also experience disability-related vulnerabilities to abuse associated with reliance on others for access to assistive devices and medication and assistance with essential personal needs such as toileting and dressing (Nosek, Foley, Hughes, & Howland, 2001).

For people with disabilities, violence serves as a prominent barrier to the full participation in society. Abuse experiences are linked with many other psychosocial problems, as identified previously. To illustrate, one analysis found that current abuse experiences were associated with greater social isolation, less social support, and higher levels of both stress and depression (Nosek, Taylor, Hughes, & Taylor, 2001). Women with disabilities may be highly vulnerable to abuse because of their dual minority status as women and people with disabilities (Nosek, Foley, et al., 2001).

Contrary to what some rehabilitation specialists may believe, disability does not serve as a protective factor against abuse for women (Nosek, Foley, et al., 2001). Our recent study of violence found that 1 out of 10 women with disabilities had experienced physical, sexual, or disability-related violence in the past year (McFarlane et al., 2001). In that study, we developed the *Abuse Assessment Screen–Disability* (AAS-D), a screening tool composed of four items that assess physical, sexual, and disability-related abuse in the past year. The AAS-D detected a 9.8% (50/511) prevalence of abuse in a sample of women with disabilities, and the two disability-related questions detected 2.0% (10/511) of abused women who would not otherwise have been identified. This study documents that four screening questions have the capability of detecting abuse in women with disabilities. Assessment for physical, sexual, and disability-related abuse must be standard care for women with disabilities.

The national survey previously mentioned detected a 13% prevalence rate of physical or sexual abuse in the past year (Nosek, Howland, et al., 2001). Of 429 women with disabilities and 421 women without disabilities, 62% of both groups reported experiencing some type of abuse during the course of their lives. Women with disabilities, however, experienced abuse at the hands of a greater number of perpetrators and for longer periods did than the women without disabilities.

Of all the abuse studies documented in the literature over the past 20 years (Schumacher, Feldbau-Kohn, Smith-Slep, & Heyman, 2001), no known empirical studies have identified characteristics of abused women with disabilities. We have begun to examine and understand these characteristics. Our preliminary findings on a cross-sectional sample of 415 women with physical disabilities suggest that five factors—age, education, mobility, social isolation, and depression—may be used to identify with 80% accuracy whether or not a woman has experienced physical, sexual, or disability-related violence or abuse within the past year (Nosek, Taylor, et al., 2001).

CONCLUSIONS

The life situation of women with disabilities is complex and permeated with attitudinal, social, and economic obstacles to psychosocial well-being. The evidence is irrefutable that women with disabilities are a substantial segment of the population and face more serious barriers to achieving their life goals than do men with disabilities or women in general. Population-based research has documented very high rates of mental and physical health problems among women with disabilities, yet efforts to develop and test interventions designed to address these problems have been minimal.

In the final analysis, it is inappropriate to compare the severity of disability-related problems faced by women to the problems faced by men. That approach reflects the masculine competitive aggressiveness that the women's movement rejects, and it pits women against men in a contest that cannot be won. More appropriately, these issues should be examined for the *ways in which* they differ, rather than *how much* they differ. Interventions that are effective for men are not necessarily effective for women. The disproportionate expenditure of resources and the bias of research directed toward the rehabilitation needs of men is testimony to the reality that we do not even know which interventions might be more effective for women. In the disciplines of cardiology, urology, immunology, psychology, and gerontology, there is now general recognition of gender-based differences. Rehabilitation, however, has been slow to rouse.

We believe that rehabilitation researchers and practitioners are ready to take action to remove these deficits in our field. It is imperative that researchers, rehabilitation counselors, and administrators heighten their awareness of and sensitivity to the commonality of these issues as they apply to all women, not solely women with disabilities, in order to make services and resources more accessible. Toward that end, we offer the following recommendations.

Recommendations to Researchers

1. Remove unnecessary enrollment criteria that would exclude or tend to exclude women with disabling conditions, such as

   limiting age to under 65, unless a working-age sample is essential to the design;
   conducting surveys or exams in inaccessible facilities;
   requiring telephone response to questions; and
   requiring attendance at a clinic or event.

2. Eliminate procedures that require manual dexterity or mobility when these are not essential for the phenomenon under investigation (e.g., minimum competency screens, intelligence tests).

3. During recruitment, take special measures to ensure that announcements reach minority, low income, low education, and sensory impaired women.

4. Set the parameters for the study carefully and state exclusion criteria in all publications of findings.

5. Always include gender as an independent variable in all data analyses.

6. Advance the careers of students who are women with disabilities by offering them scholarships, giving them opportunities to make presentations to academic audiences, and introducing them to leaders in their field.

Recommendations to Rehabilitation Counselors and Administrators

1. Be aware of gender bias when developing rehabilitation plans for women consumers.

2. Use only those assessment instruments and tools that have been validated for both genders.

3. Consider, as appropriate, the woman's life situation, and if abuse is suspected, refer her to community resources for domestic violence and sexual assault.
4. Be vigilant for signs of stress and depression and, as appropriate, refer for psychological counseling.
5. Encourage all consumers to become involved in the independent living movement or other peer support groups.
6. Include gender as a variable in analyzing consumer and program outcomes.
7. Ensure that advisory boards for rehabilitation services have equal representation of women and men with disabilities.

It is not difficult to see that some of these recommendations cannot be implemented until more research has been conducted. When assessment techniques that are common in rehabilitation settings have been proven valid for women, when counselors have available to them information and training about how disability can affect women differently than men, when success is defined by the same standards for both women and men, and when as many women as men have reached the highest levels of rehabilitation research, education, administration, and practice, then we will begin to see progress toward a truly inclusive society.

REFERENCES

Abraido-Lanza, A. F., Guier, C., & Colon, R. M. (1998). Psychological thriving among Latinas with chronic illness. *Journal of Social Issues, 54*, 405–424.

Adler, A. (1979). *Superiority and social interest.* New York: W. W. Norton.

Aikens, J. E., Reinecke, M. A., Pliskin, N. H., Fischer, J. S., Wiebe, J. S., McCracken, L. M., et al. (1999). Assessing depressive symptoms in multiple sclerosis: Is it necessary to omit items from the original Beck Depression Inventory? *Journal of Behavioral Medicine, 22*, 127–142.

Altman, B. M. (1982). *Disabled women: Doubly disadvantaged members of the social structure.* Paper presented at the meeting of the American Sociological Association, San Francisco, CA.

Altman, B. M. (1996). Causes, risks, and consequences of disability among women. In D. M. Krotoski, M. A. Nosek, & M. A. Turk (Eds.), *Women with physical disabilities: Achieving and maintaining health and well-being* (pp. 35–55). Baltimore: Brookes.

Axel, S. (1982). Spinal cord injured women's concerns: Menstruation and pregnancy. *Rehabilitation Nursing, 10*(1), 10–15.

Barnartt, S. N. (1982). The socio-economic status of deaf women: Are they doubly disadvantaged? In J. Christiansen & K. Egelston-Dodd (Eds.), *Socioeconomic status of the deaf population* (pp. 1–31). Washington, DC: Gallaudet College.

Barnwell, A. M., & Kavanagh, D. J. (1997). Prediction of psychological adjustment to multiple sclerosis. *Social Science and Medicine, 45,* 411–418.

Baruch, G. K., & Barnett, R. (1986). Role quality, multiple role involvement, and psychological well-being in midlife women. *Journal of Personality and Social Psychology, 51,* 578–585.

Becker, E. F. (1979). Sexuality and the spinal-cord-injured woman: An interview. *Sexuality and Disability, 2,* 278–286.

Beckmann, C. R. B., Gittler, M., Barzansky, B. M., & Beckmann, C. A. (1989). Gynecologic health care of women with disabilities. *Obstetrics and Gynecology, 74,* 75–79.

Bednar, R. L., & Peterson, S. R. (1995). *Self-esteem: Paradoxes and innovations in clinical theory and practice* (2nd ed.). Washington, DC: American Psychological Association.

Berard, E. J. J. (1989). The sexuality of spinal cord injured women: Physiology and pathophysiology: A review. *Paraplegia, 27,* 99–112.

Berkman, L. F., & Syme, S. L. (1979). Social networks, host resistance, and mortality: A nine-year follow-up study of Alameda County residents. *American Journal of Epidemiology, 109,* 186–204.

Bowe, F. (1984). *Disabled women in America.* Washington, DC: President's Committee on Employment of the Handicapped.

Brooks, N. A., & Matson, R. R. (1982). Social-psychological adjustment to multiple sclerosis. *Social Science and Medicine, 16,* 2129–2135.

Burckhardt, C. S. (1985). The impact of arthritis on quality of life. *Nursing Research, 34*(1), 11–16.

Burden, D. S., & Gottlieb, N. (1987). Women's socialization and feminist groups. In C. M. Brody (Ed.), *Women's therapy groups: Paradigms of feminist treatment* (pp. 24–39). New York: Springer.

Cameron, O. G. (1987). Some guidelines for a pragmatic approach to the patient with secondary depression. In O. G. Cameron (Ed.), *Presentations of depression: Depressive symptoms in medical and other psychiatric disorders* (pp. 417–423). New York: Wiley & Sons.

Carty, E. A., & Conine, T. A. (1988). Disability and pregnancy: A double dose of disequilibrium. *Rehabilitation Nursing, 13*(2), 85–92.

Charlifue, S. W., Gerhart, K. A., Menter, R. R., Whiteneck, G. G., & Manley, M. S. (1992). Sexual issues of women with spinal cord injuries. *Paraplegia, 30,* 192–199.

Cohen, S., & Williamson, G. M. (1988). Perceived stress in a probability sample of the United States. In S. Spacapan & S. Oskamp (Eds.), *The social psychology of health: Claremont Symposium on Applied Social Psychology* (pp. 31–67). Newbury Park, CA: Sage.

Cole, T. M. (1975). Spinal cord injured patients and sexual dysfunction. *Archives of Physical Medicine & Rehabilitation, 56*(1), 11–12.

Collins, J. G. (1993). Prevalence of selected chronic conditions, United States, 1986–1988: National Center for Health Statistics. *Vital Health Statistics, 10(18),* 1–5.

Cooley, C. H. (1902). *Human nature and the social order.* New York: Scribner's.

Coyle, C. P., & Roberge, J. J. (1992). The psychometric properties of the Center for Epidemiological Studies–Depression Scale (CES-D) when used with adults with physical disabilities. *Psychology and Health, 7*(1), 69–81.

Coyle, C. P., Santiago, M. C., Shank, J. W., Ma, G. X., & Boyd, R. (2000). Secondary conditions and women with physical disabilities: A descriptive study. *Archives of Physical Medicine & Rehabilitation, 81,* 1380–1387.

Craig, A. R., Hancock, K., & Chang, E. (1994). The influence of spinal cord injury on coping styles and self-perceptions two years after the injury. *Australian and New Zealand Journal of Psychiatry, 28,* 307–312.

Craig, D. I. (1990). The adaptation to pregnancy of spinal cord injured women. *Rehabilitation Nursing, 15*(1), 6–9.

Crigger, N. J. (1996). Testing an uncertainty model for women with multiple sclerosis. *Advances in Nursing Science, 18*(3), 37–47.

Crisp, R. (1996). Community integration, self-esteem, and vocational identity among persons with disabilities. *Australian Psychologist, 31,* 133–137.

Da Costa, D., Dobkin, P. L., Pinard, L., Fortin, P. R., Danoff, D. S., Esdaile, J. M., et al. (1999). The role of stress in functional disability among women with systemic lupus erythematosus: A prospective study. *Arthritis Care and Research, 12,* 112–119.

Dechesne, B. H. H., Pons, C., & Schellen, A. M. C. M. (Eds.). (1986). *Sexuality and handicap: Problems of motor handicapped people.* Springfield, IL: Charles C. Thomas.

Deegan, M. J., & Brooks, N. A. (1985). *Women and disability: The double handicap.* New Brunswick, NJ: Transaction Books.

Enns, C. Z. (1992, September–October). Self-esteem groups: A synthesis of consciousness-raising and assertiveness training. *Journal of Counseling and Development, 71,* 7–13.

Fine, M., & Asch, A. (1985). Disabled women: Sexism without the pedestal. In M. J. Deegan & N. A. Brooks (Eds.), *Women and disability: The double handicap* (pp. 6–22). New Brunswick, NJ: Transaction Books.

Fine, M., & Asch, A. (1988). *Women with disabilities: Essays in psychology, culture, and politics.* Philadelphia: Temple University Press.

Franklin, D. J. (2000). *Depression: Information and treatment.* Psychology Information Online.

Fuhrer, M. J., Rintala, D. H., Hart, K. A., Clearman, R., & Young, M. E. (1993). Depressive symptomatology in persons with spinal cord injury who reside in the community. *Archives of Physical Medicine & Rehabilitation, 74,* 255–260.

Greenspoon, J. S., & Paul, R. H. (1986). Paraplegia and quadriplegia: Special considerations during pregnancy and labor and delivery. *American Journal of Obstetrics & Gynecology, 155,* 738–741.

Griffith, E. R., & Trieschmann, R. B. (1975). Sexual functioning in women with spinal cord injury. *Archives of Physical Medicine & Rehabilitation, 56*(1), 18–21.

Hughes, R. B., Nosek, M. A., Howland, C. A., Groff, J., & Mullen, P. D. (in press). Health promotion for women with physical disabilities: A pilot study. *Rehabilitation Psychology.*

Hughes, R. B., Swedlund, N., Petersen, N., & Nosek, M. A. (2001). Depression and women with spinal cord injury. *Topics in Spinal Cord Injury Rehabilitation, 7*(1), 16–24.

Hughes, R. B., Taylor, H. B., Robinson-Whelen, S., & Nosek, M. A. (2003). *Perceived stress and women with physical disabilities*. Manuscript submitted for publication.

Jackson, A. B., & Varner, R. E. (1989). Gynecological problems encountered in women with acute and chronic spinal cord disabilities. *Abstracts Digest,* 111–112.

Jans, L., & Stoddard, S. (1999). *Chartbook on women and disability in the United States: An InfoUse report*. Washington, DC: U.S. Department of Education, National Institute on Disability and Rehabilitation Research.

Johnson, W. G. (1979). Disability, income support, and social insurance. In E. D. Berkowitz (Ed.), *Disability policies and government programs* (pp. 87–132). New York: Praeger.

Jordan, J. V., Kaplan, A. G., Miller, J. B., Stiver, I. P., & Surrey, J. L. (1991). *Women's growth in connection*. New York: Guilford Press.

Kutza, E. (1981). Benefits for the disabled: How beneficial for women? *Journal of Sociology and Social Welfare, 8,* 298–319.

LaPlante, M. P. (1988). *Data on disability from the National Health Interview Survey, 1983–1985*. Washington, DC: U.S. Department of Education, National Institute on Disability and Rehabilitation Research.

LaPlante, M. P. (1991). *Disability risks of chronic illnesses and impairments: Disability Statistics Report: Report 2*. Washington, DC: U.S. Department of Education, National Institute on Disability and Rehabilitation Research.

LaPlante, M. P., & Carlson, D. (1996). Disability in the United States: Prevalence and causes, 1992: Disability Statistics Report: Report 7. *Disability Statistics Abstract,* 1–3.

Leavesley, G., & Porter, J. (1982). Sexuality, fertility and contraception in disability. *Contraception, 26,* 417–441.

Legato, M. J. (2002). *Eve's rib: The new science of gender-specific medicine and how it can save your life*. New York: Harmony Books.

Mahat, G. (1997). Perceived stressors and coping strategies among individuals with rheumatoid arthritis. *Journal of Advanced Nursing, 25,* 1144–1150.

McFarlane, J., Hughes, R. B., Nosek, M. A., Groff, J. Y., Swedlund, N., & Mullen, P. D. (2001). Abuse Assessment Screen–Disability (AAS-D): Measuring frequency, type, and perpetrator of abuse toward women with physical disabilities. *Journal of Women's Health and Gender-Based Medicine, 10,* 861–866.

McGrath, E., Keita, G. P., Strickland, B. R., & Russo, N. F. (1990). *Women and depression: Risk factors and treatment issues: Final report of the American Psychological Association's National Task Force on Women and Depression*. Washington, DC: American Psychological Association.

McManus, P. W., Redford, J. L., & Hughes, R. B. (1997). Connecting to self and others: A structured group for women. *The Journal for Specialists in Group Work, 22*(1), 22–30.

McNeil, J. M. (1993). *Americans with Disabilities: 1991–1992, Current Population Reports P70-33*. Washington, DC: U.S. Bureau of the Census.

McNeil, J. M. (1997). *Americans with Disabilities 1994–1995: Current Population Reports P7061*. Washington, DC: U.S. Bureau of the Census.

Mead, G. H. (1934). *Mind, self, and society*. Chicago: University of Chicago Press.

Mudrick, N. R. (1988). Disabled women and public policies for income support. In M. Fine & A. Asch (Eds.), *Women with disabilities: Essays in psychology, culture, and politics* (pp. 245–268). Philadelphia: Temple University Press.

Mulder, P. L., Shellenberget, S., Streigel, R., Jumper-Thurman, P., Danda, C. E., et al. (2000, January). *The behavioral health care needs of rural women: An APA report to Congress*. Washington, DC: American Psychological Association.

Munoz, R. F., Hollon, S. D., McGrath, E., Rehm, L. P., & VandenBos, G. R. (1994, January). On the AHCPR depression in primary care guidelines: Further considerations for practitioners. *American Psychologist, 42–61*.

National Center for Health Statistics. (2002). *Healthy women with disabilities: Analysis of the 1994–1995 National Health Interview Survey: Series 10 Report* [Forward by F. Chevarley, J. Thierry, M. Nosek, & C. Gill]. Manuscript in preparation.

National Women's Health Information Center. (2002). *National Women's Health Information Center*. Retrieved from www.4woman. gov

Nosek, M. A. (1996). Wellness among women with physical disabilities. In D. M. Krotoski, M. A. Nosek, & M. A. Turk (Eds.), *Women with physical disabilities: Achieving and maintaining health and well-being* (pp. 17–33). Baltimore: Brookes.

Nosek, M. A. (2000). Overcoming the odds: The health of women with physical disabilities in the United States. *Archives of Physical Medicine & Rehabilitation, 81*, 135–138.

Nosek, M. A., Foley, C. C., Hughes, R. B., & Howland, C. A. (2001). Vulnerabilities for abuse among women with disabilities. *Sexuality and Disability, 19*, 177–189.

Nosek, M. A., Howland, C. A., Rintala, D. H., Young, M. E., & Chanpong, G. F. (2001). National study of women with physical disabilities: Final report. *Sexuality and Disability, 19*(1), 5–39.

Nosek, M. A., Hughes, R. B., O'Malley, K. W., Taylor, H. B., Howland, C. A., & Robinson-Whelen, S. (2003). *Health promoting behaviors of women with physical disabilities: The influence of physical, psychological, social, and environmental factor*. Manuscript in preparation.

Nosek, M. A., Hughes, R. B., Swedlund, N., Taylor, H. B., & Swank, P. (in press). Self-esteem and women with disabilities. *Social Science and Medicine*.

Nosek, M. A., Taylor, H. B., Hughes, R. B., & Taylor, W. P. (2001). *Demographic, disability, and psychosocial characteristics of abused women with disabilities*. Manuscript in preparation.

O'Leary, A., Shoor, S., Lorig, K., & Holman, H. R. (1988). A cognitive behavioral treatment for rheumatoid arthritis. *Health Psychology, 7*, 527–544.

Patterson, J. B., DeLaGarza, D., & Schaller, J. (1998). Rehabilitation counseling practice: Considerations and interventions. In R. M. Parker & E. M. Szymanski (Eds.), *Rehabilitation counseling: Basics and beyond* (3rd ed., pp. 269–302). Austin, TX: PRO-ED.

Perduta-Fulginiti, P. S. (1996). Impact of bladder and bowel dysfunction on sexuality and self-esteem. In D. M. Krotoski, M. A. Nosek, & M. A. Turk (Eds.), *Women with physical disabilities: Achieving and maintaining health and well-being* (pp. 287–298). Baltimore: Brookes.

Pope, A. M., & Tarlov, A. R. (1991). *Disability in America: Toward a national agenda for prevention.* Washington, DC: National Academy Press.

Ravesloot, C., Seekins, T., & Walsh, J. (1997). A structural analysis of secondary conditions experienced by people with physical disabilities. *Rehabilitation Psychology, 42*(1), 3–16.

Rintala, D. H., Hart, K. A., & Fuhrer, M. J. (1996). Perceived stress in individuals with spinal cord injury. In D. M. Krotoski, M. A. Nosek, & M. A. Turk (Eds.), *Women with physical disabilities: Achieving and maintaining health and well-being* (pp. 223–242). Baltimore: Brookes.

Russo, N. F., & Sobel, S. B. (1981). Sex differences in the utilization of mental health facilities. *Professional Psychology, 12*(1), 7–19.

Schaller, J., & DeLaGarza, D. (1995). Issues of gender in vocational testing and counseling. *Journal of Job Placement, 11*(1), 6–14.

Schlesinger, L. (1996). Chronic pain, intimacy, and sexuality: A qualitative study of women who live with pain. *The Journal of Sex Research, 33*, 249–256.

Schumacher, J. A., Feldbau-Kohn, S., Smith-Slep, A., & Heyman, R. E. (2001). Risk factors for male-to-female partner physical abuse. *Aggression and Violent Behavior, 6*, 281–352.

Schwartz, C. E., Foley, F. W., Rao, S. M., Bernardin, L. J., Lee, H., & Genderson, M. W. (1999). Stress and course of disease in multiple sclerosis. *Behavioral Medicine, 25*, 110–116.

Singh, N. A. (2000). Depression in the older woman. In M. A. F. Singh (Ed.), *Exercise, nutrition, and the older woman: Wellness for women over fifty* (pp. 395–416). Boca Raton, FL: CRC Press LLC.

Taal, E., Rasker, J. J., & Timmers, C. J. (1997). Measures of physical function and emotional well being for young adults with arthritis. *The Journal of Rheumatology, 24*, 994–997.

Tate, D. G., Forchheimer, M., Kirsch, N., Maynard, F., & Roller, A. (1993). Prevalence and associated features of depression and psychological distress in polio survivors. *Archives of Physical Medicine & Rehabilitation, 74*, 1056–1060.

Thornton, C. E. (1979). Sexuality counseling of women with spinal cord injuries. *Sexuality and Disability, 4*, 267–277.

Turner, R. J., & Beiser, M. (1990). Major depression and depressive symptomatology among the physically disabled: Assessing the role of chronic stress. *Journal of Nervous and Mental Disease, 178*, 343–350.

Turner, R. J., & Noh, S. (1988, March). Physical disability and depression: A longitudinal analysis. *Journal of Health and Social Behavior, 29*, 23–37.

U.S. Bureau of the Census. (1992). *Labor force status and other characteristics of persons with a work disability: 1981 to 1988* (Current Population Reports Series P-23, No. 160). Washington, DC: U.S. Government Printing Office.

U.S. Department of Health and Human Services. (2000). Disability and secondary conditions. In *Healthy people 2010.* Washington, DC: Author.

Verduyn, W. H. (1986). Spinal cord injured women, pregnancy and delivery. *Paraplegia, 24*, 231–240.

Walsh, A., & Walsh, P. A. (1989). Love, self-esteem, and multiple sclerosis. *Social Science and Medicine, 29*, 793–798.

Warren, L. W., & McEachren, L. (1983). Psychosocial correlates of depressive symptomatology in adult women. *Journal of Abnormal Psychology, 92*, 151–160.

Wright, B. A. (1960). *Physical disability: A psychological approach*. New York: Harper & Row.

CHAPTER ELEVEN

Female Sexuality and Spinal Cord Injury

Counseling Implications

Eva Miller and Irmo Marini

Sexual concerns are often paramount following spinal cord injury (SCI). However, despite the sexual revolution in the mid-1970s that spurred research in the area of sexuality, most of what is known about SCI on sexual function pertains to males. This is due in part to the fact that the majority of individuals with SCI are males (4:1) and because it is easier to study sexual response in males because of their external genitalia (Mona et al., 2000). Most early research regarding the sexual activity of women with SCI has also been pessimistic and narrow in focus (Sipski & Alexander, 1997). Sipski and Alexander noted that part of the problem with the lack of research relates to previously low survival rates years ago. The authors further suggested that it is difficult for some counselors to be objective about discussing sexuality due to their own values, biases, and experiences. Hwang (1997) found that females with disabilities rarely receive sex education, due in part because many such classes are offered as part of gym class where they have likely been excused from and due to the belief that "no one is going to marry them anyway" (p. 119). Hwang also noted that in a society where women are judged on their beauty

From "Female sexuality and spinal cord injury: Counseling implications," by E. Miller and I. Marini, 2004, *Journal of Applied Rehabilitation Counseling, 35*(4), 17–25. Reprinted with permission.

and desirability, many women with disabilities are excluded in matters involving sexual relationships.

The purpose of this article is to identify some of the myths associated with SCI and female sexuality, to highlight the major physiological and psychosocial implications of SCI and female sexuality, to summarize current models used to successfully work with women with SCI who are experiencing various types of sexual dysfunction, and to provide a framework for counselors in identifying and addressing sexuality concerns among women with SCI.

SEXUALITY DEFINED

Sexuality is often difficult to define because of its different and sometimes incomplete or conflicting definitions. According to Lemon (1993), sexuality involves body image, self-esteem, social reactions, myths, feelings, and interpersonal relationships. Lefebvre (1997) defined sexuality as verbal, visual, tactual, and olfactory communication which expresses intimacy and love. Medlar (1998) views sexuality as a natural and healthy part of living that encompasses physical, spiritual, emotional, and psychological dimensions that include one's sense of worth, desirability, and ability to give and receive love and affection within personal relationships. Unfortunately, the belief that people with disabilities are sexual and have sexual feelings and drives is frequently overlooked or ignored. Instead, they are often stereotyped as being asexual, lacking the same desire for sexual relationships as able-bodied persons (Sipski & Alexander, 1997). Women with disabilities are especially at risk for negative biases by others about their sexuality, and rehabilitation counselors and other human service professionals are not necessarily exempt from these attitudes.

Sexuality among women with SCI was essentially ignored until the 1990s, and what little research does exist has often been a reflection of societal bias and is frequently limited to reproductive issues instead of areas such as sexual response, activity, and satisfaction (Nosek & Hughes, 2003; Sipski & Alexander, 1995a). For example, according to Basson (1998), common beliefs in Western society about female sexuality and disability are that only independently functioning women can handle sexual relationships, women with physical disabilities who are single are celibate, all women with physical disabilities are heterosexual, and women with physical disabilities should be grateful for sexual relationships. This notion is well illustrated by the fact that women typically experience pressure to have the "perfect" body and to adhere to their gender role which includes a traditional, heterosexual marriage complete with children and possibly a job (Hwang, 1997; Livneh, 1991). According to Chenoweth (1993) it is because of these types of beliefs and attitudes that women with disabilities experience a "double strike," that is, being a woman and being disabled.

Limited education on the topic and phallocentric thinking (i.e., attitudes that a woman's sexuality exists only in relationship to her ability to satisfy her husband's [sic] needs) have also contributed to the lack of research on female sexuality and SCI. For example, Nosek et al. (1995) maintain that many adult women with physical disabilities lack basic knowledge of their reproductive health. In addition, women with disabilities are given Pap smear tests less frequently than able-bodied women due in part to the inaccessibility of gynecologists' offices and because of the assumption that they are asexual (Chance, 2002). Charlifue, Gerhart, Menter, Whiteneck, and Manley (1992) found that women with disabilities were generally satisfied with their postinjury sexual activities but reported a greater need for peer support, information, and counseling. It has also been noted that even though it is essential that rehabilitation counseling students and seasoned counselors receive adequate training on the impact of disability on sexuality issues, this is often a low priority and virtually no literature dealing with this topic is available (Boyle, 1994).

COMMON MYTHS

Despite medical advances and the feminist movement that has challenged stereotypical female roles, numerous myths regarding women with SCI and their sexuality are still in existence today. According to Tepper, Whipple, Richards, and Komisaruk (2001), accepted myths of the medical literature are that female sexuality is passive, that it is easier for a woman with a SCI to adapt to sexual changes than it is for a male, and that a loss of sexual functioning is less threatening to a woman than it is to a male. Farrow (1990) noted that individuals with SCI are assumed to be incapable, uninterested, or inactive sexually. Olkin (1999) cited several myths, including the most common one that persons with disabilities are asexual or lacking in basic sex drive. Other myths she described involve persons with physical disabilities being functionally incapable of having intercourse and not possessing the social skills and judgment to behave in a sexually appropriate manner (attributed to what Olkin believes is the result of the "spread effect"). Still another myth is that no able-bodied person will find someone with a disability desirable as a sex partner and, if they do, it is because the able-bodied person is "settling" or there is something wrong with him or her (Olkin).

Other commonly held myths by persons with SCI as well as significant others and the general public are that sex means intercourse, that sexual performance equals love, that sexual activity is natural and spontaneous, and that masturbation is sinful (Lemon, 1993). In addition, although the need to address sex and sexuality as a component of a holistic approach to the total rehabilitation process for women with SCI has been identified for over a decade, little has been done to formally educate rehabilitation counselors in these areas. Instead, counselors are often forced to learn about human sexuality and disability through vicarious experiences and may subsequently feel unprepared or uncomfortable in discussing the issue of sexuality with their clients. Burling, Tarvydas, and Maki (1994) noted that some of the most common fears and misconceptions among counselors are that they believe sexuality is beyond the purview of their care, sexuality is not an appropriate area of concern for clients, and that if clients were interested or concerned about their sexuality, they would ask questions. Parritt and O'Callaghan (2000) found that counselors reported feeling anxious about raising the issue of sexuality with clients with disabilities because they feared they might upset clients, they felt a sense of unknowing embarrassment about what people with disabilities do sexually, and they felt a need for safety in the therapeutic relationship prior to talking about disability and sex.

PHYSIOLOGICAL EFFECTS OF SCI AND SEXUALITY

The level and degree of injury must be known in order to understand the implications of SCI on a person's sexual functioning. Tetraplegia refers to partial or permanent paralysis and potential loss or dull sensation in all four limbs, whereas paraplegia is indicative of partial or permanent paralysis and probable loss or dull sensation in only the lower extremities. The specific level of injury is determined by motor strength and sensory function at specific points and is defined as the last "normal" neurologic level of both motor and sensory functions (Crewe & Krause, 2002). Injuries are also classified as complete or incomplete, depending on nerve fiber damage. The injury can also affect multiple organ systems, including diminished respiratory capacity, alterations in skin integrity, and bowel and bladder function (Sipski & Alexander, 1995a).

Genitalia are almost invariably affected by SCI. For some, sensation may be altered or limited while others may experience complete loss of sensation in that part of the body. Sipski and Alexander (1995a) reported that vaginal lubrication and the ability to achieve orgasm after SCI is maintained by many women, albeit with more difficulty and altered orgasmic quality for some women. Sipski and Alexander (1995b) also found that women with SCI had the capacity to achieve orgasm approximately 50% of the time, regardless of whether they had complete or incomplete SCI.

In addition, the authors found that females with SCI preferred some type of genital stimulation to achieve orgasm and those able to achieve orgasm scored higher on measures of sexual information and sexual drive than did female subjects who were aorgasmic. However, similar to males, women with SCI have reported decreased sexual satisfaction and decreased frequency of sexual activities following SCI (Sipski, 1997).

One reason for women's dissatisfaction and reduced sexual activity is that although sexual intercourse is neither the only nor always the most satisfying sexual activity, it is the most common (Farrow, 1990). Other types of erotic stimulation that are preferred by many women following SCI have been reported to be hugging, kissing, and touching usually just above the level of injury (Farrow). Areas that may become highly sensitive to stimulation include the neck, ears, lips, breasts, and nipples. Cuddling and massaging can also be highly pleasurable for women with SCI. For those who do choose to engage in sexual intercourse, penile-vaginal penetration can be accomplished by people with SCI in a variety of positions limited only by an individual's abilities, muscle strength, and desire. The level and severity of the injury also affect sexual activities and women with paraplegia are usually able to engage in top, bottom, and side positions whereas women with tetraplegia will more than likely need to be supine with the partner on top (Farrow).

Another area of concern for women with SCI is the appropriate contraception method. Birth control pills are typically not recommended for women with SCI due to the danger of blood clots caused by the combination of estrogen and progesterone (Farrow, 1990). The use of a diaphragm may also present several problems for women with SCI, including the need for dexterity and the ability to grasp, which is needed for insertion. In addition, weakened pelvic muscles may not allow for the diaphragm to remain in place, and the diaphragm may become dislodged. An intrauterine device (IUD) that is inserted into the uterus by a physician has sometimes been thought to be the best contraception choice; however, complications include pelvic inflammation, the possibility of a tubal pregnancy, and the fact that the expulsion of an IUD can go undetected due to the loss of sensation in the pelvic area. Levonorgestrol implants that are surgically placed in the inner upper arm have been used as a long-term contraceptive method. Levonorgestrol is a medication that does not have estrogen and requires no hand manipulation, making it appropriate for some women with SCI (Sipski, 1997). The combination spermicidal foam and condoms is one alternative that has been shown to be highly effective for women with SCI as this method does not require manual dexterity but can be used successfully for women with tetraplegia if their partner is willing to insert the foam and apply the condom. Sterilization of the male (vasectomy) or the female (tubal ligation) eliminates all worry about contraception, but serious consideration regarding this method of birth control is highly recommended since both procedures are usually permanent and irreversible (Farrow).

Although many women with SCI stop menstruating for several months postinjury, most are able to conceive and give birth. Unfortunately, most health care professionals including nurses and mental health counselors are unaware of how pregnancy affects physical disabilities (Lipson & Rogers, 2000). For those women who do become pregnant, it is important that their obstetricians are aware of the potential complications associated with pregnancy and SO. Some of the more prevalent complications include anemia, problems with transfers due to weight gain, urinary tract infections, pressure sores, and, more significantly, autonomic dysreflexia (an abnormal reflex), which frequently occurs during labor in women with injuries above the T6 vertebral level (Sipski, 1997). Pregnant women with SCI may also benefit from being hospitalized for a short time prior to their due date if they lack sensation in the abdominal or pelvic area.

PSYCHOSOCIAL ASPECTS OF SCI AND SEXUALITY

Body image is an important aspect of a person's overall self-concept and self-esteem, especially in America where the emphasis on a "beautiful body" is more apparent than in any other society (Livneh, 1991). The relationship between body satisfaction and self-satisfaction is particularly strong among females because of the emphasis our society places on attractiveness as an indicator of female worth. For women with SCIs, body image and understanding one's self may be significantly impacted by the SCI, either directly or indirectly. Despite the emphasis Western society places on physique, Wright (1983) noted how adjustment to disability may be enhanced when individuals subordinate or de-emphasize their worth based on their physique and instead begin to measure self-worth more on other personal attributes such as ones personality, intellect, or skills.

Women with SCI may also experience a sense of dependence and vulnerability because of limited financial resources, limited vocational opportunities, lack of social supports; and, an increased need for personal assistance (Tate & Forchheimer, 2001). Other secondary conditions that may affect women with SCI include mobility and accessibility concerns, pain, spasticity, fatigue, muscle atrophy and body weight issues, concerns about developing romantic relationships, isolation, and depression (Nosek, 2000; Nosek & Hughes, 2003). Nevertheless, why some women adapt to their SCI with relative ease while others struggle in their ability to understand and adjust to SCI remains questionable. Wright (1983) believed that some persons with disabilities adapt better than others due to cognitive changes in their values. Specifically, persons who are able to minimize focusing on their losses or what they no longer can do, and begin focusing on their remaining assets, goals, interests, and abilities (enlarging one's scope of values) will typically respond better to their disability. In addition, restructuring comparative status values into asset values (e.g., believing a wheelchair helps with mobility rather than it is not better than walking) also can assist in adjustment.

Mona et al. (2000) examined a number of cognitive variables relating to sexuality among men and women with SCIs who were at least two years post-injury with varying degrees of severity. The factors assessed included levels of optimism about themselves and their situation, locus of control, self-esteem, and their purpose and meaning in life. The authors found that in addition to lower severity of injury, sexual adjustment was positively correlated with an internal locus of control, an optimistic outlook, having found a sense of meaning in one's life, and high self-esteem. However, beyond the cognitive constructs identified above, sexual self-esteem was found to be the best predictor of sexual adjustment in both men and women with SCI. In another study designed to assess qualitative sexual experiences of women with complete SCIs between levels T6 and T12, Tepper et al. (2001) found a number of variables to be related to levels of sexual adjustment. For example, women who acquired their disability later in life reported lower sexual self-esteem than women who acquired their disability early in life or at birth. The authors also found that cognitive-genital dissociation or the "shutting down" of one's sexuality based on the assumption that sexual pleasure was no longer possible because of absence of sensation in the genitals was common among the women surveyed. Instead, women tended to focus their energy on physical and vocational rehabilitation, bowel and bladder management, and other activities of daily living, with sex being a relatively low priority during the first few months post-injury. A lack of or inadequate sexuality education and counseling as well as asexual attitudes toward people with disabilities, concerns about body image, and negative feedback regarding sexuality from health professionals left many women in the study feeling as if they were no longer sexually desirable. However, with time (several months to years) and experience (e.g., ability to communicate sexual needs and desires and an increasing sense of value as a human being), women became more comfortable with their sexuality and developed improved sexual self-esteem (Tepper, et al.).

Westgren and Levi (1999) found that pre-injury sexual behavior, positive attitudes toward sexuality, good communication skills, and perceived locus of control were better predictors of sexual adaptation than were age, extent of injury, and time since injury. It has also been suggested that sexual attitudes of people with SCI are more liberal than those of the general public but that females with SCI are far less experimental than males when it comes to engaging in untraditional sexual techniques (Westgren & Levi). Some of the reasons for their reticence include feeling unattractive, inadequate, and undesirable; lack of knowledge about techniques that can be used to make sexual activity a satisfying experience, and inhibitions about initiating alternative sexual techniques.

TREATMENT

The Council on Rehabilitation Education (CORE) curriculum guidelines does not require extensive training in sexuality issues; subsequently, few rehabilitation counselors are generally trained to address the "specific skills" area of sexuality among persons with disabilities. There is no reason, however, why counselors cannot be minimally prepared to grant permission to discuss and provide limited information about sexuality issues. When clients learn to trust their counselor and rapport has been developed, any question or topic may become open for discussion if the client/counselor feels comfortable and conveys this to each other.

However, before discussing various sexuality treatment methods for women with SCI, it is important to holistically understand other global adjustment issues known about women with physical disabilities which may have a direct impact on desire, affect, cognitions, and behaviors regarding sex. Specifically, Nosek and Hughes (2003) noted that women with disabilities (especially those of ethnic minority) represent the most disenfranchised group in the United States. They have higher unemployment rates and lower wages (if employed) and are more likely to be living in poverty and receiving poorer health care than non-disabled persons (Nosek, 2000). They also tend to be single more-so than males with disabilities or able-bodied persons and experience greater social isolation with accompanying higher rates of stress and depression (Hughes, Swedlund, Peterson, & Nosek, 2001). These factors have been linked to lower levels of self-esteem reported by some women with disabilities (Barnwell & Kavanagh, 1997; Walsh & Walsh, 1989).

There are a number of methods which have been successfully used to assist persons with disabilities in overcoming sexuality issues. Women with SCI, however, may not openly inquire about the effects of their injury on sexuality but instead may drop subtle hints. Therefore, it is important to plan for and provide opportunities for them to discuss their sexual concerns. Because individuals may also disguise the request for sexually-related information for fear of being rejected or embarrassed, it is important to clarify with the individual the type of information she is seeking. Although treatment models for decreased sexual desires, arousal disorders, and the inability to have orgasms have not been standardized for women with SCI, sex therapy techniques similar to those used in the non-disabled population may be appropriate for women with SCI (Sipski, 1997).

One model that is currently being used with people with SCI is the PLISSIT model of sex therapy (Lemon, 1993). This model allows professionals to participate in therapy-according to their level of skill, knowledge, and comfort. The aim of this model is to give an individual the permission to discuss sexual issues through counselor body language and verbalizations (P); to provide limited information about anatomy and physiology, dispelling myths and prevention of STDs (LI); to provide women with SCI with specific suggestions regarding sexual expression, functioning with the disability, relationships, and satisfying a partner (SS); and to provide intensive therapy (IT) including medical procedures, counseling, fertility, childbirth, and hormonal imbalances. For women with SCI, considerations might include physical appearance (e.g., wheelchair color, clothing choices), catheterization, drinking habits, sensation level and pain, lubrication methods, transferring, sexual positioning, spacticity, and learning how to identify areas of the relationship that may affect one's sexuality (e.g., role reversal). Cognitive restructuring is also used to help women identify and change maladaptive ways of viewing their disability and sexuality-related issues.

Sensate focus exercises can also be used by counselors to help women and their partners identify residual sexual functioning and enhance the couples' repertoire of sexual and sensual behaviors (Lemon, 1993). Sensate focus is based on cognitive-behavioral theory aimed at minimizing anxiety performance while increasing intimacy behaviors and is considered intensive therapy. After discussing specific sexual behaviors and cognitions couples are experiencing difficulties with (e.g., low sex desire), homework assignments designed to gradually heighten sensory/tactile awareness or foreplay as well as improved verbal and nonverbal communication techniques are practiced. When giving homework assignments, it is important for counselors to describe in detail the activity that is required, the rationale for the activity, and then to suggest problem-solving exploration to determine barriers they encounter in carrying out the assignment. For example, a woman with a SCI with little sensation in the genital area, might be counseled with her partner to have him focus more on caressing and/or kissing her neck, ears, breasts, and other areas where she has more sensation.

Using sensate focus, couples are initially given a form that is used to record specific types of sexual activity and whether the activity was pleasant and arousing. Additional exercises include visual exploration in which clients are instructed to spend approximately 30 minutes looking at their bodies with and without clothing, exploring their bodies using tactile exploration exercises, full body caresses to be completed alone or with a partner, and eventually coital activity (Lemon, 1993). Couples are continually encouraged to discuss with each other and the counselor how they feel about their sexuality, to pinpoint areas where sensation might remain, and to explore ways to enhance verbal and nonverbal communication.

The lack of training and reported discomfort of health care and rehabilitation professionals in dealing with SCI and sexuality has made the use of sexually explicit videos another attractive teaching model (Gill, 1988). Gill found that although 79% of rehabilitation professionals reported sexual adjustment was important to clients in rehabilitation, only 9% of the staff indicted feeling comfortable and having the expertise to discuss sexual issues. The use of videos and other sexually explicit materials for follow-up discussions is to communicate information and to develop more accepting attitudes about sexuality-related issues. However, caution must be used with this type of teaching because of the potential for graphic sexual images that may shock, embarrass, disgust, upset, and even block learning (Tepper, 1997). In order to avoid negative repercussions, Tepper has suggested that the videos be shown in a carefully planned sequence with time for discussion that is led by a knowledgeable and skilled facilitator.

Finally, it must be recognized that people with disabilities often internalize prevalent societal stereotypes about the nature of sexuality and disabilities and it may be difficult for them to develop a positive sexual self-concept when surrounded by negative messages about sexuality and attractiveness (Chance, 2002). Counselors must also feel comfortable with their own sexuality and must be willing to explore their attitudes and beliefs about sexuality as they relate to persons with disabilities in order to better understand how they may actually discourage client disclosure involving sexual relationships because of some of their own "hang-ups" about the subject. For example, Parritt and O'Callaghan (2000) found that therapists working with clients with disabilities thought that male partners of women with disabilities were likely to seek sex outside the relationship, they saw clients as being dependent, and they perceived clients' sexuality as "different" from that of able-bodied people. It is these types of stereotypical beliefs and attitudes that often raise doubts among people with disabilities, leaving them to question their sexuality by asking themselves "Am I normal?" and "Will I ever be normal again?" These attitudes can also lead to the exclusion of any type of discussions on sexuality-related issues during the rehabilitation process. Northcott and Chard (2000) found that although 86% of the participants in their study said their disability affected their sexual functioning, only 29% of the participants had received any formal advice or sex education from health professionals such as nurses or a psychologist.

A FRAMEWORK FOR IDENTIFYING AND TREATING SEXUALITY ISSUES IN WOMEN WITH SCI

In assisting rehabilitation counselors in better understanding the dynamics of sexuality and disability, the following five-component framework adapted from Vash (1981) is offered to help delineate specific sexuality concerns of women with SCI. Examples are provided when necessary with counseling suggestions. The five areas described below are sequentially outlined, however, often overlap when social interaction progresses to sexual intimacy on the first date or soon thereafter.

Physical Appearance

Unless first meeting over the Internet (which is gaining wider acceptance), an individual's personal appearance is the first aspect with which he or she is evaluated. Western society places a high value on physical attractiveness (Livneh, 1991; Marini, 1994; Roessler & Bolton, 1978), and women with SCI as well as other persons with disabilities are generally not perceived or portrayed by the public or media in this manner. These first impression interactions are solely based on appearance and often dictate whether a relationship will be established.

Aside from the customary beautification techniques women use to enhance appearance (e.g., hygiene, dress, make-up), women with SCI have additional factors to consider. Since a wheelchair is typically viewed as an accessory or extension of the individual, model and color become important considerations. Today, there are literally hundreds of wheelchair designs and colors to choose from. Women with SCI must consider functional use versus design. In addition, although a number of feminine colors exist today, how these colors coordinate or clash with most clothing colors should be considered. Finally, a number of manual and electric standing wheelchairs allow individuals with spinal cord injury to stand if they choose. Standing not only impacts the quality of social interactions, but also may have a positive psychological affect on one's self-esteem in avoiding instances of being looked down at.

A second consideration of physical appearance pertains to physique. In most instances, the passage of time generally atrophies legs and other paralyzed muscles in persons with SCI. Current technology involving functional electrical stimulation of the legs on stationary bikes has successfully demonstrated how muscle mass may be maintained. Conversely, the sedentary lifestyle makes weight gain more problematic; therefore, women with SCI can be encouraged to exercise whatever remaining muscle groups are left as well as adhere to a balanced diet approved by their physician and/or nutritionist. A number of exercise equipment options are available for persons with SCI including nautilus, hand cycles, and sports wheelchairs. Overall, the central question for counselors and clients in this area is "How can physical appearance be enhanced?"

Personality and Behavioral Traits

This component involves social skills such as being a good listener, appropriate eye contact, and personality traits. Counselors can assess these traits through direct observation or by utilizing psychometric tests measuring personality. For women with SCI and others with similar disabilities, it is important that they do not monopolize the conversation about their disability, how it occurred, or complications extending from it. Sagatun (1985) found, however, that when disabled and nondisabled viewers watched six different videotaped interactions between a person using a wheelchair and a person with no disability, viewers without a disability preferred the interaction where the wheelchair user acknowledged his or her disability after initiating first contact. Viewers with a disability, however, preferred the interaction where the nondisabled individual asked about the disability and initiated first contact. Although persons without disabilities liked the idea of the wheelchair user mentioning the disability to "get it out of the way," viewers with disabilities disliked this approach because they perceived that mentioning their disability did not seem to flow in the general conversation. This suggests there is a happy medium whereby briefly acknowledging one's disability appears advantageous as it serves to place non-disabled persons at ease, but dwelling on the topic can backfire and lead to what Roessler and Bolton (1978) call "prejudice inviting behavior."

Yuker (1988) analyzed the results of 318 interactions from 274 studies on interaction effects and found that attitudes toward persons with disabilities were rated more positively when these individuals were perceived as being competent, possessing good social and communication skills, and were willing to discuss their disability unemotionally. Additional well documented personality traits such as a sense of humor, extraversion, and social poise also correlated highly with positive attitude change (Yuker).

Courtship Factors

What important factors need to be considered when women with SCI begin dating? Having similar interests is a concern for everyone; however, noting probable physical limitations often precludes women with SCI from engaging in certain recreational activities such as tennis, skiing, racquetball, jogging/walking, cycling, hiking, and other similar sports. Nonetheless, women with low-level paraplegia may still be able to participate to some degree in games such as tennis, skiing (with modifications), and racquetball. In addition, assistive technology over the past decade has changed the landscape toward much greater participation possibilities in sports/recreational activities for all persons with a SCI. Today, people with low-level cervical SCI and below, with and without modified equipment, can actively participate in scuba diving, basketball, skiing, ice hockey, weightlifting, hunting, swimming, cycling, fishing, boating, billiards, and other sports.

Aside from the more physically involved leisure activities, women with SCI have a variety of other dating alternatives available to them as well. Counselors should assist women with SCI to develop a list of potential activities that they can pursue with their partner. The less demanding ones may include going to a movie, attending theater productions or concerts, going out to dinner, visiting bookstores and coffee shops, attending social gatherings, playing board or card games, and taking a walk/wheel. These activities may be especially appropriate for women with high level cervical SCI.

Available technology and legislation such as the Americans with Disabilities Act (ADA) allows persons with SCI to ski, skate, bowl, hand cycle (for low-level SCI and below, synonymous with bicycling), fish (likely offshore or on a pontoon boat), stand erect, enter/exit a swimming pool, transfer to/from a car or other vehicle, and play billiards. Titles II and III of the Americans with Disabilities Act have had a significant impact on removing barriers to socialization for persons with disabilities. Any public place, event or activity such as restaurants, theaters, parks, sporting facilities, hotels, transportation, and other publicly used facilities or services must be accessible to persons with disabilities. In short, there should be a number of options to choose from regarding possible dating ideas for women with all levels of SCI. Nevertheless, it is still a good idea to call ahead to verify accessibility since there continue to be certain businesses that have not complied with the ADA (Blackwell, Marini, & Chacon, 2001). In cases where two wheelchair users are dating, additional factors must be considered regarding transportation issues, transferring, seating arrangements in certain instances, and the need for personal assistance.

Finally, due to the recent proliferation of online dating services, chat rooms, and basic internet/e-mail capabilities, women with SCI and other disabilities can become better acquainted with a potential partner and strategically decide at what point and in what way to convey having a disability. Counselors can assist clients in determining possible ways to convey this information. Nevertheless, internet relationships established online initially work to minimize the superficial aspects of physical appearance and allow for greater intellectual intimacy to occur beforehand.

Sexual Encounter

This component of the relationship may arguably be the most difficult to explore for women with SCI. Concerns relating to body image, physical positioning, sexual self-confidence or performance issues, sensation level, myths and misconceptions about sex, bladder and bowel function, and spontaneity should be discussed. Vash (1981) noted how a perceived or actual altered body image (e.g., atrophied legs) may lead the individual with a disability to fear possible rejection once a potential mate sees her unclothed. Societal pressures regarding the perfect body are perhaps nowhere more crucial than during sex (Livneh, 1991; Vash, 1981).

Physical positioning will generally not be problematic for women with low-level SCI (e.g., T4 and below) who will most likely be able to engage in most any position unless experiencing problems with excessive weight, pain, severe muscle spasms or strength limitations (Farrow, 1990). Those with cervical or high-level thoracic SCI, however, may be limited largely to the missionary position unless physically maneuvered by an able-bodied partner or personal attendant. Relatedly, although giving oral sex to an able-bodied partner might be accomplished fairly spontaneously depending on the circumstances, sexual intercourse itself will be less spontaneous in most instances and may negatively affect immediate gratification desires.

As previously noted, intercourse will, in most cases of higher level SCI, be less spontaneous when transfers are involved or if catheterization and/or ostomy devices must be removed (Sipski & Alexander, 1995a; Tepper et al., 2001). Again, some women with SCI may fear ultimate rejection and possibly prolong or put off sexual advances by a partner for this reason. Counselors should discuss the intricacies of such issues and brainstorm ideas with their client in addressing these concerns. In addition, dispelling the myths of Hollywood movie sex (e.g., simultaneous partner orgasm, multiple orgasms) becomes important to minimizing performance anxiety. When both partners are wheelchair users and if one or both partners have a cervical SCI, the need for a personal assistant(s) or a third-party to assist in transferring, undressing, and positioning will be necessary. Unless both partners have previously discussed this alternative and negotiated this desire with a personal assistant, the encounter will be awkward at best.

Intimacy

The longevity of any intimate relationship involves much more than sexual compatibility. Partners must be able to communicate with one another as well as emotionally support each other (Sipski & Alexander, 1997; Vash, 1981). Basic marital tips generally recommended to other couples also apply here. What becomes different when having a long-term relationship with someone with a SCI depends on the severity of the injury and the need for personal assistance to carry out activities of daily living. When a partner becomes a primary caregiver (often due to financial constraints), the couple must be aware of potential caregiver burnout and role conflict between being a partner/lover and being a caregiver (McNeff, 1997). McNeff further noted that couples should establish boundaries as to what kinds of caregiving will be provided by the partner versus what type of assistance might best be provided by a personal attendant (e.g., bowel and bladder care).

Crewe and Krause (1988) found that couples who married after the onset of disability reported greater satisfaction with their sex lives, living arrangements, social lives, and emotional adjustment; whereas those already married when SCI occurred reported greater stress primarily caused by resentment and resignation. Crewe (1993) discussed role reversal in able-disabled partner relationships. For women with SCI, the role of mother, nurturer and homemaker, albeit a gender stereotype, may affect the capacity to fulfill these roles either in part or wholly. Being unable to perform one or more of these gender roles can also diminish a woman's sense of self-worth (Rolland, 1994).

Generally speaking, there may be numerous sexuality-related concerns for persons with SCI and other disabilities. For women with SCI, common concerns will include physical appearance, dating ideas, social interaction skills from a wheelchair, sexual intimacy, and long-term issues such as motherhood, employment, and caregiving. By utilizing the five-component framework, counselors can assess with clients specific issues they are experiencing to assist them in areas such as attracting potential mates, dating, and establishing a long-term relationship.

SUMMARY AND CONCLUSIONS

Despite the fact that most research on sexuality and SCI has been narrow in focus and has traditionally focused on males, developing an understanding of some of the physical and psychosocial factors associated with female sexuality and SCI can have a tremendous impact on their ability to establish and maintain intimate relationships. Dispelling some of the common myths regarding SCI and female sexuality can also have a major impact On how women with SCI perceive themselves in terms of their attractiveness and desirability.

Treatment models that emphasize the importance of providing information to individuals with SCI about their sexuality and facilitating heightened sensory awareness and improved verbal and nonverbal communication among couples have been especially helpful for assisting females in understanding overcoming their sexual reservations. The five-step counseling framework has also been shown to be an effective guide for counselors to use for assessing and treating specific client concerns regarding a woman's ability to attract, date, and develop a meaningful, romantic relationship. However, it should be noted that one of the most important counseling implications in the area of female sexuality and SCI is the counselor's ability to address sexuality-related issues in a manner that conveys to the client a level of comfort conducive to promoting opportunities for discussing a wide range of sexual topics and potential outcomes.

REFERENCES

Barnwell, A. M., & Kavanagh, D. J. (1997). Prediction of psychological adjustment to multiple sclerosis. *Social Science and Medicine, 45,* 411–418.

Basson, R. (1998). Sexual health of women with disabilities. *Canadian Medical Association, 159*(4), 359–362.

Blackwell, T. M., Marini, I., & Chacon, M. (2001). The impact of the Americans with Disabilities Act on independent living. *Rehabilitation Education, 15*(4), 395–408.

Boyle, P. S. (1994). Rehabilitation counselors as providers: The issue of sexuality. *Journal of Applied Rehabilitation Counseling, 25*(1), 6–9.

Burling, K., Tarvydas, V. M., & Maki, D. R. (1994). Human sexuality and disability: A holistic interpretation of rehabilitation counseling. *Journal of Applied Rehabilitation Counseling, 25*(1), 10–16.

Chance, R. S. (2002). To love and be loved: Sexuality and people with physical disabilities. *Journal of Psychology and Theology, 30*(3), 195–208.

Charlifue, S. W., Gerhart, K. A., Menter, R. R., Whiteneck, G. G., & Manley, M. S. (1992). Sexual issues of women with spinal cord injuries. *Paraplegia, 30,* 192–199.

Chenoweth, L. (1993). Invisible acts: Violence against women with disabilities. *Australian Disability Review, 2,* 22–28.

Crewe, N. M. (1993). Spousal relationships and disability. In F. P. Haseltine, S. S. Cole, & D. B. Gray (Eds.), *Reproductive issues for persons with physical disabilities.* Baltimore: Paul H. Brookes.

Crewe, N. M., & Krause, J. S. (1988). Marital relationships and spinal cord injury. *Archives of Physical Medicine and Rehabilitation, 69,* 435–438.

Crewe, N. M., & Krause, J. S. (2002). Spinal cord injuries. In M. G. Brodwin, F. Tellez, & S. K. Brodwin (Eds.), *Medical, Psychosocial, and Vocational Aspects of Disability* (pp. 279–291). Elliott & Fitzpatrick, Inc.: Athens, GA.

Farrow, J. (1990). Sexuality counseling with clients who have spinal cord injuries. *Rehabilitation Counseling Bulletin, 33*(3), 251–260.

Gill, K. M. (1988). Staff needs assessment data. unpublished.

Hughes, R. R., Swedlund, N., Petersen, N., & Nosek, M. A. (2001). Depression and women with spinal cord injury. *Topics in Spinal Cord Injury Rehabilitation, 7*(1), 16–24.

Hwang, K. (1997). Living with a disability: A woman's perspective. In M. L. Sispki & C. J. Alexander (Ed.), *Sexual Function and People with Disability and Chronic Illness: A Health Professionals Guide* (pp. 3–12). Gaithersburg, MD: Aspen.

Lefebvre, K. A. (1997). Performing a sexual evaluation on the person with disability or illness. In M. L. Sipski & C. J. Alexander (Eds.), *Sexual function in people with disability and chronic illness* (pp. 19–45). Aspen Publishers, Inc: Maryland.

Lemon, M. A. (1993). Sexual counseling and spinal cord injury. *Sexuality & Disability, 11*(1), 73–97.

Lipson, J. G., & Rogers, J. G. (2000). Pregnancy, birth, and disability: Women's healthcare experiences. *Health Care for Women International, 21*(1), 1–11.

Livneh, H. (1991). On the origins of negative attitudes toward people with disabilities. In R. P. Marinelli & A. E. Dell Orto (3rd ed.), *The Psychological and Social Impact of Disability* (pp. 181–196). New York: Springer.

Marini, I. (1994). Attitudes toward disability and the psychosocial implications for persons with SCI. *SCI Process* (7)4, 147–152.

McNeff, E. (1997). Issues for the partner of the person with disability. In M. L. Sipski & C. J. Alexander (Eds.), *Sexual function in people with disability and chronic illness* (pp. 19–45). Aspen Publishers, Inc: Maryland.

Medlar, T. (1998). The manual of policies and procedures of the SHIP sexuality education programme. *Sexuality and Disability, 16*(1), 21–42.

Mona, L. R., Krause, J. S., Norris, F. H., Cameron, R. P., Kalichrnan, S. C., & Lesondak, L. M. (2000). Sexual expression following spinal cord injury. *NeuroRehabilitation, 15*, 121–131.

Northcott, R., & Chard, G. (2000). Sexual aspects of rehabilitation: The client's perspective. *British Journal of Occupational Therapy, 63*(9), 2–8.

Nosek, M. A. (2000). Overcoming the odds: The health of women with physical disabilities in the United States. *Archives of Physical Medicine and Rehabilitation, 81*, 135–138.

Nosek, M. A., & Hughes, R. B. (2003). Psychosocial issues of women with physical disabilities: The continuing gender debate. *Rehabilitation Counseling Bulletin, 46*(4), 224–233.

Nosek, M. A., Rintala, D. H., Young, M. E., Howland, C. A., Foley, C. D., & Chanpong, G. (1995). Sexual functioning among women with physical disabilities. *Archives of Physical Medicine and Rehabilitation, 7*(2), 107–115.

Olkin, R. (1999). *What Psychotherapists Should Know About Disability.* New York: Guilford Press.

Parritt, S., & O'Callaghan, J. (2000). Splitting the difference: An exploratory study of therapists' work with sexuality, relationships and disability. *Sexual Relationship Therapy, 15*(2), 151–169.

Roessler, R., & Bolton, B. (1978). *Psychosocial adjustment to disability.* Baltimore: University Park Press.

Rolland, J. (1994). In sickness and in health: The impact of illness on couples' relationships. *Journal of Marital and Family Therapy, 4*(20), 327–347.

Sagatun, I. J. (1985). The effects of acknowledging a disability and initiating contact on interaction between disabled and nondisabled persons. *The Social Science Journal, 22*(4), 33–43.

Sipski, M. L. (1997). Sexuality and spinal cord injury: Where we are and where we are going. *American Rehabilitation, 23*(1), 26–29.

Sipski, M. L., & Alexander, C. J. (1997). Impact of disability or chronic illness on sexual function. In M. L. Sispki & C. J. Alexander (Eds.), *Sexual Function and People with Disability and Chronic Illness: A Health Professionals Guide* (pp. 3–12). Gaithersburg, MD: Aspen.

Sipski, M. L., & Alexander, C. J. (1995a). Spinal cord injury and female sexuality. *Annual Review of Sex Research, 6,* 224–244.

Sipski, M. L., & Alexander C. J. (1995b). Physiology parameters associated with psychogenic sexual arousal in women with complete spinal cord injuries. *Archives of Physical Medicine and Rehabilitation, 76,* 811–818.

Tate, D. G., & Forchheimer, M. (2001). Health-related quality of life and life satisfaction for women with spinal cord injury. *Top Spinal Cord Injury Rehabilitation, 7*(1), 1–15.

Tepper, M. S. (1997). Use of sexually explicit films in the spinal cord injury rehabilitation process. *Sexuality & Disability, 15*(3), 167–181.

Tepper, M. S., Whipple, B., Richards, E., & Komisaruk, B. R. (2001). Women with complete spinal cord injury: A phenomenological study of sexual experiences. *Journal of Sex & Marital Therapy, 27,* 615–623.

Vash, C. L. (1981). *The Psychology of Disability.* New York: Springer.

Walsh, A., & Walsh, P. A. (1989). Love, self-esteem, and multiple sclerosis. *Social Science and Medicine, 29,* 793–798.

Westgren, N., & Levi, R. (1999). Sexuality after injury: Interviews with women after traumatic spinal cord injury. *Sexuality & Disability, 17*(4), 309–319.

Wright, B. A. (1983). *Physical disability: A psychosocial approach.* New York: Harper & Row.

Yuker, H. E. (1988). *Attitudes toward persons with disabilities.* New York: Springer.

CHAPTER TWELVE

Cross-Cultural Counseling Issues of Males Who Sustain a Disability

Irmo Marini

The impact of a sudden traumatic disability to any individual can have profound implications in relation to his/her socialization, employment outlook, and basic independent functioning. Research pertaining to the psychosocial adjustment and reaction of persons who sustain an adventitious disability, such as spinal cord injury, often describe the individual as either going through certain stages of adjustment (Livneh, 1991; Shontz, 1975) or experiencing a continuous adaptation to the altered lifestyle (Kendall & Buys, 1998).

For males from different ethnic and cultural backgrounds, the ramifications of their disability schema, along with cultural beliefs regarding disability can significantly affect how they deal with their situations. Vash (1981) outlined the complexity of factors relating to one's reaction to disability. She identified four broad factors pertaining to the *disability, person, culture, and environment*. Determiners relating to the *disability* include time of onset (acquired vs. congenital), type of onset (accident or self-inflicted), functions impaired, severity, visibility and stability of the disability, as well as the presence of pain. *Person* factors include gender,

From "Cross-cultural counseling issues of males who sustain a disability," by I. Marini, 2001, *Journal of Applied Rehabilitation Counseling, 32,* 36–44. Reprinted with permission of The National Rehabilitation Counseling Association.

activities affected, interests/values/goals affected, remaining coping resources, personality variables, and spiritual beliefs. Factors relating to the *environment* pertain to physical barriers (curb cuts), accessible transportation, availability and cooperation from relevant support agencies. Finally, the factors relating to *culture* include community support, societal attitudes, social-political environment supporting disability issues and family dynamics.

Statistically, persons with disabilities remain the most disenfranchised population in virtually every society, no matter what their ethnicity. Over 1/3 of adults with disabilities in America have an annual income of $15,000 or less (Sue & Sue, 1999). Relatedly, the unemployment rate for persons with disabilities in the United States is estimated to be 66%–70% (Roessler & Rubin, 1998). Minorities with disabilities represent the least educated, most poverty stricken and unemployed populous in most societies. Of the approximate 49 million persons with disabilities in the United States, over five million have no health insurance coverage (Olkin, 1999).

The focus of this chapter is to first provide a brief overview of key cultural differences among European-Americans, Asian-Americans, Latino/Hispanics, African-Americans and Native-Americans. Next, the perceived masculinity of males is explored based on societal/cultural expectations. Third, an exploration of societal views toward disability is discussed, noting cultural variations. Finally, implications for counselors who work with males with adventitious disabling injuries are outlined, focusing on specific counseling recommendations and talking points during sessions.

OVERVIEW OF CULTURAL DIFFERENCES AMONG ETHNIC GROUPS

A summary of fundamental cultural values and beliefs is presented to help distinguish perceptions toward disability in various cultures. Key characteristics of European-American, Latino/Hispanic, Asian-American, African-American and Native American cultures are discussed.

Latino/Hispanic perceptions of males or masculine traits somewhat overlap with those of Western society. In fact, the Latino/Hispanic family is somewhat more patriarchal with the wife deferring to the husband as the head of the household. It is common in first generation Latino/Hispanic families for the father to work while the mother remains home with the children (Locke, 1992; Garzon & Tan, 1992). The concept of "machismo" or male pride is prevalent among Latino/Hispanic males (Gonzalez, 1997 in Sue p. 294). Latino/Hispanic males who sustain a catastrophic disability are generally devastated if their ability to earn is compromised. Many continue to work if possible until they physically can no longer do so. Conversely, some Latino/Hispanic males view disability as a punishment from God, and believe that they must accept their fate in life, thus resigning themselves from participation in rehabilitation or attempts to alter their perceived fate (Rubin, Chung & Huang, 1998). Latino/Hispanic male role conflicts may occur if the male becomes disabled. Specifically, due to the expected role of being perceived as strong, feelings of isolation and depression may occur because many males perceive they cannot share their worries/anxieties with others, for fear of this being viewed as an additional sign of weakness. Role conflict will also likely occur if the male is unable to work and the wife has to become employed (Avila & Avila, 1995).

Asian-Americans, similar to Latino/Hispanics, Native-Americans and African-Americans are family-oriented and view the needs of the family as more important than the needs of the individual (Rubin, Chung & Huang, 1998). In the United States, there are 28 nationalities represented in the Asian-American community, the largest of which include Chinese, Filipinos, Japanese, Koreans, Asian Indians and Vietnamese (U.S. Census Bureau, 1993). Traditional Chinese values embrace harmony with nature and society. This harmony constitutes a balance between the yin and yang; the two opposing forces in nature. Becoming sick or disabled is said to occur due to an imbalance between the yin and yang, often believed to be caused by God as punishment for having sinned (Lassiter, 1995). Family problems such as disability are viewed as having shamed or failed one's family, and all family members must bare the shame (Uba, 1994; Wong & Chan, 1994). Asian families tend to be secretive of family problems and often do not want to divulge the family shame. Asians also place a priority upon achievement; therefore, a disability which impedes one's ability to contribute to the family is again viewed as a devastating failure. Asian males are viewed as the head of the family power hierarchy, and the spouse is expected to take care of him, the children and the household. Asian males are the breadwinners and head of the household in Asian culture, commanding unquestionable loyalty and devotion from family members. This hierarchy follows the five Cardinal Relations rules of Confucianism (Chan, 1992). Overall, the fact that many Asian families believe disability is punishment for having sinned as well as the social stigma of failure, often leads the Asian family to keep the disability secret, and thus not actively seek out counseling (Sue & Sue, 1987). Asian, Latino/Hispanic, Native and African-American family members also generally take care of all the disabled family member's needs, often creating unnecessary dependence and possibly learned helplessness.

Among African-Americans, religion is a highly valued priority. Research has indicated that for many African-Americans, all people are believed to be God's children, including persons with disabilities. Studies indicate that the attitudes among African-Americans toward persons with disabilities tend to be more positive than European-Americans (Pickett, Vraniak, Cook, & Cohler, 1993; Rogers-Dulan & Blacker, 1995). Unlike Latino/Hispanic views, most African-American men agree that a wife should work according to her desires (Smith, 1981). Alston, McCowen, and Turner (1994) note that it is this role flexibility in addition to access to extended family members (e.g., grandparents) in the African-American household that allows for more successful adjustment when a disability occurs. It is not uncommon in African American culture for a family unit to be living with extended family, and, as with other minority groups, family comes first before individual desires.

Native-Americans also have large within group and between group differences. Over 60% of American Indians are of mixed heritage and differ in their level of acculturation (Trimble, Fleming, Beauvais, & Jumper-Thurman, 1996). Many Indians often view themselves as extensions of their tribe, which provides them with a sense of security and belonging. Personal accomplishments are acknowledged and honored if they somehow serve to benefit the whole tribe. For some Native Americans who leave the reservation, a sense of loss of self is experienced due to the detachment or loss of tribal identity (Anderson & Ellis, 1995). Women traditionally have a strong role in the family, and it is common for the extended family to include aunts, uncles, and grandparents who take part in raising the children. Since the extended family assists in child rearing and elders are held in high esteem in the family, Native males do not hold as strong a role as breadwinner or head of the household as do Latino/Hispanic and Asian husbands.

The poverty rate among Native Americans is high, as approximately one in four lives in poverty. High unemployment rates exist on the reservation as well as problems with substance abuse (Swinomish Tribal Mental Health Project, 1991). Various studies on Native American issues indicate that although there are sometimes diverse within-group differences, common issues include a basic mistrust of European-Americans, strong bonds to one's tribe, consideration of family and community needs before one's own, low levels of success with acculturation off the reservation and cultural identity conflicts leading to substance abuse, suicide and low self-esteem (Sue & Sue, 1999). Native Americans do not view disability as a punishment for having sinned, and overall tend to treat their members with a disability as they would anyone else, without judging or stigmatizing a member with a disability. Native males with disabilities on the reserve continue to contribute what they can, and regardless of their contributions, are regarded with dignity and respect (Joe & Miller, 1987).

Finally, for European Americans, autonomy and independence are highly valued as signs of achievement (Fernandez & Marini, 1995). With European-Americans being the majority in North America, the media often mirrors their views/values and beliefs. As such, television commercials and movies portray successful, physically attractive and independent people as top values to aspire toward (Livneh, 1991). Both husbands and wives often work and are approximately equally represented in the labor force (Szymanski, Ryan, Merz, Trevino, & Johnson-Rodriguez, 1996). In striving to be successful and independent, European-Americans often leave home for college or work at an early age, and family cohesiveness is not as prevalent as it is with other minority groups (Sue & Sue, 1999). For a European-American male to become disabled, the results can be devastating. Autonomy and independence become jeopardized, as does one's ability to become employed and perceived as successful. Indeed, as is next further outlined, a male's sense of self often becomes seriously compromised by a sudden catastrophic disability.

SOCIETAL PERCEPTIONS OF MASCULINE TRAITS

The concept of masculinity and masculine traits is well documented in various cultures (Bem, 1974, 1993; Brannon, 1976; Gerschick & Miller, 1995, 1997; Herek, 1986; Sprecher & Sedikider, 1993; Tepper, 1997; Zilbergeld, 1992). Zilbergeld (1992) states that most lessons about male roles have been learned by age seven. He and other researchers have defined masculinity and masculine behavior as reflecting a cluster of male competency traits, including; strength, self-reliance, success, sexual interest and prowess, active, independent, tough, no behaving like a "sissy," aggressive, dominant, stoic, never gives up, self-confident, athletic, assertive and does not express emotions or becomes upset (Bem, 1974; Herek, 1986; Spence, Helmreich, & Stapp, 1974). In the United States, movie actors who traditionally depict the societal expected behavior of the perceived "real man" have included John Wayne, Clint Eastwood, Richard Roundtree, Bruce Lee, Geronimo and Kirk Douglas to name a few.

Gender polarized traits become ingrained in us from various societal influences as projected by our culture, the media, family influences and religion. Little boys are brought up playing with toy soldiers, toy guns and contact sports; whereas, little girls are raised with dolls, toy kitchens and doll houses. Further, North American culture embraces the "body beautiful" concept which focuses on youth, health, physical/personal appearance, athletic prowess and wholeness (Livneh, 1991; Roessler & Rubin, 1982; Wright, 1983; Zilbergeld, 1992).

Several empirical studies support the concept of masculine traits. Sprecher and Sedikider (1993) found that men express less emotion than women in close relationships, attributed to male social role expectations of self-control, toughness and autonomy. Other findings indicate that men have problems asking for support and responding to such questions as "How do you feel?" Relatedly, Belle (1987) found that men tend to provide and receive less social support then women and are also less likely to seek social support to deal with problems. Other researchers have noted that many males do not seek social support because it signifies weakness and dependence, or have found self-disclosure to be inversely related to trait masculinity (Butler, Giordano, & Neren, 1985; Winstead, Derlega, & Wong, 1984). Subsequently, when a male incurs a severe disabling injury, his identity is compromised due to perceived loss of all his masculine traits.

Overall, the masculine traits described here are somewhat similarly shared across the five ethnic groups being discussed. Where subtle ethnic differences exist generally pertain to the European-American traits of independence and assertiveness. In this regard, it has typically been found that being assertive or to question authority for Asians and Latino/Hispanics is generally considered rude and/or disrespectful (Rubin, Chung, & Huang, 1998). Also, although independence and autonomy are highly valued among European-Americans, the other minority groups discussed here place a higher value on the needs of the family before the needs of the individual (Fernandez & Marini, 1995).

SOCIETAL ATTITUDES TOWARD DISABILITY

Having reviewed the masculine traits typically perceived to describe "real" men, we turn now to a brief literature review of societal views toward persons with disabilities. There exists a plethora of empirical and theoretical studies relating to the investigation of attitudes toward persons with disabilities (Anthony, 1972; Belgrave, 1984; Belgrave & Mills, 1981; Comer & Piliavin, 1975; Donaldson, 1980; English, 1971; Evans, 1976; Marini, 1992; Yuker, 1988). A critical review of the literature regarding attitudes and disability by Chubon (1982), however, found about 60% of the over 100 studies reviewed were empirical in nature. The remaining studies were conceptual or anecdotal, having little or no empirical basis.

The most compelling attitudes of able-bodied European-Americans concerning their views of persons with disabilities indicate that persons with disabilities are generally thought of as objects of pity and/or admiration and perceived to be fundamentally different from non-disabled persons (Harris, 1991). Lyons (1991) adds that Western society European-Americans perceive persons with disabilities as helpless, incapable and inferior. Although African and Native Americans may not share these perceptions, Asian and Latino/Hispanic cultures do have similar perceptions and often become overprotective of the disabled member, thus diminishing chances of the member becoming independent (Uba, 1994; Pickett et al., 1993). Aside from overprotection, Asian culture views the disability as a failure (Wong & Chan, 1994). Gething (1991) notes that societal attitudes can impact how people react toward a perceived minority. Subsequently, societal expectations can impact quality of life, job opportunities, and overall socialization as a stigmatized minority. Havranek (1991) states that the attitudes of others are often the most significant barriers that persons with disabilities encounter.

Other research suggests that many persons become anxious or tense over not knowing what to say or how to behave around someone with a disability (Albrecht, Walker, & Levy, 1982; Belgrave & Mills, 1981; Evans, 1976; Marinelli & Kelz, 1973; Yuker, 1988). Albrecht et al. (1982) found 83% of their sample reported that ambiguity or uncertainty regarding not knowing how to behave was the major reason for social avoidance of persons with disabilities. Many in the sample reported feeling anxious over the possibility of saying or doing something that would offend or upset a person 'with a disability. The Harris (1991) poll essentially confirms this sentiment as Americans' report feeling awkward around persons with disabilities. However, the same poll also suggests that previous positive familiarity with a person with a disability enhances more favorable attitudes. These findings suggest it may be difficult for persons with disabilities to attract friends and/or a mate.

Livneh (1991) classified the origins of negative attitudes toward disability into 13 categories. Two of the categories are relevant to this discussion; psychodynamic mechanisms and the spread phenomena.

"Psychodynamic mechanisms" pertaining to societal beliefs suggest that if a person does not feel badly about the disability, he/she must be in denial (Dembo, Leviton and Wright (1975). This expectation of having to mourn the loss poses a problem for males who typically attempt to hide or not show their emotions (Bem, 1993). As Olkin (1999) cities in referring to Wright's concept of requirement of mourning, this reflects society's need for members to follow proper codes of conduct regarding how one ought to act and feel. It follows then that if an individual has a disability and does not feel sad about it, this disrupts the social order of conduct. A related mechanism, the "spread phenomena," refers to society's belief that a disability affecting one aspect of an individual (e.g., paralysis) affects all other aspects such as mental abilities and emotional stability. Thus, someone with paraplegia might also be perceived as being mentally retarded. This also becomes problematic for males who want to return to work and are perceived by employers as incapable, both mentally and physically, of performing the job despite the fact they have a physical disability.

DISABILITY IMPACT ON MASCULINITY

The trauma of a physical disability upon a man's sense of masculinity compromises virtually all of the traits ascribed by most societies for males. Men struggle with two sets of social dynamics. On the one hand, they attempt to live up to the pressures of being masculine (e.g., independent, healthy, autonomous, etc.), while, on the other hand, trying to disprove society's perception of them as passive, dependent, pitiful, sick, and incapable (Gerschick & Miller, 1995, 1997).

From her interviews of men with chronic disabilities, Charmaz (1995) found that males attempt to preserve aspects of their pre-disability self by maintaining qualities or attributes that *previously* defined their self-concept. As they adapt to their disability, males "preserve self" by limiting the impact of the disability in their daily lives and develop strategies to minimize the limiting aspects of their impairment.

Charmaz (1995) also noted that some males attempted to "recapture" all aspects of their past selves by ignoring their limitations. Wright (1983) defines this behavior as "as if" behavior, whereby an individual denies his/her limitations by acting "as if" he/she does not have a disability. When these men realized that it was not possible to ignore their disabilities, they became despondent and depressed. The despondence is described by Wright as having "succumb" to the limitations of the disability rather than more appropriately coping with it.

In other studies, Gerschick and Miller (1995) conducted 10 in-depth interviews with men who sustained either a paraplegia or tetraplegia by using an analytic induction approach. They noted three patterns of coping that interviewees used in dealing with the dominant masculinity standards. The first pattern, "reformulation," characterized males who redefined *idealized* masculine traits to conform to their new abilities. Males who needed a personal attendant to assist in performing activities of daily living (e.g., grooming, dressing) continued to view themselves as independent because they "controlled" the actions of the personal attendant. They also defined the term self-reliant to mean earning capacity and the ability to work and support oneself.

The second pattern of coping, defined as "reliance," characterized those males who relied heavily on the masculine ideals of strength, independence and sexual prowess. These males were troubled by the fact that they could not live up to these ideals. Some attempted to function independently even when they needed assistance. These men refused to ask for help and, instead, struggled to complete the task. Some men played wheelchair sports to remain competitive, while others viewed wheelchair sports as not being the "real" thing and therefore did not participate. Others became involved in risk-taking behavior.

The third pattern of coping described by Gerschick and Miller (1995, 1997) was "rejection" of the masculine ideals. This group of men with disabilities rejected the traditional notion of what made the "real" man. They created an alternate masculine identity by identifying themselves as "persons" and believed that mental ability was superior to physical strength. It appears that males with disabilities either attempted to adjust their perceptions of what it meant to be a man, denied their limitations by acting as if they were able-bodied, reluctantly succumbed to their fate, or redefined themselves as a person with a disability.

Males without disabilities likely share some of these same beliefs and reformulate the definition of masculine. For some, this may mean purchasing masculine oriented material goods such as a speedboat, half-ton truck or masculine clothing. For others, it may include maladaptive means of portraying masculinity such as gang activity, spousal and/or child abuse.

COUNSELING CONSIDERATIONS WHEN WORKING WITH MALES WITH DISABILITIES

The issues men from various cultures face in general after sustaining a debilitating permanent physical disability challenges the very essence of their male identity, often creating an identity crisis. Since role expectations for males restrict or prohibit their expressing emotions, many men maintain an image of toughness, while inwardly struggling with numerous unresolved issues. Such observations are sometimes construed by counselors as client denial of disability. It is not only difficult for a male to disclose his problems for fear of being further perceived as weak, but it is also difficult to get many ethnic groups to agree to go for counseling (Sue & Sue, 1990). Sue and Sue note that approximately 50% of ethnic groups do not return for a second counseling session when the counselor is European American. African and Native Americans tend not to trust European American counselors based, in part, on past transgressions (White, 1984). Many Asians do not even make it to counseling, attempting instead to handle the disability within the family, due in-part to the embarrassment the disability brings to the family (Wong & Chan). Many Latino/Hispanics, like

Asians, also believe that disability is punishment for having sinned and the impairment should be accepted as one's lot in life without seeking correction. Any conscious attempt to improve one's situation may be perceived as going against God's wishes (Smart & Smart, 1991).

It is beyond the scope of this chapter to outline counseling strategies specific to each ethnic group discussed here, however, the reader is referred to Sue and Sue (1999) for more detailed information on the "sensitivity" and awareness of counseling culturally diverse populations. The strategies discussed below relate to overlapping counseling issues of males with disabilities from various cultures.

There are, in essence, two major schools of thought regarding how one adjusts to a traumatic severe disability. These two philosophies are complimentary, yet separate from Vash's (1981) four factors. The first is the stage model of adjustment which has been studied by many researchers and summarized by Livneh (1991). Critical to understanding the stage model of adjustment is an understanding of the fact that adjustment to a traumatic disability is dynamic, not a static process (Kahana, Fairchild, & Kahana, 1982). Further, an individual can regress to an earlier stage, progress through one stage only to revert back again later, or may skip a stage altogether. There is no predisposed time limit to the length of any one stage or stages, nor will all persons go through all stages. Some persons may never reach what might be considered an "end" stage, essentially becoming "stuck" at an earlier phase. Each defined stage carries with it certain behavioral, emotional, and cognitive correlates indicative of that stage, and the experience of various stages is usually temporary and transitional in nature (Livneh, 1991).

Livneh's (1991) five stages include *initial impact*, which generally involves extreme anxiety and shock immediately following the bodily insult. The *defense mobilization* stage involves bargaining with God for recovery and denial of the permanency of the disability. The *initial realization* stage is marked by mourning the loss, possibly leading to depression and internalized anger marked by feelings of self-blame and guilt over what has happened. The individual searches and often finds reasons (no matter how insignificant) why God has justifiably punished him (Hohmann, 1975). Suicidal ideation and verbalizations are also common at this stage. The fourth stage is *retaliation*, where the injured person turns his anger and frustration outward, sometimes lashing out at significant others, perceived incompetent medical personnel and/or God. *Reintegration* is the final stage and is divided into three successive sub-stages, namely, acknowledgement, acceptance, and final adjustment, where the individual redefines who he is as someone with a disability, and becomes accustomed to this new role. The client now acknowledges his limitations, however, focuses on remaining strengths.

The second model is *the re-current adjustment model* of disability. Davis (1987) and others have argued that although stage models of adjustment describe the linear progression of adjusting, they do not account for the ongoing recurrent nature of adjustment over time. This model is based on Beck and Weishaar's (1989) concept of cognitive schema development. Cognitive schemas are our beliefs and assumptions of self, others, and how our environment works.

Following an injury, an individual attempting to continue working from his/her pre-injury schema (Wright, 1983) exhibits "as if" behavior. When these older schema no longer work, the individual may experience anxiety, helplessness/hopelessness and despair. As time goes on, the individual begins to gradually develop new schema to function in the environment with the disability. Modification of new schemas is guided by three themes: (a) the search for meaning in this new life with a disability; (b) the need for mastery and control over the disability, environment and one's future; and (c) the effort to protect and enhance positive aspects of the disability identity. The new schema can be positive ("I can do this") or negative ("I'm a failure"). Individuals often fluctuate in their adjustment, however, over time, most persons have fewer adjustment problems (Kendall & Buys, 1998).

There are typically several areas of worry/concern for males with disabilities. These can include how to financially support one's family; lack of job alternatives; perceived employer discrimination; perceived loss of sexuality and performance ability as well as the ability to attract a mate; and, perceived social status as a poor, unemployed person with a disability. Having been previously strong and independent, many males struggle with child-like feelings of dependency from the need to ask for assistance to complete the simplest of tasks. Such issues contradict the male identity of self-reliance, success and independence as well as the ability to contribute and care for the family. Other issues pertain to loss of control of bodily functions and the fear of becoming a burden to the family with related frustrations of having to re-learn basic human functions we generally acquire by age four. This dependency is often perceived as embarrassing and shameful by many injured males.

It should be noted that although the stage and recurrent models of adjustment to disability are commonly discussed in the literature, there is scant empirical information available which suggests that racial members of underrepresented groups experience either ways of adjusting. Conversely, there is little evidence to suggest that ethnic members adjust to disability any differently than do European Americans. Cultural values and beliefs do, however, provide some insight as to what some of the concerns may be for ethnic males.

ETHNIC GROUP BASIC COUNSELING STRATEGIES

Sue and Sue (1999) recommend a number of basic counseling strategies for working with each ethnic group. For African American male clients, asking if they are uncomfortable working with a counselor from a different ethnic background (if relevant) is recommended. Exploring what their worldviews are and how they view their problem and possible solutions is also advised. It is also important to discuss how the African American male has responded to discrimination, be it due to race or disability. In addition, assessing the relative importance of the family, community and church provide clues as to how involved the family should be. Finally, note that in general, a problem-solving time-limited approach works best for this population.

In counseling Asian American males, basic strategies include using restraint in gathering information due to the norm of keeping family matters private. Assess tangible issues such as financial or assistive device needs, and as with other ethnic groups, use a more direct problem-solving approach, making sure the client generates the solutions, rather than counselor imposed values to solving client problems. Again, being aware of the client's worldviews and focusing on concrete solutions to presenting and/or future problems becomes important (Sue & Sue, 1999).

Basic counseling strategies for work with Native American males include exploring their values. Those on the reservation tend to hold more traditional values than those in the mainstream. Sue and Sue (1999) also recommend that the combination of client-centered and behavioral counseling approaches may work best with Native American clients. Exploring issues of acculturation and potential conflicts for the male client and his family is important as well as determining the strength of the family and extended family unit. Finally, remembering not to confront or stare at Native American clients (considered to be rude) and allowing the client to take his time in finishing his thoughts are key intrapersonal behaviors.

Finally, in counseling Latino/Hispanic males, counselors must be aware of the traditional male role and determine the level of acculturation. Assess whether there is an impact from racism or poverty in relation to the stated presenting problem. Discuss the desire or need for family involvement and what the impact of the client achieving his goals will have on the family. Note that Latino/Hispanic clients are generally respectful of authority, and once a strong rapport is developed, may develop a close personal bond with the counselor (Sue & Sue). With these basic ethnic group counseling strategies in mind, techniques for working with persons with acquired disabilities follow.

COGNITIVE REFRAMING RE: SOCIETAL
VIEWS OF DISABILITY

Recommendations for therapists begin with first having a thorough understanding of culture specific societal views of masculinity and disability. Many clients will harbor unresolved conflicts due to the extreme social role expectation contradictions between masculinity and disability. As noted in the recurrent model of adjustment, many males will initially strive to hold on to their pre-injury schema as if they do not have a disability (Kendall & Buys, 1998; Wright, 1983). As injured individuals continue to realize these old schemas no longer work, they may experience anxiety, depression and helplessness. Counselors should assist clients to reframe old schemas and build new schemas to function in the environment with the disability around the three themes noted earlier (Kendall & Buys, 1998). Counselors should be aware however, that some ethnic clients may not want to strive for independence or mastery of their environment. These values must be explored with minority clients and their families. For injured individuals and families who wish to see the disabled loved one become more independent, focusing on client remaining strengths while offering practical concrete suggestions to make positive changes becomes important (Kendall & Buys, 1998). Concrete strategies may include purchasing adaptive equipment, hiring personal attendants and furthering one's education to enhance employment marketability.

Another aspect to cognitive reframing relates to Albert Ellis' (1973) Rational Emotive Therapy (RET) and challenging client irrational beliefs about the presumed finality of their future. Clients who are not clinically depressed, but rather despondent and feeling hopeless/helpless about their situation could be questioned about what they believe their future holds. Those who feel their life is over should be tactfully challenged about what proof they have regarding their assertion. Counselors should be prepared to offer examples of persons with the same disabilities who have adjusted well.

SELF-INITIATING TALKING POINTS WITH CLIENTS

A second suggestion relates to the strategy that therapists will likely have to self-initiate discussions regarding the issues noted earlier. For the resistant client who continues to assert everything is "fine" and attempts to hide behind the stoic, strong male image, counselors must be able to differentiate denial versus masking what one really feels. Knowing the potential issues males with disabilities may have, counselors may begin to initiate talking points with the client. Counselors can openly address the notion of clients not wanting to burden others' with their problems so as to grant clients permission to talk about their pent-up fears. Counselors should also consider touching upon client issues such as sex, abandonment, health, career, finances, etc., then decide whether to move on or not to other issues, based on client response and nonverbal behavior. By letting clients know the counselor already understands and empathizes with the fear and anxiety clients must be feeling over these issues, clients may begin to open up and discuss their worries as well as perhaps experiencing their first catharsis, which they may have privately concealed/masked for so long.

ADDRESSING INAPPROPRIATE COPING MECHANISM ISSUES

The third issue to discuss pertains to inappropriate vs. appropriate ways of dealing with stress such as alcohol/substance abuse, avoidance and reckless behavior. Statistics regarding persons with physical disabilities indicates that as many as 68% of persons who sustain traumatic injuries have been under the influence of substances. Post-injury in many cases, substance abuse often continues for European Americans, not only because of pre-injury use, but also to mask the pain experienced from the disability (Heinemann, 1993). In extreme cases of addiction, referral to a substance abuse program will be warranted. Ironically, drinking tolerance may be considered as masculine behavior for some males and thus perceived as a way to "hang on" to some of their masculinity.

Avoidance and isolating oneself from others may be another type of inappropriate response observed, particularly for minority clients. Again, cognitions of being embarrassed and perceived as a failure can lead clients into avoiding significant others who can bring meaning back to their life. Client fears in this area should be explored and challenged regarding the differences between a person's physical appearance versus who he/she is as an individual.

A third area to observe/discuss is a client's mental status, especially pertaining to suicidal ideation. Suicide among European American males with spinal cord injury is about twice as high as the general population (Geisler, Jousse, Wynne-Jones, & Breithaupt, 1983). Persons of minority less frequently attempt suicide than European Americans, however, their rates are also higher than average. Death from unintentional injury and suicide are the leading causes of death for persons with spinal injury six months post-injury (Brown, 1998). As such, reckless behavior or suicidal ideation is another area which needs to be explored, especially during acute care rehabilitation.

UNDERSTANDING OF DISABILITY
SPECIFIC PHYSIOLOGY

A fourth suggestion is to become thoroughly familiar with the physiological changes of specific disability populations with which one is working. Aside from reading about the limitations, talk to treating therapists and physicians about an individual's functional limitations. From this, educate clients regarding sexual myths and functioning, health and wellness practices regarding taking care of oneself (e.g., managing stress, nutrition, drug/alcohol use, exercise, etc.), and the use of assistive devices for greater independence.

INTRODUCE CLIENTS TO ROLE MODELS
WITH DISABILITIES

Finally, despite a non-disabled counselor's best efforts, nothing compares to recruiting successfully adjusted persons with the same disability as your clients to interact with, and see first-hand that a quality life can still be pursued and enjoyed. This can be accomplished individually or quite effectively in group counseling. Therapists should be cautious, however, to always first ask clients if they would like to meet and talk to someone who has lived with the disability. Most newly injured persons will have a certain period (usually right after injury), where their denial of the long-term prognosis is so great, they will resent and be unwilling to meet another person with a disability. Therapists should be prepared to broach the topic occasionally until the client is finally ready to meet the individual.

Today, persons with severe physical disabilities are living longer and healthier thanks to advances in medicine, assistive technology, pharmacological developments, and in some countries, empowering legislation. As such, the quality of life for this population continues to improve, with exciting new advances on the way. Physical barriers in the community and with transportation continue to be eliminated, opening the once closed doors of engaging in social activities that give us pleasure. Indeed, it may well be that the major issues facing many males with disabilities in industrialized countries, is not so much a lack of physical access, but rather dealing with the sometime negative attitudes and societal expectations of male roles/expectations.

REFERENCES

Albrecht, G.L., Walker, V.G., & Levy, J.A. (1982). Social distance from the stigmatized. *Social Science Medical, 16,* 1319–1327.

Alston, R., McCowan, C.J., & Turner, W.L. (1994). Family functioning as a correlate of disability, adjustment for African Americans. *Rehabilitation Counseling Bulletin, 37,* 277–289.

Anderson, M.J., & Ellis, R. (1995). On the reservation. In N.A. Vacc, S.B. De-Vaney, & J. Wittmer (Eds.), *Experiencing and counseling multicultural and diverse populations* (3rd ed., pp. 179–198). Bristol, PA: Accelerated Development.

Anthony, W. A. (1972). Societal rehabilitation: Changing society's attitudes toward the physically and mentally disabled. *Rehabilitation Psychology, 19*(3), 93–203.

Avila, D.L., & Avila, A.L. (1995). Mexican Americans. In N.A. Vacc, S.B. De-Vaney, & J. Wittmer (Eds.), *Experiencing and counseling multicultural and diverse populations* (pp. 119–146). Bristol, PA: Accelerated Development.

Beck, A.T., & Weishaar, M. (1989). Cognitive therapy. In A. Freeman, K.M. Simon, L.E. Beutler, & H. Arkowitz (Eds.), *Comprehensive handbook of cognitive therapy* (pp. 21–36).

Belgrave, F. Z. (1984). The effectiveness of strategies for increasing social interaction with a physically disabled person. *Journal of Applied Social Psychology, 14*(2), 147–161.

Belgrave, F. Z., & Mills, J. (1981). Effects upon desire for social interaction with a physically disabled person after mentioning the disability in different contexts. *Journal of Applied Social Psychology, 11,* 44–57.

Belle, D. (1987). Gender differences in the social moderators of stress. In R.C. Barnett, L. Biener, & G.K. Baruch (Eds.), *Gender and stress* (pp. 257–277). New York: Free Press.

Bern, S.L. (1974). The measurement of psychological androgyny. *Journal of Consulting and Clinical Psychology, 42*(2), 155162.

Bem, S.L. (1993). *The lenses of gender: Transforming the debate on sexual inequality.* New Haven, CT: Yale University press.

Brannon, R. (1976). The male sex role: Our culture's blueprint of manhood, and what it's done for us lately. In D. David & R. Brannon (Eds.), *The forty-nine percent majority* (pp. 1–45). Reading, MA: Addison-Wesley.

Brown, W. J. (1998). Current psychopharmacologic issues in the management of major depression and generalized anxiety disorder in chronic spinal cord injury. *SCI: Psychosocial Process, 11*(3), 37–45.

Butler, T., Giordano, S., & Neren, S. (1985). Gender and sex-role attributes as predictors of utilization of natural support systems during personal stress events. *Sex Roles, 13,* 515–524.

Chan, S. (1992). Families with Asian roots. In E.W. Lynch & M.J. Hansen (Eds.), *Developing cross cultural competence: A guide for working with young children and their families* (pp. 181–257). Baltimore: Brookes.

Charmaz, K. (1995). Identity dilemmas of chronically ill men. In D. Sabo & D. Gordon (Eds.), *Men's health and illness: Gender, power and the body* (pp. 266–291). Sage: California.

Chubon, R.A. (1982). An analysis of research dealing with the attitudes of professionals toward disability. *Journal of Rehabilitation, winter,* 25–30.

Corner, R.C., & Piliavin, J.A. (1975). As others see us: Attitudes of physically handicapped and normals toward own and other groups. *Rehabilitation Literature, 36*(7), 206–221.

Davis, B.H. (1987). Disability and grief. *The Journal of Contemporary Social Work, June,* 352–357.

Dembo, T., Leviton, G., & Wright, B. (1975). Adjustment to misfortune: A problem of social psychological rehabilitation. *Rehabilitation Psychology, 22,* 1–10.

Donaldson, J. (1980). Changing attitudes toward handicapped persons: A review and analysis of research. *Exceptional Children, April,* 504–514.

Ellis, A. (1973). *Humanistic Psychotherapy: The Rational-Emotive Approach.* New York: Julian Press.

English, R.W. (1971). Correlates of stigma toward physically disabled persons. In R. P. Marinelli & A. E. Dell Orto (Eds.), *The psychological & social impact of physical disability* (pp. 162–182). New York: Springer.

Evans, J.H. (1976). Changing attitudes toward disabled persons: An experimental study. *Rehabilitation Counseling Bulletin, 19,* 572–579.

Fernandez, M.S., & Marini, I. (1995). Cultural values orientation in counseling persons with spinal cord injury. *SCI Psychology Process, 8*(4), 150–155.

Gallagher, H.G. (1994). *FDR's splendid deception.* Arlington: Vandamere.

Garzon, F., & Tan, S.Y. (1992). Counseling Hispanics: Cross-cultural and Christian perspectives. *Journal of Psychology and Christianity, 11,* 378–390.

Geisler, W.O., Jousse, A.T., Wynne-Jones, M., & Breithaupt, D. (1983). Survival in traumatic spinal cord injury. *Paraplegia, 21*(6), 364–373.

Gerschick, T.J., & Miller, A.S. (1995). Coming to terms: Masculinity and physical disability. In D. Sabo & D. Gordon (Eds.), *Men's health and illness: Gender, power, and the body* (pp. 183–204). Sage: California.

Gerschick, T.J., & Miller, A.S. (1997). Gender identities at the crossroads of masculinity and physical disability. In M. Gergen & S. Davis (Eds.), *Toward a new psychology of gender* (pp. 455–475). New York: Routledge.

Gething, L. (1991). Generality vs. specificity of attitudes towards people with disabilities. *British Journal of Medical Psychology, 64,* 55–64.

Gonzalez, G.M. (1997). The emergence of Chicanos in the twenty-first century: Implications for counseling, research, and policy. *Journal of Multicultural and Development, 25,* 94–106.

Harris, L. (1991). *Public attitudes towards people with disabilities.* New York: Louis Harris and Associates.

Havranek, J. E. (1991). The social and individual costs of negative attitudes toward persons with physical disabilities. *Journal of Applied Rehabilitation Counseling, 22*(1), 15–21.

Heinemann, A.W. (1993). An introduction to substance abuse and physical disability. In A.W. Heinemann (Ed.), *Substance abuse and physical disability* (pp. 3–10). Binghamton: NY: Haworth Press.

Herek, G.M. (1986). On heterosexual masculinity. *American Behavioral Scientist, 29*(5), 563–577.

Hohmann, G.W. (1975). Psychological aspects of treatment and rehabilitation of the spinal cord injured person. *Clinical Orthopedics, 112*, 81–88.

Joe, R.E., & Miller, D. (Eds.) (1987). *American Indian cultural perspectives on disability* (pp. 3–23). Tucson, AZ: University of Arizona, Native American Research and Training Center.

Katz, J. (1988). A theory of qualitative methodology: The social system of analytic fieldwork. In R. Emerson (Ed.), *Contemporary field research: A collection of readings* (pp. 127–148).

Kendall, E., & Buys, N. (1998). An integrated model of psychosocial adjustment following acquired disability. *Journal of Rehabilitation, Summer*, 16–20.

Lassiter, S.M. (1995). *Multicultural clients: A professional handbook for health care providers and social workers.* Westport: Greenwood.

Livneh, H. (1991). On the origins of negative attitudes toward people with disabilities. In R.P. Marinelli & A.E. Dell Orto (3rd ed.), *The psychological and social impact of disability* (pp. 181–196). New York: Springer.

Livneh, H. (1991). A unified approach to existing models of adaptation to disability: A model of adaptation. In R.P. Marinelli & A.E. Dell Orto (3rd ed.), *The psychological and social impact of disability* (pp. 111–138). Springer: New York

Locke, D.C. (1992). *Increasing multicultural understanding: A comprehensive model.* Newbury Park, CA: Sage.

Lyons, M. (1991). Enabling or disabling? Students' attitudes toward persons with disabilities. *The American Journal of Occupational Therapy, 45*(4), 311–316.

Marinelli, R.P., & Kelz, J.W. (1973). Anxiety and attitudes toward visibly disabled persons. *Rehabilitation Counseling Bulletin, 16*(4), 198–205.

Marini, I. (1992). The use of humor in counseling as a social skill for disabled clients. *Journal of Applied Rehabilitation Counseling, 23*(3), 30–36.

Olkin, R. (1999). *What psychotherapists should know about disability.* New York: Guilford Press.

Pickett, S.A., Vraniale, D.A., Cook, J.A., & Cohler, B.J. (1993). Strength in adversity: Blacks bear burden better than Whites. *Professionals Psychology: Research and Practice, 24*, 460–467.

Roessler, R., & Rubin, S.E. (1982). *Case management and rehabilitation counseling.* Austin, TX: PRO-ED.

Roessler, R., & Rubin, S.E. (1998). *Case management and rehabilitation counseling.* Austin, TX: PRO-ED.

Rogers-Dulan, J., & Blacker, J. (1995). African American families, religion, and disability: A conceptual framework. *Mental Retardation, 33*, 226–238.

Rubin, S.E., Chung, W., & Huang, W. (1998). Multicultural considerations in the rehabilitation counseling process. In R.T. Roessler & S. E. Rubin (3rd ed.),

Case Management and Rehabilitation Counseling (pp. 185–230). Austin, DC: PRO-ED.

Shontz, F.C. (1975). *The psychological aspects of physical illness and disability.* New York Macmillan.

Smart, J.F., & Smart, D.W. (1991). Acceptance of disability and the Mexican American culture. *Rehabilitation Counseling Bulletin, 34,* 357–367.

Smith, E. (1981). Cultural and historical perspectives in counseling Blacks. In D. Sue (Ed.), *Counseling the culturally different: Theory and practice* (pp. 141–185). New York: Wiley.

Spence, J.T., Helinreich. R.L., & Stapp, J. (1974). The personal attributes questionnaire: A measure of sex-role stereotypes and masculinity-femininity. *JSAS Catalog of Selected Documents in Psychology, 4,* 127.

Sprecher, S., & Sedikides, C. (1993). Gender differences in perceptions of emotionality: The case of close, heterosexual relationships. *Sex Roles, 28*(9/10), 511–530.

Sue, D., & Sue, S. (1987). Cultural factors in the clinical assessment of Asian Americans. *Journal of Counseling and Clinical Psychology, 55,* 479–487.

Sue, D.W., & Sue, D. (1990). *Counseling the Culturally Different: Theory and Practice.* New York: John Wiley & Sons.

Sue, D.W., & Sue, D. (1999). *Counseling the Culturally Different: Theory and Practice.* New York: John Wiley & Sons.

Swinomish Tribal Mental Health Project (1991). *A gathering of wisdoms.* LaConner, WA: Swinomish Tribal Community.

Szymanski, E.M., Ryan, C., Merz, M.A., Trevino, B., & Johnson-Rodriguez, S. (1996). Psychosocial and economic aspects of work: Implications for people with disability. In E.M. Szymanski & R. M. Parker (Ed.), *Work and disability: Issues and strategies in career development and job placement* (pp. 9–38). Austin, TX: PRO-ED.

Tepper, M. S. (1997). Living with a disability: A man's perspective. In M. Sipski & C. Alexander (Eds.), *Sexual function in people with disability and chronic illness* (pp. 131–146). Aspen: Maryland.

Trimble, J.E., Fleming, C.M., Beauvais, F., & Jumper-Thurman, P. (1996). Essential cultural and social strategies for counseling Native American Indians. In P.B. Pedersen, J.G. Draguns, W.J. Lonner, & J.E. Trimble (Eds.), *Counseling across cultures* (4th ed., pp. 177–209). Thousand Oaks, CA: Sage Publications.

Uba, L. (1994). *Asian Americans.* New York: Guilford.

U.S. Bureau of the Census. (1993). *1990 Census of Population: Asian and Pacific Islanders in the United States.* Washington, DC: U.S. Government Printing Office.

U.S. Bureau of the Census. (1995). *Population profile of the United States.* Washington, DC: U.S. Government Printing Office.

Vash, C.L. (1981). *The psychology of disability.* New York: Springer.

White, J.L. (1994). *The psychology of Blacks: An Afro-American perspective.* Englewood Cliffs, NJ: Prentice-Hall.

Winstead, B.A., Derlega, V.J., & Wong, P.T.P. (1984). Effect of sex-role orientation on behavioral self-disclosure. *Journal of Research in Personality, 18*, 541–553.

Wong, D., & Chan, C. (1994). Advocacy on self-help for patients with chronic illness: The Hong Kong experience. *Prevention in Human Services, 11*(1), 117–139.

Wright, B.A. (1983). *Physical disability: A psychosocial approach* (2nd ed.). New York: Harper & Row.

Yuker, H.E. (1988). *Attitudes toward persons with disabilities*. New York: Springer.

Zilbergeld, B. (1992). *The new male sexuality*. New York: Bantam Books.

CHAPTER THIRTEEN

Psychiatric and Psychological Issues in Survivors of Major Disasters

Carol S. North

DISASTER TYPOLOGY

Three main types of disasters are recognized: (1) *natural disasters,* such as earthquakes, floods, tornadoes, and volcanoes, sometimes referred to as "acts of God"; (2) *technological accidents,* such as airplane crashes, structural collapses, and major explosions, involving human error rather than intent; and (3) *terrorism,* such as the September 11 attacks, generated willfully by humans. It is generally assumed that of all types of disasters, terrorism evokes the most severe mental health effects on its victims because of the heinous, intentional nature of the event.

It may be difficult, if not impossible, to know whether these aspects of terrorism are directly linked to the mental health effects that follow, or whether it is the wide scope and intensity of terrorist attacks, such as the bombing of the Murrah Federal Building in Oklahoma City and the September 11 attacks, that have historically marked such events and

From "Psychiatric and psychosocial issues in survivors of major disasters," by C. North, 2002, *Directions in Rehabilitation Counseling, 3*(9), 105–114. Reprinted with permission by The Hatherleigh Company, Ltd.

driven the mental health effects. The utility of disaster typology in determining mental health effects of catastrophic events is further hampered because most disasters have at least some degree of overlap in typology based on the many elements involved.[1] For example, after the great midwestern floods of 1993, when the Mississippi and Missouri Rivers overflowed their banks, many people blamed the Army Corps of Engineers for allowing water to flood certain areas. After a 1999 commercial airplane crash-landed in a severe storm in Little Rock, AR litigants sued the airline, claiming that the pilot's decision to land the airplane in such adverse weather conditions was an error in judgment.

Victims of disasters are a different population from victims of individual calamities such as motor-vehicle accidents, assaults, and work-related injuries. Research has identified personal risk factors that increase the likelihood of finding oneself in harm's way,[2] defining a population preselected for exposure to trauma based on preexisting characteristics, such as low socioeconomic status, previous psychiatric illness, substance abuse, and novelty-seeking, risk-taking personality traits. *These characteristics are many of the same ones that predict poor outcomes for individuals after traumatic events.* Therefore, it can be difficult to determine the degree to which post-trauma difficulties represent aspects of preexisting characteristics leading to trauma exposure or new behaviors in response the trauma.

Disasters, on the other hand, select random cross-sections of the population on an "equal opportunity" basis (with the major exception of floods, which may select victims of lower socioeconomic status, who have chosen to live on a flood plain where land is less expensive). Research studies of human response to stress resulting from disaster may provide the most representative data on adults coping with extreme stress.

Diagnosing Post-traumatic Stress Disorder and Acute Stress Disorder

Much of what is known about human response to traumatic experiences has emerged from research on combat-veteran populations.[3] The most widely discussed psychiatric disorder that appears after traumatic events is post-traumatic stress disorder (PTSD). This diagnosis first appeared in American Psychiatric Association diagnostic nomenclature in the DSM-III in 1980,[4] largely in response need for a diagnosis to reflect the Vietnam experience, although the syndrome had been described in various forms during previous wars.

The first requirement for diagnosing PTSD is that it must occur in response to personal experience of a traumatic event that represents a threat to life or limb, either through direct personal contact, direct eyewitness

Table 1. PTSD Symptoms

Reexperiencing	Avoidance and Numbing	Hyperarousal
• Intrusive Memories	• Avoids Thoughts/Feelings	• Insomnia
• Nightmares	• Avoids Reminders	• Irritability/Anger
• Flashbacks	• Event Amnesia	• Difficulty
• Upset by Reminders	• Loss of Interest	Concentrating
• Physiologic Reactivity	• Detachment/	• Hypervigilance
to Reminders	Estrangement	• Jumpy/Easily
	• Restricted Range	Startled
	of Affection	• Sense of
		Foreshortened
		Future

of such an event, or vicariously through the sudden and unexpected experience of a loved one in such an event. To diagnose PTSD, one must identify in association with a qualifying event an illness that causes a great deal of distress or significant problems functioning, in conjunction with the presence of three types of symptoms that are new after the event. The symptoms are grouped as: (1) *intrusive recollection,* which involves symptoms such as flashbacks, nightmares of the event, and unwanted, vivid images of the event; (2) *avoidance and numbing* symptoms in individuals who are so overwhelmed by the experience that they avoid anything that would remind them of it. Their emotions may be numbed, and they may be isolated and distant from others; and (3) *hyperarousal symptoms* showing excessive vigilance against another encounter with danger, being keyed up and on edge, (being jumpy and easily startled) and having difficulty sleeping and concentrating. (Table 1 shows the complete symptom list.) Meeting diagnostic criteria requires the presence of *one* new intrusive recollection symptom, *three new* avoidance and numbing symptoms, and *two* new hyperarousal symptoms. In addition, the symptoms must persist for at least 1 month for the diagnosis to be made. *Chronic PTSD* is defined as lasting for more than 3 months, and delayed PTSD starts 6 months or more after the event.

For those who do not qualify for a diagnosis of PTSD but are symptomatic during the passage of the requisite month of symptoms required for making the diagnosis, a new diagnosis of *acute stress disorder* was added to the DSM-IV in 1994,[5] describing a similar condition that can be diagnosed in as early as 2 days. Once 4 weeks have passed, however, the diagnosis passes from acute stress disorder to PTSD in those who are still sufficiently symptomatic. Acute stress disorder also includes many of the same symptoms of all three PTSD symptom groups required for acute stress disorder, plus *dissociative symptoms*. Although the diagnosis of acute stress disorder is so new that little is known about its course or outcome,[6] research indicates that the kinds of symptoms seen in acute stress disorder may predict later development of PTSD and other psychopathology.[7–9]

Risk Factors for PTSD

Research has identified predictors of risk for PTSD. One predictor that we might expect is *severity of the disaster* itself and the *degree of individual exposure to it*. Degree of exposure to the disaster agent has been found to be associated with incidence of PTSD. People who lived closest to Mt. St. Helens volcano at the time of its eruption had higher rates of PTSD than those living farther away.[10,11] After an earthquake, severity of PTSD was found to decrease as the distance from the earthquake's epicenter increased.[12] After the Oklahoma City bombing, the degree of injury predicted development of PTSD.[13] Exposure variables are not as routinely and robustly predictive of PTSD as one might intuitively expect, however.[14] Other aspects of the disaster exposure that may be associated with the mental health consequences may include elements of terror (fear for one's life), horror (contact with the grotesque), and loss of loved ones in the event.

Mental health consequences of disasters vary in different parts of the population affected. The effects of a disaster spread outward like concentric circles; the greatest impact is at the bulls-eye or the epicenter, targeting the victims directly in the path of the disaster agent, some of whom are injured and others who fled for their lives. As the impact of the disaster spreads outward in waves, the ripples affect others with decreasing intensity as they reach the periphery. Others strongly affected are those who lose close family members or friends in the disaster, and eyewitnesses from a distance or late arrivals on the scene. Rescue workers may also be affected by exposure to gruesome aspects of body recovery and handling, danger and injury to themselves, and bereavement of colleagues or direct victims they know. Moving further outward in the concentric circle model, we encounter people affected indirectly through disruption of the usual conduct of their businesses (and business income) due to the disaster, people who lose jobs, large numbers of people whose lives may be disrupted by loss of electricity and other utilities, and people (such as commuters) who are more distant and are delayed by detours and damaged roads. More widespread economic consequences of far-reaching disasters may be followed by significant mental health consequences in the population.[15] At the furthest extreme are those who are so far removed, e.g., people halfway across the country, who only hear about the event indirectly or watch news coverage of it on television. These individuals may feel very upset by the news but are not candidates for PTSD based on just hearing or seeing news about the event. One must be directly present, an eyewitness, or a loved one of a direct victim of a disaster to develop PTSD.

The most robust and reliable predictors of PTSD after disasters have been found to be *female sex*[16−20] and *predisaster psychopathology*.[19,21,22] *It should be no surprise that women have a higher prevalence of PTSD than men after disasters, given that PTSD is classified as an anxiety disorder; in the general population that is not affected by traumatic events, anxiety and depressive disorders are more prevalent among women than men.*[23] It is well established that preexisting psychopathology is a powerful predictor of PTSD after traumatic events.[19,24−28] However, prior psychiatric illness is neither necessary nor sufficient to develop PTSD after such an event. People with no prior psychiatric difficulties regularly develop PTSD after disasters, and many people with previous psychiatric illness do not have a recurrence afterward.[13,25,26] Among people exposed to mild events or with minimal exposure to more severe events, previous psychiatric history is a particularly important predictor of PTSD. With more severe events and greater exposure, psychiatric history is less important as more and more individuals without preexisting mental health difficulties succumb to PTSD.[29]

Personality is an overlooked aspect of predisposing psychopathology. Research has shown that preexisting personality disorders predict postdisaster psychopathology.[30] A caveat is that experience of extreme events may alter people's patterns of interacting with others and the world in a way that may mimic personality disorder in the short term. In making a determination of whether the behaviors represent preexisting personality disorder, the key is to examine lifelong patterns of behavior that began long before the disaster and span the majority of the individual's life.

Other variables such as increased age, lack of education, and lower socioeconomic status have been identified as predictors of PTSD, but observations on these factors have been less uniform.[31] The apparent associations of these variables with psychopathology may lie with their confounding with significantly associated variables. For example, in two studies, lack of education was associated with PTSD only because it was a characteristic of women, who had a significantly higher incidence of PTSD than men.[13,26]

An early indicator of PTSD may be available in the form of avoidance and numbing symptoms, which in two studies have been found to serve as powerful markers of the disorder.[13,32] After the Oklahoma City bombing, 13 fulfilling PTSD's group C avoidance and numbing criteria (i.e., demonstrating three or more symptoms of this category) had 94% specificity and 100% sensitivity for PTSD. In other words, 94% of the people who met group C criteria also had full PTSD. Because the diagnostic criteria for PTSD require fulfillment of group C criteria, 100% of people with PTSD met group C criteria. In addition to predicting PTSD, and the avoidance and numbing symptom group was also associated with preexisting psychopathology, difficulties functioning, treatment-seeking, diagnostic comorbidity, and use of alcohol or drugs to cope with the disaster.

PTSD Incidence and Course

The incidence of PTSD varies considerably after different disasters. Low rates (2%–8%) were identified in studies of a volcano,[32] after torrential rain and mudslides,[34] and after flooding and exposure to dioxin contamination.[35] Rates of more than 50% have been recorded in association with an airplane crash-landing[34] and with a dam break and flood.[37]

After disasters, PTSD begins quickly. After the Oklahoma City bombing, of those who developed PTSD, 76% reported onset of symptoms the day of the bombing, 94% within the first week, and 98% within the first month.[13] Delayed PTSD (beginning more than 6 months after the incident) was not observed after the Oklahoma City bombing[13] or after a mass murder episode in Killeen, Texas.[26] The delayed PTSD that has been described after other kinds of trauma, such as in adult survivors of childhood sexual abuse[38] and combat veterans,[39] is not typical of postdisaster experience.

The course of PTSD tends toward chronicity. In a general population study of PTSD, more than one-half of all cases of PTSD continued unabated for more than 1 year.[40] Predictors of chronicity regardless of treatment, included greater severity of PTSD, psychiatric comorbidity, interpersonal numbing, emotional reactivity, female sex, and family history of antisocial behavior. In the community, the duration of PTSD averages 3 years. One-third of PTSD cases last 10 years or more.[41] Cases in women last on average four times those in men. Few studies have followed the course of PTSD longitudinally after disasters. Approximately one-half of PTSD cases had recovered 1 year after a mass-murder episode, but few predictors of chronicity versus recovery from PTSD could be identified.[26]

Other Psychiatric Disorders

Psychiatric comorbidity is important in the diagnosis and management of post-traumatic psychopathology because of its prevalence and its potential to complicate the course and treatment of PTSD and its association with functional disability.[13] It is all too easy to stop searching for psychopathology once a diagnosis of PTSD is identified, despite experience that after disasters PTSD may occur more frequently accompanied by another diagnosis than solo.[13,25] The most prevalent comorbid disorder is major depression, followed by alcohol use disorder,[13,25,26] although among some populations, such as rescue workers, alcohol use disorder may be more prevalent than major depression or PTSD.[42,43]

After disasters, the alcohol and drug use disorders identified in the affected population represent disorders that are almost always present before the event. Very few cases of alcohol or drug abuse arise anew in the postdisaster setting,[13] although substance abuse is quite prevalent among survivors of community traumas, and substances use is assumed to represent self-medication or efforts to cope with the traumatic event.[44–46] Anecdotal impressions that substance abuse surfaces after disasters may stem from people being flushed out of their private dwellings into public settings, such as on sandbagging brigades, during impending floods and in shelters housing those whose homes were destroyed. If their usual behaviors include heavy drinking in the privacy of their own homes, persistence of these behaviors in public settings during and after the disaster can expose problems not seen before that may be misinterpreted as newly developed.

Resilience

In the rush to identify psychiatric cases needing intervention after disasters, the resilience of the human spirit and the recognition that the majority of people do not become psychiatrically ill after disasters often go underappreciated. In that rush, those who do not meet diagnostic criteria for any psychiatric disorder, but who are clearly distressed by the event, may be overlooked or discounted. Strong feelings and emotional reactions are nearly universal experiences after disasters. After the Oklahoma City bombing, for example, 96% of the survivors, even those without PTSD, reported having one or more PTSD symptoms.[13] Shortly after the September 11 terrorist attacks, a Pew poll of the general public[47] found that 7 out of 10 people acknowledged feeling depressed, nearly 1 in 2 reported trouble concentrating, and 1 in 3 had trouble sleeping. These experiences can hardly be considered pathological, given that they are the norm, reported by the majority after such extreme events. Some describe these responses as "normal responses to abnormal events." These highly prevalent symptoms tend to consist of PTSD group B (intrusive recall) and group D (hyperarousal) items that do not correspond to comorbidity or problems functioning.[13] Studies have shown that with time these symptoms generally diminish on their own as the process of healing proceeds.

Other findings that may also be easily neglected in considering mental health consequences of disasters represent positive outcomes, benefit, or growth after experiencing such a cataclysmic event. Despite the massive harm disasters bring to people and communities, some people do well or find positive elements in the experience that they would never have discovered otherwise.[48,49] A study of three different disaster sites found that 35%–95% of individuals interviewed reported such positive effects,[48] and a study of sexual assault survivors found that 85% identified a positive change in their lives as a result of the incident.[50]

Mental Health Intervention After Disasters

Management of postdisaster mental health problems begins by identifying individuals at highest risk for PTSD and other psychopathology through early screening. Special attention should be paid to individuals with known risk factors: greater exposure to more severe disaster events, women, and individuals with previous psychopathology.[51] Because symptoms start early, efforts to identify potential cases may also start early, even in the first few days when a diagnosis of PTSD cannot yet be made. Although delayed PTSD is generally not seen after disasters, delay in seeking treatment and failure to seek treatment are common.[52] Therefore, along with screening cases, a goal of intervention is outreach to the affected population that typically is reluctant to venture outside its community or to accept help from strangers.[53,54]

The main key to management of mental health effects after disasters is to subdivide the affected population into those who are psychiatrically ill versus those who are not psychiatrically ill but are subdiagnostically distressed. Because these two subpopulations are likely to require different interventions, they need triage for treatment tailored to their situation. Therefore, no one treatment approach is right for everyone. Treatment needs to be individualized.

PHARMACOTHERAPY FOR PTSD

A number of pharmacotherapeutic options are available for treatment of postdisaster psychopathology.[55] Because PTSD can cause considerable functional disability and pharmacotherapy reduces symptoms and improves comfort and functioning, use of medication in the treatment of this disorder is as vital as it is to the treatment of major depression. Antidepressant medications are the mainstay of pharmacotherapy for PTSD.

Although tricyclic antidepressant and monoamine oxidase inhibitor agents have been documented to be efficacious in PTSD, the selectiveserotonin reuptake inhibitors (SSRIs) are more widely used and studied currently, in large part because of their less toxic and more tolerable side-effect profiles. Other agents, such as benzodiazepines, sedative-hypnotics, and mood stabilizers, are not first-line agents of pharmacotherapy for PTSD.[56]

Currently, only one antidepressant agent has been indicated by the Food and Drug Administration for the treatment of PTSD, and only recently. Sertraline (Zoloft) was approved for treatment of PTSD in 1999,[57] but only for women because the supporting studies failed to demonstrate convincing benefit in male populations. Paroxetine subsequently received FDA approval for the treatment of PTSD. Many of the studies assessing these agents have failed to include instruments measuring hyperarousal, making it difficult to determine effectiveness of the medications with this symptom group.[56] Studies have shown that the therapeutic effects of these agents in the treatment of PTSD are independent of antidepressant properties.[58]

The antidepressant agents used to treat PTSD are also effective for the conditions that most often are comorbid with PTSD, and this is an important benefit. Not only do SSRIs benefit PTSD, but they are also mainstays of treatment for major depression, panic disorder, generalized anxiety disorder, and other anxiety disorders. Thus the patient with comorbid PTSD may benefit in multiple ways from the same pharmacologic intervention. It is important to search for other disorders besides PTSD because they tend to be very treatable as well.

Effective pharmacotherapy in the treatment of PTSD is best provided in conjunction with supportive and cognitive psychotherapy.[59] *Clinicians are cautioned that psychotherapies requiring patient confrontation of emotional memories and other material related to experience of the traumatic event may produce negative outcomes at least in some individuals.*[60] The reason for this may lie with the prominent avoidance and numbing profiles that characterize disaster victims with full PTSD. These individuals may be so overwhelmed that they are unable to face memories or reminders of the event, distancing themselves to reduce the emotional impact. Immersing these individuals in memories and confronting them squarely with reminders of the disaster in the therapy setting may retraumatize them and be more than they can cope with.

NONPHARMACOLOGIC INTERVENTIONS FOR PTSD

Different approaches are needed for those who do not fulfill criteria for PTSD after disasters. While it would be a disservice to these individuals to pathologize them by diagnosing them with a psychiatric disorder based on behaviors that are normative in the context of a highly unusual event and fail to meet diagnostic criteria, *their distress should not be discounted,* and some intervention may be appropriate. Distressed individuals not meeting criteria for a psychiatric diagnosis sometimes contact mental health professionals seeking information and reassurance about what their symptoms mean and requesting assistance with short-term symptom management. Psychoeducation approaches help provide the information and reassurance these people seek. These individuals can be reassured that their troublesome symptoms and unpleasant reactions do not necessarily mean that they are becoming psychologically unraveled or mentally ill. They can be told that, for most people, these experiences tend to lose intensity and fade away with the natural process of healing and the passage of time. Most survivors of disasters tend to cope by turning to their trusted loved ones for sharing, support, and starting the process of trying to make meaning of their experience and gain some perspective on it. This "natural talk" may help to reduce discomfort and speed healing, although there is no evidence for its effects on preventing or ameliorating psychiatric illness after disasters.

For those who desire to share and begin to process their experience cognitively with other survivors of the disaster, *group formats* may be helpful. Some of these groups meet fairly spontaneously in loosely structured memorial services and workplace meetings after disasters. A form of talking through an experience is a more organized activity termed *debriefing,* which is widely used in many contexts from spontaneously informing someone about something that happened to a highly formalized and structured psychological debriefing format called *Critical Incident Stress Debriefing,* developed by Jeffrey Mitchell.[61] This debriefing can take on elements of narrative revisitation of an experience, crisis intervention (critical-incident-stress debriefing), education or psychoeducation, prevention, stress management, and psychotherapy.[62] Debriefing has been widely applied far beyond its original intended goals[60] to apply to diverse life experiences, and provide a "magic bullet" of preventive intervention and the keystone of a "new 'trauma' industry" (Raphael and Wilson, p. 2).[62]

Debriefing may not be for everyone. It must also be tailored to an individual's needs and to the setting and the time frame.[62] If debriefing is not suited to the individuals and the setting, prolongation or intensification of distress may occur. The rising popularity of debriefing has elicited messages of caution by professionals[63] against engaging in blanket application of this kind of intervention without a number of preliminary considerations. Despite a number of published articles claiming effectiveness of debriefing, methodological and conceptual difficulties have seriously limited the comparison to the extent that no database systematically evaluates the acute and long-term effectiveness of debriefing in randomized, controlled trials.[63,64] *At present, debriefing procedures have not been shown to prevent or reduce PTSD.*

Bioterrorism

Terrorism involving biological and chemical agents—bioterrorism—occupies a class by itself due to unique elements that are not shared by other disasters. An inherent aspect of bioterrorism that heightens fear and panic is that people cannot appraise their level of exposure because the effects may be delayed and the direct exposure may leave no acutely observable stigmata. The disaster agent in bioterrorism may go undetected for some time after the exposure, with the emotionally traumatic aspect occurring only when it comes to light that the individual may have been exposed. It is difficult for individuals to assess their own risk when they do not even know the status or the extent of their exposure to a hazardous agent. In bioterrorism, inability to appraise one's exposure to the agent leaves estimation of illness or damage to the imagination, easily influenced by the level of panic in the individual potentially exposed. The psychiatric effects of bioterrorism thus become disarticulated from the level of exposure.

Two recognized models of human behavior are pertinent to understanding psychological responses to bioterrorism; both involve a phenomenon previously known as *hysteria* and now termed *somatization*. Both also involve uncertainty about exposure and its potential effects. The first model pertains to acute response to bioterrorism. When people learn that they were possibly exposed to a biohazard, many will panic and turn to the health system for protection, flooding emergency rooms and other portals of care, seeking vaccines, antidotes, and treatments for symptoms they present and for reassurance of their worries about future illness. This is behavior reminiscent of mass panic or mass hysteria epidemics that spread in an infectious diseaselike pattern[65] and disperse upon separation of involved people from one another and from inciting environmental cues.[66]

The second pattern involves responses more distant in time to the exposure. Models involving toxic chemical spills and contamination accidents may be relevant to these kinds of events. Previous studies of chemical spills and attacks have suggested that post-traumatic, anxiety, mood, and somatization symptoms may follow, as well as "cancer phobia" syndromes.[17,67–69]

When managing psychological threats arising from bioterrorism and toxic contamination incidents, it's important to provide practical, accurate, and reassuring information and useful direction to avoid panicking the public.[70,71] Good risk communication and provision of such information may actually reduce the impact of bioterrorism by directing the public away from panic that fuels the problem and moving them toward accurately informed problem solving.[72,73]

REFERENCES

1. World Health Organization. Psychosocial Guidelines for Preparedness and Intervention in Disaster. MNH/PSF/91.3. Geneva: World Health Organization; 1991.
2. Breslau N, Kessler RC, Chilcoat HD, et al. Trauma and post-traumatic stress disorder in the community. *Arch Gen Psychiatry.* 1998;55:626–632.
3. Brewin CR, Andrews B, Valentine JD. Meta-analysis of risk factors for post-traumatic stress disorder in trauma-exposed adults. *J Consult Clin Psychiatry.* 2000;68:748–766.
4. Robins LN, Helzer JE, Croughan J, Williams JBW, Spitzer RL. *NIMH Diagnostic Interview Schedule. Version 3.* Bethesda MD: National Institute of Mental Health; 1981.
5. Robins LN, Cottler L. Bucholz K., Compton W., North CS, Rourke KM. *Diagnostic Interview Schedule for DSM-IV.* St. Louis, MO. Washington University: 1999.
6. Solomon Z, Mikulincer M. Combat stress reactions, post-traumatic stress disorder, and social adjustment: A study of Israeli veterans. *J Nerv Ment Dis.* 1987;175:277–285.
7. Solomon Z, Mikulincer M, Kotler M. A two year follow-up of somatic complaints among Israeli combat stress reaction casualties. *J Psychosomatic Res.* 1987;31:463–469.
8. Carde1:463–469.ncer M, Kotler M. A two year follow-up of somatic complaints among Israeli com*Am J Psychiatry.* 1993;150:474-478.
9. Weisæth L. The stressors and the post-traumatic stress syndrome after an industrial disaster. *Acta Psychiatr Scand.* 1989;80:25–37.
10. Shore JH, Vollmer WM, Tatum EL. Community patterns of posttraumatic stress disorders. *J Nerv Ment Disord.* 1989;177:681–685.
11. Shore JH, Tatum EL, Vollmer WM. Psychiatric reactions to disaster: The Mount St Helens experience. *Am J Psychiatry.* 1986;143:590–595.
12. Abdo T, al-Dorzi H, Itani AR, Jabr F, Zaghloul N. Earthquakes: Health outcomes and implications in Lebanon. *J Med Liban.* 1997;45:197–200.
13. North CS, Nixon SJ, Shariat S, et al. Psychiatric disorders among survivors of the Oklahoma City bombing. *JAMA.* 1999;282:755–762.
14. Sungur M, Kaya B. The onset and longitudinal course of a man-made post-traumatic morbidity: survivors of the Sivas disaster. *Int J Psychiatry Clin Pract.* 2001;5:195–202.
15. Bland RC. Psychiatry and the burden of mental illness. *Can J Psychiatry.* 1998;43:801–810.

16. Moore HE, Friedsam HJ. Reported emotional stress following a disaster. *Social Forces*. 1959;38:135–138.
17. Lopez-Ibor JJ, Jr., Canas SF, Rodriguez-Gamazo M. Psychological aspects of the toxic oil syndrome catastrophe. *Br J Psychiatry*. 1985;147:352–365.
18. Steinglass P, Gerrity E. Natural disasters and posttraumatic stress disorder: Short-term vs. long-term recovery in two disaster-affected communities. *J Appl Soc Psychol*. 1990;20:1746–1765.
19. Weisæth L. Post-traumatic stress disorder after an industrial disaster. In: Pichot P, Berner P, Wolf R, Thau K, eds. *Psychiatry—The State of the Art*. New York, Plenum Press; 1985:299–307.
20. Kasl SV, Chisholm RE, Eskenazi B. The impact of the accident at Three Mile Island on the behavior and well-being of nuclear workers. *Am J Public Health*. 1981;71:472–495.
21. Steinglass P, Weisstub E, De-Nour AK. Perceived personal networks as mediators of stress reactions. *Am J Psychiatry*. 1988;145:1259–1264.
22. Feinstein A, Dolan R. Predictors of post-traumatic stress disorder following physical trauma: An examination of the stressor criterion. *Psychol Med*. 1991;21:85–91.
23. Blazer DG, Hughes D, George LK, Swartz M, Boyer R. Generalized anxiety disorder. In: Robins LN, Regier DA, eds. *Psychiatric Disorders in America: The Epidemiologic Catchment Area Study*. New York: The Free Press; 1991:180–203.
24. Bromet EJ, Parkinson DK, Schulberg HC. Mental health of residents near the Three Mile Island reactor: A comparative study of selected groups. *J Prev Psychiatry*. 1982;1:225–276.
25. Smith EM, North CS, McCool RE, Shea JM. Acute postdisaster psychiatric disorders: Identification of persons at risk. *Am J Psychiatry*. 1990;147:202–206.
26. North CS, Smith EM, Spitznagel EL. Posttraumatic stress disorder in survivors of a mass shooting. *Am J Psychiatry*. 1994;151:82–88.
27. Ramsay R. Post-traumatic stress disorder: A new clinical entity? *J Psychosomatic Res*. 1990;34:355–365.
28. McFarlane AC. The aetiology of post-traumatic morbidity: Predisposing, precipitating and perpetuating factors. *Br J Psychiatry*. 1989;154:221–228.
29. Hocking F. Psychiatric aspects of extreme environmental stress. *Dis Nerv Syst*. 1970;31:542–545.
30. Southwick SM, Yehuda R, Giller EL. Personality disorders in treatment-seeking combat veterans with posttraumatic stress disorder. *Am J Psychiatry*. 1993;150:1020–1023.
31. North CS. Human response to violent trauma. *Baliére's Clinical Psychiatry*. 1995;1:225–245.
32. McMillen JC, North CS, Smith EM. What parts of PTSD are normal: Intrusion, avoidance, or arousal? Data from the Northridge, California earthquake. *J Traum Stress*. 2000;13:57–75.
33. Shore JH, Tatum EL, Vollmer WM. The Mount St. Helens stress response syndrome. In: Shore JH, ed. *Disaster Stress Studies: New Methods and Findings*. Washington, DC: American Psychiatric Press; 1986:77–97.

34. Canino G, Bravo M, Rubio-Stipec M, Woodbury M. The impact of disaster on mental health: Prospective and retrospective analyses. *Int J Ment Health.* 1990;19:51–69.

35. Smith EM, Robins LN, Przybeck TR, Goldring E, Solomon SD. Psychosocial consequences of a disaster. In: Shore JH, ed. *Disaster Stress Studies: New Methods and Findings.* Washington, DC: American Psychiatric Association, 1986:49–76.

36. Sloan P. Posttraumatic stress in survivors of an airplane crash-landing: A clinical and exploratory research intervention. *J Traum Stress.* 1988;1:211–229.

37. Green BL, Lindy JD, Grace MC, et al. Buffalo Creek survivors in the second decade: Stability of stress symptoms. *Am J Orthopsychiat.* 1990;60:43–54.

38. McNally RJ, Clancy SA, Schacter DL, Pitman RK. Cognitive processing of trauma cues in adults reporting repressed, recovered, or continuous memories of childhood sexual abuse. *J Abnorm Psychol.* 2000;109:355–359.

39. Prigerson HG, Maciejewski PK, Rosenheck RA. Combat trauma: Trauma with highest risk of delayed onset and unresolved posttraumatic stress disorder symptoms, unemployment, and abuse among men. *J Nerv Ment Dis.* 2001;189:99–108.

40. Breslau N, Davis GC. Posttraumatic stress disorder in an urban population of young adults: Risk factors for chronicity. *Am J Psychiatry.* 1992;149:671–675.

41. Kessler RC, Sonnega A, Bromet E, Hughes M, Nelson CB. Posttraumatic stress disorder in the National Comorbidity Survey. *Arch Gen Psychiatry.* 1995;52:1048–1060.

42. North CS, Tivis L, McMillen JC, et al. Psychiatric disorders in rescue workers of the Oklahoma City bombing. *Am J Psychiatry. Am J Psychiatry* 2002;159:857–859.

43. Boxer PA, Wild D. Psychological distress and alcohol use among fire fighters. *Scand J Work and Environmen Health.* 1993;19:121–125.

44. Zatzick DF, Roy-Byrne P, Russo JE, et al. Collaborative interventions for physically injured trauma survivors: A pilot randomized effectiveness trial. *Gen Hosp Psychiatry.* 2001;23:114–123.

45. Jacobsen LK, Southwick SM, Kosten TR. Substance use disorders in patients with posttraumatic stress disorder: A review of the literature. *Am J Psychiatry.* 2001;158:1184–190.

46. Saxon AJ, Davis TM, Sloan KL, et al. Trauma, symptoms of posttraumatic stress disorder, and associated problems among incarcerated veterans. *Psychiatric Services.* 2001;52:959–964.

47. Associated Press. Poll: Americans depressed, sleepless. *MSNBC.* 9-19-2001. Washington, DC.

48. McMillen JC, Smith EM, Fisher RH. Perceived benefit and mental health after three types of disaster. *J Consult Clin Psychiatry.* 1997;6:733–739.

49. McMillen JC. Better for it: How people benefit from adversity. *Soc Work.* 1999;44:455–468.

50. Resilience among sexual assault survivors. New York City: Presented at the annual meeting of the American Psychological Association, 1995.

51. Smith EM, North CS, Spitznagel EL. Post-traumatic stress in survivors of three disasters. *J S Behav Pers.* 1993;8:353–368.

52. Weisæth L. Acute posttraumatic stress: Nonacceptance of early intervention. *J Clin Psychiatry.* 2001;62:35–40.

53. North CS, Hong BA. Project C.R.E.S.T.: A new model for mental health intervention after a community disaster. *Am J Public Health.* 2000;90:1–2.

54. Lindy JD, Grace MC, Green BL. Survivors: Outreach to a reluctant population. *Am J Orthopsychiatry.* 1981;51:468–478.

55. Davidson JR. Pharmacotherapy of posttraumatic stress disorder: Treatment options, long-term follow-up, and predictors of outcome. *J Clin Psychiatry.* 2000;61(Suppl):52–59.

56. Cyr M, Farr MK. Treatment for posttraumatic stress disorder. *Ann Pharmacother.* 2000;34:366–376.

57. Schatzberg AF. New indications for antidepressants. *J Clin Psychiatry.* 2000;61(Suppl):9–17.

58. Davidson JRT, Rothbaum BO, van Der Kolk BA, Sikes CR, Farfel GM. Multicenter, double-blind comparison of sertraline and placebo in the treatment of posttraumatic stress disorder. *Arch Gen Psychiatry.* 2001;58:485–492.

59. Southwick SM, Yehuda R. The interaction between pharmacotherapy and psychotherapy in the treatment of posttraumatic stress disorder. *Am J Psychother.* 1993;47:404–410.

60. Pitman RK, Altman B, Greenwald E, et al. Psychiatric complications during flooding therapy for posttraumatic stress disorder. *J Clin Psychiatry.* 1991;52:17–20.

61. Mitchell JT, Everly GS. Critical Incident Stress Debriefing (CISD). Ellicott City, MD: Chevron Publishing, 1995.

62. Raphael B, Wilson JP. Introduction and overview: Key issues in the conceptualization of debriefing. In: Raphael B, Wilson JP, eds. *Psychological Debriefing: Theory, Practice and Evidence.* Cambridge: Cambridge University Press, 2000:1–14.

63. Ursano RJ, Fullerton CS, Vance K, Wang L. Debriefing: Its role in the spectrum of prevention and acute management of psychological trauma. In: Raphael B, Wilson J, eds. *Psychological Debriefing: Theory, Practice and Evidence.* Cambridge: Cambridge University Press, 2000.

64. Raphael B, Meldrum L, McFarlane AC. Does debriefing after psychological trauma work? *BMJ.* 1995;310:1479–1480.

65. Kharabsheh S, Al-Otoum H, Clements J, et al. Mass psychogenic illness following tetanus-diphtheria toxoid vaccination in Jordan. *Bul WHO.* 2001;79:764–770.

66. Jones TF. Mass psychogenic illness: Role of the individual physician. *American Family Physician.* 2000;62:2649–2653, 2655–2656.

67. Bowler RM, Mergler D, Huel G, Cone JE. Psychological, psychosocial, and psychophysiological sequelae in a community affected by a railroad chemical disaster. *J Traum Stress.* 1994;7:601–624.

68. with technological disaster: An application of the conservation of resources model to the Exxon Valdez oil spill. *J Traum Stress.* 2000;13:23–39.

69. Bowler RM, Mergler D, Huel G, Cone JE. Aftermath of a chemical spill: Psychological and physiological sequelae. *Neurotoxicology.* 1994;15:723–729.
70. Moscrop A. Mass hysteria is seen as main threat from bioweapons. *BMJ.* 2001;323:1023.
71. Marks TA. Birth defects, cancer, chemical, and public hysteria. *Regul Toxicol Pharmacol.* 1993;2(Pt 1):44.
72. Covello CT, Peters RG, Wojteki JG, Hyde RC. Risk communication, the West Nile virus, and bioterrorism: Responding to the challenges posed by the intentional or unintentional release of a pathogen in an urban setting. *J Urban Health.* 2001;87:382–391.
73. National Research Council. Chemical and Biological Terrorism: Research and Development to Improve Civilian Medical Response. Washington, DC: National Academy Press; 1999.

CHAPTER FOURTEEN

Quality of Life and Psychosocial Adaptation to Chronic Illness and Acquired Disability

A Conceptual and Theoretical Synthesis

Malachy Bishop

In contrast to persons with congenital disabilities, for whom research suggests that the process of body image and identity development is likely to be similar to that of children without disabilities (Grzesiak & Hicok, 1994; Livneh & Antonak, 1997; Wright, 1983), persons who experience later-onset chronic illness or acquired disability (CIAD) may find their sense of self suddenly and dramatically challenged or altered. These persons may be faced with significant changes in their social and familial relationships and life roles while dealing concurrently with psychological distress, physical pain, prolonged medical treatment, and gradually increasing interference in or restriction of the performance of daily activities (Charmaz, 1983; Livneh & Antonak). Understanding how people navigate this process of adapting to CIAD-related changes, and applying this understanding in the form of effective clinical interventions has been

From "Quality of life and psychosocial adaptation to chronic illness and acquired disability: A Conceptual and theoretical synthesis," by M. Bishop, 2005, *Journal of Rehabilitation*, 71, 5–13. Printed with permission from *Journal of Rehabilitation*.

an important focus of rehabilitation research for several decades (Elliott, 1994; Wright & Kirby, 1999).

Yet despite the decades of research committed to understanding the dynamics of psychosocial adaptation, a review of the rehabilitation literature suggests a surprising lack of conceptual clarity and limited consensus about such fundamental questions as the nature of the process of adaptation and the appropriate conceptualization of outcome (Frank & Elliott, 2000; Livneh, 1988; Livneh & Antonak, 1997; Smart, 2001; Wright & Kirby, 1999). Further, in terms of the ultimate goal of this theoretical development, the translation of theory into practice, there is little evidence that adaptation theory has effectively translated into clinical intervention (Parker, Schaller, & Hansmann, 2003).

It has been suggested, for example, that few rehabilitation counselors either utilize the various existing measures of adjustment or adaptation in the counseling process, or assess the client's adaptation in terms of any extant theory (Bishop, 2001; Kendall & Buys, 1998). Rather, outside of the research context, measures specifically designed to assess adaptation rarely play a significant role in rehabilitation assessment, counseling, or planning. The failure of rehabilitation counselors to evaluate and address psychosocial adaptation in the counseling relationship likely results from a number of factors, including: (a) failure to understand the potential influence of adaptation on rehabilitation outcome; (b) failure to see the clinical utility of extant theories of adaptation in the rehabilitation relationship; and (c) a lack of familiarity with, or confusion over, the many and frequently contradictory theories or models of adaptation found in the rehabilitation counseling literature. The present article presents a model of adaptation to CIAD that may address some of these problems.

In the course of the decades long exploration of the adaptation to disability process theories from fields of study outside of rehabilitation counseling have frequently contributed to both rehabilitation counseling practice and theoretical understanding. Such applications include, for example, that of Lewin's field theory (Lewin, 1951), operant learning principles (Elliott, 1994), and research from the medical sociology literature concerning the implications of chronic illness for the sense of self (Charmaz, 1983). Consistent with this approach, over the last two decades rehabilitation researchers have suggested with increasing frequency that concepts from quality of life (QOL) research may provide an appropriate framework in which to understand the adaptation process (Crewe, 1980; Livneh, 2001; Livneh, 1988; Livneh, Martz, & Wilson, 2001; Viney & Westbrook, 1982; Wright, 1983).

The twofold purpose of this article is (a) to explore this frequently proposed but underdeveloped relationship between adaptation to disability and QOL, and (b) to propose a QOL-based model of adaptation to

CIAD that has significant potential for enhancing both theoretical understanding and clinical application. This article begins with a review of those theoretical approaches to adaptation that have been prevalent in the rehabilitation counseling literature, and the theoretical and clinical limitations associated with them. It is then proposed that a QOL perspective on adaptation may be seen to both encompass the important features of these extant approaches and address many of the limitations. Following this, a specific QOL-based model of adaptation, termed disability centrality, is proposed. This model integrates concepts drawn from the QOL literature with existing models of adaptation from the rehabilitation literature. Because the proposed model relies on specific and contextual definitions of both QOL and adaptation, the definitions that are used in the proposed model are presented. Finally, the clinical implications of the proposed model are discussed.

DEFINING PSYCHOSOCIAL ADAPTATION

Although considerable disagreement exists concerning the specific nature of psychosocial adaptation (Livneh, 2001; Livneh & Antonak, 1997); Wright & Kirby, 1999), at a fundamental level adaptation may be conceived as a process of responding to the functional, psychological, and social changes that occur with the onset and experience of living with a disability, chronic illness, or associated treatments. This process has been characterized in terms of movement toward some variously described outcome. Researchers have conceived both the process and the outcome in a great variety of ways (e.g., DeLoach & Greer, 1982; Kendall & Buys, 1998; Linkowski, 1971; Livneh & Antonak, 1997; Wright, 1983; Wright & Kirby, 1999).

In order to suggest that QOL represents an appropriate framework for defining and understanding the adaptation process, it is first necessary to understand how adaptation has been conceptualized to date. The following discussion reviews the current and historical approaches prominent in the rehabilitation literature, the limitations that have been associated with these approaches, and some points of theoretical consensus.

Current and Historical Approaches and their Limitations

Early approaches to understanding the process of psychosocial adjustment to CID were based on a medical, or psychopathological model, and on the idea that "specific types of disabilities brought about specific types of personality characteristics or psychological problems" (Shontz, 2003), p. 178). It was believed that there existed "a direct relationship between the condition and psychosocial impairment" (Elliott, 1994, p. 231). Such theories failed, however, to reflect either the individuality or the complexity of the process of adaptation. Further, these early models neglected to consider the interaction between the individual and his or her social and physical environment. Over time, as it was increasingly observed that neither diagnosis nor degree of impairment, irrespective other factors, served as important predictors of an individual's overall adaptation (Williamson, Schulz, Bridges, & Behan, 1994) such theories were increasingly recognized as incomplete and lacking empirical support or clinical utility.

Sequential or stage theories, in which adaptation is described in terms of movement through a predictable and terminal series of stages of adjustment, gained increasing acceptance in the 1970's and 1980's. The premise of such theories has been questioned in recent years. For example, the concept of a final stage of adjustment has repeatedly been rejected as unrealistic (Kendall & Buys, 1998; Parker et al., 2003). In addition, Kendall and Buys suggested that counselors working from this perspective may come to expect and identify as normal such reactions as depression and denial, and withhold or delay services until the client exhibits these responses according to the counselor's expectations. Stage theories have also been criticized as lacking both empirical validity (Elliott, 1994; Parker et al.), and sufficient complexity to accurately represent the adaptation process, particularly in terms of progressive conditions (Kendall & Buys; Wortman & Silver, 1989).

More recent conceptualizations represent a more complex and comprehensive approach in which emphasis is placed on the interaction between the individual and the environments in which he or she lives. The conceptual framework of adaptation proposed by Livneh and Antonak (1997) and Livneh (2001) has been described as illustrative of the differences between early and modern approaches (Shontz, 2003). Livneh and Antonak proposed that four groups of variables influence adaptation outcomes, including social-demographic variables, disability-related variables, personality attributes, and physical/social environment. The comprehensive nature of such ecological or interactive models is more congruent with the observation that psychosocial adaptation is a highly complex and individual process. However, as has been suggested about stage or phase models (Kendall & Buys, 1998), ecological models are primarily descriptive rather than predictive. Because they fail to identify the motivating force behind the generally recognized movement toward adaptation (Kendall & Buys; Linkowski, 1971), such models have limited utility in terms of informing counseling intervention.

In terms of psychometric approaches to defining and measuring adaptation outcome, the measures most commonly used in research have been criticized for their unidimensional and atheoretical nature, and their conceptual vagueness (Livneh & Antonak, 1997; Wright & Kirby, 1999). In the most frequently used measures adaptation is operationalized as a unidimensional construct, measured as, for example: (1) pathological dimensions of personality (primarily the presence of depression or anxiety); (2) physical or behavioral complaints; (3) changes in productivity or reduction in performance; or (4) degree of disability acceptance (Livneh & Antonak). These unidimensional approaches to defining adaptation fail to encompass the complex and multidimensional nature of the individual's experience.

Other criticisms of existing theories of adaptation include their relative silence with regard to the individual differences that may be associated with gender and culture. Extant measures of adaptation have also been criticized for having a negatively skewed perspective (Smart, 2001; Wright & Kirby, 1999). That is, although individuals frequently report psychologically positive aspects of living with a disability (e.g., Smart, 2001; Wright, 1983; Wright & Kirby, 1999), unidimensional and deficit-oriented measures of adaptation are unable to register this aspect of experience.

Theoretical Consensus

Despite the ongoing debate about the adaptation process and appropriate conceptualization of outcome, two points of general consensus have consistently emerged across theories. The first is that the process of adaptation to the onset of disability involves a multidimensional response. The second is that this process is highly individual and unique.

Adaptation as a Multidimensional Construct

Because the onset of chronic illness and disability may potentially affect a range of psychological, physical, environmental, and social domains, rehabilitation researchers have consistently suggested that adaptation to chronic illness be measured multidimensionally (e.g., Jacobson et al., 1990; Livneh & Antonak, 1997; Shontz, 1965). For example, Jacobson et al. described adaptation to chronic illness in terms of self-esteem, psychological symptoms, behavioral problems, demonstrated skills in educational and social situations, and attitudes regarding the condition. Livneh and Antonak described adaptation as comprising "(1) active participation in social, vocational, and avocational pursuits; (2) successful negotiation of the physical environment; and (3) awareness of remaining strengths and assets as well as existing functional limitations" (p. 8).

Adaptation as a Subjective Process

Research has also consistently indicated that significant variation exists within and across individuals in the adaptation process (Kendall & Buys, 1998). Inherent in more recent approaches to understanding the adaptation process is the subjective and phenomenological nature of the individual's response. That is, just as the condition itself fails to act as a predictor of adaptation, neither can the individual's response be predicted based on an objected analysis of specific features of either the person or the environment. Rather, the individual's personal and subjective analysis of his or her total situation appears to be the most important factor in guiding his or her response.

Adaptation Defined

Based on these points of current consensus, for the purpose of this article adaptation to CIAD is defined as the individual's personal and highly individual response to disability or illness-related disruptions across a wide range of life domains. These disruptions may be experienced, for example, in interpersonal relationships, in interaction with the physical environment, and as changes in psychological or emotional health and function.

Because adaptation is both multidimensional and subjective, it is suggested that an appropriate measure of adaptation to CIAD is necessarily one that (a) is sufficiently broad to assess change across a range of life domains, and (b) is able to portray the individual's subjective experience of changes within those domains. For the purpose of this article it is suggested that QOL, appropriately defined, represents such a measure.

QUALITY OF LIFE DEFINED

Because QOL has been defined in numerous ways and applied in a variety of contexts, it is incumbent on researchers to identify the specific definition for their purpose. Quality of life has been defined in terms of both subjective and objective indices. Traditionally, researchers have focused on the objected indicators. These include such externally manifested and measurable indices as employment status, income, socioeconomic status, and size of support network (Bishop & Feist-Price, 2001). However, focusing solely on objective indicators has been found to account for only a small amount of the variance in overall QOL ratings (Diener, Suh, Lucas, & Smith, 1999), and there appears to be little correlation between objective indicators and subjective measures of overall well-being, QOL, life satisfaction, or personal happiness (Michalos, 1991; Myers & Diener, 1995).

Such findings have lead to the suggestion that overall QOL is largely regulated by internal mechanisms (Gilman, Easterbrooks, & Frey, 2004) and researchers have increasingly focused on more subjective components of QOL, including for example, self-reported attitudes, perceptions, and aspirations (Gilman et al.). This focus is increasingly prevalent in the rehabilitation counseling literature (Frank-Stromberg, 1988; Noreau & Sheppard, 1995; Rubin, Chan, & Thomas, 2003).

Based on the above noted consensus that adaptation to disability represents a subjective and multidimensional process, for the present purpose QOL is defined in terms of the same characteristics. Specifically, QOL is defined as the subjective and personally derived assessment of overall well-being that results from evaluation of satisfaction across an aggregate of personally or clinically important domains. This specific definition of the broader QOL construct has alternately been referred to as subjective QOL (Frisch, 1999; Michalos, 1991) and subjective well-being (Ormel, Lindenberg, Steverink, & Verbrugge, 1999).

Inherent in this definition is the assumption that overall QOL is associated with satisfaction across a finite number of domains, or areas of life. Research on the QOL construct increasingly supports this assumption (Bowling, 1995; Cummins, 1997; Felce & Perry, 1995; Frisch, 1999). Over the last two decades, researchers in different fields of human study, and using different methodological approaches, have identified a fairly consistent set of core domains as important determinants of QOL Bishop & Allen, 2003). Although the number of domains varies somewhat, those typically identified include (a) psychological well-being (defined in such terms as life satisfaction, and freedom from depression or anxiety); (b) physical well-being; (c) social and interpersonal well-being; (d) financial and material well-being; (e) employment or productivity, and (f) functional ability (Bishop & Allen; Felce & Perry; George & Bearon, 1980; Jalowiec, 1990).

THE DISABILITY CENTRALITY MODEL

It is clear that, while not synonymous, subjective QOL and psychosocial adaptation may be said to share a number of conceptual similarities, including their multidimensional and subjective character. Based on a linking of these similar constructs, and the inclusion of additional concepts drawn from the QOL literature, the disability centrality model for measuring and understanding the impact of CIAD is proposed. The model's underlying conceptual tenets are listed below. This is followed by a brief discussion of the rationale for each tenet. Because the proposed model represents, to a great extent, an integration of existing theories, these underlying theories are described in the course of this discussion.

Conceptual Tenets

1. First it is proposed that an individual's overall QOL represents a summative evaluation of satisfaction or well-being in a number of life domains, and particularly those that are of greater personal importance (or are more highly central) to the individual.
2. Through mechanisms originally identified by Devins (Devins et al., 1983), the onset of CIAD is proposed to result in a change in overall QOL. (Although this effect may typically be experienced as a reduction, this is not universally the case). A reduction in overall QOL occurs to the extent that the disability, illness, or associated treatments act to reduce satisfaction in centrally important domains either by reducing the ability to participate in valued activities, roles, or relationships, or by reducing perceived control over valued outcomes.
3. People seek (and actively work) to achieve and maintain a maximal level of overall QOL, in terms of an internal and personally derived set-point. This is achieved by working to close perceived gaps between the present and the desired level of QOL.
4. As a result of this homeostatic mechanism, when an individual experiences significant negative impact from the onset of a CIAD, three potential responses, or outcomes may result: (a) importance change- People experience a shift in the importance of domains so that previously central, but highly affected domains become less central to overall QOL, and peripheral but less affected domains, in which more satisfaction may be realized, become more central; (b) control change- Through processes that increase perceived control, such as self-management, treatment, or environmental accommodation, the negative impact in important domains is reduced and these domains remain central, or; (c) neither change situation occurs, and the person continues to experience a reduced overall QOL.

Quality of Life and Centrality

To a great extent, the first tenet simply summarizes the above discussion of the definition of QOL as a subjective and multidimensional construct. There is, however, an additional idea that is critical to the proposed model and concerns the concept of importance, or centrality. In the QOL literature this concept has been referred to as domain importance.

Although there is growing consensus that people equate overall QOL with satisfaction within a limited set of life domains, it stands to reason that individuals will differ with regard to which domains are more personally meaningful or important. An individual may report a high overall level of QOL or life satisfaction, despite being dissatisfied with some specific life domains. For this reason many researchers have suggested that a single rating of overall QOL has limited practical and clinical utility (Cummins, 1996). Rather, QOL researchers have suggested that satisfaction in more highly valued areas of life will "have a greater influence on evaluations of overall [QOL] than areas of equal satisfaction but lesser importance" (Frisch, 1999, p. 56). A critical assumption underlying this perspective is that satisfaction in more important domains may mitigate, or compensate for, dissatisfaction in other areas (Campbell, Converse, & Rogers, 1976; Gladis, Gosch, Dishuk, & Crits-Christoph, 1999).

The concept of domain importance provides rationale for the use of the term "centrality" in the proposed model. This term has been used in the social psychology, sociology, and rehabilitation literature to refer to the importance that a person attributes to a role or life domain (Quantanilla, 1991; Rosenberg, 1979; Wheaton, 1990). For example, work centrality has been defined as "the degree of general importance that working has in the life of an individual at any given point in time" (Quantanilla, p. 85). In the proposed model, the term centrality refers to the importance an individual attributes to an area of life that is altered by the onset of CIAD.

The Impact of CIAD on QOL

Among the theories in which the impact of CIAD is described in terms of QOL, Devins' theory of illness intrusiveness is perhaps the best established and the most comprehensively researched in the rehabilitation literature. In essence, Devins has posited that chronic illness acts to disrupt an individual's life, and that this disruption may be interpreted in terms of its impact on well-being, or QOL (Devins et al., 1983). Specifically, chronic illness-induced lifestyle disruptions are proposed to compromise psychosocial well-being by reducing (a) positively reinforcing outcomes of participating in meaningful and valued activities, and (b) feelings of personal control, by limiting the ability to obtain positive outcomes or avoid negative ones (Devins et al., 1983; Devins & Shnek, 2001). Devins has further suggested that this impact can be assessed in terms of QOL domains. To assess this dynamic, Devins developed the Illness Intrusiveness

Ratings Scale (IIRS; Devins, et al., 1983), a self-report instrument that obtains ratings of the degree to which an illness or its treatment interfere with each of 13 life domains that were identified by Flanagan (1978) as being important to QOL. Significant empirical support for this theory has been established by Devins and other researchers over the last two decades (Devins, 1994; Devins et al., 1983; Mullins et al., 2001).

Extension of the Illness Intrusiveness Model

The present model begins with Devins' fundamental assumption that QOL domains represent an appropriate format for assessing the impact of the impact of CIAD. However, based on current research in the QOL literature suggesting the importance of weighting more personally important domains, an extension of Devins' approach is proposed. Specifically, in addition to assessing the impact of CIAD in terms of QOL domains, it is also critical to understand the relative importance of each domain to the individual.

Because individuals differ in the value they place on various areas of their life, simply assessing the extent of CIAD-related disruption across a range of domains fails to take into account the differential importance of domains, and therefore provides an incomplete picture of the individual's experience. Rather, in order to effectively help an individual to adapt to these changes it is critical to understand the extent to which central versus peripheral aspects of one's QOL, and one's identity, are affected (Ryff & Essex, 1992). To a great extent the concept of domain importance, of centrality, explains why two individuals who appear objectively similar may express very different responses to the same condition.

Domain Control

Devins has suggested that the impact of CIAD on QOL occurs through two mechanisms; by reducing satisfaction and by reducing control. Related to this latter mechanism, Devins further suggested that interventions that increase the individual's control over the CIAD or its treatment will act to ameliorate this impact (Devins, 1994; Devins & Shnek, 2001). This second value also has significant implications for clinical intervention.

The onset of CIAD, and its associated treatments, can affect personal control in myriad ways. Treatment schedules, functional limitations, changes in cognitive function and mood, and other CIAD-associated changes can lead to limitations and restrictions that reduce opportunities to engage in valued activities or achieve desired outcomes (Sidell, 1997). Conversely, research among persons with chronic illnesses suggests that interventions that increase perceived control are associated with increased psychological and behavioral well-being (Endler, Kocovski, & Macrodimitris, 2001).

With regard to such interventions, a clinically useful distinction has been suggested between primary and secondary control (Heckhausen & Schulz, 1995). Primary control refers to behaviors or cognitions that are aimed at altering the external environment and efforts to change the environment to meet the changing needs of the individual. Secondary control refers to changes in internal cognitive or psychological processes. These changes act to reduce the impact of uncontrollable and aversive realities through mechanisms such as altering expectations, disengaging from or changing unachievable goals, or reframing a negative experience in a positive way (Misajon, 2002). Rehabilitation counseling interventions aimed at assisting the client to increase control may be directed at both the external environment through, for example, environmental modification and accommodations, and the internal environment, through cognitive counseling techniques that enhance the individual's sense of control. Specific interventions in both areas are further discussed below.

Potential Response to the Impact of CIAD on QOL

Thus far it has been suggested that CIAD-related changes frequently lead to reduced overall QOL by reducing satisfaction and control in personally important domains. The final component of the disability centrality model proposes the mechanisms by which people adapt to this reduction in QOL. Specifically, based on research suggesting that a positive level of QOL is not only normative but adaptive, it is proposed that people respond to this reduction in QOL by making adaptive changes in either domain importance or domain control.

Quality of life research with adults suggests that maintaining a positive level of QOL may be vital to adaptation. For example, Diener and Diener (1995) argued that a positive subjective QOL baseline is necessary from an evolutionary perspective in that it allows for greater opportunities for social and personal advancement, exploratory behavior, and reliable coping resources. The idea that people naturally seek to improve their perceived position with regard to their goals and aspirations is suggested generally in the work of many personality theorists, including, for example, Alfred Adler (in Ansbacher & Ansbacher, 1956). Carl Rogers (1963), and Abraham Maslow (1964), all of whom described people as inherently seeking to overcome perceived personal and situational deficits. Because people seek to maintain a relatively high level of QOL, when CIAD impacts QOL an adaptive response is to be expected. In the present model it is proposed that an individual's response takes the form of one of three processes or, more likely, some combination thereof.

Importance Change

When significant negative change is experienced in centrally important domains the person may engage in or experience an adaptive shift, in which the central domain becomes less valued and previously peripheral, but less affected domains gain more importance, or become more central. This form of value change was originally suggested in the acceptance of loss theory, initially described by Dembo, Leviton, and Wright (1956) and later further explicated by Wright (1960; 1983). This value change "represents an awakening interest in satisfactions that are accessible, and facilitates coming to terms with what has been lost" (Wright, 1983, p. 163).

This phenomenon of an adaptive shift has also received attention in the QOL literature, and has alternately been referred to as "preference drift" (Groot & Van Den Brink, 2000), "domain compensation" (Misajon, 2002), and, most frequently "response shift" (Schwartz & Sprangers, 1999, 2000). Similar to the concept of value change, response shift represents a change in an individual's evaluation of his or her QOL resulting from either (1) a change in the individual's internal standards of measurement, (2) a change in the individual's values (i.e., in the important of domains constituting QOL), or (3) a redefinition of life quality (Schwartz & Sprangers, 1999). There is a growing body of literature and increasing empirical support associated with the response shift concept in the QOL literature (e.g., Andrykowski, Brady, & Hunt, 1993; Bach & Tilton, 1994).

Control Change

The second potential response is referred to as control change. In this case, through various processes that increase personal control, the impact in central domains is reduced and these domains remain important. Whereas the loss of perceived control is associated with decreased QOL, "feelings of vulnerability and helplessness can be offset by generating a sense of personal control over the illness" or disability (Misajon, 2002, p. 48). Both of these potential responses, importance change and control change, have important clinical implications which are further discussed below.

No Change

The third potential outcome is that despite a reduced level of satisfaction, no change occurs in either domain importance or sense of control and the individual continues to experience a reduction in his or her overall QOL. In this situation the individual may become involved in a cycle of increasing loss of control, decreased satisfaction, and decreasing QOL. Because the process of adapting to CIAD, as to other changes, is a continuously evolving and cyclical one (Kendall & Buys, 1998; Livneh, 2001), it is likely that all people experience a phase of inertia for some duration before the types of changes described above occur.

CLINICAL IMPLICATIONS

Abraham Maslow (1966) once quipped that when the only tool one owns is a hammer, every problem begins to resemble a nail. The rehabilitation counselor's perspective on the process of psychosocial adaptation plays a significant role in guiding both service delivery and outcome expectations. The models and theories of adaptation prevalent in the rehabilitation literature (i.e., the counselor's tools) have frequently been criticized for engendering potentially limiting or otherwise problematic counseling approaches. The following discussion describes how, as a means of assisting counselors to understand and explore adaptation with their clients, the QOL perspective in general, and the disability centrality model in particular offers a number of important advantages.

Advantages of a Quality of Life Approach

As opposed to traditional unidimensional measures of adaptation, the multidimensional QOL-framework offers counselors and their clients the opportunity to view the client's life holistically, and understand the impact of CIAD in the context of the complex interactions of personal, social, and environmental domains. This approach also has significant potential for furthering understanding of individual differences in the response to disability. For example, analyzing the impact of CIAD on QOL in terms of the unique values that may emerge from gender differences, cultural background differences, and different disability or illness types may lead to the development of more effective interventions based on these differences.

Finally, assessing adaptation across QOL domains may help counselors distinguish between positive and negative experiences in response to disability, addressing the previously identified limitation of measures that focus on and are capable of assessing only the negative aspects of disability. Thus, it may be seen that as a general framework for assessing and understanding the impact of disability, QOL assessment has the potential to offer a more realistic, comprehensive, and informative approach.

Advantages of the Disability Centrality Approach

In addition to these general advantages, the disability centrality model offers counselors a specific approach for understanding and developing individually-based counseling interventions. Essentially, the disability centrality model suggests that in order to comprehensively assess the impact of and response to disability, it is important to understand not only the level of impact experienced in different areas of life, but the importance placed upon these areas by the individual.

Rehabilitation counselors should explore the client's experience in the domains of mental health, physical health, family relations, social relations, relationships with partner or spouse, economic situation, leisure activity, and the religious or spiritual domain. Although information about the client's experiences in each of these domains is frequently discussed as a party of the intake interview, the present model offers a means of organizing this information in a way that allows for the prioritizing of interventions. For example, if work is discovered to be highly central for a client, and is also highly affected by the disability or illness, counselors may prioritize addressing work-related problems over concerns in less central areas. If, however, family relations are of primary importance, and are currently being significantly impacted, it is important that this area receive counseling attention. Indeed, until these more important issues are addressed it is less likely that vocational planning will be successful.

Counseling Interventions

The proposed model suggests that counselors can assist clients in the adaptation process by (1) helping clients to experience increased control, and (2) by exploring avenues for increasing satisfaction in currently peripheral domains. A number of interventions may be identified to enhance personal control over the illness or disability, the associated treatments, and the impact of the condition in important areas of a person's life. For example, Devins (1994; Devins and Shnek, 2000) and others have suggested the importance of self-management, or actively taking responsibility and informed control over managing one's disability or illness. Corbin and Strauss (1988) suggested that in order to effectively manage a CIAD, one must become knowledgeable about, and a participant in, one's own care. Self-management means that the client is an active and informed participant in the relationship with health care providers, adheres to and understands treatment regimens, and communicates adverse effects and questions. From the counselor's perspective, this involves helping the client (a) to actively monitor and evaluate physical and psychological well-being, and (b) to be knowledgeable about their condition and its treatment.

Counselors may also increase the client's sense of control by helping the client to first clarify and then reach domain-specific goals. For example, if the client reports experiencing little control in the dimension of social relationships, the counselor may employ social skills training to increase the client's confidence and competence in social skills. Simultaneously, the counselor can help the client identify opportunities for social interaction. This process of enhancing the sense of personal control involves promoting success by initially developing measurable and achievable subgoals, and encouraging the client for successful efforts. Finally, identifying functional and environmental accommodations at work or at home also represents a way to help the client experience increased control and mastery.

Counselors can also play a role in assisting clients in the process of adaptation by helping them to reevaluate the range and form of their participation in life domains. That is, by assisting the client to develop new interests, new social outlets, and new ways of engaging life, counselors may enable clients to increase the importance of, or satisfaction within previously peripheral domains.

CONCLUSION

The importance of addressing the individual's adaptation to the onset of chronic illness and disability has consistently been highlighted as an essential component in the rehabilitation process. Dell Orto (1991) underscored the importance of addressing adaptation in the clinical relationship when he suggested that the enormity of chronic illness and disability "is so pervasive, powerful, and all-encompassing that coping with, challenging, and overcoming it cannot be left to chance" (p. 333).

This article provides a practical QOL-based framework for assessing adaptation in the counseling process. This framework also provides rehabilitation counselors specific interventions for enhancing clients' control over the impact of CIAD. Although the model presented in this article is not meant to represent a finished product, this synthesis of constructs is seen as a potentially useful beginning. Research specifically aimed at assessing the validity and utility of the combined model is currently underway and further refinement of these ideas will be an important next step.

REFERENCES

Andrykowski, M.A., Brady, M.J., & Hunt, J.W. (1993). Positive psychosocial adjustment in potential bone marrow transplant recipients: Cancer as a psychosocial adjustment. *Psycho-Oncology, 2,* 261–276.

Ansbacher, H.L., & Ansbacher, R.R. (1956). *The Individual psychology of Alfred Adler.* New York: Basic Books.

Bach, J.R., & Tilton, M.C. (1994). Life satisfaction and well-being measures in ventilator assisted individuals with traumatic tetraplegia. *Archives of Physical Medicine and Rehabilitation, 75*, 626–632.

Bishop, M. (2001). The recovery process and chronic illness and disability: Applications and implications. *Journal of Vocational Rehabilitation, 16*, 47–52.

Bishop, M., & Allen, C.A. (2003). Epilepsy's impact on quality of life: A qualitative analysis. *Epilepsy & Behavior, 4*, 226–233.

Bishop, M., & Feist-Price, S. (2001). Quality of life in rehabilitation counseling: Making the philosophical practical. *Rehabilitation Education, 15*(3), 201–212.

Bowling, A. (1995). What things are important in people's lives? A survey of the public' judgment to inform scales of health related to quality of life. *Social Science and Medicine, 41*, 1447–1462.

Campbell, A., Converse, P.E., & Rogers, W.L. (1976). *The quality of American life: Perceptions, evaluations, and satisfaction.* New York: Russell Sage.

Charmaz, K. (1983). Loss of self: A fundamental form of suffering in the chronically ill. *Sociology of Health and Illness, 5*, 168–195.

Corbin, J., & Strauss, A. (1988). Unending work and care: *Managing chronic illness.* San Francisco: Jossey-Bass.

Crewe, N.M. (1980). Quality of life: The ultimate goal in rehabilitation. *Minnesota Medicine, 63*, 586–589.

Cummins, R. A. (1996). The domains of life satisfaction: An attempt to order chaos. *Social Indicators Research, 38*, 303–328.

Cummins, R.A. (1997). *Comprehensive Quality of Life Scale-Ault (5th ed.-ComQol-A-5).* Melbourne: Deakin University School of Psychology.

DeLoach, C., & Greer, B.G. (1981). *Adjustment to severe physical disability: A metamorphosis.* New York: McGraw-Hill.

Dell Orto, A.E. (1991). Coping with the enormity of illness and disability. In R.P. Marinelli & A.E. Dell Orto (Eds.), *The psychological and social impact of disability* (3rd ed., pp. 333–335). New York: Springer Publishing Co.

Dembo, T., Leviton, G.L., & Wright, B.A. (1956). Adjustment to misfortunte: A problem of social-psychological rehabilitation. *Artificial Limbs, 3*(2), 4–62.

Devins, G.M. (1994). Illness intrusiveness and the psychosocial impact of lifestyle disruptions in chronic life-threatening disease. *Advances in renal replacement therapy, 1*, 125–263.

Devins, G.M., Blinik, Y.M., Hutchinson, T.A., Hollomby, D.J., Barre, P.E., & Guttmann, R.D. (1983). The emotional impact of end-stage renal disease: Importance of patients' perceptions of intrusiveness and control. *International Journal of Psychiatry in Medicine, 13*, 327–343.

Devins, G.M., & Shnek, Z.M. (2001). Multiple Sclerosis. In R.G. Frank & T.R. Elliott (Eds.), *Handbook of Rehabilitation Psychology* (pp. 163–184). Washington, D.C.: American Psychological Association.

Diener, E., & Diener, C. (1995). Most people are happy. *Psychological Science, 7*, 181–185.

Diener, E., Suh. E.M., *Lucas, R.E., & Smith, H.L.* (1999). Subjective well-being: Three decades of progress. *Psychological bulletin, 125*, 276–302.

Elliott, T.R. (1994). A place for theory in the study of psychological adjustment among persons with neuromuscular disorders: A reply to Livneh and Antonak. *Journal of Social Behavior and Personality, 9,* 231–236.

Endler, N.S., Kocovsky, N.L., & Macrodimitris, S.D. (2001). Coping, efficacy, and perceived control in acute versus chronic illness. *Personal and Individual Differences, 30,* 617–625.

Felce, D., & Perry, J. (1996). Exploring current conceptions of quality of life: A model for people with and without disabilities. In R. Renwick, I. Brown, & M. Nagler (Eds.), *Quality of life in health promotion and rehabilitation: Conceptual approaches, issues, and applications* (pp. 52–62). Thousand Oaks, CA: Sage.

Flanagan, J.C. (1978). A research approach to improving our quality of life. *American Psychologist, 33,* 138–147.

Frank, R.G., & Elliott, T.R. (2000). Rehabilitation psychology: Hope for a psychology of chronic conditions. In R.G. Frank & T.R. Elliott (Eds.), *Handbook of Rehabilitation Psychology* (pp. 3–8). Washington D.C.: American Psychological Association.

Frank-Stromberg, M. (1988). *Instruments for clinical nursing research.* Norwalk, CT: Appleton & Lange.

Frisch, M.B. (1999). Quality of life assessment/intervention and the Quality of Life Inventory (QOLI). In M.R. Maruish (Ed.), *The use of psychological testing for treatment planning and outcome assessment* (2nd ed. pp. 1227–1331). Hillsdale, NJ: Lawrence-Erlbaum.

George, L., & Bearon, L. (1980). *Quality of life in older persons.* New York: Human Sciences Press.

Gilmon, R., Easterbrooks, S., & Frey, M. (2004). A preliminary study of multidimensional life satisfaction among deaf/hard of hearing youth across environmental settings. *Social Indicators Research, 66,* 143–166.

Gladis, M.M., Gosch, E.A., Dishuk, N.M., & Crits-Christoph, P. (1999). Quality of life: Expanding the scope of clinical significance. *Journal of Consulting and Clinical Psychology, 67,* 320–331.

Groot, W., & Van Den Brink, H.M. (2000). Life satisfaction and preference drift. *Social Indicators Research, 50,* 315–328.

Grzesiak, R.C., & Hicok, D.A. (1994). A brief history of psychotherapy and disability. *American Journal of Psychotherapy, 48,* 240–250.

Heckhausen, J., & Schulz, R. (1995). A life-span theory of control. *Psychological Science, 102(2),* 284–304.

Jacobson, A.M., Hauser, S.T., Lavori, P., Woldsdorf, J.I., Herskowitz, R.D., Milley, J.E., Bliss, R., Gelfand, E., Wertlieb, D., & Stein, J. (1990). "Adherence among children and adolescents with insulin-dependent diabetes mellitus over a four-year longitudinal follow-up" 1. The influence of patient coping and adjustment. *Journal of Pediatric Psychology, 15,* 511–526.

Jalowiec, A. (1990). Issues in using multiple measures of quality of life. *Seminars in Oncology Nursing, 6,* 271–277.

Keany, K.C., & Glueckauf, R.L. (1999). Disability and value change. In R.P. Marinelli & A.E. Dell Orto (Eds.), *The psychological and social impact of disability* (4th ed.; pp. 139–151). New York: Springer Publishing Co.

Kendall, E., & Buys, N. (1998). An integrated model of psychosocial adjustment following acquired disability. *Journal of Rehabilitation, 64*(3), 16–20.

Lewin, K. (1951). *Field theory in social science: Selected theoretical papers.* New York: Harper & Row.

Linkowski, D.C. (1971). A scale to measure acceptance of disability. *Rehabilitation Counsling Bulletin, 14*, 236–244.

Livneh, H. (1980). The process of adjustment to disability: Feelings, behaviors, and counseling strategies. *Psychosocial Rehabilitation Journal, 4*(2), 26–35.

Livneh, H. (1988). Rehabilitation goals: Their hierarchical and multifaceted nature. *Journal of Applied Rehabilitation Counseling, 19*(3), 12–18.

Livneh, H. (2001). Psychosocial adaptation to chronic illness and disability: A conceptual framework. *Rehabilitation Counseling Bulletin, 44*(3), 151–160.

Livneh, H. & Antonak, R.F. (1997). *Psychosocial adaptation to chronic illness and disability.* Gaithersburg, MD: Aspen.

Livneh, H., Martz, E., & Wilson, L.M. (2001). Denial and perceived visibility as predictors of adaptation to disability among college students. *Journal of Vocational Rehabilitation, 16*, 227–2234.

Maslow, A.H. (1966). *The psychology of science: A reconnaissance.* New York: Harper and Row.

Maslow, A.H. (1964). The superior person. *Transaction, 1*, 17–26.

Michalos, A.C. (1991). *Global report on student well-being: Volume 1, Life satisfaction and happiness.* New York: Springer-Verlag.

Misajon, R.A. (2002). *The homeostatic mechanism: Subjective quality of life and chronic pain.* Unpublished doctoral dissertation, Deakin University, Australia.

Mullins, L.L., Cote, M.P., Fuemmeler, B.F., Jean, V.M., Beatty, W.W., & Paul, R.H. (2001). Illness intrusiveness, uncertainty, and distress in individuals with multiple sclerosis. *Rehabilitation Psychology, 46*, 139–153.

Myers, D.G., & Diener, E. (1995). Who is happy? *Psychological Science, 6*, 10–19.

Nasar, S. (1998). *A beautiful mind: the life of mathematical genius and Nobel Laureate John Nash.* New York: Touchstone.

Noreau, L., & Sheppard, R.J. (1995). Spinal cord injury, exercise and quality of life. *Sports Medicine, 20*, 225, 250.

Ormel, J., Lindenberg, S., Steverink, N., & Verbrugge, L.M. (1999). Subjective well-being and social production functions. *Social Indicators Research, 46*, 61–90.

Parker, R.M., Schaller, J., & Hansmann, S. (2003). Catastrophe, chaos, and complexity models and psychosocial adjustment to disability. *Rehabilitation Counseling Bulletin, 46*, 234–241.

Quintanilla, S.A.R. (1991). Introduction: The meaning of work. *European Work and Organizational Psychologist, 1*, 81–89.

Rogers, C.R. (1963). The concept of the fully functional person. *Psychoterhapy: Theory, Research, and Practice, 1*, 17–26.

Rosenberg, M. (1979). *Conceiving the self.* New York: Basic Books Inc.

Rubin, S.E., Chan, F., & Thomas, D.L. (2003). Assessing changes in life skills and quality of life resulting from rehabilitation services. *Journal of Rehabilitation, 69*(3), 4–9.

Ryff, C.D., & Essex, M.J. (1992). The interpretation of life experiences and well-being: The sample case of relocation. *Psychology and Aging, 7,* 507–517.

Shontz, F.C. (1965). Reaction to crisis. *Volta Review, 67,* 364–370.

Shontz, F.C. (2003). Rehabilitation Psychology, Then and now. *Rehabilitation Counseling Bulletin, 46,* 176–181.

Schwartz, C.E., Sprangers, M.A.G. (1999). The challenge of response shift for quality of life based clinical oncology research. *Annals of Oncology, 10,* 747–749.

Schwartz, C.E., Springers, M.A.G. (2000). *Adaptation to changing health: Response shift in quality of life research.* Washington, DC: American Psychological Association.

Sidell, J. (2001). Adult adjustment to chronic illness: A review of the literature. *Health and Social Work, 22*(1), 5–12.

Smart, J. (2001). *Disability, Society, and the Individual.* Gaithersburg, MD: Aspen.

Viney, L.L., & Westbrook, M.T. (1982). Patients' psychological reactions to chronic illness: Are they associated with rehabilitation? *Journal of Applied Rehabilitation Counseling, 13*(2), 38–44.

Wheaton, B. (1990). Life transitions, role histories, and mental health. *American Sociological Review, 55,* 209–223.

Williamson, G.M., Schulz, R., Bridges, M.W., & Behan, A.M. (1994). Social and psychological factors in adjustment to limb amputation. *Journal of Social Behvaior and Personality, 9,* 249–268.

Wright, B.A. (1960). *Physical disability: A psychological approach.* New York: Harper & Row.

Wright, B.A. (1983). *Physical disability: A psychological approach.* New York: Harper & Row.

Wright, S.J., & Kirby, A. (1999). Deconstructing conceptualizations of "adjustment" to chronic illness: A proposed integrative framework. *Journal of Health Psychology, 4,* 259–272.

CHAPTER FIFTEEN

Six Principles Relating Disability and Psychological Adjustment

Franklin C. Shontz

Recently, I agreed to write a brief article summarizing the principles that describe the psychological aspects of physical disability and handicap. The article is to appear in a forthcoming professionally-oriented encyclopedia, the readership of which will probably consist of physicians and psychologists who know little or nothing about the topic. My problem was to select the most important things that such a group should know. Although that task seemed impossible at first, I ultimately found that the mass of things that should be said were reducible to six general propositions.

The thought then occurred to me that the propositions might be interesting to people who are professionally identified with rehabilitation psychology, either for their own information or for presentation to others. At the very least, a public statement of the propositions should provoke discussion and stimulate their revision and improvement.

The first two propositions are confutative; they assert that some commonly held beliefs are false. These propositions describe stereotyped ideas that are not confirmed by systematically collected data; in fact, careful

From "Six principles relating disability and psychological adjustment," by F. Shontz, 1977, Presidential Address, Division 22, Rehabilitation Psychology, American Psychological Association, Washington, DC, September 1976, *Rehabilitation Psychology*, 24(4), 207–210. Reprinted by permission. Also published in *The Psychological and Social Impact of Illness and Disability*, 3rd Edition. NY: Springer, 1999.

observation provides an ample supply of cases that clearly contradict the stereotypes.

The other four propositions are affirmative. They assert relations that are probably true, according to the best information and most authoritative opinion currently available. To people who are familiar with the field of rehabilitation psychology, the propositions may seem to state the obvious. I hope so, for that will mean we agree on several most important points.

CONFUTATIVE PROPOSITIONS

1. *Psychological reactions to the onset or imposition of physical disability are not uniformly disturbing or distressing and do not necessarily result in maladjustment.*

A corollary to this is that *psychological reactions to the removal of physical disabilities are not uniformly or necessarily pleasant and do not necessarily lead to improved adjustment.* Some consequences of physical illnesses and disabilities on behavior are direct and consistent; for example, completely severing the optic nerves blocks behavioral responses to visual stimuli. Properly speaking, however, direct consequences such as these are *effects* of rather than *reactions* to disabilities, and reactions are the only concern of this proposition. Though many efforts have been made to correlate disability with overall personality maladjustment, no systematic evidence has yet been published to show that reactions involving psychiatric disturbance occur any more frequently within a truly representative sample of people with disabilities than within the general population. In fact, overall personal adjustment improves when disability, or a handicap, solves life problems. The personality resources of an individual may be strengthened, not weakened, when the stresses that disability imposes are successfully managed.

The corollary to the first proposition is supported by reports that removal of physically disabling conditions sometimes increases guilt, anxiety, or maladjustment. Guilt may stem from the belief that one is unworthy, particularly in cases where the beneficiary believes that personal benefit has been gained at the expense of the health or welfare of others. Anxiety arises when a recovered person is forced to face problems that never arose before or that could be successfully avoided during the period of disablement.

2. *Reactions (favorable or unfavorable) to disabilities are not related in a simple way to the physical properties of the disabilities.*

In massed data, studies of persons with physical illnesses suggest that, as a group, such persons show a tendency to experience heightened body anxiety and depression. However, these studies provide no reason to believe that such responses differ from what would occur under equally strong stress of psychological origin. Well-designed research, testing the relationship between degree or type of disability and strengths of personality traits or types of personality organizations, is practically nonexistent. What studies there are have produced no correlations of any appreciable magnitude or dependability. Knowledge of the type or degree of a person's physical disability provides virtually no information about that person's personality.

AFFIRMATIVE PROPOSITIONS

1. *The shorter and less complex the causal linkage between the body structure affected by disability and the behavior in question, the more predictable the latter is from the former.*

When a cause-effect network consists of physiochemical processes alone, the linkage is direct and predictability is high. For example, neurological damage usually has fairly consistent and predictable effects on reflexive responses.

When a cause-effect network concerns instrumental skills, such as dressing and ambulation, that involve learned components, linkage is less direct and predictability diminishes accordingly.

Cause-effect networks that affect emotional states are even less direct than those involving instrumental acts, so predictability is correspondingly lower. At this level, the analysis of the psychological aspects of disability crosses the line from being mainly concerned with the effects of disability to being mainly concerned with the person's reactions or adjustment to disability.

Finally, when the cause-effect network involves such complex matters as the meaning of disability in the total life situation of the person or the place of disability in the self-concept, predictability virtually disappears. At this level of analysis, so many factors other than the body state are operative that correlation between disability is not only minimal but would be truly amazing if it occurred.

2. *The less direct the linkage between the body structure affected by disability and the behavior in question, the more appropriate it is to describe the influence of disability as facilitative, rather than as causal or coercive.*

The term *facilitative* implies that, while a disability may make one particular trait or type of psychological adjustment easier to adopt or more attractive than others, no disability requires any specific type of molar reaction. Suppose, for example, that a person with a spinal cord injury who can no longer engage in conventional sexual activities reacts by becoming bitter or despondent. Reactions like these are made more probable (i.e., facilitated) by the occurrence of spinal cord injury in a person of a certain age and sex who has certain ideas about the importance of sexual identity in the self-concept. But the reactions are not forced upon the person, they do not arise automatically, and they are not a direct product of the spinal cord injury. Teaching persons with spinal cord injuries to find new means to gain sexual satisfaction or intimacy often restores emotional balance, even though it does not remove or alter the physical disability.

> 3. *Environmental factors are at least as important in determining psychological reactions to disabilities as are the internal states of the persons who have the disabilities.*

Obvious illustrations of the meaning of this proposition are to be found everywhere in the adversities that architectural barriers impose upon the mobility and the educational, vocational, and interpersonal adjustment of persons with disabilities. Barriers such as these contribute to the overall message often communicated to persons with disabilities that they are judged as inferior and will be kept that way. Maladjustment surely follows when someone accepts that judgment as accurate and fair. The effects of attitudes of devaluing pity or of stigmatization are more subtle but are equally important. These lead to the portrayal of persons with disabilities in the media either as miserable, suffering, helpless creatures whose greatest need is for charity or as supercourageous beings who deserve medals merely for traveling from one place to another or attending college. Anyone who is constantly exposed to such ideas about himself will find it extremely difficult to accept himself as a competent, worthwhile, normal person.

> 4. *Of all the factors that affect the total life situation of a person with a disability, the disability itself is only one, and often its influence is relatively minor.*

This proposition is stated affirmatively. However, it also confutes the commonly held belief that a physical disability is of necessity the most important thing in a person's life. When a disability interferes with, stops, or actually reverses psychological growth, it is a source of worry and concern.

It may even lead to maladjustment; however, the forms that maladjustment takes among persons with disabilities do not differ from the forms it takes in others. By contrast, when a disability opens up opportunities for learning, challenges the persons to achieve successfully, in short, promotes ego growth, it is a source of growth and ultimate maturity.

This is the most important of the six propositions. It implies that, in the final analysis, the understanding of psychological reactions to physical disability requires the understanding of individual human beings in all their complexity.

PART II

Discussion Questions

1. Is it true that with the onset of a physical disability or chronic illness an individual will emotionally react according to a patterned sequence, implying that there are sequential steps leading to personal adjustment?
2. Do different events, such as accidents or natural disasters, precipitate different emotional reactions in the affected individual? Why?
3. Is it possible that the quality of life for someone with a severe disability could improve, more so than the quality of life before disability onset? How?
4. Although the article on female sexuality and spinal cord injury discusses the psychosocial effects for a woman with SCI, are these effects the same for a woman with multiple sclerosis, or muscular dystrophy?
5. What do you believe is a specific aspect of one's culture that can be a strong influence on a person's emotional reaction to a physical disability?
6. How does gender make a difference in one's psychosocial adaptation to a disability?
7. Are the six principles identified by Shontz as relevant to the world of disability in 2007 as they were in 1977?
8. Discuss how a person's role and identity can affect their disability experience.
9. How can a disability impact and alter coping mechanisms?
10. Discuss how the disability experience can challenge a person's assumptions about life and living.

PART II

Personal Perspective

Albert Ellis

One of the most well-known counseling therapists in the world speaks of his own life living with and in spite of illness and disabilities and how he coped with the physical and mental implications of his experiences. His process of adaptation is a fascinating journey. Of interest, Dr. Ellis's own physical disabilities add to his effectiveness as a therapist. He explains those behavioral strategies that emerge from his disability, such as self-disclosure and combating irrational thoughts, and how they can be included in intervention strategies. Dr. Ellis provides another thought-provoking perspective on the realities of psychosocial adaptation. This was reprinted from the fourth edition.

USING RATIONAL EMOTIVE BEHAVIOR THERAPY TECHNIQUES TO COPE WITH DISABILITY[1]

Albert Ellis

I have had multiple disabilities for a long number of years and have always used Rational Emotive Behavior Therapy (REBT) to help me cope with these disabilities. That is one of the saving graces of having a serious disability—if you really accept it, and Stop whining about having it, you can turn some of its lemons into quite tasty lemonade.

I started doing this with my first major disability soon after I became a practicing psychologist in 1943, at the age of 30. At age 19 I began to have trouble reading and was fitted for glasses, which worked well enough for sight purposes but left me with easily tired eyes. After I read or even looked steadily at people for no more than 20 minutes, my eyes began to feel quite fatigued, and often as if they had sand in them. Why? Probably because of my prediabetic condition of renal glycosuria.

Anyway, from 19 years onward I was clearly handicapped by my chronically tired eyes and could find no steady release from it. Today, over a half-century later, it is still with me, sometimes a little better, sometimes a little worse, but generally unrelieved. So I stoically accepted my tired eyes and still live with them. And what an annoyance it is! I rarely read, especially scientific material, for more than 20 minutes at a time—and I almost always keep my eyes closed when I am not reading, working, or otherwise so active that it would be unwise for me to shut them.

My main sight limitation is during my work as a therapist in the world. For at our clinic at the Institute for Rational Emotive Behavior Therapy in New York, I usually see individual and group clients from 9:30 am to 11:00 pm—with a couple of half hour breaks for meals, and mostly for half hour sessions with my individual clients. So during each week I may easily see over 80 individual and 40 more group clients.

Do I get tired during these long days of working? Strangely enough, I rarely do. I was fortunate enough to pick high-energy parents and other ancestors. My mother and father were both exceptionally active, on-the-go people until a short time before she died of a stroke at the age of 93 and he died, also of a stroke, at the age of 80.

Anyway, for more than a half-century I have conducted many more sessions with my eyes almost completely shut than I have with them open. This includes thousands of sessions I have done on the phone without ever

[1] From *Professional Psychology: Research and Practice,*1997, 28(1), pp. 17–22. Reprinted with permission. Included in 4th Edition of *The Psychological & Social Impact of Disability*, Springer, 1999.

seeing my clients. In doing so, I have experienced some real limitations but also several useful advantages. Advantages? Yes, such as these:

1. With my eyes shut, I can focus unusually well on what my clients are telling me and can listen nicely to their tones of voice, speech hesitations and speed-ups, and other aspects of their verbal communications.
2. With my eyes closed, I can focus better, I think, on what my clients are telling themselves to make themselves disturbed: on their basic irrational meanings and philosophies that are crucial to most of their symptoms.
3. When I am not looking at my clients I am quite relaxed and can easily avoid bothering myself about how well I am doing. I avoid rating myself and producing ego problems about what a great therapist and noble person I am—or am not!
4. My closed eyes and relaxed attitude seem to help a number of my clients relax during the session themselves, to open up to concentrating on and revealing their worst problems.
5. Some of my clients recognize my personal disabilities: They see that I refuse to whine about my adversities, work my ass off in spite of them, and have the courage to accept what I cannot change. They therefore often use me as a healthy model and see that they, too, can happily work and live in spite of their misfortunes.

Do not think, now, that I am recommending that all therapists, including those who have no ocular problems, should often shut their eyes during their individual therapy sessions. No. But some might experiment in this respect to see what advantages closing their eyes may have, especially at certain times.

Despite the fact that I could only read for about 20 minutes at a time, I started graduate school in clinical psychology in 1942, when I was 28, finished with honors, and have now been at the same delightful stand for well over a half-century—still with my eyes often shut and my ears widely open. I am handicapped and partially disabled, yes—but never whining and screaming about my disabilities, and always forging on in spite of them.

In my late 60s my hearing began to deteriorate; and in my mid-70s I got two hearing aids. Even when working in good order, they have their distinct limitations and have to be adjusted for various conditions, and even for the voice loudness and quality of the voices of the people I am listening to. So I use them regularly, especially with my clients, but I am still forced to ask people to repeat themselves or to make themselves clearer.

So I put up with all these limitations and use rational emotive behavior therapy to convince myself that they are not awful, horrible, and terrible but only a pain in the ass. Once in awhile I get overly irritated about my hearing problem—which my audiologist, incidentally, tells me will definitely get a little worse as each year goes by. But usually I live very well with my poor auditory reception and even manage to do my usual large number of public talks and workshops every year, in the course of which I have some trouble in hearing questions and comments from my audiences but still manage to get by. Too bad that I have much more difficulty than I had in my younger years.

I was diagnosed as having full-blown diabetes at the age of 40, so that has added to my disabilities. Diabetes, of course, does not cause much direct pain and anguish, but it certainly does lead to severe restrictions. I was quickly put on insulin injections twice a day and on a seriously restricted diet. I, who used to take four spoons of sugar in my coffee in my prediabetic days, plus half cream, was suddenly deprived of both. Moreover, when I stuck with my insulin injections and dietary restrictions, I at first kept my blood sugar regularly low but actually lost 10 pounds off my usually all-too-thin body. After my first year of insulin taking, I became a near-skeleton!

I soon figured out that by eating 12 small meals a day, literally around the clock, I could keep my blood sugar low, ward off insulin shock reactions, and maintain a healthy weight. So for over 40 years I have been doing this and managing to survive pretty well. But what a bother! I am continually, day and night, making myself peanut butter sandwiches, pricking my fingers for blood samples, using my blood metering machines, carefully watching my diet, exercising regularly, and doing many other things that insulin-dependent diabetics have to do to keep their bodies and minds in good order.

When I fail to follow this annoying regimen, which I rarely do, I naturally suffer. Over the many years that I have been diabetic, I have ended up with a number of hypoglycemic reactions, including being carried off three times in an ambulance to hospital emergency wards. And, in spite of my keeping my blood sugar and my blood pressure healthfully low over these many years, I have suffered from various sequelae of diabetes and have to keep regularly checking with my physicians to make sure that they do not get worse or that new complications do not develop. So, although I manage to keep my health rather good, I have several physicians whom I regularly see, including a diabetologist; an internist; an ear, nose, and throat specialist; a urologist; an orthopedist; and a dermatologist. Who knows what will be next? Oh, yes: Because diabetes affects the mouth and the feet, my visits to the dentist and podiatrist every year are a hell of a lot more often than I enjoy making them. But, whether I like it or not, I go.

Finally, as a result of my advancing age, perhaps my diabetic condition, and who knows what else, I have suffered for the last few years from a bladder that is easily filled and slow to empty. So I run to the toilet more than I used to do, which I do not particularly mind. But I do mind the fact that it often takes me much longer to urinate than it did in my youth and early adulthood. That is really annoying!

Why? Because for as long as I can remember, I have been something of a time watcher. I figured out, I think when I was still in my teens and was writing away like a demon, even though I had a full schedule of courses and other events at college, that the most important thing in my life, and perhaps in almost everyone else's life, is time. Money, of course, has its distinct value; so does love. But if you lose money or get rejected in your sex—love affairs, you always have other chances to make up for your losses, as long as you are alive and energetic. If you are poor, you can focus on getting a better income; if you are unloved and unmated, you can theoretically get a new partner up until your dying day. Not so, exactly, with time. Once you lose a few seconds, hours, or years, there is no manner in which you can get them back. Once gone, you can in no way retrieve them. Tempus fugit—and time lost, wasted, or ignored is distinctly irretrievable.

Ever since my teens, then, I have made myself allergic to procrastination and to hundreds of other ways of wasting time, and of letting it idly and unthinkingly go by. I assume that my days on earth are numbered and that I will not live a second more than I actually do live. So, unless I am really sick or otherwise out of commission, I do my best to make the most of my 16 daily hours; and I frequently manage to accomplish this by doing two or more things at a time. For example, I very frequently listen to music while reading and have an interesting conversation with people while preparing a meal or eating.

This is all to the good, and I am delighted to be able to do two things at once, to stop my procrastinating and my occasional day dreaming and, instead, to do something that I would much rather get done in the limited time that I have to be active each day and the all too few years I will have in my entire lifetime. Consequently, when I was afflicted by the problem of slow urination in my late seventies, I distinctly regretted the 5 to 15 minutes of extra time it began to take me to go to the toilet several times each day and night. What a waste! What could I effectively do about saving this time?

Well, I soon worked out that problem. Instead of standing up to urinate as I had normally done for all my earlier life, I deliberately arranged for most of the times I went to the john to do so sitting down. While doing so, I first settled on doing some interesting reading for the several minutes that it took me to finish urinating. But then I soon figured out that I could do other kinds of things as well to use this time.

For example, when I am alone in the apartment that I share with my mate, Janet Wolfe, I usually take a few minutes to heat up my regular hot meal in our microwave oven. While it is cooking, I often prepare my next hot meal as well as put it in a microwave dish in the refrigerator, so that when I come up from my office to our apartment again, I will have it quickly ready to put in the oven again. I therefore am usually cooking and preparing two meals at a time. As the old saying goes, two meals for the price of one!

Once the microwave oven rings its bell and tells me that my cooked meal is finished, I take it out of the oven, and instead of putting it on our kitchen table to eat, I take it into the bathroom and put it on a shelf by the side of the toilet, together with my eating utensils. Then, while I spend the next 5 or 10 minutes urinating, I simultaneously eat my meal out of the microwave dish that it is in and thereby accomplish my eating and urinating a the same time. Now some of you may think that this is inelegant or even boorish. My main goal is to get two important things— eating and urinating—promptly done, to polish them off as it were, and then to get back to the rest of my interesting life. As you may well imagine, I am delighted with this efficient arrangement and am highly pleased with having efficiently worked it out!

Sometimes I actually can arrange to do tasks while I am also doing therapy. My clients, for example, know that I am diabetic and that I have to eat regularly, especially when my blood sugar is low. So, with their permission, I actually eat my peanut butter and sugarless jelly sandwiches while I am conducting my individual and group sessions, and everyone seems to be happy.

However, I still have to spend a considerable amount of time taking care of my physical needs and dealing with my diabetes and other disabilities. I hate doing this, but I accept the fact that I have little other choice. So I use rational emotive behavior therapy (REBT) to overcome my tendencies toward low frustration tolerance that I may still have. I tell myself whenever I feel that I am getting impatient or angry about my various limitations:

> Too damned bad! I really do not like taking all this time and effort to deal with my impairments and wish to hell that I didn't have to do so. But alas, I do. It is hard doing so many things to keep myself in a relatively healthy condition, but it is much harder, and in the long run much more painful and deadly, if I do not keep doing this. There is no reason whatsoever why I absolutely must have it easier than I do. Yes, it is unfair for me to be more afflicted than many other people are. But, damn it, I should be just as afflicted as I am! Unfairness should exist in the world—to me, and to whomever else it does exist—because it does exist! Too bad that it does—but it DOES! (Ellis, 1979, 1980)

So, using my REBT training, I work on my low frustration tolerance and accept—yes, really accept—what I cannot change. And, of course, barring a medical miracle, I cannot right now change any of my major disabilities. I can live with them, and I do. I can even reduce them to some extent, and I do. But I still cannot get rid of them. Tough! But it is not awful.

REBT, as you may or may not know; posits that there are two main instigators of human neurosis: First, low frustration tolerance (e.g., I absolutely must have what I want when I want it and must never, never be deprived of anything that I really, really desire). Second, self-denigration (e.g., when I do not perform well and win others' approval, as at all times I should, ought, and must, I am an inadequate person, a retard, a nogoodnik!).

Many disabled people in our culture, in addition to suffering from the first of these disturbances, suffer even more seriously from the second. People with serious disabilities often have more performance limitations in many areas (e.g., at school, at work, and at sports) than those who have no disabilities. To make matters worse, they are frequently criticized, scorned, and put down by others for having their deficiencies. From early childhood to old age, they may be ridiculed and reviled, shown that they really are not as capable and as "good" as are others. So not only do they suffer from decreased competence in various areas but also from much less approval than more proficient members of our society often receive. For both these reasons, because they notice their own ineptness and because many of their relatives and associates ignore or condemn them for it, they falsely tend to conclude, "My deficiencies make me a deficient, inadequate individual."

I largely taught myself to forgo this kind of self-deprecation long before I developed most of my present disabilities. From my early interest in philosophy during my teens, I saw that I did not have to rate myself as a person when I rated my efficacy and my lovability. I began to teach myself, before I reached my mid-20s, that I could give up most of my feelings of shame and could unconditionally accept myself as a human even when I did poorly, especially at sports. As I grew older, I increasingly worked at accepting myself unconditionally. So when I started to practice REBT in 1955, I made the concept of unconditional self-acceptance (USA) one of its key elements (Baiter, 1995; Dryden, 1995; Ellis, 1973, 1988, 1991, 1994, 1996; Hauck, 1991).

As you can imagine by what I stated previously in this chapter, I use my REBT-oriented high frustration tolerance to stop myself from whining about disabilities and rarely inwardly or outwardly complain about this. But I also use my self-accepting philosophy to refrain from ever putting myself down about these handicaps. For in REBT one of the most important things we do is to teach most of our clients to rate or evaluate only their thoughts, feelings, and actions and not rate their self, essence, or being. So for many years I have followed this principle and fully acknowledged that many of my behaviors are unfortunate, bad, and inadequate, because they do not fulfill my goals and desires. But I strongly philosophize, of course, that I am not a bad or inadequate person for having these flaws and failings.

I must admit that I really hate growing old. Because, in addition to my diabetes, my easily tired eyes, and my poor hearing, old age definitely increases my list of disabilities. Every year that goes by I creak more in my joints, have extra physical pains to deal with, slow down in my pace, and otherwise am able to do somewhat less than previously. So old age is hardly a blessing!

However, as I approach the age of 82, I am damned glad to be alive and to be quite active, productive, and enjoying life. My brother and sister, who were a few years younger than I, both died almost a decade ago, and just about all my close relatives are also fairly long gone. A great many of my psychological friends and associates, most of who were younger than unfortunately have died, too. I grieve for some of them, especially for my brother, Paul, who was my best friend. But I also remind myself that it is great that I am still very much alive, as is my beloved mate, Janet, after more than 30 years of our living together. So, really, I am very lucky!

Do my own physical disabilities actually add to my therapeutic effectiveness? I would say, yes—definitely. In fact, they do in several ways, including the following.

1. With my regular clients, most of whom have only minor disabilities or none at all, I often use myself as a model and show them that, in spite of my 82 years and my physical problems, I fully accept myself with these impediments and give myself the same unconditional self-acceptance (USA) that I try to help these clients achieve. I also often show them, directly and indirectly, that I rarely whine about my physical defects but have taught myself to have high frustration tolerance (HFT) about them. This kind of modeling helps teach many of my clients that they, too, can face real adversities and achieve USA and HFT.

2. I particularly work at teaching my disabled clients to have unconditional self-acceptance by fully acknowledging that their deficiencies are unfortunate, bad, and sometimes very noxious but that they are never, except by their own self-sabotaging definition, shameful, disgraceful or contemptible. Yes, other people may often view them as horrid, hateful people, because our culture and many other cultures often encourage such unfair prejudice. But I show my clients that they never have to agree with this kind of

bigotry and can actively fight against it in their own lives as well as help other people with disabilities to be fully self-accepting.

I often get this point across to my own clients by using self-disclosure and other kinds of modeling. Thus, I saw a 45-year-old brittle, diabetic man, Michael, who had great trouble maintaining a healthy blood sugar level, as his own diabetic brother and sister were able to do. He incessantly put himself down for his inability to work steadily, to maintain a firm erection, to participate in sports, and to achieve a good relationship with an attractive woman who would mate with him in spite of his severe disabilities.

When I revealed to Michael several of my own physical defects and limitations, such as those I mentioned previously in this chapter, and when I showed him how I felt sad and disappointed about them but stubbornly refused to feel at all ashamed or embarrassed for having these difficulties, he strongly worked at full self-acceptance, stopped denigrating himself for his inefficacies, shamelessly informed prospective partners about his disabilities, and was able to mate with a woman who cared for him deeply in spite of them.

In this case, I also used REBT skill training. As almost everyone, I hope, knows by now, REBT is unusually multimodal. It shows people with physical problems how to stop needlessly upsetting themselves about their drawbacks. But it also teaches them various social, professional, and other skills to help them minimize and compensate for their hindrances (Ellis, 1957/1975, 1988, 1996; Gandy, 1995). In Michael's case, in addition to teaching him unconditional self-acceptance, I showed him how to socialize more effectively; how to satisfy female partners without having perfect erections; and how to participate in some sports, such as swimming, despite his physical limitations. So he was able, although still disabled, to feel better and to perform better as a result of his REBT sessions. This is the two-sided or duplex kind of therapy that I try to arrange with many of my clients with disabilities.

3. Partly as a result of my own physical restrictions, I am also able to help clients, whether or not they have disabilities, with their low frustration tolerance (LFT). As I noted earlier, people with physical restrictions and pains usually are more frustrated than those without such impediments. Consequently, they may well develop a high degree of LFT. Consider Denise, for example. A psychologist, she became insulin dependent at the age of 30 and felt horrified about her newly acquired restrictions. According to her physicians, she now had to take two injections of insulin and several blood tests every day, give up most of her favorite fat-loaded

and salt-saturated foods, spend a half-hour a day exercising, and take several other health-related precautions. She viewed all of these chores and limitations as "revolting and horrible," and became phobic about regularly carrying them out. She especially kept up her life-long gourmet diet and gained 20 extra pounds within a year of becoming diabetic. Her doctors' and her husband's severe criticism helped her feel guilty, but it hardly stopped her in her foolish self-indulgence.

I first worked with Denise on the LFT and did my best to convince her, as REBT practitioners often do, that she did not need the eating and other pleasures that she wanted. It was indeed hard for her to impose the restrictions her physical condition now required, but it was much harder, I pointed out, if she did not follow them. Her increased limitations were indeed unfortunate, but they were hardly revolting and horrible; I insisted that she could stand them, though never necessarily like them.

I at first had little success in helping Denise to raise her LFT because, as a bright psychologist, she irrationally but quite cleverly parried my rational arguments. However, using my own case for an example, I was able to show her how, at my older age and with my disabilities greater than hers, I had little choice but to give up my former indulgences or die. So, rather than die, I gave up putting four spoons of sugar and half cream in my coffee, threw away my salt shaker, stopped frying my vegetables in sugar and butter, surrendered my allergy to exercise, and started tapping my fingers seven or eight times a day for blood tests. When Denise heard how I forced my frustration tolerance up as my pancreatic secretion of insulin went down, and how for over 40 years I have thereby staved off the serious complications of diabetes that probably would have followed from my previous habits, and from her present ones, she worked on her own LFT and considerably reduced it.

Simultaneously, I also helped Denise with her secondary symptoms of neurosis. As a bright person and as a psychologist who often helped her clients with their self-sabotaging thoughts, feelings, and behaviors, she knew how destructive her own indulgences were, and she self-lambasted and made herself feel very ashamed of them, thereby creating a symptom about a symptom: self-downing about her LFT. So I used general REBT with her to help her give herself unconditional self-acceptance (USA) in spite of her indulging in her LFT. I also specifically showed her how, when I personally slip back to my pre-disability ways and fail to continue my antidiabetic exercise and other prophylactic routines, I only castigate my behavior and not my self or personhood. I therefore see myself as a goodnik who can change my no-goodnik actions, and this USA attitude helps me correct those actions. By forcefully showing this to Denise, and using myself and my handling of my disabilities as notable examples, I was able to help her give up her secondary symptoms—self-deprecation—and go back to working more effectively to decrease her primary symptom—low frustration tolerance.

I have mainly tried to show in this chapter how I have personally coped with some of my major disabilities for over 60 years. But let me say that I have found it relatively easy to do so because, first, I seem to be a natural born survivor and coper, which many disabled (and nondisabled) people are not. This may well be my innate predisposition but also may have been aided by my having to cope with nephritis from my 5th to my 8th years and my consequent training myself to live with physical adversity. Second, as noted earlier, I derived an epicurean and stoic philosophy from reading and reasoning about many philosophers' and writers' views from my 16th year onward. Third, I originated REBT in January 1955 and have spent the great majority of my waking life teaching it to clients, therapists, and members of the public for over 40 years.

For these and other reasons, I fairly easily and naturally use REBT methods in my own life and am not the kind of difficult customer (DC) that I often find my clients to be. With them, and especially with DCs who have disabilities and who keep complaining about them and not working too hard to overcome and cope with them, I often use a number of cognitive, emotive, and behavioral techniques for which REBT is famous and which I have described in my book, *How to Cope With a Fatal Illness* (Ellis & Abrams, 1994) and in many of my other writings (Ellis, 1957/1975, 1985, 1988, 1994, 1996).

Several other writers have also applied REBT and cognitive behavior therapy (CBT) to people with disabilities, including Rochelle Balter (1995), Warren Johnson (1981), Rose Oliver and Fran Bock (1987), and J. Sweetland (1991). Louis Calabro (1991) has written a particularly helpful chapter showing how the anti-awfulizing philosophy of REBT can be used with individuals suffering from severe disabilities, such as those following a stroke, and Gerald Gandy (1995) has published an unusual book, *Mental Health Rehabilitation: Disputing Irrational Beliefs.*

The aforementioned writings include a great many cognitive, emotive, and behavioral therapy techniques that are particularly useful with people who have disabilities. Because, as REBT theorizes, human thinking, feeling, and acting significantly interact with each other, and because emotional disturbance affects one's body as well as one's physical condition affects one's kind and degree of disturbance, people who are upset about their disabilities often require a multifaceted therapy to deal with their upset state. REBT, like Arnold Lazarus' (1989) multimodal therapy, provides this kind of approach and therefore often is helpful to people with disability-related problems.

Let me briefly describe a few of the cognitive REBT methods that I frequently use with my clients who have disabilities and who are quite anxious, depressed, and self-pitying about having these handicaps. I bring out and help them dispute their irrational beliefs (IBs). Thus, I show these clients that there is no reason why they must not be disabled, although that would be distinctly desirable. No matter how ineffectual some of their behaviors are, they are never inadequate persons for having a disability. They can always accept themselves while acknowledging and deploring some of their physical and mental deficiencies. When other people treat them unkindly and unfairly because of their disabilities, they can deplore this unfairness but not damn their detractors. When the conditions under which they live are unfortunate and unfair, they can acknowledge this unfairness while not unduly focusing on and indulging in self-pity and horror about it.

Preferably, I try to show my disabled clients how to make a profound philosophical change and thereby not only minimize their anxiety, depression, rage, and self-pity for being disadvantaged but to become considerably less disturbable about future adversities. I try to teach them that they have the ability to consistently and strongly convince themselves that nothing is absolutely awful, that no human is worthless, and that they can practically always find some real enjoyment in living (Ellis, 1994, 1996; Ellis & Abrams, 1994). I also try to help them accept the challenge of being productive, self-actualizing, and happy in spite of the unusual handicaps with which they may unfortunately be innately endowed or may have acquired during their lifetime. Also, I point out the desirability of their creating for themselves a vital absorbing interest, that is, a long-range devotion to some cause, project, or other interest that will give them a real meaning and purpose in life, distract them from their disability, and give them ongoing value and pleasure (Ellis, 1994, 1996; Ellis & Harper, 1975).

To aid these goals of REBT, I use a number of other cognitive methods as well as many emotive and behavioral methods with my disabled clients. I have described these in many chapters and books, so I shall not repeat them here. Details can be found in *How to Cope With a Fatal Illness* (Ellis & Abrams, 1994).

Do I use myself and my own ways of coping with my handicaps to help my clients cope with them? I often do. I first show them that I can unconditionally accept them with their disabilities, even when they have partly caused these handicaps themselves. I accept them with their self-imposed emphysema from smoking or with their 100 extra pounds of fat from indulging in ice cream and candy. I show them how I bear up quite well with my various physical difficulties and still manage to be energetic and relatively healthy. I reveal some of my time-saving, self-management, and other discipline methods that I frequently use in my own life. I indicate that I have not only devised some sensible philosophies for people with disabilities but that I actually apply them in my own work and play, and I show them how. I have survived my handicaps for many years and damned well intend to keep doing so for perhaps a good number of years to come.

CONCLUSION

I might never have been that much interested in rational or sensible ways of coping with emotional problems had I not had to cope with a number of fairly serious physical problems from the age of 5 years onward. But rather than plague myself about my physical restrictions, I devoted myself to the philosophy of remaining happy in spite of my disabilities, and out of this philosophy I ultimately originated REBT in January 1955 (Ellis, 1962, 1994; Wiener, 1988; Yankura & Dryden, 1994). As I was developing REBT, I used some of its main principles on myself, and I have often used them with other people with disabilities. When I and these others have worked to acquire an anti-awfulizing, unconditional self-accepting philosophy, we have often been able to lead considerably happier and more productive lives than many other handicapped individuals lead. This hardly proves that REBT is a panacea for all physical and mental ills. It is not. But it is a form of psychotherapy and self-therapy especially designed for people who suffer from uncommon adversities. It points out to clients in general and to physically disadvantaged ones in particular that however much they dislike the harsh realities of their lives, they can manage to make themselves feel the healthy negative emotions of sorrow, regret, frustration, and grief while stubbornly refusing to create and dwell on the unhealthy emotions of panic, depression, despair, rage, self-pity, and personal worthlessness. To help in this respect, it uses a number of cognitive, emotive—evocative, and behavioral methods. Its results with disabled individuals have not yet been well researched with controlled studies. Having used it successfully on myself and with many other individuals, I am of course prejudiced in its favor. But controlled investigations of its effectiveness are an important next step.

REFERENCES

Balter, R. (1995. Spring). Disabilities update: What role can REBT play? *IRETletter*, 1–4.

Calabro, L. E. (1991). *Living with disability.* New York: Institute for Rational—Emotive Therapy.

Dryden, W. (1995). *Brief rational emotive behavior therapy.* London: Wiley.

Ellis, A. (1962). *Reason and emotion in psychotherapy*. Secaucus, NJ: Citadel.

Ellis, A. (1973). *Humanistic psychotherapy: The rational—emotive approach*. New York: McGraw-Hill.

Ellis, A. (1975). *How to live with a neurotic: At home and at work* (rev. ed.). Hollywood, CA: Wilshire Books. (Original work published 1957)

Ellis, A. (1979). Discomfort anxiety: A new cognitive behavioral construct. Part 1. *Rational Living, 14*(2), 3–8.

Ellis, A. (1980). Discomfort anxiety: A new cognitive behavioral construct. Part 2. *Rational Living, 15*(1), 25–30.

Ellis, A. (1985). *Overcoming resistance: Rational—emotive therapy with difficult clients*. New York: Springer.

Ellis, A. (1988). *How to stubbornly ref use to make yourself miserable about anything—yes, anything!* Secaucus, NJ: Lyle Stuart.

Ellis, A. (1991). Using RET effectively: Reflections and interview. In M. D. Bernard (Ed.), *Using rational—emotive therapy effectively* (pp. 1–33). New York: Plenum Press.

Ellis, A. (1994). *Reason and emotion in psychotherapy* (revised and updated). New York: Birch Lane Press.

Ellis, A. (1996). *Better, deeper and more enduring brief therapy*. New York: Brunner/Mazel.

Ellis, A., & Abrams, M. (1994). *How to cope with a fatal illness*. New York: Barricade Books.

Ellis, A., & Harper, R. A. (1975). *A new guide to rational living*. North Hollywood, CA: Wilshire Books.

Gandy, G. L. (1995). *Mental health rehabilitation: Disputing irrational beliefs*. Springfield, IL: Thomas.

Hauck, P. A. (1991). *Overcoming the rating game: Beyond self-love—beyond self-esteem*. Louisville, KY: Westminster/John Knox.

Johnson, W. R. (1981). *So desperate the fight*. New York: Institute for Rational—Emotive Therapy.

Lazarus, A. A. (1989). *The practice of multimodal therapy*. Baltimore, MD: Johns Hopkins University Press.

Oliver, R., & Bock, F. A. (1987). *Coping with Alzheimer's*. North Hollywood, CA: Melvin Powers.

Sweetland, J. (1991). *Cognitive behavior therapy and physical disability*. Point Lookout, NY: Author.

Wiener, D. (1988). *Albert Ellis: Passionate skeptic*. New York: Praeger.

Yankura, J., & Dryden, W (1994). *Albert Ellis*. Thousand Oaks, CA: Sage.

PART II

Perspective Exercise 2

Prime of Life

PERSPECTIVE

Illness and disability rarely occur at a "convenient" time in a person's life. Try to imagine what your life would have been like if you experienced an injury when you were a young adult.

EXPLORATION

1. If you were severely injured, would your girlfriend or boyfriend remain with you? Husband, wife, parents, grandparents, relatives significant others?
2. Would you have preferred to be at home or away from home during your rehabilitation? Why?
3. Would your family respond differently if the person with a disability was female or male? Why?
4. What would you have needed to maintain a sense of control, independence and dignity?
5. Should people who do not wear helmets when riding a motorcycle be covered by insurance or eligible to sue if injured?
6. How would you respond if your son were brain injured as a result of a motorcycle accident, made great gains, and wanted to buy another motorcycle so he could feel normal again? Your daughter?
7. What is the moral and financial responsibility and liability of a person who gives a ride to someone and they are disabled? Killed? Would it make a difference to you if the person was drunk?

8. Do parents have the right to request that a severely brain injured child not be resuscitated? Brought to a hospital? If such a request is made and the child is given medical care over the objections of the parents, who should be responsible for the life long-care of the child?

Family Issues in Illness and Disability

Introduction to Part III

In recent years, there has been increased attention in the professional literature and rehabilitation practice to the vital role of the available family in the life adjustment of the family member with a disability. The literature has particularly alerted health service providers to those specific family dynamics that play a role in the person's rehabilitation. Family members are speaking out, moreover, and participating in research that provides different and unique perspectives on caring responsibilities and opportunities during the disability experience. The articles in Part III identify and explain these perspectives, as well as offer insights that can facilitate timely and appropriate interventions.

The six articles in Part III cover a wide range of disabilities of both children and parents. The notable difference among the articles is the persons who have incurred the disability, namely, children or mothers and fathers with a chronic medical condition or severe disability. Yet there are also distinctive themes emerging from all of the articles, such as (a) family stress is an ever-present reality in all families living with chronic disease and disability, and such stress represents a threat to family functioning; (b) disability is a family affair and when disability occurs or a chronic illness is diagnosed, there is usually over a period of time a shift in family roles; (c) psychosocial factors existing within the family influence the emotional function of the family member with a disabling condition; (d) there are numerous relationship issues emerging from the family disability experience, and (e) a family member's self-identity is challenged and perhaps reformulated during care-giving responsibilities. Each theme, consequently, encourages the development of an integrated understanding of what happens within a family in their journey to adapt to the disability situation.

Tilden and her colleagues, in their article "Family Decision Making in Foregoing Life-Extending Treatments" discuss a painful reality on this journey when they identify the complicated issues for the family when individuals act as surrogate decision makers for their hospitalized, dying family member. Through interviews with family members, they found that the family members had varied cognitive beliefs when seeking explanations from clinicians, as well as mixed emotions for coming to terms with the life-ending decision. These interviews also revealed several surprising reactions to this difficult decision-making responsibility. Of particular interest in the article was the information gathered from the families' 6 months post decision and the recommendations for clinicians.

Prilleltensky, in her article "My Child Is Not My Carer: Mothers With Physical Disabilities and the Well-Being of Children," also like Tilden, Tolle, Nelson, Thompson, and Eggman, engaged in a qualitative study, focusing on the experiences of mothers with physical disabilities as a mother with muscular dystrophy. She wanted to explore the meaning of motherhood for this group of women and also their experiences, issues, and priorities. Her findings suggest useful guidelines for health professionals when working with families. The numerous direct quotes from those mothers not only reveal their expectations but also delineate the important needs and significant issues for parents with a disability when caring for their children.

The literature has identified several perspectives for parents caring for a child living with a severe illness. Case-Smith in her article, "Parenting a Child With a Chronic Medical Condition," gives the reader another viewpoint as a nondisabled mother caring for a chronically ill child. She collected information from in-depth interviews of parents and extended observations of the families. From this data collection, those themes emerged that can assist practitioners to help families maintain a balance of family functions, such as being aware of assistive technology, providing accurate information, and suggesting sources for social and recreational activities. There are additional recommendations, all of which can give guidance to parents and helping professionals on how to sustain a productive family life while coping with a child with a severe disability.

The reader's attention is shifted to adult disability and chronic illness with the article: "In the Midst of a Hurricane: A Case Study of a Couple Living with AIDS." Buki, Kogan, Keen, and Uman pursued an in-depth case study into one heterosexual couple's experience with AIDS. The husband was in the advanced stages of the disease, and his wife was the primary caregiver. Several themes emerged from their study, and these factors generate many of the important aspects, such as the emotional impact of the diagnosis, the role shifts in a family, and the coping strategies of family members, that should be considered when planning interventions for families experiencing a severe disability. The article also offers a discussion of another coping dimension, namely, spirituality, which is receiving more attention in the literature. Understanding the ramifications of spirituality can assist the practitioner, when appropriate, to provide a source of support for caregivers in their efforts to care for themselves.

Pederson and Revenson offer still another intervention perspective when exploring the issue of family dynamics and the disability experience. They discuss parental illness and its impact on adolescents. In their article, "Parental Illness, Family Functioning, and Adolescent Well-Being: A Family Ecology Framework to Guide Research," the authors critically evaluate existing research on their topic and present a family ecology framework that shows that interrelationships among the variables of parental illness characteristics, family functioning, and adolescent well-being. In their explanation of this framework, they identify several moderators of parental illness as, for example, gender, family roles, and family coping styles, and their effects both on families and on adolescents. The study of these moderators is adding to the growing body of family literature. The authors further discuss the dynamics of the relationship between parental illness and family functioning and adolescent well-being. The effects of the illness-related moderators on the family and adolescents, such as role distribution, daily hassles, threats to the family's identify, and stress responses, provide a blueprint for future research on adaptation to parental illness. They also give the reader a focus for developing effective family interventions.

The psychosocial concepts detailed in the five family articles of Part III are reemphasized in the "classic" article by M. Hulnick and H. Hulnick, "Life's Challenges: Curse or Opportunity? Counseling Families of Persons With Disabilities," reprinted from the third edition of this book. The article reiterates the belief that the flow of time has not eroded the significance of the truth that the occurrence of disability within a family is a demanding and unique challenge. But the families' challenges become the counselor's challenges, and many insights are provided in their article on how the family can be assisted to cope with the illness or disability-related trauma. The authors further indicate the importance for family members of accepting personal responsibility for both their feelings and their actions. Such acceptance becomes foundational for the exercise of the coping methods of reframing, self-forgiveness, and self-talk. Each coping strategy is carefully explained, and suggestions are offered to counselors on how family members can be assisted to use successfully those techniques. Practitioners are also given "empowering" questions that may facilitate a family member's awareness of possible choices during care-giving responsibilities.

CHAPTER SIXTEEN

Family Decision Making in Foregoing Life-Extending Treatments[1]

Virginia P. Tilden, Susan W. Tolle, Christine A. Nelson,
Maye Thompson, and Susan C. Eggman

As is custom in the United States and the law in some states, families serve as decision-making surrogates when gravely ill patients cannot make decisions to forego aggressive treatments at the end of life. Despite growing public awareness of advance directives, few gravely ill hospitalized patients have executed them (SUPPORT, 1995). Therefore, negotiations in the hospital between families and clinicians about treatment decisions for dying patients are commonplace.

The clinical bioethics literature (e.g., Blustein, 1993; Brock, 1991; Hardwig, 1990; Jecker & Schneiderman, 1995; Reckling, 1997) and the critical care literatures of both medicine and nursing (e.g., Emanuel & Emanuel, 1992; Kleiber et al., 1994; Nelson, 1994) extensively discuss family roles, rights, and responsibilities. However, little empirical research

From "Family decision making in foregoing life-extending treatments," by V. Tilden, S. Tolle, Nelson, C., et al., 1999, *Journal of Family Nursing, 5*(4), 426–442, Copyright 1999 by Sage Publications, Inc. Reprinted by permission of Sage Publications, Inc.

[1] This research was supported by a grant from the National Institute of Nursing Research (R01 NR03526). We are grateful to Michael Garland, D.Sc.Rel, Associate Director, Center for Ethics in Health Care, Oregon Health Sciences University, for assistance with coding and assessments of reliability, and to Marina Rios-Daley for transcription of data.

has been done from the family's perspective about their experiences and processes in surrogate decision making. Also, although historically families have served as surrogate decision makers, periodic reexamination of the family's experience is warranted given the rapid changes in organization and financing of health care services.

By understanding family processes of decision making within the context of a changing health care climate, clinicians can more effectively avoid miscommunications and decisional conflict and facilitate more positive outcomes for families.

Changing profiles both in population demographics and in acute treatment service delivery influence family decision making. Advances in medical technologies and gains in standards of living have combined to create a large number of people whose end-of-life course unfolds slowly from long-term chronic illnesses at an advanced age (Field & Cassel, 1997). For example, 50% to 70% of deaths in the United States have a lengthy prodrome related to such conditions as cancer, heart disease, or lung disease (Emanuel & Emanuel, 1998). These are the types of patients for whom questions about how long to pursue aggressive treatment commonly arise after they themselves no longer have decisional capacity, thus families usually become involved in the decision making. On the other hand, changes in provider reimbursement methods and the increased use of hospital specialists often result in providers and families who do not have long-standing relationships or have not met each other until the index hospitalization of the patient. Also, the lay public has come to fear that a business ethic versus a humanitarian ethic will pervade their interactions with hospitals and providers. This can make families wary of clinicians' motives and distrustful of bedside negotiations when the question of futility of treatment arises.

Clinicians, on the other hand, hold a wide range of opinions about what their proper role should be in facilitating discussions to forego treatments (Baggs & Schmitt, 1995; Morrison, Morrison, & Glickman, 1994; Solomon et al., 1993; Terry & Korzick, 1997). For example, how certain should they be of futility before calling the question? What factors should most affect the level of aggressiveness of treatment? How much of clinicians' own opinions and values are appropriate to indicate to the family? Debate on this topic (e.g., Oddi & Cassidy, 1998) followed the widely publicized findings of the SUPPORT (1995) study that showed the widespread reluctance of inpatient physicians to fully know patients' or families' wishes, the frustrations of nurses who often feel sandwiched in a go-between position, and the low rate in hospitals of both physicians and nurses to correctly judge patients' desires for CPR or DNR.

Families also hold a full range of opinions about how to and who should initiate discussions, what the tenor of the discussions should be, what is the right balance of hope versus realism, and what behaviors and communications from clinicians are helpful or unhelpful (Rothchild, 1994; Tilden, Tolle, Garland, & Nelson, 1995). Past research of family decision making has noted that the two most important decisional factors influencing family members are the patient's prognosis and the patient's own preferences about quality of life (Reckling, 1994; Swigart, 1994). Also, involvement in decision making is described months later by family members as an emotionally difficult but meaningful experience (Jacob, 1998). The phases of decision making have been described as the recognition of a dilemma, followed by a period of vacillation that moves to a turning point and ends in letting go (Hiltunen, Medich, Chase, Peterson, & Forrow, in press). Another investigation also noted "letting go" as the core process, with steps necessary to achieve it that included seeking information, seeking meaning about the patient's life, and working within the family to gain a sense of "doing the right thing" (Swigart, Lidz, Butterworth, & Arnold, 1996).

In order to further explore the processes involved in hospital-based family decision making, we interviewed families shortly after the death of hospitalized adult patients who were decisionally incapacitated (e.g., cognitive confusion, coma) and whose deaths followed the withdrawal of life-sustaining treatments. In this chapter, we report findings from interviews with family members of 18 adult patients who died between 1996 and 1998 in acute care at a major university teaching hospital in the Pacific Northwest.

The mean age of the 18 decedents was 59 years ($SD = 14$ years; $range = 34$ to 78 years). They came from varied ethnic backgrounds (61% Caucasian non-Hispanic, 28% African American, 5.5% Asian American, and 5.5% Native American). A little over half were male (56%) and lived in a major metropolitan area (56%). The majority were married or partnered (67%), and all but three had assistance with payment coverage (22% private insurance, 33% public sponsorship, 39% a combination of both public and private support). The length of hospitalization varied from 1 to 34 days ($mean = 11.7$, $SD = 10.9$), but 61% of the patients were hospitalized for less than 10 days. All of the patients spent time in an intensive care unit (ICU); the mean length of the ICU stay was 7 days ($SD = 8.5$ days). Diagnoses included cerebrovascular disease ($n = 3$), liver disease ($n = 3$), trauma ($n = 3$), cardiac disease ($n = 2$), cancer ($n = 2$), renal failure ($n = 2$), sepsis ($n = 2$), and pneumonia ($n = 1$). Over half (61%) were managed by the medical service, while the remainder were with the surgical service or a combination of both medical and surgical services during their hospitalization. Patient death occurred within minutes to days following the withdrawal of such life-extending treatments as mechanical ventilation and renal dialysis.

We interviewed 30 family members of these 18 deceased patients at two time periods: shortly after the patient's death and then 6 months later.

Family participants ranged from one to three per family. This resulted in 30 family interviews during the first time period and 25 interviews during the second time period, with five family members lost to follow-up after the initial interview. The first interview occurred within a month following the patient's death and focused on the medical situation and the family's experience of decision making prior to the patient's death. Interviews were done by experienced research associates in a private location of the family member's choice (usually the home), lasted about 45 minutes, and followed accepted ethnographic techniques of using a semistructured interview guide augmented by probe questions to elicit details of respondents' perspectives (Fontana & Frey, 1994). Interview questions explored the circumstances of the case, focusing on how the family reached decisions about life-sustaining treatment. We asked family respondents to describe who brought up the question of withdrawing treatment, how it was presented, how they and their family responded, and who took the leadership role within the family in negotiations.

We reinterviewed family respondents 6 months after the patient's death in order to gain retrospective views about the decision. These second interviews generally were briefer and focused on overall satisfaction with the decision and the experience of reaching it. We asked respondents to reflect on the process of reaching decisions, describe anything about the process or the decision that lingered in their memories, delineate anything they would do differently, and give advice to clinicians and other families facing similar end-of-life decisions.

Interviews were tape-recorded with permission and tapes were transcribed verbatim. We used content analysis methods (Krippendorff, 1980) to analyze transcripts. Multiple readings led to agreement on main categories of data and subcodes within them. For example, in a category we named *context of the decision*, we noted numerous themes that seemed to influence family process, such as knowing the patient (e.g., knowing the patient's values and lifestyle) and patient suffering (e.g., family observations and speculations about patient distress). To ensure reliability in coding, we selected specific segments of the transcripts of every fifth interview for a re-review for consistency and completeness by an outside expert in qualitative data who was not a member of the team. Once full agreement on the coding scheme was reached, final coding was completed and coded segments were sorted and analyzed.

RESULTS

In this article, we report findings that pertain to family processes leading to the decision and the family's reflection on the decision 6 months later. Study data indicated a core set of phases through which families passed before arriving at the decision to withdraw aggressive life-extending treatments. Although, as would be expected, there was variation in the nature and timing of these phases, we found a great deal of similarity despite obvious differences in patient-related factors such as cause of death and family composition, socioeconomic backgrounds, and values. Even with their own individual variations, families moved through four fairly distinct phases that usually occurred in a relatively linear sequence: (a) *recognition of futility*, (b) *coming to terms*, (c) *shouldering the surrogate role*, and (d) *facing the question*. Half a year later, they reflected on the process as one of seeking a triangulation of certainty.

Recognition of Futility

Despite a wide variety of medical situations, level of family understanding, and length of time prior to the point at which a decision was necessary, families described a period of gradual recognition that, despite aggressive medical efforts, the outcome was bleak. In our earlier study (Tilden et al., 1995), we referred to the unfolding recognition of futility as a "dawning awareness" because of its gradual, steady, and incremental nature that often reflected a dawning or unfolding of realization that the patient is unlikely to regain cognition or function or to leave the hospital.

Family members' cognitive activities that underlay recognition of futility included their efforts to seek explanations from clinicians and intensely observing and interpreting clinicians' behaviors. Families wanted as much information as possible to help them understand their loved one's situation. One wife, who made it a point to be present each morning during medical rounds, recalled:

> The thing that kept me sane was that my daughter and I were there every time the doctors came in and we could see what was going on— we could see the highs and the lows and what they were doing. [At the end] we went into a conference room and I asked the doctor questions about what they were doing and if it was doing any good and if it was going to last. I wouldn't have come to the same conclusion if I hadn't been there the whole time.

Families described becoming "exquisitely attuned" to clinicians' behaviors and to a myriad of subtle cues that might contain a message about prognosis. For example, in one family, recounting a visit to the bedside by the anesthesiologist:

> I talked to my stepson who works for a hospital and he said anesthesiologists never go up and talk to the family if there's any hope, but they always do if there isn't any hope so I realized that when this particular doctor sought us out that hope was over.

A son, interpreting the doctor's behavior, said, "They could have continued aggressive treatment, but by his tone and his attitude it was apparent that [the lead doctor] was not feeling good about [continuing treatment]."

Recognition of futility, especially in the timing of recognition, was influenced by whether the medical situation was acute or chronic. When a patient's medical condition related to a progressive decline, recognition had started long before the final hospitalization and was reflected in comments such as these from a wife: "I knew before that he [her husband] . . . didn't have long, and he did too. And so—whenever we would discuss, you know, what we would do if he died first . . . he always said that whatever decision you make will be fine with me." But when a patient's condition resulted from an acute illness or trauma, the family's recognition of futility was abrupt and often followed a period of denial, cognitive dissonance, and difficulty "hearing." For example, a wife whose husband was severely injured in a motor vehicle accident said:

> I was just in such a stupor that [the doctor] kept answering my questions and then I would just turn around and really ask him the same question and he would answer it in different words but I kept thinking, is it really as bad as he is implying?

Such acute situations tended to be laced with family resistance to recognizing futility. For example, the following is a wife's insightful reflection regarding her own resistance:

> I really think that what Dr. P. was telling me early on was that he was not going to make it. And I didn't want to hear that and so I don't think that was what I was hearing . . . I knew that [disconnecting life support] was the thing I should do, but I just kept hoping that it wasn't true.

As the recognition of futility unfolded and the need for a decision became apparent, the family process shifted toward resignation to an unfavorable outcome, which we labeled *coming to terms*.

Coming to Terms

Families usually came to terms when they recognized the patient's suffering and realized that ongoing medical treatments contributed to suffering. All study families were adamant that they did not want their loved one to suffer when recovery was unlikely. One sister described her analysis of suffering when her brother with cancer returned from surgery on mechanical ventilation:

> We could save him to suffer later, when his cancer kicked in, or we could just let him go now [crying]. And so we all decided that we didn't want him to suffer later, so we chose to turn off life support.

Another family member, when considering a decision to withdraw mechanical ventilation from the patriarch of the family, reported: "All of us agreed. The whole family said that we don't want to see him [the father] suffering that long."

Families used several strategies to assess suffering. Many respondents related their efforts to imagine what the patient was experiencing, thinking, knowing, or feeling. Some reported that they imagined themselves in the patient's place and how they would feel. Several families spoke of learning how to read the medical equipment: "After we learned to read all the little registers on the wall, we could see how the pressure on his brain was so high."

Others used their knowledge of the patient as a person. Knowing the person meant knowing their values, character, personality, and life experiences. Key areas of knowing the person centered around knowing what their physical and emotional responses had been to previous health problems, knowing their feelings about the death of other family members, and knowing what gives life meaning for that individual. Most respondents talked about living as the ability to engage in favorite activities, to care for him- or herself, to communicate with loved ones, and not to be unduly hampered by complex medical regimens.

Although most families believed the patient would not want to be dependent on machines, sometimes a past experience influenced the family in a different direction. For example, one family member recalled that her disabled but very independent brother had, as a young man, survived polio in an iron lung. She felt that he would want to rely on a ventilator, even for an extended period of time, as long as any chance remained of even a minimum level of recovery.

As they weighed the balance of suffering and continued treatment, the availability of advance directives made an important difference. If a written advance directive from the patient was available, it lent the most security to the family in coming to terms. However, in the absence of formal advance directives, knowing the patient's values and wishes helped, especially when patients had verbally expressed preferences. In almost half of the families ($n = 8$, 45%), informal advance directives had been expressed by patients. Family respondents made numerous comments that relayed the security this gave them, for example: "...we had talked about it for years and I knew what she wanted. . . . "; "he said many times 'I don't want to be a vegetable if it comes down to that. . . . ' or 'I don't want to live like that . . . I don't want to just be a thing lying there breathing.' "In only four cases were formal written advance directives available to guide decision making, and in two additional cases, the family believed the patient had an advance directive but it was not available. Families of six of the patients had not talked about their loved one's preferences to receive or avoid aggressive treatments when recovery was unlikely. Thus, as is generally true in a cross section of hospital decision making in the country, patient preferences and values had earlier been expressed informally to families. Even these informal directives provided guidance that was helpful and comforting. For example, one wife looking back on the decision said, "I know I did what he wanted me to do, and that makes it easier." A daughter recounting her father's decision-making process about her mother's care said, "My dad knew very strongly my mother's wishes. In the end, that's probably what helped him most. He didn't have to guess what she would have wanted."

Some families expect more direction from advance directives than they generally provide. One family member described wishing the patient had expressed formal advance directives because " . . . if we had had one, it would have cut down on the confusion and we wouldn't have had to guess about the specifics of what he wanted." This comment reflects both the burden on families who did not have prior guidance from the patient, as well as the common lay misunderstanding about the scope of advance directives. The comment implies the family's expectation that, had the patient completed an advance directive, it would have provided a definitive prescription of the treatment plan. In another example of family misunderstanding about advance directives, a wife reported that she believed it was necessary for her to sign her husband's advance directive when he completed it a year ago. She had not wanted to "because I felt that if I signed it, he would have felt that he really wasn't going to be with us long." Thus, she had discouraged him from completing an advance directive in order to avoid the topic, which she said "was a poor choice to make because then he didn't have it when we needed it."

Sometimes an advance directive was difficult to locate:

> We had an awful time finding that thing [the written advance directive]. We thought it would come over with all of his medical records, but it didn't, so we made them dig it out of there and send it up.

Another family described a situation in which the patient's primary doctor was not willing to append the written advance directive to the chart because he did not think the patient was actually terminal yet.

Over time, coming to terms influenced readiness to take on or shoulder the responsibility of being the patient's representative. With or without advance directives, coming to terms led to becoming the surrogate decision maker on behalf of the patient, which we called *shouldering the surrogate role.*

Shouldering the Surrogate Role

With a great deal of spontaneous emphasis, most respondents described accepting this responsibility as the hardest thing family members ever have to do. Again and again, respondents used such terms as "difficult," "intense," "painful," "overwhelming," "devastating," and "traumatic." They often said that words failed to communicate the difficulty. In their words, "Who wants to say to someone you love, it's time to go?"; "I hope I never do anything that hard in my life again."; "It left me feeling like I was telling him life or death... like I was pronouncing his death."; "I didn't want to pull those life supports and I kept thinking every day: maybe, maybe, maybe...."

In describing the surrogate role, several respondents used the term "work." For example, "I never realized how much work it would be and how draining... how it takes its toll on you." Another respondent said, "It just wears you to a pulp," and still another noted, "... all the stress and pressure..." while another said, "... it was a lot on one person...." Families varied in how prepared they felt for the surrogate role. Some maintained that "... it's not something that anything can prepare you for...", others felt somewhat or greatly prepared by events such as earlier deaths in the family or the chronic, long-standing medical condition of the patient.

The burden of shouldering the surrogate role was, for some, mitigated or counterbalanced by a sense of duty and pride in fulfilling a family obligation. Several respondents spoke of the duty as an honorable one that left them enriched: "I was honored to speak for him because I knew what he wanted." Eventually, having assumed the responsibility of the surrogate, the family turned to face the question and make the decision.

Facing the Question

Eventually, a turning point either in the patient's condition or the family's readiness arrived and was followed shortly thereafter by either the family or clinicians pressing toward a decision. We called this stage *facing the question.* We explored facing the question from the standpoint of whether family or clinicians "called" the question, how it was discussed, and whether the family had comments about the process. Clinicians called the question in 11 of the 18 cases; in 5 of the 18 cases, family members thought they had initiated the conversation, and in 2 cases, family members and clinicians mutually initiated the discussion.

Most families felt the clinicians acted with tact and sensitivity. If any criticism was offered about the clinicians' approach, usually it was that clinicians were too circumspect or tentative. One family member said:

> ...the doctors have a hesitancy about coming right out point blank and telling you their actual feelings...I think they're trying to mask what they tell you so you don't lose hope, but they know the situation is basically hopeless...they don't want to tell you point blank because maybe they can't stand the pain.

When the family called the question, they were more likely to feel the clinician should have been more direct.

Regarding the timing of calling the question, families generally expressed being quite ready to engage in the discussion:

> [The doctors] left it totally up to us. [The doctor] said this is the seriousness of the moment and laid out the problems, expectation, and probabilities. He said, "I'm going to leave you alone to discuss this among yourselves." So we shut the door and, let's see, there were 10 of us. We just knew it was time.

Once having faced the question, families generally were ready to act, and most made the decision to withdraw treatment within 24 hours after the question was called. "They told us they could leave him on life support but it would only be 24 to 48 hours...we just figured since it was going to be a short amount of time anyway why make him suffer." When the family asked to delay, this related most often to waiting for distant family members to gather at the bedside, "I think it was important to keep her alive until all the kids could be there," or to inform distant relatives about the situation and gain their support.

> I woke up saying to myself, "I've got to do this...." But first I called his brother and sister and then I called the kids, each one of them. Because it's their father and they loved him and they had to know what was going on if nothing else.

However, several families took longer to make the decision after the question was called. Some respondents reported they just could not face their loved ones' certain death. While there seemed to be little difference in the level of support these respondents felt from their extended family, they appeared less able to take comfort in that support or use it to mobilize more quickly.

Six Months Later: Looking Back

A main theme reflected from the perspective of 6 months postdecision was the quest for certainty, which we called seeking a *triangulation of certainty*. The term *triangulation* refers to accessing more than one source of information and combining multiple pieces of information to increase certainty in the decision. Many respondents spoke of their need for corroborating data, data that confirmed other data. For example, "We asked a lot of questions, and then we gave [the patient] our own physical. We'd climb on top of him and look in his eyes every day and try to understand. . . . "

In general, reflections after 6 months were more positive if the family felt they had acted in their loved one's best interest: "That's why basically I have no regrets. I was carrying out her wishes. And her wishes were not to lie there on a machine." After 6 months, many again spoke of the importance of advance directives. Some respondents reported guilt arising from feeling that they had prolonged suffering. They felt that perhaps they should have made the decision to terminate treatment sooner. These respondents worried that they had hesitated because they were uncertain about the correct course of action, or because they were trying to gather family members together. One family member said:

> What would the outcome be by delaying it? Is [he] going to get better, or is it because you don't want to let them go? Maybe it's just that I don't want [him] to leave me. There is the selfishness . . . you just don't want them to go, but you have to let them go.

After 6 months, family members had reflected on what advice they would give other families faced with a similar situation. The most common theme was to focus on the patient's quality of life should they survive: "You need to look at the whole person. My brother loved to talk and he wouldn't have been able to talk if he had lived." Other respondents referred to such aspects of quality of life as "touching grandchildren" or "listening to music." These reflections echoed the themes of *knowing the person* and *living* is what we had noted after 1 month. Advice to clinicians often centered on a plea that clinicians be as open and direct as possible. Shouldering the surrogate role rested in large part on becoming convinced of futility. Family respondents expressed that they felt better about the decision if they were convinced of futility, but because of the foreign world of acute care units, much translation from clinicians was needed. A daughter said, "Don't encourage me that there is life when there is not...make sure I know exactly where things stand...."

Another family member said clinicians often were too tentative:

> I wanted the doctors to come out and tell me more what they think. They were so scared to say "I don't think he's going to make it—do you want to continue this?" They never said that to me—they seemed to wait until I gave them an opportunity, an opening.

DISCUSSION

In reaching the decision to terminate aggressive treatments, families transition through a fairly predictable series of stages that begins with recognition and, in time, ends in the withdrawal decision. Present societal expectations of tertiary care likely contribute to this being a process rather than an event. Prior to the mid-1900s, end-of-life decisions were infrequent; nature took its course. Now the majority of those who die in U.S. hospitals do so under circumstances where decisions must be made about how long to pursue life-extending treatments. Television portrayals of miraculous recoveries foster citizens' expectations that death may be optional. Americans are accustomed to miraculous advances in biomedical technology, and reaching a decision that ends in the death of a loved one is extraordinarily difficult.

Families feel a heavy weight of responsibility, which Rothchild (1994) suggested parallels executioner's guilt. When clinicians are willing to actively share the responsibility, family views of the experience tend to be more positive overall. Thus, we encourage clinicians to use language that implies shared decision making (e.g., "In our best clinical judgment, your loved one has essentially no chance to regain the quality of life you say he would want"), in contrast to language that implies a completely neutral stance (e.g., "It's up to you to decide").

Uncertain prognosis is a major element in lengthening the process of decision making and causing family distress. An important finding from SUPPORT (1995) is that on average, just 2 days before a patient's death, there is still a 50% chance of living 2 more months. Uncertainty is a source of anguish for surrogates as they weigh suffering and consider earlier expressions by the patient such as, "don't keep me alive on machines." Although the term *"futility"* is fraught with definitional complexity (Jecker & Schneiderman, 1992) and clinicians consider it ambiguous, the term seemed less ambiguous to families. In both the first and second interviews, families concentrated on the quality of life for the loved one, and used the term "futility" to mean zero or low probability of return of minimal functioning to achieve a required level of quality of life. Quite simply, families said "he would not want to live like this."

The SUPPORT (1995) study indicated that many families of hospitalized, seriously ill patients think that patients' preferences are not well respected, and that about half of all families of conscious patients report that patients are in significant pain in the final days of life. In contrast to that study, we noted few instances in which families in our study thought the level of aggressive treatment was inappropriate or that patients' pain was not well managed. Our findings may reflect the national trend toward improving end of life care, a trend triggered in large part by the findings of SUPPORT.

As advanced biomedical technology increasingly makes the timing of death negotiable, clinicians should attend to the family's progression through the phases necessary to move from an expectation of the patient's recovery to the certainty of patient death, and finally, to the decision to withdraw the aggressive medical treatments that allows death to occur. The major findings of this study point to the family's understanding of the patient's quality of life, and of the importance of patient advance directives in relieving family anxiety. Families generally prefer clinicians to be as direct, honest, and realistic as possible as they guide and facilitate the family through these sequential tasks leading to the decision.

REFERENCES

Baggs, J. G., & Schmitt, M. H. (1995). Intensive care decisions about level of aggressiveness of care. *Research in Nursing and Health, 18*, 345–355.

Blustein, J. (1993). The family in medical decision making. *Hastings Center Report, 23*(3), 6–13.

Brock, D. W. (1991). What is the moral basis of the authority of family members to act as surrogates for incompetent patients? *The Journal of Clinical Ethics, 3*, 121–123.

Emanuel, E., & Emanuel, L. (1992). Proxy decision making for incompetent patients. *Journal of the American Medical Association, 267*(15), 2067–2071.

Emanuel, E., & Emanuel, L. (1998). The promise of a good death. *Lancet, 351*, SII21–SII29.

Field, M. J., & Cassel, C. K. (1997). *Approaching death: Improving care at the end of life*. Washington, DC: Institute of Medicine Committee on Care at the End of Life, National Academy Press.

Fontana, A., & Frey, J. H. (1994). Interviewing: the art of science. In N. Denizen & Y. Lincoln (Eds.), *Handbook of qualitative research* (pp. 361–376). Thousand Oaks, CA: Sage.

Hardwig, J. (1990). What about the family? *Hastings Center Report, 20*(2), 5–10.

Hiltunen, E. F., Medich, C., Chase, S., Peterson, L., & Forrow, L. (in press). Family decision making for end of life treatment: The SUPPORT nurse narratives. *The Journal of Clinical Ethics.*

Jacob, D. A. (1998). Family members' experiences with decision making for incompetent patients in the ICU: A qualitative study. *American Journal of Critical Care, 7*, 30–36.

Jecker, N. S., & Schneiderman, L. J. (1992). Futility and rationing. *American Journal of Medicine, 92*, 189–196.

Jecker, N. S., & Schneiderman, L. J. (1995). When families request that 'everything possible' be done. *The Journal of Medicine and Philosophy, 20*, 145–163.

Kleiber, C., Halm, M., Titler, M., Montgomery, L., Johnson, S. K., Nicholson, A., Craft, M., Buckwalter, K., & Megivern, K. (1994). Emotional responses of family members during a critical care hospitalization. *American Journal of Critical Care, 3*, 70–76.

Krippendorff, K. (1980). *Content analysis: An introduction to its methodology* (4th ed.). Newbury Park, CA: Sage.

Morrison, R. S., Morrison, E. W., & Glickman, D. F. (1994). Physician reluctance to discuss advance directives. *Archives of Internal Medicine, 154*, 2311–2318.

Nelson, J. L. (1994). Families and futility. *Journal of the American Geriatrics Society, 42*, 879–882.

Oddi, L. F., & Cassidy, V. R. (1998). The message of SUPPORT: Change is long overdue. *Journal of Professional Nursing, 14*(3), 165–174.

Reckling, J. (1994). *Deciding whether to withhold or withdraw life-sustaining treatment.* Unpublished doctoral dissertation, University of Kansas, Lawrence.

Reckling, J. B. (1997). Who plays what role in decisions about withholding and withdrawing life-sustaining treatment? *The Journal of Clinical Ethics, 8*, 39–45.

Rothchild, E. (1994). Family dynamics in end-of-life treatment decisions. *General Hospital Psychiatry, 16*, 251–258.

Solomon, M. Z., O'Donnell, L., Jennings, B., Guilfoy, V., Wolf, S. M., Nolan, K., Jackson, R., Koch-Weser, D., & Donnelley, S. (1993). Decisions near the end of life: Professional views on life-sustaining treatments. *American Journal of Public Health, 83*, 14–23.

SUPPORT Principal Investigators. (1995). A controlled trial to improve care for seriously ill hospitalized patients. *Journal of the American Medical Association, 274*, 1591–1598.

Swigart, V., Lidz, C., Butterworth, V., & Arnold, R. (1996). Letting go: Family willingness to forgo life support. *Heart and Lung, 25*(6), 483–494.

Swigart, V. (1994). *A study of family decision making about life support using the grounded theory methods.* Unpublished doctoral dissertation, University of Pittsburgh, Pittsburgh, PA.

Terry, P. B., & Korzick, K. A. (1997). Thoughts about the end-of-life decision-making process. *The Journal of Clinical Ethics, 8,* 46–49.

Tilden, V. P., Tolle, S. W., Garland, M. J., & Nelson, C. A. (1995). Decisions about life sustaining treatment: Impact of physicians' behaviors on the family. *Archives of Internal Medicine, 155,* 633–638.

CHAPTER SEVENTEEN

My Child Is Not My Carer

Mothers With Physical Disabilities and the Well-Being of Children

Ora Prilleltensky

This article is based on a study that explored the intersection of motherhood and physical disability. My own experience as a mother with Muscular Dystrophy has provided the impetus for this research. Elsewhere (Prilleltensky, 2003, in press), I depict the pregnancy and early parenting experiences of mothers with disabilities, and their access (or lack thereof) to formal and informal supports. In this article, I focus on the relationship between disabled mothers and their children, and on the efforts of the former to enhance the well-being of the latter.

My use of the term *disability* is consistent with its reframing by disability scholars as a socially constructed disadvantage (Gill et al., 2003). There are some substantive variations between the British social model of disability and the minority group model in the Unites States and it is beyond the scope of this article to explain them. Nonetheless, both models highlight issues of power, oppression and civil rights, and share the premise that many of the barriers associated with disability are socially constructed and thus preventable. The impact of structural and attitudinal barriers on the lives of people with disabilities is manifest in the

From "My child is not my carer: Mothers with physical disabilities and the well being of children," by O. Prilleltensky, 2004, *Disability and Society,* 2004, *19,* 209–223. Reprinted with permission of Taylor & Francis, Ltd.

realm of parenting. Kirshbaum and Olkin (2002) refer to parenting as the 'last frontier', where discrimination due to impairment is enacted. As a group, parents with disabilities and particularly mothers with disabilities have encountered others' skepticism regarding their capacity to function as parents. Prejudicial assumptions about their ability to provide care and about the psychological well-being of their children often underpin the resistance that many encounter (Campion, 1995; Kocher, 1994; Wates, 1997; Wates & Jade, 1999).

People with learning difficulties are particularly vulnerable to societal misconceptions that the mere presence of such impairments is inevitably counter-indicated with the ability to parent. Work by Booth and Booth (1994) and others (Tymchuk, 1992, cited in Campion, 1995) has emphasized the need to deconstruct such assumptions, rather than hold them as truisms. However, whereas individuals with intellectual and physical impairments share some common experiences of discrimination, this should not obscure important distinctions that may be of relevance to policy and practice. This article specifically explores the intersection of motherhood and physical disabilities, and reviews literature that is specific to physical impairment. Whereas it cannot automatically be extrapolated to parents with other types of disabilities (e.g., intellectual, emotional), some of its implications and conclusions may be of relevance, and can thus advance work in these fields. Of course, the category of physical disabilities is not a uniform one either and encompasses a wide range of conditions varying in severity, stability, and health status.

Despite the growing numbers of disabled adults who are having children, parents with disabilities continue to be primarily ignored by research and social policy (Olkin, 1999; Meadow-Orlans, 2002). The sparse literature that can be found on the topic typically focuses on the relationship between parental disability and children's well-being. In some cases, a negative impact is hypothesized, studied and 'verified' (Peters & Esses, 1985); in other cases, the correlation between indices of dysfunction in children and parental disability is explored (LeClere, & Kowalewski, 1994); and in others yet, the negative impact on children and the need to counsel them is taken as a given (Kennedy & Bush, 1979). Much of this literature has been critiqued on various grounds including unexamined assumptions, methodological flaws, and lack of differentiation between disability situations (Kelley et al., 1997; Kirshbaum & Olkin, 2002; Meadow-Orlans, 2002; Prilleltensky, in press).

In the past decade, a body of literature on children who provide care to ill and disabled relatives (dubbed young carers) has gained prominence. One article emphasized the negative impact of such caring, referring to it as 'a curse on children' (Sidall, 1994, p. 15). This issue has received increased attention not only from the popular media, but from researchers and policy analysts, as well, most notably in Britain. Based on research carried out by Aldridge and Becker (1993) and others, arguments have been made regarding societal neglect of young carers, and their social, economic and educational disadvantage. A host of recommendations for respite services, drop-in centres and emotional support to these youngsters have emanated from this research (Aldridge & Becker, 1996).

The focus on young carers has been critiqued on a number of fronts. Olsen (1996) has drawn attention the artificial divide between this body of literature and one that explores the lives of parents with disabilities. He argues that researchers who have focused on young carers have neglected to emphasize the inadequacy of funded supports to meet the needs of their parents. He further objects to the unchallenged assumption that caring on the part of children is unquestionably associated with negative outcomes. Keith and Morris (1996) point to poverty, insensitive attitudes, and inadequate services as impediments to parental access to resources. Parents with disabilities are often reluctant to disclose their needs for services due to fear that their parental competence will be questioned (Thorne, 1991; Keith & Morris, 1996; Thomas, 1997).

Keith and Morris (1996) contend that the very terminology of young carers connotes taking charge of the individual requiring assistance. In other words, the child is assumed to be taking responsibility for the parent or even to be in the reversed role of parenting the parent. Not only is this association between the provision of assistance and role reversal harmful to children and parents alike, it is also an inaccurate description of the relationship dynamic in many such families. The misguided perception where disability is inevitably associated with dependency tends to undermine the parenting role of people with disabilities. Thus, parents who are unable to independently fulfill all of the physical tasks of child rearing may encounter skepticism regarding their ability to function as parents. Those requiring assistance with personal care are even more vulnerable to this kind of criticism (Keith, 1992; Keith & Morris, 1996; Olsen, 1996; Lloyd, 2001; Morris, 2001).

Those who have voiced concerns with some of the research and policy development on young carers also point to the danger of institutionalizing this phenomenon as an acceptable practice. After all, it is much cheaper to provide respite services and emotional support to young carers than to ensure that the entire family is properly serviced (Olsen & Parker, 1997). Indeed, a recent report on young carers in Australia (2002) contends that they need to be acknowledged and supported, given that there will never be sufficient resources to meet the needs of those who require care. Arguments of this nature, coupled with instances where services are withdrawn based on the availability of a young carer, are cautious reminders of the potentially disablist policies that may ensue from this discourse. The reader is referred to Aldridge and Becker (1996) and Olsen and Parker (1997) for a thorough understanding of the controversy that surrounds this issue.

Researchers who align themselves with disabled parents emphasize the importance of the overall family constellation, as well as sources of risks and protective factors external to the parental disability. The family's level of isolation versus support, the impact of poverty and disincentives for gainful employment, and inaccessible environments faced by many parents with disabilities are being raised as important contributing factors that should be considered in research (Kelley et al., 1997; Blackford, 1999; Kirshbaum & Olkin, 2002). Furthermore, some studies have found positive psychological adjustment amongst parents with Cerebral Palsy (Greer, 1985); lack of adverse effects of paternal disability (spinal cord injury) on the well-being of children (Buck & Hohmann, 1981, 1982); and similar interaction patterns between disabled and non-disabled mothers and their daughters (Crist, 1993).

What helps some families cope well despite the presence of risk factors, and what can be learned from their success in the presence of illness and disability? What supports do parents require that will assist them in caring for their children? These are some of the questions that warrant researchers' attention. Indeed, some studies have been instrumental in highlighting factors associated with positive functioning. For example, one study found that the family's ability to reflect on its performance and make adjustments in the face of illness was associated with a positive outcome (Hough et al., 1991; Lewis et al., 1989). Another study of parents with multiple sclerosis identified specific coping mechanisms that were utilized by well adjusted versus poorly adjusted families (Power, 1985).

An encouraging trend among some researchers and service providers is one of approaching these families with the purpose of identifying strengths. One such example is *Talking it Out in the Family*, a video portraying real life situations of parental disability where the actors are the people living the experience (Blackford, 1990). Work conducted at Through the Looking Glass (TLG) in California also operates from a strength-based orientation. Some examples are research that explores the impact of assistive technology on the transition to parenthood, an in-depth study of families that have positive parenting experiences and an investigation of factors that promote positive child outcomes, as well as those that increase risk (Kirshbaum, 1996; Kirshbaum & Olkin, 2002).

These types of studies can advance knowledge about specific coping strategies associated with positive outcome. They have clear implications for practice that can be used by professionals, parents with disabilities and those who are considering parenthood. Rather than minimizing difficulties or potentially problematic family situations, work of this nature attempts to identify and reduce socially created constraints to optimal functioning. Furthermore, as more research that explicitly sets out to 'document the spectrum of capability in parents with disabilities' (Kirshbaum & Olkin, 2002, p. 70) is amassed, professional and public perceptions will continue to shift in a more favourable direction.

STUDY DESCRIPTION

This article draws on a larger study that focused on the intersection of motherhood and physical disability, and included women with disabilities with and without children (Prilleltensky, in press). The main objective was to explore the meaning of motherhood for this group of women and their mothering-related experiences, issues, and priorities. For the purpose of the present article, I focus on mothers with disabilities.

I conducted two focus groups for mothers at a symposium on mothering with a disability. One group was for mothers of young children (under eight) and one for mothers of older children. Most of the women in the latter group had teenagers at home, while two had adult children. I also held 16 in-depth interviews with eight mothers, some of whom also participated in the focus groups. All mothers had a physical impairment and most were wheelchair users. All but one interview took place in participants' homes. Participants were well educated as a group, with approximately two-thirds of those interviewed holding a post-secondary degree. Some of the focus group participants, but none of the interviewees belonged to a visible minority group.

Informed by the literature and by a pilot study, I constructed an interview guide that was used loosely and flexibly during the first interview. The interviews were approximately 90 minutes in length, and were audiotaped, transcribed and sent to participants for review along with a 3–5-page summary. This served as the basis for the second interview. My approach to data analysis was informed by the work of Glesne & Peshkin (1992), Merriam (1988) and Seidman (1991), and consisted primarily of thematic organization of the data. Each transcript was carefully reviewed, excerpts were labeled according to categories, and categories were clustered into broader themes.

FINDINGS

Promoting Growth and Enhancing Well-Being in Children

Parenting is largely about the creation of a nurturing and caring atmosphere where children's physical and emotional growth can take place.

This entails facilitating the expression of feelings, maintaining open lines of communication, and ensuring that children feel loved and protected. It also involves meeting children's physical and emotional needs, and making sure that the challenges they face are appropriate to their developmental phase.

Promoting their children's growth and enhancing their well-being was a central theme in most of the interviews and focus groups. At the most basic level, this includes measures to ensure that children are safe and out of harm's way. For one mother (and given the nature of her impairment), this meant that she was never alone with her children for more than a few minutes when they were infants. Once they were old enough to sit on the footrest of her wheelchair and could respond to verbal instructions, she greatly enjoyed taking them for short outings on her own. As the children are maturing she increasingly relies on verbal instructions to keep them safe:

> From a young age I taught them that if they listen to me I can keep them safe ... like if a fire alarm goes, if they just listen to what I tell them they'll be safe you know, they're not going to burn to death. I think it's very important for children to feel safe. I don't want them to feel anxious like if they're home alone with me that there's more of a threat to their security than if they're home alone with their dad. Because even though there are things that I can't do, they still see that I get it done somehow. Like I know who to call or what to do or I can teach them to do things themselves.

Another mother of now-adult children had a number of surgeries when they were young. She knew that her then husband who was not involved in the children's care could not be trusted to look after them in her absence. Having no reliable co-parent, and devoid of other formal and informal supports, this mother had to make a very difficult decision:

> I couldn't leave them with him ... God knows what would have happened to them. So when I had to go into the hospital I had to make a big decision. I called Children's Aide ... I called them and they took the children into care while I was in the hospital because I was there sometimes 6 to 8 months (at a time). My kids spend practically their whole childhood going in and out of the Children's Aide.

The ramifications of these children being in and out of foster care will be discussed later; relevant to the present discussion is this participant's belief that she had to temporarily relinquish her mothering role in order to ensure her children's safety and physical well-being.

Other participants noted their use of formal and informal supports as a way of ensuring that children's needs are always met, even if they are at times unable to fulfill those needs themselves. One single mother, whose health precludes her from being consistently available, assertively advocated for and was finally granted funded assistance. This assured her that 'no matter how bad I feel I manage to come through or have someone else who is always there for the children'.

A related theme that ran across a number of interviews and focus group discussions is the attempt to shield children from any burden related to maternal disability. A number of participants emphasized that they do not want their disability to become a source of hardship for their children. One mother noted that, although she encourages her children to help out, she doesn't want them to feel that they need to look after her:

> They are developing skills to be a little more independent. But I don't want them to be adultified children. I don't want my children to take care of mommy. To be kind and respectful and to listen and to be responsible for their actions and to do simple things sometimes—that's great. To me, that's teaching morals and values of life. But for my children to take care of me I think is wrong. I think children should not be taking care of their parents.

Another mother expressed very similar sentiments:

> I don't want my children to take on or have a sense that they have to take care of me. I am their parent. I think that a child has to be able to feel that they can be kids. And I guess you need to be able to say to yourself I'm going to take care of myself if it means getting the resources out there to help me take care of myself but to set a limit on what you expect of your children.

A third woman who utilizes attendant services for personal care emphasized the importance for her of having this service performed by a paid assistant. She expressed a concern that attendant services that are now publicly funded may be targeted for cuts in the future. She noted that her 7-year-old daughter helps out with the laundry. However, this was instituted with the goal of promoting the youngster's independence and sense of self-efficacy rather than as a necessity related to the mother's disability.

A related topic that came up in one of the focus groups is the attempt to protect children from the burden of worry. Interestingly, several women noted that the "super mom" role model that their own mothers provided as they were growing up made it difficult for them as mothers with disabilities:

> When I was growing up the image that my mother portrayed is that you have to let your kids think that everything is fine ... to constantly portray the image that everything is okay even though you feel like shit ... That was the image that I grew up with and that was the image I also felt I had to continue with my own kids and I think that caused a really severe depression because I couldn't do it ... I couldn't be that super mom.

In response, another participant made eloquent connections between women's reflections on how they were parented and their similar attempts as mothers to shield their children from burden:

> We talk about our parents who looked as if they are so strong and everything is just fine and then behind it we realize that we try to do that too sometimes with our own kids simply because we don't want to burden them with the worry. We're there to make their life better.

THE CHALLENGE OF SETTING BOUNDARIES AND MANAGING CHILDREN'S BEHAVIOUR

Nurturing a caring relationship goes hand in hand with managing behavior in a constructive way. Discipline and control are not ends in themselves; they are part of fostering congenial and harmonious relationships with youngsters. Parenting in the context of a physical disability may have specific implications for discipline and behavior management. Some parents with disabilities may not be able to catch a toddler who is trying to get away or pick up a child in the midst of a temper tantrum. Furthermore, the ongoing demands of parenting that are energy taxing for most parents, may be especially challenging for those whose energy is already in short supply.

Some participants discussed the disciplinary challenges they have come across, as well as strategies and techniques to overcome them. One mother found the toddler stage particularly taxing until she and her husband took a parenting course, and came up with a consistent approach:

> We needed to come to some kind of a compromise and some consistency ... because how he dealt with it had implications for how I could deal with it.

They subsequently implemented a system of contracts and consequences giving as many choices as possible in accordance with the children's stage of development and maturation.

Another participant who has some funded assistance occasionally
uses this support to implement consequences such as taking a young child
to her room for 'time-out'. This would all be discussed ahead of time to
ensure that the support person is indeed prepared to follow through on
the mother's decision. As much as possible, this mother deals with mis-
behavior on a verbal level: '... I'm much more of an explainer and I try
to reason with them even when they're quite little. I always wanted them
to be able to deal with me on that verbal level'. Now that the children
are older it is increasingly easier to rely on verbal explanations and logical consequences as demonstrated by the following scenario at a public
swimming pool:

> Can you imagine talking a kid out of a pool in July? Like the last thing
> they want to do is leave the water. But you know, they do, because the
> first time one of them wouldn't come when I called, then the next day
> it's like 'I'm not taking you swimming today and this is why'. I have
> to be (consistent). It's the kiss of death if I'm not. And they go 'Oh,
> we'll be good today, we'll go out' and I say 'no, that's what you said
> yesterday so today you won't go swimming. Tomorrow I'll give you
> another chance.

This participant gave various other examples that attest not only to
her consistent parenting style but also to her attempts to accentuate the
positive and reinforce desirable behaviour whenever possible. Her strong
parenting skills notwithstanding, she jokingly indicated that 'believe me,
I don't do it as perfectly as it might sound that I do ... (sometimes) it just
all falls apart and I scream at them'.

Another participant who also relies on verbal communication and
logical consequences encourages her young children to solve problems
with words:

> It's a totally non-violent atmosphere that I have here. You have an
> anger problem, let's sit down and talk about it. I'll actually get them
> together and I'll say: 'okay, you sit here and you sit there and I'll sit
> here. Now what is it that you're upset about? How can we make this
> better?' ... The other day, the seven year old says 'mom, you sound
> like a judge'.

In addition to her solid parenting skills, this mother's ability to deal
with conflicts and misbehaviour in an effective manner is likely enhanced

by the funded assistance she was able to secure as a single disabled mother. She conserves her energy by having someone else carry out household tasks, as well as provide direct care when she is in need of rest. Being able to get the rest she requires to replenish her strength allows her to be a more effective and compassionate parent. This point was further accentuated in a focus group by a participant who reflected on the years that she raised her son as a single mother:

> Around the discipline issue, there are two things. One is the energy level, again depending on what your situation is. I couldn't be consistent to follow through on stuff because I was just wiped out. I felt that if I asked for help around that stuff I was giving up my child and in fact on one occasion someone did suggest the Children's Aide. I had wonderful help but not enough of it. Part of it was that it's not out there automatically and part of it was that I was afraid to disclose the need.

In the same group, a mother to teenagers shared the significant behavioural challenges she experienced when her daughter was a pre-schooler:

> She'd come home at lunch and she'd walk through the door and start screaming ... just screaming about stuff ... it got to the point where I didn't talk to her hardly because it didn't matter what I said, it made her mad ... I can remember thinking: 'I'm not surprised some children get the shit kicked out of them by their parents', you know, because I can think of two or three times where I was just ready to strangle her.

Most parents who are honest with themselves can relate to this candid description of a highly intense situation where emotions run amok. Such scenarios are by no means unique to families of disabled parents, nor can they be said to characterize them. Nonetheless, it is perhaps significant that this mother experienced frequent change of homemakers when her children were very young and little involvement in the day to day running of the house.

The mother whose children were in care during her hospitalizations experienced major disciplinary challenges. I asked her what it was like when her children returned home from care:

> It was very hard when they came back. Of course, whoever they were staying with had rules and regulations, and things that they did and then I would have to try to get them to do what I wanted. It was really difficult. Then you had a man there that did a lot of yelling and spanking.

This mother spoke about the negative impact of frequent changes, an unstable family environment, and harsh and inconsistent disciplinary measures by the children's father. Consequently, she felt that her children were often out of control as adolescents.

The combined experience of study participants suggests that having access to appropriate resources and supports can have a facilitative impact on discipline and behaviour management. Mothers who are inadequately supported are more likely to experience challenges while those who have access to formal and informal supports are better equipped to set boundaries, follow through and promote cooperative behaviour.

RELATIONSHIP WITH CHILDREN

The preceding sections on enhancing children's well-being and providing structure and behavioural boundaries provide a backdrop for the types of relationships that study participants have with their children. The participant who successfully lobbied for funded assistance noted that it enabled her to play a more significant role in her children's life. She further commented on the diverse ways of carrying out parenting activities:

> My kids at a very young age, if they wanted me to read to them they knew they could either sit on my lap or beside me on the bed or if it was a heavy book they knew they'd have to help me hold it up. And they just did that quite spontaneously.

Now that her children are older and the relationship is based less and less on the provision of physical care, this mother feels that she can play an even greater role in the children's lives. She jokingly referred to this period in their lives as the 'golden years' when they are no longer toddlers and have yet to enter the potentially rocky adolescent phase. In the focus group for mothers of older children, participants emphasized the more difficult and challenging adolescent years and made humorous references to 'raging hormone syndrome' and 'wonderful adolescent roller coaster ride'.

For a number of participants, the fulfillment derived from motherhood is particularly magnified given the barriers that may have prevented them from experiencing it. Having been told early in life that she would not become a mother, one woman reflected on the joy of motherhood:

> I really treasure it when my eight year old still, you know, when I'm sitting on the couch, will curl up on my lap and put his head on my shoulder. Or my eleven year old when we're walking down the street,

will put his arm around me. I think I'm so lucky to be where I am at this date and time because I may not have ever had the opportunity to enjoy this.

Another woman, who resisted pressures to undergo an abortion, gave a number of examples of the strong bond and intimacy that she has with her baby and the sense of 'oneness' that new mothers often describe:

I always think that it's too good to be true. I love him so much ... and I feel so protective of him. I know what he needs. I know when he's complaining. I always know what he wants. I know exactly what he wants.

Recognizing the dynamic nature of a mother–child relationship she reflected on what it may be like years from now when her infant son grows up:

You know what I think? I wonder if his friends will make fun of me. I wonder about that and I wonder if it'll be hard for him having a mom who is in a wheelchair. I wonder if he'll be embarrassed. But then I think, maybe he'll stick up for me.

The issue of how children respond to a mother's disability came up in a number of interviews and focus groups. One woman related a conversation she overheard just the other day as she came to pick up her son from day care:

He said something yesterday. I went to pick him up from day care. I was just watching him play with other kids in the sandbox and he was getting up to leave. One of the little girls whom I didn't recognize said: 'Why is your mom in a wheelchair?' And he just said: 'Oh, she broke her back as a kid.' That's all he said. It was sort of like matter of fact. I was so proud of him the way he said that, you know, I thought: you couldn't give a better answer to another kid than that. It was just so matter of fact.

This mother, and several others, emphasized the importance of mothers with disabilities being visible and involved in children's schools and activities. A few mothers came to their children's class to speak about disabilities. In one case this put an end to the teasing of an 11-year-old boy by some classmates. Of course, the inaccessibility of some venues restricts disabled parents from full participation in their children's lives: one mother attributed her husband's greater involvement in extracurricular activities to accessibility issues.

Contrary to the above indications of acceptance and comfort with mother's disability, another participant recounted a phase when her daughter refused to be out in public with her:

> I had the scooter then. She'd sit on my lap but she'd never go for a walk. You know, my husband could take her to the park but I couldn't. I think she was embarrassed even when she was 4 years old.

This is the same little girl who had frequent and unexpected changes in care givers for the first few years of her life, a factor to which the mother attributes various difficulties throughout the years. Being disagreeable and uncooperative as a young child she became somewhat distant as a teenager preferring to spend most of her time at friends' houses.

The participant whose (now adult) children spent time in foster care during her hospitalizations reflected on the impact of these separations on their emotional well-being. She noted with sadness the somewhat distant nature of her relationship with her adult children:

> They will call and ask how I feel. But if I need help, I definitely won't pick up the phone and call my kids. This is where I phone my friends.

Her frequent hospitalizations as a young mother provided a formidable barrier to the formation of a close alliance with her children. Having spent a lot of time in hospital as a young child, she drew the following parallels between her relationship with her siblings and her children:

> The bonding that I was talking about when I went away to the hospital and I didn't bond with my siblings, I think the same thing pretty much happened with my kids, depending on which kid and what operation ... And with them being pulled away all the time, I don't think they had a chance to bond with anybody either because they were going to different homes and everything. So we really both lost.

In the two cases noted above, the mother's impairment was a precursor to some degree of inconsistency in the children's care. Hence, it is not the impairment itself but the context in which it is embedded that can have a potentially adverse affect on the relationship between mothers with disabilities and their children. Where the contact with mother is stable and continuous, and the children receive consistent and nurturing care in her absence, the relationship has a greater chance of being a close and fulfilling one. Furthermore, it is important to emphasize the obviously complex and dynamic relationship between all parents and their children, regardless of disability status. By their very nature, relationships go through ebbs and flows, peaks and valleys. Even the closest of relationships experience periods of greater distance and lessened intimacy. Clearly, maternal disability is but one of many factors that could affect the relationship between mother and child.

DISCUSSION

Women who participated in this study provide us with a glimpse into the lived experience of parenting with a physical disability. As one would expect in any group of mothers, a range of parenting practices, experiences and relationships were reported. This diversity cannot be attributed to any specific factor pertaining to the nature, severity, or age of onset of the mother's disability. The variability of experiences notwithstanding, participants' life stories demonstrate a strong commitment to children, actions to ensure their care and well-being in different circumstances, and attempts to shield them from any burden related to the maternal disability. While challenges and barriers were candidly reported, by and large, they do not overshadow the joy and fulfillment that these women derive from motherhood.

The issue of children caring for disabled parents was noted in the theoretical overview. The present study did not find any indication of this phenomenon amongst the children and families of participants. If anything, there were indications of participants' desire to shield their children from the burden of care. There is little doubt that being burdened with excessive, developmentally inappropriate responsibility and worry is not conducive to children's well-being. Nonetheless, there is a price to be paid for a hedonistic, self-indulgent upbringing where reciprocating and contributing to the well-being of others is not fostered.

Children whose lives are restricted by caring for a parent with a disability deserve our attention and concern. However, there is a big difference between a teenager who has little choice about providing intimate care to a parent and one who may be expected to assist more with household chores than some of his peers. Both the quality and quantity of tasks need to be considered, as well as the child's age and the overall dynamic of the parent–child relationship. Even when assistance in personal care is provided, this does not mean that a reversal of roles has occurred.

Research on young carers clearly indicates that this is rarely seen as an acceptable solution by parents themselves (Aldridge & Becker, 1996). Hence, the fact that this phenomenon exists at all is a reflection of the inadequacy and insufficiency of funded services to meet the personal-care needs of parents with disabilities. Of course, there may well be situations where children are expected to carry out tasks that are inappropriate, burdensome and restricting. Just as the presence of a disability does not impair the ability to function as a responsible parent, neither does it safeguard anyone from poor decision-making and possible deficits in parental competence. Without minimizing the plight of some children who may be overburdened with caring tasks, I am concerned about the possible equating in some people's minds of parental disability with overworked, emotionally burdened children.

Related to the topic of enhancing children's well-being is participants' accounts of the child-rearing practices they utilize and their overall relationship with their children. The emphasis on consistent parenting practices, and reliance on verbal explanations and instructions was noted by a number of mothers. This is consistent with narrative accounts found in the literature suggesting that such children tend to respond to verbal instructions from an early age. I began to take my (now 16-year-old) son out on my own as soon as he was able to climb into the car seat on his own. Although he was assertive and strong willed from a young age and would frequently negotiate parental limits, I knew I could count on his following my verbal instructions even as a young child.

In my work as a counsellor and a psychologist I have often come across parents who struggle with how to enforce limits with teenagers. Clearly, physical strength is irrelevant in getting older children to respond to limit setting. Solid and consistent parenting practices from a young age go a long way toward preventing unmanageable situations and disregard for parental authority. Indeed, a number of participants showed a good deal of ingenuity in fostering an enjoyable yet manageable family atmosphere. These mothers can be a source of knowledge and inspirations to disabled and non-disabled parents alike.

An important consideration is the relationship between child-rearing practices, and level of formal and informal supports. One woman noted the difficulty with being consistent, and following through in the context of fatigue and limited supports. In other cases, insufficient, inadequate or non-existent supports were implicated in adversely affecting the ability to handle behavioural issues. In extreme situations, this can have a lasting effect on the overall nature of the relationship between parents and children. Relationships are not formed and maintained in a vacuum, nor can they be nourished by good intentions alone. Although the people involved in the relationship enact the lived experience of being together, their behaviours are not just a reflection of personal intentions, but of extraneous forces as well. Negative distal and proximal factors like economic deprivation, crowded housing, and insufficient formal and informal supports penetrate the interactions between otherwise loving individuals. These powerful influences can slowly erode ties created by much individual effort on the part of parents and children. Indeed, one particular case exemplified the lasting impact that these factors can have on the relationship between a mother and her children

I believe that this study can advance our understanding of the relationship between parental disability and child well-being. The experience of study participants suggests that the welfare of children need not be compromised due to parental disability. Study participants gave numerous examples from their daily lives that describe their attempts to ensure their children's welfare. They also described loving relationships and positive communication with the children, as well as their pride in children who are well adjusted, caring, and appreciative of human diversity. Alongside these accounts, and sometimes intertwined with them, are indications of how stressors such as poverty and lack of support can compound difficulties related to the disability. It is safe to say that in the presence of internal and external resources and supports, parental disability in and of itself need not present a significant risk factor. On the other hand, the high rate of poverty, single parenthood and attitudinal barriers that characterize the lives of many women with disabilities, may indeed, if unmitigated, present a risk to family well-being.

ACKNOWLEDGEMENTS

This research was supported by a scholarship from the Social Sciences and Humanities Research Council of Canada.

REFERENCES

Aldridge, J. & Becker, S. (1993). Punishing children for caring, *Children and Society, 7*(4), 277–278.

Aldridge, J. & Becker, S. (1996). Disability rights and the denial of young carers: the dangers of zero-sum arguments, *Critical Social Policy, 48*(16), 55–76.

Blackford, K. (1990). A different parent, *Healthsharing,* 20–25.

Blackford, K. (1999). A child's growing up with a parent who has multiple sclerosis: theories and experiences, *Disability & Society, 14*(5), 673–685.

Booth, W. & Booth, T. (1994). Working with parents with mental retardation: lessons from research, *Journal of Physical and Developmental Disabilities, 6*(1), 23–41.

Buck, F.M. & Hohmann, G.W. (1981). Personality, behavior, values, and family relations of children of fathers with spinal cord injury, *Archives of Physical Medical Rehabilitation, 62,* 432–438.

Buck, F.M. & Hohmann, G.W. (1982). Child adjustment as related to severity of paternal disability, *Archives of Physical Medical Rehabilitation, 63,* 249–253.

Campion, M.J. (1995). *Who's fit to be a parent?* (London, Routledge).

Crist, P. (1993). Contingent interaction during work and play tasks for mothers with multiple sclerosis and their daughters, *American Journal of Occupational Therapy,* 47(2), 121–131.

Gill, C., Kewman, D. & Brannon, R. (2003). Transforming psychological practice and society: policies that reflect the new paradigm. *American Psychologist,* 58(4), 305–312.

Glesne, C. & Peshkin, A. (1992). *Becoming qualitative researchers* (White Plains, Longman). Greer, B.G. (1985) Children of physically disabled parents: some thoughts, facts and hypotheses, in: S. K. Thurman (Ed.). *Children of handicapped parents: research and clinical perspectives* (Orlando, Academic Press).

Hough, E.E., Lewis, F.M. & Woods, N.F. (1991). Family response to mother's chronic illness: case studies of well and poorly adjusted families, *Western Journal of Nursing Research,* 13(5), 568–596.

Keith, L. (1992). Who cares wins? Women, caring and disability, *Disability, Handicap & Society,* 7(2), 167–175.

Keith, L. & Morris, J. (1996). Easy targets: a disability rights perspective on the 'children as carers' debate, in: J. Morris (Ed.). *Encounters with strangers: feminism and disability* (London, Women's Press).

Kelley, S., Sikka, A. & Venkatesan, S. (1997). A review of research on parental disability: Implications for research and counselling, *Rehabilitation Counseling Bulletin,* 41(2), 105–116.

Kennedy, K.M. & Bush, D.F. (1979). Counselling the children of handicapped parents, *Personnel and Guidance Journal,* 58(4), 267–270.

Kirshbaum, M. (1996). Mothers with physical disabilities, in: D.M. Krotoski, M.A. Nosek & M.A. Turk (Eds). *Women with physical disabilities: achieving and maintaining health and well-being* (Baltimore, Paul Brooks Publishing).

Kirshbaum, M. & Olkin, R. (2002). Parents with physical, systemic or visual disabilities, *Sexuality & Disability,* 20(1), 65–80.

Kocher, M. (1994). Mothers with disabilities, *Sexuality and Disability,* 12(2), 127–133.

LeClere, F.B. & Kowalewski, B.M. (1994). Disability in the family: the effects on children's well-being, *Journal of Marriage and the Family,* 56(May), 457–468.

Lewis, F.M., Woods, N.F., Hough, E.E. & Bensley, L.S. (1989). The family's functioning with chronic illness in the mother: the spouse's perspective, *Social Science Medicine,* 29(11), 1261–1269.

Lloyd, M. (2001). The politics of disability and feminism: discord or synthesis? *Sociology,* 35(3), 715–723.

Meadow-Orlans, K.P. (2002). Parenting with a sensory or physical disability, in: M.H. Bornstein (Ed.). *Handbook of Parenting, Volume IV. Social conditions and applied parenting* (New Jersey, Lawrence Erlbaum Associates, Publishers).

Merriam, S.B. (1988). *Case study research in education* (San Francisco, Jossey-Bass).

Morris, J. (2001). Impairment and disability: constructing an ethics of care that promotes human rights, *Hypatia, 16*(4), 1–16.

Olkin, R. (1999). *What therapists should know about disability* (New York, Guilford Press).

Olsen, R. (1996). Young carers: challenging the facts and politics of research into children and caring. *Disability & Society, 11*(1), 41–54.

Olsen, R. & Parker, G. (1997). A response to Aldridge and Becker—'Disability rights and the denial of young carers: the dangers of zero-sum arguments', *Critical Social Policy, 50*(17), 125–133.

Peters, L.C. & Esses, L.M. (1985). Family environment as perceived by children with a chronically ill parent, *Journal of Chronic Diseases, 3 8*(4), 301–308.

Power, P.W. (1985). Family coping behaviours in chronic illness: a rehabilitation perspective, *Rehabilitation Literature, 46*(3–4), 78–82.

Prilleltensky, O. (2004). *Motherhood and disability: children and choices* (New York, Palgrave Macmillan).

Prilleltensky, O. (2003). A ramp to motherhood: the experiences of mothers with physical disabilities, *Sexuality and Disability, 21*(1), 21–47.

Seidman, I.E. (1991). *Interviewing as qualitative research* (New York, Teachers College Press).

Sidall, R. (1994). Lost childhood, *Community Care, 9–15* June, 14–15.

Thomas, C. (1997). The baby and the bath water: disabled women and motherhood in social context, *Sociology of Health & Illness, 19*(5), 622–643.

Thorne, S.E. (1991). Mothers with chronic illness: a predicament of social construction. *Health Care for Women International, 11,* 209–221.

Wates, M. (1997). *Disabled parents: dispelling the myths* (Cambridge, National Childbirth Trust Publishing).

Wates, M. & Jade, R. (1999). *Bigger than the sky: disabled women on parenting* (London, Women's Press).

Young Carers Research Project (2002). *Final report: a carers Australia Project.* Available online at: www.carers.asn.au

CHAPTER EIGHTEEN

Parenting a Child With a Chronic Medical Condition

Jane Case-Smith

The demands and responsibilities of caring for children who have disabilities appear to be different from those of parents with typical children (Burke, Harrison, Kauffmann, & Wong, 2001; Gallimore, Coots, Weisner, Gamier, & Guthrie, 1996; Innocenti & Huh; King, King, & Rosenbaum, 1996). Although most researchers agree that caregiving for children with disabilities can be stressful (Dyson, 1996; Smith, Oliver, & Innocenti, 2001), the overall effect on families' well-being seems to vary across time and across individual families (Knafl, Breitmayer, Gallo, & Zoeller, 1996; Scorgie, Wilgosh, & McDonald, 1998; Tak & McCubbin, 2002). Early research (e.g., Tizard & Grad, 1961) focused on the psychological effects and the social isolation and adversity associated with raising a child with disabilities (Barnett & Boyce, 1995). More recent studies have demonstrated that families with children with disabilities face complex issues; however, the overall impact on the family is not necessarily negative (Harris & McHale, 1989; Patterson & Blum, 1996; VanLeit & Crowe, 2002). For some families, the impact is positive, strengthening the family as a unit. To implement a model of family-centered care in pediatric practice, professionals need to acknowledge and understand how a child's disability affects the entire family.

From "Parenting a child with a chronic medical condition," by J. Case-Smith. *The American Journal of Occupational Therapy, 58*(5), 551–560. Reprinted with permission of *The American Journal of Occupational Therapy.*

Turnbull and Turnbull (1997) use a family systems model to examine how a child's disability affects family functions. The economic function of the family is affected because parents generally work fewer hours outside the home in order to care for their child and costs for treatment and medication are high. Therefore parents' earning ability decreases at the same time that their costs increase. Additionally, the child care demands on parents' time increases as daily care of the child rises above that required for typical children (Dunlap & Hollinsworth, 1977; Harris & McHale, 1989; Helitzer, Cunningham-Sabo, VanLeit, & Crowe, 2002). For example, parents may regularly implement numerous therapeutic procedures, engage in feeding for long periods of time or frequently throughout the day, administer medications or medical procedures (e.g., suctioning, gastrostomy feedings), and attend therapy and clinic appointments. Because more time is spent in daily care activities, less time is available for other activities, such as recreation and socialization (Helitzer et al., 2002; Turnbull & Turnbull). Barnett and Boyce (1995) found that mothers with children with Down syndrome were unable to maintain employment and spent less time in social activities. Their survey results demonstrated that socialization and work activities were replaced with child-care activities. Fathers also reported more child-care time and less time in social activities.

Turnbull and Turnbull (1997) explain that when parents' socialization is limited, the entire family is affected. Families are the bases from which children learn to interact with others; therefore, children's first experiences with friends and family are vital to their social-skill development. Loss of social activity opportunities early in life can have long-term implications for building friendships and social supports.

Other researchers have investigated the types of accommodation that the family system must make when it includes children with developmental disabilities (Gallimore et al., 1996). These authors define accommodation as the family's functional responses or adjustments to the demands of daily life with a child with special needs (Gallimore et al., 1996; Gallimore, Weisner, Kaufman, & Bernheimer, 1989). Every accommodation is presumed to have costs as well as benefits to the individuals of the family and to the family as a whole. The types of accommodations that families make change throughout the life cycle. Some investigators report that adjustments are greatest when first learning about the disability (Weisner, 1993); other authors propose that coping becomes more difficult and greater adaptations are needed as children get older and performance discrepancies increase (Bristol & Schopler, 1983; Suelzle & Keenan, 1981). Examples of accommodations made by families are that the mother arranges for flexibility in work or works at home, the family's home is altered to improve safety or accessibility, and the caregiving responsibilities of both parents increase (Gallimore et al., 1996; Helitzer et al., 2002).

A few studies have examined the impact of children with medical diagnoses who require ongoing intervention and medical technology on parents (see Patterson & Blum [1996] for a review). Caring for a child who requires routine use of medical technology; such as respirators, gastrostomy pumps, suctioning equipment, can be socially isolating for parents. Some parents report that they are virtually housebound (Andrews & Nielson, 1988). For example, parents may not be able to find babysitters, the child's behaviors may create uncomfortable social situations, the logistics of leaving the house for nonessential events may be overwhelming, as when equipment, medical supplies, and medical technology needs to be packed and unpacked. Kirk (1998) and Murphy (1997) reported that most families with children with chronic medical problems must rely on nurses and other health care professions for respite care. In addition, the home environment is not as conducive to social activities when it is filled with medical technology and supplies, taking on the appearance of an intensive care unit (ICU). Although parents seem to accommodate to the presence of medical technology, friends and extended family may feel less comfortable. Concerns about the child's exposure to viruses and bacteria may also limit social opportunities.

Parents have reported that their experiences with a child who requires continual medical care is exhausting and at times overwhelming (Jennings, 1990; Kirk, 1998). The uncertainty of chronic illness and the child's prognosis can produce ongoing anxiety for parents (Andrews & Nielson, 1988; Murphy, 1997). The stress associated with a child's chronic illness can create problems in the mother's relationships with her other children and in the marriage (Kirk, 1998; Murphy, 1997).

Other areas of family function that are often affected when a child has chronic medical problems are parents' self-identity and social–emotional well-being (Turnbull & Turnbull, 1997). When all or most family activities revolve around the exceptionality (e.g., therapies, meetings with professionals, caregiving, hospitalizations), the exceptionality may become the major identifying characteristic to the parents (Patterson & Blum, 1996). For example, the parents may introduce themselves as the parents of a child with a congenital heart condition or a neurological syndrome.

The degree of family stress appears to partially relate to the amount of support available. Families without access to respite and services are more likely to feel overburdened, emotionally exhausted, and socially isolated (Kirk, 1998; Murphy, 1997; Tak & McCubbin, 2002). Support in the form of friends, extended family, financial security, professional services, and community resources can help families maintain healthy, balanced lives (Gallimore et al., 1993; Humphry & Case-Smith, 2001; Turnbull & Turnbull, 1997; VanLeit & Crowe, 2002).

Understanding how parents' occupations and experiences differ when they include a child with chronic medical problems can help occupational therapy practitioners focus on the issues that matter most to families. Professionals need a deep understanding of the experiences of these families in order to fit their interventions into the family's daily life and to help them make accommodations that are of low cost and high benefit. The purpose of this study was to examine in depth the caregiving, social occupations, and self-identities of parents with children with significant disabilities and chronic medical conditions. We examined these occupational areas because the literature suggests that these family functions are substantially affected by young children with serious medical issues and intense caregiving needs (Barnett & Boyce, 1995; Crowe, 1993; Kirk, 1998; Patterson, Jernell, Leonard, & Titus, 1994).

METHOD

Design

We implemented an ethnographic approach to examine the caregiving, social occupations, and self-identities of families with preschool-age children with chronic medical conditions and disabilities. The design used multiple sources for data about the families, including in depth interviews with the parents and extended observations of the families. The informants were mothers and fathers, and almost all observations included the entire nuclear family. As part of an interdisciplinary early intervention training project in a Midwest university, the parents consented to allow graduate students to participate with them in 60 hours of family activities and outings. I selected data from 8 of the 22 participating families for analysis because their children had ongoing and complex medical concerns, were dependent on technology, or had significant disabilities that affected all areas of development, or all. Each graduate student conducted an in-depth interview with one set of parents, transcribed the interview, and subsequently participated in 60 hours of activities with the family over a 6-month period. The students described the family outings and activities in depth and detail, generating between 12 and 15 field notes. Following description of the activity and the interactions, each student wrote journal entries that interpreted her experiences based on coursework readings on family occupations and interactions.

Participants

The training project coordinator, who is the mother of a child with cerebral palsy, recruited the families ($n = 22$) with children with disabilities from her school and hospital contacts. Each signed informed consent to

Table 1. Medical Diagnoses of the Children With Chronic
Medical Conditions

Name*	Participants' Medical Diagnoses and Risk Factors
Annie	Twin, anoxia at birth, cerebral palsy, seizures, cortical blindness
Sean	Congenital heart defect, digestive problems, on transcutaneous peritoneal nutrition (TPN), genetic syndrome
Katie	Premature birth, gastrostomy tube, blind, seizures
Michael	TPN, jejunostomy tube, gastrostomy tube, genetic syndrome: velocardiofacial disorder, heart defects
Carlie	Premature, gastrostomy tube, hypersensitive to sounds and oral stimulation
Jeremy	Near strangling, severe brain injury, cortically blind, seizures, severe cerebral palsy
David	Hypoplastic left heart, cerebral vascular accident following heart surgery
Kevin	Severe spastic quadriparesis cerebral palsy, seizures, mental retardation

*All names are pseudonyms.

participate in the study. The eight families in this study had children with combinations of complex medical issues and significant developmental delays. The children were 4 to 6 years of age. All of the families were married couples and six of the eight had other children. Two of the children with disabilities were adopted at birth. All of the families were Caucasian and middle class. Five of the eight children received 40 or more hours per week of nursing services. The graduate students who interviewed and observed the families were four occupational therapists, one nurse, one special educator, and two speech pathologists. Table 18.1 lists the diagnoses of the children whose families participated in the study.

Instrumentation/Procedures

The faculty and staff of the training project designed the interview guide, based on family systems concepts defined in Turnbull and Turnbull (1997). Parents were asked to describe a typical day, their family routines, social supports, interventions and their satisfaction with those interventions, and their hopes and dreams for the future. The interviews were transcribed verbatim. Field notes regarding nonverbal responses and the environment during the interviews were recorded. During the 60 hours that the students spent with the families, they accompanied the family to therapy, clinic, and physician visits, Individualized Educational Program meetings, family outings, respite, and typical activities as defined by the family. Examples of family outings and activities were touring the science museum, eating at restaurants, swimming, and bowling. The students attended baseball games, picnics, birthday parties, and church events with their families. Each student described his or her experiences, focusing on the family's occupations and their interactions with medical and educational professionals.

Data Analysis

Following several readings of the interviews, field notes, and journals, I coded each statement or group of statements with a label that defined its theme. These labeled sections were combined and organized into common and related themes. Data within the thematic categories were analyzed to identify concepts. An iterative process was implemented to reorganize the themes and concepts to obtain the best fit using all of the data. The concepts were interpreted using related literature and reflection based on my experiences with families over 25 years in early intervention programs. Two mothers from the study reviewed the themes and concepts to provide member checks and validate the findings. Two graduate students and three project faculty served as peer reviewers by examining the data and the interpretation. The peer reviewers and member checks resulted in slight modification of the themes and reorganization of the data; this process also served to confirm the truth-value of the themes.

RESULTS

Three themes emerged related to caregiving. "The challenge of always being there" describes mothers' constant efforts to provide for their children's medical, educational, and recreational needs given their total dependency on their parents. "Change in career plans" describes how in each family, one parent gave up his or her career plans to stay home and care for the child with special needs. "Making decisions and tolerating compromises" describes compromises that the parents made in caring for their children. The themes that emerged related to the families' social lives were "Where do we find a sitter?" which describes the lack of resources for respite care and the difficulties the parents experienced when leaving the house, and "anticipating the unanticipated," which describes the elaborate planning required when families did venture from their homes. A third set of themes described issues in the families' self-identify and illustrated how each family's identity was defined by the child with special needs. The parents explained how their experiences with their children helped them to appreciate life and demonstrate more sensitivity to and tolerance of individual differences. They had become strong advocates for their children and other children with similar needs.

Managing Caregiving Responsibilities

Each parent described a typical day, revealing the level of caregiving required of the child with a medical condition. In most of the families, the parents maintained a rigorous, highly scheduled day of medical procedures and caregiving responsibilities. Sean's [all names are pseudonyms] father describes their typical routine:

> We get up at 6:15. We get ready for work. Sean gets up by 7 and gets unhooked from his TPN [transcutaneous peritoneal nutrition]. He gets a bottle and his diaper changed. When the nurse is not there, we draw up his meds . . . . It takes about an hour to get all the medications together for the day and then we lay them out. All of the meds are given over the course of the day . . . . He probably gets some meds every half hour or so. Then he gets a break [at 3:30]. We start the evening meds around 7. He gets insulin at 9 a.m., 3 p.m., and again at 9 p.m. We put him down to bed between 9 and 9:30.

Michael is the youngest of five children. He has "a G-tube [gastrostomy], a J button [jejunostomy], and a broviak [for the TPN], and a trach." His mother describes her day of caregiving:

> During the week, Michael gets up between 7 and 7:30. I have already taken my shower, two of the kids are already gone, two of the kids are getting ready. We kind of sponge him down because he wakes up soaking wet from his diaper. We disconnect his TPN, give him his breathing treatments, his meds, change dressings . . . . After the first wet diaper, we put his pants and shoes on him and hook up his pump, and then we get ready for school.
> He gets tube fed for 4 hours a day . . . . Then he comes home, and he gets more medicine, more breathing treatments, another diaper change, goes to bed for a nap. Then we have to wake him up for therapy . . . so we get him up, change him again, and it's either speech, OT or PT, depending on which day of the week it is. Some days it's doctor's appointments . . . . We do that and then usually between 4 and 7 we're driving everyone else to their stuff, taking them to piano lessons or choir or scouts or whatever it is, ice skating lessons . . . . A couple times a week we give him a bath in the evening, and when we do that, we have to go through changing all of the dressings, which takes about an hour. About 8:30 he goes to bed. I'm usually up two or three times in the night suctioning him or something like that . . . so that is a typical Michael day.

These descriptions reveal highly structured days, filled with many caregiving tasks. Although most families with young children lead busy, highly scheduled days; these families' activities revolved around caregiving tasks and medical procedures, not recreational and social activities. The five families who received nursing care expressed how grateful they were to have professional assistance in caregiving, yet numerous medical and therapeutic procedures remained to be administered by the parents. The families seemed to have incorporated these intensive caregiving responsibilities into their daily lives.

The Challenge of Always Being There

The children's medical issues seemed to require the constant attention and energy of the families. Five of the children cycled through infections brought on by their immobility, shallow breathing, and suppressed immune systems. The parents expected periods of illness and relied heavily on their nurses for care during these periods. When the children were ill, therapies and routine appointments had to be put on hold. The parents' activities were also cancelled, so that they could be home with their children. These times were discouraging because often the children would lose skills, and progress in learning new skills was put on hold.

Beyond the medical procedures and caregiving routines, the parents were concerned about their children's developmental growth and their abilities to engage in interaction with others. This concern about the child's involvement in play seemed to present the greater challenge to the parents. The parents recognized that time spent with the child in caregiving and medical procedures did not fulfill the child's need to play and socially interact.

Because these children had limited ways of expressing their feelings, interaction and communication required constant effort by the parents. Jeremy's mother said, "Our biggest challenge with him right now is trying to find a way for him to interact more independently and to communicate with us." The student with this family observed that when the mother played physical games with Jeremy, it was important, "to look for subtle signs, like a slight furrow of his brow or the pursing of his lips" to know when he was tired and ready to stop.

One student explained with empathy how Annie's mother worried about how she felt when she showed signs of illness:

> I was struck by the stress of wondering what was wrong with Annie. It is so hard to know since her communication is so impaired. She can't answer questions, speak, or communicate her thoughts using a device. She can activate switches with voice output ... but her understanding of language seems to be limited to a small set of familiar words and phrases.

> I wonder if it would be beneficial to somehow to teach her words related to pain and discomfort.... I would find this [lack of communication] upsetting and terribly frustrating, knowing that a seizure was likely on the way and being unable to do anything to stop it.

Perhaps because Jeremy, Annie, and Katie could not play independently, their parents expressed that they felt guilty when their children were left alone. They tried many methods to engage them in independent play given their severely limited movement and vision. For example, several families had borrowed or owned switch-activated toys and easy-to-activate toys. Despite these efforts, the families had yet to discover methods for their children to play independently.

Katie's mother explained, "[the challenge is] keeping her entertained because she can not do anything for herself.... she likes to be entertained.... We're trying to find something that she can do independently ... "The student noted that Jeremy's "participation in the world is through his family members." At age 6, "he is completely dependent on them for his every need."

The literature has identified the importance of a balance between meeting the child's developmental needs and managing the illness (Patterson & Blum, 1996; Tak & McCubbin, 2002; Turnbull & Turnbull, 1997). The parents seemed to make great efforts to maintain this balance, keeping the child's developmental skills a priority.

Change in Career Plans

Primarily due to their children's frequent medical appointments, illness, and hospitalizations, the parents changed their career goals. In six of the eight families, the mother left paid employment to become a full-time mother. In the family with five children, one with a rare genetic disorder, the father held three jobs to help pay for the medical expenses and allow his wife to stay home. In another family, the mother left her job to be home full time, and the father changed jobs to be home more of the time. One mother explained that she did not work outside the home because, "When [my daughter] is sick ... everything stops because we don't know how sick she's going to get ... she has seizures and sometimes she ends up in the hospital for a couple days, and if the respite worker calls off, I don't have anyone to watch her." These unpredictable events were not compatible with maintaining a job.

In one exception, a mother held a part-time position that allowed her and her husband to alternate days at home so that one or the other was at home with their child everyday. In a second exception, the father left his work to become a stay-at-home dad while his physician wife continued her practice. This father stated, "There were three people trying to deal with Carlie's feeding issues. So we made a decision that one of us had to stay home so that she would have a little more consistency." Both parents were pleased with the progress she had made since her father has been at home full time.

As in previous research (Barnett & Boyce, 1995; Crow, VanLeit, Berghmans, & Mann, 1997; Dunlap & Hollinsworth, 1997; Helitzer et al., 2002), these eight families had shifted their family occupations, devoting more time and energy to caregiving and less to socialization and work. When caregiving for children with specific needs requires that one parent stay home, the family's financial well-being, and the parents' social network and self-identity can be negatively affected (Barnett & Boyce; Turnbull & Turnbull, 1997).

Making Decisions and Tolerating Compromises

Parents in this study were asked to make difficult decisions for their children on a regular basis—decisions about services, medications, and treatments that had important effects on their children. The parents were also frequently given advice and offered alternative treatments. Sometimes when asked to make decisions about treatments, they did not always feel that they were knowledgeable about the potential effects, risks, and benefits. Generally these decisions involved compromise that weighed the costs and benefits of several options.

For example, Jeremy had intractable seizures that needed to be controlled by medication. However, the medication made him drowsy, lethargic, and nonresponsive; therefore, his parents asked for less potent medication. As a result Jeremy was more alert, responsive, and communicative; however, he also had 30–40 seizures a day. His parents valued the ability to have daily positive interaction with their son at the risk of possible long-term consequence of the seizure activity.

Kevin's parents and physician agreed to the insertion of a baclofen pump to decrease his spasticity. By decreasing his muscle tone, his parents could easily position him with good alignment in his wheelchair. Unfortunately, the muscle tone inhibitor also affected his arm movement, such that he could no longer use his arms to reach and hold objects. Despite his loss of strength, his mother decided to continue the baclofen and hoped that he would regain some of his arm strength.

Another context for family decision making was the Individualized Education Program (IEP) meeting. In Kevin's IEP meeting, his mother decided that due to his seizure meds, sleep needs, and endurance, she would bring him to school late, that is, between 9:30 or 10:00. Although this later arrival time meant that Kevin would miss 2 hours of instruction, his mother negotiated this arrangement because she knew that if he became overly tired, his seizures would increase, and he would not benefit from the instruction he did receive.

In family-centered intervention, professionals recognize that parents are the primary decision makers when planning services for their child (Dunst, Trivette, & Deal, 1994; Humphry & Case-Smith, 2001). The Individuals With Disabilities Education Act Amendments (1997) reinforce this concept by specifically including the parents in every educational decision that is made for the child. Although professionals recognize that parents have these rights, they also acknowledge that good decision making requires deep understanding of the issues. At times, the parents felt that they were being asked to weigh options without adequate information and without knowledge of the costs associated with each option. The parents in our study discussed the compromises that they had needed to make when planning medical and educational interventions. These decisions seemed to weigh on the parents and they expressed anxiety regarding whether or not they had made the best choice.

Maintaining a Social Life

As discussed in the previous section, socialization was affected by the parents' inability to find a sitter and the lack of respite care. When families, including the child with a medical condition, attended recreational or social events outside their home, extraordinary planning and creative adaptability were required.

Where Do We Find a Sitter?

Most of the families did not use child-care providers given the extensive caregiving demands of their children; therefore, the parents had limited options for leaving home. Five of the children had poorly controlled seizures, four had compromised immune systems, two vomited frequently, and two had very low endurance for activity. In several of the families, one extended family member took care of the child for short periods if the parents needed some respite. For Annie's parents, "Basically the only people that help are Dan's parents ... no one else has taken the time to learn how to do the medicines."

Although several of Jeremy's extended-family members had indicated an interest in learning his medical treatment to help care of him, these arrangements had not been made. Sean's family also did not have any help with respite other than nurses; "I would say the only extended family that really helps is [my husband's] mother, and mostly when we are not home and people need to drop off supplies. When we are in the hospital [with Sean], she will watch our daughter ... so the only respite that we have had is the nurse." In general, the families only attended community activities in which the entire family could participate.

These parents, like those described by Kirk (1998) and Murphy (1997), rarely accessed respite. The parents did not complain about lack of respite and seemed to accept their situations. In some cases, the child's care could be taught to others, but the parents seemed reluctant to take the chance that problems may occur.

Anticipating the Unanticipated

Because the children in this study had multiple and often unpredictable needs, parents felt that they had to carefully and extensively plan each activity outside the home. Unanticipated events and preparing for them was a dominant theme in each family's social life.

When Jeremy's family went swimming or bowling, the parents had to check the facilities' accessibility before the visit. His father prepared for a bowling outing by researching the facility's accessibility and its least busy times. This family organized the equipment and supplies needed before every event. They developed plans "A" and "B"—"A" hoping that Jeremy would tolerate the activity or "B" fearing that he would not and they would need to return home. Carlie's reflux, required that her parents take two to three changes in clothes with them on outings. They always had an "escape plan" in case she began to vomit. Carlie had a very low tolerance to noise so her parents used headphones at birthdays and in restaurants. The headphones allowed Carlie to enjoy the activity without being overwhelmed.

David's parents often had to curtail social events and outings because his endurance was poor. "We mainly have problems because David gets tired faster, he gets colds easier, and if he gets any type of cold we pretty much have to stay in the house. We have to do what he can do. So if he gets worn out we just have to go home ... he has asthma and when you can't breathe and you have a weak heart, it is double trouble." David's mother further explained:

> You make plans with friends, but you really don't know if you're going to be there until you're there ... because he can get sick, he can have a seizure, his respite provider may not show up ...

In general the families made careful decisions about their outings and the social events they attended. They weighed the costs and benefits, they decided whether or not they had the energy, then they planned carefully what supplies and equipment would be needed. Each had mastered packing all of the equipment and supplies that may be needed, including headphones, medications, extra clothing, and medical supplies. As well-supplied as they were, they also prepared to return home quickly, curtailing their attendance when problems arose. Several parents voiced that they hoped that relatives and friends understood their frequent early departures.

Perhaps these parents persevered in making efforts to participate in social events in order to maintain a balance and a semblance of typical family functioning. Gallimore et al. (1996) discussed the ongoing importance of family flexibility and adaptability to balance family functions when children have developmental disabilities or medical chronic conditions.

Maintaining a Self-Identity

With the level of care required by these children, it is not surprising that the disability became a prominent aspect of the family's identity and social–emotional selves. Through many of the conversations with the parents, it became apparent that the families viewed their self-identity in a positive way, to the extent that they made opportunities to support others in similar situations.

Celebrating Life

An important element of the parents' attachment to and feelings about their child was that each had faced the very real possibility that the child would die. Each child, at some point, and usually not at the time of birth, had reached a state of critical medical condition. These times, when their children were critically ill and in ICUs, left the parents with indelible memories. Although the students did not specifically ask about these traumatic times, the parents provided detailed accounts of medical crises when they thought they would "lose" their child.

David's parents described his heart surgeries during his first 2 years. During the last heart surgery, he had a stroke and was in a coma for several days. Michael's genetic disorder is known to result in early death, and he has been critically ill a number of times. Carlie spent the first 2 months in the neonatal ICU "barely holding on to life." Jeremy had been a typically developing infant until an accident in which he was almost strangled by slipping through his highchair. He was very close to death in the 24 hours following the accident.

Parents seemed to respond to these experiences of critical illness or severe injury by vowing to be continually grateful for their child's survival and life. Several of the parents referred to their child as a gift who allowed them to appreciate life. About half of the parents continued to live with the knowledge that they may yet lose their child. However, rather than grieving, this knowledge seemed to make them to appreciate the time that they had with their child and the joys that he or she brought to the family. Michael's mother explained; "Michael has given us so much. His brothers and sisters love him. They've learned about what it's like to be different.... They've changed. My husband and I have changed ... because Michael has these issues, we enjoy every little thing he does."

The parents described ways that they had become more sensitive to and tolerant of individual differences. They seemed to appreciate life more, having almost lost a child and knowing how tenuous life is.

Becoming an Advocate

The families actively participated in advocacy for children with disabilities and had joined advocacy organizations or support groups. For example, Sean's mother belonged to two support groups, a transcutaneous peritoneal nutrition support group and a support group for children with genetic disorders.

Two other mothers worked part-time for advocacy groups. Mary, Jeremy's mother, worked part time for a state family advocacy agency. Her role was to maintain a Web site for families with children with disabilities. She also belonged to a parent organization that matched parents throughout the United States who had similar children and established long-distance communication. Michael's mother also worked a few hours a week for an advocacy group. "You know, I finally feel like I have a purpose. I'm on the family advisory council at the hospital."

Helitzer et al. (2002) suggested that mothers of children with disabilities assume roles that bridge the world of medical and educational professional with everyday home life. These support groups may replace some of the social activities that the parents have lost or cannot sustain. The personal satisfaction that they achieve through their advocacy occupations may fulfill their interests in leadership and professional interaction that they may have otherwise experienced in a career.

The findings of this study suggest that the identities of these parents revolved around their preschool children with chronic medical conditions. The parents felt competent in caring for their children, who had survived life-threatening trauma or illness. They had accessed a full range of services and had joined advocacy and support groups. Each family felt that sharing their stories and their experiences was important as they told their stories in detail to the students and opened their homes to the students for 6 months. Parents communicated that the child had a positive effect on family members who had become more sensitive to and accepting of disabilities. They also seemed to feel more appreciative of each other and of life itself.

Occupational Therapy Practice Implications

Practitioners can help families maintain a balance of family functions, by problem solving to find ways to enable children with severe disabilities to play and interact and suggesting efficient ways for parents to manage their daily caregiving routines. For example, recommending use of assistive technology, such as adapted switches or augmentative communication devices, can allow children with limited motor function to access toys that provide auditory and visual stimulation. Assistive technology is most helpful when it fits well into the families' values and style of communication and provides meaningful play to the child (Deitz & Swinth, 1997).

The medical and educational decisions these parents faced were difficult to make, and often the parents felt that they were without one clearly best choice. Sometimes these parents had to choose the least detrimental option among several potentially negative scenarios. Professionals can support parents in their decision making by providing them accurate, relevant information (King et al., 1999; Patterson et al., 1994) and supporting their decision once it has been made. Parents should be prepared and informed as much as possible when asked to prioritize intervention and treatment options. Once parents have made a decision, professionals should not only honor it, but embrace and implement the decision so that it can serve the best interests of the child and family. Parents in early intervention have expressed that they wished professionals were nonjudgmental and would think the best of the choices they made as parents (McWilliam, Tocci, & Harbin, 1998).

To help parents balance their caregiving responsibilities with social and recreational activities, practitioners can identify sources of respite that parents can use, acknowledging that competence in nursing and medical procedures would be necessary. Professionals can encourage parents to teach the child's care to extended family members. Extended family often want to help but do not know how. When they participate in the child's care, they gain a better understanding of the parents' experiences and can offer more emotional support.

Practitioners should encourage families to participate in recreational and social activities (Dunst et al., 1994). Practitioners can help by identifying community recreational facilities that are accessible and suggest methods to make outings successful. An occupational therapist's role is to listen and to provide parents with information on support and advocacy groups, including those on the Internet. They can also encourage families to establish identities in organizations and with social groups beyond those focused on disability (Dunst et al.; Turnbull & Turnbull, 1997).

Limitations

This sample of families was homogeneous across a number of dimensions, including race, socioeconomic status, and composition. The homogeneity allowed for in-depth exploration of their similar experiences and functions. The strong cohesion among family members may be unique to the participants who were studied and who volunteered to participate in a graduate student training project. All of the families had financial resources and medical insurance; the study's findings can not be generalized to families without these resources.

Recommendation for Future Research

Inclusion of a larger and more heterogeneous group of participants would increase the generalizability of the study's findings. Future qualitative research should explore family occupations when children have other types of disabilities, such as behavioral problems. The siblings' experiences should also be explored because the research literature investigating sibling experiences is minimal. The shifts in parents' roles and their methods of adapting to their children's caregiving needs should be further analyzed using quantitative research methods. Analysis of measures of coping strategies, social supports, perception of stress, and adaptability in parents with children with chronic conditions can produce predictive models of family adaptation and resiliency to further extend and validate the findings of this study.

CONCLUSIONS

These families had round-the-clock demands and responsibilities to care for children with significant chronic medical conditions and developmental disabilities. The parents had shifted their occupations from work outside the home and social activities to caregiving activities and frequent interaction with health care professionals. When children have chronic medical conditions, practitioners can help families balance the child's medical needs and developmental needs. They can also support families in balancing caregiving responsibilities with social and recreational activities. Resilient families, such as those who participated in this study, give us lessons to pass onto other families in similar circumstances.

ACKNOWLEDGMENTS

I appreciate the families' willingness to share their lives with The Ohio State University IMPACTS graduate students and faculty. I thank the IMPACTS students and families who allowed me to use the data from their experiences together. I also acknowledge the IMPACTS faculty for their assistance in collecting and interpreting the data. This study and the IMPACTS project were funded by a U.S. Office of Special Education and Rehabilitative Services personnel preparation grant, H325A010114.

REFERENCES

Andrews, M. M., & Nielson, D. W. (1988). Technology dependent children in the home. *Pediatric Nursing, 14,* 111–114.

Barnett, W. S., & Boyce, G. C. (1995). Effects of children with Down syndrome on parent's activities. *American Journal on Mental Retardation, 100,* 115–127.

Bristol, M. M., & Schopler, E. (1983). Stress and coping in families with autistic adolescents. In E. Schopler & G. B. Mesibov (Eds.), *Autism in adolescent and adults* (pp. 251–278). New York: Plenum.

Burke, S. O., Harrison, M. B., Kauffmann, & Wong, C. (2001). Effects of stress point intervention with families of repeatedly hospitalized children. *Journal of Family Nursing, 7*(2), 128–158.

Crowe, T. K. (1993). Time use of mothers with young children: The impact of a child's disability. *Developmental Medicine and Child Neurology, 35,* 621–630.

Crowe, T. K., VanLeit, B., Berghmans, K. K., & Mann, P. (1997). Role perceptions of mothers with young children: The impact of a child's disability. *American Journal of Occupational Therapy, 51,* 651–661.

Deitz, J. C., & Swinth, Y. (1997). Accessing play through assistive technology. In L. D. Parham & L. S. Fazio (Eds.), *Play in occupational therapy with children.* St. Louis, MO: Mosby.

Dunlap, W. R., & Hollinsworth, J. S. (1977). How does a handicapped child affect the family? Implications for practitioners. *The Family Coordinator, 26,* 286–293.

Dunst, C. J., Trivette, C. M., & Deal, A. G. (Eds.). (1994). *Supporting and strengthening families: Methods, strategies, and practices.* Cambridge, MA: Brookline.

Dyson, L. L. (1996). The experiences of families of children with learning disabilities: Parental stress, family functioning, and sibling self-concept. *Journal of Learning Disabilities, 29,* 280–286.

Gallimore, R., Coots, J., Weisner, T, Gamier, H., & Guthrie, D. (1996). Family responses to children with early developmental delays II: Accommodation intensity and activity in early and middle childhood. *American Journal on Mental Retardation, 101*, 215–232.

Gallimore, R., Weisner, T., Bernheimer, L., Guthrie, D., & Nihira, K. (1993). Family responses to young children with developmental delays. Accommodation activity in ecological and cultural context. *American Journal of Mental Retardation, 98*, 185–206.

Gallimore, R., Weisner, T., Kaufman, S., & Bernheimer, L. (1989). The social construction of ecological niches. Family accommodation of developmentally delayed children. *American Journal of Mental Retardation, 94*, 216–230.

Harris, V. S., & McHale, S. M. (1989). Family life problems, daily caretaking activities, and the psychological well-being of mothers and mentally retarded children. *American Journal on Mental Retardation, 94*, 231–239.

Helitzer, D. L., Cunningham-Sabo, L. D., VanLeit, B., & Crowe, T K. (2002). Perceived changes in self-image and coping strategies of mothers of children with disabilities. *Occupational Therapy Journal of Research, 22*, 25–33.

Humphry, R., & Case-Smith, J. (2001). Working with families. In J. Case-Smith (Ed), *Occupational therapy for children* (4th ed.). St. Louis, MO: Mosby.

Individuals With Disabilities Education Act Amendments of 1997. Pub. L. 105-117, 34 C.ER.

Innocenti, M. S., & Huh, K. (1992). Families of children with disabilities: Normative data and other considerations on parenting stress. *Topics in Early Childhood Special Education, 12*, 403–427.

Jennings, P. (1990). Caring for a child with a tracheostomy. *Nursing Standard, 4*(32), 38–40.

King, G. A., King, S. M., & Rosenbaum, P. L. (1996). How mothers and fathers view professional caregiving for children with disabilities. *Developmental Medicine and Child Neurology, 38*, 397–407.

Kirk, A. (1998). Families' experiences of caring at home for a technology-dependent child: A review of the literature. *Child Care, Health, and Development, 24*, 101–114.

Knafl, K., Breitmayer, B., Gallo, A., & Zoeller, L. (1996). Family response to childhood chronic illness: Description of management styles. *Journal of Pediatric Nursing: Nursing Care of Children and Families, 11*, 315–326.

McWilliam, R. A., Tocci, L., & Harbin, G. L. (1998). Family centered services: Service providers' discourse and behavior. *Topics in Early Childhood and Special Education, 18*, 206–221.

Murphy, K. E. (1997). Parenting a technology assisted infant: Coping with occupational stress. *Social Work in Health Care, 24*, 113–126.

Patterson, J., & Blum, R. W. (1996). Risk and resilience among children and youth with disabilities. *Archives of Pediatric and Adolescent Medicine, 150*, 692–698.

Patterson, J., Jernell, J., Leonard, B., & Titus, J. C. (1994). Caring for medically fragile children at home: The parent-professional relationship. *Journal of*

Pediatric Nursing, 9, 98–106.

Scorgie, K., Wilgosh, L., & McDonald, L. (1998). Stress and coping in families of children with disabilities: An examination of recent literature. *Developmental Disabilities Bulletin, 26*, 22–42.

Smith, T. B., Oliver, M. N., & Innocenti, M. S. (2001). Parenting stress in families of children with disabilities. *American Journal of Orthopsychiatry, 71*, 257–261.

Suelzle, M., & Keenan, V. (1981). Changes in family support networks over the life cycle of mentally retarded persons. *American Journal of Mental Deficiency, 86*, 267–274.

Tak, Y. R., & McCubbin, M. (2002). Family stress, perceived social support and coping following the diagnosis of a child's congenital heart disease. *Journal of Advanced Nursing, 39*, 190–198.

Tizard, J., & Grad, J. C. (1961). *The mentally handicapped and their families.* New York: Oxford University Press.

Turnbull, A. P., & Turnbull, H. R. (1997). *Families, professionals, and exceptionality: A special partnership* (2nd ed.). Columbus, OH: Merrill.

VanLeit, B., & Crowe, T. K. (2002). Outcomes of an occupational therapy program for mothers of children with disabilities: Impact on satisfaction with time use and occupational performance. *American Journal of Occupational Therapy, 56*, 402–410.

Weisner, T. S. (1993). Siblings in cultural place. Ethnographic and ecocultural perspectives. In Z. Stoneman & P. Berman (Eds.), *Siblings of individuals with mental retardation, physical disabilities, and chronic illness* (pp. 51–83). Baltimore: Brookes.

CHAPTER NINETEEN

In the Midst of a Hurricane

A Case Study of a Couple Living With AIDS

Lydia P. Buki, Lori Kogan, Bethanne Keen, and Patti Uman

That is the big thing I have learned from this illness. The time is *now*, if you have people that you love and care about, you take that time. You have to live each day like you have a lifetime, and each day like you have just a short period of time. It's *now*, it's *today*.

—*Rosalie*

There are an estimated 1 million people living with HIV infection in the United States (Kalichman, 2000). As a result of new drug technologies, the life expectancy of these individuals has increased steadily (Kalichman, 2000; Trainor & Ezer, 2000). The transition from living with the HIV virus to dealing with AIDS, and the resultant physical and mental deterioration, brings numerous changes in the patient's lifestyle. Partners, friends, spouses, and other family members often become the primary caregiver for the person with AIDS, sometimes providing in-home care for 10 years or more (Kalichman, 2000; Richards, Acree, & Folkman, 1999).

Research on nonprofessional caregivers has generally focused on parents or gay partners (Williams & Stafford, 1991). Heterosexual couples,

From "In the midst of a hurricane: A case study of a couple living with AIDS," by L. Buki, L. Kogan, B. Keen, and P. Uman, 2005, *Journal of Counseling & Development, 83,* 470–479. ACA. Reprinted with permission. No further reproduction authorized without written permission from the American Counseling Association.

however, represent a group with distinctive needs that are not always addressed in services oriented to gay couples. In a national survey of HIV-related mental health needs for persons with AIDS (PWAs), Lamping and Sachdev (1993) found several differences in the identified top concerns described by heterosexual and gay PWAs. Examples of top concerns reported by heterosexual PWAs, but not gay PWAs, include concerns about confidentiality; feelings of anger toward the health care system; and feelings of loneliness, isolation, and discrimination. Furthermore, compared with gay PWAs, heterosexual PWAs noted higher levels of distress associated with feeling rejected by others, problems accessing help, and telling others about their disease. Very little has been written specifically about heterosexual couples in which the partner is the primary caregiver for the PWA. The majority of case studies in the literature focus on the experiences of the PWA only (e.g., Gordon & Shontz, 1990), a limitation we sought to overcome in this study by interviewing not only a man with AIDS but also his wife, who was his full-time caregiver. This case study provides an illustration of this unique relationship and the special counseling needs that it creates.

Depending on the stage of their illness, PWAs experience varying levels of stress. One of the most prevalent of these stressors is coping with changes in their social support system (Somlai & Heckman, 2000). There is evidence that many PWAs, because of their illness, are rejected by at least one family member, are abandoned by friends due to fear or discrimination, and/or lose their lovers (Crystal & Jackson, 1989). Some of the people in the PWAs' support system might also have AIDS and may die before the PWA, further reducing their available support (Bloom, 1997). PWAs and their caregivers often lose valuable social support due to the social stigma surrounding HIV transmission (Kalichman, 2000; Tross & Hirsch, 1988). Friends and family may become fearful of associating with individuals who have a disease perceived to be related to at-risk behavior. In fact, gay patients in gay communities, although marginalized, are usually more informed and have greater social support than heterosexual individuals living in communities in which AIDS is not as prevalent (Turner, Pearlin, & Mullan, 1998).

An additional source of stress for PWAs is the cycle of sickness and health experienced with this illness (Kalichman, 2000). The cycle is often marked by periods of uncertainty, renewed hope, and readjustments (Trainor & Ezer, 2000). As time goes on, progressive loss of physical functioning creates an experience of multiple losses and an increasing need to ask for external help (Bloom, 1997; Holt, Houg, & Romano, 1999). The HIV replication process and adaptive qualities of the virus may require concurrent use of numerous medications to manage symptoms. In recent years, medications have become more effective, and medical management of the illness has improved. Nonetheless, PWAs may find medication adherence difficult if their regimens change too often or become more complex (Roberts & Mann, 2000). It is not unusual for PWAs to make changes in their daily routine to accommodate medication schedules and the side effects their medications cause (Trainor & Ezer, 2000). However, some PWAs do experience positive changes as a result of their illness. Many infected persons develop new coping skills, learn to live in the "here and now," and have more meaningful lives after the diagnosis (Vaughan & Kinnier, 1996). Their relationships have the potential to deepen as they come to rely on those in their support system to a greater extent and place more emphasis on the quality of their relationships (Trainor & Ezer, 2000).

As the illness advances, caregiving needs of PWAs become more involved and pose new challenges for caregivers (Kalichman, 2000). In a study of 642 caregivers in Los Angeles and San Francisco, Turner et al. (1998) found that higher levels of external support helped caregivers deal with daily stressors. However, in contrast with friends and other family members, partners and spouses were the least likely of all caregivers to receive informal assistance with daily activities. It is possible that visitors and friends may offer less help to partners and spouses, perhaps feeling it is that person's unique role to care for the patient. Likewise, caregivers who live with the PWA may perceive their activities as a duty and may find less gratification and meaning in those daily activities than caregivers who experience their work as nurturing and reciprocal (Ayres, 2000).

In addition to performing unremitting caregiving duties without external support, full-time caregivers may experience frequent conflict with the PWA in their life (Turner et al., 1998). Conflict often arises when the PWA and caregiver disagree over the handling of side effects from medication, the medication regimen to follow, or about how much autonomy to allow the PWA in certain situations. This conflict can be particularly distressing to a caregiver for whom the patient was an important source of support prior to the onset of the illness (Turner et al., 1998). The combination of minimal external support, reduced gratification, and conflict can put tremendous strain on the caregiving relationship (Kalichman, 2000; Turner et al., 1998).

PWAs and their caregivers must develop coping strategies in order to reduce stress. One such strategy often discussed in the literature is the solace offered by spiritual practices (Holt et al., 1999; Moneyham et al., 1997; Somlai & Heckman, 2000). The majority of PWAs engage in some sort of daily spiritual activity, usually in the form of prayer, meditation, or breathing exercises (Holt et al., 1999; Somlai & Heckman, 2000). Both PWAs and caregivers rely on their spirituality to provide emotional and cognitive resources during stressful times and to bring a sense of meaning to their lives (Ayres, 2000; Richards et al., 1999). Enhanced meaning can often bring a sense of hope, equilibrium, and resolution to daily challenges (Trainor & Ezer, 2000). Caregivers also find comfort in their spiritual beliefs during and after the death of their loved one, insofar as spirituality provides solace during the grieving process (Richards et al., 1999).

In this article, we present a case study based on the daily activities, challenges, coping strategies, and relationship dynamics of a heterosexual, HIV-serodiscordant (mixed HIV status) couple in which the male partner has AIDS and the female partner is his primary caregiver. Rather than looking for specific determinants of behavior, our goal was to gain a holistic understanding of what it meant to this couple to live with AIDS. Finally, we sought to identify specific counseling recommendations for individuals who work with HIV-serodiscordant couples.

METHOD

Participants

At the time of the interviews for this article, John was 42 years old and in the advanced stages of AIDS. Rosalie, who was not infected with HIV, was John's primary caregiver. He and Rosalie had been married for 22 years and had two children, a 19-year-old son and a 17-year-old daughter. John had begun to show physical signs of his illness approximately 4 years after his diagnosis, and when his physical condition deteriorated, Rosalie left her job to care for him. After this life change, Rosalie received some training and financial compensation for working as John's hospice caregiver. The couple was referred to us by a local psychotherapist who worked with AIDS patients and their families. We had no preexisting relationship with John and Rosalie prior to our assessment of their interest in participating in this study.

Design and Analysis

Using predetermined variables to test established hypotheses can some-times influence the outcome of the research and fail to uncover meaning-ful events (Coyle, 1998; Glachan, 1998; Polkinghorne, 1991). Although counseling psychology has tended to underutilize qualitative research, researchers are increasingly recognizing it as the preferred way of ob-taining in-depth knowledge and insights regarding the human experience (e.g., Coyle, 1998; Hill, Thompson, & Williams, 1997; Morrow & Smith, 2000; Polkinghorne, 1991, 1996). It may be said that we developed the study's methodology in collaboration with John and Rosalie, insofar as the couple not only requested that their real names be used in the study but agreed to be interviewed only with the condition that their stories be published to help others in similar circumstances. As described by many PWAs (e.g., Gordon & Shontz, 1990; Trainor & Ezer, 2000) and clearly stated by John and Rosalie, people have a need to tell their stories. We believed that the best way to communicate their stories was through a case study.

Case studies are used in the social sciences because of their power "to convey vividly the dimensions of a social phenomenon or individual life" (Reinharz, 1992, p. 174). Typically, a case study is conducted to present uniqueness; our choice to conduct a case study was based on the relatively limited attention focused on the experiences of HIV-serodiscordant, heterosexual couples. Three semistructured interviews were conducted with each participant over a period of 1 week, with each interview taking place on a different day of the week. We (i.e., the first and third authors) developed a tandem interview session in which John and Rosalie were interviewed at the same time in their home, but in different rooms. This procedure was preferred for a variety of reasons: (a) It allowed each of the participants freedom to express his or her own story; (b) it reduced the possibility of Rosalie answering questions for John, given that he had physical difficulty talking; (c) both respondents could feel that their stories were equally valued; and (d) perceptions of events could be presented from both points of view. Also, having two researchers interview both members of the couple, as opposed to John or Rosalie only, allowed for investigator triangulation of the data (Huberman & Miles, 1998). In other words, it allowed for the verification of data collected from both informants (i.e., by obtaining two perspectives on the phenomenon) as well as for the convergence between the two researchers regarding the interpretation of the data.

We each prepared an interview guide with questions to ask our assigned informant (i.e., John or Rosalie). We adopted a nondirective, nonevaluative Rogerian (Rogers, 1951) stance as recommended by Flick (1998) "to prevent the interviewer's frame of reference being imposed on the interviewee's viewpoints" (p. 77). We introduced structured questions as required to attain conversational depth and understanding of the impact or meaning of living with AIDS for the interviewees (see Flick, 1998). Because of our experience as crisis counselors, we felt comfortable eliciting sensitive material. This allowed the informants' accounts to go beyond general statements and delve into multiple levels of experience. Toward the end of each interview, we orally summarized key themes that had emerged during that meeting and invited feedback from our informant that would ensure an accurate understanding of his or her experience. Therefore, patterns began taking shape during the data collection process and, in turn, informed the questions we developed for our next interview (see Patton, 2002).

We developed both sets of interview questions based on the literature on living with AIDS and caregiving and a professional consultation with a nurse who had extensive experience with caregiving and end-of-life issues. The questions John's interviewer prepared for him inquired about his daily activities, such as "What do you do each day?" and "How do you organize your life?" We discovered early on, however, that following an interview guide was generally ineffective with John because the prepared questions seemed to miss the point of the story he wished to tell. For example, he was perplexed by the question "What is a typical day like for you?" He responded, "Do you mean what do I *do*? Well, the first thing is try to get in touch with my Higher Power." John's interviewer began to see that his life wasn't about *doing* anymore, it was about *being*—living with pain, meditating and praying, and feeling the loving presence of Rosalie. Consequently, John's interviewer adjusted the questions, with the goal of learning what was important to John in his life. Although the prepared questions did not address John's experience, the flexibility of the qualitative process allowed us to adjust the questions and thereby open the way for him to present a more relevant story.

Rosalie's interviewer also prepared questions to guide her interviews with Rosalie. The theme of inquiry centered on learning about a partner's diagnosis with HIV and caregiving. For example, questions included "How did you find out about the diagnosis, and how did you feel then?" "What keeps you going?" and "Has your ability to cope changed as the disease progressed?"

All interviews were audiotaped, taking about 1.5 hours each. Themes were extracted by reviewing the audiotapes systematically to answer the following research questions: "What aspects of the experience of AIDS are salient to the informant?" "How has the informant reacted to these experiences?" "What challenges were identified by the informant?" and "What is the meaning of the experiences to the informant?" These questions follow the structure proposed by Denzin (1989) to allow an understanding of the "existentially problematic moments in the lives of individuals" (p. 129). We first each analyzed the series of interviews we had conducted with our informant (i.e., either John or Rosalie) and, subsequently, weaved together the two analyses for the writing of this publication.

RESULTS

Four common themes emerged from John and Rosalie's narratives: the emotional impact of learning about the diagnosis, new roles and experiences in daily life, the need for social support, and the spiritual journey.

Emotional Impact of the Diagnosis

Six years prior to the interviews, and after 16 years of marriage, John and Rosalie had initiated a marital separation. They were separated for approximately 9 months, and during this time John contracted HIV. John learned of his diagnosis 8 months after he and Rosalie had reunited to rebuild their marriage. Rosalie was tested for the virus shortly after learning of John's diagnosis. At the culmination of the most terrifying 2 weeks of her life, she found out with great relief that she was not infected.

John told Rosalie about the diagnosis the same day he found out. Rosalie received a phone call at work, and John asked her to come home. He said he had something to tell her. Although Rosalie had no reason to suspect that he could be HIV positive, she explained that when she saw his face, she intuitively knew what he was going to tell her. John said, "I told my wife the very first day that I found out. She said she knew already, for some reason. She accepted me right off the bat.... She let me know that there's no difference, nothing's changed." Rosalie remembered how she felt when she heard about the diagnosis:

> How I see it is like a big puzzle that was kind of tossed in the air and all these puzzle pieces are now falling into place. The closer those pieces get down to the bottom, the more there is an understanding of what's happening.

Soon after receiving the diagnosis, John was forced to resign from his job, resulting in the loss of his health insurance coverage. For the first time in her life, Rosalie, who worked as a staff member in a home for children with developmental disabilities, became the primary breadwinner in the household. She recalls this period as a very difficult time in which the family was "scattered." Just beginning to learn how to deal with the intensity of her feelings, Rosalie often cried in the shower or on her way to work. In contrast, John experienced feelings so overwhelming that they led to several suicide attempts. Convinced that his illness would rob Rosalie of the best years of her life, John recalled,

> I wanted her to divorce me because she could never have a full life as long as I was alive. But she wouldn't see it, which caused a lot of grief in my heart. Just knowing that she could not live out her most fruitful years with her husband, or a husband, or—another way of looking at it—a dysfunctional husband, which I am. So, I guess she must have evaluated...what she thought was [highest] on her list, and keeping me on was the better decision. And it was, for me [also]. But it took me a long time, of hurt and guilt on my part, to overcome....I know if you do something wrong, you feel guilty. But this was years before, and I can't even single out what event occurred, you know. So I bear the brutality of it..., but not the guilt any longer.

The most significant change in the marriage was the shifting roles Rosalie and John experienced because of the illness. Prior to the illness, John had played the traditional role of head of the household. As John's illness progressed and Rosalie was forced to take on more responsibility in supporting the family, it was difficult for her to accept that John could not work anymore. She wondered, "Why couldn't he? He looked fine, didn't he?" In time, she developed a greater understanding of the fatigue that accompanies the experience of AIDS:

> You couldn't visually see how physically sick he was, so a lot of times our nature says, "Well, you are okay, you are all right. Why don't you get a little job?" or "Why don't you try to do things around the house? Why don't you do something? Don't just lay there." That was how my intellect was until I could really get an understanding of this disease. This is just a real physical sickness, that even if you didn't look sick, you really have this horrible, horrible tiredness in your body that just zonks you out, and just doing small things takes a lot of energy out of you.

Learning how to care for John was not easy. According to Rosalie, John was stubborn, and when he had trouble doing simple physical tasks such as lifting a glass, he refused help. Although she understood that he was still capable of making his own decisions, she often had to remember to respect her husband's right to think and act for himself:

> He won't want any help, unless he asks for it. And that is something I've become sensitive to. And I think that's really been the whole thing. Just really respecting John...respecting his wants and his needs....And also I find myself not only being his wife, but this person that helps him, his caregiver. [When it comes to his health,] it's not my decision. It's John's decision. And that's something that has really come to me in the last couple of months. It's not what I want. It's what John wants. Because I kind of think, what would I do for myself if I try to put myself in that position? But I'm not in that position, *John* is in that position, and I have to go by what he thinks.

Intimacy between John and Rosalie changed during the course of his illness. Although the relationship deepened and the bond between them strengthened, they floundered for a period of time, not knowing how to replace the sexual intimacy that had necessarily been stripped from their marriage. They learned together how to increase the intensity of the other kinds of love they had for each other. John explained,

> It's unfortunate that we have just one word for so many [kinds of love] because we get things twisted. The Greeks had four or five words for love....The loves that [I'm referring to] are fulfilling in a very

miraculous way. They seem to kick into gear in a greater way, to compensate, you know. But you have to cultivate them, too.

One of their favorite things to do together was to play a tape of meditative music and quietly hold each other.

John could not remember a time when Rosalie was not taking care of him in his illness. Even before she was being paid as a hospice nurse, she was always there for him. At the time of the interview, when she was not administering to his physical needs, she was often tending to his emotional and spiritual needs. Rosalie noted, "In a situation like this you can really lose yourself in the other person and their needs, but I'm going to be here and I'm going to stay here."

John expressed that what he wanted most for Rosalie's future was happiness, and he did not want her to grieve for him. "Maybe she'll be lucky enough to find the man of her dreams," he said, "and get remarried." When the interviewer asked if it was hard for him to imagine her being with another man, John responded, "No, it's been hard with me sick, and her being alone."

Rosalie and John's experience with his illness did not occur in isolation. Their two teenage children, a daughter and a son, were also deeply affected by news of John's diagnosis. When Rosalie tested negative for HIV she was relieved, but her first thought was for her children. She said,

> There was also the problem of, okay, was *I* HIV positive? And we had to go through that turmoil for a while. But I'm not HIV positive, you know. So that was the hardest thing for me. Because I knew the kids were eventually going to lose their father, and I didn't want to do it to them too. I didn't want to be HIV positive and have the children lose me too.

Rosalie soon realized she would be the surviving parent of their two children. She noted that it was a rough transition for the family. At first the kids believed John would die right away. After several years passed and they saw him recover from a number of crises, they started to take his illness more in stride. Life became a little more normal for them, and their friends often came by to visit. As John became more ill, however, the children began to realize that he would not be with them much longer. One night their son broke down. Rosalie and John helped him begin the grieving process, offering him comfort as he realized the painful reality that his father would soon die. As a family, they confronted these challenging times successfully, and Rosalie felt that the family was finally able to come together because they could no longer deny that the illness was taking John's life. "We've kind of come to this place, John and I, of being in harmony with each other and in harmony with our family and with our children. Just real bonding between us."

Daily Life: New Roles, New Experiences

Upon entering John and Rosalie's home, one would not have guessed all of the challenges they had experienced in the past 5 years. Their home was in a modest neighborhood and was warm and cozy. Furnished in soft colors, it seemed very lovingly cared for. In the living room, the sofa was covered with a lovely spread made up of fabrics with various designs, and pictures were displayed in frames of various types and sizes. Some of the children's friends were often visiting when the interviewers arrived, and the home was filled with a sense of life and anticipation. Few would have realized that this home was officially John's hospice during his illness.

At the time of the interviews, John was a small man, emaciated and fragile. He walked in a slow, teetering manner, as if in pain from slow starvation. Although his hair was thinning, it was long and woven into a pencil-thin braid at the back of his neck. He and his interviewer spoke in a small room that appeared to have been furnished for his comfort during the illness. It included a hospital bed, a leather recliner, a small television, and a set of bookshelves. The shelves held books on a wide variety of top-ics, including psychological, literary, scientific, inspirational, and medical titles. This room also housed a multitude of reminders that John's life was medically bound: numerous prescription bottles occupying various places in the room, many pills in different shapes and sizes; menacing-looking machines near the bed with lights, knobs, and hoses; and a volume of the *Physician's Desk Reference.*

Although Rosalie was his primary caretaker, a nurse visited John in their home twice a week to take vital signs and check on his general health. John explained, "I have flare-ups about twice a year. Each time I have a flare-up, it takes 3 or 4 months to recover. So you might say that I'm always recovering and on the brink of [being] sick." Together, John and his doctor had endlessly adjusted, and gradually whittled down, his assortment of prescription drugs. John could not remember exactly all of the pills he was taking. He admitted that, over time, he had come to devalue knowledge of what drugs his doctor had prescribed to him because the list was so long and had changed so frequently.

As his pain increased, John began taking morphine. Initially he had not wanted to use morphine because he considered it to be a dangerous drug and was concerned that it would affect the functioning of his mind. By the 5th year of his illness, however, the pain in his bones and joints had become so intense, especially upon awakening in the morning, that he needed the morphine "just to take the edge off." Other daily challenges included the effort it took to balance when standing or walking, because the bottoms of his feet were often numb, and watching his gums shrink and his teeth deteriorate.

John's wife Rosalie was a very gentle and kind woman with beautiful sparkling eyes. Pleasant and smiling, she had a lively enthusiasm in her voice. Although to the casual observer everything might have seemed fairly normal, Rosalie shared with the interviewer her feeling that much of her life was "up in the air":

> When everything is over, I think I will be able to really sum up a lot of the feelings that I have inside that I find hard to express or I don't have the words for. When everything is over, I think I'll probably have a lot of things inside of me. Isn't that what happens? Like when you are in the midst of a hurricane it's real hard to kind of...figure out everything. But once you are out of it, you can kind of go, "Hey, yeah, I was in the middle of that hurricane, and this is what happened." So it's just real hard for me to kind of sum up...or really express, a lot of the things I have inside of me. And...and I keep saying that will happen once everything is over.

Knowing that even small tasks exhausted John, Rosalie spent a great part of her day administering to his physical needs. She helped him eat, take his medicine, and communicate (often by telephone) with doctors, friends, and family.

John explained that he mostly read, slept, watched television, and spent time with Rosalie. He hadn't felt hungry lately but tried to heed the doctor's advice about drinking lots of fluids. He also tended to family matters around the home. However, when speaking to John, it was clear that his life was not about *doing* anymore; it was about *being*. On particularly difficult days, when he felt drained, in severe pain, and had trouble staying awake due to the morphine, he would search for the Higher Power within himself. He would meditate and recall the many good things that had happened in his life, and he would pray for help in weathering the storm.

The Need for Social Support

As do many PWAs, John experienced a decline in social relationships as his illness progressed. He explained that maintaining contact with people was important to him, but even though a number of good friends stayed in touch, others had stopped visiting or making contact. He wondered if it had something to do with his physical appearance. John recognized that he had "that look" that publicly identified him as an AIDS patient: sunken eyes, an emaciated frame, an unbalanced walk. At the time of the interviews, he weighed 94 pounds. When he had first seen that number on his scale a few months earlier, he could not believe it. When he received what he called "the news" about his illness 5 years before, he had weighed about 145 pounds. Having lost in excess of 50 pounds from his 5'7" frame, more than one third of his total body weight, it was not surprising that he said he felt astonished when he saw himself in the mirror. He commented that he did not see a reflection of himself, but rather the face and body of a concentration camp victim.

Rosalie also experienced social support difficulties, often feeling judged by others. In particular, she did not like being questioned about how John had contracted HIV. When people asked "How did he get it?" she would reply, "Who cares how he got it?! He is HIV positive and that is all that matters." There was friction, too, with visitors who did not know John very well. For example, John often struggled with simple tasks like walking or lifting a glass. Others would look at Rosalie as if to say, "Do something!" when in fact Rosalie was caring for John by allowing him the independence he desired. She respected his need for autonomy and his ability to make decisions about what he could or could not do.

Despite these difficulties, John and Rosalie strove to remain as socially active as possible. John and his pastor worked together to create a coffeehouse, a place where AIDS patients could gather 1 day a week, enjoy free coffee and food, and socialize with one another. Close to the time of the interviews, John and Rosalie went to the coffeehouse, speculating that it might be his last visit. The realities of his illness and of his anticipated death were emphasized by the absence of those who had once been companions in weathering the storm but now had reached the final calm after the hurricane.

> We did drop in last Thursday, just at the right time. We stayed for a half hour and saw that, of everybody that was there when we started the program, we had three still alive. Almost everybody I knew was dead. It kind of makes you feel like a survivor. However, you are bonding with people who die, and it happens over and over again. Pretty soon, you'd just like to sidestep the AIDS people. But I can't do that, because by facing them now, I'm facing my own situation.

John admitted his desire to "sidestep the AIDS people" in an effort to flee from the face of death, yet he knew that confronting such fear was necessary for him to reach acceptance and inner peace.

The Spiritual Journey

John's spiritual journey consisted of coming to terms with his own mortality and coping with his illness. When asked how he got through the difficult days, John said he was always searching for the Higher Power within himself by practicing meditation and prayer. He explained, "I have to look at this as a spiritual adventure, for my own sanity. Because if I didn't, it would be morbid." During meditation, he tried to recall the many good things that had happened in his life. Meditating, in turn, brought him to a place where he could "place a face" on his spirituality and his Higher Power. He explained that he no longer prayed for a healing or cure as he first did. Instead, he prayed for help in "weathering the storm." Comparing himself with Paul the Apostle, John attained some peace of mind "in God's words to Paul, 'My grace is sufficient unto you.'" Just as Paul had prayed three times that his thorn be removed from the flesh, John also felt, "I've been told [for] the third time these last few years [that healing would not come]. Now I am set, accepted and relaxed." Actually, John considered himself lucky, in a way. "You don't know when you are going to die," he said to the interviewer, "but I have a far clearer idea."

Rosalie also drew strength from spirituality as she cared for John and prepared herself for life after John's death. Rosalie explained that God helped her survive all the changes she had endured. She took comfort "in the scripture that assures 'all works out for those who love God and act according to His purpose.'" She believed she had been called on by God to care for John, and therefore she knew that everything would work out for good. Several times each day, Rosalie set aside a few minutes for herself to read, meditate, or listen to inspirational music. Her goal was to quiet herself, listen to what was inside her, and to get in touch with her present experience. Rosalie explained,

> That is the big thing I have learned from this illness. The time is *now*, if you have people that you love and care about, you take that time. You have to live each day like you have a lifetime, and each day like you have just a short period of time. It's *now*, it's *today*.

In her own words, Rosalie experienced "a profound realization" when she understood that her relationship with John was not really ending with his death. She believed that the illness was taking John's life, "but [it isn't] taking John, just his body. This is a short time in a real existence."

DISCUSSION

The relationship between John and Rosalie was a dominant theme in both of their interviews. The couple was just in the midst of reestablishing their relationship after a short time apart and had to bear the weight of John's diagnosis. As discovered by Brown and Stetz (1999), decisions about caregiving are strongly dependent on the relationship status prior to an AIDS diagnosis, and although the diagnosis may initially overshadow preexisting relationship difficulties, these difficulties resurface over time. These preexisting difficulties are then compounded by the role changes that often mark PWAs' relationships (Williams & Stafford, 1991). Rosalie alluded to some of the challenges they encountered when she discussed John's stubbornness and her initial resistance to letting him struggle, for example, as he picked up and drank from a glass. Yet her strong commitment to John and to their relationship eventually led her to understand John's need to do what he could for himself, and subsequently she remained respectful of his choice, despite the effort it took for her to adopt this observer role. In addition to role changes, couples often struggle with alternative ways to demonstrate intimacy and affection when sexual contact is no longer possible (Williams & Stafford, 1991). As the couple dealt with the dilemma of wanting to be sexual but not being able to do so (except at great risk of infecting Rosalie with HIV, a chance they were not willing to take), they turned to alternatives and reframed the meaning of love, broadening its definition to fit their new reality.

As partners struggle to adapt to their new roles when a partner is diagnosed with AIDS, children of parents with AIDS likewise experience turmoil and are at a high risk for psychological difficulties (Williams & Stafford, 1991). It is therefore important for parents to remain committed to their parenting roles and help their children understand the illness and initiate the grieving process. John and Rosalie, despite their own difficulties with adjusting to AIDS, remained committed to meeting their children's needs and continued to be a source of strength and learning for them. Their parenting role appeared to remain stable in the midst of many other role changes.

John, like many PWAs, struggled to redefine himself after learning about his illness. No longer able to contribute to society and his family in traditionally accepted ways (e.g., through work and by providing financial support), he fought strong feelings of inadequacy. Because of the necessary changes in the couple's sexual expression, John reported feeling like a "dysfunctional" husband, a negative self-assessment that culminated in several suicide attempts. This is consistent with previous research, which has suggested that PWAs have elevated rates of depressive disorders and are especially vulnerable to feelings of despair and guilt (Pakenham & Rinaldis, 2001). In time, however, John was able to focus his cognitions on positive aspects of his life, to avoid dwelling on the negative, and to take control whenever possible (e.g., making decisions about medication in conjunction with his doctor). Consistent with previous research indicating that PWAs' cognitive appraisal of their situation is an important predictor of coping success (Pakenham & Rinaldis, 2001), John experienced an improvement in his quality of life and relationships after he changed the negative way in which he was appraising his situation. In redefining himself and reprioritizing what was important, day-to-day living became John's focus and educating himself about pills or other such tasks became unimportant. Although this could be interpreted as learned helplessness, we believe that John would have seen it as reflective of a shift in priorities.

Similarly, many overwhelming feelings (e.g., anger, guilt, sadness) often accompany the initial news of a partner's diagnosis. Because these feelings are often seen as "inappropriate," caregivers may not feel comfortable expressing them to other people or even to themselves (Williams & Stafford, 1991). This was true of Rosalie, who cried in the shower as a way to grieve privately, even secretly, particularly upon finding out that John was infected with HIV and she was not. The presence of children added complexity to Rosalie's emotional reaction given her initial fear that she might also die, leaving the children alone.

Rosalie also contended with the reality of becoming the sole family provider for the first time in 22 years of marriage. Many caregivers report developing new confidence, gaining additional competencies, taking better care of themselves, and becoming advocates for others in similar situations as they assume new responsibilities (Brown & Stetz, 1999; Viney, Allwood, Stillson, & Walmsley, 1992). The role changes that Rosalie was forced to make, however, illustrate both positive and negative aspects of this type of challenge. Within a short period of time, she was forced to perform new roles for which she was ill-prepared (i.e., primary breadwinner, full-time hospice caregiver), requiring her to gain many new skills and make radical changes in her daily life. On the other hand, this shift in responsibilities helped her to gain the confidence that she would be able to take care of her family after John's death, allowed her to strengthen her spiritual beliefs, and prompted her to learn to take better care of herself. Perhaps what was most significant, Rosalie believed that she had learned what was important to her in life, suggesting that she underwent a kind of values clarification process that would have a positive impact on her psychological well-being for the foreseeable future.

Facing the reality of an AIDS diagnosis demands significant adjustment (Brown & Stetz, 1999), although initial physical changes are often unnoticed by people outside the home. Even though a lack of outwardly apparent illness can help couples maintain a sense of normalcy, it also creates difficulties (Trainor & Ezer, 2000). As did Rosalie, some people may struggle to understand why an outwardly healthy PWA cannot work or assume other responsibilities. Through educational experiences, however, she came to understand that although many physical symptoms (e.g., tiredness) were not apparent, they impaired John's ability to perform mundane tasks. Also, in the developmental adaptation process, PWAs and their caregivers come to understand that AIDS does not progress as a gradual decline of physical health but is an illness marked by a succession of ups and downs. Until fairly recently, people diagnosed with AIDS prepared to die within a relatively short period of time. With the advances in medical care, however, PWAs are living longer, thereby dealing with an unavoidable cycle of opportunistic infections (Trainor & Ezer, 2000). This cycle has been described as a descending staircase with a series of increasingly lower landings (Brown & Stetz, 1999), a situation that forces PWAs and their partners to face death several times throughout the course of the disease. John's physical flare-ups illustrate this phenomenon. The downward cycle with small plateaus of stability presents unique challenges, yet it can also help people develop new adaptive habits and coping skills. During these times, John and Rosalie learned how to talk about John's illness and, at the same time, how to talk about the future. The couple's house, a combination of living and death artifacts, was symbolic of these two diametrically opposed realities existing under one roof.

A caregiver's contact with family and friends usually decreases as the illness progresses, even as the need for support increases (Turner et al., 1998; Williams & Stafford, 1991). John and Rosalie both reported that contact with people outside the family had slowly decreased over the course of his illness. Despite these changes in the support system, John and Rosalie used some common coping strategies to reduce their social isolation. For example, they discussed the importance of talking about and sharing their perspectives with other people struggling to live with AIDS. Created by John and his pastor, the coffeehouse that the couple frequented was a place where PWAs could gather and socialize. This type of gathering may have also been a vehicle for other therapeutic elements more traditionally associated with support groups or group therapy (e.g., Yalom, 1995). For instance, John's discussion about feeling like a "survivor" when most of the initial members of the coffeehouse had died was possibly a reflection of downward comparison, in which people compare themselves to others who are in a worse state. This cognitive strategy has been suggested as one way in which people can feel more positive about their own standing (Lazarus & Folkman, 1984; Trainor & Ezer, 2000). Moreover, being with others who struggle with parallel issues can contribute to a feeling of not being alone (i.e., universality of experience). As John explained, there are both positive and negative aspects to connecting with other PWAs. Although it is important for PWAs to feel understood and connected to others undergoing similar experiences, it is painful to experience losses when these companions die. Facing these losses, as well as many other concurrent losses experienced by the couple (e.g., changing roles, physical deterioration, erosion of social support system), made John's and Rosalie's grieving process more complex.

Many PWAs and their caregivers draw strength from their spiritual beliefs (Koenig & Larson, 2001; Somlai & Heckman, 2000). Religion can help people derive meaning from their experiences as they attempt to come to terms with their own mortality. This coping strategy is clearly depicted in John's discussion of the relationship with his Higher Power and in Rosalie's meaningful and comforting spiritual breakthrough that her relationship with John will continue after his death. Their shift in priorities, by which the depth of their feelings toward each other assumed the greatest position and other more mundane issues (i.e., material possessions) shifted to the background, was viewed by both as a positive spiritual change.

Contributions and Limitations of the Study

As traditional avenues of contributing to society are curtailed, PWAs and their caregivers often feel the desire to comfort and counsel others who are experiencing similar situations as one way to find meaning in their own pain (Brown & Stetz, 1999; Gordon & Shontz, 1990). The couple felt these sentiments strongly as expressed by John, "I would very much like to make a contribution to the world's knowledge about what it is like to live with AIDS, and see publication of this report as an opportunity to do this."

Every person's experience of living with AIDS is unique. As human beings, all of us handle challenging situations differently, drawing from our past experiences, our personality characteristics, our current relationships, and various environmental contexts in which our lives are embedded. Moreover, we may heed social desirability to different degrees. Therefore, John and Rosalie's subjective experiences will not be representative of the subjective experiences of all other HIV-serodiscordant, heterosexual couples. In particular, our findings may not reflect the experiences of couples who are willing to discuss the mode of HIV transmission. John alluded to having a very vague sense of how he became infected, and Rosalie felt strongly that this information was irrelevant. Therefore, we cannot ascertain the impact of the mode of transmission on their adaptation to living with AIDS. Their stories, however, have given us a glimpse into distinct themes as perceived by a couple going through a unique life changing experience. There is much we can learn from what John and Rosalie have told us, as was suggested by their intention to share their story so that others may profit from it.

WORKING WITH PWAs AND THEIR CAREGIVERS: OUR PERSONAL REFLECTIONS

Witnessing our informants' experiences and documenting their journeys had a profound effect on us, the interviewers, as well. Our assumptions about the grieving process and about living with a chronic and often fatal disease were challenged. We marveled at the strength of the human spirit, particularly the affirming way in which Rosalie and John learned to live within the context of the disease. To observe their zest for life in the middle of death was very moving.

As investigators and observers, we helped create their reality, and we were changed by it in the process. Although this type of empathy is a common element of the counseling process, it was compounded in this situation because of the particularly intimate views and complete honesty offered by both Rosalie and John. We were honored to be a part of the process by which they would leave a legacy, and we could not avoid examining our own spiritual beliefs, our comfort levels in dealing with life and death, and our own life priorities during various stages of this project. By acknowledging and honoring our emotional reactions, we gained better insight into the factors that arise for counselors working with PWAs and with their caregivers.

RECOMMENDATIONS FOR COUNSELORS WORKING WITH PWAs AND THEIR CAREGIVERS

As counselors, we help PWAs and their caregivers weather the winds of the hurricane. We help PWAs reconstruct the self and reprioritize their lives to improve their quality of life. We aid caregivers during both the caregiving and the grieving processes. We provide the communities of PWAs with the education and support needed to embrace families living with AIDS, thus helping communities to enhance the quality of life of PWAs and their families. Several recommendations for counselors working with PWAs and with their caregivers emerged from our interactions with John and Rosalie and our experience with the research process. These recommendations address the needs of PWAs, their caregivers, their families, and their communities.

1. Consider the benefit of including the entire family in the therapy process. Members of a PWA's family have specific needs that will vary according to their own personality traits, ways of coping and grieving, and the intensity of their relationship with the PWA.

2. Because of the uncertainty brought about by the nature of the disease, be cautious when setting therapeutic goals with PWAs and their caregivers. Goals should be crafted through a cooperative effort with the couple, carefully choosing time frames within which the couple can be comfortable.

3. Assist couples in renegotiating roles within the marriage, especially if new roles challenge that couple's gender and/or cultural norms. For couples with children, it is important to retain the parenting role as a critical collaborative task.

4. Remain aware of where people are in the stages of the disease and help them explore how much information and responsibility they can handle (or desire) in terms of making decisions about their medical status and other personal issues.

5. Bear in mind the inherent risk involved when couples living with AIDS tell others about their disease. Discuss with clients their expectations of disclosure as well as ways to address possible negative reactions from others.

6. Recognize that partners of PWAs may need some period of time to adjust to the diagnosis. They may benefit from normalizing the amount of time they need to accept news of this nature and should not be forced to make any immediate decisions that would affect either themselves or others.

7. Support caregivers in their efforts to care for themselves. Although caregivers for people with short-term illnesses can sometimes delay taking time for themselves until after a patient's death, this is not practical for caregivers of PWAs. Because of the cyclic and prolonged nature of the illness, caregivers should be encouraged to discover and maintain self-care habits early on in the adaptation process.

8. Provide additional guidance and support as caregivers' responsibilities shift from caring for a chronically ill partner to supporting a partner as he or she dies.

9. Recognize that most PWAs and their caregivers desire the opportunity to talk about their feelings, either one-on-one or in a group setting. Assist them in finding avenues for expression, such as creating a "coffeehouse" setting or through writing, painting, or other creative outlets.

10. Help couples learn how to express intimacy in new ways, when sexual intimacy is no longer possible.

Living with AIDS is an unremitting challenge for PWAs and their caretakers, but as John and Rosalie so eloquently demonstrated, it does not have to be a dark, lonely journey. It can, in fact, be a transcendental one, allowing for a tremendously enriching spiritual experience. John and Rosalie exemplify the unlimited potential of the human spirit in the face of adversity. As counselors, it is our responsibility to help PWAs, their caregivers, and families tap their inner resources and gain strength from their unique histories and interpersonal relationships. Let us use the growing knowledge and research in this area to help PWAs and their caretakers realize this potential.

REFERENCES

Ayres, L. (2000). Narratives of family caregiving: The process of making meaning. *Research in Nursing and Health, 23*, 424–434.

Bloom, F. R. (1997). Searching for meaning in everyday life: Gay men negotiating selves in the HIV spectrum. *Ethos, 25*, 454–479.

Brown, M., & Stetz, K. (1999). The labor of caregiving: A theoretical model of caregiving during potentially fatal illness. *Qualitative Health Research, 9*, 182–197.

Coyle, A. (1998). Qualitative research in counseling psychology: Using the counseling interview as a research instrument. In P. Clarkson (Ed.), *Counseling psychology: Integrating theory, research and supervised practice* (pp. 57–73). London: Routledge.

Crystal, S., & Jackson, M. (1989). Psychosocial adaptation and economic circumstances of persons with AIDS and ARC. *Family and Community Health, 12*, 77–88.

Denzin, N. K. (1989). *Interpretive interactionism.* Newbury Park, CA: Sage.

Flick, U. (1998). *An introduction to qualitative research.* London: Sage.

Glachan, M. (1998). Balancing the qualitative and the quantitative in counseling psychology research. In P. Clarkson (Ed.), *Counseling psychology: Integrating theory, research and supervised practice* (pp. 182–188). London: Routledge.

Gordon, J., & Shontz, F. C. (1990). Living with theAIDS virus: A representative case. *Journal of Counseling & Development, 68*, 287–292.

Hill, C. E., Thompson, B. J., & Williams, E. N. (1997). A guide to conducting consensual qualitative research. *The Counseling Psychologist, 25*, 517–572.

Holt, J. L., Houg, B. L., & Romano, J. L. (1999). Spiritual wellness for clients with HIV/AIDS: Review of counseling issues. *Journal of Counseling & Development, 77*, 160–170.

Huberman, A. M., & Miles, M. B. (1998). Data management and analysis methods. In N. K. Denzin & Y. S. Lincoln (Eds.), *Collecting and interpreting qualitative materials* (pp. 179–210). Thousand Oaks, CA: Sage.

Kalichman, S. C. (2000). Couples with HIV/AIDS. In K. B. Schmaling & T. G. Sher (Eds.), *The psychology of couples and illness: Theory, research, and practice* (pp. 171–189). Washington, DC: American Psychological Association.

Koenig, H. G., & Larson, D. B. (2001). Religion and mental health: Evidence for an association. *International Review of Psychiatry, 13*, 67–78.

Lamping, D. L., & Sachdev, I. (1993). Psychological needs and services for heterosexuals with HIV infection. In L. Sherr (Ed.), *AIDS and the heterosexual population* (pp. 199–221). London: Harwood Academic Publishers.

Lazarus, R. S., & Folkman, S. (1984). *Stress, appraisal, and coping.* New York: Springer.

Moneyham, L., Demi, A., Mizuno, Y., Sowell, R., Seals, B., & Guillory, J. (1997). Development and testing of a contextually and culturally relevant measure of coping for use with women infected with HIV. *Omega, 36*, 359–374.

Morrow, S. L., & Smith, M. L. (2000). Qualitative research for counseling psychology. In S. D. Brown & R. W. Lent (Eds.), *Handbook of counseling psychology* (3rd ed., pp. 199–230). New York: Wiley.

Pakenham, K. I., & Rinaldis, M. (2001). The role of illness, resources, appraisal, and coping strategies in adjustment to HIV/AIDS: The direct and buffering effects. *Journal of Behavioral Medicine, 24*, 259–279.

Patton, M. Q. (2002). *Qualitative research and evaluation methods* (3rd ed.). Thousand Oaks, CA: Sage.

Polkinghorne, D. E. (1991). Qualitative procedures for counseling research. In C. E. Watkins, Jr., & L. J. Schneider (Eds.), *Research in counseling* (pp. 163–204). Hillsdale, NJ: Erlbaum.

Polkinghorne, D. E. (1996). Narrative knowing and the study of lives. In J. E. Birren, G. M. Kenyon, J.-E. Ruth, J. J. F. Schroots, & T. Svensson (Eds.), *Aging and biography: Explorations in adult development* (pp. 77–99). New York: Springer.

Reinharz, S. (1992). *Feminist methods in social research.* New York: Oxford University Press.

Richards, T., Acree, M., & Folkman, S. (1999). Spiritual aspects of loss among partners of men with AIDS: Post-bereavement follow-up. *Death Studies, 23*, 105–127.

Roberts, K. J., & Mann, T. (2000). Barriers to antiretroviral medication adherence in HIV infected women. *AIDS Care, 12*, 377–386.

Rogers, C. R. (1951). *Client-centered therapy.* Boston: Houghton Mifflin.

Somlai, A. M., & Heckman, T. G. (2000). Correlates of spirituality and well-being in a community sample of people living with HIV disease. *Mental Health, Religion, and Culture, 3*, 57–70.

Trainor, A., & Ezer, H. (2000). Rebuilding life: The experience of living with AIDS after facing imminent death. *Qualitative Health Research, 10*, 646–660.

Tross, S., & Hirsch, D. A. (1988). Psychological distress and neuropsychological complications of HIV infection and AIDS. *American Psychologist, 43*, 929–934.

Turner, H. A., Pearlin, L. I., & Mullan, J. T. (1998). Sources and determinants of social support for caregivers of persons with AIDS. *Journal of Health and Social Behavior, 39*, 137–151.

Vaughan, S. M., & Kinnier, R. T. (1996). Psychological effects of a life review intervention for persons with HIV disease. *Journal of Counseling & Development, 75*, 115–123.

Viney, L. L., Allwood, K., Stillson, L., & Walmsley, R. (1992). Caring for the carers: A note on counseling for the wider impact of AIDS. *Journal of Counseling & Development, 70*, 442–444.

Williams, R. J., & Stafford, W. B. (1991). Silent casualties: Partners, families, and spouses of persons with AIDS. *Journal of Counseling & Development, 69*, 423–427.

Yalom, I. D. (1995). *The theory and practice of group psychotherapy* (4th ed.). New York: Basic Books.

CHAPTER TWENTY

Parental Illness, Family Functioning, and Adolescent Well-Being

A Family Ecology Framework to Guide Research[1]

Sara Pedersen and Tracey A. Revenson

Parental illness is a stressful experience for young people, constituting a potential threat to physical and mental health and normative development. Although it is difficult to obtain statistics, available data suggest that a substantial number of young people, approximately 13–14% of adolescents, experience serious parental illness (Centers for Disease Control and Prevention, 2001; Masten, Neeman, & Andenas, 1994). Still, research literature examining the effects of parental illness on the child's development and well-being remains underdeveloped in contrast to the substantial literatures on families adjusting to a child's illness (see, e.g., Barakat & Kazak, 1999) and on the relation of stressful life events to child and adolescent pathology (see review by Grant et al., 2003).

From "Parental illness, family functioning, and adolescent well being: A family ecology framework to guide research," by S. Pederson and T. A. Revenson, 2005, *American Psychological Association, 19*(3), 404–409. Copyright by the American Psychological Association. Reprinted with permission.

[1] We thank Diane L. Hughes, Anne E. Kazak, and Edward Seidman for their helpful feedback on previous versions of this article.

Living with a physically ill parent may be especially challenging for adolescents. An adolescent's greater cognitive development enables an understanding of the implications of the illness for oneself and one's family, which may result in greater psychological distress than would be experienced by a younger child. Further, an adolescent's ability to take on additional family responsibilities or roles during parental illness may compromise the normative development of social ties and competencies outside the home. Despite this heightened risk, there are few studies of adolescents' adaptation to serious parental illness.

One explanation for this gap may be the absence of a comprehensive theoretical framework to guide research. This article proposes such a framework, as well as a research agenda based on that framework.

We offer a *family ecology framework* that illustrates the interrelationships among parental illness characteristics, family functioning, and adolescent well-being. To provide a foundation for this framework, we reviewed the existing research literature in developmental, clinical, and community psychology, as well as in family medicine. Because of the dearth of studies on families coping with parental illness, we also turned to theoretical, clinical, and empirical work on families with ill children, particularly research that is grounded in family systems and developmental perspectives. In particular, Kazak's (1989) family systems model of family adaptation in the context of childhood illness guided our thinking (see also Kazak, Simms, & Rourke, 2002). Using the family ecology framework, we describe a set of mediating and moderating pathways through which serious parental illness affects adolescent well-being and family functioning, reviewing the available evidence for each pathway. In the final section, we present guidelines to direct future research on parental illness in adolescence that is consistent with the family ecology framework.

The experiences of childhood and parental illness have many similarities but are not identical: There are critical differences in the coping tasks, role redistribution, and long-term sequelae for families coping with parental versus childhood illness. Thus, we do not review the literature on families coping with a child's illness, although we acknowledge the conceptual contribution that research on families who are coping with a child's illness has made to researchers' thinking about the effects of parental illness on adolescent well-being and family functioning.

FAMILY ECOLOGY FRAMEWORK

The proposed family ecology framework finds its underpinnings in general systems theory (e.g., von Bertalanffy, 1968) as well as human ecology (e.g., Bronfenbrenner, 1977). Four basic principles underlie the framework:

(a) Individual behavior can only be understood within its social context; (b) Individuals exist within a number of interdependent systems or contexts; (c) The *reciprocal* relationships between individuals and the social systems with which they interact are essential for understanding development and adaptation; and (d) Variables beyond the level of individual attributes (i.e., social and cultural variables), particularly those that specify the relations between individuals and systems, must be included in order to understand adaptational processes (Revenson, 1990). The framework is loosely based on stress and coping theories (e.g., Lazarus, 1999; Scheier & Carver, 2003) but does not adhere to them strictly. That is, the concepts of stress, cognitive appraisal, and coping are invoked, but because the framework involves the interplay of the adolescents' and other family members' appraisals and reactions to the illness, it goes beyond the traditional individual-level stress and coping approach (see also Degotardi, Revenson, & Ilowite, 1999; Revenson, 1994, 2003).

The specific pathways by which parental illness is expected to affect adolescent well-being and family functioning are depicted in Figure 1. In general, characteristics of the parent's illness, such as type and severity of illness, are hypothesized to affect family functioning and adolescent well-being (distal effects) indirectly through a number of individual- and family-level mediators (proximal effects). More specifically, illness severity is expected to impact appraisals of stigma and threat, physiological stress responses, the distribution of roles and responsibilities within the family, and daily hassles. These processes, in turn, will shape family functioning and adolescent well-being. The individual- and family-level mediators also interact with each other; for example, the nature of the parent's illness may create particular perceptions of stigma, which may affect the adolescent's and the family's life in the form of increased physiological stress responses, which ultimately affect health and well-being. It is also important to note that within this framework, the adolescent's illness appraisals or coping strategies may not be congruent with those of other family members', creating additional stress and family dysfunction.

The mediational, or indirect, pathways in the framework may be affected by a number of contextual or moderator variables that will alter the direction or magnitude of illness effects on the mediating variables. Contextual moderator variables include whether the parent and adolescent are the same gender, the family's attachment style, and cultural norms concerning emotional responses to stress; Table 1 presents a more complete list of potential moderator variables. Although we have chosen not to include moderational processes in Figure 1, the proposed moderators affect specific and multiple pathways in the Figure 1 and are more interlinked than we have depicted graphically. For example, the youth's developmental stage and gender may moderate the path between parental illness

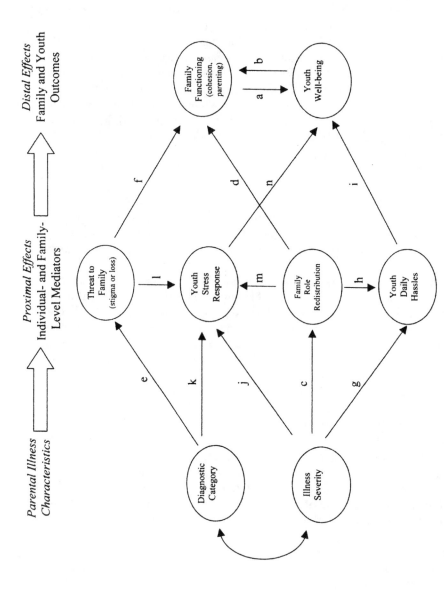

Figure 20.1. Mediating pathways within a family ecology framework for research on parental illness.

Table 1. Proposed Moderators of Parental Illness Effects on Families and Adolescents

Level of analysis	Moderator
Individual	Youth developmental stage
	Parent's age at onset of illness
	Ill parent's gender
	Ill parent's family role
	Individual (youth and parent) coping style
	Other youth and parent psychological resources
Dyadic and family	Parent–youth gender congruence
	Marital relationship quality
	Family coping style
	Family attachment style
Extrafamilial/societal	Social support
	Cultural norms
	Access to care

Note. Not all of the potential moderators listed in Table 1 are discussed in detail in the text. We chose to highlight those that have received the least attention in the literature to date.

severity and family role redistribution (Path c), which is itself a mediator of the relationship between parental illness severity and family functioning (Paths c–d). The mediating and moderated pathways proposed in the framework are not exhaustive but reflect a wide range of intra- and extrafamilial factors that may elucidate the underlying processes. In the next section we will review studies that have tested the major pathways in the family ecology framework, noting the strength of the evidence, the types of illnesses that have been studied, and whether the evidence is based on child, adolescent, or mixed-aged samples.

SUPPORTING EVIDENCE FOR THE FAMILY ECOLOGY FRAMEWORK: STUDIES OF THE EFFECT OF PARENT ILLNESS ON YOUTH DEVELOPMENT AND FAMILY FUNCTIONING

Scope and Organization of the Evidence

In this section we review those studies that provide support for the major pathways in the family ecology framework. We started with four existing literature reviews of how parental illness impacts family functioning and adolescent well-being (Armistead, Klein, & Forehand, 1995; Finney & Miller, 1999; Korneluk & Lee, 1998; Worsham, Compas, & Ey, 1997) and the studies that composed those reviews. We then turned to *PsycINFO*, the psychology database, to search for published, peer-reviewed literature using the following terms and combinations of these terms: *parental illness, maternal illness, paternal illness, chronic, physical, disease, family functioning, adolescent functioning*, and *adolescent well-being*. We also searched using the specific illness terms *cancer, HIV, AIDS, diabetes, heart disease*, and *spinal cord injury*.[2] We then checked the references of the sources identified using this search procedure for any relevant keywords. Publications containing the keywords in their titles were also retrieved.

Although we drew on the literature examining family and parental reactions to a child's illness in building the theoretical framework, we excluded these studies from the current literature review. We also excluded studies that sampled only parents with a mental illness or an acute illness with no long-term health implications. Although we targeted empirical articles for review, we also retrieved theoretical articles, literature reviews, and clinical reports. In addition, because research that specifically addresses the effects of parental illness effects on families with adolescents was limited, we included studies of parental illness in families with young children when they addressed an underresearched area.

In the following section, we describe the ways in which the central construct of interest—parental illness—has been conceptualized. We then review the literature that examines direct effects of parental illness on two outcomes: family functioning and adolescent well-being. Although the family ecology framework is explicitly transactional (i.e., it assumes that family functioning and youth development are mutually influential), the effects of parental illness on family functioning and on adolescent well-being are considered separately in an effort to highlight the state of the research on each pathway within the proposed model. The final part of the section reviews evidence for the mediating and moderated pathways in the family ecology framework.

Defining and Measuring Parental Illness

For the most part, researchers have relied on two dimensions by which to characterize parental illness: type of illness (diagnosis) or severity

---

[2] These illnesses and conditions were chosen because the Centers for Disease Control (Kochanek & Smith, 2004) has identified them as 5 of the 10 most common causes of death for adults in the age ranges during which they are most likely to raise children (25–44 years and 45–65 years). Unlike other common causes of death, such as accidents, homicide, and suicide, the illnesses that we selected are associated with chronic disability and may impair one's ability to maintain daily routines. Spinal cord injury was added to the list in an effort to adjust for any gender bias in the targeted illnesses, which mostly affect women. This bias remains in the literature and the current review, however, as very few articles have addressed familial adjustment to parental heart disease or spinal cord injury—conditions that are more likely to affect men.

(Patterson & Garwick, 1994; Rolland, 1999).[3] Contrasting the experiences of families in which the ill parents have different diagnoses suggests that one illness impacts family life more negatively or in a different way than another, regardless of cross-cutting dimensions such as prognosis or level of disability. The dimensions of diagnosis and severity are not orthogonal, however; some diagnoses may be less stigmatizing or threatening in part because these illnesses are associated with less disability than other illnesses, for example, diabetes compared with AIDS.

Studies that operationalize parental illness as diagnosis and those that operationalize illness as severity require different sets of assumptions about the causal mechanisms linking parental illness to adjustment. For example, a cancer diagnosis generally carries more life threat than diabetes, although many forms of cancer are less life threatening because of advances in treatment and detection. Thus, most youth coping with a parent's cancer are coping with the issue of parental loss to some degree and in a qualitatively different fashion than youth coping with a parent's diabetes or arthritis. Moreover, no diagnosis is monolithic; for example, different types or stages of cancer pose different degrees of life threat, so even the label of "cancer" tells little about potential parental loss. Unless the adaptive tasks of particular diagnoses are spelled out (Moos & Schaefer, 1984), using diagnosis as a marker of stress is limited.

Conceptualizing parental illness by its severity, rather than diagnostic type, implies a different mediating mechanism, one that involves familial role redistribution (Reiss, Steinglass, & Howe, 1993). Irrespective of diagnosis, more severe illnesses have a greater impact on the parent's ability to fulfill familial roles and responsibilities, placing greater demands on family members. For example, a mother diagnosed with breast cancer at an advanced stage may not only experience more debilitating symptoms of illness but also undergo more frequent treatments over a longer period of time—interfering to a greater degree with parenting tasks and thus affecting the child's well-being—than a mother diagnosed with early-stage breast cancer.

One particularly important aspect of severity is onset, or the rapidity with which the illness symptoms develop. The adaptive tasks demanded of a family facing a parental illness with a sudden and traumatic onset, such as spinal cord injury resulting from an accident, may be different from those faced by a family in which a parent is diagnosed with an illness that also results in physical debilitation but develops gradually

---

[3] On the basis of earlier work by Rolland (1984), Kazak (1989) proposed that an analogous set of illness characteristics—onset, course, and outcome—affect family adaptation in the context of childhood illness.

over a long period of time, such as Parkinson's disease. To complicate matters, many of the chronic illnesses addressed in the literature that we used to build our framework, such as breast cancer and HIV/AIDS, have both gradual and rapid aspects to their onset. For example, a mother may experience symptoms such as exhaustion and frequent infections that lead her to request an HIV test. A positive result on the test may result in a rapid change in the life of the mother and her family as they cope with the diagnosis and a complex regimen of medications and doctor visits. The progression of the illness symptoms in this case is gradual, but the diagnosis and the treatment-related life changes that ensue are rapid and traumatic.

Empirical work rarely contrasts these different illness dimensions. Perhaps because of convenience, most study a single parental illness in an effort to establish the association between illness severity and adjustment (e.g., Armistead, Tannenbaum, Forehand, Morse, & Morse, 2001; Compas et al., 1994; Compas, Worsham, Ey, & Howell, 1996; Dutra et al., 2000; Ell, Nishimoto, Mantell, & Hamovitch, 1988; Grant & Compas, 1995; Lewis, Hammond, & Woods, 1993; Murphy, Steers, & Dello Stritto, 2001; Rotheram-Borus & Stein, 1999; Steele, Forehand, & Armistead, 1997). Only a few studies have compared family functioning across different illnesses (e.g., Dura & Beck, 1988; Lewis, Woods, Hough, & Bensley, 1989; Stetz, Lewis, & Primomo, 1986; Yates, Bensley, Lalonde, Lewis, & Woods, 1995), compared physical versus mental illnesses (e.g., Anderson & Hammen, 1993; Hirsch, Moos, & Reischl, 1985; Johnson & Lobo, 2001; Mikail & von Baeyer, 1990; Pelton, Steele, Chance, Forehand, & the Family Health Project Research Group, 2001; Peters & Esses, 1985), or compared families with illness to families without known illness (e.g., Harris & Zakowski, 2003; Kotchick et al., 1997).

Association Between Parental Illness and Family Functioning

In the family systems literature, families characterized as well-functioning are described as cohesive, flexible, and self-reflective (Walsh, 2003). Markers of positive family functioning during parental illness include high levels of communication, a family identity that is not defined by the illness, and the ability to redistribute family roles in ways that do not compromise the development of individual members (Patterson & Garwick, 1994; Reiss et al., 1993; Rolland, 1999). In contrast, poorly adapting families have been characterized as those that use extensive family reorganization as a coping response. Reorganization is defined as the extent to which the intrafamilial transactions are altered to meet the needs of the sick individual. Although short-term reorganization during acute illness or a crisis phase of a chronic illness is adaptive, maintaining a family structure, organization, and identity that revolve around the ill parent for an extended length of time compromises the family's ability to meet the developmental needs of other members, especially children (Reiss et al., 1993). Reiss et al. (1993) provided support for this in a case study of one family's response to the father's end-stage renal disease, where reorganization contributed to increased psychological distress in each family member.

Few empirical studies of parental illness, however, have assessed reorganization directly. One cross-sectional study that compared family organization among impoverished families in which the mother was HIV– to impoverished families in which the mother was HIV+ revealed no association between maternal HIV serostatus and the extent to which family routines were consistent and organized (Kotchick et al., 1997).

A greater number of studies have assessed aspects of family functioning, such as cohesion and conflict. In a series of interrelated studies of the families of women with either breast cancer, fibrocystic breast disease, or diabetes, family functioning was measured using self-report scales assessing family adaptability, cohesion, and/or the family's satisfaction with the quality of the family's interactions (Lewis et al., 1989, 1993; Yates et al., 1995). These measures of family functioning were modestly related to illness severity, with some families at risk for low cohesion and increased conflict when the illness was more severe. In a study that used only the subsample of families with maternal breast cancer, Lewis et al. (1989) found a negative correlation between illness severity (operationalized as frequency of illness demands on the family) and spousal reports of family functioning. However, this significant finding was not replicated when the women's reports of functioning were substituted for their husbands' reports (Lewis et al., 1993). In addition, women's reports of family functioning did not differ among the three diagnoses (breast cancer, fibrocystic breast disease, and diabetes; Yates et al., 1995).

Two additional studies suggest that more severe illnesses are associated with poorer family functioning. In a study of parents with chronic headaches, parental perceptions of the extent to which the illness interfered with daily life were inversely associated with perceptions of family cohesiveness, and perceptions of pain severity were inversely associated with family organization (Mikail & von Baeyer, 1990). Dura and Beck (1988) found that families with maternal diabetes or chronic pain reported lower cohesiveness than families with no illness, although only families in which the mothers had chronic pain reported greater conflict than the families without illness. The authors suggest that these findings are best explained not by diagnosis, however, but by levels of disability. Mothers with chronic pain reported the most disability—particularly in the area of family and home responsibilities—followed by mothers with diabetes; mothers with no illness reported the least disability.

Not all studies, however, have identified a negative relation between illness severity and family functioning. Kotchick et al.'s (1997) study of HIV+ mothers and their children found that disease severity was unrelated to either parent–child relationship quality or parental monitoring, although mothers who were HIV+ tended to score lower than mothers who were HIV– on these measures of parenting. It should be noted, however, that the socioeconomic conditions under which the impoverished, inner-city participants in this study lived are substantially different from samples in many of the other studies we reviewed, which may have limited the variance in the variable tapping the organization of family routines. In sum, although how parental illness is conceptualized (diagnosis vs. severity), who is reporting on the quality of family functioning, and other unstudied dimensions (e.g., level of disability) are critical constructs in understanding the effects of parental illness on family well-being, the nature and extent of the impact of parental illness on family functioning remains undetermined.

Association Between Parental Illness and Adolescent Well-Being

Some scholars have suggested that parental illness exerts devastating effects on the behavioral and psychosocial well-being of adolescents (Hollingsworth, 1982; Patenaude, 2000). Yet only a relatively small number of empirical studies have considered the unique challenges posed by parental illness to families with adolescents. We examine three domains of youth well-being that have been addressed in the empirical literature: psychological distress, problem behaviors, and positive well-being.[4]

Psychological Distress

Contrary to Hollingsworth's (1982) expectations that adolescents' advanced cognitive development would protect them from psychological distress during parental illness, the empirical evidence suggests that adolescents are at *greater* risk than young children (Armistead et al., 1995; Worsham et al., 1997). A substantial proportion of adolescents with HIV+ mothers have been observed to exhibit high levels of depression (Gardner & Preator, 1996). In several studies, illness severity has been associated with internalizing symptoms among youth whose fathers had

---

[4] This article provides evidence for unidirectional effects of parental illness on adolescent and family functioning. It is equally important, however, to test the competing hypothesis that families with members susceptible to physical illness are also families with members susceptible to psychological dysfunction over the course of that illness.

hemophilia or both hemophilia and HIV/ AIDS (Steele et al., 1997), urban adolescents whose parent (usually the mother) was diagnosed with AIDS (Rotheram-Borus & Stein, 1999), and middle childhood youth whose mothers were HIV+ (Hough, Brumitt, Templin, Saltz, & Mood, 2003). Illness severity also was related to externalizing symptoms of psychological distress in the Hough et al. (2003) study. Another study of parent–adolescent pairs in which the parent was HIV+ found that parental distress associated with illness-related pain positively predicted adolescent reports of somatic symptoms (Lester, Stein, & Bursch, 2003). Finally, one study of the children (ages 9–17) of chronic headache sufferers found that these young people experienced more symptoms of anxiety and depression than a comparison sample of adolescents with no parental illness (Mikail & von Baeyer, 1990).

Adolescent children of parents with cancer—particularly girls whose mothers are ill—may also be at greater risk for anxiety and depression than younger children (Compas et al., 1994, 1996; Grant & Compas, 1995). In the series of studies by Compas and colleagues, the severity of the parent's illness was associated with a heightened stress response (characterized by intrusive thoughts, anxiety, and depression) among adolescents. Another group of researchers examining the psychological symptoms (including anxiety and depression) of adult daughters of women with breast cancer failed to find a significant difference between these daughters and a matched sample with no maternal history of breast cancer. However, daughters of women with breast cancer were more likely to feel uncomfortable about their involvement with the mother's illness *if* the illness had occurred during childhood or adolescence (Wellisch, Gritz, Schain, Wang, & Siau, 1991, 1992). Harris and Zakowski (2003), however, found no evidence of risk among adolescents experiencing parental cancer. In this study of 50 youth, adolescents experiencing parental cancer reported lower anxiety and fewer PTSD symptoms than a comparison group of adolescents with no history of parental cancer.

Problem Behavior

The effect of parental illness on conduct problems, drug use, and other risk-taking behaviors has rarely been addressed, and the existing literature is equivocal. Patenaude (2000) suggested that children of parents with cancer would react by acting out. In contrast, Christ, Siegel, and Sperber (1994) argued that acting out occurs only if the adolescent exhibited problem behaviors prior to the illness. Gardner and Preator (1996) similarly concluded that increased conduct problems among children of parents with HIV/AIDS stems from the accumulation of risk factors associated with the illness rather than the illness per se. For example, young people experiencing maternal HIV/AIDS may be at risk for dysfunction because of the cumulative impact of other stressors, such as poverty. Women diagnosed as HIV+ and their families tend to live in economically disadvantaged circumstances, exacerbating illness-related stress on the family and, potentially, the economic ramifications of parental loss (Gardner & Preator, 1996).

In the empirical literature, one study of mothers with HIV found that HIV-related stressors on the mother (e.g., HIV-related physical symptoms, opportunistic infections, and CD4 counts) were directly related to child behavior problems among youth aged 7–14 (Hough et al., 2003). In contrast, in another study of maternal HIV/AIDS, Rotheram-Borus and Stein (1999) did not find an association between maternal health status and adolescent problem behaviors, such as drug use, sexual risk, and conduct problems. Maternal risk behaviors and substance use were associated with youth problem behaviors, suggesting that adolescents with ill parents may exhibit greater risk behaviors than youth whose parents are not ill only to the extent that parental illness co-occurs with parental risk behaviors. Thus, youth risk behaviors are not a direct outcome of parental illness, but they result from the modeling of parental risk behaviors. In contrast, studies of younger children find parental illness is associated with problem behaviors. Armistead et al. (2001) observed a significant correlation between illness severity and aggressive behavior in children aged 6–11 whose mothers were HIV+. A more in-depth analysis of 15 mothers in this sample found that mothers perceived increased behavior problems following disclosure of their HIV status to their children (Shaffer, Jones, Kotchick, Forehand, & the Family Health Research Project Research Group, 2001).

Positive Well-being

Four studies identified differences in self-esteem (one aspect of positive well-being) between children and adolescents facing parental illness and children and adolescents who were not experiencing parental illness. Hirsch et al. (1985) conducted a study of adolescents whose parents were diagnosed with either physical illness (arthritis) or mental illness (depression) and compared them with adolescents of parents with no known health disorder. Adolescents with an arthritic or depressed parent reported lower self-esteem than comparison youth. Armsden and Lewis (1994) similarly found that, among youth in middle childhood, those experiencing maternal breast cancer and diabetes reported lower self-esteem than a comparison sample with no known parental illness. One study of children of parents with coronary heart disease found that boys, but not girls, of parents with coronary heart disease reported lower self-esteem than a matched comparison sample (Räikkönen, Keltikangas-Järvinen, & Pietikäinen, 1991). Finally, Siegel, Raveis, and Karus (2000) found that the self-esteem of young people experiencing parental cancer (40% of whom were adolescents) tended to be lower than that which is found in surveys with normative samples of youth.

Other aspects of positive well-being are rarely addressed in the parental illness literature. In particular, personal growth associated with the parental illness experience has not been studied, despite empirical support for the hypothesis that many young people report psychosocial benefits following a traumatic experience (e.g., Milam, Ritt-Olson, & Unger, 2004). Milam et al. (2004) also identified individual differences in the extent to which the adolescents in their cross-sectional study reported that they had experienced growth following a negative life event. For example, older adolescents endorsed the growth measure more highly than younger adolescents. In contrast, substance use was negatively associated with scores on the posttraumatic growth scale. These findings suggest not only that young people can use a negative event to enhance their skills or psychological resources but also that individual and contextual characteristics may influence the degree to which adolescents capitalize on the opportunity for growth through the challenge of parental illness.

It should be noted that we had hoped to find evidence to support the hypothesis that some young people would find the parental illness experience to be a challenge that leads to personal growth. The small empirical literature in this area, however, focuses almost exclusively on negative outcomes associated with parental illness. Thus, we were unable to include studies that examined competence development or positive growth in our review. We hope that such outcomes will be addressed in future empirical research with families living with parental illness.

Summary

The literature provides support for the hypothesis that parental illness negatively impacts some aspects of adolescent well-being. Adolescent children of ill parents are at greater risk for anxiety, depression, and low self-esteem (Compas et al., 1994; Hirsch et al., 1985; Siegel et al., 2000). Parental illness may also lead to increased problem behaviors among youth evidencing such behaviors before diagnosis (Christ et al., 1994). Empirical research in this area, however, is limited and often does not address conflicting hypotheses reported in theoretical and clinical research. For example, Christ et al. (1994), Gardner and Preator (1996), and Patenaude (2000) disagree regarding the extent to which adolescents are at risk for problem behaviors during parental illness. Only one empirical study, however, examined problem behaviors among adolescents with ill mothers (e.g., Rotheram-Borus & Stein, 1999), and although the findings support Gardner and Preator's (1996) observations, the extent to which these results generalize to other populations of youth experiencing parental illness is unknown. The literature also rarely examines how adolescents may view parental illness as a challenge from which they may learn more about themselves and their skills and abilities. Finally, few studies take into account moderating variables—such as cognitive development, gender, and age of onset of parental illness—that may buffer or exacerbate illness effects on adolescent outcomes.

MEDIATING MECHANISMS

In the following section, we propose a series of mediating mechanisms to account for the observed associations among parental illness, family functioning, and adolescent well-being. In particular, we focus on mediating pathways that can be incorporated into interventions. These mediators are the alphabetically labeled paths in Figure 1. Mediators of illness effects on family functioning include familial role redistribution and threat to the family's identity through stigma and potential loss. Mediators of illness effects on youth well-being include daily hassles and the stress response. Family functioning and adolescent well-being are also assumed to be mutually influential, although these pathways are not described explicitly below (see Paths a and b in Figure 1).

Mediators of Illness Effects on Family Functioning

Role Redistribution

Stetz et al. (1986) observed that role redistribution was the most common coping mechanism used by families experiencing parental illness. If an ill parent is incapable of fulfilling the roles that he or she previously filled, other family members may be required to adopt those roles (see Path c). Whether or not roles are reassigned fairly (with clear communication and with concern for well family members' developmental needs) may affect family functioning (see Path d; Patterson & Garwick, 1994; Rolland, 1999).

For example, one parent in a family may be responsible for picking the children up from after-school activities. If that parent develops a movement disorder or if medications and other treatments affect the parent's cognitive and perceptual functioning, that parent may no longer be able to operate a car safely, interfering with this role. The family may utilize a number of behavioral strategies to cope with this role limitation. In the case of a two-parent family, the well parent may adjust his or her schedule to accommodate the children's transportation needs. Arrangements may be made for another adult to bring the children home, an older sibling may become responsible for bringing the children home, or the children may stop engaging in after-school activities in order to take the school bus home. None of these solutions automatically results in family dysfunction. Some teens may be happy to assist, gaining new responsibilities and respect. Familial relationships may be adversely affected, however, when one or more family members feel overly or unfairly burdened by the family's response to the illness.

The role redistribution mediational hypothesis is supported by a few empirical studies. In one study of HIV+ mothers, maintaining stable family routines was associated with better parent–child relationship quality (Dutra et al., 2000). Lewis et al. (1989), in one study of maternal breast cancer, also implicitly assessed a role redistribution hypothesis. The family's use of introspective coping mediated the association between illness demands and family functioning, although the statistical significance of the indirect effect was not reported. This finding could imply that families that use more introspective coping techniques are more successful in readjusting to the demands of the parent's illness without compromising the development of well family members; however, our ability to interpret this finding is limited because the relations among illness demands, introspective coping, and family reorganization have not been tested in other studies.

Threat to the Family's Identity

Weihs and Reiss (2000) suggested that illness in a family member threatens the "life course of the family" (p. 19). The family's relational processes are shaped by the extent to which that system is threatened by the potential loss of the ill family member. If the family views the illness as a serious threat to the ill member's life (see Path e), family functioning may be affected such that the patterns of transactions among family members will become reorganized around the illness (see Path f). In this way, illness may compromise the normative identity development and transactional processes of the family system (Reiss et al., 1993). Illnesses that are stigmatized may also threaten the family's belief systems—the shared conceptions of the qualities that define the family's identity (see Path e; Reiss et al., 1993)—and, in turn, family functioning.

No empirical studies have examined changes in family identity brought about by parental illness, nor have investigators elucidated how such changes relate to family functioning. More specifically, no empirical studies have examined the stigma or level of life threat associated with an illness as a mediator of the association between illness and family functioning.

Mediators of Illness Effects on Youth Well-Being

Daily Hassles

Parental illness may impact youth well-being by creating a surplus of daily hassles experienced by the adolescent. Daily hassles are "stresses and strains of daily life" (Rowlison & Felner, 1988, p. 433; DeLongis, Folkman, & Lazarus, 1988) and have been associated with depression, anxiety, antisocial behavior, and academic achievement (DuBois, Felner, Meares, & Krier, 1994; Masten et al., 1994; Rowlison & Felner, 1988). To the extent that parental illness increases the difficulties associated with daily life (e.g., increased chores, nagging from parents), greater dysfunction among youth with ill parents should be observed.

We hypothesize that daily hassles mediate the effects of parental illness on youth well-being and that this individual-level pathway is related to the family-level process of role redistribution in the context of parental illness (Patterson & Garwick, 1994; Rolland, 1999). Illness demands may lead directly to increased hassles when youth are asked to adopt new roles associated with the illness, such as accompanying the ill parent to medical appointments (see Path g). Alternately, the redistribution of existing family roles, such as household responsibilities, may lead to greater daily hassles for adolescents (see Path h). These new or increased familial responsibilities may then affect adolescent well-being by interfering with the development of peer relationships and attachment to important others outside the family system (see Path i; Compas et al., 1994; Feeney & Ryan, 1994; Rolland, 1999; Weihs & Reiss, 2000). Indeed, Lewis et al. (1989) observed that husbands' perceptions of maternal illness demands on the family were inversely associated with the quality of the child's peer relationships.

Grant and Compas (1995) most explicitly addressed the issue of perceived hassles by asking adolescents with ill parents to report the stressors associated with their family responsibilities. An earlier publication with the same sample found that girls with ill mothers reported greater anxiety and depression than girls with ill fathers and boys with ill mothers or fathers (Compas et al., 1994). Later analyses indicated that greater family responsibilities fully accounted for this interaction (Grant & Compas, 1995), suggesting that adolescent girls bear the burden of role restructuring in families experiencing illness.

Stress Response

The stress response pathway suggests that parental illness contributes to youth maladjustment to the degree that parental illness represents, and is appraised as, a discrete, negative, and uncontrollable life event (Compas,

1987; Masten et al., 1994). Appraisals of the event's stressfulness create feelings of threat and helplessness (and even decreased immune function; McEwen, 1998). In other words, the mediating process driving the association between parental illness and youth well-being is cognitive-emotional. Perceived stress among the adolescent children of ill parents may arise because of worry about parental death associated with a very severe illness (see Path j), worry about the child's own risk of illness and death if the parent's illness is associated with genetic susceptibility (see Path k), or the family-level perceived stigma associated with particular diagnoses (see Path l). Finally, perceived stress may result from illness demands associated with familial role redistribution that the adolescent perceives as adversely affecting his or her peer, school, and family relationships (see Path m; Compas et al., 1994). The extent to which the adolescent appraises the parent's illness as stressful determines his or her response to the illness (see Path n; Contrada & Guyll, 2000), including emotions, coping behaviors, or both.

Few studies have tested the perceived stress hypothesis in the context of parental illness. In a study of children of cancer patients, Compas et al. (1994) found that perceived stress attributed to the parent's illness predicted adolescents' anxiety, depression, and stress-response symptoms. In contrast, studies examining disclosure effects on children's well-being in families with maternal HIV/AIDS—which could constitute an approximate measure of perceived threat or stigma associated with diagnosis—have not found differences between children who know about their mothers' health status and those who do not (e.g., Armistead et al., 2001; Murphy et al., 2001), although one study found that mothers perceived increased child behavior problems and decreased parent–child relationship quality following disclosure (Shaffer et al., 2001). Similarly, in a study of families in which the father had hemophilia and was HIV+, although bivariate analyses revealed that disclosure of the father's HIV+ status was related to lower grades and greater depression among the children in the sample, no association between disclosure and child well-being was observed after adjusting for parent–child relationship quality (Armistead, Klein, Forehand, & Wierson, 1997).

The children in these studies of adjustment to parental HIV, however, tended to be in middle childhood, rather than adolescence, raising the possibility that cognitive development may moderate the association between parental illness and perceived stress. Alternately, the children in the disclosure and nondisclosure samples may have appeared similar on the outcomes studied because the youth nondisclosure samples were aware of the parent's diagnosis—or, at least, that the parent was seriously ill—without having been told and subsequently experienced levels of threat and stress similar to that of youth in the disclosure samples.

Parenting

Parental illness may also affect youth well-being through its impact on family functioning. One aspect of family functioning that has received attention in the empirical literature is parenting. Illness may affect parenting in two ways. First, as a chronic illness becomes more serious, the illness may impact the parent's ability to fulfill his or her usual role responsibilities (see Path c). The subsequent redistribution of family roles may affect the family's functioning as a whole and, specifically, the parent's relationship with the child (see Path d). Second, a particular diagnosis may lead the parent to experience perceived stigma and threat (see Path e). The distress associated with this experience may also interfere with parenting.

Kotchick et al. (1997) suggested that illness may affect such aspects of the parent–child relationship as the quality of that relationship and the extent to which the parent monitors the child's behaviors. Indeed, in their study, poor, urban HIV+ mothers rated themselves lower on indices of positive parenting, including mother–child relationship quality and monitoring, than a comparison sample of poor, urban mothers who had not been diagnosed as HIV+. Reyland, McMahon, Higgins-Delessandro, and Luthar (2002) similarly found that inner-city adolescents (ages 11–16) living with an HIV+ mother experienced less positive mother–child relationships (e.g., more hostility and indifference from the mother) than a comparison sample from the same community. Although mediation analyses assessing the significance of the indirect effect of HIV serostatus on youth outcomes were not conducted in these studies, other analyses using the same sample of children and mothers, as in the Kotchik et al. (1997) study, found that the children of HIV+ mothers had more externalizing and internalizing symptoms and lower social and cognitive competence than children from the comparison sample (Forehand et al., 1998).

Summary

The theoretical literature suggests that daily hassles and perceived stress mediate the effects of parental illness effects on adolescent well-being, but very few empirical studies have tested mediators of parental illness effects on family functioning. Studies that examine perceived stress as a mediator yield mixed results, suggesting that this pathway is conditional on other variables, such as cognitive development. Finally, there is some evidence to suggest that parental illness impacts youth adjustment through aspects of family functioning, such as parenting.

Contextual Moderating Factors

Are the associations among parental illness characteristics, family functioning, and youth well-being the same or different across populations and contexts? Developmental theorists have emphasized the importance of developing models that incorporate factors that could alter the nature of the associations among the variables studied (Rutter, 1990). Identifying intra- and extrafamilial factors that color the family's experience of a parent's illness is a crucial step in the development of a framework to guide research. In this section, a number of potential family- and individual-level moderators of the relations among parental illness, family functioning, and youth well-being are proposed, and empirical evidence for these moderators is presented.

Developmental Stage

The developmental stage at which a young person experiences parental illness represents a critical yet understudied moderator of the association between illness and youth well-being. Older children may experience greater threat of loss because they are more knowledgeable about the potential consequences of disease and more capable of conceptualizing death. Further, older children are more capable of adopting additional household responsibilities. Such responsibilities may prohibit involvement in extrafamilial contexts that promote positive development and in which youth become more interested as they age, such as their peer group (Berndt, 1996).

Alternately, older children may adapt to the illness experience more easily because of greater cognitive resources and prior exposure to stressors. They may also accomplish tasks that require a high level of responsibility with more ease and less stress than younger children would experience when confronted with the same task. Thus, older children may find additional familial responsibilities associated with parental illness to be a challenge that promotes positive growth, rather than an impediment to the development of peer ties. Indeed, Milam et al. (2004) found that age was associated with positive growth following a negative life event in a large sample of Latino adolescents. Older adolescents were more likely than younger adolescents to identify benefits associated with their traumatic experience. One potential explanation for this finding is that older youth are more equipped by their maturity, social development, and cognitive development to view negative experiences as opportunities for personal growth.

Only the studies of children of cancer patients by Compas and his associates (e.g., Compas et al., 1994, 1996; Grant & Compas, 1995) bring developmental stage into the equation. Their findings suggest that adolescent and young adult children of people with cancer exhibit greater anxiety and depression than preadolescent children. These associations are further moderated by other variables, such as gender.

Ill Parent's Gender or Family Role

The ill parent's gender has seldom been studied as a moderator. Most studies sample ill parents of only one gender—usually mothers (e.g., Dura & Beck, 1988; Lewis et al., 1989, 1993; Yates et al., 1995). One study of cancer patients and their spouses (Compas et al., 1994) revealed that the perceived seriousness of the illness varied by the adult's gender and status as patient or (healthy) spouse: Women perceived the cancer as more stressful than men, as did spouses (vs. patients). A study of coronary heart disease patients and their spouses also found that women were more distressed than men and that this gender difference was more pronounced among spouses than patients (Rohrbaugh et al., 2002). In other studies, wives of rheumatic disease patients were more likely to bear the burden of familial role redistribution than ill women, ill men, or husbands of patients (Revenson, 1994, 2003).

Of course, family role rather than—or in addition to—gender per se is likely a strong contributing factor to any differences in family or youth adjustment to parental illness. In a more traditional two-parent family in which the mother has assumed most of the caretaking responsibilities and the father is primarily responsible for the family's income, maternal illness may necessitate the father and children assuming more childcare and housekeeping roles. Paternal illness may result in other family members seeking out new employment situations to maintain the family's economic solvency. For families in which both parents are of the same gender, the effect of the illness on the family and child would likely depend more on the family roles adopted by the ill parent than on the parents' gender. In a single-parent family, parental illness could require reassignment of both caretaking and breadwinner roles within the family.

Parent and Youth Gender Congruence

The congruence between the gender of the ill parent and that of the child may moderate the association between parental illness and youth well-being. When the ill parent is the same gender as the child, the child would be more likely to assume some of the parent's roles; for example, daughters of ill mothers might be more likely than sons to take on housekeeping chores (Compas et al., 1994). Only studies by Compas and his colleagues address this explicitly. Compas et al. (1994) found support for the hypothesis that the gender of the sick parent and his or her child interact to predict child well-being: Adolescent girls reported greater anxiety and depression than adolescent boys, and this finding was most robust among girls with sick mothers. This finding was accounted for by the increased household responsibilities adopted by girls experiencing maternal illness (Grant & Compas, 1995).

It is also possible that poorer adjustment by same-sex dyads is colored by perceived risk. Some illnesses—for example, certain types of breast cancer—may be partially determined by genetic factors such that same-sex children are more likely to develop the illness themselves. Research on healthy adult women's breast-cancer-related distress indicates that a maternal history of breast cancer puts a woman at risk for heightened breast-cancer-related distress, particularly if she cared for her mother during the illness and if her mother died of the illness (Erblich, Bovbjerg, & Valdimarsdottir, 2000).

Family Coping Style

Coping has rarely been conceptualized at a family level. Instead, this construct has most often been viewed as reflective of an internal cognitive–emotional process of decision-making that culminates in behavior designed to ameliorate the perceived stress associated with a particular situation or experience (Lazarus, 1999). Only recently has coping been conceptualized and studied as an interpersonal or dyadic process (e.g., Bodenmann, 1997; Lyons, Mickelson, Sullivan, & Coyne, 1998; Revenson, 1994, 2003; Revenson, Kayser, & Bodenmann, 2005; Schmaling & Sher, 2000). When family-level coping is examined in the context of illness, researchers most often study families with an ill child rather than an ill parent (e.g., Degotardi, 2000; Hauser, DiPlacido, Jacobson, Willett, & Cole, 1993).

No studies could be found that explicitly examined individual- or family-level coping as a moderator of the association between parental illness and family functioning. The results of one study of families with adolescents experiencing juvenile rheumatoid arthritis, however, support the hypothesis that family coping moderates illness effects on family functioning and youth well-being (Degotardi, 2000). Still, if parental illness leads to a redistribution of roles in the family (affecting the balance of relationships established among family members), family coping style may determine the extent to which adolescents are the recipients of "unfair" redistributions that leave them feeling overburdened or resentful. Open dialogue about the illness also may make families less likely to view the illness as a threat to the family's development.

Intervention research suggests that coping plays an important role in determining youth adjustment during parental illness. An evaluation of a 24-session cognitive–behavioral intervention targeting the coping skills of parents living with HIV/AIDS and their adolescent children found both short-term and long-term benefits associated with participation in the intervention. The intervention was successful at reducing youth rates of childbearing over 4 years and resulted in short-term reductions in youth problem behaviors and emotional distress, relative to a randomized control group (Rotheram-Borus, Lee, Gwadz, & Draimin, 2001; Rotheram-Borus et al., 2003).

Family Attachment Styles

Weihs and Reiss (2000) suggested that fear of separation from the ill parent depends on the quality of the attachment relationships in the family. Just as individuals may exhibit secure or insecure styles of attachment in their relationships (Ainsworth, 1979), so may families. Attachment at the family level is defined as the holistic pattern of attachment exhibited within the intrafamilial relationships over time (Weihs & Reiss, 2000). Families may be securely attached or may exhibit ambivalent, avoidant, or disorganized patterns of attachment among members. To date, the empirical literature has not examined family-level attachment styles in studies of parental illness experiences.

Social Support

Support from both within and outside of the family system may moderate the mediational processes described in Figure 1. A wealth of research over the past 2 decades has demonstrated that the quality of interpersonal relationships is a strong predictor of adjustment to illness among adult populations (Sarason, Sarason, & Gurung, 2001; Schmaling & Sher, 2000; Stanton & Revenson, in press; Wills & Fegan, 2001). Most of the coping tasks of illness require help from others. Thus, people faced with a serious illness need an available network of interpersonal relations on which they can count for both emotional sustenance and practical help during periods of pain, disability, and uncertainty. Children of ill parents serve on this frontline. In essence, then, they occupy a dual role in the adjustment process: as a primary provider of emotional and instrumental support to the ill parent and as a family member who needs (additional) support in the face of a major and often long-lasting life stressor.

Support received by the adolescent may come from many sources, including the ill parent, other family members, peers, teachers, religious mentors, and other adolescents in a similar situation. Such support may involve demonstrations that the adolescent is loved, valued and cared for as well as the provision of helpful information or tangible assistance. Receiving support should enable adolescents to use effective coping strategies by helping them come to a better understanding of the problem faced, increasing motivation to take instrumental action, and reducing emotional stress, which may impede coping.

As described earlier, many adolescents take over parental responsibilities, particularly during acute or early phases of illness, reducing the amount of time adolescents spend socializing with their own peer networks, one potential source of support. Further, even long-standing peers may not understand the challenges the adolescent faces. Support groups or Internet chat groups can be helpful at these times. Discussing stressful events in a supportive, uncritical social environment allows people to process emotions, maintain or reestablish a positive self-concept, and find meaning (Lepore, 2001). Disclosure of stressful experiences may regulate emotion by changing the focus of attention, increasing habituation to negative emotions, or facilitating positive cognitive re-appraisals of threats (including for adolescents facing parental illness with a genetic component, the threat associated with the fear of developing the same illness as the parent). Recent research, however, suggests that support groups are not uniformly effective (e.g., Helgeson, Cohen, Schulz, & Yasko, 2000).

Within a family ecology framework, it is important to remember that adolescents living with parental illness occupy many social roles in addition to family member and parent caregiver—they are friends, students, athletes, and community members. Especially when there is a great amount of role restructuring in the family, role conflict is likely to occur, and the amount of support the child is able to provide to either the ill parent (or to the healthy spouse, who may be falling apart) may be limited by the need to perform well or derive satisfaction from other social roles. Thus, role conflict and role overload, a result of familial role restructuring, may not only interrupt ongoing social relationships but also increase daily hassles and the physiological stress response. Clearly, social support may operate to bisect many of the arrows in Figure 1.

Cultural Norms

Most studies have been conducted on samples of White, middle-class, two-parent families. The "universal" models of family-level effects of parental illness that support this research ignore the influence of cultural background on the way in which individuals and families perceive illness and disabilities (Landrine & Klonoff, 1992). Family and youth expectations of the youth's emotional and instrumental contributions to family life are also related to cultural norms (Fuligni & Pedersen, 2002). Cultural norms may influence the extent to which the adolescent's family responsibilities increase during parental illness and the extent to which the responsibilities contribute to youth maladjustment or distress. Cultural norms may also shape coping, emotional expression, and other aspects of the response to illness.

Access to Care

Much of the health psychology and prevention literatures have identified striking racial and socioeconomic disparities in morbidity, mortality, and the use of health-related services. Research has documented that access to care is one of the major contributors to these differences in health care use and health-related outcomes (Smedly, Stith, & Nelson, 2003). Such discrepancies are apparent across a variety of forms of health care, including both treatment and prevention. In particular, racial or ethnic background, education, income, and health insurance are related to the receipt of services that may prevent the onset of chronic health conditions or allow for early intervention that minimizes the effect of the health condition on the individual and his or her family (Sambamoorthi & McAlpine, 2003). Although we were unable to identify any examples of research that specifically addressed issues related to access to care and family or adolescent adjustment to parental illness, we suggest that this is one potentially important moderator of illness effects on the family. We expect that greater access to care and access to the highest quality of care would both minimize the inconvenience of treatment (reducing the extent to which families must adjust their daily routines to accommodate the illness) and minimize the functional disability associated with the illness (reducing the extent to which the illness impedes the parent's ability to fulfill his or her role in the family).

Summary

Research on parental illness conducted within a family ecology framework requires a greater understanding of how aspects of the family's experience may alter the effects of the illness on family and youth well-being. However, moderator or contextual variables have seldom been studied. Gender—of the ill parent and of the adolescent—seems to play a crucial role in determining the effects of the illness. Other factors at the family and extrafamilial levels, including coping style, culture, social support, and access to care, may also affect the direction and magnitude of the association between parental illness and family/youth well-being.

BLUEPRINT FOR FUTURE RESEARCH ON ADAPTATION TO PARENTAL ILLNESS

Reviewing the literature on parental illness suggests not simply that the field needs more research in this area—which it does—and that prospective, longitudinal studies are needed to disentangle the directionality of effects—which they are—but that future studies should move from asking *whether* there is an effect toward uncovering variables that mediate or moderate the association between parental illness and adjustment. We offer some more specific guidelines for researchers who are interested in designing studies of youth and family adaptation to parental illness. These guidelines stem from limitations in the existing literature as well as the multiple, interconnected mediational and moderational pathways suggested by the family ecology framework.

1. *Measures must capture the quality of family-level processes.* Few studies assessed family-level constructs, such as reorganization, that may elucidate the nature of the illness effects or integrate data from multiple family members. Most studies used single- or dual-informant reports of illness effects, which may not be sufficient to capture family-level processes and which may present different perceptions of "reality." Differences between mothers', fathers', and children's reports of family functioning suggest that individuals view the family environment differently depending on age, gender, or role in the family. For example, men and women perceive illness severity differently (Revenson, 1994, 2003). Research that uses multiple informants—mothers, fathers, and children—may begin to capture processes occurring at the family level (Compas et al., 1994; Degotardi, 2000; Dura & Beck, 1988; Hauser et al., 1993). An important first step toward this goal is the design and validation of reliable, multiple-informant measures of family-level processes critical to the illness response, such as cohesion, adjustment, and role redistribution. The work by Hauser and his colleagues (Hauser et al., 1993) is a first step.

2. *Comparisons within and across illnesses should be more nuanced, focusing on the adaptive tasks and cascading set of changes in the family's transactions necessitated by the illness.* Comparisons across illnesses may yield more fruitful information than single

illness studies for several reasons. First, they allow researchers to disentangle the confounded effects of illness severity and diagnosis. Second, multiple-illness studies may illustrate both common coping tasks of chronic illness and those that are specific to particular diagnoses. Both general and illness-specific coping tasks are important to understanding *how* an illness leads to particular outcomes (Moos & Schaefer, 1984). Third, multiple-illness studies provide an indication of the generalizability (and specificity) of research findings across diagnoses.

Other aspects of any particular diagnosis, such as rapidity of onset and disease progress, degree of illness intrusion (Devins, Edworthy, Guthrie, & Martin, 1992) and life threat also may affect the family's adaptational process and warrant greater attention in future research. Family and adolescent adjustment may be shaped by the length of time that a parent experiences physical symptoms of an illness without a diagnosis, the prognosis of the illness at the point of diagnosis, how fast or slow the disease worsens, and whether there are symptomatic and asymptomatic periods (and how long they last). Family adaptation to an illness may be smoother in cases in which the disease progresses steadily and slowly, as each family member has time to adjust to his or her new roles and tasks and anticipate mechanisms for coping with future problems. Families may find the rapid readjustment required by an illness with cyclical symptomatic and asymptomatic stages more challenging. Alternately, cycles of relative health may make the cycles marked by greater disability easier for some families to bear. These are all hypotheses that could be—but have not yet been—tested empirically.

3. *Studies of ethnically, racially, and economically heterogeneous samples of families are needed to disentangle the confounded effects of socioeconomic status, ethnic group membership, and illness.* Most studies of cancer patients are conducted with White, middle class samples, and most studies of HIV/AIDS patients are conducted with economically disadvantaged African American samples. Therefore, it is impossible to determine whether differences in study findings are observed because the types of illnesses studied affect families and youth differently, because members of different racial/ethnic categories view illness differently, or because the samples experience differing levels of social and economic disadvantage independent of the illness. The far-reaching changes in population demographics that are expected to occur over the next decade have important implications for psychological research (Yali & Revenson, 2004). Ignoring the historic, economic, and

sociocultural contexts in which individuals are situated limits our knowledge and our ability to create effective, culturally anchored research, interventions, and policy for families with parental illness.

4. *Studies should include more positive or growth-related outcomes in addition to traditional indices of psychopathology.* Parental illness and other forms of adversity may offer families and young people the opportunity to develop strengths and competencies (Walsh, 2003). No studies to date have examined positive outcomes among adolescents experiencing parental illness, although many studies show that adults facing severe life stressors, such as illness, find benefits or growth in their experience (e.g., Tennen & Affleck, 2002). Some adolescents may find that parental illness allows them to acquire skills, such as self-reliance, that promote positive development. It is important not only to document these positive outcomes but also to identify factors that may enhance such outcomes (Seligman & Csikszentmihalyi, 2000). One of the major limitations of the existing literature is that studies of youth outcomes associated with parental illness tend to focus on indicators of negative development or maladjustment. The literature in this area would benefit from a refocusing of efforts toward understanding the situations under which adolescents are able to use the challenge of parental illness as a springboard to positive growth and development. Conducting qualitative studies of adolescents' parental illness experiences and using the results to develop and pilot measures of positive growth through parental illness are necessary first steps toward incorporating valid and reliable measures of positive adaptation into large-scale, longitudinal empirical studies.

5. *Research efforts should have a distal goal of prevention and intervention.* Given the strong public health implications of research in the area of parental illness and family and youth adjustment, it is important for researchers to design studies with their "eyes on the prize." It is a given that the literature on parental illness would benefit from more well-designed, prospective, and longitudinal studies. Such studies would help identify the most effective targets for intervention by action-researchers seeking to enhance posttraumatic growth and ameliorate any negative effects of parental illness on youth and families. We do not suggest, however, that action-researchers should wait for those studies to be published before developing and evaluating interventions in this area of research. Rather, preventive interventions and other forms of action-research are essential complements to basic and

developmental research in areas with strong clinical and public health implications, such as parental illness. Rigorously evaluated interventions, developed on the basis of well-constructed theory and existing research, not only have the potential to help young people challenged by parental illness but, if the interventions incorporate a random-assignment strategy, could also elucidate the hypothesized causal mechanisms underlying our proposed framework. For example, an evaluation of an intervention designed to reduce stigma and threat may reveal fewer negative youth outcomes among a randomly assigned intervention group, relative to a treatment-as-usual control group. Such a finding would not only help the youth who received the intervention but also provide supporting evidence for one major pathway in our proposed frame-work. Alternately, the intervention could reveal null findings—or no convincing evidence that the intervention was effective in enhancing youth outcomes by reducing stigma or threat. In this situation, researchers could begin to test alternate pathways in the proposed framework that may yield more fruitful results.

CONCLUSION

Theories in health psychology, child development, and family medicine, as well as a small body of empirical and clinical research, indicate that adolescents appear to be at heightened risk for maladjustment as a result of parental illness. These findings have both conceptual and methodological limitations that impede the translation of research findings into practice. We advocate that research is needed to identify the mediating mechanisms by which parental illness affects families and youth, as well as moderating contextual factors that may shape those mediating processes. The family ecology framework presented here has the potential to serve as a blueprint for research in this area, elucidating the causal pathways linking illness to family and youth well-being while remaining sensitive to variation in individual families' needs and experiences. As empirical support is found for some of the framework's pathways and disconfirming evidence is found for others, a more comprehensive understanding of the parental illness experience will emerge. Such knowledge will aid researchers and clinicians in the design and implementation of effective interventions that can achieve the ultimate goal of assisting at-risk youth and families cope with and learn from the experience of parental illness.

REFERENCES

Ainsworth, M. S. (1979). Infant-mother attachment. *American Psychologist, 34,* 932–937.

Anderson, C. A., & Hammen, C. L. (1993). Psychosocial outcomes of children of unipolar depressed, bipolar, medically ill, and normal women: A longitudinal study. *Journal of Consulting and Clinical Psychology, 61,* 448–454.

Armistead, L., Klein, K., & Forehand, R. (1995). Parental physical illness and child functioning. *Clinical Psychology Review, 15,* 409–422.

Armistead, L., Klein, K., Forehand, R., & Wierson, M. (1997). Disclosure of parental HIV infection to children in the families of men with hemophilia: Description, outcomes, and the role of family processes. *Journal of Family Psychology, 11,* 49–61.

Armistead, L., Tannenbaum, L., Forehand, R., Morse, E., & Morse, P. (2001). Disclosing HIV status: Are mothers telling their children? *Journal of Pediatric Psychology, 26,* 11–20.

Armsden, G. C., & Lewis, F. M. (1994). Behavioral adjustment and self-esteem of school aged children of women with breast cancer. *Oncology Nursing Forum, 21,* 39–45.

Barakat, L. P., & Kazak, A. E. (1999). Family issues. In R. T. Brown (Ed.), *Cognitive aspects of chronic illness in children* (pp. 333–354). New York: Guilford Press.

Berndt, T. J. (1996). Transitions in friendships and friends' influence. In J. A. Graber, J. Brooks-Gunn, & A. C. Petersen (Eds.), *Transitions through adolescence: Interpersonal domains and context* (pp. 57–84). Hillsdale, NJ: Erlbaum.

Bodenmann, G. (1997). Dyadic coping: A systemic-transactional view of stress and coping among couples: Theory and empirical findings. *European Review of Applied Psychology, 47,* 137–141.

Bronfenbrenner, U. (1977). Toward an experimental ecology of human development. *American Psychologist, 32,* 513–531.

Centers for Disease Control and Prevention. (2001). *Morbidity and Mortality Weekly Report, 50,* 120–125.

Christ, G. H., Siegel, K., & Sperber, D. (1994). Impact of parental terminal cancer on adolescents. *American Journal of Orthopsychiatry, 64,* 604–613.

Compas, B. E. (1987). Stress and life events in childhood and adolescence. *Clinical Psychology Review, 7,* 275–302.

Compas, B. E., Worsham, N. L., Epping-Jordan, J. E., Grant, K. E., Mireault, G., Howell, D. C., & Malcarne, V. L. (1994). When mom or dad has cancer: Markers of psychological distress in cancer patients, spouses, and children. *Health Psychology, 13,* 507–515.

Compas, B. E., Worsham, N. L., Ey, S., & Howell, D. C. (1996). When mom or dad has cancer: II. Coping, cognitive appraisals, and psychological distress in children of cancer patients. *Health Psychology, 15,* 167–175.

Contrada, R. J., & Guyll, M. (2000). On who gets sick and why: The role of personality and stress. In A. Baum, T. A. Revenson, & J. E. Singer (Eds.), *Handbook of health psychology* (pp. 59–84). Mahwah, NJ: Erlbaum.

Degotardi, P. B. (2000). Stress, family coping and adjustment in adolescents with juvenile rheumatoid arthritis (Doctoral dissertation, City University of New York, 2000). *Dissertation Abstracts International, 61,* 2240B.

Degotardi, P. J., Revenson, T. A., & Ilowite, N. (1999). Family-level coping in juvenile rheumatoid arthritis: Assessing the utility of a quantitative family interview. *Arthritis Care and Research, 12,* 314–324.

DeLongis, A., Folkman, S., & Lazarus, R. S. (1988). The impact of daily stress on health and mood: Psychological and social resources as mediators. *Journal of Personality and Social Psychology, 54,* 486–495.

Devins, G. M., Edworthy, S. M., Guthrie, N. G., & Martin, L. (1992). Illness intrusiveness in rheumatoid arthritis: Differential impact on depressive symptoms over the adult lifespan. *The Journal of Rheumatology, 19,* 709–715.

DuBois, D. L., Felner, R. D., Meares, H., & Krier, M. (1994). Prospective investigation of the effects of socioeconomic disadvantage, life stress, and social support in early adolescent adjustment. *Journal of Abnormal Psychology, 103,* 511–522.

Dura, J. R., & Beck, S. J. (1988). A comparison of family functioning when mothers have chronic pain. *Pain, 35,* 79–89.

Dutra, R., Forehand, R., Armistead, L., Brody, G., Morse, E., Morse, P. S., & Clark, L. (2000). Child resiliency in inner-city families affected by HIV: The role of family variables. *Behaviour Research and Therapy, 38,* 471–486.

Ell, K., Nishimoto, R., Mantell, J., & Hamovitch, M. (1988). Longitudinal analysis of psychological adaptation among family members of patients with cancer. *Journal of Psychosomatic Research, 32,* 429–438.

Erblich, J., Bovbjerg, D. H., & Valdimarsdottir, H. B. (2000). Looking forward and back: Distress among women at familial risk for breast cancer. *Annals of Behavioral Medicine, 22,* 53–59.

Feeney, J. A., & Ryan, S. M. (1994). Attachment style and affect regulation: Relationships with health behavior and family experiences of illness in a student sample. *Health Psychology, 13,* 334–345.

Finney, J. W., & Miller, K. M. (1999). Children of parents with medical illness. In W. K. Silverman & T. H. Ollendick (Eds.), *Developmental issues in the treatment of children* (pp. 433–442). Needham Heights, MA: Allyn & Bacon.

Forehand, R., Steele, R., Armistead, L., Morse, E., Simon, P., & Clark, L. (1998). The Family Health Project: Psychosocial adjustment of children whose mothers are HIV infected. *Journal of Consulting and Clinical Psychology, 66,* 513–520.

Fuligni, A. J., & Pedersen, S. (2002). Family obligations and the transition to adulthood among youths from Asian, Latin American, and European backgrounds. *Developmental Psychology, 38,* 856–868.

Gardner, W., & Preator, K. (1996). Children of seropositive mothers in the U.S. AIDS epidemic. *Journal of Social Issues, 52,* 177–195.

Grant, K. E., & Compas, B. E. (1995). Stress and anxious-depressed symptoms among adolescents: Searching for mechanisms of risk. *Journal of Consulting and Clinical Psychology, 63,* 1015–1021.

Grant, K. E., Compas, B. E., Stuhlmacher, A. F., Thurm, A., McMahon, S. D., & Halpert, J. A. (2003). Stressors and child and adolescent psychopathology:

Moving from markers to mechanisms of risk. *Psychological Bulletin, 129,* 447–466.

Harris, C. A., & Zakowski, S. G. (2003). Comparisons of distress in adolescents of cancer patients and controls. *Psycho-Oncology, 12,* 173–182.

Hauser, S. T., DiPlacido, J., Jacobson, A. M., Willett, J., & Cole, C. (1993). Family coping with an adolescent's chronic illness: An approach and three studies. *Journal of Adolescence, 16,* 305–329.

Helgeson, V. S., Cohen, S., Schulz, R., & Yasko, J. (2000). Group support interventions for women with breast cancer: Who benefits from what? *Health Psychology, 19,* 107–114.

Hirsch, B. J., Moos, R. H., & Reischl, T. M. (1985). Psychosocial adjustment of adolescent children of a depressed, arthritic, or normal parent. *Journal of Abnormal Psychology, 94,* 154–164.

Hollingsworth, C. (1982). Adolescents' reactions to parental illness or death. In R. O. Pasnau (Ed.), *Psychosocial aspects of medical practice: Children and adolescents* (pp. 201–209). Menlo Park, CA: Addison Wesley.

Hough, E. S., Brumitt, G., Templin, T., Saltz, E., & Mood, D. (2003). A model of mother-child coping and adjustment to HIV. *Social Science & Medicine, 56,* 643–655.

Johnson, M. O., & Lobo, M. L. (2001). Mother-child interaction in the presence of maternal HIV infection. *Journal of the Association of Nurses in AIDS Care, 12*(1), 40–51.

Kazak, A. E. (1989). Families of chronically ill children: A systems and social-ecological model of adaptation and challenge. *Journal of Consulting and Clinical Psychology, 57,* 25–30.

Kazak, A. E., Simms, S., & Rourke, M. T. (2002). Family systems practice in pediatric psychology. *Journal of Pediatric Psychology, 27,* 133–143.

Kochanek, K. D., & Smith, B. L. (2004). Deaths: Preliminary data for 2002. *National Vital Statistics Reports, 52*(13), 28.

Korneluk, Y. G., & Lee, C. M. (1998). Children's adjustment to parental physical illness. *Clinical Child and Family Psychology Review, 1,* 179–193.

Kotchick, B. A., Forehand, R., Brody, G., Armistead, L., Morse, E., Simon, P., & Clark, L. (1997). The impact of maternal HIV infection on parenting in inner-city African American families. *Journal of Family Psychology, 11,* 447–461.

Landrine, H., & Klonoff, E. A. (1992). Culture and health-related schemas: A review and proposal for interdisciplinary integration. *Health Psychology, 11,* 267–276.

Lazarus, R. S. (1999). *Stress and emotion: A new synthesis.* New York: Springer.

Lepore, S. J. (2001). A social-cognitive processing model of emotional adjustment to cancer. In A. Baum & B. L. Andersen (Eds.), *Psychosocial interventions for cancer* (pp. 99–116). Washington, DC: American Psychological Association.

Lester, P., Stein, J. A., & Bursch, B. (2003). Developmental predictors of somatic symptoms in adolescents of parents with HIV: A 12-month follow-up. *Journal of Developmental and Behavioral Pediatrics, 24,* 242–250.

Lewis, F. M., Hammond, M. A., & Woods, N. F. (1993). The family's functioning with newly diagnosed breast cancer in the mother: The development of an explanatory model. *Journal of Behavioral Medicine, 16*, 351–370.

Lewis, F. M., Woods, N. F., Hough, E. E., & Bensley, L. S. (1989). The family's functioning with chronic illness in the mother: The spouse's perspective. *Social Science & Medicine, 29*, 1261–1269.

Lyons, R. F., Mickelson, K. D., Sullivan, M. J., & Coyne, J. C. (1998). Coping as a communal process. *Journal of Personal and Social Relationships, 15*, 579–605.

Masten, A. S., Neeman, J., & Andenas, S. (1994). Life events and adjustment in adolescents: The significance of event dependence, desirability, and chronicity. *Journal of Research on Adolescence, 4*, 71–97.

McEwen, B. S. (1998). Protective and damaging effects of stress mediators. *New England Journal of Medicine, 338*, 171–179.

Mikail, S. F., & von Baeyer, C. L. (1990). Pain, somatic focus, and emotional adjustment of children of chronic headache sufferers and controls. *Social Science & Medicine, 31*, 51–59.

Milam, J. E., Ritt-Olson, A., & Unger, J. B. (2004). Posttraumatic growth among adolescents. *Journal of Adolescent Research, 19*, 192–204.

Moos, R. H., & Schaefer, J. A. (1984). The crisis of physical illness. In R. H. Moos (Ed.), *Coping with physical illness: Vol. 2. New perspectives* (pp. 3–25). New York: Plenum Press.

Murphy, D. A., Steers, W. N., & Dello Stritto, M. E. (2001). Maternal disclosure of mothers' HIV serostatus to their young children. *Journal of Family Psychology, 15*, 441–450.

Patenaude, A. F. (2000). A different normal: Reactions of children and adolescents to the diagnosis of cancer in a parent. In L. Baider, C. L. Cooper, & A. K. De-Nour (Eds.), *Cancer and the family* (pp. 239–254). Chichester, England: Wiley.

Patterson, J. M., & Garwick, A. W. (1994). The impact of chronic illness on families: A systems perspective. *Annals of Behavioral Medicine, 16*, 131–142.

Pelton, J., Steele, R. G., Chance, M. W., Forehand, R., & the Family Health Project Research Group. (2001). Discrepancy between mother and child perceptions of their relationship: II. Consequences for children considered within the context of maternal physical illness. *Journal of Family Violence, 16*(1), 17–35.

Peters, L., & Esses, L. (1985). Family environment as perceived by children with a chronically ill parent. *Journal of Chronic Diseases, 38*, 301–308.

Räikkönen, K., Keltikangas-Järvinen, L., & Pietikäinen, M. (1991). Type A behavior and its determinants in children, adolescents and young adults with and without parental coronary heart disease: A case-control study. *Journal of Psychosomatic Research, 35*, 273–280.

Reiss, D., Steinglass, P., & Howe, G. (1993). The family's organization around the illness. In R. E. Cole & D. Reiss (Eds.), *How do families cope with chronic illness?* (pp. 173–213). Hillsdale, NJ: Erlbaum.

Revenson, T. A. (1990). All other things are *not* equal: An ecological perspective on the relation between personality and disease. In H. S. Friedman (Ed.), *Personality and disease* (pp. 65–94). New York: Wiley.

Revenson, T. A. (1994). Social support and marital coping with chronic illness. *Annals of Behavioral Medicine, 16*, 122–130.

Revenson, T. A. (2003). Scenes from a marriage: Examining support, coping, and gender within the context of chronic illness. In J. Suls & K. A. Wallston (Eds.), *Social psychological foundations of health and illness* (pp. 530–559). Malden, MA: Blackwell.

Revenson, T. A., Kayser, K., & Bodenmann, G. (Eds.). (2005). *Emerging perspectives on couples coping with stress.* Washington, DC: American Psychological Association.

Reyland, S. A., McMahon, T. J., Higgins-Delessandro, A., & Luthar, S. S. (2002). Inner-city children living with an HIV+ mother: Parent-child relationships, perceptions of social support, and psychological disturbance. *Journal of Child and Family Studies, 11*, 313–329.

Rohrbaugh, M. J., Cranford, J. A., Shoham, V., Nicklas, J. M., Sonnega, J. S., & Coyne, J. C. (2002). Couples coping with congestive heart failure: Role and gender differences in psychological distress. *Journal of Family Psychology, 16*, 3–13.

Rolland, J. S. (1984). Toward a psychosocial topology of chronic and life threatening illnesses. *Family Systems Medicine, 2*, 245–262.

Rolland, J. S. (1999). Parental illness and disability: A family systems framework. *Journal of Family Therapy, 21*, 242–266.

Rotheram-Borus, M. J., Lee, M. B., Gwadz, M., & Draimin, B. (2001). An intervention for parents with AIDS and their adolescent children. *American Journal of Public Health, 91*, 1294–1302.

Rotheram-Borus, M. J., Lee, M., Leonard, N., Lin, Y., Franzke, L., Turner, E., et al. (2003). Four-year behavioral outcomes of an intervention for parents living with HIV and their adolescent children. *AIDS, 17*, 1217–1225.

Rotheram-Borus, M. J., & Stein, J. A. (1999). Problem behavior of adolescents whose parents are living with AIDS. *American Journal of Orthopsychiatry, 69*, 228–239.

Rowlison, R. T., & Felner, R. D. (1988). Major life events, hassles, and adaptation in adolescence: Confounding in conceptualization and measurement of life stress and adjustment revisited. *Journal of Personality and Social Psychology, 55*, 432–444.

Rutter, M. (1990). Psychosocial resilience and protective mechanisms. In J. Rolf, A. S. Masten, D. Cicchetti, K. H. Nuechterlein, & S. Weintraub (Eds.), *Risk and protective factors in the development of psychopathology* (pp. 181–214). New York: Cambridge.

Sambamoorthi, U., & McAlpine, D. D. (2003). Racial, ethnic, socioeconomic, and access disparities in the use of preventive services among women. *Preventive Medicine, 37*, 475–484.

Sarason, B. R., Sarason, I. G., & Gurung, R. A. R. (2001). Close personal relationships and health outcomes: A key to the role of social support. In B. R.

Sarason & S. Duck (Eds.), *Personal relationships: Implications for clinical and community psychology* (pp. 15–41). Chichester, England: Wiley.

Scheier, M. F., & Carver, C. S. (2003). Self-regulatory processes and responses to health threats: Effects of optimism on well-being. In J. Suls & K. A. Wallston (Eds.), *Social psychological foundations of health and illness* (pp. 395–428). Malden, MA: Blackwell.

Schmaling, K. B., & Sher, T. G. (2000). *The psychology of couples and illness.* Washington, DC: American Psychological Association.

Seligman, M. E. P., & Csikszentmihalyi, M. (2000). Positive psychology: An introduction. *American Psychologist, 55,* 5–14.

Shaffer, A., Jones, D. J., Kotchick, B. A., Forehand, R., & the Family Health Project Research Group. (2001). Telling the children: Disclosure of maternal HIV infection and its effects on child psychosocial adjustment. *Journal of Child and Family Studies, 10,* 301–313.

Siegel, K., Raveis, V. H., & Karus, D. (2000). Correlates of self-esteem among children facing the loss of a parent to cancer. In L. Baider, C. L. Cooper, & A. K. De-Nour (Eds.), *Cancer and the family* (pp. 223–238). Chichester, England: Wiley.

Smedley, B. D., Stith, A. Y., & Nelson, A. R. (Eds.). (2003). *Unequal treatment: Confronting racial and ethnic disparities in health care.* Washington, DC: National Academies Press.

Stanton, A., & Revenson, T. A. (in press). Progress and promise in research on adaptation to chronic illness. In H. S. Friedman & R. C. Silver (Eds.), *The Oxford handbook of health psychology.* New York: Oxford University Press.

Steele, R., Forehand, R., & Armistead, L. (1997). The role of family processes and coping strategies in the relationship between parental chronic illness and childhood internalizing problems. *Journal of Abnormal Child Psychology, 25,* 83–94.

Stetz, K. M., Lewis, F. M., & Primomo, J. (1986). Family coping strategies and chronic illness in the mother. *Family Relations, 35,* 515–522.

Tennen, H., & Affleck. G. (2002). Benefit-finding and benefit-reminding. In C. R. Snyder & S. Lopez (Eds.), *Handbook of positive psychology* (pp. 584–597). New York: Oxford University Press.

von Bertalanffy, L. (1968). *General systems theory: Foundations, developments, applications.* New York: Braziller.

Walsh, F. (2003). Family resilience: A framework for clinical practice. *Family Process, 42,* 1–18.

Weihs, K., & Reiss, D. (2000). Family reorganization in response to cancer: A developmental perspective. In L. Baider, C. L. Cooper, & A. K. De-Nour (Eds.), *Cancer and the family* (pp. 17–40). Chichester, England: Wiley.

Wellisch, D. K., Gritz, E. R., Schain, W., Wang, H., & Siau, J. (1991). Psychological functioning of daughters of breast cancer patients. Part I: Daughters and comparison subjects. *Psychosomatics, 32,* 324–336.

Wellisch, D. K., Gritz, E. R., Schain, W., Wang, H., & Siau, J. (1992). Psychological functioning of daughters of breast cancer patients. Part II: Characterizing the distressed daughter of the breast cancer patient. *Psychosomatics, 33,* 171–179.

Wills, T. A., & Fegan, M. F. (2001). Social networks and social support. In A. Baum, T. A. Revenson, & J. E. Singer (Eds.), *Handbook of health psychology* (pp. 139–173). Mahwah, NJ: Erlbaum.

Worsham, N. L., Compas, B. E., & Ey, S. (1997). Children's coping with parental illness. In S. A. Wolchik & I. N. Sandler (Eds.), *Handbook of children's coping: Linking theory and intervention* (pp. 195–213). New York: Plenum Press.

Yali, A. M., & Revenson, T. A. (2004). How changes in population demographics will impact health psychology: Incorporating a broader notion of cultural competence into the field. *Health Psychology, 23*, 147–155.

Yates, B. C., Bensley, L. S., Lalonde, B., Lewis, F. M., & Woods, N. F. (1995). The impact of marital status and quality on family functioning in maternal chronic illness. *Health Care for Women International, 16*, 437–449.

CHAPTER TWENTY-ONE

Life's Challenges

Curse or Opportunity? Counseling Families of Persons With Disabilities

Mary R. Hulnick and H. Ronald Hulnick

It is interesting to go back and reread a similar article we wrote 10 years ago (Prescott & Hulnick, 1979). Most interesting was the realization that our basic approach is essentially the same. Our philosophical orientation that all of life's experiences are, in fact, opportunities for personal growth and learning is unchanged. We are more convinced than ever that counselor empathy is of paramount importance, as is the need to communicate genuine caring to clients, the importance of carefully addressing the issue of personal responsibility, and the value of effectively dealing with judgment of self and others. And we continue to recognize the validity of having a well-developed information and referral network. These, then, are the fundamentals that enhance the effectiveness of any counseling relationship as much today as 10 years ago.

There are, however, changes that have occurred and that are still in process that speak for the value of an update. For one, the language recommended for referring to individuals with disabilities reflects a fundamental shift. The special issue of *The Personnel and Guidance Journal*

From "Life's challenges: Curse or opportunity? Counseling families of persons with disabilities," by M. Hulnick and H. R. Hulnick, 1989, *Journal of Counseling and Development*, *86*, 9–22. Also published in *The Psychological and Social Impact of Disability*, 3rd Edition. NY: Springer, 1991.

in 1979 was titled *Counseling Handicapped Persons and Their Families*. The 1989 issue on the same theme is called *Counseling Persons With Disabilities*. The former referred to *handicapped persons*, while the latter speaks of *persons with disabilities*. It is encouraging to see the language focusing on the person rather than the limitation. As counselors, it is essential that we retain a person-centered rather than a problem-centered approach.

PERSONS AS SEPARATE FROM DISABILITIES

Taking this concept a step further in establishing a context for this chapter, we recognize the importance of further refining our language by defining disabled as *differently abled*. Each of us as human beings has unique challenges as well as unique gifts. As we see it, *disability* is a term referring to functional limitation. Such limitation may occur at different levels; that is, there may be a functional limitation in the physical body, the mind, or the emotions. These limitations can be seen as an individual's challenges and are not to be confused with a person's intrinsic worth or value. As a good friend of ours who is a rehabilitation counselor has said, "We all have our challenges. Some of us wear them on the outside and some on the inside. Down deep, we're all whole and complete, and thank God, we're all worthy."

While a particular person may have a physical limitation, he or she may also have a profound sense of the value of himself or herself and others. Another person may be "physically abled" yet have an extremely low sense of self-esteem and be functionally unavailable to give and receive love. Which person is truly more disabled?

And then there are those like our good friend Kathy, who passed away about a year ago. Kathy used her 8-year battle with cancer to transform herself from an extremely angry and judgmental lady into a most beautiful and lovely soul. We will probably never forget her sitting there at her master's graduation during her last days all hunched over in her wheelchair, looking about 20 years older than she was. She spoke from her heart of the need for us all to learn to love one another and of her loving for us. Her sharing was sacred. She achieved this quality of awareness by successfully dealing with all that her "disability" had brought forward. She became the victor over it rather than the victim of it.

Viewing disability in this way is paradoxical, as it is difficult to know whether one's condition is a curse or an opportunity. As we see it, the only difference is in the way we respond to the challenge. As counselors, we have the opportunity to hold a focus that supports individuals and families in meeting challenges with an empowering perspective that sees all people as worthwhile and responsible players fully capable of actively and successfully participating in the game of life.

Thus a counselor's challenge in working with families of persons with disabilities remains the same today as it was 10 years ago. Fundamentally, it is to assist people in learning the mental and emotional skills and attitudes necessary for dealing effectively with life's gifts as well as life's challenges. What has changed is public sensitivity to the issue of disability, as well as a maturing in the counseling field, which has spawned a new generation of skills and techniques enabling us to stand on the shoulders of those who taught us what we knew 10 years ago. Today we know more about assisting clients in the psychological healing process of applying caring and compassion to the places inside that hurt.

CRISIS AS OPPORTUNITY

In the Chinese language, the written character for *crisis* and *opportunity* is the same. In other words, Chinese culture recognizes that opportunity is inherent in crisis. It all depends entirely on how you look at a given situation. We have a saying in our classes: "How you relate to the issue *IS* the issue;" or perhaps more to the point: "How you relate to yourself while you go through an issue IS the issue." Are there, then, ways we can incorporate this attitude into our counseling with families who have a person with disability within their structure? We have found several that we would like to share here.

REFRAMING ISSUES AS CHALLENGES

Reframing is a skill made popular by the founders of neurolinguistic programming (Bandler & Grinder, 1979). Essentially, it is a technique for learning another way of seeing any particular situation. This can include recontexting the issues raised by the presence of a disability. For example, families with a person who has a disability often come to counseling with the orientation (view) that they have a "problem" that by definition tends to be perceived as negative. Because they are I pain, the preferred treatment, as initially seen through their eyes, is eradication. Trying to "get rid of" problems is actually an ineffective approach to life's challenges since, as we have said before, the real issue is *not what* is happening but *how we relate to what is happening.*

What counselors can do is caringly assist family members in learning how to shift, or reframe, their view of the situation. In particular, a shift is usually required in the direction of learning new ways for successfully responding to "what is" rather than magically wishing current reality would change (Wright, 1983). We as counselors can caringly demonstrate how a shift of attitude can be very beneficial in successfully coping with what is. We refer to those types of shifts as moving to a position of positive outlook. Positive outlooks are characterized by the following attitudes: "What new learning is in store for me now?" "What are the opportunities and blessings present in this unique situation?" A positive attitude can provide the inspiration necessary to move forward (Egan, 1988).

An effective counselor's initial responsibilities include establishing a safe space for client expression of feelings and concerns while communication acceptance, understanding, and empathy. Once this quality of relationship is consistently experience, then there are four empowering questions the client and counselor can gently explore together, which can be very fruitful for family members:

1. "Can you see any way you can use this situation to your advancement?"
2. "What can you learn from all this?"
3. "What can you do that might result in a more uplifting experience for everyone involved?"
4. "How can you relate to yourself right now in a more loving way?"

These questions in the context of a caring counseling relationship provide an exploratory focus that supports both individuals with disabilities, as well as their relatives, in making peace with the realities of their situation in a way that implies true acceptance rather than embittered resignation. Real healing occurs in the presence of genuine caring. The painful challenges in time become parts of valuable lessons experienced as worth learning (Miller, 1988).

Once a situation has been empathically reframed to a more positive context, then more choices become available for coping with both the emotional the logistical challenges that may be involved. When more options are seen, tensions and pressures associated with seemingly burdensome situations are often alleviated.

CLARIFYING MISINTERPRETATIONS
OF PERSONAL RESPONSIBILITY

Accepting personal responsibility for both their feelings and actions is probably the most challenging step family members face in coming to terms mentally and emotionally with the advent of a loved one's disability. As a concept, responsibility seems to have several nonconstructive meanings, which often emerge in working with families of individuals with disabilities. For instance, some family members consider themselves and others "responsible" for their actions in much the same way that a driver is responsible for steering a car off the road. If an "accident" occurs resulting in a family members becoming disabled, this is often viewed mentally, and experienced emotionally, by the other family members involved as evidence that they are not only at fault but "bad" as well.

Seen in this way, person responsibility becomes twisted and is nothing more than a form of self-judgment, self-punishment, and self-abuse. Since we are "at fault," we must punish ourselves in retribution. It is as if somehow this will make things okay. In some way it evens the score. Guilt and a compensatory desire to do more, to atone for not having done enough, are often part of this pattern. Sometimes clients feel somehow they deserve the "disaster" (Miller, 1988).

Another variation on this type of reasoning occurs when someone, although not directly involved in the disabling process, nevertheless feels responsible. They somehow take another's disability as evidence of their own failure or shortcomings. If an experience, such as a loved one developing a disability, violates one of the family member's beliefs, such as "things like this don't happen to good people," then he or she blames and punishes himself or herself. A result of this type of self-destructive behavior is beating oneself up mentally when our loved one is not physically, mentally, or emotionally "normal" in some way. We judge ourselves as wrong for not measuring up to some unhealthy idea of "goodness." This is often reflected by attitudes or statements such as "What did I do to deserve this?" Or, "If I'd only done something different, this wouldn't have happened."

The error in this approach is, of course, that it has a completely negative focus. The process of engaging in this judgmental activity invariably results in the opposite of uplifting and constructive behavior by family members. It rarely results in a greater willingness to approach the situations constructively, since it only erroneously reinforces the experience of personal failure by associating a family member's disability with the pain of self-judgment. Clients sometimes fool themselves by falsely thinking they are making themselves "right" by judging themselves for "wrongdoing."

Encouraging family members to find a more compassionate definition of personal responsibility is imperative.

RESPONSIBILITY—THE WILLINGNESS TO CHOOSE

Seeing issues as opportunities presupposes a constructive definition of personal responsibility. Here responsibility is defined simply as the ability to respond, and, more specifically, to respond differently and more constructively than the way we have been responding if it has not been truly working for, us. In this sense, we are talking about the willingness to consciously make constructive choices rather than to unconsciously react with resentment, disappointment, irritation, or anger. When events characterizing an opportunity for personal growth present themselves, such as a family member developing a disability, demonstrating willingness to accept individual responsibility is, for many families, perhaps the most challenging step. Consciously or not, choices are made by all involved. Exploring choices is an important part of the healing process.

At this point, personal responsibility divides into two areas, outer choices and inner choices. Examples of outer choices include "Will I go to the hospital to visit my son who is going through rehabilitation for serious and disabling injuries, or would I be better off going home and going to bed?" "Will I reach out to my son as well as to those who can support me, or will I withdraw and isolate myself nursing my hurt and self-pity?" Choosing these, or other alternatives, is the process of taking responsibility. It is only when a family member has chosen a course of action and is doing it that they have taken responsibility. And, of course, each separate action will have its consequences. When the consequences appear, the choice in how to respond at that time will be the next opportunity for taking responsibility.

Inner choices are similar. "How will I choose to be with myself over the fact that I have a son who's paralyzed from the waist down?" "And how will I choose to be with myself while I go through the process of dealing with the fact that he has a serious physical disability?" "Will I hold myself 'responsible' for my son's disability, judge myself, and suffer guilt and remorse?" "Or will I move into acceptance that he now has this condition, be loving with myself, and outwardly do those things I need to do in order to assist myself and him?" "Will I take good care of myself and honestly share my feelings and needs for support with other family members?"

In these types of emotionally laden situations, willingness to take inner responsibility in the moment would suggest that it is the choice of each family member whether or not to take 100% responsibility for his or her own internal emotional reaction, independent from what seems to have caused it (e.g., their relative's disability). Viewed in this way, situations are simply triggering devices that surface unresolved issues needing healing within (Power, 1988).

For family members, there is a very human temptation to assign responsibility for their feelings and emotional reactions to what is going on outside, to the "because" in life. Often it sounds like, "I am upset because . . . ," and a laundry list of justifiable reasons follows. "I am upset because my child or spouse has a disability." Being caught in this stance is a process of self-victimization. Family members may unknowingly be victimizing themselves by blaming their upset on outside events. Are there alternatives? Although upset is always understandable and acceptable, if there are no justifiable causes for being upset, how can we constructively proceed?

SELF-FORGIVENESS: COMPASSION FOR ONESELF

In fact, we may or may not be at all responsible for circumstances that life brings to us. There are mixed opinions on this subject, and we think it is important to remember that that is exactly what they are, opinions. Only God knows for sure. It is precisely this vantage point of realizing "Only God knows for sure," which gives counselors a most important tool as family members must be assisted in facing and healing any deep feelings of rage, sadness, loss, and guilt. Emotional suffering is only exacerbated by holding oneself accountable in a negative way for a loved one's disability. Any unwillingness to let go of blame and judgment one has placed against oneself must be challenged. But how?

We have observed many times that there is a sequence that always seems to be present at times of emotional upset. It goes like this. Whenever anger is present and we look beneath the anger, we always find hurt. Anger turns out to largely be a reaction occurring when we feel hurt. And when we look beneath the hurt, we always find caring. We are only hurt when something or someone we care about has been, in some way, desecrated or violated.

This sequence gives us the key for effectively handling these types of situations. It is this. Give a client full permission to express his or her deepest pain. In fact, assist clients by actively encouraging them in expressing it. If the pain is at the anger level, encourage them in safely expressing their anger. This may involve the use of an encounter bat, rolled-up towel or newspaper, or even a tennis racquet or length of rubber hose directed against a soft object such as a mattress or large pillow. Care must be taken to provide guidelines stressing safety, and a willingness to "not hurt oneself or others in the process" should actually be verbalized and committed to by the client.

As a client risks fully expressing his or her anger, he or she will naturally tend to drop down into the hurt that is always beneath. As with anger, this expression should be actively encouraged. To the degree that clients are willing to risk expressing their hurt, this expression will tend to be characterized by deep sobbing, the deeper the better. It is at this point that a counselor has an opportunity for truly making a serious intervention. It is to encourage the client to begin working with self-forgiveness. For what? We need to forgive ourselves not for our anger and not for our hurt, but for any *judgments* we may have placed against ourselves or our disabled loved one. It is simply an act of realizing "Only God knows for sure what any disability is all about." Regardless of what we may think or feel, we must admit the obvious: We really do not know what any human condition is truly about. We just do not know. The act of judging implies that we do know. By forgiving ourselves, we release the judgments we have placed and we pass through the hurt level into the caring that lies just' below. By walking across the bridge of self-forgiveness, hurt gives way to peace, and the client is released from his or her self-induced hell. The healing process has begun.

Assisting clients in evoking their own compassion for themselves as human beings is essential. In this way, they can courageously embrace themselves as worthwhile persons with both strengths and weaknesses. By entering into this quality of caring relationship with themselves, they come into greater willingness and ability to work with the realities of their current situation.

Over the years, we have found that it matters little whether one is disabled or is a family member of a disabled person. The process we have just described is effective regardless.

RESPONSIBILITY—THE CARING CHOICE

Once a client is at peace within himself or herself, it is crucial to assist him or her in recognizing that little has changed regarding outside circumstances. We still must respond to the circumstances coming our way (Frankl, 1963). However, being willing to take responsibility from a place of "caring" inside is a much different story from taking responsibility from a place of "anger or hurt" inside. If we are to be victors, we must be willing to face our choices "caringly." This involves nothing more than assisting families with disabilities in acknowledging not only the choices they are currently making but also inviting consideration of potentially more constructive choices they could be making that might produce more beneficial results. In this context, it may be useful to remember one definition of insanity is: Doing the same thing over and over while expecting a different result. Clients often recognize the truth of this statement and experience renewed motivation to move beyond the limitations of previous attitudes and actions.

EMPOWERING QUESTIONS FACILITATING
AWARENESS OF CHOICES

We have designed a series of questions for use in assisting family members in looking at both their inner and outer choices in the context of a caring and supportive counseling relationship.

1. "What choices are you making that tend to perpetuate this situation?"
2. "Are you aware of any other choices you might make which would tend to have a different result? Keep in mind that you are only looking at possibilities and you are not committing to doing anything."
3. "Let's look at each choice you have brought forward in more detail. What would it really look like if you were really to do it? Describe yourself in the present tense as if you are actually doing it now."
4. "Has considering these questions resulted in any new possibilities for you?"

In addition to maintaining an empathic attitude, there are two important aspects to keep in mind while doing this process. The first aspect is the importance of emphasizing that families are not committing to actually doing anything other than looking at choices. We have found that parents, spouses, and siblings all tend to be much more creative when they are given permission to freely explore, knowing that they are not committing to actually doing anything other than consider what they bring forward as alternatives.

The second aspect is to encourage family members in detailing each choice "as if" they were actually doing it here and now. We invite and encourage them to enthusiastically describe themselves in the present tense *having, being,* and *doing* the experience of their choice. Research is clearly showing that the psyche does not seem to differentiate very well between a well-imagined fantasy and physical reality. By imagining doing something in detail, we have found that many family members often then tend to spontaneously take that action in physical reality. Clients sometimes delightedly report finding themselves doing the new actions that are more supportive of themselves as well as of the family member with the identified disability even though no commitment was actually made.

Part of a counselor's challenge is assisting family members in more consistently choosing the attitudes and actions that support them in creating the quality of inner and outer life preferred. Many times this is a process that requires conscious commitment to moving ahead on the part of all involved, as many responses are well-ingrained habits and it takes time to develop the awareness that allows for more conscious constructive choices.

POSITIVE SELF-TALK—A MAJOR FORCE

Often family members are caught in a mental habit of catastrophizing imagined negative consequences of their situation and the health of their relative with the disability. This kind of inner dialogue repeated internally can become a negative self-fulfilling prophecy. Albert Ellis hit the nail on the head (Ellis, 1988) when he discussed how people tend to get themselves into trouble by continuing to indoctrinate themselves with their own limiting beliefs.

These days this concept can be demonstrated easily through the use of an applied kinesiology technique called *muscle-testing*. This method can be especially powerful in working with families where the disability is physical. When we ask family members to hold out their arm and instruct them to resist our downward pull on their wrist, we most likely will find it somewhat difficult to pull their arm down. We then instruct them to visualize a situation where they entered into judgment or negative self-talk about themselves, another, or a situation, and, while continuing the negative dialogue in their mind, we ask them to once again resist our downward pull. Invariably, we find the muscle has weakened considerably, and it is quite easy to pull their arm down.

We then ask them to tell themselves that, while the situation in question might have been difficult, how they handled it really has very little to do with their value or lovableness as a person. In fact, we have them say out loud something like "I know I am a lovable and worthwhile person." While continuing a positive mental dialogue, we again ask them to resist our downward pull, and we find the muscle usually not only has returned to its original strength but also, in most cases, is actually stronger than when we started.

It seems, then, that what we tell ourselves has a tremendous effect not only on our psyche but also on our physical body as well. In a recent article (Rosellini, 1988), the U.S. Surgeon General, Dr. C. Everett Koop, commented on the mind-body relationship: "There is no question that the things that we think have a tremendous effect upon our bodies. If we can change our thinking, the body frequently heals itself" (p. 64). A good friend or ours who knows the validity of this information has put it wisely, "It's foolish not to win in your own fantasies!"

Positive self-talk is a skill that every counselor can readily teach since, in some ways, the mind is easier to work with than the body or the emotions. It is relatively easy to consciously redirect our thoughts once it dawns on us that we can do so. We find that many people have a critical inner dialogue going on in their minds a great deal of the time. The muscle-testing demonstration shows that this is a physically debilitating process. By consciously choosing to redirect this dialogue so both the content and context (attitude) are positive, we facilitate a more nurturing, supporting, and uplifting relationship inside our self, not to mention the physical benefits. Consciously engaging in this process tends to *automatically* result in more positive outcomes in our lives.

Again, we have designed another series of questions to assist clients in learning to do "positive self-talk." Let us assume a client is complaining about having to spend so much time and effort taking care of his wife who has had a stroke. The steps for assisting him in learning positive self-talk follow:

1. Assist the client in identifying his or her current pattern of self-talk regarding the situation: "What are you telling yourself about this situation?"
2. Encourage the possibility of a more positive and nurturing pattern of self-talk: "What *could* you tell yourself right now which would be more self-supporting to you as well as uplifting to your wife?"
3. Encourage the client in taking responsibility for redirecting self-talk into a more positive pattern: "Would you be willing to begin *right now* and tell yourself this positive self-talk?"
4. Give the client permission to do it and support and encourage as he or she does so: "OK, go ahead and do it!"

THEN AND NOW

Ten years ago we implied, and now we are even more sure, that there is really only one issue with which we are all dealing. It is becoming clearer that earth is a school for learning how to become more loving within ourselves as individuals and between each other. Viewed in this way, there really is very little difference between the so-called disabled person and the equally so-called able-bodied person. They are both simply conditions with which we must deal. And how we deal with them is everything. If we abuse ourselves complaining about our condition, blaming ourselves and others, and generally expressing negativity, then our life, with disability or without, will be a curse. And if we use our life to transform our pain into loving then our time, disabled or not, will be a blessing. There is a prayer attributed to an unknown Confederate soldier (Cleland, 1980) that seems to sum up what we are saying beautifully:

> I asked God for strength that I might achieve,
> I was made weak, that I might learn humbly to obey.
> I asked for health, that I might do greater things,
> I was given infirmity that I might do better things.
> I asked for riches, that I might be happy,
> I was given poverty, that I might be wise.
> I asked for power, that I might have the praise of men,
> I was given weakness, that I might feel the need of God.
> I asked for all things, that I might enjoy life,
> I was given life, that I might enjoy all things.
> I got nothing I asked for—
> but everything I had hoped for.
> Almost despite myself,
> my unspoken prayers were answered.
> I am among all men,
> most richly blessed.

REFERENCES

Bandler, R., & Grinder, J. (1974). *Frogs into princes*. Moab, UT: Real People Press.

Cleland, M. (1980). *Strong at the broken places*. TX: Chosen Books.

Egan, P. (1988). Personal statement: My life with a disability—continued opportunities. In P. W Power, A. E. Dell Orto, & M. B. Gibbons (Eds.), *Family interventions throughout chronic ill ness and disability* (pp. 44–46). New York: Springer Publishing Co.

Ellis, A. (1988). *How to stubbornly refuse to be miserable about anything—yes anything*. Secaucus NJ: Lyle Stuart.

Frankl, V. (1963). *Man's search for meaning*. New York: Pocket Books.

Miller, J. (1988). Personal statement: Mechanisms for coping with the disability of a child—a mother': perspective. In P. W. Power, A. E. Dell Orto, & M. B. Gibbons (Eds.), *Family intervention: throughout chronic illness and disability* (pp. 136–147). New York: Springer Publishing Co.

Power, P. W. (1988). An assessment approach to family intervention. In P. W. Power, A. E. Dell Orto, & M. B. Gibbons (Eds.), *Family interventions throughout chronic illness and disability* (pp. 5–23). New York: Springer Publishing Co.

Prescott, M. R., & Hulnick, H. R. (1979). Counseling parents of handicapped children: An empathic approach. *The Personnel and Guidance Journal, 28,* 263–266.

Rosellini, L. (1988, May). Rebel with a cause: Koop. *U.S. News & World Report*; pp. 55–64.

Wright, B. (1983). *Physical disability: A psychosocial approach* (2nd ed.). New York: Harper & Row.

PART III

Discussion Questions

1. One of the articles discussed the issues with a mother who has a disability and the effects on the well-being of her children. If the father is the one with a disability, would the same issues exist?
2. What do you believe is the role of the allied health professional when assisting family decision making directed toward the termination of life-extending treatments?
3. To assist in the recovery of children who are severely injured, what do you believe is the most effective way for a helping professional, such as a nurse or counselor, to develop a positive helping relationship with the child's family during the beginning of treatment?
4. When parenting a child with a chronic, medical condition, how would you prioritize care-giving efforts, related to economic considerations, socialization opportunities, and parental self-identity needs, so that parental energy is appropriately and constructively expended?
5. One of the articles in Part III explained the care-giving needs and concerns for the wife of a spouse with HIV/AIDS. Suppose it was the wife who has HIV/AIDS. Would such issues as emotional impact of the disability, needs for social support, and the context of one's spiritual journey be the same as the husband's?
6. Do such moderators as the ill parent's gender and family role, family-coping style, and parents' age at onset of his or her illness have differential effects on the family according to different serious illnesses or chronic conditions?
7. Discuss the issues related to the following statement: "A family is better able to cope with a seriously ill child during the early years of marriage."

8. Does the gender of a child living with illness or disability impact the response of the family to the child and the situation? If so, how?

9. What are the issues that are unique to children with a serious condition, for example, cancer as compared to adults?

10. What are the factors that place a family at risk when coping with a child with a chronic medical condition?

PART III

Personal Perspectives

Robert Winske and Janet Lingerman

The statement by Robert Winske adds still another perspective to understanding family dynamics in illness and disability. It focuses on the devastating effects of family secrets and on how the absence of communication across family generational lines can cause lingering uncertainty and thwart necessary coping efforts. When the secret is discovered, the impact of the discovery fuels anger and resentment. When the family secret concerns the origin of a genetic disability, its discovery induces a more powerful sense of loss and a call for possible forgiveness. Robert Winske's statement is about this secret, and its continually unfolding demand on the family member's ability to achieve life adjustment. It also captures and reflects some of the issues addressed in Prillentensky's article in Part III. Adding another perspective on the family is the personal statement by Janet Lingerman. Janet carefully describes what happens to a married couple when the sudden event of a medical crisis with a newborn occurs. Her story identifies the many coping methods utilized when unexpected traumas associated with illness and disability emerge. Sibling dynamics are also discussed. Importantly, Janet Lingerman's family journey shows that despite the many serious disruptions and crises a family can survive and even grow in spiritual health and maturity. This personal perspective is reprinted from "Families Living With Chronic Illness and Disability" (Power & Dell Orto, Springer 2004).

MY LIFE WITH MUSCULAR DYSTROPHY:
LESSONS AND OPPORTUNITIES

Personal Perspective: Robert P. Winske

I am 41 and the middle son of three boys born with a rare form of muscular dystrophy known as Nemaline Rod Myopathy. To date there is still little information known about the disease, as was the case at the time when we were born in the early to mid-1960s, though it is clear that it is a progressive condition and is passed from mother to son. At the time of each of our births, what made the case more baffling to the doctors was how this occurred. As I stated, muscular dystrophy is a congenital impairment that is passed through the X-chromosomes of the mother. To my mother's knowledge, however, she herself didn't have the disability.

When my older brother was born, the doctors requested that my parents check the family tree and see if there was anyone on either side of the family that may have had muscular dystrophy. However, as requested, my parents with the assistance of their parents did check each side and their efforts proved unsuccessful. To their knowledge no one on either side of the family had ever been diagnosed and treated for any form of the impairment. Though my mother did have a physical disability, to her knowledge it was polio, not muscular dystrophy. She became sick as a young child in the late 1940s, which was at the height of the polio epidemic that extended into the early fifties. Growing up, my mother always talked about being a young girl getting sick in which her muscles got weak, especially in her lower extremities and was told by her parents that it was polio. She had no reason to doubt this information because her mother was a registered nurse. She was also treated in hospital wards, where several children her age were being treated for the same condition and some were worse that she was. My mother was still able to walk which was not so for most of the children.

As there were no signs of the disease found on either side of the family, the doctors believed the occurrence of muscular dystrophy was a fluke. There was no reason why it occurred and they informed my parents that to their understanding, the odds to their having another child with the birth defect were unlikely. This led them to decide to have another child. Like my brother, I also was born with the same form of muscular dystrophy. This really perplexed the doctors, not only because my parents had another baby with the disease, but also because I wasn't as severely impacted by its limitations.

However, following the birth of a second child with the neuromuscular condition, the doctors again insisted someone on one side of the family had to have had the condition. They even wondered if a family member had a baby with the same or similar condition, but never took the baby home. This was common at that time as children with birth defects were generally institutionalized because it was an embarrassment to families to have children with impairments. It was also believed that parents couldn't provide the needed, specialized care. If this were the case, the doctors believed that whoever in the family may have had a child with muscular dystrophy wouldn't want to admit to it, being ashamed or embarrassed, along with the belief that everyone wants the perfect baby.

Following the doctor's recommendation, my parents again went back to their parents to examine both sides of the family. It was emphasized that it was important to know if there was any family history of muscular dystrophy so the doctors could more efficiently treat me and my brother. Again, as with the previous search the second attempt to identify anyone in the family who may have had the same or similar condition also proved unsuccessful. No one in the family reported having any family members with any physical disabilities. Because of the absence of any disclosure, it was suggested that my parents not have any more children because it couldn't be guaranteed that they wouldn't have another child with the physical impairments. With each of our births it was also recommended that they not bring us home, as the doctors attempted to tell my parents that we would never grow up to be anything, to have independent lives, and would demand a lot of care. Such communication was especially true after I was born. The doctors tried to explain that my parents already had their hands full with taking care of a child with a severe physical impairment. In trying to take care of two, that would be too much and too overwhelming. In both cases my parents opted not to listen to the doctors so they took me home with them, and about two years later would have a third child. Again, a boy was born with the same physical impairments but with less impairment that I had.

Following the birth of my parents' third child, the physicians were perplexed as to how parents who had no history of muscular dystrophy on either side of the family could have three children with the condition. The only thing they were left to believe is that my mother as a child had been misdiagnosed as having polio. They believed it could have been an easy mistake because at the time many children were getting sick with polio, and the symptoms my mother recalled experiencing as a child were similar to the impairments experienced with polio. This perception existed for several years until my younger brother was fifteen years old. Around that time my mother and he both had concurrently a muscle biopsy, a process in which they each had a small piece of muscle removed from their thigh to be analyzed. This analysis revealed that each had the same condition and then these results were compared to biopsy results my older brother and I had as young children. Thus, as had long been expected, my mother did in fact have muscular dystrophy.

But our lives continued and my parents successfully raised three children with muscular dystrophy. Each of us completed high school and went on to college. My older brother obtained a job as an advocate of individuals with various impairments after leaving Boston University; I was a senior at Northeastern University; and my younger brother entered the first year at U Mass Amherst after earning an AA degree from Newbury Jr. College. However, after my brothers and I had begun to move forward with our lives, my mom found that her mother started to have slight problems with memory which in the early days was minimal but then slowly progressed. This would eventually lead her to bring her mother to be seen by a doctor because she was concerned that there may be something more serious than that of aging. She was told that her mother did in fact have major health problems and that she was in the early stages of Alzheimer's.

As the disease would progress my mom would be faced with one of the most difficult decisions that no child ever looks forward to making regarding one's parent. She would realize that despite existing support systems her mother was no longer safe living on her own, and my mom would have to make the decision that she was unable to care for her mother's needs and would have to put her in a nursing home. She knew her mother wouldn't want that as she'd always made it clear that she wanted to remain and die in her own home with her dignity. However, my mom knew a nursing home was the only real option available, fearing that not acting so would result in her mother doing something that would result in serious injury or worse yet, put a neighbor at risk in the elderly housing complex where she was living.

During this process of placing her mother in a nursing home, my mother needed to obtain a variety of information about her mother for the nursing home, which included a determination of eligibility for Medicaid, which is the insurance company that covers the nursing home expenses. One item needed was my grandmother's birth certificate, leading my mother to call the city hall of the town of Kennebunkport, Maine. That is the town where my grandmother had always reported as being born and raised. However, this would prove unsuccessful because when speaking with the town's city hall administrator, my mother would be told that there was no record of anyone with the name my mother had provided. A bit confused, my mother followed the recommendation of the city hall employee, which was to check neighboring towns in the event my grandmother had been mistaken. Though my mother found it difficult to believe her mother wouldn't know the town where she'd been born, she wondered whether maybe she had been born in a different city and just raised in Kennebunkport. My mother would spend days calling numerous city halls in those cities and towns surrounding Kennebunkport. All of these calls were unsuccessful, as none of the cities or towns had any record of anyone being born there with her mother's name.

After days of numerous phone calls and feeling frustrated, my mother contacted her mother's sister to ask for assistance inquiring where her mother was born. To my mother's shock, she found out that her mother was adopted as a child. This frustrated my mother. She could only think of why her mother never mentioned this, especially during the early years in which she and my father were checking both of their family's background to see if there was any history of muscular dystrophy on either side of the family. In further conversation with her aunt, my mother would indeed discover that her mother was aware that she did in fact have muscular dystrophy. But for reasons my own mother will never understand, her mother was apparently embarrassed by this diagnosis, and her mother told the doctors treating my mother as child to tell her it was polio, not muscular dystrophy.

After this revelation, my mother was extremely confused, understandably frustrated, as well as angry that her mother would keep this information from her. Her mother was a registered nurse and should have known that muscular dystrophy is a genetic disorder and not the result of something she or my mother had done wrong that resulted in this impairment. Even more aggravating for my mother was wondering how her mother could remain silent about this information when she, my father and the doctors were working with both sides of the family to explore if there was any history of the impairment on either side of the family. My mother found herself not knowing how she should feel or how to approach this topic with her mother. Her mother probably wouldn't have a clear understanding of her reasoning behind the decision or understand the frustration my mother was dealing with. Alzheimer's had robbed her mother of an ability to comprehend anything beyond simple childlike questions and reasoning She had to figure out herself how to deal with the anger and frustration she had towards her mother, which she knew would be difficult. My mom was unable to resolve questions regarding her mother's decision making, as well as how to set aside these feelings. She knew she had to do this, because she could see her mother quickly withering away day by day as the Alzheimer's progressed, and knew that things were only going to get worse. Thus, for her mother to be properly cared for at that time as well in the later years of her life, and knowing the effects Alzheimer's would continue to have, she had to put these feelings aside if she were to make sure that her mother's needs were met.

Though my mother didn't and probably never will totally understand or forgive her mother for what she did at that time, my mother was able to put these feelings aside and put her mother into a nursing home where she was properly cared for during the final few years of her life. I don't know how my mother was able to do this as I knew how she felt, thought I do know it took a great deal of strength. She would be able to draw on the same strength and courage it took to raise three children with physical impairments during a time when most parents would have had their children placed in an institution. This was recommended when my brother and I were born.

During my lifetime I've gone through numerous changes due to the progression of my impairment. I started as an individual who was able to walk, then to walking and using a manual wheelchair when having to go for any distances or when my legs were sore and weak due to fatigue, then to using a manual chair at all times because I was no longer able to walk, though I was able to perform all activities of daily living, to currently both requiring the use of an electric wheelchair for mobility and relying on a Personal Care Attendant to assist me with all activities of daily living.

Though I have dealt with and will continue to deal with rough times that are associated with a progressive form of a physical impairment, I truly can't complain about my life. I have completed both Bachelor's and Master's degrees from two major universities in Boston and have always had a great job. In most instances such accomplishments are not true for individuals with major impairments. When people first meet me, whether they are personal care attendants, colleagues, students, or clients, they tend to be surprised at my positive outlook on life. I think they believe they probably be angry if they were in my situation. But perhaps they would not be angry, since I believe that most people with various limitations learn to make the most out of life. Of course there will always be some people who will never be able to accept their life, choosing instead to be bitter and angry about their situation and wishing they were dead. Some of these people will indeed die, whether through willing themselves to die or from self-induced or assisted suicide.

Concerning my positive outlook on life, I attribute most of this attitude to my parents. They wouldn't allow me or my two brothers to sit back and feel sorry for ourselves, or use our disability as an excuse for not doing something. My mother particularly served as a personal inspiration for us. Though she also has muscular dystrophy, our mother taught us through example how to live and make the most out of life. She believes that having a disability doesn't entitle one to look for pity from others, or to feel sorry for oneself.

My mother even advocated early in my life, fighting with the local school board that my brothers and I be integrated and mainstreamed into regular classes with our nondisabled peers, actually doing so years before the Massachusetts public law, Chapter 766, was enacted that guaranteed equal public education for children with disabilities.

Feeling sorry for ourselves was not an option. While in high school it was instilled in us that we were expected to go to college, and that to get ahead in life and to get a good job continued education was a necessity. Though I received social security benefits as an individual with a disability, my parents made it clear that it was only while in school would I collect benefits and not do so for life. Having a job was an important value for my parents, and they insisted that my brothers and I were to have jobs every summer, with a majority of the money to be set aside to pay for college. This value is one that stuck with me. Since earning a bachelor's degree I've always had a job, even when because of a dramatic change in my impairment I had to take time off from work. Each time I knew I would return to work. Not working was never an option in my mind, though the doctors would have preferred that I only collect disability benefits. I believe that having a job is important because it allows people to understand that individual's with disabilities are capable of working and can be productive members of society who shouldn't feel sorry for themselves because of their limitations.

Another belief I value that allows me to have a positive outlook on life is that this is always someone worse off then myself. When I was eleven years old and had recently undergone surgery for scoliosis. I was sent for 4 years to a residential school for children with disabilities. Because this school was wired via television cameras to the classrooms, allowing me to participate in the school curriculum while recuperating from the surgery and because the local junior high school, where I was born and raised, was inaccessible to individuals with physical impairments, I attended this "hospital school." While attending the school I went home on weekends and holidays. I realized that half of the students lived there like myself because their family wanted nothing to do with them, choosing to make them wards of the state and to be forgotten about. But as a young boy I hated to be away from my family and during this time I gained an appreciation of how fortunate I was. I realized that my parents cared for and loved me and only sent me to this "hospital school" because it was the only viable option for my junior high education.

Many at this school had no one and would be there until they were 21. Then they would leave the school and at that time not know what would happen to them. I also feel fortunate because I was born with my disability and it's the only life I've known. Compared to those who acquire an impairment due to a traumatic event or any illness, I've always said that if I had to have a disability I'm glad I was born with it. Yes, there have been changes in my condition, resulting in a loss of independence. But I grew up knowing that I was going to experience exacerbations in this neuromuscular impairment. The only thing I had to live with was not to know when the condition would get worse, and to what extent would be the change. If an individual acquires their impairment later in life, with one's life turned upside down with no warning that the life they were used to be suddenly taken away, for that person the adjustment is extremely difficult if they do make any adjustment at all.

In addition, I've always been thankful that my impairment affects my body and not my mind. I do not consider myself better than someone else with a different condition. But I'd rather have it the way that I am though I depend a great deal on assistance from others. Importantly, despite my physical limitations I'm able to understand my needs, direct others on how to assist me with my needs, and with my intact cognitive functions I have earned two college degrees and maintain a great job. These are just my personal beliefs, and I do not ever intend to insult those who have severe, cognitive impairments, such as traumatic brain injuries or Alzheimer's disease.

My final belief that has allowed me to maintain a positive attitude is the conviction that God doesn't put more on one's plate than one is able to manage. Though I am not a very religious individual, I do not want to convey the impression that I've never been angry about my situation, bitter, and depressed wishing that I was dead. There have been numerous times when I wonder why I don't understand what it's all about, and why it happened to me, and I can't wait to ask God what it was all about. However, in time I always come around to the beliefs that have allowed me to adjust and make the most out of my life and realize how lucky I am.

I have always been asked, "If there was a cure for muscular dystrophy would I take it?" People are usually amazed when I state that I would decline. Why I decline a hypothetical cure is because this is the only life I know and I feel, because of the reasons discussed, that I am truly blessed with my life. I believe that having this impairment allows me, despite my limitations, to serve as an example that one is still able to have a happy and productive life.

DEALING WITH SPINA BIFIDA: MOTHER'S PERSPECTIVE

Personal Statement: Janet Lingerman

Maintaining a Balanced Attitude. Maintaining a balanced attitude as a family member while experiencing the continued impact of a chronic illness or severe disability is crucial to effective coping. Achieving this balanced outlook while confronting the many realities associated with a serious medical condition is an endless struggle. In this chapter these realities have been conceptualized as perspectives, such as vulnerability, family challenges, stress, family change, and relationships with health care professionals. In turn, these realities also become a foundation for family understanding, resilience, and affirmation. The mother's story in the following account identifies the many perspectives highlighted in the chapter, and illustrates how the awareness of changes, stressors, and one's vulnerability can stimulate understanding and resilience.

Both my husband and I have come from upper-middle class families of four children; he is the youngest of four boys, and I am the oldest child in my family. Each of us has also compensated for a mild form of disability. Although I remember almost no direct conversations regarding my congenital hearing loss, I was taken regularly to Boston for tests and treatments. Probably before my school years I had taught myself to read lips and to stay close to people whose words I wanted to hear. Reading difficulties plagued my husband during his school years, and he received tutoring and summer help. He, too, was able to succeed in school, intellectually able to fine-tune his auditory learning abilities. We each made a practice of "passing" as normal, choosing instead to work around the difficulties.

At the time of our marriage I was 21 1/2 years old and my fiancé was 29. Our courtship had been a relatively short 10 months. Although we attempted to expand our family shortly after marriage, there were problems. Pregnancy difficulties over 6 years were the first problems that either of us had really come across that could not be resolved by working harder. Action oriented, we tried all medical possibilities from tests to surgeries, capitalizing on the hope of each. We became closer than most couples, I think, but the closeness was largely nonverbal, as we rarely discussed our disappointments but could see it in each others' faces, especially during the many times in the hospital, sitting quietly, sometimes holding hands. We considered it a sign of strength that we could maintain our optimistic facade, especially with others, even members of our families of origin who visited but were not overly attentive.

The most difficult trial during our early marriage occurred when I had to have emergency surgery for a ruptured ectopic pregnancy that could have ended my life. I was more concerned that the surgery ended not only the pregnancy but also our chances for having children at all. Aware only of a sense of defeat and questions about what to do with my life, I sought no further than my husband and the doctor for support for my bruised self-esteem. Initiating adoption procedures and keeping busy did help to fend off some of the discouragement.

The following fall another pregnancy began against all medical odds. This pregnancy, like the others, got off to a troublesome start, and we didn't dare hope it would continue. It did continue, however, even without any medical intervention, for which we would later be glad. As each month passed, and we could feel the baby moving, we became more and more sure that our troubles were over. By 7 months we felt as if we were home free, because even babies born that early often survived unscathed. We went through Lamaze classes together. Those months in the last half of the pregnancy will probably always be remembered as our happiest, closest, and most deliciously carefree with both of us wrapped up in the event to come. Beth's delivery was "medically unremarkable." For us it was a most remarkable achievement, all the more worthy because we had warded off all anesthesia and even the threatened forceps. Yet even as we congratulated each other and snapped a photo or two in the delivery room, we registered the silence of the staff that came only moments before the doctor told us what he had just discovered: Beth had been born with a meningomyelocele (open spine).

The obstetrician was kind and gentle, putting his hand on my arm as he told us of the meningomyelocele. He told us nothing more, and my strong biology background registered a thud in the back of my mind but did not connect. All I could ask was whether Beth would be all right, whether she would live, to which I received affirmative answers. On a maternal high, I found the nurses to be annoyingly businesslike and was glad to finally return to my room to make phone calls. My husband was back with me when we were told the baby would be sent by ambulance to Boston, and even then we assumed that Beth would be hospitalized for whatever was necessary and would come home later fine. The pediatrician arrived and began the jumble of what was to be our introduction to spina bifida. Although I recall that he gave a long description of the many organs and functions affected by the condition, I remember little else except his kindness and brutal honesty. A voice in my head kept repeating, "My baby won't be like that," and I was worrying about my husband, who had also been up all night and was expected to accompany the baby to Boston.

My husband will never forget that trip to Boston, being asked whether to treat the baby—a decision, really, whether to let her live. He was told she was paralyzed from the waist down, would never walk, and would be retarded if she lived at all—and then he had to return to me to go through it all again. With essentially no guidance from anyone, we were asked to make a decision regarding a child for whom we had waited for 6 years and about a condition we had never heard of until just hours earlier. Coming to an agreement was only the first of many extreme difficulties, as we juggled our high value on this child against a future we could not begin to imagine. Beth's back was closed at the age of 24 hours. With this commitment I resolved that if she were to be disabled, at least I would see to it that she maximized every potential.

In those early days we did not cope; we existed. Minute followed minute and crisis followed crisis. We tried to keep up with our social life in an effort to maintain some semblance of an old reality, but I found those times dreamlike and irrelevant, because I was unable to think of anything but Beth and us. My husband appeared to me to be intensely emotional, but he kept it in tight control; it was too big for us to discuss in anything but small snatches.

Our families were in their own shock and did not know how to help. Nor did we know how to ask for help. Our mothers visited Beth and me in the hospital, and I was grateful, especially sensing that they were ill equipped to deal with the horror stories of others packed in around us at the nursery. I at least had had a medical background and could better understand both the hope and the limits of care given in answer to the insistent beeping of monitors. Meanwhile, our siblings received contradictory misinformation and tended either to minimize or exaggerate the facts of Beth's condition. Many people, family included, came to us with success stories about other children with spina bifida. Although I acknowledged their intent to help with hope, I also made a very conscious effort to put out of my mind these other stories, knowing that Beth was an individual and would be in her own way different from any others.

Within days of Beth's birth, our entire value system changed abruptly. All issues, problems, and questions were related to matters of life and death. Nothing seemed more important than survival. Concurrently, the value we placed on friendship skyrocketed, as there seemed so few people who could even begin to understand what we were going through. I seemed to live at a layer many levels deeper and more vulnerable than ever before and became acutely sensitive, while at the same time attempting an incongruous facade of strength. We learned quickly that others needed to be put at ease with us, because they felt inadequate to help. Most did not know whether to send us a baby gift or flowers for condolence, whereas what was really important was that they cared enough to send anything. As time went on, I found, and still find, more and more people with problems of many kinds turning to me for solace, because they know somehow that I have grown sensitive ears.

In her first 18 months, Beth had nine operations, including brain surgery for a shunt and two revisions for the hydrocephalus that developed at 3 weeks. She seemed to spend more time in the hospital than out of it. Two or three times when she had severe urinary tract infections, I opted to keep her at home and give her injections around the clock to avoid another hospitalization. Carrying out a relentless litany of medical procedures, equipment applications, exercises, treatments, and medication administrations, I have never ceased to be amazed at what one can learn to consider an ordinary part of life. Part of what was most difficult was keeping track of the constant changes. When she first came home at the age of six weeks, I initially had little confidence in caring for this small girl. It felt as if she belonged more to the hospital than to us. The staff had been very supportive in teaching me, though, and by the end of the first year I had gained some considerable expertise. My life was lived more moment-to-moment than day to day, with a motto of, "Tomorrow may not be any better, but at least it'll be different," or, "At least I'll never be bored." Planning even a day in advance was difficult because there were so many appointments and changes. But by the end of the first year I had developed a technique I called "putting my worries on hold." I was able to make an observation of impending crisis, set a reasonable time for a new evaluation of the problem, and mentally put aside anxiety on the issue until the appointed time and the new information. I would then (1) act, (2) decide it was a false alarm, or (3) go back on hold until the next assessment. I was determined to "accept" her condition and to avoid foisting my hangups on her, and to the extent that even at my worst I have managed to keep her independence in sight as my first priority for her, I have been fairly successful in maintaining an attitude of optimism and open honesty. Emotionally speaking, however, the first year was relatively easy, with numbness and denial carrying me along.

My husband, meanwhile, pulled together after the initial weeks into a stable strength. His attitude is generally more pessimistic and fatalistic than my complementary optimist activism. To this day, he starts with the worst possibilities and works toward reality, whereas I look to the most hopeful, backtracking toward reality where we meet minds. Although I do not entirely understand his ability to mentally analyze a problem and work toward a solution alone, I do see that this method works for him. Says he about problems, "I think about them alone, in the car, uninterrupted, and I break the cycle" of going round and round on the same issue. On the other hand, he does not entirely understand my need to, as he puts it, "Sit around and talk about the same things."

When Beth was 18 months old, she had to have double hip surgery, necessitating use of a spica cast and a Bradford frame for two months. Concurrently, my husband was laid up with what was later diagnosed as a broken back, which could have left him a paraplegic as well. Both were in body casts at the same time. It was then that I began to seriously doubt my ability to continue. We had also just begun Beth's program of intermittent catheterization primarily to avoid what we considered to be destructive surgery on her bladder. Although I became tied to the schedule and even the urologist was skeptical, Beth had far fewer infections. More tired than I ever knew was possible, I also felt especially lonely with my husband seeming to be someone else when he was on high doses of painkillers. My life seemed to consist of nothing besides constant nursing duties, and I knew that I was not functioning at all well.

Until this time I had had very little in the way of external support besides medical expertise and a few select baby-sitters on whom I depended

heavily for some time out. My husband and I have insisted on maintaining some semblance of a social life, with some time set aside for just
the two of us. We have both found it essential to our sanity and to our
marriage in spite of financial pressures and hassles in getting sitters. We
have had extraordinarily good luck with training students in high school
or college. I hide nothing from them and describe what is involved to
check their reactions before actually teaching them and putting them to
work. For privacy's sake we have insisted on having only girls involved
with the catheterization and find that once they have matured a bit beyond their own self-consciousness over puberty, they accept our medical
regime matter-of-factly.

Through our Lamaze teacher I became involved with an organization
of parents of special-needs children. I had, of course, met many other
parents of disabled children and had had meaningful conversations at
clinics, in hospital corridors, and occasionally on the phone, but there was
no sense of continuity with these people who were not otherwise parts
of our lives. After a lecture sponsored by Parent to Parent on the subject
of birth defects, I discovered a sense of warm, interested, understanding
community spirit among the local parents in over an hour of conversation.
The parents were as varied as the special needs their children represented.
It was exhilarating to be face-to-face with a group of sane people who
could cope (something I very much needed to know how to do), people
who were just as much in awe of my situation as I was of theirs. Parent to
Parent also helped open many doors to worlds of assorted resources. Even
though I had since the beginning specialized in becoming an expert on the
subjects of spina bifida and hydrocephalus from a medical standpoint,
through the parent group I began to learn of consumer services, sources
of adaptive equipment and clothing, and helpful hints to facilitate the
translation of medical treatment into individual family living.

By the time Beth was 2 1/2, our lives had stabilized some—with my
husband back on his feet and Beth home for a whole year without hospitalization. I went to an exercise class and became satisfyingly involved
with Parent to Parent, matching families for phone support. With assistance through an Early Intervention program Beth had begun to walk
with a walker and braces to the waist, and her developmental age was
gaining on her chronological age. During this time, we got a call from
the adoption agency telling us that they had a 3-week-ld baby girl for us
to pick up in just 4 days. She was adorable and very much wanted, even
so suddenly, but those first months were awfully hectic for me, because
Lindsey had her own set of problems; colic from the start, pneumonia
requiring hospitalization at the age of 10 weeks, four months of incessant
crying, and finally the discovery of her allergy to milk that lasted until
she was over two years old. Actually, now I am glad for these problems

because they established immediately a place for Lindsey in our family, which might otherwise have tended to put aside her needs for Beth's, which still seemed so urgent. Always, even during the hardest times, I knew that Lindsey's assertive presence was beneficial to all of us, although I worried about whether she got enough attention. I felt somewhat saddened and slightly cheated that Lindsey and I would never be as intimately involved as Beth and I had been. It was my husband who helped me see that I was overinvolved with Beth, not that Lindsey was lacking my attention. Both girls were thriving, Beth as the oldest, Lindsey with the attentions of a big sister.

Once I gained some time and the distance that Beth's schooling provided at age 3 $1/2$, I was able to see our enmeshment more clearly. I had not been prepared for the sense of responsibility I would feel toward a child, perhaps even an able-bodied one. The enmeshment had been understandably born out of our desires for a child and the related needs of this particular one. Enmeshment was also fostered by the system that taught me all the care and treatments. I once realized that I was expected to carry out 9 hours of assorted treatments per day, while meals, baths, groceries, a social life, laundry, errands and recreation were to come out of the little remaining time. The diluting effect of Lindsey's arrival had been very healthy. My husband's role and mine did not change a great deal, but they expanded instead to include more tasks, some of which were traded or shared. He spent many hours each week on the paper work and financial mix-ups of insurance, handicapped license plates, taxes, and the like.

By the time Beth was five and Lindsey two and a half, I was mired in depression. My previously optimistic ability to make the most of a hard situation had burned out in negative musings on how badly we would lose this game of life with a disabled child in spite of all the hard work. To my credit, I knew even then that Beth's disability was far from the whole problem (scapegoating), but I also knew that I needed professional help. I had read many times about the grief surrounding the birth of a child with defects, but the literature did not ring true for me. My life certainly included denial, anger, bargaining, depression, and acceptance. But for me these were not milestones on a timeline, but were aspects of every day, sometimes every hour. Furthermore, there was little grief attached to the "expected baby." The grief was tied up in the whole mental picture I had had for my family, our future, and myself. Feeling I had failed myself, my husband, Beth, the family, and even society itself, what I really had lost was my whole sense of self-worth, which I defined in terms of what I could do.

The most significant help came to me through a fine clinical psychologist who worked individually with me, primarily on the issue of self-esteem, helping me to better integrate my thinking with my feelings.

From the start he offered me respect, as if I had as much to teach him as he had to teach me, and he responded with compassion and human reactions, from time to time with tears in his eyes. His positive regard for me supported his assumption that I could grow through this, and that, indeed, I already had. I was certain that I had crossed the line into insanity, wishing I could quietly evaporate. He got me an antidepressant, which helped me to go on and see that all of the overwhelming things I was feeling were, even in all their intensity, normal reactions to abnormal circumstances. The counselor taught me a whole new perspective on worth and value, one that rested on who I am, not on what I do. From this viewpoint then, failures or disapproval could not change my value as a person.

Crucial to the counseling was my somewhat private but strong faith in God, a faith shared by the counselor but not by my husband. Rigidly clinging to various misconceptions, I was less able to utilize effectively the resources of my faith. For instance, guilt was not an issue for me intellectually or even spiritually, because I believe in forgiveness. But emotionally I felt I deserved this disaster, not realizing I also had to forgive myself. I learned about peace and pacing as well as about my own human limitations, and I relearned a sense I had had long ago, that there is something to be learned in every situation. Knowing I was doing the best I could under the circumstances, I could let God take over the responsibility for the end results and put aside long-term worries. The counselor helped me gain a perspective, a broader sense of time and meaning for my life. Contemplating the biblical concept of unconditional love also helped bolster my sense of self-esteem. By the time we terminated, I was able to see myself as a special and unique individual, equipped with my own set of strengths and weaknesses, grown and growing. These gifts could actually be used for the benefit of others, and a future began to form for the first time in five years. I had never before seen myself in this light, and it was a monumental turning point for me. Also, a growing involvement with our local church provided not just spiritual sustenance, but practical assistance and a warm, new support network as well.

The interaction between the girls has been decidedly normal, although frequently they seem closer than do many sisters, sharing well and at times showing surprising consideration for each other. Beth's time in school has given me a chance to be with just Lindsey and to delight in her development, which, although less studied than Beth's, has been remarkable in its own right. The two of them fight and squabble like any other siblings and also gang up against us parents. It is a loud, irritating nuisance, but I realize a sense of gratefulness that they can be so normal. That each has an effect on the other is clear. In a burst of independence and perhaps competition with her sister, Beth learned to catheterize herself last fall, but tries on occasion to go "like Lindsey" without a catheter. Lindsey in the meantime was very slow in toilet training, and I wondered if she craved the attention Beth got at the toilet. Although I have made a concerted effort to help each view herself as an individual, I am seldom sure of how life looks from their angle.

I have also tried to direct disability-related anger at the equipment or the spina bifida itself, as opposed to Beth herself. I don't know yet whether she can herself make the distinction. She said several months ago, "I hate meatballs, applesauce, and myself," then paused while my ears pricked up and added, "I don't know why I said that, Mummy." As casually as I could, I asked her what she didn't like about herself. "Oh." she thought, "casts and braces and catheters and stuff." We talked it out, cried it out, as I tried to help her separate these things from whom she is. A few weeks later she asked, "Mummy, how come you always like to talk to me about braces and crutches and spina bifida?" Perception is perhaps Beth's greatest strength, and I knew as I chuckled that I'd been had. Yet it wasn't much later that she said, "You know, Mum, there are some good things about spina bifida. I get lots and lots of extra attention."

In the meantime, Lindsey is becoming quite the athlete, and I have wondered how Beth would take to her sister's prowess on bikes, skis and roller skates. Beth has opted to try each to the best of her ability with our help, and since Lindsey's first steps "without anything," Beth has so far been quite proud of her sister. In a thousand little ways, such as grocery shopping (Who rides in the cart? Who walks?), my husband and I have also had to face Lindsey's passing Beth in abilities, and we are reminded that it is personhood that is important, not abilities. With this in mind, I can freely encourage Lindsey's weekly swimming with more enthusiasm that I might otherwise have.

My husband and I, like Beth and Lindsey, lead parts of our lives together and other parts more separately. We have mustered a fairly united front in house rules and discipline. Now that I am out of the house more, having returned to school with the goal of eventually rejoining the work force, my husband has to pick up more of the childcare and household chores. Conversely, I hope in time to provide some income to offset the pressures on him. Although it is still difficult to predict the future for either of our children, we have a hopeful coinciding picture of independence for each. We may be wrong, but we have probably considered a full spectrum of possible outcomes, although we don't look too far ahead. The more I study, the more I come to the comforting conviction that, despite some asynchrony, our family is indeed generally functional. It is far from perfect, and nothing is ever that simple. However, a strong alliance in our marriage, our flexibility, and the healthy dyads in each direction can all help build our coping strengths. These years, although frequently overwhelming, have been a challenge to growth for each of us. Frankly, I am proud of the maturity we have each gained. I become more and more convinced that the lessons most worth learning are also the most painful ones. The pain will undoubtedly continue, but so, too, I think, will the growth.

Perspective Exercise 3

My Family and Disability: Where Do We Stand?

1. List five ways your family could be additive to the care of a family member with an illness or disability.
2. If you had a contagious disease, would you want your family involved in your care? Why or why not? Would you care for a family member with a contagious disease?
3. What would be the most difficult aspect of family involvement for you?
4. What has been, is, or would be most difficult for your family in caring for a child who has a disability? Would there be a difference if it was physical, emotional, and developmental? An adult?
5. List the characteristics of your family that could help in the care of a member with an illness and or a disability
6. What are the characteristics of your family that hinder the care-giving process?
7. Do you feel that you are fully functioning in your own life so that you are a role model for other family members?
8. Would this change if you had a physical disability? A psychiatric disability?
9. Which family member would "understand" if you had AIDS?
10. Who would not be able to understand? Why?
11. Who in your family would be least able to cope with or adapt to illness or disability?
12. Can disability be prevented?
13. If disability can be prevented, why does it occur?
14. Would you be in favor of placing a limit on financial awards in personal injury cases?

15. Should lawyers be limited to a 6% "commission" on all personal injury cases? What do you think is reasonable and why?

16. What is your position on sharing large awards, via a tax, with persons who were injured by an uninsured motorist who had no financial resources?

17. What are the benefits of a $5 million settlement in a personal injury case?

18. What are the liabilities of a $5 million settlement for the injured person and their family?

PART IV

Interventions and Resources

Introduction to Part IV

For decades, intervention strategies have been developed to respond to complex and challenging family life experiences. More recently, however, with the repeated occurrence of extraordinary and traumatic incidents such as natural disasters, illness epidemics, and terrorist activities, catastrophic injuries and severe disabilities have resulted. These disability and illness conditions call for specially tailored interventions. Such crafted assistance has three factors in common: counseling, education, and support. With counseling approaches the family members share their feelings and begin to understand their own perceptions of their ability and willingness to provide care for themselves, when possible, and care for other family members. Education involves teaching individuals with a disability and family member's productive coping skills, how to use available resources, and how to deal constructively with health care professionals. Support has many dimensions. It can extend to assisting family members to utilize their personal strengths to assist others in the family both emotionally and physically. It can also mean the many different daily care care-giving activities performed by families and friends that enhance a person's quality of life.

The seven articles and personal perspective in Part IV build on these established interventions and create additional options for family members to live their life as fully as possible. They provide enlightening helping perspectives for coping with illness and disability. Three of the articles explain the power of spirituality as a coping resource in very difficult disability related situations. The personal perspective illustrates the force of spirituality during a critical time in one's life. Two of the articles discuss the effects of sudden, possibly devastating traumas on individuals and what interventions could be appropriate. The remaining articles either bring to the reader's attention the human factor when utilizing assistive technology or review the enduring concepts for attitudinal changes toward people with handicaps. All of the articles are in step with those developing distinctive intervention strategies that are receiving increasing attention in the literature. Moreover, though they generally identify the different origins and consequent effects of disability and illness, the articles have several common themes:

1. The incidence of severe disability and illness brings loss to the affected individuals, and interventions should include loss resolution.
2. Interventions in severe disability and chronic illness situation usually must be ongoing and will change during the course of adjustment.
3. Intervention efforts directed toward an individual and the family is hopefully a joint venture shared by helping professionals and the individuals themselves.
4. The focus of intervention goals is on introducing and implementing, when possible, more productive, effective, and realistic coping methods.

The coping theme as a resource for adaptation to disability and illness is illustrated in three articles that elaborate on the concept of spirituality. Two of the articles, however, introduce different dimensions for understanding spirituality namely, as a process from loss through determination to hope, the acknowledgement spirituality as a coping mechanism and the construct of forgiveness as a means of coping.

The importance of maintaining hope during the rehabilitation process is emphasized in Collins and Kuehn's article, "The Construct of Hope in the Rehabilitation Process." These authors explain that hope is related to many factors in any rehabilitation process, and then identify both the constructs related to hope and the situational challenges inspiring hope. Hope focuses on spiritual well-being, and the authors believe that higher levels of hope are correlated with better coping skills. The article urges helping professionals to understand the importance of this concept when offering medical and/or physical care to individuals with a disability or illness. An interesting and helpful discussion is provided on whether rehabilitation specialists should allow consumers to work through their grieving, thus usually prolonging a dependency period, or to discourage consumers from dealing with their negative emotions and instead to focus on skills training. Perhaps an integrated strategy is more effective.

But the article by J. Kaye and S. Raghaven, "Spirituality in Disability and Illness," offers a comprehensive literature review that supports spirituality as a coping method among individuals attempting to manage a variety of illnesses and disabilities. The authors explain the several implications for practice related to the literature findings. Though interventions need to be individualized, claim these authors, in order to be helpful to the person dealing with a disability situation, the article provides general information on the many spiritual activities that bring purpose and meaning to people facing these illness/disability conditions.

The role of specific spiritual factors in rehabilitation is discussed in Webb's article, "Spiritual Factors and Adjustment in Medical Rehabilitation: Understanding Forgiveness as a Means of Coping." Because medical rehabilitation often brings human error, apparent, unfair circumstances, and, at times, violence, forgiveness can assume a distinctive importance and have a positive role in encouraging recovery or health. The author explains the concepts of spirituality and forgiveness, discusses the steps and dynamics of forgiveness, and then points out selected empirical relationships between forgiveness and health variables. Suggestions are also offered to rehabilitation professionals on how to encourage and facilitate the practice of forgiveness in rehabilitation. The author asserts that forgiveness can be a powerful coping force during medical rehabilitation and can decidedly contribute to improved quality of life.

Two articles bring to the reader's attention how both extraordinary and war-related events cause a unique psychosocial impact on survivors. Interventions should be developed in the perspective of the individual needs emerging from these traumas. Stebnicki, in his article, "The Psychosocial Impact on Survivors of Extraordinary, Stressful, and Traumatic Events: Principles and Practices in Critical Incident Response for Rehabilitation Counselors," proposes many roles for the rehabilitation professional, identifies the shifting definitions and assumptions regarding a crisis response, and comprehensively outlines the psychosocial response of survivors. Essential to life adjustment from these traumatic events are community and individual interventions. Both are clearly explained and a model is proposed for Group Crisis Intervention. The article makes a distinctive contribution to the literature when explaining the psychosocial dynamics of sudden trauma situations and proposing how rehabilitation professionals can have a specialized role during intervention efforts when linking the survivor with other community services.

Grief takes on a special feature when it emerges from a death related to a war effort. In these circumstances grief resolution entails a number of steps. Beder, in her article, "War, Death, and Bereavement: How Can We Help," outlines clearly these steps, and discusses why war bereavement is complicated. Each step is carefully explained and suggestions are offered about bereavement counseling in groups. The persons who suffer these war-related losses have special needs, and the author urges helping professionals to take the responsibility to understand the unique dynamics of this loss situation, and then "to help restore them in whatever ways they can."

The context in which coping strategies can develop is clearly identified in Brodwin, Star, and Cardozo's article on "Users of Assistive Technology: The Human Component." They explain that the specific characteristics of self-esteem, positive attitudes, self-efficacy, and strong motivation can contribute to successful use of assistive technology. The utilization of this technology is in itself a productive coping strategy. The authors further discuss how the consumer's cognitive functioning plays an important role in one's response and application to using assistive devices. All of the provided information offers significant insights for the helping professional into those afore-mentioned individual characteristics that should be identified when planning to use this technical resource for those with a physical disability.

One of the most legendary, historic, and well-known names in the psychosocial aspects of disability literature is Beatrice Wright. Almost forty years ago she wrote a "classic" article, "Changes in Attitudes Toward People With Handicaps," that identified a few of the beliefs and principles that provided guidelines for rehabilitation of people with disabilities. This identification was a summary of 18 value-laden beliefs and principles published a year earlier. In this article, reprinted from the second edition of this book in 1984, Dr. Wright develops from her previous summary many implications of these guidelines for practice opportunities. Examples are increasing accommodation of children who are handicapped within regular schools, the greater involvement of people with a disability in leadership positions in agencies serving them, and the importance of speaking out to affirm their dignity as persons with a disability. The article also highlights the ideals of human dignity and basic civil rights. Interventions should be developed within society to implement these ideals. Progress toward the recognition of basic civil rights of those with disabilities has been slow, but with gradual changing attitudes in society, the author believes that continued progress might be counted on.

CHAPTER TWENTY-TWO

The Construct of Hope in the Rehabilitation Process

Amy B. Collins and Marvin D. Kuehn

Hope is a significant and complex psychological construct that is integrally related to many aspects of any rehabilitative process in which psychological or physical loss occurs. Hope can be defined from many perspectives, and its importance can be misunderstood and overlooked in the rehabilitation process. The inability to establish hope in the process of adjusting to loss or illness may be a critical issue for an individual experiencing disability.

Stotland (1969) defines hope as looking forward to something with desire and confidence, or having an expectation of something desired, with the level of hope being contingent upon the person's perceived level of probability of the desired outcome. As a verb, hope is wishing and expecting, and is usually related to a specific situation in regard to an outcome. As a noun, hope is an emotion (Reeve, 2004), or feeling one has, such as confidence in an event or outcome (Stotland). Snyder (2003) conducted extensive research and refined a cognitive theory of hope that explained hope as a thinking process in which a person conceptualizes goals and can initiate and sustain movement toward the objectives or pathways identified.

Hope also can be seen as a trait that individuals possess to varying degrees and that interacts with other psychological constructs. When

From "The construct of hope in the rehabilitation process," by A. Collins and M. Kuehn, 2004, *Rehabilitation Education, 18*(3), 176–183. Reprinted with permission of Rehabilitation Education.

understood as a fairly stable characteristic, it becomes clear that hope may affect individuals, particularly young people with a disability, in profound ways as they experience various developmental stages in their lives.

Carifio and Rhodes (2002) asserted that while hope is a personality trait, there is also a pathway or state aspect of hope, which is the collection of response strategies a person possesses. Anyone working in the rehabilitation field should be aware that influencing a client's level of hope entails more than cheering someone up; it involves altering underlying thought processes and attributions.

CONSTRUCTS RELATED TO HOPE

To understand the developmental implications of hope, a brief review of the relationship of related constructs is important. The construct of hope involves understanding attitude formation, the change process, and cognitive thinking which may be distorted or false; it may also include issues related to attachment, spirituality and meaning in life, and maintenance of self-concept (Snyder, 2000). Each construct suggests an orientation or paradigm that may influence the response of an individual struggling with the establishment or attainment of hope.

Construct	Interpretation or Orientation
Hope	Looking forward to something with desire and confidence, or having an expectation of something desired.
Learned Helplessness	Unable to control or predict outcomes of a situation regardless of the level of effort exerted and often involving passivity, demoralization, and depression.
Hopelessness	Adopting negative attitudes that do not lead to predictable or controllable outcomes.
Locus of Control	A general expectancy that outcomes are controlled by personal behavior and choices versus internal or external factors.
Self-Efficacy	A subset of hope that focuses on a person's belief that he/she will be successful in specific situations or activities.
Self-Defeating Thoughts	Cognitive thoughts involving negative self-talk tendencies not permitting success or achievement.

CONSEQUENCES OF HOPELESSNESS

A consequence of the inability to develop hope is the concept of hopelessness. Hopelessness is often directly related to the term "learned helplessness," a psychological state of expectation that one will be unable to control or predict outcomes of a certain situation regardless of the level of effort exerted (Shnek, Foley, LaRocca, Smith, & Halper, 1995; Seligman, 1998). Sometimes, individuals have learned that, no matter what they do, there is no expectation of fulfillment from success. Learned helplessness also refers to the concerns that arise in the wake of uncontrollability and is observed in a variety of human behaviors entailing inappropriate passivity and demoralization (Peterson, Maier, & Seligman, 1995). Depression and pessimism are generally the manifestations of learned helplessness; most frequently it is cited as an explanation of depression.

Not surprisingly, hopelessness is caused by experiences in which the person's efforts did not lead to a predictable or controllable outcome; but, not everyone reacts by giving up or adopting negative attitudes (Shnek et al., 1995).

Considering Stotland's (1969) explanation of hope as an expectation of something desired, the effect that learned helplessness has on hope quickly becomes apparent. When someone has no expectation of being able to predict or control a situation to produce a positive outcome, or any outcome for that matter, it is difficult for that person to be hopeful. In a study involving patients with multiple sclerosis (MS) (Shnek et al., 1995), learned helplessness was found to be associated with other negative psychological constructs such as depression, cognitive distortions, and self-efficacy. Falvo (1999) characterized depression that results from hopelessness as involving fatigue, negative cognition, disinterest in previously enjoyed activities, as well as discouragement and hopelessness.

Depression is thus tied to the concept of learned helplessness and cognitive distortion, or, thoughts about a situation that may be the result of depression and helplessness rather than the result of rationally appraising the situation (Robertson & Brown, 1992). Interestingly, when Shnek et al. (1997) conducted a study similar to that of Shnek et al. in 1995 that included patients with spinal cord injuries (SCI) as well as multiple sclerosis patients, they found that the people with MS had higher levels of helplessness and depression and lower levels of self-efficacy. The authors concluded that this was because MS is more unpredictable than SCI, and individuals therefore feel less control over their situation, which could lead to depression and lowered self-efficacy (Shnek et al., 1997).

Although these studies did not find a direct correlation between disability and depression, the results do suggest that the predictability of a disability will have an impact upon learned helplessness, which can then lead to depression. People with MS, a less predictable disease, had higher levels of learned helplessness than people with SCI (Shnek et al., 1995, 1997).

SITUATIONAL CHALLENGES INSPIRING HOPE

In unpredictable situations, people may have varying levels of hope due to the interaction of factors such as coping style, self-efficacy, and religious beliefs. When Stanton, Danoff-Burg, and Huggins (2002) studied how hope predicted adjustment among women diagnosed with breast cancer, they found that hope interacted with coping styles. Hope and approach-oriented coping strategies combined to predict higher levels of psychological and physical adjustment than were present with women who did not possess these traits (Stanton et al.).

Surprisingly, relying on religion for comfort or support improved adjustment levels for women low in hope, but decreased adjustment for women high in hope. This may be because religion provides comfort and reassurance (Stanton et al), even in situations perceived to be uncontrollable. However, people with high levels of hope are more likely to believe they can do something to improve the situation, and to employ approach-oriented coping strategies (Stanton et al.).

People with a high level of hope may also tend to have an internal locus of control in addition to higher levels of self-efficacy, both of which would lead them to adjust best through active coping, which could potentially be hindered by reliance on God, or any other entity or person. Internal locus of control, which is more generalized than self-efficacy, has been found to be an important concept in rehabilitation. It is the expectancy that outcomes are the result of personal choices and decisions. Individuals with an internal locus of control are not controlled by either internal factors, such as how hard a person works, or by external forces, such as luck or fate (Moore & Stambrook, 1995).

According to Carifio and Rhodes (2002), Bandura defined self-efficacy as a subset of hope that focuses on a person's belief that he or she will be successful in specific activities or situations. The interaction of hope with other factors shows how important it is for rehabilitation professionals to understand several psychological characteristics of their clients before attempting to help them adjust to an illness or disability.

For example, some clients may react to suggestions to take a more active role in their recovery by choosing not to comply, or they choose to exhibit denial because they do not feel that they can control what happens to them. Other people may react to the same suggestion by being assertive, taking charge, and feeling less depressed or frustrated with the situation.

There is a growing body of evidence documenting the positive relationship between patients' religious and spiritual lives and their experiences with illness and disease (Puchalski, 1999). Hope, in the context of religious belief, focuses on spiritual well-being that emphasizes confidence in dealing with future outcomes and challenges. In times of severe and disabling injury, passion for the possible may be mediated through ritual, meditation, and prayer. Puchalski concluded from studies on spirituality in the rehabilitation and lives of those with disability that spiritually-based hope is the single most important variable in patient adjustment. Therefore, rehabilitation professionals should develop an awareness of how relevant spirituality constructs may affect levels of hope.

After an injury or diagnosis, medical professionals are sometimes cautious about encouraging what they fear could be false hope. The promotion of a positive outlook is always desired; however, it is often a challenge to achieve since hoping does not mean success will always follow. Medical professionals want to foster motivation while at the same time protect the individual from the potential for future psychological trauma or distress.

Anthony (1993) described the process of mental health recovery and the factors that influence constructive behavior change from the perspective of the consumer (client). Anthony identified recovery as a unique process of changing one's attitudes, values, feelings, goals, skills and/or roles. It is a way of living a satisfying, contributing life even with the limitations caused by an illness: Literature on the recovery process has focused on what facilitates or helps recovery from mental illness.

Anthony listed specific factors that consumers identified as having been important in their recovery. One factor was hope, which Anthony described as a desire that is accompanied by an attitude of confident expectation. Hope is an intrinsic belief that things can get better. Anthony summarized what helps individuals establish hope. He indicated that hope can be facilitated by helping individuals develop a sense of meaning, identifying role models, appreciating personal strengths, and establishing positive perspectives about self-determination.

SELF-DEFEATING THOUGHTS

Although an individual tends to perceive situations in a relatively consistent manner, it is possible to change problematic thought, processes or attributions. Robertson and Brown (1992) discussed self-defeating thoughts that undermine adjustment and rehabilitation. Individuals may not even be aware of these thoughts because they often exist at the sub-cortical level, and their effect on the self-talk that influences perceptions of situations and self-efficacy can be subconscious (Robertson & Brown). While clients are usually unaware of their own self-defeating thoughts and negative self-talk, professionals can identify them with interviews and by asking clients if they agree with self-defeating thoughts commonly associated with disabilities (Robertson & Brown). Robertson and Brown identified

10 self-defeating thoughts in the form of self-talk, such as "asking for help is a sign of personal weakness," and "it is impossible for a person with a disability to be happy" (p. 88).

Robertson and Brown (1992) said they agree with Albert Ellis's belief that once clients understand how self-defeating thoughts affect themselves, they are usually able to recognize detrimental thought patterns and begin to change them with the help of a professional. Changing thought patterns that have existed since childhood can be difficult. However, considering that many of these negative self-talk tendencies are developed at a young age and have become ingrained and automatic by the time people are old enough to evaluate them rationally, after clients learn to identify these irrational thoughts, they can substitute positive self-talk (Robertson & Brown).

Hope may seem to be unrelated to self-defeating thoughts because thoughts are cognitive, whereas hope is an emotion. However, thought processes are a key determinant of emotions (Reeve, 2004) and, in that hope consists of an expectation or optimism toward a positive result (Stotland, 1969), it is dependent upon positive thoughts. People who undermine their own success by subconsciously telling themselves that nothing they do matters will not have a high level of hope because they have no expectation of a positive outcome and are likely to suffer from learned helplessness. Such people also will be less able to adopt approach-oriented coping styles because of the perception that they cannot do anything to control the situation.

ENHANCING HOPE

Addressing negative thought processes is a valid approach to long-term adjustment, but some situations may require more specific or immediate attention: In these cases physiological factors, which also affect cognitions and attitudes, may be relevant considerations. Teaching people to modify their physiological responses can have an important role in the establishment of hope in the rehabilitative process. For example, biofeedback and relaxation can be useful in increasing perceived control and decreasing anxiety (Burish & Bradley, 1983). In a study conducted on cancer patients undergoing chemotherapy and struggling with nausea and anxiety, Burish, Shaffner and Lyles (1981) found that biofeedback and progressive muscle relaxation training interacted to reduce physiological arousal, anxiety, and nausea.

Allowing people to take an active role in coping with distressing situations by teaching them self-relaxation techniques would be especially helpful to people who have high levels of hope because it would provide them with a means for achieving goals and staying in control. Research has shown that people who have lower levels of hope at the onset of their illness adjust better when they turn to religion (Stanton et al, 2002), or any comforting belief system. Relaxation and biofeedback may also be helpful, as they may be considered passive, comforting activities involving minimal non-threatening thinking that they may help these people as well. They may even increase levels of hope by providing a means of control that does not require levels of initiative or activity that would be stress-provoking for most individuals. Conceivably, if people highly value religion or a belief system, these also could be supportive and reassuring, and could be incorporated into relaxation techniques to provide optimal adjustment to distressing circumstances.

Regardless of whether people receive any type of counseling that deals with self-talk, cognitive processes and attitudes can be affected by many variables. One important factor is the attitudes of others, especially people close to the individual. Stotland (1969) explained that both hope and anxiety can be influenced by positive expectations and encouragement from others. Kobler and Stotland's study (as cited in Stotland, 1964) showed that people who commit suicide are nearly hopeless and only kill themselves after attempting to find hope "through the communicated expectations of others." It is important to understand how the expectations of others influence people, especially because expectations and attitudes can be communicated through subtle behaviors, and may have a devastating effect on people who are already in stressful situations and in need of social support.

Rosenbaum and Rosenbaum (1998) said if individuals are living with an illness or the debilitating results of an accident, those close to them undoubtedly empathize with their expressed thoughts and emotions. In the process of reestablishing personal autonomy, individuals who have experienced loss usually try to accept responsibility for their physical and emotional well-being (Snyder, 1998). They recognize that their attitudes toward loss or illnesses and the way in which they have portrayed them to others may determine how friends, family, and colleagues would react to them (Snyder).

Rosenbaum and Rosenbaum believed that the process of achieving this positive attitude allows for the construct of hope to develop. Responding to loss and participating in a rehabilitation program challenges individuals. But if they are successful in the process, they will have begun to nurture the will to live and to convey the attitudes and behaviors commonly associated with hope (Rosenbaum & Rosenbaum). Individuals manifest hope by living in the present. They accept their new problems and attempt to solve them through introspection, understanding, and sharing. They set reasonable goals and focus on feelings of love while downplaying negative emotions. They surround themselves with supportive friends, and they actively search for ways to help others (Rosenbaum & Rosenbaum).

Hope is the overall perception that one's goals can be achieved (Snyder, 2000). Goals need to be of sufficient value to the individual so as to occupy conscious thought; they should be challenging yet attainable. Goals that are certain to be achieved do not by themselves give individuals hope. Snyder (2000) suggested that the level of hope individuals have is related to their perceptions about themselves and their goals.

Individuals with higher levels of hope remember more positive comments and events involving themselves and feel challenged by goals, whereas individuals with lower levels remember more negative comments and events and feel demoralized by failure to achieve goals. Individuals with higher levels of hope have higher feelings of self-worth.

The implications from this study provide evidence that higher levels of hope are correlated with better coping skills and higher levels of pain tolerance, less depression, and few harmful-to-recovery behaviors. Engendering high levels of hope may be significant in goal setting, facilitating behavior change, and adjustment in the rehabilitation process. In addition to being aware of a client's locus of control, professionals should also consider investigating clients' self-talk, which may take more effort to understand, but could provide important clues regarding how individuals perceive their circumstances, approach situations, and identify goals.

FAMILY INFLUENCES

Involving family members, and even close friends, in the establishment of hope in the rehabilitation process may be crucial. Supplying these people with an understanding of the situation and with ways they can help will decrease their anxiety by providing knowledge and giving them some degree of control over their loved one's rehabilitation.

In addition, family members and friends cannot be as supportive if their own emotions and concerns are not taken seriously, or if they are expected to devote all of their time and emotional energy to dealing with the individual with a disability or illness.

Counseling should be provided to these people not only to teach them how to help individuals with disabilities, but also to help them adjust to the situation for their own well-being. This includes siblings, who may be too young to understand the situation or feel left out and ignored. By working together, an effective rehabilitation team should be able to facilitate an atmosphere of hope and provide an optimal rehabilitation plan for the entire family that addresses all aspects of the adjustment and rehabilitative processes.

One group of people who may be especially influenced by the attitudes and expectations of others is children (Eisenberg, Sutkin, & Jansen, 1984). Children learn about themselves and their environment by observing role models; childhood experiences also shape how a child views his or her world. As Robertson and Brown (1992) pointed out, most self-defeating thoughts are developed during childhood, and children are less capable than adults of rationally appraising situations. This makes it vital for family members to provide a supportive and stable environment. Pless, Roghmann, and Haggerty (1972) found that families with low indices of functioning were nearly twice as likely to have poorly adjusted, sick children as families that functioned well. This finding creates a problem because even families that function well under normal circumstances may not know how to cope with the illness or disability of a child. Parents have to adapt to the situation and deal with stress of their own, and must also help each other and siblings of the individual with a disability cope with their feelings (Eisenberg et al.).

Another set of problems can occur when parents become chronically ill or disabled. Although it is detrimental for anyone to lose autonomy or a sense of independence and self-determination (Reeve, 2004), adults who are used to taking care of their families may have an especially difficult time allowing others to take over some of their former responsibilities and may be more likely to experience learned helplessness under these circumstances (Walker, 1992). Therefore, it is essential that all family members be well-informed and seek counseling and social support for themselves. This ensures that they will be able to deal with the situation effectively on a personal level, while providing the environment that best supports autonomy and rehabilitation for either their child or an adult family member (Reeve).

FOCUS OF REHABILITATION APPROACHES

The construct of hope cannot be analyzed or addressed in isolation if one is examining its importance to adjustment and rehabilitation. Just as physiological systems constantly interact with each other, hope interacts with factors such as cognitive processes, locus of control, self-efficacy, beliefs, attitudes, expectations of the self and others, and behavioral and physiological responses (Robertson & Brown,1992; Eisenberg, et al., 1984). Different psychological constructs, situations, and treatments interact to affect each person differently.

Hope would also apply similarly to situations that do not necessarily involve illness or disability. Coping with everyday situations, as well as distressing circumstances, requires the ability to deal with situations effectively while maintaining emotional stability. This is not likely to be accomplished without a healthy level of hope.

Hope and related concepts need to be understood by all people in helping professions, including those who deal primarily with the medical or physical care of clients. It is ineffective to attempt to treat only one part of a person without taking into consideration who they are and what attitudes and reactions they have experienced.

Professionals need to be made aware that their behaviors, attitudes, and expectations, even those that they do not intend to communicate, can have an impact on a client's adjustment. If all professionals have even minimal training in psychological aspects of their clients' rehabilitation, such as hope and cognitions, they will be able to increase the effectiveness of all domains of recovery. A physical therapist teaching exercises and activities that individuals can do independently at times convenient for them with an approach-oriented coping style may find that clients recover more quickly and are more compliant with treatment than if the same clients had been required to do all physical therapy under supervision at scheduled times.

Groopman (2003) explored the way hope affects one's capacity to cope with serious illness. He pointed out the power that doctors and other health care providers have to instill or kill hope. Groopman cited studies on placebo effect as evidence that positive beliefs (hope) can be extremely helpful in motivating people to initiate or continue painful, debilitating treatment. The author provided a convincing rationale for the connections between mind and body, and between mental state and illness, and how these relationships affect one's ability to heal physically and also to have the strength to fight back.

Dodds, Bailey, and Yates (1991) speculated that there may be critical flaws in two common rehabilitation approaches often utilized in dealing with the development of hope. Some rehabilitation specialists believe that depression is a normal response to loss and that grieving is a natural process that occurs with serious illnesses or disabilities involving permanent loss (Dodds et al). This belief leads these professionals to postpone physical or cognitive aspects of training until their clients work through this emotional stage (grieving) either on their own or with psychological counseling, thus prolonging the period during which patients are dependent on others. This delay may result in increasing the possibility of learned helplessness (Dodds et al). This approach is invalidated by the findings that not everyone experiences the predicted stages of grief in the same manner (Dodds et al.). There is the possibility that well-intended rehabilitation professionals or psychologists in an attempt to help the client uncover repressed feelings, may actually create a self-fulfilling prophecy in which individuals become depressed because they are told they should feel this way (Dodds et al.).

An almost opposite approach is to discourage clients from dealing with their negative emotions and to emphasize skills training instead. This strategy is based on the theory that feelings of helplessness and depression are caused by loss of control over daily activities, and focusing on skills that can improve control and independence will therefore be more constructive than psychologically-oriented rehabilitation (Dodds et al, 1991).

Because so many factors influence recovery and adaptation during the rehabilitation process, it is likely that both approaches have valid contributions to make, but neither is holistic enough. There is no reason why a rehabilitation plan cannot include an integrative strategy that combines skills training with psychological counseling. Rehabilitation personnel should be trained to work together to provide both types of rehabilitation, especially because it is important for individuals to learn activities of daily living. However, even if they do learn important skills, most people will have to deal with an altered self-concept and modify their lifestyle to some extent, which can be a difficult transition.

A study by McGuigan (1995), which found no relationship between levels of depression, attribution style, and perception of pain in men undergoing treatment for chronic back pain, demonstrated the importance not only of skills training but also of cognitive and psychological treatment as soon as possible. These results may contradict the findings of many similar studies related to hope, but McGuigan believed that this is because the men in this study had been experiencing chronic pain for about four to six years. However, learned helplessness is a more important factor at the onset of an illness or disability, and therefore has more of an impact on people in the beginning of their rehabilitation.

Another explanation is that the men in this sample provided a restricted range of data, which minimized any correlations between these constructs merely because they were in treatment. All of these men may have had similarly high levels of hope and low levels of helplessness that caused them to continue seeking treatment even after they had not found a solution in the past four to six years. This theory is supported by Sterling, Gottheil, Weinstein, Lundy, and Serota (1996 study). Sterling et al. found that the length of time cocaine addicts entering a treatment program would stay in the program, and therefore, their chance of recovery could be predicted by the Learned Helplessness Scale (LHS) that they completed upon entering rehabilitation. This research shows the detrimental implications of denying clients rehabilitation that focuses on reducing helplessness by improving skills and promoting psychological adjustment.

CONCLUSION

The construct of hope acts as a buffer that prevents individuals from experiencing hopelessness and depression when they are faced with loss, failure, unexpected challenges, and lack of success. Individuals who have hope perceive adversity and setbacks as temporary. Most individuals naturally assume a significant recovery after a disabling injury or diagnosis of a chronic or progressive disease. Hope allows the individual to perceive failure and loss as normal consequences. Helping individuals to acquire hope and see problems as situations with multiple solutions or options is desired. Individuals should be permitted and encouraged to take responsibility for their own lives.

Without hope there is no incentive for an individual to deal with loss in the rehabilitation process. Hope should facilitate rational, constructive thinking and optimistic behavior. The developmental antecedents of hope, the existence of false hope (hopelessness), and issues that involve coping, attitude formation, self-concept affirmation, and spirituality may all be important factors in the development and maintenance of hope in adjustment to disability.

Analyzing the construct of hope, in the course of perusal of the extant literature, resulted in additional questions about the meaning of and measurement of hope. Understanding the positive and negative indicators of hope that influence an individual's response should contribute to meaningful interpretation of and constructive attitude formation related to individual adjustment. The relationship of hope to the integration of optimistic, hopeful behavior and attitudes requires further inquiry and research. The assessment of personal, environmental, and situational factors must be considered as this evaluation may be crucial for added insight and decision-making by the individual experiencing a disability. It also would assist the rehabilitation professional seeking to facilitate the attainment of hope.

The implications of reviewing the construct of hope are multifaceted and provide a rationale for inclusion in the professional preparation of students in academic programs in rehabilitation counseling/education. Discerning the numerous variables that support the development of hope for consumers and practitioners should result in increased sensitivity and awareness of adjustment issues in the rehabilitation process.

Without hope one can experience frustration and lack of direction and commitment. Attaining an expectation of hope that enhances the development of meaningful rehabilitation, positive adjustment, and overall success can facilitate the adoption of a positive attitude by an individual with a disability.

REFERENCES

Anthony, W. A. (1993). Recovery from mental illness: The guiding vision of the mental health service system in the 1990's. *Psychosocial Rehabilitation Journal, 16*, 11–23.

Burish, T. G., & Bradley, L. A. (Eds.). (1983). *Coping with chronic disease research and applications.* New York: Academic Press.

Burish, T. G., Shartner, C. D., & Lyles, J. N. (1981). Effectiveness of multiple-site EMG biofeedback and relaxation training in reducing the aversiveness of cancer chemotherapy. *Biofeedback and Self-Regulation, 6*(4), 523–535.

Carifio, J., & Rhodes, L. (2002). Construct validities and the empirical relationship between optimism, hope, self-efficacy, and locus of control. *Work: A Journal of Prevention, Assessment, and Rehabilitation, 19*(2), 125–136.

Dodds, A. G., Bailey, P, Pearson, A., & Yates, L. (1991). Psychological factors in acquired visual impairment: The development of a scale of adjustment. *Journal of Visual Impairment and Blindness, 85*(7), 306–310.

Eisenberg, M. G., Sutkin, L. C., & Jansen, M. A. (Eds.). (1984). *Chronic illness and disability through the life span.* New York: Springer Publishing Company.

Falvo, D. R. (1999). *Medical and psychosocial aspects of chronic illness and disability* (2nd ed.). Gaithersburg, MD: Aspen Publishers.

Groopman, J. (2003). *The Anatomy of hope: How people prevail in the face of illness.* New York: Random House.

Kobler, A. L., & Stotland, E. (1964). *The end of hope: A social-clinical study of suicide.* New York: Free Press.

McGuigan, J. B. (1995). Attributional style and depression in men receiving treatment for chronic pain. *Journal of Applied Rehabilitation Counseling, 26*(4), 21–25.

Moore, A. D., & Stambrook, M. (1995). Cognitive moderators of outcome following a traumatic brain injury: A conceptual model and implications for rehabilitation. *Brain Injury, 9*(2), 109–130.

Peterson, C., Maier, S. F., & Seligman, M. E. (1995). *Learned helplessness: A theory for the age of personal control.* Oxford: Oxford University Press.

Pless, I. B., Roghmann, K., & Haggerty, R. F. (1972). Chronic illness, family functioning, and psychological adjustment: A model for the allocation of preventive mental health services. *International Journal of Epidemiology, 1*, 271–277.

Puchalski, C. M. (1999). Touching the spirit: The essence of healing. *Spiritual life.* Washington, DC: Discalced Carmelite Friars of the Washington Province.

Reeve, J. (2004). *Understanding motivation and emotion* (4th ed.). New York: Wiley.

Robertson, S. E., & Brown, R. I. (Eds.). (1992). *Rehabilitation counselling approaches in the field of disability.* London: Chapman & Hall Publishing.

Rosenbaum, E. H., & Rosenbaum, I. R. (1999). *Inner fire: Your will to live: Stories of courage, hope, and determination.* Austin, TX: Plexus.

Seligman, M. E. (1998). *Learned optimism* (2nd ed.). New York: Simon & Schuster.

Shnek, Z. M., Foley, F. W., LaRocca, N. G, Gordon, W. A., DeLuca, J., Schwartz-
    man, H. G., Halper, J., Lennox, S., & Irvine, J. (1997). Helplessness, self-
    efficacy, cognitive distortions, and depression in multiple sclerosis and spinal
    cord injury. *Annals of Behavioral Medicine, 19*(3), 287–294.
Shnek, Z. M., Foley, F. W., LaRocca, N. G., Smith, C. R., & Halper, J. (1995).
    Psychological predictors of depression in multiple sclerosis. *Journal of Neu-
    rologic Rehabilitation, 9*(1), 15–23.
Snyder, C.R. (1998). A case for hope in pain, loss, and suffering. In J. H. Harvey, J.
    Omarzy, & E. Miller (Eds.), *Perspectives on loss: A sourcebook*. Washington,
    DC: Taylor & Francis, Ltd.
Snyder, C. R. (2000). The past and possible futures of hope. *Journal of Social and
    Clinical Psychology, 19*, 11–28.
Snyder, C.R. (2003). *The psychology of hope: You can get there from here*. New
    York: The Free Press.
Stanton, A.L., Danoff-Burg, S., & Huggins, M.E. (2002). The first year after breast
    cancer. diagnosis: Hope and coping strategies as predictors of adjustment.
    Psycho-Oncology, 11, 93–102.
Sterling, R.C., Gottheil, E., Weinstein, S.P., Lundy, A., & Scrota, R.D. (1996).
    Learned helplessness and cocaine dependence: An investigation. *Journal of
    Addictive Diseases, 15*(2), 12–24.
Stotland, E. (1969). *The Psychology of hope*. San Francisco: Jossey-Bass.
Walker, J. M. (1992). Injured worker helplessness: Critical relationships and sys-
    tems level approach for intervention. *Journal of Occupational Rehabilita-
    tion, 2*(4), 201–209.

CHAPTER TWENTY-THREE

Spirituality in Disability and Illness

Judy Kaye and Senthil Kumar Raghavan

REVIEW OF THE LITERATURE

Spirituality has been described as the central philosophy of life which guides people's conduct and is the core of individual existence that integrates and transcends the physical, emotional, intellectual, moral-ethical, volitional, and social dimensions (Colliton, 1981; Dombeck & Karl, 1987; Ellerhorst-Ryan, 1985; Fish & Shelly, 1978; Heriot, 1992). Spirituality may be perceived as personal views and behaviors that express a sense of relatedness to a transcendent dimension or to something greater than the self that empowers, values, and integrates the self (Kaye, 2000; Reed, 1987). Psychiatrist John F. Hiatt (1986) described the concept of spirituality in psychological terms and related it to a health care perspective: "Spirit refers to that non-corporeal and non-mental dimension of the person that is the source of unity and meaning, and spirituality refers to the concepts, attitudes, and behaviors that derive from one's experience of that dimension" (p. 742). Spirituality is viewed as being at the core of the individual's existence, integrating and transcending the physical, emotional, intellectual, and social dimensions (Landrum, Beck, Rawlins, Williams, & Culpan, 1984).

From "Spirituality in disability and illness," by J. Kaye and S. K. Raghavan, 2002, *Journal of Religion and Health*, *41*(3), 231–242. Reprinted with permission.

In recent years, the concept of spirituality has appeared with increasing frequency in the literature (Aldridge, 1993; Emblen, 1992; Reed, 1987). Spirituality has been described as an emerging paradigm for investigation (Reed, 1992) and is a developing area of inquiry involving mind-body-spirit interaction (Goleman & Gurin, 1993; Leskowitz, 1993; Moyers, 1993). The traditional, mechanistic biomedical paradigm is being replaced by a broader holistic perspective encompassing bio-psychosocial-spiritual factors of health and illness (Dossey, 1995; Wiedenfeld et al., 1990).

SPIRITUALITY VS. RELIGION

The spiritual nature of individuals needs to be differentiated from the religious aspects of an individual's life (Mansen, 1993). Spirituality is a broader term and may be viewed as an umbrella concept under which one finds religion. Religiosity is an expression of one's spiritual perspective and refers to an external, formal system of beliefs, values, rules of conduct, and rituals (Heriot, 1992; Mickley, Soeken & Belcher, 1992). The word religion has as its root the Latin term *relegare*, which means "to bind fast, or tie together" (Mansen, 1993, p. 141). Religion is concerned with public participation in a faith community with specific practices and doctrines (Walker, 1992). Research supports religion (an expression of a person's spiritual perspective) as a primary means of coping with stress of illness and disability (Kaye & Robinson, 1994; Wykle & Segal, 1991).

SPIRITUALITY AND TRANSCENDENCE

A common thread found in definitions of spirituality is the universal human desire for transcendence and connectedness (Carson, 1993; Haase et al., 1992; Reed, 1991a, 1992). Transcendence is defined as a level of awareness that exceeds ordinary, physical boundaries and limitations, yet allows the individual to achieve new perspectives and experiences (Klass & Gordon, 1978–9; Reed, 1982). Spirituality may be seen as an expression of the capacity for self-transcendence. Spirituality is the nature of human beings, spans the entire developmental life process, and is viewed as diverse worldwide phenomenon (Reed, 1992).

A spiritual perspective is antecedent to self-transcendence (Haase et al., 1992). Awareness of self-transcendence refers to "the developmental maturity whereby there is an expansion of self-boundaries and an orientation toward broadened life perspectives and purposes" (Reed, 1991, p. 64). Awareness of transcendence involves a transformation of perception, in that the problems of meaninglessness, fear of nonbeing, and separation anxiety are overcome (Belcher, Dettmore & Holzemer, 1989). Spiritual transcendence does not imply a detachment from other dimensions of ones' life, rather it emphasizes an openness to the perceived environment that extends beyond spatial-temporal boundaries (Conrad, 1985). Transcendent experiences include participation in worship, prayer, and a sense of closeness to something greater than the self (Koestenbaum, 1977).

Klass and Gordon (1978–9) describe transcendence as a transformation of the perception of the human condition. Transformation of perceptions, such as hopelessness and helplessness, experienced with disability and illness may provide some comfort and aid among adults trying to deal with these conditions. Klass & Gordon (1978–9) used qualitative methodology to study 30 people diagnosed in three categories: dying, had almost died, or were grieving a significant person's death. The researchers concluded that transcendence was "a generalization of the many ways human beings have found to move beyond the banal, the profane, or the transitory into the meaningful, the sacred, or the eternal" (p. 19).

Hood and Morris (1983), in a series of qualitative studies, proposed a preliminary theory of death transcendence based on Lifton's (1975) work. Transcendence was supported as experiential and occurred through identification with phenomena more enduring than oneself. Persons were capable of experiencing union with others, nature, or God when this experience occurred and a sense of transcendence was assured.

Reed (1986) focused spirituality as an empirical indicator of the capacity for transcendence among terminally ill persons. The terminally ill patients reported greater spirituality than the healthy adults (t (112) of 3.11, $p < .001$). The spiritual perspective of transcendence was supported as having the capacity to overcome a person's concepts of inevitable biological losses and death. Spirituality provides the person with the capacity for healthy outlooks through transcendence of ordinary boundaries despite illness and potential death (Reed, 1992).

SPIRITUALITY AND COPING WITH DISABILITY AND ILLNESS

Spirituality has been found to be an important variable when coping with illness. Since the 19th century, over 250 published empirical studies have appeared in the epidemiological and medical literature in which spirituality has been statistically associated in many ways with particular health outcomes (Levin, 1993). Studies, which identified spirituality as a resource, included a wide variety of disability and illness situations.

Spirituality was described as a resource in several studies related to life threatening illness. Spirituality was found to be profoundly related to decreased fear of death ($p < .05$), decreased discomfort, decreased loneliness ($p < .0 16$), increased emotional adjustment, and positive death perspective ($p < .001$) among seriously ill patients (Gibbs & Achterberg-Lawlis, 1978; Miller, 1983; Reed, 1986). Terminally ill patients realistically aware of a prognosis of less than six months to live reported greater number of spiritual activities ($t (4.16) = 2.19, P < .05$) than those unaware of their prognosis (Sodestrom & Martinson 1987).

In a qualitative study, Emblen and Halstead (1993) interviewed 19 surgical patients regarding their views of spirituality. They described prayer, spiritual assistance, and a transcendent view of needing a more powerful than earthly being and not feeling abandonment as important spiritual perspectives. Saudia and associates (1991) studied prayer, a component of spirituality, among a population of 100 cardiac surgery patients using the Helpfulness of Prayer Scale, a likert-type scale with a range of 0–15. Ninety Six percent of the patients indicated that prayer was extremely helpful as a spiritual activity utilized as a coping strategy to deal with the stress of cardiac surgery. In another correlative study, Pressman, et al. (1990) showed that among the elderly women hospitalized for hip fractures ($n = 30$), those with stronger spirituality had better ambulation status at discharge ($F = 12.15, df = 1.26, p < 0.002$).

A number of researchers found spirituality to be a primary resource among persons dealing with chronic disability and illness. These included hypertension, chronic obstructive pulmonary disease, diabetes, chronic renal failure, rheumatoid arthritis, multiple sclerosis, and Polio (Miller, 1985; O'Brien, M.E., 1982; Smith, 1995; Young, 1993).

Miller (1985) administered the Abbreviated Loneliness Scale (ABLS) and the Spiritual Well Being Scale (SWB) to 64 chronically ill adults with rheumatoid arthritis and 64 randomly selected healthy adults to determine the relationship between loneliness and spiritual well-being. The chronically ill patients ($M = 94.25$) had significantly higher spiritual well-being compared to the healthy group ($M = 83.72$) ($p < 0.01$). Spiritual well-being had an inverse relationship to loneliness in both groups.

O'Brien (1982) in a three-year longitudinal study examined spirituality and the association with adjustment to hemodialysis and end-stage renal failure. Perceptions of the importance of spiritual faith and social functioning were evaluated using the Interactional Behavior Scale. Results indicated that patients who attended church services once a week or more achieved the highest mean scores for interactional behavior ($F (3, 122) = 15.30 p < 0.01$), and quality of interaction ($F (3, 122) = 8.20 p < 0.01$). Patients who attended church more regularly were also more compliant in adhering to the prescribed hemodialysis regime.

Smith's (1995) comparative study on spirituality and perceptions of power among polio survivors showed that power was positively related to spirituality ($r = .34$, $p < 0.005$). Polio survivors manifested the same power on the Power of Knowing Participation in Charge Test ($t = .44$, $p < 0.33$) and significantly greater spirituality on the Spiritual Orientation Inventory than people who had not dealt with polio ($t = 3.79$, $p < 0.001$).

Young (1993) used an ethnographic qualitative method to study spirituality among 12 chronically ill elderly with various diagnoses including arthritis, chronic obstructive pulmonary disease, diabetes mellitus, heart disease, presbycusis, presbyopia, hypertension, and stroke. Informants indicated that their spirituality increased as they aged and became elderly. A feeling of well-being emanated from the belief that God knew their needs and empowered them to continue to survive through difficult times.

Several studies addressed the importance of spirituality as a resource when dealing with terminal illness and end of life issues (Gotay, 1984; Mickley, Soeken, & Belcher 1992; O'Connor, Wicker, & Germino 1990). In Gotay's study (1984) on coping mechanisms among cancer patients dealing with the advanced stages of cancer, faith and prayer was ranked as first in importance of coping mechanisms. Similarly, their mates ranked faith and prayer as second in importance among coping mechanisms. Individuals dealing with advanced stages of cancer were more apt to share their fears with other people and their God.

Mickley et al. (1992) utilized the constructs of spiritual well being (Spiritual Well Being Scale—Ellison, 1983), religiousness (Feagin Intrinsic/Extrinsic Religiousness Scale—Feagin, 1964), and hope (The Nowotny Hope Scale) to clarify spiritual health among 175 women diagnosed with breast cancer. Hierarchical regression indicated that existential well-being, a component of SWB, was the primary contributor of hope (b .037, $p < 0.001$). A semistructured interview conducted by O'Connor et al. (1990) on thirty cancer patient revealed that faith, prayer, and the healing power of God helped 50% of the respondents' cope, while faith was described as "the strongest support." Almost one-third (30%) described their spirituality or God as a source of hope.

A sense of power, among populations dealing with end of life issues and terminal illness, was achieved through prayer, and a belief in afterlife provided hope for the future. Believing that their life has real purpose, seeking understanding and meaning in their lives, their suffering, and their impending death were among the spiritual perspectives reported.

Spirituality was reported to affect positive outcomes with addictive illnesses (Carroll, 1993; Corrington, 1989). Corrington (1989) identified the relationship between levels of spirituality and contentment during recovery from Alcoholism among 30 members of Alcoholics Anonymous.

Spirituality as measured by the Spirituality Self-Assessment Scale (SSAS) (Whitfield, 1984) had a direct linear relationship to contentment in life as measured with Hudson's Generalized Contentment Scale (GCS) (Hudson, 1982). Carroll's (1993) study on the importance of spirituality and purpose in life in Alcoholism Recovery among 100 Alcoholics Anonymous (AA) members revealed that Spirituality (practice of AA Step 11) had a significant positive relationship to The Purpose in Life Test (Crumbaugh and Maholick, 1964) scores ($r = .59, p < 0.001$) and the length of sobriety ($r = .25, p < 0.01$).

Spiritually has historically been a major part of treatment plans for alcoholism. Recovering alcoholics use spirituality as a positive method for processing stress and expressing feelings, whereas alcohol had previously been the means to suppress feelings aroused by stressors. Higher levels of spirituality have been correlated with greater contentment with life and duration of sobriety.

Several studies of clients experiencing immunosuppressive related illnesses and disabilities support spirituality as a primary coping mechanism (Carson & Green, 1992; Guillory, Sowell, Moneyham, & Seals, 1997; Sowell, Moneyham, Hennessy, Guillory, Demi, & Seals, 2000). Spiritual well-being was found to be significantly related to hardiness ($R = .4165$, $p < 0.001$) among individuals diagnosed as HIV positive (Carson & Green, 1992).

Guillory and colleagues (1997) studied the meaning of spirituality among 45 women infected with HIV/AIDS, 12 white and 33 black, using a focus group methodology. The most frequently identified theme evident in the data was the need for personal relationship or connectedness with a Supreme Being. Prayer was the most frequent spiritual activity identified. The researchers concluded that as a result of the women facing a stigmatized and terminal illness, the need for peace of mind and a sense of love were especially important components of spirituality.

Sowell and associates (2000) examined the role of spiritual activities as a moderator of the impact of HIV-related stressors (functional impairment, work impairment, and HIV-related symptoms) on two stress-related adaptative outcomes (emotional distress and quality of life) on a clinic-based sample of 184 HIV-positive women. Using a theoretically based causal model, the researchers demonstrated that HIV-related stressors had a significant positive effect on emotional distress ($b = .52, p < 0.05$) and significant negative effect on quality of life ($b = -.38, p < 0.05$) while spiritual activities had essentially no effect on HIV-disease-related stressors (physical condition—functional ability) ($b = -.02$), $p < 0.75$). However spiritual activities reduced emotional distress ($b = -.21, p < .05$) and enhanced quality of life ($.19$ ($t = 1.88$) even when the physical conditions of the respondent were statistically controlled.

Belcher et al. (1989), in a qualitative study of persons with AIDS found that their spirituality was reported to have changed after the onset of AIDS. Spirituality was a resource that enhanced personal control, provided a source of comfort, a way of understanding, and ordering their AIDS experience.

Research has demonstrated that the use of spirituality as a resource resulted in improved overall physical outcomes. Psychosocial factors of spiritual coping (i.e., prayer, devotional reading, and church attendance) were found to ameliorate the autonomic consequence of stress and its effect on health (Tanzy, 1991). In a randomized double-blind study (Byrd, 1988) of 393 hospitalized cardiac clients, use of intercessory prayer (prayers to God to intercede on another person's behalf) was demonstrated as beneficial to recovery. The experimental group that were prayed for had better outcomes requiring less ventilatory assistance, antibiotics, and diuretics than did patients in the control group that had no prayers.

Family members dealing with a critical illness report use of greater spiritual perspective. Kaye, Heald, and Polivka (1996) studied spirituality among family members of critically ill adults. After controlling for the demographic variables of age, education, gender, and religious background, family members ($n = 100$) described significantly greater spirituality ($p = 0.001$) and greater frequency of conversation about spiritual matters, reading of spiritually related materials, and private prayer ($p < 0.001$), compared to a set of healthy adults ($n = 97$). Kaye (2000) also demonstrated the use of spiritual perspective by wife caregivers ($n = 11$) of persons with Alzheimer's disease as a method of coping. The caregiver's spiritual perspective included thoughts of God or a "higher power" being in charge of and present during the stressful situation of dealing with disability and illness of the afflicted person.

In summary, many different populations facing disability and illness were described in the literature who utilize spirituality in their coping process. Research literature supports spirituality as an important resource when facing disability and illness.

DISCUSSSION

People experiencing disability and illness described prayer, transcendence perspectives and connectedness as important spiritual needs. These studies support Clinebell's (1966) theological framework of spiritual needs: (a) finding meaning and purpose in life; (b) giving and receiving love; and (c) maintaining hope and creativity.

The stress of illness and disability often causes a disequilibrium of mind, body, and spirit that requires coping resources (Soeken & Carson,

1987) and research supports spirituality as a valuable resource for dealing with the stress of various types of disabilities and illnesses. Bargament (1990) described how spirituality relates to the stress and coping process in Lazarus and Folkman's (1984) theoretical framework. Spirituality helps the person cope with the stressful situation especially through relationship with God and their faith community. It can be a part of the elements of primary and secondary appraisal of the stressful situation that helps the person make some sense out of pain and suffering. The search for meaning in the illness situation involves a spiritual process (Frankl, 1963). Actually spiritual growth can be a product of the stress and coping experienced during disability and illness.

IMPLICATIONS FOR HEALTH CARE PRACTICE

There are many implications for practice related to the findings in the literature. Studies support that spirituality has important relationships to psychological and physical recovery from illness among persons suffering from various disabilities and diseases (Belcher et al., 1989; Byrd, 1988; Carroll, 1993; Carson et al., 1992; Guillory et al., 1997; Kaye, 2000; Pressman, 1990; Smith, 1995; Sowell et al., 2000; Young, 1993). Perceptions of God as source of strength and comfort and church attendance had positive relationships to recovery from illness and coping with disabilities. Therefore, these relationships should be encouraged and facilitated by health care providers.

Ill persons reported being distressed when unable to attend worship and other faith community services (Pressman et al., 1990; Tanzy, 1991). Additionally, attendance at faith community activities decreased alienation (O'Brien, 1982) and spirituality had an inverse relationship to loneliness (Miller, 1985). Since faith communities are such a significant part of individual's lives and a resource for combating alienation and loneliness, health care providers need to facilitate attendance to these activities (O'Brien, 1982).

Family members of the afflicted also need spiritual resources while caring for the sick person and dealing with the disability and illness (Kaye et al., 1996). Lay volunteers within faith communities may be trained to assist the family with the physical needs of the ill person and to provide respite care while the family members shop, run errands, participate in recreation, or attend church. Faith community members should be encouraged to phone and visit on a regular basis to provide social and spiritual support. Asking people from the faith community to prepared meals to bring to the ill person's home and eating with them and their family is another example of using the caregiver's faith congregation to help decrease loneliness and increase social support satisfaction. Utilizing the faith community to providing social support to the ill person and their family incorporates their spiritual faith into their care and may be a more satisfying resource to many people suffering from disability and disease.

Studies indicate that persons facing disability and illness use various spirituality activities to find purpose and meaning and a sense of hope for the future (Carroll, 1993; Guillory et al., 1997; O'Connor et al., 1990; Sowell et al., 2000; Young, 1993). Additionally, seeking forgiveness was an important part of their spirituality (Kaye, Heald, & Polivka, 1996). Health care providers can work with other members of the multidisciplinary team such as chaplains and clergy to help the ill person find purpose and meaning in their current state of living. Exploring discussions and thoughts of hope as well as asking God or others for forgiveness may help alleviate feelings of guilt and provide a futuristic view of life despite the illness (Young, 1993). Belief in afterlife may be a part of the person's spiritual perspective that provides a source of comfort and hope for the future, especially those experiencing end of life and terminal illnesses.

Studies indicate that spirituality relates to coping and facilitates transcending perceptions of helplessness (Kaye, 2000). Perceptions of God being in control of the overall universe, when an illness has resulted in loss of function and control within one's current life, may help transcend feelings of helplessness. Some patients report that praying and "turning it over to the Lord" provides feelings of peace and comfort (Kaye, 2001, p. 41). Spiritual activities such as prayer and meditation (Byrd, 1988; Saudia et al., 1991) and communication with God may provide a sense of an omnipotent being having overall control during illness or disability situations where the person has lost control (Kaye et al., 1996). Prayer and meditation have been shown to be valuable resources during illness and may reduce stress (Byrd, 1988; Saudia et al., 1991). Therefore, prayer and meditation should be encouraged when it is an important part of the person's spirituality.

Additionally, attendance at church activities decreased alienation (O'Brien, 1982) and spirituality had an inverse relationship to loneliness and depression (Pressman et al., 1990; Miller, 1985; Tanzey, 1991). Since spirituality is such a significant part of individual's lives and a resource for combating alienation, loneliness, and depression health care providers need to facilitate important spiritual activities and attendance at to faith community or church programs (O'Brien, 1982). Identifying and implementing interventions related to the individual's spiritual perspectives may be extremely important to combat feelings of helplessness and depression.

Religious items and rituals symbolic and important to one's individual faith often provide comfort to the ill person and their families. Reading favorite spiritually related materials, candles, and other various faith symbols important to the person's faith should be made available. Placing an important personal faith item such as a cross, rosary, or other symbol in a semi-conscious terminal individual's hand may to contribute to a sense of calmness. Encouraging family members to read favorite spiritual verses to the ill person who is too sick to read for themselves may provide a sense of connectedness and peace.

The studies throughout the literature supporting spirituality as having an important relationship to overall well-being and health are notable. However, it is evident that interventions and treatments utilizing spirituality need to be individualized to be acceptable and helpful to the person experiencing disability and illness. Use of spirituality is a personal resource that may actually help reduce vulnerability, and morbidity and mortality. However, further research and investigation into variables, significant relationships, and conceptual model testing is needed to understand more fully the causal relationships between spirituality and psychological and physical health outcomes.

IMPLICATIONS FOR FUTURE RESEARCH

Considering the paucity of research investigating spirituality, results of this literature review reveal a clear need for further investigation in this area, particularly as it relates to outcomes of depression and health. Specifically, how spirituality affects depression, whether it is through mechanisms of improved perceptions of control or cognitive reframing of stressful events, is an important question for future investigation. Future research is needed to further define spirituality's relationship to stress. How spirituality relates to health through the psychoneuroimmunology response is a promising new horizon of study. Whether spiritual perspectives relates to physiologic measures of stress such as cortisol and immune suppression are important questions for future research.

Longitudinal studies are needed to evaluate how spirituality and its relationship to the variables of stress, life satisfaction, social support satisfaction, depression and health are affected over time. Experimental studies using spirituality and spiritual activities as an intervention as well as spiritually focused support groups need testing.

Positive imaging has been used as an intervention among stressed patients effectively. Images of God and perspectives of relationship to a supreme power or the divine being among individuals facing the stress of illness and disability need investigation. Use of positive spiritual images and how they relate to depression and health are important questions not answered. Prayer and meditation needs further investigation to understand its relationship to psychological and physiological health.

The entire spectrum of spirituality, illness, and disability, from different cultures, faiths, and races, as it relates to health outcomes has not been researched. Examples include: spirituality and health outcomes of African American, Hispanic, Native American, Asian Americans and Pacific Islander caregivers as well as caregivers with different faiths that are not found in the literature.

Future research in spirituality and health is only limited by the vision and resources available to researchers. However, with the National Institutes of Health's new center for Alternative and Complementary Medicine, more funding is available for studies that are not exclusively biomedical in focus, and spirituality research may be one area considered for funding.

REFERENCES

Aldridge, D. (1993). Is there evidence for spiritual healing? *Advances: The Journal of Mind-Body Health, 9*(4), 4–21.

American Psychiatric Association (1994). *Diagnostic and statistical manual of mental disorders*, 4th ed. Washington, DC.

Belcher, A.E., Dettmore, D., & Holzemer, S.P. (1989). Spirituality and sense of well-being in persons with AIDS. *Holistic Nursing Practice, 3*(4), 16–25.

Byrd, R. (1988). Positive therapeutic effects of intercessory prayer in a coronary care unit population. *Southern Medical Journal, 81*(7), 826–929.

Carroll, S. (1993). Spirituality and purpose in life in alcoholism recovery. *Journal of Studies on Alcohol*, May, 297–301.

Carson, V.B. (1993, Winter). Spirituality: Generic or Christian? *Journal of Christian Nursing*, 24–27.

Carson, V.B. & Green, H. (1992). Spiritual well-being: A predictor of hardiness in patients with Acquired Immunodeficiency Syndrome. *Journal of Professional Nursing, 8*(4), 209–220.

Clinebell, H.J. (1966). *Basic types of pastoral counseling: New resources for ministering to the troubled*. New York: Abingdon.

Colliton, M.A. (1981). The spiritual dimension of nursing. In Beland & Passos (Eds.), *Clinical Nursing* (4th ed.). New York: Macmillan.

Conrad, N.L. (1985). Spiritual support for the dying. *Nursing Clinics of North America, 20*, 415–426.

Corrington, J.E. (1989). Spirituality and recovery: Relationships between levels of spirituality, contentment and stress during recovery from alcoholism and AA. *Alcoholism Treatment Quarterly, 6*(3/4), 151–165.

Crumbaugh, J.C. & Maholick, L.T. (1964). An experimental study in existentialism: The psychometric approach to Frankl's concept of noogenic neurosis. *Journal of Clinical Psychology, 20*, 200–207.

Dombeck, M. & Karl, J. (1987). Spiritual issues in mental health care. *Journal of Religion and Health, 26*, 183–197.

Dossey, L. (1995). Whatever happened to healers? *Alternative Therapies, 1*(5), 6–13.

Ellerhorst-Ryan, J. (1985). Selecting an instrument to measure spiritual distress. *Oncology Nursing Forum, 12*,(2), 93–99.

Ellison, C.W. (1983). Spiritual well-being: Conceptualization and measurement. *Journal of Psychology and Theology, 11*(4), 330–340.

Emblen, J.D. (1992). Religion and spirituality defined according to current use in nursing literature. *Journal of Professional Nursing, 8*(1), 41–47.

Emblen, J.D. & Halstead, L. (1993). Spiritual needs and interventions: Comparing the views of patients, nurses, and chaplains. *Clinical Nurse Specialist, 7*(4), 175–182.

Feagin, C.M. (1987). Stress: Implications for nursing research. *IMAGE, 19*(1), 38–41.

Fish, S. & Shelly, J. (1978). *Spiritual Care: The Nurses Role.* Downers Grove, IL: Intervarsity Press.

Frankl, V. (1963). *Man's Search for Meaning.* Boston: Beacon.

Gibbs, H.W. & Achterberg-Lawlis, J. (1978). Spiritual values and death anxiety: Implications for counseling with terminal cancer patients. *Journal of Counseling Psychology, 25*, 563–569.

Goleman, D. & Gurin, J. (1993). *Mind Body Medicine: How to Use Your Mind for Better Health.* Yonkers, NY: Consumer Reports Books.

Gotay, C.C. (1984). The experience of cancer during early and advanced stages: The views of patients and their mates. *Social Science Medicine, 18*(7), 605–13.

Guillory J.A., Sowell R., Moneyham L. & Seals, B. (1997). An exploration of the meaning and use of spirituality among women with HIV/AIDS. *Alternative Therapies 3*(5), 55–60.

Haase, J.E., Britt, T., Coward, D.D., Leidy, N.K., & Penn, P.E. (1992). Simultaneous concept analysis of spiritual perspective, hope, acceptance, and self-transcendence. *IMAGE, 24*(2), 141–147.

Heriot, C.S. (1992). Spirituality and aging. *Holistic Nursing Practice, 7*(1), 22–31.

Hiatt, J.F. (1986). Spirituality, medicine, and healing. *Southern Medical Journal, 79*(6), 736–743.

Hood, R.W. & Morris, R.J. (1983). Towards a theory of death transcendence. *Journal of the Scientific Study of Religion, 22*, 353–365.

Hudson, W. (1982). *The clinical measurement package: A field manual.* Homewood, Illinois: Dorsey Press.

Kaye, J. (2000). Spirituality and the emotional and physical health of Black and White southern caregivers of persons with Alzheimer's disease and other dementias. *Doctoral Dissertation.* Medical College of Georgia, Augusta, GA.

Kaye, J., Heald, G., & Polivka, D. (1996). Spirituality among family members of critically ill adults. *American Journal of Critical Care, 5*(3), 242, National Teaching Institute abstracts.

Kaye, J. & Robinson, K. (1994). Spirituality among caregivers. *IMAGE, 26*(3), 218–221.

Klass, D. & Gordon, A. (1978–79). Varieties of transcending experiences in death: A videotape-based study. *OMEGA, 9,* 19–36.

Koestenbaum, R.J. (1977). Death and development through the life span. In H. Feifel, *New Meanings of Death.* New York: McGraw-Hill.

Landrum, P.A., Beck, C.M., Rawlins, R.P., Williams, S.R. & Culpan, F.M. (1984). The person as a client. In Beck, C.M., Rawlins, R.P., & Williams S.R., (Eds.), *Mental Health-Psychiatric Nursing: A Holistic Life-Cycle Approach.* St. Louis: Mosby.

Lazarus R. & Folkman, S. (1984). *Stress Appraisal, & Coping.* New York: Springer Publishing.

Levin, J.S. (1993). Esoteric vs. exoteric explanations for findings linking spirituality and health. *Advances, The Journal of Mind-Body Health, 9*(4), 54–56.

Lifton, R.J. (1975). On death and the continuity of life: A psychohistorical perspective. *OMEGA, 6*(2), 143–157.

Mansen, T.J. (1993). The spiritual dimension of individuals: Conceptual development. *Nursing Diagnosis, 4*(4), 140–147.

Mickley, J.R., Soeken, K., & Belcher, A. (1992). Spiritual well-being, religiousness and hope among women with breast cancer. *IMAGE, 24*(4), 267–272.

Miller, J.F. (1983). *Coping with chronic illness: Overcoming powerlessness.* Philadelphia: F.A. Davis.

Miller, J.F. (1985). Assessment of loneliness and spiritual well-being in chronically ill and healthy adults. *Journal of Professional Nursing,* March–April, 79–85.

Moyers, B. (1993). *Healing the mind.* New York, Doubleday.

O'Brien, M.E. (1982b). Religious faith and adjustment to long-term hemodialysis. *Journal of Religion and Health, 21,* 68–80.

O'Connor, A.P., Wicker, C.A., & Germino, B.B. (1990). Understanding the cancer patient's search for meaning. *Cancer Nursing, 13,* 167–175.

Pressman, P., Lyons, J.S., Larson, D.B., & Strain, J.J. (1990). Religious belief, depression, and ambulation status in elderly women with broken hips. *American Journal of Psychiatry, 147*(6), 758–760.

Reed, P.G. (1992). An emerging paradigm for the investigation of spirituality in nursing. *Research in Nursing & Health, 15,* 349–357.

Reed, P.G. (1991). Toward a nursing theory of self-transcendence: Deductive reformulation using developmental theories. *Advances in Nursing Science, 13*(4), 64–77.

Reed, P.G. (1987). Spirituality and Well-being in terminally ill hospitalized adults. *Research in Nursing & Health, 10,* 335–344.

Reed, P.G. (1986). Religiousness among terminally ill and healthy adults. *Research in Nursing and Health, 9,* 35–41.

Reed, P.G. (1982). Well-being and perspectives on life and death among death-involved and nondeath-involved adults. *Doctoral Dissertation,* Wayne State University.

Saudia, T.L., Kinney, M.R., Brown, K.C., & Young, W.L. (1991). Health locus of control and helpfulness of prayer. *Heart & Lung, 20,* 60–65.

Smith, D.W. (1995). Power and spirituality in polio survivors: A study based on Roger's science. *Nursing Science Quarterly 8*(3), 133–9.

Sodestrom, K.E. & Martinson, I.M. (1987). Patient's spiritual coping strategies: A study of nurse and patient perspectives. *Oncology Nursing Forum, 14*(2), 41–46.

Soeken, K. & Carson, V. (1987). Responding to the spiritual needs of the chronically ill. *Nursing Clinics of North America, 22*(3), 603–611.

Sowell, R.L., Moneyham, L., Hennessy, M., Guillory, J., Demi, A., Seals, B. (2000). Spiritual activities as a resistance resource for women with Human Immunodeficiency Virus. *Nursing Research, 49*(2).

Tanzy, J.S. (1991). Stress-related change in health status: Relationship between psychological and physiological adjustment (Psychological Adjustment). (Doctoral dissertation, Fuller Theological Seminary, School of Psychology, 1991). *Dissertation Abstracts International, 52-08*, AAI9132224.

Walker, M.T. (1992). Spirituality: Implications for nursing care. *American Association of Rehabilitation Nurses, 48*(6), 17–18.

Whitfield, C.L. (1984). Stress management and spirituality during recovery: A transpersonal approach. Part 1: Becoming. *Alcoholism Treatment Quarterly 1*, 3–54.

Wiedenfeld, S., Bandura, A., Levine, S., O'Leary, A., Brown, S., & Raska, K. (1990). Impact of perceived self-efficacy in coping with stressors on components of the immune system. *Journal of Personality and Social Psychology, 59*(5), 1082–1094.

Wykle, M. & Segal, B. (1991). Increasing the longevity of minority older adults through improved health status. In *Minority Elders: Longevity, Economics and Health.* Washington, D.C.: Gerontological Society of America.

Young, C. (1993). Spirituality and the chronically ill Christian elderly. *Geriatric Nursing, 14*(6), 298–303.

CHAPTER TWENTY-FOUR

Spiritual Factors and Adjustment in Medical Rehabilitation[1]

Understanding Forgiveness as a Means of Coping

Jon R. Webb

The role of spirituality in the process of adjustment and as a means of coping is but one of the many areas of responsibility health care providers are faced with in modern medical rehabilitation. Yet, little attention has been paid to spirituality and the influence of religion, including forgiveness, on the health and well-being of people with disabilities (Selway & Ashman, 1998). The psychology of religious and spiritual issues in relation to rehabilitation (Kim, Heinemann, Bode, Sliwa, & King, 2000), and in general (Richards & Bergin, 1997), has not always been viewed as worthy of attention. However, it is apparent that spiritual issues have long been and continue to be important to most people in America (Gallup, 2001; Gallup Poll, 2001), as well as most people in need of rehabilitation (Kim et al.).

From "Spiritual factors and adjustment in medical rehabilitation: Understanding forgiveness as a means of coping," by J. Webb, 2003, *Journal of Applied Rehabilitation Counseling*, *34*(3), 16–23. Reprinted with permission.

[1] Note: Supported by Department of Education grant H133P990014 and National Institutes of Health grant T32AA07477

The purpose of this chapter is twofold. The first purpose is to bring increased attention and understanding to spiritual factors in the process of adjustment in rehabilitation, and the second is to focus on the ability to forgive *others* as a specific psycho-spiritual coping mechanism available to rehabilitation professionals.

Rehabilitation psychology, long known for its expertise in addressing the psychosocial factors associated with chronic illness and disability (Wegener, Elliott, & Hagglund, 2000), has, until recently, essentially overlooked spirituality as a factor in rehabilitation. While spirituality has now been recognized as a viable factor in rehabilitation and adjustment (Rybarczyk, Szymanski, & Nicholas, 2000), and healthcare in general (George, Larson, Koenig, & McCullough, 2000), at best it has received broad brush strokes on the canvas of holistic treatment in rehabilitation, as "much more work remains to be done in understanding the religious and spiritual dimensions of disability and rehabilitation" (Kilpatrick & McCullough, 1999, p. 399). In sum, spirituality is too important in the process of rehabilitation to be overlooked (Riley et al., 1998).

The need for medical rehabilitation often arises from human error, violence, and/or seemingly unfair circumstances, resulting in a variety of negative emotions. Left unaddressed, negative emotions can lead to significant health problems, both physically (see Seeman, McEwen, Rowe, & Singer, 2001) and mentally. As such, forgiveness can be a powerful tool in the rehabilitative healing process.

Nevertheless, the psychology of forgiveness has been overlooked (McCullough, 2000) due to its subjective nature and close association to religion (Enright & Zell, 1989; Levin & Vanderpool, 1991). Yet, forgiveness is highly relevant to a variety of health issues and medical conditions (Worthington, 1998). In discussing the connection between forgiveness and health, Worthington, Berry, and Parrott (2001) discuss the direct impact of forgiveness and unforgiveness on health with unforgiveness, through rumination, involving the following emotions: resentment, bitterness, hatred, hostility, residual anger, and fear. There are many ways to address unforgiveness, including retaliation, revenge, justice, denial, and forgiveness (Worthington & Wade, 1999). Forgiveness involves the contamination or prevention of unforgiveness with strong, positive, love-based emotions (Worthington et al.). When describing the emotions of forgiveness and unforgiveness, Worthington et al., citing others, are careful to point out that these are not just subjective feelings, but, like all emotions,

> ...involve thoughts, memories, associations (Lazarus, 1999), neurochemicals in the brain (Damasio, 1999), pathways through various brain structures (LeDoux, 1996), hormones in the bloodstream

(Sapolsky, 1994, 1999), 'gut feelings' (Damnsio, 1999), facial musculature (Plutchik, 1994), gross body musculature (Plutchik, 1994), and
acts of emotional expression (Damasio, 1999). (p. 109)

The negative effects of unforgiveness on health have received more
attention in the empirical literature than the positive effects of forgiveness
on health (Berry & Worthington, 2001).

While forgiveness is likely to have a direct and positive role in promoting health, it is also likely that this relationship will be indirect with
health behavior acting as a mediating variable (Temoshok & Chandra,
2000; Worthington et al., 2001). Health behavior (HB) or the practice of
health promoting behavior is commonly associated with and predictive
of actual health (Bausell, 1986). An important component in the relationship between HB and health outcome is understanding what leads one
to engage in HB (Becker, Stuifbergen, Ingalsbe, & Sands, 1989). Waite,
Hawks, and Gast (1999) found a significant relationship between spiritual health and performance of HBs. It may very well be that forgiveness
impacts health through an indirect relationship with HB. In other words,
if one is able to forgive one is more likely to engage in HB thereby leading
to improved health.

SPIRITUALITY

Introduction

One reason why spiritual (and religious) issues have been overlooked in
scientific literature is the difficulty associated with defining and quantify-
ing undeniably subjective variables. Rybarczyk et al. (2000) state that it is
only recently that these issues have begun to find resolution, through the
development of functional conceptualizations and valid instruments of
measurement. The functional conceptualization of spirituality necessarily
involves an accurate definition, particularly in terms of clarifying its relationship to other closely associated terms, such as religion or religiosity
and existentialism.

Spirituality, Religiosity, and Existentialism

Spirituality typically refers to a connection with the divine without reference to organized religion or religiosity. Spirituality usually includes a
search for meaning and purpose and an underlying connection with nature
or the universe (Sperry & Giblin, 1996) and tends to be highly individualistic (Miller & Thoresen, 1999). While spirituality and religiosity overlap

in their connection with the divine (George et al., 2000), the reference to organized religion forms the basis of the differentiation. One can "be religious without being spiritual and spiritual without being religious" (Richards & Bergin, 1997, p. 13).

Religiosity is defined as established beliefs and practices (Fowler, 1996; Sperry & Giblin, 1996) and is commonly associated with organized religion. Much of what is assessed in the measurement of religiosity involves how much or how often one participates in their religion. Additionally, religiosity has been broken into two sub-constructs; intrinsic and extrinsic (Allport & Ross, 1967). *Intrinsic religiosity* is defined as religion practiced for altruistic purposes and *extrinsic religiosity* is defined as religion practiced for selfish reasons (e.g., social status).

Overlapping with spirituality, *existentialism* is primarily concerned with finding meaning and purpose in one's life (Yalom, 1998). Frankl (1992) defines existential in three ways: existence itself, the meaning of existence, and the striving to find a specific meaning in one's own existence, or the will to meaning. While existential spirituality is nontheistic (Richards & Bergin, 1997), it can also include an underlying connection with nature or the universe.

Existentialism and religiosity appear to be at opposite ends of the spectrum of spirituality. Nevertheless, there is a relationship between the two. While existentialism is not dogmatic (Mahrer, 1996), but is clearly rooted in the quest for meaning and purpose in life and religiosity is clearly rooted in the organized practice of religious principles, teachings, and doctrines, it is fair to say that they share a common theme of observance of established principle.

It may be helpful to incorporate the discussion of spirituality, religiosity, and existentialism into a multi-dimensional continuum (see Figure 1). As such, the construct of spirituality may best be described as a trio of interrelated concepts ranging from existential to spiritual to religious.

Furthermore, the spiritual subtype of the construct of spirituality may better be described as theistic spirituality, both to clarify its meaning and relationship to the others and to avoid redundancy. While not always the case, it is important to note that the points of overlap highlighted in Figure 1 are not commonly associated with the perpendicularly corresponding type of spirituality in its strict form (e.g., the divine is not commonly associated with existential spirituality). Lastly, the relationships illustrated in Figure 1 are conceptualized to be largely multidirectional and proportional (i.e., more of one equals less of another) and it is reasonable to conclude that healthy spirituality would be reflected by a relatively balanced point somewhere in the middle of the triangle.

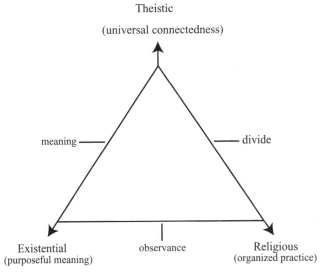

Figure 1. A multi-dimensional continuum of spirituality.

Understanding if and where a person falls on this continuum will be helpful to rehabilitation professionals when seeking to facilitate the benefits of spirituality. Not only will it foster the therapeutic relationship to accurately understand and address one's spirituality, but also it may be the case that different types of spirituality will respond differently to different interventions (see Riley et al., 1998).

Spirituality and Forgiveness

The recent development of spirituality as a more objectively defined and measurable construct has led to an increase in its credibility in the scientific literature. Nevertheless, the study of spirituality is still in its infancy, as it has primarily focused on it at a general level. While this is valuable, the study of spirituality needs to include specific components, such as; faith, hope humility, and forgiveness, as these, too, are relevant issues in the lives of many people.

Forgiveness is highly relevant to a variety of medical issues, including disabling conditions and aggressive and accidental trauma (Worthington, 1998). While forgiveness is commonly associated with religion and spirituality, it is not confined to religion, as it is also central to psychology and philosophy (McCullough & Worthington, 1994). As such, and consistent with the aforementioned conceptualization of the construct of spirituality, forgiveness can be thought of and applied in existential, spiritual, and/or religious terms.

Similarly, a secular, perhaps purely existential, assessment of one's capacity for forgiveness may prove useful for those people without religiospiritual affiliation. Forgiveness and spirituality are related concepts for many people, but not necessarily for all. Furthermore, it is not necessary for forgiveness and spirituality to be connected in one's conceptualization. Forgiveness can exist outside of spirituality. As forgiveness is central to psychology and philosophy, as well as mainstream world religion (Webb, 1999), it is a boundless concept and construct, unlimited by culture, time, and geography.

FORGIVENESS

Introduction

The concept of forgiveness is accepted and practiced in the field of psychology and practice of psychotherapy, albeit in different terms, such as; working through, acceptance (Hope, 1987; Pingleton, 1989), letting go (Davenport, 1991; Wahking, 1992), refraining (Cunningham, 1985), mourning (Durham, 1990), resolving conflict and mitigating loss (Lundeen, 1989), as a synonym for techniques that reduce conditioned anticipatory fear responses (Shontz & Rosenak, 1988), and coming to terms with. Nevertheless, the process is not sufficiently understood. While DiBlasio (1992) states that "few would argue with the benefits of forgiveness" (p. 182), scientific psychology has essentially not explored the concept of forgiveness (McCullough, 2000), as it is too closely associated with religion (Enright & Zell, 1989; Levin & Vanderpool, 1991). Nevertheless, there are many commonalties between psychology and religion (Tjeltveit, 1991) including the concept of forgiveness (McCullough & Worthington, 1994). While the value of scientifically investigating general spirituality (Richards & Bergin, 1997), including forgiveness (McCullough), has been on the rise, there continues to be a lack of and need for an understanding of the dynamics of forgiveness (McCullough), including the development of theory (McCullough & Worthington; Richards & Bergin). An accurate understanding and appreciation of forgiveness is vital if it is to be accepted as an important tool in the service of assisting rehabilitation professionals in facilitating the process of adjustment and overall healing in people with disabling and chronic conditions.

Definition

Forgiveness has been defined in a variety of ways. A constant theme in the definition of forgiveness involves decreasing negative attitudes and actions toward the offender (Gassin & Enright, 1995; Hargrave, 1994), while not seeking retribution (Rosenak & Hamden, 1992) or restitution (Wahking, 1992). Additionally, forgiveness does not relieve the offender of fault or responsibility, does not require the victim to return to a state of vulnerability, and does not necessarily include reconciliation (Enright, Freedman, & Rique, 1998). As such, in order to forgive one need not believe that an offense is now okay or even a good event. When the cause of one's disability or chronic condition is attributable to another or others, one can still forgive without feeling a need to befriend the offender. Similarly, one can forgive while still holding the offender accountable for the incident; criminally, personally, or otherwise.

Forgiveness can be studied as a trait or state variable. That is, forgiveness can be viewed as a trait or an enduring and generally non-malleable characteristic of an individual and yet, can also be studied as state dependent or a response to an event. As previously mentioned, Worthington et al. (2001) propose a model regarding the effects of religion on health, including forgiveness having direct and indirect effects on health. Thus, forgiveness can provide an avenue to resolve negative emotions and may also lead to improved health outcomes through promoting healthy behavior.

Forgiveness and Healing

While the salutary effects of forgiveness are likely to be complex, including direct and indirect pathways, an outcome central to forgiveness seems to include healing (Bonar, 1989; Canale, 1990; Worthington & DiBlasio, 1990). David Viscott, as quoted by S. L. Zelen (personal communication, 1995), stated that, "Most feelings can be traced back to the hurt, the loss, telling the person who has hurt you and then forgiving them. Often you also need to forgive yourself." O'Neill (1994, December 1) relates how a victim of rape began to recover when she was able to forgive the rapist. McCullough and Worthington (1994) discuss potential benefits of forgiveness as including; positive change in affect and well-being, improved physical and mental health, restoration of a sense of personal power, and reconciliation of offendee and offender. Hope (1987) states that forgiveness can serve as a powerful therapeutic tool and may well be a core element in the therapeutic process.

Evidence is building regarding the positive effects of forgiveness on mental and physical health (see Table 1). Levels of forgiveness have been shown to be negatively associated with physiological stress arousal (including blood pressure), cortisol reactivity, psychological distress, anxiety, depression, anger, negative self-esteem, and psychopathology. Also, levels of forgiveness have been shown to be positively associated with

Table 1. Empirical Relationships Observed Between Forgiveness and Health Variables

Negative Relationships	Author(s)
Physiological Stress Arousal, Iincluding Blood Pressure	Witvliet, Ludwig, & Vander Laan (2001)
Cortisol Reactivity	Berry & Worthington (2001)
Psychological Distress	Toussaint, Williams, Musick, & Everson (2001)
Anxiety	Freedman & Enright (1996); Hebl & Enright (1993); Mauger et al. (1992); Subkoviak et al. (1995)
Depression	Freedman & Enright; Hebl & Enright; Mauger et al.; Toussaint et al.; Toussaint & Webb (2002)
Anger	Berry & Worthington; Mauger et al.; Toussaint & Webb
Negative Self-Esteem and Psychopathology	Mauger et al.
Positive Relationships:	
Physical Health Status	Toussaint et al.; Webb, Toussaint, Kalpakjian, & Tate (2002)
Mental Health Status	Berry & Worthington
Self-Esteem	Hebl & Enright
Life Satisfaction	Hargrave & Sells (1997); Poloma & Gallup (1991); Toussaint et al.; Webb et al.
Sleep Quality	Toussaint & Webb
Adjustment to Spinal Cord Injury	Willmering (1999)

physical health status, mental health status, self-esteem, life satisfaction, sleep quality, and adjustment to spinal cord injury. Researchers have also argued for the beneficial effects of forgiveness in aiding recovery from clinical depression, coronary heart disease, and cancer (Fitzgibbons, 1986; Kaplan, 1992; Pingleton, 1989). Furthermore, forgiveness is anecdotally reported to relieve anger and resentment (Canale, 1990; Donnelly, 1984), relieve feelings of rage, resentment, fear, and distrust (Wahking, 1992), resolve emotional, physical, and sexual abuse (Rosenak & Hamden, 1992), turn failure into power and possibility (Lundeen, 1989), enable harmony with life, courage for vitality, and to live in risk (Cunningham, 1985), lead to past hurts being healed as current hurts are addressed (Pingleton, 1989), heal relationships, in general (Rogers, 1989), be central to family healing and healthy functioning (Rogers, 1989; Rosenak & Harnden, 1992), benefit offender, offended, and community (The Educational Psychology Study Group, 1990), be a generator of positive change (Bergin, 1988), enable a higher level of life (Allen & Bachelder, 1985), and help the psychotherapeutic process (Brandsma, 1982). As such, the benefits of forgiveness hold great potential in improving the outcomes of people in need of rehabilitation, both physically and psychosocially.

Forgiveness and Personal Control in Medical Rehabilitation

There also seems to be a relationship between control and forgiveness. While Benson (1992) and Hope (1987) discuss a positive relationship between forgiveness and personal control over one's life, Witvliet et al. (2001) have found empirical evidence in support of this relationship.

As the ability to forgive seems related to perceptions of control and thereby assumptions of one's personal responsibility for the future, it follows that it will lead one to engage in healthy behavior, which, in turn, will lead to improved health. Through forgiveness, one may have more energy, both physically and mentally, to dedicate toward healthy behavior, rather than focusing said energy on holding a grudge or externalizing control and responsibility and waiting for an outside resolution to one's problems.

In sum, forgiveness has been shown to have a salutary effect on mental and physical health variables and may also play an important role in medical rehabilitation. The value of forgiveness almost seems to be common sense. Yet, most of the articles published regarding forgiveness have been published in religiously oriented journals (Hargrave & Sells, 1997).

Steps and Dynamics of Forgiveness

Much of the literature that discusses forgiveness in detail tends to describe the steps or how-to's of forgiveness (Bauer et al., 1992; Enright et al., 1998; Enright & The Human Development Study Group, 1994; Gorsuch & Hao, 1993; Lundeen, 1989) rather than to sufficiently explore its dynamics or what enables one to do the steps. Enright et al. provide a summarization of 20 steps or units of forgiveness described in the literature. They further divide the 20 units into four broad phases: uncovering, decision, work, and deepening. Uncovering refers to the awareness of the problem and emotional pain following an offense, such as anger and insight, decision includes realizing the need for an alternate resolution, work includes processes, such as; reframing, empathy, and acceptance of pain, and deepening includes finding meaning and universality. They are careful to point out that the overall process of forgiveness is not likely to be linear.

McCullough (2000) provides an overview of the current status of the study of forgiveness including determinants of the ability to forgive. He discusses; empathy and perspective-taking, rumination and suppression of rumination, relational closeness, commitment, and satisfaction, and apology as factors shown to influence forgiveness. Nevertheless, he further states that our understanding of this vital factor in the process of healing continues to be limited and in need of investigation.

While the process of forgiveness has been outlined and the outline makes intuitive sense, there seems to be little empirical evidence supporting said hypothesized steps or units of forgiveness. In addition to the empirical validation of the steps, it would also be helpful to expand our understanding of the dynamics of forgiveness or what enables a person to complete its steps and to clarify another commonly hypothesized factor in the process of forgiveness, or the role of perceived control, as discussed above. Furthermore, while forgiveness is commonly associated with religion and spirituality, it will likely be helpful to investigate which type of spirituality, if any, is actually associated with the ability to forgive.

Facilitating forgiveness and its dynamics likely will lead to improved outcomes in rehabilitation. If forgiveness is related to greater levels of internal locus of control, for instance, it follows that forgiveness will improve patient outcomes, both psychosocially *and* physically, as one is more likely to be pro-active in their self-care. Through forgiveness one can find resolution and relief from psychosocial stressors and reap the benefits to physical and mental health thereof. Additionally, it follows that one will be more likely to tend to their physical needs (see Temoshok & Chandra, 2000; Worthington et al., 2001), such as; compliance with medical advice, including; medication, activities of daily living, exercise, and nutrition.

Utility and Implications of Forgiveness in Medical Rehabilitation

Understanding the ability to forgive others will assist rehabilitation professionals in the treatment of disability and chronic conditions. Often the individual need for rehabilitation arises from accidents, whether personal, interpersonal, or societal, due to risk taking, alcohol/drug use, poor judgement, human error, or pure chance, resulting in debilitating conditions, such as; spinal cord injury, traumatic brain injury, and chronic pain. Additionally, those with disabling conditions, such as; multiple sclerosis, polio, spina bifida and other conditions not necessarily associated with human error, may have issues with forgiving family, society, God, nature, or the universe. Self-forgiveness may also be an issue for those with disabilities or chronic conditions. Lastly, not only patients, but family members of people with disabilities may need to forgive, as well.

The need for forgiveness implies the existence of negative emotions. While not automatic, negative emotions often arise in response to an offense or set of negative circumstances. For example, in response to accidents and acts of violence, it follows that many people may be struggling with issues of responsibility (Richards, Elliott, Shewchuk, & Fine, 1997), blame (Bulman & Wortman, 1977), hostility (Mayou, Ehlers, & Hobbs, 2000), anger, anxiety, depression, fear, and irritability (Bisson & Shepherd, 1995) as well as with related issues of vengeance, resentment, and post-traumatic stress. Left unaddressed, negative emotions increase the risk for psychological stress and dysfunctional behavior, thereby leading to diminished physical (see Seeman et al., 2001) and mental health. As such, forgiveness can be a powerful force in resolving negative emotions and their associated consequences.

For rehabilitation professionals to encourage and facilitate the practice of forgiveness in rehabilitation, it is not only necessary to have a functional conceptualization of the concept and its steps, but also an empirical understanding of the underlying process, or what it is about a person that will enable him/her to forgive. During the initial stages of evaluation and treatment of people in rehabilitation, providers can include an assessment of the patient's spirituality, including capacity for forgiveness, and incorporate this assessment into the overall treatment plan, which assessment may, in fact, be welcomed by patients (Fitchett, Rybarczyk, DeMarco, & Nicholas, 1999). While issues presented by people in rehabilitation vary, some common issues seem particularly amenable to forgiveness and its aforementioned dynamics. If a person is found to primarily approach life from a perspective of external locus of control, or perhaps, playing the blame game, it may be helpful to explore and develop attributes of internal locus of control. If a person is struggling with questions of, why did this happen to me or why did somebody do this to me, it may be helpful to develop insight and facilitate the process of understanding the realities of random events or plausible explanations of events, being careful not to exonerate responsibility, as well as fostering empathy and identification with the offender. Often times an objective sense of understanding can facilitate resolution of stress and anger associated with offense. Additionally, it could be helpful to monitor one's level of preoccupation or rumination regarding the offense and work to minimize this, being careful to avoid denial. Once it is established which components, if any, of spirituality are associated with forgiveness, it will likely be helpful to foster those spiritual qualities. For example, if intrinsic or altruistic components of spirituality are found to be related to the ability to forgive then it may be helpful to encourage, develop, and facilitate said components.

Spirituality is highly personal both in terms of experience and expression. Thus, it can be, and often is, a sensitive issue in the therapeutic relationship. Accurately understanding and addressing it will foster the therapeutic relationship, while misunderstanding and misconstruing one's spirituality will likely have a negative effect and hinder the relationship.

With the recent increase in the scientific investigation of spirituality has come a variety of resources addressing its effective and competent incorporation into therapeutic treatment (see Miller, 1999; Richards & Bergin, 1997, 2000; Shafranske, 1996).

As different types of spirituality may respond differently to different interventions (see Riley et al., 1998), it is important to consider variations in the interface between the promotion and facilitation of forgiveness and type of spirituality as modeled in Figure 24.1. In each case, the effect of forgiveness may take a direct and/or indirect pathway (Worthington et al., 2001). Increased levels of forgiveness may decrease levels of negative health outcomes themselves (i.e., more forgiveness equals less stress) or increased levels of forgiveness may lead to increased levels of healthy behavior (as a function of increased levels of perceived personal control resulting in increased mental and physical energy), which in turn will lead to improved health outcomes (i.e., more forgiveness leads to increased compliance with medical advice which leads to improved health outcomes) and vice versa. A person espousing a primarily theistic spirituality may benefit from being encouraged to think of forgiveness as a means of developing one's individualistic sense of universal connectedness and equality. A person espousing a primarily religious spirituality, for example, Judeo-Christian or Islamic, may benefit from being encouraged to think of forgiveness as a means of emulating the divine (see Webb, 1999). A person espousing a primarily existential spirituality may benefit from being encouraged to think of forgiveness as a means of affirming meaning and purpose and thereby avoiding an existential vacuum (see Frankl, 1992), or an absence of fundamental direction in one's life. While these broad examples are tailored to facilitate acceptance of forgiveness by people with corresponding types of spirituality, it is also quite possible that the prospect of forgiveness will be rejected. A theistically spiritual person may view forgiveness as a threat to individual growth and autonomy, a religiously spiritual person may assume a holier-than-thou position and expect the offender to have known better, and an existentially spiritual person may choose to find meaning and purpose in *not* forgiving.

While rehabilitation professionals must provide education to patients and families regarding a myriad of issues such as the course and nature of injury/illness, pain and stress management, mood and cognition, etc., education must be provided regarding forgiveness as well. The ability to forgive will likely be hampered if one misunderstands what is involved. Having a clear understanding that the act of forgiving another does not involve absolving the offender of responsibility nor opening oneself up for further offense will be of great service in facilitating the ability to forgive.

CONCLUSION

Understanding and facilitating spirituality and spiritual factors, including forgiveness, can play a significant role in medical rehabilitation. As such, forgiveness can be a powerful force in the process of adjusting to and coping with disability and chronic conditions, thereby leading to improved outcomes both physically and psychosocially and enabling one to avoid a pitfall implicit in the need to forgive, that is, holding a grudge hurts the holder much more than who or what it is held against (see Worthington, 2001). Rehabilitation professionals and scientists can serve a vital function through the delivery of quality care informed and driven by high-quality research in this emerging and fertile field.

REFERENCES

Allen, D. F., & Bachelder, R. (1985). Psychiatry and religion: Judeo-Christian theism and Fromm's humanism. *Journal of Religion and Health, 24,* 49–59.

Allport, G. W., & Ross, J. M. (1967). Personal religious orientation and prejudice. *Journal of Personality and Social Psychology, 5,* 432–443.

Bauer, L., Duffy, J., Fountain, E., Hailing, S., Holzer, M., Jones, E., Leifer, M., & Rowe, J. O. (1992). Exploring self-forgiveness. *Journal of Religion and Health, 31,* 149–160.

Bausell, R. B. (1986). Health-seeking behavior among the elderly. *The Gerontologist, 26,* 556–559.

Becker, H. A., Stuifbergen, A. K., Ingalsbe, K., & Sands, D. (1989). Health promoting attitudes and behaviors among persons with disabilities. *International Journal of Rehabilitation Research, 12,* 235–250.

Benson, C. K. (1992). Forgiveness and the psychotherapeutic process. *Journal of Psychology and Christianity, 11,* 76–81.

Bergin, A. E. (1988). Three contributions of a spiritual perspective to counseling, psychotherapy, and behavior change. *Counseling and Values, 33,* 21–31.

Berry, J. W., & Worthington, E. L., Jr. (2001). Forgiveness, relationship quality, stress while imagining relationship events, and physical and mental health. *Journal of Counseling Psychology, 48,* 447–455.

Bisson, J. I., & Shepherd, J. P. (1995). Psychological reactions of victims of violent crime. *British Journal of Psychiatry, 167,* 718–720.

Bonar, C. A. (1989). Personality theories and asking forgiveness. *Journal of Psychology and Christianity, 8,* 45–51.

Brandsma, J. M. (1982). Forgiveness: A dynamic, theological and therapeutic analysis. *Pastoral Psychology, 31,* 40–50.

Bulman, R. J., & Wortman, C. B. (1977). Attributions of blame and coping in the "real world": Severe accident victims react to their lot. *Journal of Personality and Social Psychology, 35,* 351–363.

Canale, J. R. (1990). Altruism and forgiveness as therapeutic agents in psychotherapy. *Journal of Religion and Health, 29,* 297–301.

Cunningham, B. B. (1985). The will to forgive: A pastoral theological view of forgiving. *The Journal of Pastoral Care, 39*, 141–149.

Davenport, D. S. (1991). The functions of anger and forgiveness: Guidelines for psychotherapy with victims. *Psychotherapy, 28*, 140–144.

DiBlasio, F. A. (1992). Forgiveness in psychotherapy: Comparison of older and younger therapists. *Journal of Psychology and Christianity, 11*, 181–187.

Donnelly, D. (1984). Forgiveness and recidivism. *Pastoral Psychology, 33*, 15–24.

Durham, M. S. (1990). The therapist and the concept of revenge: The law of the talion. *The Journal of Pastoral Care, 44*, 131–137.

Enright, R. D., Freedman, S., & Rique, J. (1998). The psychology of interpersonal forgiveness. In R. D. Enright & J. North (Eds.), *Exploring forgiveness* (pp. 46–62). Madison, WI: The University of Wisconsin Press.

Enright, R. D., & The Human Development Study Group. (1994). Piaget on the moral development of forgiveness: Identity or reciprocity? *Human Development, 37*, 63–80.

Enright, R. D., & Zell, R. L. (1989). Problems encountered when we forgive one another. *Journal of Psychology and Christianity, 8*, 52–60.

Fitchett, G., Rybarczyk, B. D., DeMarco, G. A., & Nicholas, J. J. (1999). The role of religion in medical rehabilitation outcomes: A longitudinal study. *Rehabilitation Psychology, 44*, 333–353.

Fitzgibbons, R. (1986). The cognitive and emotive uses of forgiveness in the treatment of anger. *Psychotherapy, 23*, 629–633.

Fowler, J. W. (1996). Pluralism and oneness in religious experience: William James, faith-development theory, and clinical practice. In E. P. Shafranske (Ed.), *Religion and the clinical practice of psychology* (pp. 165–186). Washington, DC: American Psychological Association.

Frankl, V. E. (1992). *Man's search for meaning: An introduction to logotherapy* (I. Lasch, Trans. 4th ed.). Boston: Beacon Press.

Freedman, S. R., & Enright, R. D. (1996). Forgiveness as an intervention goal with incest survivors. *Journal of Consulting and Clinical Psychology, 64*, 983–992.

Gallup, G., Jr. (2001). Americans more religious now than ten years ago, but less so than in 1950s and 1960s. Retrieved October 30, 2001, from http://www.gallup.com/poll/releases/pr010329.asp.

Gallup Poll. (2001). Religion. Retrieved October 30, 2001, from http://www.gallup.com/poll/indicators/indreligion3.asp.

Gassin, E. A., & Enright, R. D. (1995). The will to meaning in the process of forgiveness. *Journal of Psychology and Christianity, 14*, 38–49.

George, L. K., Larson, D. B., Koenig, H. G., & McCullough, M. E. (2000). Spirituality and health: What we know, what we need to know. *Journal of Social and Clinical Psychology, 19*, 102–116.

Gorsuch, R. L., & Hao, J. Y. (1993). Forgiveness: An exploratory factor analysis and its relationships to religious variables. *Review of Religious Research, 34*(333–347).

Hargrave, T. D. (1994). *Families and forgiveness: Healing wounds in the intergenerational family.* New York: Brunner/Mazel Publishers.

Hargrave, T. D., & Sells, J. N. (1997). The development of a forgiveness scale. *Journal of Marital and Family Therapy, 23*, 41–62.

Hebl, J. H., & Enright, R. D. (1993). Forgiveness as a psychotherapeutic goal with elderly females. *Psychotherapy, 30*, 658–667.

Hope, D. (1987). The healing paradox of forgiveness. *Psychotherapy, 24*, 240–244.

Kaplan, B. (1992). Social health and the forgiving heart: The type B story. *Journal of Behavioral Medicine, 15*, 3–14.

Kilpatrick, S. D., & McCullough, M. E. (1999). Religion and spirituality in rehabilitation psychology. *Rehabilitation Psychology, 44*, 388–402.

Kim, J., Heinemann, A. W., Bode, R. K., Sliwa, J., & King, R. B. (2000). Spirituality, quality of life, and functional recovery after medical rehabilitation. *Rehabilitation Psychology, 45*, 365–385.

Levin, J. S., & Vanderpool, H. Y. (1991). Religious factors in physical health and the prevention of illness. *Prevention in Human Services, 9*, 41–64.

Lundeen, L. T. (1989). Forgiveness and human relationships. In L. Aden & D. G. Benner (Eds.), *Psychology and Christianity series: Vol. 3. Counseling and the human predicament: A study of sin, guilt, and forgiveness*. Grand Rapids, MI: Baker Book House Company.

Mahrer, A. R. (1996). Existential-humanistic psychotherapy and the religious person. In E. P. Shafranske (Ed.), *Religion and the clinical practice of psychology* (pp. 433–460). Washington, DC: American Psychological Association.

Mauger, P. A., Perry, J. E., Freeman, T., Grove, D. C., McBride, A. G., & McKinney, K. E. (1992). The measurement of forgiveness: Preliminary research. *Journal of Psychology and Christianity, 11*, 170–180.

Mayou, R. A., Ehlers, A., & Hobbs, M. (2000). Psychological debriefing for road traffic accident victims. *British Journal of Psychiatry, 176*, 589–593.

McCullough, M. E. (2000). Forgiveness as human strength: Theory, measurement, and links to well-being. *Journal of Social and Clinical Psychology, 19*, 43–55.

McCullough, M. E., & Worthington, E. L., Jr. (1994). Encouraging clients to forgive people who have hurt them: Review, critique, and research prospectus. *Journal of Psychology and Theology, 22*, 3–20.

Miller, W. R. (Ed.). (1999). *Integrating spirituality into treatment: Resources for practitioners*. Washington, DC: American Psychological Association.

Miller, W. R., & Thoresen, C. E. (1999). Spirituality and health. In W. R. Miller (Ed.), *Integrating spirituality into treatment: Resources for practitioners* (pp. 3–18). Washington, DC: American Psychological Association.

O'Neill, L. (1994, December 1). Fear, pain return for 2 victims of rape. *Los Angeles Times*, pp. B1, B3.

Pingleton, J. P. (1989). The role and function of forgiveness in the psychotherapeutic process. *Journal of Psychology and Theology, 17*, 27–35.

Poloma, M., & Gallup, G. (1991). *Varieties of prayer*. Philadelphia: Trinity Press.

Richards, J. S., Elliott, T. R., Shewchuk, R. M., & Fine, P. R. (1997). Attribution of responsibility for onset of spinal cord injury and psychosocial outcomes in the first year post-injury. *Rehabilitation Psychology, 42*, 115–124.

Richards, P. S., & Bergin, A. E. (1997). *A spiritual strategy for counseling and psychotherapy.* Washington, DC: American Psychological Association.

Richards, P. S., & Bergin, A. E. (Eds.). (2000). *Handbook of psychotherapy and religious diversity.* Washington, DC: American Psychological Association.

Riley, B. B., Perna, R., Tate, D. G., Forchheimer, M., Anderson, C., & Luera, G. (1998). Types of spiritual well-being among persons with chronic illness: Their relation to various forms of quality of life. *Archives of Physical Medicine and Rehabilitation, 79,* 258–264.

Rogers, R. G. (1989). Forgiveness and the healing of the family. In L. Aden. & D. G. Benner (Eds.), *Psychology and Christianity series: Vol. 3. Counseling and the human predicament: A study of sin, guilt, and forgiveness.* Grand Rapids, MI: Baker Book House Company.

Rosenak, C. M., & Hamden, G. M. (1992). Forgiveness in the psychotherapeutic process: Clinical applications. *Journal of Psychology and Christianity, 11,* 188–197.

Rybarczyk, B., Szymanski, L., & Nicholas, J. J. (2000). Limb amputation. In R. G. Frank & T. R. Elliott (Eds.), *Handbook of rehabilitation psychology* (pp. 29–48). Washington, DC: American Psychological Association.

Seeman, T. E., McEwen, B. S., Rowe, J. W., & Singer, B. H. (2001). Allostatic load as a marker of cumulative biological risk: MacArthur studies of successful aging. *Proceedings of the National Academy of Sciences of the United States of America, 98,* 4770–4775.

Selway, D., & Ashman, A. F. (1998). Disability, religion and health: A literature review in search of the spiritual dimensions of disability. *Disability and Society, 13,* 429–439.

Shafranske, E. P. (Ed.). (1996). *Religion and the clinical practice of psychology.* Washington, DC: American Psychological Association.

Shontz, F. C., & Rosenak, C. (1988). Psychological theories and the need for forgiveness: Assessment and critique. *Journal of Psychology and Christianity, 7,* 23–31.

Sperry, L., & Giblin, P. (1996). Marital and family therapy with religious persons. In E. P. Shafranske (Ed.), Religion and the clinical practice of psychology (pp. 511–532). Washington, DC: American Psychological Association.

Subkoviak, M. J., Enright, R. D., Wu, C.-R., Gassin, E. A., Freedman, S., Olson, L. M., & Sarinopoulos, I. (1995). Measuring interpersonal forgiveness in late adolescence and middle adulthood. *Journal of Adolescence, 18,* 641–655.

Temoshok, L. R., & Chandra, P. S. (2000). The meaning of forgiveness in a specific situational and cultural context: Persons living with HIV/AIDS in India. In M. E. McCullough, K. I. Pargament, & C. E. Thoresen (Eds.), *Forgiveness: Theory, research, and practice* (pp. 41–64). New York: The Guilford Press.

The Educational Psychology Study Group. (1990). Must a Christian require repentance before forgiving? *Journal of Psychology and Christianity, 9,* 16–19.

Tjeltveit, A. C. (1991). Christian ethics and psychological explanations of "religious values" in therapy: Critical connections. *Journal of Psychology and Christianity, 10,* 101–112.

Toussaint, L., & Webb, J. R. (2002). [Forgiveness and well-being following the September 11th, 2001 terrorist attacks on America]. Unpublished raw data.

Toussaint, L. L., Williams, D. R., Musick, M. A., & Everson, S. A. (2001). Forgiveness and health: Age differences in a U.S. probability sample. *Journal of Adult Development, 8,* 249–257.

Wahking, H. (1992). Spiritual growth through grace and forgiveness. *Journal of Psychology and Christianity, 11,* 198–206.

Waite, P. J., Hawks, S. R., & Gast, J. A. (1999). The correlation between spiritual well-being and health behaviors. *American Journal of Health Promotion, 13,* 159–162.

Webb, J. R. (1999). Forgiveness and control: Toward an understanding of the dynamics of forgiveness (Doctoral dissertation, California School of Professional Psychology, Los Angeles, 1998). *Dissertation Abstracts International, 60*(1-B), 0379.

Webb, J. R., Toussaint, L., Kalpakjian, C. Z., & Tate, D. G. (2002). [The role of forgiveness in promoting health and well-being among persons with spinal cord injury]. Unpublished raw data.

Wegener, S. T., Elliott, T. R., & Hagglund, K. J. (2000). On psychological identity and training: A reply to Thomas and Chan (2000). *Rehabilitation Psychology, 45,* 74–80.

Willmering, P. P. (1999). Forgiveness as a self-reported factor in adjustment to disability (Doctoral dissertation, University of Wisconsin, Madison, 1998). *Dissertation Abstracts International, 60*(6-B), 3009.

Witvliet, C. V. O., Ludwig, T. E., & Vander Laan, K. L. (2001). Granting forgiveness or harboring grudges: Implications for emotion, physiology, and health. *Psychological Science, 12,* 117–123.

Worthington, E. L., Jr. (1998). Empirical research in forgiveness: Looking backward, looking forward. In E. L. Worthington, Jr. (Ed.), *Dimensions of forgiveness: Psychological research and theological perspectives* (pp. 321–339). Philadelphia: Templeton Foundation Press.

Worthington, E. L., Jr. (2001). Everett L. Worthington, Jr.: Should we, can we forgive? Retrieved September 14, 2001 from http://www.dallasnews.com/religion/470916_column_15rel.A.html.

Worthington, E. L., Jr., Berry, J. W., & Parrott, L., III. (2001). Unforgiveness, forgiveness, religion, and health. In T. G. Plante & A. C. Sherman (Eds.), *Faith and health: Psychological perspectives* (pp. 107–138). New York: The Guilford Press.

Worthington, E. L., Jr., & DiBlasio, F. A. (1990). Promoting mutual forgiveness within the fractured relationship. *Psychotherapy, 27,* 219–223.

Worthington, E. L., Jr., & Wade, N. G. (1999). The psychology of unforgiveness and forgiveness and implications for clinical practice. *Journal of Social and Clinical Psychology, 18,* 385–418.

Yalom, I. D. (1998). *The Yalom reader: Selections from the work of a master therapist and storyteller.* New York: Basic Books.

CHAPTER TWENTY-FIVE

The Psychosocial Impact on Survivors of Extraordinary, Stressful, and Traumatic Events

Principles and Practices in Critical Incident Response for Rehabilitation Counselors

Mark A. Stebnicki

INTRODUCTION

Extraordinary, stressful, and traumatic events such as natural events (e.g., hurricanes, earthquakes, floods); crimes (e.g., school shootings, robbery), or catastrophic injury and illness (e.g., SCI, HIV, AIDS) are common experiences in the lives of many Americans.[1] In fact, it is estimated that the typical American will spend nearly 12 years of his or her life in a state of limited psychosocial functioning because of chronic illness and disability acquired through disease or injury.[2] Regardless of how close one is to the

From "The psychosocial impact on survivors of extraordinary, stressful, and traumatic events," by M. Stebnicki, 2001, *Directions in Rehabilitation Counseling*, 12(6), 57–71. Reprinted with permission by The Hatherleigh Company, Ltd.

"epicenter" of a critical event, the "aftershocks" significantly effect the physiological, social, emotional, psychological, and social functioning of the survivor, family members, the community, and the professional helpers.[3]

Extraordinary stressful and traumatic events also occur in the workplace and contribute to the syndrome known as occupational stress. For example, Bachman[4] reports that the U.S. Department of Justice has documented more than 2,406 deaths due to violent crimes between 1995 and 1996. Additionally, more than 1 million people per year are survivors of work-related rapes, physical assaults, and robberies.[5] These figures may be underreported because many victim/survivors do not report crimes immediately, or at all, after they have occurred.

The defining characteristics of most critical incidents are the individual's perception of the potential threat to their survival and the perception that the event itself is both uncontrollable and unpredictable.[6] Psychosocially, it is recognized that individuals who are directly affected by traumatic events must try to adjust and adapt physically, psychologically, socially, vocationally, and economically, as well as in many other ways.[7] Consequently, some survivors are at risk of experiencing clinical symptoms identified with posttraumatic stress disorder (PTSD).[8] Interventions that promote survivors to communicate their reactions to traumatic events in detail will decrease the severity, intensity, and frequency of long-term PTS.[9] Accordingly, many schools, human resource departments, and victim assistance programs have called upon professionally trained crisis counselors to provide critical incident stress debriefings to small and large groups of people who have been affected by traumatic events.

Role of the Rehabilitation Counselor

Many Red Cross volunteers and other mental health counselors have been trained in crisis response and critical incident stress debriefing. However, rehabilitation counselors have had little preparation for the role of assisting survivors of critical incidents. Rehabilitation counselors, by virtue of their training and expertise in dealing with issues of loss, grief, psychosocial adaptation, and adjustment to chronic illness and disability, appear to be uniquely qualified to provide crisis response to small and large groups of individuals once they have undertaken some further training in crisis intervention.[5,10]

Providing small and large group critical incident response to deal with the psychosocial aftershocks of individuals in crisis appears to be a new direction of training and research for rehabilitation professionals in the twenty-first century. Hence, this lesson aims to: (a) provide rehabilitation professionals with an understanding of the significant impact of group-related critical incidents and the psychosocial response of survivors, family members, counseling professionals, and the sociocultural community environment; and (b) offer brief, solution-focused strategies for coping with the acute, post-, and secondary traumatic stressors associated with crisis events.

Shifting Definitions and Assumptions Regarding Crisis Response

Crisis response is not a new phenomenon in the counseling and mental health field. In the early 1970s, the psychology and counseling literature was replete with brief and immediate interventions for clients who were in crisis.[11-13] Because of increasing trends in violence against groups of people (e.g., minority groups, school children, work-related violence) there is a need for trained and qualified crisis responders who can intervene with people who are directly *(primary survivors)* or indirectly *(secondary survivors)* affected by the aftermath of extraordinary stressful and traumatic events. These acts of interpersonal violence require a unique understanding and set of strategies to facilitate brief and immediate interventions. Accordingly, the terminology, concepts, and strategies used to characterize principles and practices in crisis response appear to have shifted. The focus in crisis response has changed primarily because of the following:

- Nature and severity of critical incidents (e.g., increase in school and workplace violence resulting in multiple deaths)
- Types of interventions and services provided (e.g., group stress debriefings, defusings with public and private entities)
- Shift toward serving different groups of primary and secondary survivors (e.g., paramedics, police, nurses, counselors)
- Research suggesting that immediate and brief interventions will decrease the negative long-term symptoms associated with PTS (e.g., depression, suicide, nightmares)

Definitions

The following is a brief list of definitions that refer to more recent principles and practices in crisis response.[14]

Extraordinary Stressful and Traumatic Event (also referred to as a Critical Incident or Crisis Event)

A sudden stressful or traumatic event that is typically outside the normal range of ordinary human experience and is so overwhelmingly stressful to an individual or group that, initially, they have little or no coping skills they can use in dealing with the event.

Critical Incident Stress Debriefing (CISD). CISD refers to a formal, structured protocol originally developed by Mitchell[15] as a direct, action-oriented crisis intervention process designed to prevent traumatic stress symptoms for both primary and secondary survivors. CISD is recognized as the most widely used among disaster response teams and military and emergency service personnel.[16] CISD is a team-oriented approach, a group process, and should not be a substitute for psychotherapy. The purpose of using a CISD approach is to provide stabilization for the group, mobilizing the groups resources, and to restore function to the group members.

Critical Incident Stress Management (CISM). CISM uses a comprehensive team approach of stress management education, programs, interventions, and strategies designed to prevent PTS and Secondary Traumatic Stress (STS) in primary and secondary survivors. The function of the CISM team is to serve as the "first line of defense" against traumatic stress.[14] After a critical incident, the CISM team can be called into action rapidly to provide group debriefings.

Debriefing

Debriefing is a generic term, originally used by military personnel, to describe an approach that involves forming small and large groups of primary and secondary survivors to educate and discuss one specific critical incident. Debriefings typically last 60–90 minutes and are facilitated by trained and qualified group leaders. Sessions focus primarily on the ventilation and validation of the individuals' and groups' emotional and psychological health as impacted by the traumatic event. Debriefings also use prediction and preparation interventions to help facilitate resources and coping skills among the group of survivors. The National Organization for Victims Assistance (NOVA) uses a group debriefing model as the primary intervention.[17]

Defusing

Defusings are basically a shortened version of the CISD model. They are designed to either eliminate the need for a formal debriefing or enhance the CISD. Defusings take place immediately or relatively soon after the critical incident and include three parts: introduction, exploration, and information.[14]

Assumptions

It is currently recognized that both the primary and secondary survivors of extraordinary stressful and traumatic events are at risk for PTSD and

STSD.[3,14] Figley distinguishes PTSD from STSD stating: "STSD is a syndrome of symptoms nearly identical to PTSD, except that exposure to knowledge about a traumatizing event experienced by a significant other is associated with the set of STSD symptoms, and PTSD symptoms are directly connected to the sufferer, the person experiencing primary traumatic stress."[3 (p. 8)] Accordingly, crisis responders should be knowledgeable and mindful of the following factors when providing interventions.

1. *Recognize the person as a survivor.* Viewing people as "victims" of traumatic events discounts their survival skills and negatively reinforces the stereotype of being helpless, hopeless, dependent, and defenseless. Although the person may be a victim of a crime, perceiving and intervening with individuals in this role will hinder their ability to cope and adapt.

2. *Accept that the stressors accompanying traumatic events are real and legitimate for survivors.* People involved with extraordinary stressful and traumatic events will typically be physiologically and psychologically affected and will require some short-term therapeutic interventions. This does not mean that the person is "going crazy" or "emotionally weak." Rather, the physiological and psychological effects are normal responses to an extraordinary stressful event.

   - *There is a high incidence of PTS and STS that affects secondary survivors as well.* The phenomenon of "vicarious victimization" suggests that persons can acquire posttruamatic stress disorder (PTSD) or STS by having indirect exposure to violent events.[17]

   - *Depending on how close the professional counselor is to the "epicenter" of the crisis event, he or she may also be at risk of experiencing the stressors associated with being a secondary survivor.* If these stressors go unrecognized, professional counselors may experience the emotional, mental, and physical exhaustion associated with empathy or compassion fatigue.[18]

   - *Interventions should be person centered, as opposed to treating a diagnostic category.* The DSM-IV[19] does not allow PTS "disorder" to be diagnosed until 30 days after exposure to traumatic events. Regardless, primary and secondary survivors are affected by traumatic events and respond in many different ways. People who report a history of trauma are not members of a homogenous population. Thus, treatment efforts must consider unique individual and environmental characteristics by focusing on symptom relief of the person's acute stress and coping strategies.[20] Regardless of the results of the person's DSM-IV clinical assessment (i.e., PTSD), the individual's previous response and coping mechanisms after prior traumatic events may offer more insight for brief or solution-focused interventions.

- *Professional counselors must view the survivor in relationship to his or her cultural, sociopolitical, and institutional environment, and assess which factors may hinder the ability of the person (or group of people) to cope and adjust.* Rehabilitation has always emphasized the role environment plays in dealing with the stress of and emotional response to disability.[21] Thus, mental health problems associated with the traumatic event do not reside solely within the individual.

- *Empowering survivors with multiple resources and support systems will facilitate better coping abilities and recovery.* Family, friends, churches, and other support groups can be a major source for coping and psychosocial adaptation.

- *Individuals heal at different rates.* Coping abilities and adjustment to the grief and loss associated with traumatic events vary from person to person and do not fit neatly into a theoretical stage model of adaptation or adjustment. Victor Frankl[22] sums up this point by suggesting that it is not necessarily the nature of the trauma itself that will most affect one's ability to cope psychologically with its consequences, but rather, the person's own attitude toward the trauma.

- *Preexisting physical, emotional, cognitive, or financial limitations may intensify a crisis event and produce more complex reactions of grief and loss.* People with disabilities, such as life-threatening illnesses, may be at risk of increased psychological and emotional trauma following a critical incident.[23] Thus, preexisting chronic illnesses and disabilities will complicate issues of adjustment and adaptation.

  Primarily, exposure to critical incidents for people with disabilities may be "trigger events" that can exacerbate current medical conditions and cause some people to relapse; thus, there are unique characteristics of facilitating crisis interventions for people with disabilities.

- *Regardless of disability, survivors of previous traumatic events may be retraumatized by critical incidents.* When people who have existing mental or physical disabilities experience a traumatic event, the crisis event may combine with these other issues to produce a synergistic effect, which may intensify the person's response to the extraordinary stressful and traumatic event.[24]

Extraordinary Stressful or Traumatic Events and PTS

Emotional stress is a part of everyday life. Most of us attempt to maintain a balance between healthy and unhealthy stress, which have four primary sources, from one's:[25]

- Ecological environment
- Family/social situations
- Physiological level of health and functioning
- Cognitions and thought patterns

When individuals do not cope well with the cumulative primary life stressors and "daily hassles," then chronic stress can occur. An unhealthy response to dealing with chronic stress may result in chemical dependency, depression, and even suicide.[26] Mind—body research (i.e., physiological and psychometric measures combined) has also demonstrated that when chronic stress has not been dealt with effectively, our internal biological functioning is frequently affected.[21]

It is important for rehabilitation counseling professionals to make the distinction between everyday emotional stress and extraordinary stressful or traumatic events that may result in more long-term clinical symptoms, such as those associated with PTS. Traumatic and enormously painful events vary in their psychological and emotional impact. While not all painful events are traumatic for the individual, some survivors become physically, psychologically, or emotionally overwhelmed and may require assistance from a professional counselor or peer-support group.

PTS differs from acute (nontrauma-induced) and chronic stress in that it is provoked by events that occur outside the normal range of most human experience and may be totally disabling to the person physiologically as well as psychologically. The DSM-IV[19] indicates that PTS occurs as the result of exposure to a traumatic event in which the person (a) experienced, witnessed, or was confronted with an event that involved actual or threatened death or serious injury; and (b) has responded with intense feelings of fear, helplessness, or horror. Individuals have difficulty cognitively processing and emotionally responding to the overwhelming event. Soon the event becomes an overpowering sensory experience as the person continues to attempt to make "ordinary" sense from an extraordinary event.

It is suspected that there may be many other groups of people that do not meet the criteria for PTS (e.g., adult children of alcoholics, victims of racism, victims of sexual harassment), but who do exhibit evidence of acute stress or PTS. Ivey and Ivey[8] propose a Developmental Counseling and Therapy (DCT) model that offers an approach using the PTS classification system of the DSM-IV. These authors advocate expanding the view of trauma by reframing the client's severe distress, or acute stress episodes, as a response to their environment and developmental history. They further propose that "In the framework of DCT, trauma can be extended to include repeated sexual or racial harassment, a physical beating as a result of homophobia, poverty, and repeated issues of discrimination for reason of physical disability or challenge."[8] (p. 343) For example, it has been estimated that 80% of people exhibiting symptoms of PTS are survivors of rape, physical injury, or other life-threatening traumatic events.[27]

The prevalence of PTS symptomatology in people with cancer and other life-threatening illnesses has lead to a new direction in PTS research. The psychological sequelae of cancer survivors have focused almost exclusively on feelings of anxiety, anger, or depression. However, a growing body of research suggests that people with acquired life-threatening illnesses exhibit intrusive, persistent, and traumatic thoughts related to their disease.[23] Overall, it appears that the diagnostic category of PTS has too narrow an assessment focus and does not give full environmental considerations for persons with chronic illnesses and mental, emotional, or physical disabilities.[8]

Ecological Environmental Considerations

It is critical to understand the impact the environment has on the psychosocial functioning of people with PTS. The "person-in-the-environment" focus has long been a theoretical precept within the rehabilitation counseling literature.[28] Many authors suggest that the use of the word "disorder," as in PTSD, is misleading because it tends to focus on issues of stress within the person rather than recognizing that the environment may be a precipitating factor.[8,29,30] More recently, Hershenson[31] proposed a systemic, ecological model that rehabilitation counselors can use to view the rehabilitation process and choose appropriate interventions. I include this model because of its application to the adjustment and adaptation process in coping with extraordinary stressful and traumatic events.

Hershenson proposes the examination of systems and subsystems that comprise:

- Values and attitudes
- Behavioral expectations and skill demands of the person
- Potential resources and supports
- Presenting physical and attitudinal barriers
- Opportunities and reinforcers that the system has to offer

It is critical that rehabilitation counselors be mindful of how all of these systems and subsystems interact and affect the individual before choosing any interventions that might be used in a crisis-demand situation.

Psychosocial Response of Survivors

In this section, a discussion of the psychosocial response to traumatic events will be presented as it relates to: (a) survivors (b) family members, (c) the sociocultural community environment, and (e) rehabilitation counseling professionals.

Psychosocial Stages of Adjustment and Adaptation

Aiding in the synthesis of grief and loss experiences appears to be at the heart of serving people who[62] have experienced extraordinary stressful or traumatic events. Individuals who are confronted with such adversity experience a multitude of losses. For example, some individuals who are survivors of violent crimes may feel the loss of a sense of fairness or justice with the legal system.[32] Those who experience life-threatening illnesses may feel a loss of their faith in God or a higher power.[33] People who have acquired a chronic illness or disability may feel the loss of their future as it relates to their vocation, emotional, social, or physical health, and many other life areas.[34]

The sense of loss and grief requires that the individual adapt and adjust for survival. The terms psychosocial adaptation and psychosocial adjustment often overlap, and the concepts are often indistinguishable in the literature.[7] Generally, psychosocial adaptation is a dynamic process, a subjective experience that involves both internal and external factors. Adaptation describes the degree to which the person functions successfully physiologically, psychologically, and socially after a traumatic event, such as an acquired disability. The concept of adjustment typically refers to a specific phase of experiences or psychosocial reactions to the chronic or disabling condition and relates to how the individual and others perceive the actual loss or trauma sustained.

There are a number of stage models offered in the literature regarding psychosocial adaptation and adjustment to disability, trauma, crisis, grief, and loss.[14,29,32,35-37] These models emphasize that the prolonged course of treatment, often uncertain prognosis, constant intense psychological stress, limited daily functioning, and the psychological impact on family and friends all combine to create complications in adjustment and adaptation to extraordinary stressful and traumatic events. Stage models also make it clear that:

- There is no universal experience or response to chronic illness, trauma, or disability

- A state of final adjustment (sometimes referred to as resolution, acceptance, assimilation, or reintegration) is not always achieved by the individual
- Based on the available clinical and empirical evidence, psychological recovery does not follow an orderly sequence of reaction phases. Thus, individuals may experience phases of adjustment on a continuum and may regress to an earlier phase, skip one or more phases, or may overlap with other phases.[7]

Overall, it is suggested that each stage of adjustment:

- Requires different coping patterns
- May be both maladaptive and adaptive
- Has a variety of emotional triggers that hinder the survivor's ability to adapt to the experience of trauma, loss, or disability

Common Phases in Reaction to Extraordinary Stressful or Traumatic Events

The following section briefly describes common phases of reactions associated with psychosocial adaptation to chronic illness, trauma, and disability as offered by Livneh and Antonak's research.[7] These authors hypothesize and suggest that as the person completes or gains closure within a particular phase, that they reach some level of meaning, emotional growth, and understanding regarding their disability which will help them transition into the next phase.

Shock

The individual's initial emergency reaction to the onset of sudden and severe trauma. Shock is characterized by psychic numbness, overwhelming physiological experience, and cognitive disorganization.

Anxiety

Viewed as a panic reaction, anxiety is marked by confused thinking, cognitive flooding, and numerous physiological correlates.

Denial

Denial is one of the more problematic reactions because its subtle, often conflicting aspects make it difficult to verify. Denial is marked by defensiveness, minimizing, or unrealistic thinking.

Depression

Depression is a reactive response as a result of the trauma; the degree of depression depends upon family history, predisability trauma, reaction to the stressors involved with the trauma, and biological or neurochemical changes attributable to the disability. People who are depressed typically report feelings of helplessness, hopelessness, isolation, and despair.

Internalized Anger

This emotion is perceived to be the person's self-directed resentment and bitterness, often associated with feelings of self-blame or guilt. This reaction is often most evident in people who realize that the impairment is a chronic and disabling condition.

Externalized Hostility

This behavior may be the individual's attempt at retaliation and is marked by hostility directed at other people or objects, or aggressive or passive-aggressive acts.

Acknowledgment

This phase is regarded as the first indication that the person has a cognitive awareness of the losses that have occurred in his or her life. There is a cognitive reorganization toward self and the external environment. The individual begins to accept him/herself as a person with a permanent impairment, gains a new sense of self, and has the ability to reappraise life goals and seek new meanings.

Adjustment

Characterized as the theoretical or final phase of the adaptation process, the person who reaches this theoretical phase reestablishes self-worth, realizes the existence of remaining or newly discovered potentials, actively pursues and implements social and vocational goals, and successfully overcomes obstacles encountered in the pursuit of his or her goals.

The Family's Response

Families of the twenty-first century are culturally and socially very different from those of any other time and it seems that the stress in today's family unit is unparalleled by that of any other generation. Traditional family roles and values have changed, economic factors have required two household incomes, and the emotional antecedents and aftermath of "divorce-wars" have a significant impact on the family. Some statistics on divorce indicate that as many as 60% of youth will spend a portion of childhood or adolescence in a single-parent environment.[38] These factors, when combined with extraordinary stressful and traumatic events, make it increasingly difficult to use family members as a support mechanism. However, the family as a social institution remains the most important factor influencing how well survivors of trauma or disability adapt. The family's resources (e.g., financial status, emotional and other support networks) have a significant impact on how individuals within the family survive adversity;[26] yet, the best resource that family members have is each other. The marital relationship is key, and is considered one of the most important elements for surviving traumatic events within the family system.[39] Marital distress tends to evoke, maintain, and exacerbate the family's response to trauma. If the marital relationship is not dealt with in a therapeutic manner, both partners often have a decreased ability to cope with the acute and long-term emotional effects of trauma.

Ideally, the family should provide each member with protection, love, security, identity, self-esteem, and a value system that emphasizes the positive qualities of life.[40] Generally, families cope with extraordinary stressful and traumatic events in the same way and with the same success as past life crises.[41] Some families that have experienced trauma and disability report that they have coped quite well with little or no outside intervention. Protective factors that can reduce stress and traumatic responses included adequate rule setting and structure, family cohesion, lower parental conflicts, open communication, warmth toward the child, and being patient in parenting interactions.[42]

Dysfunctional family behaviors are especially critical in the child's growth and development and can be the source of difficulties carried into adulthood. Feelings that are prevalent among dysfunctional families include anger, sadness, shame, and fear. Families that have not coped well with past crisis events tend to exhibit alcohol and substance abuse behaviors, physical violence, physical, emotional, and sexual abuse, emotional and physical neglect, separation, and divorce.[24,43,44] Children observe older siblings, as well as the adults within their family, as examples of how they should respond emotionally to stressful events and family crisis.[40] Unhealthy coping responses such as not verbalizing feelings, long-term denial, or active avoidance of a crisis event will likely result in more severe problems later in life.[45] The family can be strengthened as family members learn to increase and encourage disclosure of feelings and emotions associated with the traumatic experience. Parents must give permission openly for their children to grieve the traumatic experience by creating an environment of trust and support which encourages the children to verbalize their feelings and experiences. Overall, a more securely attached family and an increased level of social support can help successful adaptation on many levels. Further, rehabilitation counselors who specialize in substance abuse treatment as a co-existing disability with other trauma issues related to the family dynamic can help bring this system back into balance.

The Sociocultural Community's Response

Recently, researchers have begun to examine the psychosocial responses of communities who have been exposed to violent and traumatic events. Individuals within communities can experience psychological trauma through indirect knowledge of, or exposure to a crisis event.[46] In my experience counseling people in communities where school violence and natural disasters (i.e., hurricanes, tornadoes) have occurred, it is evident that the community-at-large is a secondary survivor of crisis events. The phenomenon of "vicarious victimization" describes this experience, which is associated with seven specific factors that increase its likelihood.[17] These factors are:

- A realistic threat of death to all members of the community
- Extraordinary carnage
- Strong community affiliation
- Witnessing of the event by community members
- Symbolic significance of victims to the community (i.e., children)
- Need for numerous rescue workers
- Significant media attention

Generally, qualitative research suggests that PTS as a result of extraordinary stressful or traumatic events has psychological consequences that are more far-reaching for the community as a whole than was once thought.

Social and cultural factors such as gender, ethnicity, race, disability, socioeconomic status, level of acculturation, and urban vs. rural culture also have an impact on how emotions are expressed collectively by a community. Knowledge of the person's cultural and social norms for expressing emotion during trauma, grief, death, and dying is critical. For example, in the Amish culture, there is a calm acceptance of trauma, grief, death, and dying, which is marked by a high level of support given to bereaved family members. In New Orleans, some African Americans engage in funeral rituals that include marching or parading through the streets with music and dancing. Mexican Americans, because of language, cultural, and socioeconomic barriers, are often cut off from traditional western professional medical and mental health services, especially in rural areas.[47] Thus, they are more dependent on the family or folk medicine to assist in the emotional healing process. Counselors need to respond to the client by recognizing the person's individuality (e.g., race, ethnicity, gender) and common coping abilities (e.g., family, socioeconomic, and community support) through a holistic multicultural approach.[48,49]

Certain segments of the community, such as children, older persons, or different cultural groups that may have feelings of being victimized, are particularly vulnerable to the psychosocial impact of traumatic events. For example, research indicates that people who live in rural settings felt safer in their homes than persons, especially older adults, who live in urban settings.[50] When violent crime occurs in rural areas, the person's feeling of emotional security is upset and the community becomes out of balance. When violent crime occurs in urban areas, particularly, people who work in institutions such as schools, churches, or social clubs may exhibit symptoms of PTS that include depression, fear, sleeping or eating disorders, or substance abuse behaviors. These feelings may be intensified and exacerbated by extensive media coverage of the community's crisis event, lengthy police investigations, or civil litigation.

Community Interventions

Most extraordinary stressful and traumatic events do not occur in isolation. Rather, critical incidents act as "shock waves" that affect the community as a whole, regardless of whether the critical incident stems from a natural disaster, school shooting, or a neighborhood shooting. There is much that community leaders can do to offer social support and increase the therapeutic environment during times of a community crisis. However, interventions require building relationships within the community through police, mental health professionals, schools, teachers, and administrators, as well as spiritual and religious groups.[51] An organized effort among these institutions can help develop a sense of community empowerment.[52] For example, promoting commendations and awards to rescue workers, counselors, and other volunteers who have been part of the community crisis response team is an important part of the healing process. Public leaders (i.e., city, state, federal officials) also have a powerful influence in the community. These leaders should be encouraged to express their own grief which will in a sense, signal permission for others to grieve the community's loss.[53]

When others outside a region recognize and acknowledge community members grief, then the affected community will generally feel a sense of support and connection to the outside world. This support is necessary in the healing process. For example, after the Westside Middle School shootings that took place in Jonesboro, Arkansas, children from other middle schools around the nation sent cards, letters, and posters to express their deepest sympathy for the loss sustained by the Westside students. Miller[54] emphasizes that a support network of outside mental health consultants and other service providers also serves an important function during community disasters. They can assist the affected community in developing a plan for education and prevention which will promote safety and security. Planning actions such as these and instituting them can help people within the community feel that they can gain some control over their lives again. As a member of the Westside crisis response team, the present author experienced first-hand how outside help could provide additional support, energy, and assistance in the crisis debriefings with the large numbers of students, teachers, and parents who were affected by this crisis event. It may be a natural response for members of a community in crisis to feel that no one outside their community can understand or relate to their tragedy. However, communities in crisis should not hesitate to ask for outside assistance because there are many talented individuals who can assist in the recovery process.

Rehabilitation counselors are uniquely qualified to assist as members of a crisis response team due to their academic training with issues related to loss and grief, which are integral to the process of psychosocial adaptation and adjustment to chronic illness, disability, and life after a crisis event. Through counseling and case coordination activities, the rehabilitation professional can utilize community resources to assist with the survivor's physical, emotional, psychological, social, vocational, and independent functioning needs.

The Counselor's Response

Recent and accumulating research related to trauma and disability,[3,55] along with the applied experiences of mental health and rehabilitation counseling professionals[56] indicate that there is a natural secondary traumatic stress response that is associated with providing services to individuals and groups who are directly and indirectly affected by traumatic events. This response is known as the phenomenon of empathy fatigue[10,19] or compassion fatigue.[3,57] *Empathy fatigue* is the grief reaction, or the psychological, emotional, and physical exhaustion that occurs during helping interactions. Dealing with another person's traumatic experience has a definite impact on the professional's behavior and personal life.[58] Many rehabilitation professionals who work with survivors of trauma and those with chronic life-threatening illness and disability are frequently exposed to their client's life story and experiences. Counseling professionals must be empathically available to individuals or family members; in fact, the

Code of Professional Ethics for Rehabilitation Counselors[59] emphasizes that rehabilitation counselors are compelled by ethical obligation to place their clients' needs and interests above their own.

The nature of STS has been illustrated by Figley[3] in the traumatology and psychology literature. He suggests that STS is equivalent to PTS. STS is the natural emotional and physiological response resulting from learning about, or knowing about, a traumatizing event that has been experienced by another person. In other words, the professional helper can experience similar feelings without actually being physically harmed or threatened with harm. The DSM-IV[20] notes specific characteristics and features of PTSD, but the underlying premise is that people can be traumatized either directly or indirectly as either primary or secondary survivors.

Counselors or caregivers who may not be aware of this parallel process or the experience of counter-transference may be at risk for increased levels of anxiety, depression, or substance abuse behaviors. Counseling professionals who are just beginning their career have little preparation for dealing with people in trauma. Studies have shown that younger, less experienced counselors report higher levels of STS than those who are more seasoned professionals.[60,61] This is primarily because the experienced professional has learned different ways of coping with his or her job and working more efficiently. When the cumulative effects of STS go unrecognized, or the individual or organization has little capacity for dealing with a traumatic event, this may lead to a secondary stress reaction and increased levels of emotional, mental, and physical exhaustion.

Adaptive Coping, Prevention, and Intervention Strategies

Survivors of extraordinary stressful or traumatic events typically spend a lot of time and energy avoiding the feelings, thoughts, and activities that are associated with the critical event. This is a normal response. Some avoidance of past crisis events may be an important coping strategy. However, too much emotional avoidance or suppression may result in numbness or dissociation from the cognitive and emotional experience of past stressful events.[62] Thus, dealing with the psychological and emotional impact of a critical incident early on will ultimately benefit individuals, family members, organizations, and the community in adaptation and healing. The following strategies are recommendations which can be given to survivors to initiate or continue the adjustment process to extraordinary stressful or traumatic events.

Adaptive Coping Strategies for Survivors:

1. Allow time for the transition back into a day-to-day routine, such as school or work.

2. Identify friends and family members who may be physically, psychologically, or emotionally at risk.
3. Be familiar with the resources available in your community that will support your recovery.
4. Support your peers and allow them to talk about their loss and reinforce their positive steps toward recovery.
5. Focus on the routine things that you are able to do, as well as some positive things that you have done in the past.
6. Establish ongoing support and contacts with friends and family members.
7. Be mindful that the most important resource you have is one another—the other individuals that have been through the same or a similar experience.

Strategies for Coworkers, Friends, and Family to Support the Survivor:

1. Be an active listener for the survivor but do not get "hooked" into the role of counselor.
2. Identify when the survivor is emotionally overwhelmed and suggest professional help.
3. As difficult as it may be for you, allow and invite the survivor to talk about his or her feelings of loss or fear of future critical events.
4. Establish regular contact with the survivor to ensure that he or she is safe and has adequate emotional and social support.

Strategies for Organizations and Employers to Support the Survivor:

1. After the survivor has been through a critical incident, it is likely that the person will have a difficult time focusing on job performance. Allow the survivor time to transition back to the day-to-day work routine. Take a "time-out" from your regular structure for an "emotional check-in" with the survivor. You may want to begin the work day or a meeting by giving permission and allowing the survivor to ventilate feelings concerning a recent past extraordinary stressful experience. Verbalizing thoughts and emotions has therapeutic benefits.
2. Be sensitive to the emotional needs of the survivor during work. While you are not (and do not need to be) a professional helper, you can offer to be a good listener.
3. Familiarize yourself with and promote educational or wellness-type resources for survivors. Be aware of employees who may be at risk for additional emotional or psychological stress.

4. Be aware that you may be experiencing some stress-related symptoms associated with the emotional aftershocks. Also, be mindful that secondary stress is a natural artifact of just being around or overhearing the survivor's stories of extraordinary stressful experiences.

5. Emphasize the survivor's strengths by reinforcing positive aspects of current functioning or productivity level.

NOVA Model of Group Crisis Intervention

The National Organization for Victim Assistance (NOVA) offers an excellent model for group crisis intervention.[32] This model uses a similar protocol to that of CISD models and is composed of three phases of intervention which can typically be accomplished in one 90-minute session. The strategies and approaches used to facilitate group debriefings allow crisis responders to work with large groups of both primary and secondary survivors. NOVA has adopted the term "group crisis intervention" rather than "group debriefing" because the term "debriefing" is often confused with models used with military and law enforcement personnel, which may create confusion or inhibit participation among civilian survivors of traumatic incidents. The NOVA model differs from typical debriefings and therapeutic or support groups that are ongoing in nature because this (and other) crisis intervention groups are usually formed immediately after a critical event.

Group crisis interventions often take place at or near the site of the critical incident. Strategies in this model allow group facilitators to consider group size as well as sociocultural aspects of the group or organization. Peer groups should ultimately be arranged in separate sessions with the survivors who were closest to the epicenter. Those groups who were indirectly affected by the critical event, such as counselors or trauma rescue or crisis response personnel should be debriefed in a separate group. Timing of the group crisis intervention is also critical, as it relates to a crisis event (e.g., several hours postcrisis, day after, one week later).

Safety and Security

The first phase of the model, *Safety and Security*, usually begins with introductions of the group facilitator(s), providing parameters for building an environment based on trust, safety, confidentiality, and personal disclosure. The goal of this phase is to provide a safe environment for survivors to release intense emotions after a traumatic event.

Ventilation and Validation

The second phase of the model, Ventilation and Validation, allows survivors to ventilate and review physical, emotional, and sensory experiences they associated with the critical incident. Some key questions that the group facilitator(s) may use during this phase include:

- Where were you when this incident happened?
- Who were you with?
- What did you see, hear, smell?
- What did you do next?
- How did you react at the time?

This phase of intervention provides an opportunity for survivors in the group to become aware that others have had similar experiences. This is also an opportunity to educate the survivors on common emotional reactions to extraordinary stressful and traumatic events, reinforcing the belief that they are not "going crazy" and that other people in the group have similar feelings and emotions. During this phase, survivors should be provided with factual information regarding the traumatic event that has taken place to dispel any misinformation and counter any myths or rumors. A second set of questions that would be beneficial in this phase includes:

- Since the time of the event, what are some of the memories that stand out for you?
- What has happened in the last 48 hours?
- How has this event affected your life?

Prediction and Preparation

The last phase, *Prediction and Preparation*, should be a time for group members to cultivate seeds of hope for the future. Goals for this phase are for survivors to prepare for future emotions and identify any critical life areas that would hinder their recovery. This is also a time for survivors to identify resources and supports that will facilitate coping and healing. The third series of questions that the group facilitators may use includes:

- After all that you have been through, what do you think will happen in the next few days or weeks?
- Do you think that your family, friends, and community will continue to be affected?
- Do you have any concerns about what will happen next?

CONCLUSION

Extraordinary stressful and traumatic events such as fires, floods, hurricanes, or school shootings have a significant impact on survivors' physical, emotional, psychological, social, spiritual, and financial well-being. Regardless of how close we may be to the epicenter of such an event, it is quite normal and expected that emotional aftershocks can affect survivors weeks and even months after experiencing the critical incident. Thus, it is important and necessary to deal with interventions early-on and be mindful of how to cope with possible future emotional triggers.

Presently, the literature does not specifically address the role and function of the rehabilitation counselor as part of a crisis response team. However, I have personally worked along side other rehabilitation counselors during critical incident stress debriefings and have found these professionals to be well-trained, skilled, and competent in dealing with the psychosocial adjustment needs of persons in crisis. Historically, rehabilitation professionals have functioned in the roles of case manager, counselor, and consultant for persons with acquired chronic illness and disability. Indeed, rehabilitation professionals "wear many hats" and have a breadth of knowledge and skills to deal with the individual's physical, emotional, psychological, social, vocational, and independent functioning needs. Accordingly, persons directly affected by physical and emotional trauma will likely become part of the "disability community" and will require ongoing services and commitments from many other helping professionals. Thus, by virtue of the rehabilitation counselor's academic training and the diversity of job settings, these professionals can provide both direct services (i.e., mental health and substance abuse counseling), as well as acting as the "case coordinator" to directly link the person with a variety of other community resources.

REFERENCES

1. Elliott D. (1997). Traumatic events: Prevalence and delayed recall in the general population. *J Consult Clin Psych, 1997*;65:811–820.
2. Eisenberg MG, Glueckauf RL, Zaretsky HH. *Medical Aspects of Disability: A Handbook for the Rehabilitation Professionals.* New York: Springer Publishing; 1999.
3. Figley CR. *Compassion Fatigue: Coping with Secondary Traumatic Stress Disorder in Those Who Treat the Traumatized.* Bristol, PA: Brunner/Mazel; 1995.
4. Foa E, Hearst-Ikeda D, Perry, K. Evaluation of a brief cognitive behavioral program for prevention of PTSD in recent assault victims. *J Consult Clin Psychol. 1995*;63:948–955.

5. Ivey, A. E., & Ivey, M. B. (1998). Reframing DSM-IV: Positive strategies from developmental counseling and therapy. *Journal of Counseling & Development, 76,* 334–350.

6. Bachman R. *Crime Data Brief: Violence and Theft in the Workplace.* (NCJ-148199). Washington, DC: U.S. Department of Justice, Office of Justice Programs; 1994, July.

7. Keim J. *Workplace violence and trauma: A 21st century rehabilitation issue. J Rehabil.* 1999;65(1):16–20.

8. Friedman MJ, Marsella AJ. Posttraumatic stress disorder: An overview of the concept. In: Marsella AJ, Friedman, MJ, Gerrity, ET, Scurfield RM, eds. *Ethnocultural Aspects of Posttraumatic Stress Disorder: Issues, Research, and Clinical Applications.* Washington, DC: American Psychological Association; 1996:11–32.

9. Livneh H, Antonak RF. *Psychosocial Adaptation to Chronic Illness and Disability.* Gaithersburg, MD: Aspen; 1997.

10. Ivey AE, Ivey MB. Reframing DSM-IV: Positive strategies from developmental counseling and therapy. *J Counsel Devel.* 1998;76:334–350.

11. Stebnicki MA. *Grief Reactions Among Rehabilitation Professionals: Dealing Effectively with Empathy Fatigue.* Presentation made at the NRCA/ARCA Alliance Annual Training Conference. Dallas, TX: 1999, April.

12. Lester, D., & Brockopp, G. W. (1974). *Crisis intervention and counseling by telephone.* Springfield, IL: Charles C Thomas.

13. Specter, G. A., & Claiborn, W. L. (1973). *Crisis intervention: A topical series in community—Clinical psychology.* New York: Behavioral Publications.

14. Mitchell JT, Everly GS. *Critical Incident Stress Debriefing: An Operations Manual for the Prevention of Traumatic Stress Among Emergency Services and Disaster Workers.* 2nd ed. Ellicot City, MD: Chevron Publishing; 1996.

15. Mitchell J.T. When disaster strikes: The critical incident stress debriefing process. *J Emergency Medic Services.* 1983;(1):36–39.

16. Meichenbaum D. *A Clinical Handbook/Practical Therapist Manual for Assessing and Treating Adults with Post-Traumatic Stress Disorder (PTSD).* Waterloo, Ontario, Canada: Institute Press; 1994.

17. Young MA. Crime, violence, and terrorism. In: Gist R, Lubin B, eds. *Psychosocial Aspects of Disaster.* New York: Wiley; 1989:61–85.

18. Stebnicki MA. Stress and grief reactions among rehabilitation professionals: Dealing effectively with empathy fatigue. *J Rehabil.* 2000;66(1):23–29.

19. American Psychiatric Association. *Diagnostic and Statistical Manual of Mental Disorders.* 4th ed. Washington, DC: Author; 1994.

20. Naugle AE, Follette WC. A functional analysis of trauma symptoms. In: Follette VM, Ruzek JI, Abueg FR, eds. *Cognitive Behavioral Therapies for Trauma.* New York: Guildford Publications, Inc; 1998:48–73.

21. Trieschmann RB. The energy model: A new approach to rehabilitation. *Rehabil Educ.* 1995;9(2):217–227.

22. Frankl VE. *Man's Search for Meaning: An Introduction to Logotherapy.* New York: Touchstone-Simon Shuster; (Original work published by Beacon Press 1959) 1984.

23. McGrath P. Posttraumatic stress and the experience of cancer: A literature review. *J Rehabil. 1999;65*(3):17–23.
24. Goodwin LR, Holmes GE. Counseling the crime victim: A guide for rehabilitation counselors. *J Appl RehabilCounsel. 1988;19*(2):42–47.
25. Davis M, Robbins-Eshelman E, McKay M. *The Relaxation & Stress Reduction Workbook.* 4th ed. Oakland, CA: New Harbinger Publications, Inc; 1995.
26. Moore KA, Cooper CL. Stress in mental health professionals: A theoretical overview. *Intl J Soc Psychiatry. 1996;42*(2):82–89.
27. Kilpatrick DG, Saunders B, Amick-McMullan A, et al. Victim and crime factors associated with the development of crime-related post-traumatic stress disorder. *Behav Ther. 1989;20*:199–214.
28. Arokiasamy CV. A theory for rehabilitation. *Rehabil Educ. 1993;7*:77–98.
29. Shontz FC. *The Psychological Aspects of Physical Ilness and Disability.* New York: MacMillan; 1975.
30. Vash CL. *Personality and Adversity: Psychospiritual Aspects of Rehabilitation.* New York: Springer Publishing; 1994.
31. Hershenson DB. Systemic, ecological model for rehabilitation counseling. *Rehabil Counsel Bul. 1998;42*(1):40–50.
32. Young MA. *The Community Crisis Response Team Training Manual.* 2nd ed. Washington, DC: National Organization for Victim Assistance (NOVA); 1998.
33. Kushner H. *When Bad Things Happen to Good People.* New York: Avon Books; 1981.
34. Marinelli RP, Dell Orto AE. *The Psychological and Social Impact of Disability.* 4th ed. New York: Springer Publishing; 1999.
35. Antonak RF, Livneh H. A hierarchy of reactions to disability. *Intl J Rehabil Res. 1991;14*:13–24.
36. Garfield CA. *Stress and Survival: The Emotional Realities of Life-Threatening Ilness.* St. Louis: C.V. Mosby Company; 1979.
37. Kubler-Ross E. *On Death and Dying.* New York: Macmillan; 1969.
38. Norton A, Glick P. One-parent families: A social and economic profile. *Family Relations. 1986;35*:9–17.
39. Johnson SM, Williams-Keeler L. Creating healing relationships for couples dealing with trauma: The use of emotionally focused marital therapy. *J Marital Fam Ther. 1998;24*(1):25–40.
40. Sigelman CK, Shaffer DR. *Life-Span Human Development.* Pacific Grove, CA: Brooks/Cole Publishing; 1991.
41. Rando TA. *Grief, Dying, and Death: Clinical Interventions for Caregivers.* Champaign, Il: Research Press Company; 1984.
42. Miars RD. Stress and trauma: Coping in today's society. In: Capuzzi D, Gross DR, eds. *Youth at Risk: A Prevention Resource for Counselors, Teachers, and Parents.* 3rd ed. Alexandria, VA: American Counseling Association; 2000:167–191.
43. Carey AL. Survivor revictimization: Object relations dynamics and treatment implications. *J Counsel Devel. 1997;75*:357–365.

44. Glover NM, Janikowski TP, Benshoff JJ. The incidence of incest histories among clients receiving substance abuse treatment. *J Counsel Devel.* 1995;73:475–480.

45. Burrows-Horton C, Cruise TK. Clinical assessment of child victims and adult survivors of child maltreatment. *J Counsel Devel.* 1997;76:94–104.

46. Herkov MJ, Biernat M. Assessment of PTSD symptoms in a community exposed to serial murder. *J Clin Psychol.* 1997;53:809–815.

47. Lopez-De Fede A. Rural America and persons with disabilities. In: Smith TF, ed. *Rural Rehabilitation: A Modern Perspective.* Arnaudville, LA: Bow River Publishing; 1998:12–39.

48. Ridley CR, Mendoza DW, Kanitz BE. Multicultural training: Reexamination, operationalization, and integration. *Counsel Psychologist.* 1994;22:227–289.

49. Stebnicki MA, Rubin SE, Rollins C, Turner T. A holistic approach to multicultural rehabilitation counseling. *J Appl Rehabil Counsel.* 1999;30(2):3–6.

50. Mann WC. Assistive technology and the rural elderly. In: Scott TF, ed. *Rural Rehabilitation: A Modern Perspective.* Arnaudville, LA: Bow River Publishing; 1998:313–326.

51. Osofsky, JD. Community-based approaches to violence prevention. *Devel Behav Pediatr.* 1997;18(6):405–407.

52. Harley DA, Stebnicki MA, Rollins CW. Applying empowerment evaluation as a tool for self-improvement and community development with culturally diverse populations. *J Commun Devel.* (in press; Special Issue).

53. Ursano RJ, Fullerton CS, Norwood AE. Psychiatric dimensions of disaster: Patient care, community consultation, and preventative medicine. *Harvard Review of Psychiatry.* 1995;3:196–209.

54. Miller, L. *Shocks to the system: Psychotherapy of traumatic disability syndrome.* New York: W.W. Norton & Company; 1998.

55. Carbonell JL, Figley CF. When trauma hits home: Personal trauma and the family therapist. *Journal of Marital and Family Therapy.* 1996;22(1):53–58.

56. Stebnicki MA. *Psychosocial Adjustment and Adaptation to Trauma and Disability.* Presentation made at the American Counseling Association's World Conference. San Diego, CA: 1999, April.

57. Joinson C. Coping with compassion fatigue. *Nursing.* 1992;22(4):116–122.

58. Green BL. Psychosocial research in traumatic stress: An update. *J Traumatic Stress.* 1994;7(1):341–362.

59. Code of Professional Ethics for Rehabilitation Counselors. *J Appl Rehabil Counsel.* 1987;18(4):26–31.

60. Corey MS, Corey G. *Becoming a Helper.* 3rd ed. Pacific Grove, CA: Brookes Cole Publishing; 1998.

61. Cranswick K. Burnout: A study of level of burnout and factors responsible for burnout in rehabilitation workers. *J Rehabil Admin.* 1997;21(2):119–134.

62. Walser RD, Hayes SC. Acceptance and trauma survivors: Applied issues and problems. In: Follette VM, Ruzek JI, Abueg FR, eds. *Cognitive-Behavioral Therapies for Trauma.* New York: Guilford Publications, Inc; 1998:256–277.

CHAPTER TWENTY-SIX

War, Death, and Bereavement

How We Can Help

Joan Beder

IN 2002, MY ARTICLE ENTITLED Mourning the Unfound: How We Can Help was published in Families in Society. The article was prompted by the destruction of the World Trade Center in September 2001. As was the rest of the world, I was deeply affected by this event and hoped that through the article I could offer some guidance to those in the helping professions in their work with bereaved adults, especially those who had suffered their loss without physical confirmation of death.

Now, over a year after September 11th, I'd like to offer suggestions to those who will be helping individuals—spouses, partners, or family members—who have lost or will lose loved ones in the war effort. The casualties will surely mount, and the adult survivors face bereavement situations that may be fraught with many emotions. For those of us who will be helping these adult mourners, we may be venturing into some new and challenging territory.

From "War, death and bereavement: How we can help," by J. Beder, 2003, *Families in Society: The Journal of Contemporary Human Services* (www.familiesinsociety.org), *84*(2), 163–167. Published by Alliance for Children and Families.

GRIEF AND WAR: WHAT WE KNOW

The bereavement of parents, spouse or partner, or other family members who have lost an adult is a traumatic form of grief, especially when the death is related to a war effort. For all, it is a vivid reminder that the world is not a safe and ordered place. For older parents, it highlights the untimeliness of such deaths: parents are supposed to predecease their children. For the older parent, the relationship with their adult children has gone through the many phases, trials, and tribulations of growing up and an adult-to-adult relationship has emerged. Loss of an offspring at this time occurs after years of parental investment and involvement and at a time when it is unlikely that they will be replaced; it is thus felt as a devastating loss (Archer, 1999). For spouses or partners, the level of upset and turmoil is huge, as one's partner in life has died, leaving a vast hole in the fabric of life for all involved. There are many other forms of loss during wartime: soldiers who mourn comrades, those who lose friends, loss of innocence by those who are forced to impose death on others, and families with children. Considering the vast body of literature on bereavement, there are few studies that address bereavement based on war death, for any of the above mentioned groups. The available studies have looked at parents and their specific reactions to this form of loss. No studies document the reaction of spouses or partners. The studies that have been reported about adults will be detailed.

Gay (1982) measured the self-concept of parents who had lost an adult son during the 1973 Yom Kippur War in Israel. Her findings, when comparing bereaved parents' adjustment and grief scores with the norms of Israeli adults in general, showed that the bereaved ranked poorly in overall self-concept. There was a high frequency of somatic complaints and a higher tendency toward depression.

Rubin (1989–1990) compared 42 Israeli parents who had lost sons in a war an average of 9 years before, with a sample of 13 parents who had lost 1-year-old children around the same time. He found that the bereaved parents of adults showed higher current levels of grief and higher levels of recalled earlier grief than parents who had lost a young child. He concluded, "Overall, parents who have lost younger children to illness are functioning better than are parents who have lost adult sons to war" (p. 316). While a small sample, these findings may reflect the reality that for the older parents, the ability to produce another child has passed while younger parents have the capacity to replace the deceased, which mitigates the intensity and prolonged aspect of the loss.

In a follow-up study of 102 parents who had lost sons in war 4 and 13 years before, Rubin (1991–1992) found that the bereaved parents showed higher levels of grief and anxiety than a control sample of 73 nonbereaved adults, even after this length of time. These findings suggest that the grief does not completely abate, even after many years have passed.

Florian (1989–1990) studied 102 married couples—52 bereaved couples who lost their son during combat and 50 couples who had not experienced the loss of a son who served as a control group. In the bereaved group, 26 parents had lost their sons during the Yom Kippur War in 1973 and 26 in the 1982 Lebanon Campaign. At the time of the study the range of years from soldier death was 2–11 years. The bereaved parents, both mothers and fathers, experienced less meaning and purpose in life compared to the nonbereaved on the Meaning in Life Scale. The bereaved parents evaluated their health status as poorer compared to the control group. More troubling for the bereaved cohort in this study was that the parents expressed a sense of meaninglessness and a lack of purpose in life that did not improve with the passage of time. This was measured by the Purpose in Life Test. Florian concluded, "The fact that no differences on the low level of meaning and purpose in life was found after 2 and 11 years following the loss of the child may serve as an indication of the 'devastating' nature of this type of bereavement" (p. 100).

In a more recent study, Malkinson and Bar-Tur (1999) looked at long-term grief of older parents whose sons were killed during military service in Israel. The study was conducted with 29 older adults—60 to 87 years old—in a group setting. The length of bereavement was 11 to 33 years. Forty percent were widowed, there were 4 couples and the rest were single parents. Findings support earlier studies: the authors note that within their group, grief continued along the lifespan unaffected by other developmental processes or life events and that the inner attachment to the deceased child was not relinquished. Additionally, "It seems that the grief becomes painful and more difficult to tolerate as the parent weakens and becomes more fragile and isolated" (p. 424).

WAR BEREAVEMENT: WHY IT IS COMPLICATED

We know that with the loss of an adult child, a significant portion of the parent's life energy can effectively die with the child (Rubin & Malkinson, 2001). We know the power of the loss when a spouse or partner has died, leaving family and loved ones behind. But what are the variables with wartime death that exaggerate this reaction and prolong bereavement, sometimes for a lifetime?

The death of a service person has multiple meanings, not just for the family and spouse or partner but for society as well. "The extent of the mourner's adjustment not only depends on personal strengths or psychic vulnerability but also is integrally linked to the cultural context and value system of that society" (Rando, 1993, p. 520). The meaning, both cultural and personal, that the war holds is inherent in the reaction to this loss of life.

From a social constructionist perspective, everything that we experience is shaped by our current sociocultural environment (Rosenblatt, 2001). If we live in a society in which war is occurring, there are threats to person and country, massive numbers of people are involved in a war effort and there is the potential loss of many lives (Raphael, 1983). In this environment, one imagines that the inevitability of violent dying makes it expected and more acceptable—a risk rather than an abhorrent act. After all, slaying the enemy is what war is all about and soldiers are valued for their bravery in killing. Many people in military service are trained to do battle and to kill; dying in battle is often retold as heroic (Rynearson, 2001). With the high expectation of death and the impersonality of violent death during war, again the question, why is it that this form of death creates such a difficult bereavement experience?

There are a variety of factors that impact and/or complicate the bereavement experience. The service person's and mourner's philosophical agreement with war in general and the specific reasons for this war are a strong predictive factor. If the family or service person is philosophically against the war effort, a level of bitterness will enter the bereavement experience. Likewise, if the family is supportive of the war effort and the service person is not, acrimony about participating in the war may be present. Raphael (1983) notes that wars have special meaning in that a cause is fought for, and the responses of the bereaved may reflect their values. Their responses may be especially bitter if they perceive the death as having no point, as serving no purpose or a purpose they cannot support.

In addition, for the mourner, the service person's attitudes about going to war (Did he or she volunteer or get drafted? Were they reluctant to serve?) will either vindicate the death or exacerbate the pain of the loss. If the service member was there against his or her will, parents and surviving family members will surely feel the uselessness of the death and experience heightened anger over the dying. The type of death and circumstance (in battle, with torture, in a noncombatant situation) will impact the survivors as they picture the last moments of the soldier's life and replay their beliefs about these final moments. Was the soldier alone, in a battlefield, or in pain or anguish? The country's political climate and degree of support for the war will make the soldier's effort more or less meaningful. After the Vietnam War, for example, many soldiers returned home feeling that they had risked their lives while the country was unsupportive of their effort and unsupportive of them personally. This attitude can undermine the bereavement experience. It should be noted that, in spite of personal political views about the war, many will still respect the efforts of the service persons and will still honor their death. In this current war, while the country is somewhat divided on the rational for the war, there has been support for those who are risking their lives to protect the United States. However, not everyone will be respectful.

The stress of separation experienced by the mourner while the service person was deployed and the length of deployment can be an additional factor. If the person was deployed and it created a level of hardship at home, the separation and anticipated return will have been aborted by the death, extending the hardship and possible resentment.

The extent of support available to the mourner is always a buffering aspect of any bereavement situation. If there is general support for the war effort, deceased heroes are celebrated; if the war is not supported, deceased heroes are denied adequate recognition and the bereavement may be experienced in more troubled ways (Rando, 1993, p. 521). Bereavement may be especially potent if there has been any "unfinished business" between the mourner and the deceased service person. Unfinished business refers to those issues between the deceased and the mourner that were never addressed or lacked successful closure in the relationship. It includes the expression of things unsaid issues that were unresolved, conflicts that needed resolution (Rando, 1984, p. 50). If there are a lot of loose ends, especially emotional ones, the mourner may struggle mightily over the lost opportunity to address the loose ends. These factors, above and beyond any the "usual" anticipated reactions, can influence the bereavement trajectory for the survivors.

What the above description suggests is that the societal and personal milieu of the mourner is a significant variable in the after-death experience. While the loss of an adult person is devastating for parents and spouses or partners, the attitudes and reactions to war play a major role in the grief of these survivors.

HOW WE CAN HELP

Grief resolution is not a linear process; it entails a number of steps. For some, these steps need to be facilitated and encouraged through counseling with a mental health professional/grief counselor for the best outcome (Beder, 2002). In the counseling situation of wartime bereavement, following Worden's Task Model (2002), with some modification and explanation, is a sound choice. I have found this approach to be useful in many situations and like the notion of the mourner being directed to take action on their own behalf. For the counselor, it is useful because it creates a path and plan for us to follow while allowing a good deal of latitude and helps us locate the mourner in their bereavement process. The Tasks of Mourning, as outlined in a book by Worden (2002) are:

- Task 1. To accept the reality of the loss;
- Task 2. To work through the pain of grief;
- Task 3. To adjust to an environment in which the deceased is missing; and
- Task 4. To emotionally relocate the deceased and move on with life (pp. 27–37).

Each of these tasks will be explained with additional comments related to wartime bereavement. Accepting the reality of the loss means that the mourner must face the fact that the person is dead and will not return—that reunion is impossible. This is both an intellectual and emotional acceptance; while intellectually, the mourner recognizes that the deceased is gone forever, accepting the overwhelming emotion that is provoked by this realization is much more difficult. The funeral ritual, for many, facilitates the beginning of the emotional acceptance. With wartime death, this phase may be a greater struggle for the mourner, as frequently there are no remains to bury or the remains may take a long time to arrive, thus delaying the funeral rituals and delaying the acceptance. In addition, since the service member has been gone for a certain amount of time, it is possible to almost pretend that he or she is still involved in the fighting. The counseling effort has to help the mourner break down their denial to be able to begin accepting their loss. It should be noted, however, that most individuals who are seen in counseling have begun this process of emotional acceptance and are experiencing the pain of their loss. This is often the motivating factor in seeking help.

Denial occurs because for some, the contemplation of the death is too stressful and overwhelming to contemplate. It is the mind's way of insulating the individual from the emotional impact of the knowledge of the death and their loss (Kalish, 1985). The strategy for the counselor to help those who are in denial is to attempt to keep the mourner talking about the deceased, to have the counselor use the name of the deceased whenever possible, and to have the counselor ask questions about the deceased. The underlying concept is to gently pierce the denial by bringing the deceased into the counseling room and counseling effort.

The second task, working through the pain of the grief, involves experiencing the sadness and emptiness of life without the deceased. The negation of this task is not experiencing the pain by not feeling. This can have serious long-term emotional consequences. Sometimes the pain is physical, a wrenching pain that will not go away; mostly, the pain is emotional as the mourner recognizes that the deceased will never be seen again, never touched, their voice will never be heard, their smile and presence are gone.

In the counseling it is important for the mourner to give voice to their emotional pain; grief counseling is based on the assumption that emotions needs a voice or the individual may carry this pain throughout life, creating periods of depression and anguish (Rando, 1993). In general counseling efforts, not only bereavement counseling, there is the goal of encouraging the expression of emotions, especially powerful emotions, as a way of easing the intensity of certain feelings. It has been acknowledged that keeping in anger, for example, can lead some to levels of depression. The same concept prevails in bereavement work: the pain of loss needs expression and can be facilitated by the counselor. This is done through questioning about reactions to their loss, to imagining life without the deceased, to what was special about the deceased that will be missed. Our sometimes-overused question—How are you feeling about that?—may need to be evoked to stimulate the mourner to discussion at an emotional level. If the mourner is struggling with unfinished business, encourage the griever to say aloud the things that were unsaid to the deceased; encourage the griever to finish the unfinished business by voicing it. This second task may be heavily impacted by society's reaction to the mourner and their social system; it is here that the impact of society's reaction to the wartime effort will be felt. As noted above, if society is generally supportive of the war effort, the response to a soldier's death and to those who are grieving will be more supportive. If the prevailing mindset is against the war effort, people may be less supportive and even disdainful of the grief of a soldier's family. If the soldier served against his or her will, the anger of the griever may be hard for others to tolerate. Also, in wartime, the number of soldiers who die can, in time, inure society to personal loss making much-needed social support less and less available as the war effort continues.

Task 3, adjusting to an environment in which the deceased is missing, touches three areas of adjustment: external, internal, and spiritual. External adjustments are the day-to-day roles and tasks that the mourner has to assume with the absence of the deceased. Internal adjustments are more complex and are more concerned with a new definition of self as a widow or bereaved parent. These new self-definitions require internal reorganization and may impact self-esteem and a sense of identity regarding how one sees oneself. This is not unique to bereavement after war; whenever there is a loss of someone close, individuals have to redefine their roles and relationships around the void. Sometimes, this contributes to lowering of self-esteem. Counselors need to be alert to this dynamic as we might make the assumption that the depression we observe in our client(s) is due exclusively to the death while it may be equally related to the loss of self-esteem and position created by death.

In the area of spiritual adjustment, the mourner has to make peace with their revised view of the world, trying to make sense of a world that does not necessarily reward good and doesn't always make sense. Again, this is not unique to bereavement after war deaths. In most situations that involve violent and unexpected death, individuals tend to question their assumptions about the stability of the world and the benevolence of the world. This realigning of the worldview to incorporate the death and loss takes time and cannot be easily addressed in the counseling.It is important to recognize this as a death reaction and know that for most mourners this casts an additional pall on their understanding of life.

Oddly, Task 3 may be facilitated for the wartime griever: some of the adjustments may have been made, although believed to be temporary, because of the absence created by their service. As the soldier is absent for an extended amount of time before their death, the mourner or others might have assumed some of the day-to-day roles and shifted some of their emotional needs to others. The final area, spiritual, can also be somewhat easier as wartime is a time of chaos and revision of priorities, alliances, power, and control. In this atmosphere of changing assumptions, the personal revision of the world-view is happening nationally or internationally and coincides with that of the mourner.

Task 4, the final task of emotionally relocating the deceased and moving on with life is especially difficult for anyone who has sustained a loss. For many, the confusion of this task is that they feel guilty that they have moved on, and moving on, for some, means closing the chapter on the deceased and negating their existence. The counseling effort is geared to help the mourner to be able to find a special and secure spot for the deceased in their emotional life while at the same time being able to go forward with their life and plans. For grievers in wartime, especially parents, this is very difficult. As the review of the studies on bereaved wartime parents showed, this may never be fully accomplished but steps toward it can be realized. For the spouse or partner, moving ahead may be associated with moving away and this may prevent forward motion into their own future.

Worden (2002) has provided a template from which we can work in helping parents and spouses or partners. It must be understood that this is not a smooth, linear process occurring in a fixed progression with tidy completion of one task before moving onto the next. Tasks can be partially completed and can be reworked and revisited; grieving is a fluid process with many stopping and starting points.

SOME THOUGHTS ABOUT GROUPS

Bereavement groups are an excellent method of working with mourners. The support, sense of connection between and among members, the opportunity to help others and be helped by others, and the hope that can be engendered by seeing others who have overcome some of their grief make groups a viable, and sometimes preferable, counseling option. Two cautions are suggested: the groups should be led by a trained professional and should be comprised only of those struggling with wartime bereavement issues. This form of grief, with its multiple meanings and struggles, could overwhelm a self-help group. The benefit of the group being homogeneous—only those struggling with wartime death—is because the wartime aspect of the loss creates a gestalt of reactions that are not generic to all losses. As understood from the section in this article on why the bereavement is complicated, there are certain societal and familial issues that confront the wartime mourner which do not exist in other bereavement situations.

CONCLUSION

The finality of death is inescapable and in most situations; so is the pain of loss. If we engage with another, if we feel close to them, we risk the pain of loss. As parents, we birth and love our children whether they are 3 months or 53 years old and we hope that we will not have to bury them. But life is not predictable and some events impact us in ways over which we have no control. War is such an event. With war comes hardship, death, sadness, and pain for those left behind. As grief counselors and mental health practitioners, we have a responsibility to help those who suffer with their losses and to help restore them in whatever ways we can. Hopefully, some of the suggestions in this article will be useful in that effort. War is hell.

REFERENCES

Archer, J. (1999). The nature of grief. London: Routledge. Beder, J. (2002). Mourning the unfound: How we can help. *Families in Society, 83*(4), 400–403.

Florian, V. (1989–1990). Meaning and purpose in life of bereaved parents whose son fell during active military service. *Omega, 20*(2), 91–102.

Gay, M. (1982). The adjustment of parents to wartime bereavement. In N. A. Milgram (Ed.), *Stress and anxiety* (Vol. 8, pp. 47–50). New York: Hemisphere.

Kalish, R. (1985). *Death, grief, and caring relationships* (2nd ed.). Monterey, CA: Brooks-Cole.

Malkinson, R., & Bar-Tur, L. (1999). The aging of grief in Israel: A perspective of bereaved parents. *Death Studies, 23*(5), 413–433.

Rando, T. (1984). *Grief, dying, and death*, Champaign, IL: Research Press.

Rando, T. (1993). *Treatment of complicated mourning.* Champaign, IL: Research Press.

Raphael, B. (1983). *The anatomy of bereavement.* NY: Basic Books.

Rosenblatt, P. (2001). A social contructionist perspective on cultural difference in grief. In M. Stroebe, R. Hansson, W. Stroebe, & H. Schut (Eds.), *Handbook of bereavement research* (pp. 285–300). Washington, DC: American Psychological Association.

Rubin, S. S. (1989–1990). Death of the future: An outcome study of bereaved parents in Israel. *Omega, 20*(4), 323–339.

Rubin, S. S. (1991–1992). Adult child loss and the two track model of bereavement. *Omega, 24,* 183–202.

Rubin, S. S., & Malkinson, R. (2001). Parental response to child loss across the life cycle: Clinical and research perspectives. In M. Stroebe, R. Hansson, W. Stroebe, & H. Schut (Eds.), *Handbook of bereavement research* (pp. 219–240). Washington, DC: American Psychological Association.

Rynearson, T. (2001). *Retelling violent death.* Philadelphia, PA: Brunner-Routledge.

Worden, J. W. (2002). *Grief counseling and grief therapy* (3rd ed.). New York: Springer.

CHAPTER TWENTY-SEVEN

Users of Assistive Technology

The Human Component

Martin G. Brodwin, Tristen Star, and Elizabeth Cardoso

The importance of assistive technology (AT) for consumers with disabilities cannot be overestimated. Technology offers opportunities for increased self-sufficiency, greater independence, and enhanced employment potential. It extends into the realms of daily living, social functioning, recreational activities, and work opportunities, thus decreasing a consumer's functional limitations and helping to "level the playing field" between people with disabilities and those without disabilities. A primary purpose of this article is to discuss the human component of AT, and the relationship between consumers and technological devices and equipment. The first part describes acceptance and use of AT by consumers. In the AT process, a consumer's self-worth, sense of belonging, and the attitudes of others play a dynamic role. Therefore, consumer involvement needs to be at the forefront of this process. Initially, in the assessment/evaluation phase of rehabilitation, the rehabilitation counselor should help the consumer identify the priorities and motivation for requesting assistive technology. These should be in the forefront throughout the entire process as they are key to successful implementation and use of AT. By carefully

From "Use of assistive technology: The human component," by M. Brodwin, T. Star, and E. Cardoso, 2003, *Journal of Applied Rehabilitation Counseling, 34,* 23–29. Reprinted with permission of The National Rehabilitation Counseling Association.

defining goals of the consumer, the counselor will be able to more clearly define what the consumer wants to accomplish by using technology. This involves the activities that motivate a consumer to use AT, and is crucial to successful adaptation and use.

Self-esteem, self-efficacy, and motivation are described as central elements in increasing a consumer's confidence and belief in self. High outcome and efficacy expectations, as well as strong motivation, help lead to successful adaptation to AT. The role of cognitive functioning in the use of technology is discussed. Additionally, recommendations are offered to assist rehabilitation professionals in helping the consumers they work with in accepting, utilizing, and benefiting from AT.

Assistive technology was defined in the "Technology-Related Assistance of Individuals with Disabilities Act of 1988" (Tech Act; P. L. 100-407) as "any item, piece of equipment, or product system, whether acquired commercially off the shelf, modified, or customized, that is used to increase, maintain, or improve functional capabilities of individuals with disabilities" (Scherer, 2000, p. 185). These devices and equipment may be low-tech (mechanical) or high-tech (electromechanical or computerized) and can compensate for sensory and functional losses. Assistive technology provides the means to move (e.g., wheelchairs, scooters, lifts), speak (e.g., augmentative and alternative communication devices), read (e.g., Braille input, voice recognition devices), hear (e.g., telecommunication devices for the Deaf [TDD], hearing aides), or manage self-care tasks (e.g., remote environmental control systems, prosthetic and orthotic devices). Technology service is "any service that directly assists an individual with a disability in the selection, acquisition, or use of an assistive technology device" (Scherer, p. 185).

Assistive technology increases functional abilities, independence, and access to mainstream society by individuals with disabilities. Currently, more than 17 million Americans with disabilities are using AT; however, a national survey on AT abandonment found that 29% of devices obtained were later discarded (Riemer-Reiss & Wacker, 2000). These researchers found "that individuals who continued to use their technology had significantly higher mean scores than those who discontinued use of their technology in relation to relative advantage, consumer involvement, and compatibility" (p. 48).

ASSISTIVE TECHNOLOGY ACCEPTANCE AND USE

Riemer-Reiss and Wacker (2000) researched AT use and abandonment issues by consumers. Their findings inferred that little documentation existed from the consumer's perspective as to why assistive devices had been abandoned. These authors' goal was to determine factors associated with

AT continuance or discontinuance using Roger's (1995) theory of diffusion, based on a consumer's initial decision to accept a device and later reject it. According to Riemer-Reiss and Wacker, discontinuance happens in two ways: (a) replacement, where one device is discarded for an improved one, and (b) user disenchantment or dissatisfaction. The researchers derived the following as crucial factors for consumers' continued use of AT: advantage, compatibility, trialability, and re-invention.

Carroll and Phillips (1993), in a survey on abandonment of AT by 25 new users, concluded that characteristics of relative advantage (effectiveness, reliability, ease of use, comfort, and enhancement of the user's performance) were significantly related to not abandoning technology. Compatibility, a factor related to use, is the extent to which the device is perceived by consumers to meet their needs. Trialability was defined as the degree to which the consumer could experiment with the AT device or equipment before acquisition. Reinvention occurs when a new model replaces an older one. Riemer-Reiss and Wacker (2000) hypothesized that the relationship between continuance/discontinuance involved a combination of compatibility, advantage, support, trialability, consumer involvement, and changes when making decisions or setting goals. These authors concluded that further research is necessary in areas of evaluation and whether the provision of technology is meeting the needs and desires of the consumer.

USE OR NON-USE OF ASSISTIVE TECHNOLOGY

The degree to which a device is essential for a consumer's desired function includes his or her personal needs, and becomes crucial in determining whether the consumer uses or abandons the product (Scherer, 2000, 2002). To avoid nonuse, rehabilitation counseling professionals need to identify and consider matching of technology with aspects of the person's personality and temperament, characteristics of the setting, and the material traits of the assistive device itself.

Scherer (2000) further described optimal characteristics of the setting where the AT will be used to include: support from others (family, peers, employer), realistic expectations of family/employer and a setting/environment that fully supports and rewards use of AT. Positive consumer personality variables involve: motivation (how AT will help the consumer accomplish desired tasks), coping skills, capability to use the device, pride in using AT, patience, and self-discipline. Characteristics of the technology that influence consumer use include: compatibility with and enhancement of other technologies that the consumer is using, reliability, ease of use, problem-free and timely maintenance, and desirable transportability.

Benefit Expectations

These expectations involve what the consumer wants to accomplish by using AT – the desired tasks that are most important to the consumer. Aspects of technology that will benefit consumers are influenced by the positive and negative attitudes of others. Other areas that may influence continued use of AT are the following: social support, loneliness, isolation, and cultural identity. Research has shown that individuals who do not have social support have an increased chance of discontinuing use of recently acquired technology (Riemer-Reiss & Wacker, 2000; Scherer, 2000). The characteristics related to consumers' acceptance and use of AT include level of technical comfort, cognitive (intellectual) skills, personality traits, adjustment, and outlook, including pre-existing temperament and ways of coping. In addition, technological characteristics to consider include design factors, such as weight, ease of set-up, compatibility with other devices, as well as the consumer's level of comfort when using AT (Cook, 2002; Reed, 2002).

The emotions of consumers' who use AT vary widely and the social environment contributes to feelings of being viewed as conspicuous, labeled in a negative way, or stigmatized as being different than what is considered "normal" (Scherer, 2000). Consumers need social support when attempting to use technological devices and equipment. However, essential to AT acceptance are the need and use of support services to assist the consumer to gain knowledge and training in using the devices or equipment, including the option of having an emergency backup system (Langton & Ramseur, 2001). An important consideration for providers includes a genuine belief that consumers are capable of learning new things and are able to change and adjust.

THE HUMAN COMPONENT

Self-Worth

Schaller and DeLaGarza (1999) affirmed that the self-concepts of consumers with disabilities are influenced by the social context in which they interact, validating either positively or negatively, self-worth. Supportive relationships for consumers promote a sense of belonging and are necessary for the development of positive self-images and self-acceptance. Positive social support promotes more stability, less emotional stress, and greater psychological well-being by buffering negative life events and easing environmental pressures. Consumers with disabilities usually have knowledge of their needs, but have a difficult time expressing and attaining feelings of belonging.

Schaller and DeLaGarza (1999) studied relationship perspectives of individuals with cerebral palsy, noting that there was a recurring theme concerning individual perceptions of belonging. Emotional affect and response perception was determined by early life experiences, such as interaction between family and the environment. For instance, participants with cerebral palsy described feeling different from others at some point in their youth. The emotional components varied based on individual perceptions of acceptance and support. This research also indicated that important to self-acceptance was the need for children with disabilities to learn that they had a right to interact with children without disabilities. Technology can both heighten feelings of being different (in a negative way) and, at the same time, enhance the ability to interact with others. As noted by Taylor and Kopriva (2002), children with cerebral palsy who use AT are more capable of interacting with children without disabilities.

Attitudes

Attitudes professionals exhibit are crucial factors in establishing trust and confidence in the counselor/consumer relationship. When a consumer forms a relationship with a professional involving how to effectively use AT, the consumer takes the position of initiating a help-seeking role. This role requires developing a level of courage toward, and trust and confidence in, the professional relationship. The rehabilitation counselor needs to maintain the consumer's best interests and have a positive, humanistic attitude. Humanistic, person-centered approaches focus on consumers' subjective experiences (Garske & Soriano, 1997). The goal is to approach providing AT services from a consumer's own perspective when defining specific objectives, needs, and desires. Above all else when providing AT, the focus needs to be on the consumer. According to Scherer (2000), "assistive technologies are used when consumers have goals and see the devices as valuable to goal achievement. When users have significant input into selection of the devices, they become more invested in using them successfully" (p. 131).

SELF-ESTEEM AND SELF-EFFICACY

Self-Esteem

Behavior and cognition are essential elements that contribute to learning, with an emphasis on learning through observation of others. This is certainly true when consumers are adapting to the use of AT. Self-esteem is highly related to an individual's ability to accomplish tasks and goals. The concepts of self-esteem, self-worth, and self-image are defined as the total dimension of the self, with self-concept relating to a specific area in which individuals self-evaluate their knowledge, capabilities, and skills (Santrock, 2002).

Development of positive self-esteem occurs early in children's developmental processes (Santrock, 2002). An ability to cope with a problem rather than avoid it contributes to positive self-evaluative thoughts, which generate self-approval, thus enhancing one's self-esteem. Bandura's (1982) theory of individuals believing that they can master a situation and produce a positive outcome is labeled self-efficacy. It is based on the principle that cognitive events are induced and altered by efforts and persistence demonstrated in a task. Personal experience reinforced by successful performance of a task, including use of AT, increases an individual's belief that goals attempted can be accomplished (Conyers, Enright, & Strauser, 1998; Cook & Hussey, 2002).

Self-Efficacy Theory

Efficacy Expectations and Outcome Expectations

Self-efficacy beliefs consist of two components: efficacy expectations and outcome expectations (Conyers et al., 1998). Efficacy expectations concern a person's beliefs about the ability to undertake a given task (in this case, learning to use assistive technology), and range from high to low. Outcome expectations involve whether a person knows what to do in a given situation and believes that the outcomes of effort will be beneficial or not, and also have a range of high to low. Both efficacy and outcome expectations need to be relatively high for people to attempt and succeed at using AT. Self-efficacy includes four essential elements that can be related to the use of AT (Bandura, 1982; Mitchell & Brodwin, 1995):

1. In a given situation, an individual knows what to do and how to do it. In the case of AT, the consumer needs the knowledge on how to successfully use the device.
2. The person has the confidence that he or she can succeed in the activity. This relates to a consumer being self-assured that, if given sufficient instruction, he or she can successfully learn to use the AT device or equipment.
3. The individual believes that what he or she does will have an impact on the end result. This element involves a consumer believing that he or she can learn to use the technology and that this will result in a positive outcome, in that the consumer will be able to accomplish the desired tasks with use of technology.

4. The outcome is of sufficient importance for the person to want what the outcome will provide. The consumer believes that what the device or equipment provides in decreasing functional limitations and enhancing capabilities is what he or she wants.

Self-efficacy theory proposes that expectations vary in level of challenge (high or low degree), in strength (ability to persevere), and flexibility of self-efficacy (whether it will transfer from one area to another). The above four essential elements affect the level of self-efficacy and the extent to which an individual is able to cope with obstacles, and is applicable to technology. In the first element, a consumer feels confident in knowing what to do with AT and how to do it. The second element involves a belief that, if tried out, success will be achieved. A belief that the chosen behavior will have an effect on the outcome (adaptation to AT), is the third element. The final element brings successful reinforcement to the consumer as he or she believes that the device or equipment is of importance; thus, the enhancement of activities and reduction of functional limitations provides adequate incentives for performing the behavior in the future (Conyers et al., 1998; Cook & Hussey, 2002; Scherer, 2000). Consequently, the level of self-efficacy a consumer maintains will determine, in part, whether he or she will accept, try out, and continue to use assistive technology in the future.

When the levels of these four components are high, the consumer typically demonstrates goal-oriented, self-assured, and persistent behavior when dealing with the technology. The higher the consumer's self-efficacy, the greater the likelihood of successful adaptation to and use of AT.

Bandura (1982) defined individual expectations as information based on data retrieved from the environment: emotional arousal, overt experiences, verbal persuasion, and performance accomplishments. Choice-making decisions are influenced by expectations an individual has about an anticipated outcome, based on prior outcome experiences. Successful use of and adaptation to AT is partially dependent on consumer expectation. Self-efficacy is centered on personal beliefs and perceptions that are influenced by the quality of coping skills over which one has power. Low self-efficacy triggers an individual's choice to avoid situations and environments, in this case a desire to try out and use AT. The consumer with low self-efficacy avoids the task and seeks other environments that are perceived to provide more adequate feelings of accomplishment (Conyers et al., 1998; Cook & Hussey, 2002; Scherer, 2002).

Motivation

The term motivation is defined as an inner urge or desire that prompts an individual to perform a behavior; motivation produces a particular action or manifests itself as any influence that promotes positive performance (Scherer, 2000). Self-efficacy provides the foundation for motivation by establishing actions that result in positive, repetitive reinforcement. In the process of delivering AT services to a consumer, motivation may result from any point within the process: the consumer, the activity engaged in, the environment, or the AT system components (Cook & Hussey, 2002; Reed, 2002). As noted by Rubin and Roessler (2001), in dealing with consumers and assistive technology, motivation always must be maintained for there to be a successful end result.

Generally, human behavior may be inspired, intrigued, satisfied, or provide feelings of accomplishment at any point in task engagement that reinforces an intrinsic element expressed as motivation. Assistive technology can provide motivation in many ways. Social rewards, such as increased interpersonal interaction, may provide the necessary motivation and desire to use technology. For example, when a student derives pleasure from playing games on a computer, he or she will be more motivated and interested in using the computer for homework. By carefully defining the goals of the potential user, devices can be selected that are meaningful and motivating to the particular consumer.

Achievement Motivation. This kind of motivation is based on the need for achievement, and defined by the desire to accomplish some purpose or reach a level of excellence by expending an amount of effort to excel. Achievement-oriented individuals are less likely to have fear of failure; they have stronger hopes for success and are moderate risk takers. To learn to use AT involves taking risks that may result in failure. Factors that influence achievement motivation have been identified as early independence training by parents and interaction within an environment with others engaging in strong social modeling of achievement behavior (Santrock, 2002). One can postulate that consumers with this background will more readily adapt to and persist in using AT devices.

Intrinsic and Extrinsic Motivation. According to Santrock (2002), there are two types of motivation components that have been identified: intrinsic and extrinsic. Intrinsic motivation is defined as confidence in one's ability to be competent and to accomplish something for its own sake, such as a personal standard of excellence in meeting a desired goal. Feeling good about meeting or exceeding that desired goal is an example of intrinsic motivation. Extrinsic motivation is based on external rewards and punishments. Working hard in school with the goal of a higher paying job is an example of extrinsic motivational behavior. Learning to operate a computer to do better in school or work is another example. The use of a computer to interact socially, using e-mail, chat rooms, playing games, or listening to music is a third example.

Researchers (Rogers, 1995; Santrock, 2002) have identified the roll of the environment in promoting high intrinsic motivation. Factors that contribute to internal motivation are the variety of experiences and the extent to which the family or caregiver encourages competence and curiosity. Extrinsic motivation may include those resulting from social outcomes or successful completion of an activity. Examples of social outcomes involving AT acquisition include conversational discourse, achievement of a goal (moving to a desired location in a power wheelchair), or reinforcement (getting higher grades in school) (Herman & Hussey, 1998). As outcomes are more clearly identified and understood, a consumer may increase goal-directed behavior towards acquiring AT.

Beliefs also influence motivation to use AT. A system needs to be consistent with a consumer's beliefs for there to be sufficient motivation to use it (Cook & Hussey, 2002). A simple example is offering an athlete a more streamlined wheelchair to enhance motivation and desire to use it. The provider of assistive technology should carefully assess the consumer for both intrinsic and extrinsic motivators. As reported by Scherer (2000), motivation is one of the key personality traits pertinent to successful learning and using technological devices. If motivational factors are low and remain low, it is unlikely the consumer will follow through and persist at learning and using AT (Cook, 2002).

Mastery Orientation

An underlying attribute that sustains mastery-oriented individuals is the personal level of self-efficacy and satisfaction that they achieve from effective interaction with their respective environments. An intrinsic factor that motivates all individuals is a desire to succeed (Bandura, 1982). Motivation is an essential factor for successfully learning and using AT devices (Herman & Hussey, 1998). Service providers emphasize the importance of motivation in order accept and use technology. Technology outcome efforts partially depend on definitiveness of assessment and evaluation phases that identify skills, abilities, capabilities, and the personality traits of self-esteem, self-efficacy, and motivational factors (Rizer, 1999; Santrock, 2002).

Cognitive Function

A consumer's cognitive functioning and response to technology plays a significant role in the application of assistive technology (Cook, 2002). The functioning of the brain depends on perception, cognition, and motor

control. The perception of an event is necessary before cognition can provide meaning to that event. Cognitive reasoning processes use knowledge,
abilities, and skills to identify, understand, and make decisions. They
encompass environmental interaction, communicate in meaningful language, and change when new information is introduced. Motor control
depends on both cognition and the consumer's physical and sensory capabilities and limitations (Cook & Hussey, 2002; Herman & Hussey,
1998).

For example, a consumer with speech and mobility limitations who
accesses the environment with use of a power wheelchair (an AT device)
must visually interpret the environment, make decisions regarding spatial
dimensions, and activate a control-interface to manipulate the wheelchair
(Herman & Hussey, 1998). At the same time, communication can take
place by the use of an augmentative and alternative communication device
(AAC), technology that "enable persons with limited speech or no usable
speech to visually display their words or speak through the assistance
of electronic communication devices with voice input" (Scherer, 2000,
p. 185). An AAC requires capabilities and skills, such as motor function,
interpretation of scanning codes, and selection of appropriate schema and
response (Reed, 2002; Santrock, 2002).

Cognitive Skill Development

Skills used in AT acquisition depend on a combination of physiological,
psychological, social, and environmental components. Developmental researchers have interpreted a basic understanding of the developmental
process over the lifespan. They have theoretically documented how the acquisition of sensorimotor skills and symbolic representation influence the
maturation of a child's central nervous system. Both physical growth and
learning contributes to the formation of cognitive organization (Santrock,
2002). When learning and applying AT systems, cognitive skill levels and
motor development play an essential role (Cook & Hussey, 2002). A consumer who learned sufficient skills related to AT use as a child, will find
it easier to adapt to new and unfamiliar technology.

Symbolic Representation. This involves directly responding to the
ability to use language concepts to access augmentative communication
devices. Capability to "sequence" correlates with skills needed to use various step-control systems in multiple symbol communication. The term
"centration" applies to a focus on shapes, sizes, and colors rather than
needing a language conception of function (Cook & Hussey, 2002). Many
technologies become an extension of the person; a strategy to personalize

a device, "animism," is when a device is given a name. The strategy of "play equals reality" uses play to accomplish functional goals, identifying what motivates a consumer and incorporating those aspects in applying AT. An example is the "universal design" concept of using video games for educational purposes. Practitioners need to carefully match the developmental level of the individual to the available tools of technology (Cook, 2002; Herman & Hussey, 1998).

BENEFITS AND EXAMPLES OF ASSISTIVE TECHNOLOGY

Assistive technology enables consumers with disabilities to reduce, and perhaps minimize, functional limitations. Many of these consumers become able to participate more fully in mainstream society. In reality, technology helps equalize the capacities of those individuals with disabilities compared to those without disabilities. Technology has many social and recreational applications, enhancing the ability of the consumer to participate in meaningful activities. For example, a wheelchair with balloon tires allows a consumer to travel on the beach and traverse other rough, outdoor terrain. Greater independence in daily living, including leisure-time activities, becomes enhanced with AT. Remote environmental control allows a consumer to do such tasks as turning on lights, a computer, television or radio, answering a telephone, and unlocking the front door. Through reasonable accommodations, many consumers are able to remain on their jobs, and others can seek employment, if not working. A power chair or scooter at work may allow a consumer mobility without the use of excess energy required when walking. An adaptive computer at work may permit a consumer to perform required work functions that were previously time consuming or not possible. For example, applications of technology can extend communication capabilities. Consumers with expressive communication deficits may be capable of performing work or school functions with increased and enhanced use of computer-based communication (Brodwin, Parker, & DeLaGarza, in press).

Another form of technology, custom-designed prosthetic and orthotic devices, help consumers with upper extremity limitations. These devices enhance manual dexterity, bilateral dexterity, and tasks involving eye-hand coordination. Consumers with upper extremity difficulties may be helped by enlarged keyboards, key guards, miniature keyboards, and various specialized user interface switches (optical head pointers, light beams, touch screens) (Rubin & Roessler, 2001). Prosthetic and orthotic devices help consumers with lower extremity limitations perform such activities as standing and walking.

Accommodations for consumers with visual deficits include both optical and nonoptical low vision devices. Examples of optical devices are magnifiers, specially coated lenses, and telescopes. Nonoptical visual aids include talking clocks, talking calculators, closed-circuit televisions that enlarge print electronically, and personal computers and peripherals with the capability of print magnification, speech output, and optical scanning (Brodwin et al., in press). In addition, hearing aids, telecommunication devices for the Deaf (TDD), cochlear implants, electronic ears, amplified telephones, and audioloops are helpful AT devices for consumers who are Deaf or hard-of-hearing.

RECOMMENDATIONS FOR REHABILITATION COUNSELING PROFESSIONALS

1. Consumer involvement, from initial assessment through selection and adaptation, is essential to the success of assistive technology. A consumer-driven model provides a feeling of ownership and responsibility and is directly related to continued use of AT (Riemer-Reiss & Wacker, 2000).
2. By having the consumer identify priorities and desires he or she wants to accomplish through the use of AT, the rehabilitation counselor learns what is foremost in motivating the consumer to use technology.
3. A careful analysis of costs and benefits of AT from the perspective of the consumer prior to selection should be made. The advantage a device provides must outweigh the costs of using it or the device will probably not be used (Riemer-Reiss & Wacker, 2000).
4. Basic, minimal (low-tech) cost solutions should be considered before expensive high-tech ones. Simple devices may be as effective as more complex ones.
5. The devices should be durable, reliable, and effective (Rubin & Roessler, 2001).
6. Provisions need to be in place for technical assistance, repairs, and routine maintenance (Rubin & Roessler, 2001).
7. To ensure increased functioning and independence (the ultimate goals of using AT), the correct match between consumer and the AT must occur. If not, the chances of continued consumer use of the device or equipment will be minimized (Reed, 2002).
8. When recommending AT, the consumer should be presented with any possible alternative choices (Star, 2001).
9. Each consumer has his or her own preferences, perspectives, and expectations. The counselor needs to realize that professionals

and consumers see things from very different perspectives (Scherer, 2000).

10. The degree to which an AT is essential for desired functioning, the more likely it will be used (Carroll & Phillips, 1993; Star, 2001).

11. The counselor needs to make sure the consumer really does want the device and that it is not just something someone else really wants him or her to have (Scherer, 2000).

12. The consumer needs the skills, to use the device; it should be easy to operate, and require little assistance from others for everyday use (Scherer, 2002).

A change in a consumer's needs can result in product discontinuance (Cook, 2002; Scherer, 2000). Therefore, follow-up and periodic re-assessment of a consumer's desires and abilities are crucial for continued use of AT devices.

CONCLUSION

The goal of AT is to increase functional independence for consumers who have disabilities (Cook & Hussey, 2001; Langton & Ramseur, 2001). The focus, therefore, is not on the disability but on the remaining functional (residual) abilities that individuals use to accomplish their chosen objectives and their daily tasks. When AT systems are considered for use, the rehabilitation counselor needs to evaluate the various characteristics of the consumer that will effect successful adaptation. According to Scherer (2000), the single most significant factor associated with technology abandonment is a failure to consider the user's opinions and preferences in device selection – *in other words, the device is abandoned because it does not meet the person's needs or expectations'* (p. 118). Other reasons that AT may be abandoned include a lack of motivation, insufficient training, ineffective device performance, and accessibility problems (Phillips & Zhao, 1993). There needs to be a close and appropriate fit (match) between technological device and consumer. Therefore, the need for the rehabilitation counselor to actively listen and engage the consumer in the process is essential to the effectiveness and outcome of AT success. The closer the rehabilitation counselor matches the consumer's various characteristics to the appropriate AT device, the greater the chance it will continue to be used. Additionally, the counselor and consumer need to be knowledgeable and trained in the specific AT device in order for it to be used efficiently.

REFERENCES

Bandura. A. (1982). Self-efficacy mechanism in human agency. *American Psychologist, 37*, 122–147.

Brodwin, M. G., Parker, R. M., & DeLaGarza, D. (in press). Disability and accommodation. In E. M. Szymanski & R. M. Parker (Eds.), *Work and disability: Issues and strategies in career development and job placement* (2nd ed.). Austin, TX: Pro-ed.

Carroll, M., & Phillips, B. (1993). Survey on assistive technology abandonment by new users (Cooperative Agreement No. H133E0016). Washington, DC: National Institute on Disability and Rehabilitation Research.

Conyers, L. M., Enright, M. S., & Strauser, D. R. (1998). Applying self-efficacy theory to counseling college students with disabilities. *Journal of Applied Rehabilitation Counseling, 29*(1), 25–30.

Cook, A. M. (2002). Future directions in assistive technology. In M. J. Scherer (Ed.), *Assistive technology: Matching device and consumer for successful rehabilitation* (pp. 269–280). Washington, DC: American Psychological Association.

Cook, A. M., & Hussey, S. M. (2001). *Assistive technologies: Principles and practice* (2nd ed.). St. Louis, MO: Mosby.

Garske, G. G., & Soriano, M. (1997). Client perceptions of the rehabilitation counseling relationship: Humanistic approaches and related outcomes. *Journal of Applied Rehabilitation Counseling, 28*(2), 10–14.

Herman, J. H., & Hussey, S. M. (1998). Module II: Clinical fundamentals. In Rehabilitation Engineering Society of North America (RESNA) (Ed.), *Fundamentals in assistive technology* (2nd ed., pp. II-1–II-36). Arlington, VA: RESNA.

Langton, A. J., & Ramseur, H. (2001). Enhancing employment outcomes through job accommodation and assistive technology resources and services. *Journal of Vocational Rehabilitation, 16*, 27–37.

Mitchell, L. K., & Brodwin, M. G. (1995). Self-efficacy and rehabilitation counseling. *Directions in Rehabilitation Counseling, 6*, 1–4.

Phillips, B., & Zhao, H. (1993). Predictors of assistive technology abandonment. *Assistive Technology, 5*(1), 36–45.

Reed, B. J. (2002). Assistive technology. In J. D. Andrew & C. W. Faubion (Eds.), *Rehabilitation services: An introduction for the human services professional* (pp. 198–237). Osage Beach, MO: Aspen Professional Services.

Riemer-Reiss, M. L., & Wacker, R. R. (2000). Factors associated with assistive technology discontinuance among individuals with disabilities. *Journal of Rehabilitation, 66*(3), 44–50.

Rizer, B. (1999, March). *Overview of assistive technology.* Symposium presented at the conference of Technology and Persons with Disabilities sponsored by the Center on Disabilities, California State University, Northridge, CA.

Rogers, E. M. (1995). *Diffusion of innovation* (4th ed.). New York: Free Press.

Rubin, S. E., & Roessler, R. T. (2001), *Foundations of the vocational rehabilitation process* (5th ed.). Austin, TX: Pro-ed.

Santrock, J. W. (2002). *Life-span development* (8th ed.). New York: McGraw-Hill.

Schaller, J., & DeLaGarza, D. (1999): "It's about relationships:" Perspectives of people with cerebral palsy on belonging in their families, schools, and rehabilitation counseling. *Journal of Applied Rehabilitation Counseling, 30*(2), 7–18.

Scherer, M. J. (2000). *Living in the state of stuck: How technology impacts the lives of people with disabilities* (3rd ed.). Cambridge, MA: Brookline Books.

Scherer, M. J. (Ed.) (2002). *Assistive technology: Matching devices and consumers for successful rehabilitation.* Washington, DC: American Psychological Association.

Star, T. (2001). *Matching assistive technology for consumer rehabilitation: Match guidebook and referral index.* Unpublished master's thesis, California State University, Los Angeles.

Taylor, J. R., & Kopriva, P. G. (2002). Cerebral palsy. In M. G. Brodwin, F. A. Tellez, & S. K. Brodwin. (Eds.), *Medical, psychosocial, and vocational aspects of disability* (2nd ed., pp. 387–400). Athens, GA: Elliott & Fitzpatrick.

CHAPTER TWENTY-EIGHT

Changes in Attitudes Toward People With Handicaps[1]

Beatrice A. Wright

Attitudes toward people with handicaps are not isolated phenomena that stand apart from the general sweep of social change. Two of the most vital general developments since World War II have been the increased emphasis on human and civil rights for all people and the determination on the part of disadvantaged groups to speak out and act on their own behalf. Many instances could be reported illustrating these developments in the case of race, religion, sex, prisoners, ethnic groups, and the poor. The present review cites examples that apply to people with physical and mental handicaps.

AFFIRMATION OF HUMAN RIGHTS

A most important document appeared in 1948 when the General Assembly of the United Nations adopted the Universal Declaration of Human

---

From "Changes in attitudes toward people with handicaps," by B. Wright, 1973, *Rehabilitation Literature, 34,* 354–368. Copyright 1973 by the National Easter Seal Society for Crippled Children and Adults. Reprinted by permission of the Editor. Also published in *The Psychological and Social Impact of Disability,* 1st Edition, 1977.

Rights. That Declaration not only affirmed that it is possible for all of humanity to agree in general on what is important to every human being, but, more than that, it forthrightly stated that "every individual and every organ of society" has a responsibility to promote the matters contained in the Declaration.

Since then, in fact, different persons and organs of society have formulated principles to serve as guidelines for action to insure the fuller realization of human dignity. In 1973, the American Hospital Association published a "Patient's Bill of Rights" consisting of 12 points. These rights are considered to be so fundamental that every patient in a hospital setting is to be informed of them. The rights include such items as the right of the patient to respectful care and to consideration of privacy, the right to receive information necessary to give informed consent to any procedure or treatment, and the right to be advised if the hospital proposes to engage in human experimentation affecting his care. The document concludes with this significant emphasis. "No catalog of rights can guarantee for the patient the kind of treatment he has a right to expect.... [For such treatment] must be conducted with an overriding concern for the patient, and, above all, the recognition of his dignity as a human being."[3]

In addition to the rights of patients in general, a formulation of the basic rights of the mentally ill and the mentally retarded was published in 1973.[8] These rights are articulated in three broad categories, namely, the right to treatment, the right to compensation for institution-maintaining labor, and the right to education. Prototype court cases are presented to show that litigation can be a valuable tool and catalyst in protecting the rights of the mentally handicapped.

A set of 18 value-laden beliefs and principles published in 1972 provides guidelines for rehabilitation of people with disabilities.[12] The general tenor of these principles may be conveyed by citing a few of them:

1. Every individual needs respect and encouragement; the presence of a handicap, no matter how severe, does not alter these fundamental rights.
2. The assets of the person must receive considerable attention in the rehabilitation effort.
3. The active participation of the client in the planning and execution of his rehabilitation program is to be sought as fully as possible.
4. The severity of a handicap can be increased or diminished by environmental conditions.
5. Involvement of the client with the general life of the community is a fundamental principle guiding decisions concerning living arrangements and the use of resources.

6. All phases of rehabilitation have psychological aspects.
7. Self-help organizations are important allies in the rehabilitation effort.

For each of these principles, implications for action are elaborated. For example, principle 1 further asserts that "A person is entitled to the enrichment of his life and the development of his abilities whether these be great or small and whether he has a long or short time to live." "A Bill of Rights for the Disabled,"[1] published in 1972, highlights 16 rights that apply to such areas as health, education, employment, housing, transportation, and civil rights. To take transportation as an example, it is resolved that programs and standards be established for the "modification of existing mass transportation systems and the development of new specially designed demand-schedule transportation facilities."

"A Bill of Rights for the Handicapped" was recently adopted by the United Cerebral Palsy Association.[11] Among the 10 rights listed are the right to health and educational services, the right to work, the right to-barrier-free public facilities, and the right to petition social institutions and the courts to gain such opportunities as may be enjoyed by others but denied the handicapped because of oversight, public apathy, or discrimination.

Also in accord with the stress on civil rights is the recent declaration of intent by the Canadian Rehabilitation Council for the Disabled, which delineates 14 areas to which these rights pertain.[4] These areas include treatment, education, recreation, transportation, housing, spiritual development, legal rights, and economic security.

Accepting the handicapped person as a full human being means accepting him as having the full range of human needs, including those involving the sexual areas of life. The past few years have witnessed a much greater awareness of the importance of this matter. A brief summary of specialized studies and conferences in a number of countries was presented at the Twelfth World Congress of Rehabilitation International in 1972.[5] In this enlightening presentation, Chigier listed six rights with regard to sexual behavior of individuals in general and then traced the extent to which persons with disabilities are assisted or prevented from achieving these rights. Among the rights examined were the right to be informed about sexual matters, the right to sexual expression, the right to marry, and the right to become parents. While recognizing certain problems that come with greater freedom in these areas, the thrust of the analysis is directed toward constructive solutions that will enable severely disabled and mentally retarded persons to realize these rights more fully. Also in 1972, a beautiful article appeared on management of psychosexual readjustment in the cord-injured male.[7] It deals specifically with the kinds of sexual activities open to the cord-injured person and how the possibilities for sexual fulfillment can be enhanced between two people who care for each other.

Legislation helps to give reality to principles of human rights by making provision for the financing and administration of relevant services. The First International Conference on Legislation Concerning the Disabled was held in 1971. The principles guiding the recommendations reflect changing attitudes toward people with handicaps. For example, it is pointed out that "the ultimate objective of all legislation for the disabled is complete integration of the disabled in the community and to enable the disabled person to lead as normal a life as possible regardless of productive capacity."[6] The conference further emphasized that real progress can be achieved only when legislation is designed to foster "respect for the personality and human rights of the individual."[6]

MANIFESTATIONS IN PRACTICE

Fortunately, the explicit expression of principles and ideals set forth in the aforementioned documents is increasingly becoming manifest in practice. Let us consider, as an example, the concept of integration, which has been regarded as a principle that can more fully insure the realization of human rights for most people. What is necessary to appreciate is that, once integration becomes a guiding principle, certain matters were not at issue until they quickly assume vital importance. The location of institutions and the houses in which handicapped people can live becomes important, because their location within communities enables participation of the handicapped in community offerings. Architectural barriers become an issue, because their elimination enables people with a wide range of physical abilities to have access to events within buildings at large. The organization of services becomes a challenge, because integration rather than segregation is fostered when special needs can be met within general community facilities, such as hospitals, comprehensive rehabilitation centers, schools, recreation areas, churches, and community centers. Transportation assumes special significance, because integration requires that the person have a way to get to the integrated facilities that exist. And, when these issues receive sufficient attention, ways to improve the situation become apparent.

A case in point is the increasing accommodation of handicapped children within regular schools. Helping to make such integration a reality are special classes, resource teachers, and teacher aides. The following conclusion, based on a review of children with hearing impairments, is also applicable to children with other handicapping conditions: "Recent experience indicates that children can manage in the ordinary school with more severe hearing impairments than has been generally considered possible."[9] Lest there be a too-ready overgeneralization, however, I hasten to add that this conclusion does not obviate the need for special groupings of children in particular instances and for special purposes.

Integration is not an answer for all circumstances. It will ill serve handicapped children unless their special needs are met through necessary accommodations within the community setting that nurtures a climate of full respect for the dignity of each individual. Nor must integration imply that, where handicapped people are integrated within general community settings, there is no need for handicapped people to get together. Sharing and solving mutual problems, participating in specially designed activities together, and finding needed companionship are some of the rewards that can be provided by self-help, recreation, and other groups. This does not mean that people should be forced to join such groups, that the groups are appropriate for all people with handicaps, or that these groups should preempt association with people who are not handicapped. But it does mean that such groups should not be discredited as fostering segregation, as limiting adaptation to a nonhandicapped world, or as implying overconcern with personal problems. It does mean that groups like these should be valued for providing the opportunity for people to meet together, have fun together, and to affirm and assert themselves together.

A second example of change in practice is the greater involvement of people with handicaps in leadership positions in agencies working on their behalf. Agencies are increasingly recognizing that handicapped people themselves have special contributions to make in the development of services directed toward meeting the needs and enriching the lives of clients. The United Cerebral Palsy Association (UCPA), for example, has enumerated the kinds of roles that adults with cerebral palsy are especially equipped to fill by virtue of their special vantage point.[10] It is explicitly pointed out that adults with cerebral palsy should serve on boards of directors and on *all* committees, that they can help with educating parents, that they can provide constructive role models and share personal experiences with young cerebral palsied children and teenagers, and that in-service training programs for such leadership roles are important just as are other in-service training efforts. A recent survey conducted by UCPA of New York on "The Status of the Cerebral Palsied Adult as a Board, Committee, or Staff Member in UCP Affiliates" revealed that one or more cerebral palsied adults were on the Board of Directors in 24% of the 227 local agencies who replied and served as staff members in 16 percent.[10] It was urged that these percentages be increased.

A third reflection in practice of the affirmation of human dignity is the enormously significant effort on the part of people with handicaps to speak out and act on their own behalf, an effort that so clearly parallels the efforts of other minority groups. Sometimes the effort has taken the form of individual action, as in the case of a blind woman who, in 1964, filed a complaint in criminal court against being refused restaurant service because of her seeing-eye dog. Sometimes the protest involved civil disobedience, as in 1967 when a group of seven persons were refused restaurant service because four of them were blind and had guide dogs. They refused to leave the premises until, after the owner contacted the Health Department, they were allowed to remain. Sometimes the effort involved street demonstrations, as in 1970, when a group of university paraplegic students undertook a 100-mile wheelchair trek to promote employment of the handicapped.

Sometimes the effort was extended beyond a single issue to include wide-ranging problems of concern to large numbers of people with handicaps. Thus, in 1970, after winning the case of a young woman confined to a wheelchair who had been refused a teaching license, the Law institute that was involved extended its services to all cases of infringement of civil rights of the handicapped. Among these new cases were a bedridden man who was refused an absentee ballot in a federal election and a blind man who was denied a teacher's license. Recently a National Center for Law and the Handicapped was established. Sometimes the effort on the part of the handicapped solicited the support of an entire community as in the case of the Committee for the Architecturally Handicapped, organized by two University of Kansas students. Curb cuts in town and on campus, the remodeling of buildings, the revamping of architectural plans for new construction, and the appearance of the international symbol of access attest to the success of this effort.

Parent groups have had a long and impressive history of involvement on behalf of children with disabilities; currently people with handicaps themselves are gaining the sense of strength and accomplishment that comes from actively participating in advancing their own cause. The number of self-help and mutual aid groups keeps growing. There are publications by people with handicaps for people with handicaps, such as *Accent on Living, Rehabilitation Gazette* (formerly *Toomey j Gazette*), *Paraplegia News*, and *The Braille Technical Press. Stuttering*, published for specialists in the field of speech pathology, primarily consists of papers presented at an annual conference by speech pathologists who stutter. All of these efforts reflect a greater readiness on the part of people with handicaps to acknowledge their own handicaps and to become actively involved with improving their circumstances and increasing understanding of their problems.

PROSPECTS

Attitudes toward the handicapped have seen such marked change since World War II that I believe the reader will be able to guess whether the article from which the following is quoted was published before 1950 or after. It deals with the birth of a child with Down's syndrome (mongolian mental retardation):

> The problems presented by the arrival into a family of one of these accidents of development are many. . . . Because the mongolian is so incompetent in the ordinary technics of living, his mother soon becomes a complete slave to his dependency. As a result, she devotes all of her time to his necessary care, neglecting her other household duties, her other children . . . , and inevitably, her husband. The effect of all this is that all other satisfying areas of living are blotted out. . . . With the passing years, . . . [the mongol's] brothers and sisters refuse to bring other children into the house, . . . and are obsessed with a feeling of family shame no matter how unjustifiable it may be. . . . There is only one adequate way to lessen all this grief, fortunately a measure which most experienced physicians will agree to, and that is immediate commitment to an institution at the time of diagnosis. . . . When the diagnosis has been made in a newborn the mother is told that the baby is not strong enough to be brought to her at present. . . . Next, the father is asked to meet the physician immediately, bringing with him any close relatives . . . the nature of the problem is explained, . . . emphasizing its seriousness . . . and that immediate placement outside the family provides the only hope of preventing a long series of family difficulties. . . . [The mother] is asked, not to make the decision, but to accept the one which has already been made by the close relatives. . . . It means that the physician must take the lead in precipitating an immediate crisis in order to prevent much more serious difficulties later on. This is preventive medicine.[2]

The cues that one had in guessing correctly? There were many. In that article the emphasis was on institutionalizing the child rather than on seeking ways to make it feasible for him to remain with his family, at least during his early years; the main responsibility for deciding the issue rested with the physician rather than with those directly concerned, i.e., the family; gross devaluating generalizations were made concerning the devastating effects of having such a child; no consideration was given the capacity of families, with the help of community resources, to be able to accept and adapt to new circumstances. It is not likely that the article in question could be published in a responsible professional journal today, an indication of how attitudes have changed in the past quarter of a century even though, to be sure, there continue to be frequent breeches of the new directions in actual life settings.

We have seen how the ideals of human dignity and basic civil rights are being reflected in what is being said and done regarding people with handicaps. But how much can we count on continued progress? Not very much, I would argue. To assert otherwise would be to invite apathy. There is no guarantee that the right of each individual to respect and encouragement in the enrichment of his life will increasingly be honored, or that people with handicaps will increasingly have an important voice in influencing conditions that affect their lives. Although we can affirm that the changing attitudes described above are durable insofar as they are regarded as expressions of basic human rights, we must also recognize that they are fragile insofar as they are subject to the vicissitudes of broad-sweeping social and political circumstances. The lives of handicapped people are inextricably a part of a much wider socio-economic-political and ethical society affecting the lives of all people. It is therefore essential for all of us to remain vigilant to protect and extend the hard-won gains of recent decades and to be reedy to counter undermining forces. Vigilance requires thoughtful action guided by continuing reevaluation of the effectiveness of present efforts and alertness to needs of changing conditions.

REFERENCES

1. Abramson, Arthur S. and Kutner, Bernard. A Bill of Rights for the Disabled. *Arch. Phys. Med. and Rehab.* Mar., 1972. *53* :3 :99–100.

2. Aldrich, C. Anderson. Preventive Medicine and Mongolism. *Am. J. Mental Deficiency.* Oct., 1947. *52* :2 :127–129.

3. American Hospital Association. *A Patient's Bill of Rights.* Chicago : 1973. Also published as: *Statement on a Patient's Bill of Rights*; Affirmed by the Board of Trustees, Nov. 17, 1972. *Hospitals.* Feb. 16, 1973. *47* :4 :41.

4. Canadian Council for Rehabilitation of the Disabled. A Declaration of Intent. *Rehab. Digest.* Spring, 1973. *4* :4 :4–5.

5. Chigier, E. Sexual Adjustment of the Handicapped, p. 224–227, in: *Proceedings Preview: Twelfth World Congress of Rehabilitation International, Sydney, Australia.* 1972, vol. 1.

6. First International Conference on Legislation Concerning the Disabled. *Internatl. Rehab. Rev.* Second Quarter, 1972. *23* :2 :18–19, 23.

7. Hohmann, George W. Considerations in Management of Psychosexual Readjustment in the Cord Injured Male. *Rehab. Psychol.* Summer, 1972. *19* :250–58.

8. Mental Health Law Project. *Basic Rights of the Mentally Handicapped.* Washington, D.C.: Mental Health Law Project (*1751 N St., N.W., 20036*), 1973.

9. Telford, Charles W. and Sawrey, James M. *The Exceptional Individual.* (ed. 2) Englewood Cliffs, N.J.: Prentice-Hall, 1972.

10. United Cerebral Palsy Associations. Survey Shows Few CP Adults Involved in UCP Decision Making. *Crusader.* No. 6, 1971. p. 2.
11. United Cerebral Palsy Associations. A Bill of Rights for the Handicapped. *Crusader.* No. 3, 1973. p. 1, 2, 3, 4, 5, 6. Also published separately.
12. Wright, Beatrice A. Value-Laden Beliefs and Principles for Rehabilitation Psychology. *Rehab. Psychol.* Spring, *1972. 19* :1 :38–45.

PART IV

Discussion Questions

1. Outline a psychosocial intervention approach for the parents of a 19-year-old soldier who was killed in a war that they all strongly opposed. If he were disabled?
2. How can one's spirituality be a vital, ongoing, realistic resource when this individual is confronting a life-threatening illness?
3. What position are you more comfortable with: Postpone physical or cognitive aspects of rehabilitant training until those with severe disabilities work through their grieving; or, discourage those with disability from dealing with any negative emotions and stress instead the required rehabilitation training?
4. When someone realizes that a medical error has been made during rehabilitation, and this error only prolongs the period of recuperation, how can one forgive the health service providers responsible for the mistake? Is it really possible and how would the person on whom the error has been made actually proceed?
5. What would be a difference in the psychosocial intervention approaches for someone who became seriously disabled as a result of a severe hurricane and an individual who become severely disabled because of a specific terrorist activity?
6. How would an individual's level of self-esteem make a difference in the utilization of assistive technology?

PART IV

Personal Perspective

James T. Herbert

The value of tapping into one's spiritual beliefs is engagingly illustrated in Dr. Herbert's essay on his personal journey in recovering from open-heart surgery. The concepts and intervention strategies presented in the different articles of Part IV assume an everyday impact and understanding when someone is confronted with life-and-death issues. The story of Dr. Herbert's recovery experience is not necessarily told for inspiration but for its teaching and other intervention values. He provides a refreshing perspective on how to cope with the daily hassles of life postsurgery and how to gain a renewed appreciation of the ordinary and unexpected. The lessons emanating from his recovery experience resonate with all of us who are vulnerable to the uncertain effects of the unexpected.

RECOVERY AND THE REHABILITATION PROCESS: A PERSONAL JOURNEY[1]

James T. Herbert

Pennsylvania State University

On Thursday, November 7, 2002, I underwent quintuple by-pass, open heart surgery, or as my cardiac surgeon and new best friend characterized, the "grand slam of heart surgery." I am not sure if he is a baseball fan, but since this procedure was my first surgical experience, I had nothing to compare it with. Given that he was the surgeon and I was the reluctant "designated hitter," I took him at his word. While I am happy to report that my initial and subsequent recovery continues to go well, this experience provided me with an opportunity to conduct a serious inventory of my life and decide whether some changes were in order. This inventory led me to assess life lessons that I either failed to embrace or simply ignored altogether.

I thought this forum might provide the opportunity for me to share some of these lessons as they relate to being a rehabilitation counselor educator. Frankly, I am not sure whether anything that I write on this topic will have the intended impact but, at the very least, I hope what I share provides the opportunity for each of us to stop for a moment and take quick inventory of our professional lives. For some, I suppose what I share will already be obvious. For others, what I share may be dismissed quickly as personal ramblings that have no application to their lives. With apologies to educators in both groups, I am directing my thoughts to the rehabilitation counselor educator who fits somewhere in between.

CALLING ON GOD—WHERE ARE YOU?

One consequence of facing life-threatening or life-altering surgery is that it provides an opportunity to reflect on your life. For the first time, I began to think of my mortality and, in particular, my personal relationship with God. As a rehabilitation counselor educator, I do not talk about God with my students. For reasons of political correctness, religious freedom, personal insecurity, and lack of informed opinion, I have purposely stayed

From "Recovery and the rehabilitation process: A personal journey," by J. T. Herbert. *Rehabilitation Education, 17*(2), 125–132. Reprinted with permission of Rehabilitation Education.

[1] I want to thank the reviewers and co-editors for their helpful comments on the initial draft of this article.

away from any serious engagement on this topic with students. Other than the anecdotal comment that "discussing client spirituality is an important aspect of the rehabilitation process," in retrospect, I provided no clear idea of what this statement involved, how to do it, or why it may be true.

Concerning my own rehabilitation, I realize now that having a personal relationship with God was an important aspect in preparing for surgery and the recovery process. This renewed relationship started with prayer. By prayer, I am not referring to the recital of the "Lord's Prayer" and then waiting for some divine intervention to occur. Certainly, this tried and true approach works for many, but in my case, I had to find a different prayer. More often my prayers were associated with fears and doubts regarding what I was about to face, facing it, and then trying to enhance my spiritual relationship with God. There were times throughout my rehabilitation that prayer provided an important comfort to me and helped me to deal with the emotional, physical, and social aspects of illness. I would ask for comfort and peace and somehow through prayer I found it. There were other times, however, that my prayers did not provide comfort. My intentions were the same as before, but I did not achieve the same results. It was as if I was having a one-way conversation with the "Big Spirit in the Sky." I would pray for spiritual guidance and then I would wait for something—some indication for me to do something. Maybe a voice in the wind would provide a divine response ("Hey God—was that you whispering something to me?" No, it was just our two cats scratching the furniture). Maybe my "inner voice" would say something profound, but often it seemed the voice was simply me having a conversation with me ("Hey God—was that you talking to me or me talking to me?").

Listening to my inner voice was never easy given that I was always unsure who was talking and on whose authority the comments were being made. Still, if I believe that I am made in God's image then I guess it was God talking to me. (O.K., I recognize this statement reflects my personal religious belief, so we can agree to disagree on its validity.) During particularly difficult times when I would get despondent (most men do not like to use the word depressed), I would sometimes wait for a sign from God that would hopefully help. A multicolored, flashing neon sign dropping from the sky that read, "Jim, I am pleased with you—keep up the good work" would provide clear indication that God was with me. However, even this proof might be asking a bit too much from God. Lowering my expectations of divine intervention, I was willing to settle for a ceiling light flickering off and on when I asked for evidence that God did care about me. Although neither electrical communication method has occurred, I am gradually recognizing how God communicates to me by being more open to spiritual opportunities in my everyday dealings with others. My interactions to share or not share love with others, to take time and acknowledge blessings, to recognize the limits of things I cannot control, and to forgive myself and others were all opportunities to experience a spiritual connection with God. It is not my intention to confuse the issue of religious versus spiritual beliefs and impose my personal beliefs of whom and what God means in this narrative (earlier exception noted). History is replete with examples of personal and social tragedies with each side believing that "God is with us."

On a smaller scale and having direct relevance to my work as a rehabilitation counselor educator, my recent personal experience with illness provided me with new spiritual insights and how I might incorporate them when working with students. For instance, in my supervised clinical practicum, I plan to ask questions that, up to now, were left unexplored. Examples of questions include:

1. What are your views about a higher spiritual power? Have they remained the same over your life? If they have changed, what events have impacted on them?
2. How do your spiritual views impact your daily interactions with people you work with and the people you plan to serve during your professional careers?
3. Are there situations where it is appropriate or inappropriate to discuss your personal spiritual beliefs with your clients or have them discuss their views with you?
4. What aspects are uncomfortable when discussing spiritual beliefs with others?

As I have not addressed these questions in prior supervision experiences, I have no idea what might follow. At the very least, I hope that asking such questions will lead to a better understanding of how spiritual beliefs are as fundamental as inquiring about other personal, social, medical, and vocational aspects of disability and illness. Regardless of one's spiritual or religious beliefs, it is an area that can have tremendous importance to individuals we work with and, if rehabilitation counselors are willing to open the door on the topic, it offers promise for helping others.

TIME KEEPS ON TICKING

Exploring one's spiritual beliefs eventually leads to the issue of mortality, a difficult topic to address with colleagues, family, and friends when facing serious illness. Each of us recognizes that we have finite time to be here, yet there is an undeniably irrational aspect that suggests the contrary. Just like the old Timex© watch commercial, we assume that we will just "keep on ticking." Suspending the belief of reincarnation for a moment, if one assumes that the present lifetime is your one and only chance to "get it right," I started considering questions such as: "Why did I get this illness and what happens if things do not work out as planned?" "What kind of life have I made for myself and the people I love?" "What did I value throughout my life and how did I recognize its importance?" "Who loves me and how have I loved them in return?" "What kinds of changes do I want to make and what obstacles stand in the way of making beneficial changes?" and "How will I find ways to overcome these obstacles?"

To the extent you have supportive family and friends and your willingness to examine these questions provides you with an opportunity for sobering answers. Some of the rediscovered answers made me realize that I spent too much time and energy on things I could not control. I found that I worried too much and too often about small matters that caused a great deal of personal and professional angst. I allowed work to comprise too much of my personal identity and account for too much of my life activities. Having a healthy career is one thing, but when the hospital social worker asks how you spend your free time and you can't come up with a single avocational activity that provides personal joy, it may be time to reconsider your life balance.

An important step in reevaluating my professional identity and the effort to achieve and maintain it started with the recognition that I do not have all the time in the world: When you start thinking about your life clock and accept the notion that you have limited control on life longevity, you tend to approach the future differently. For a start, you question whether, in fact, there will be a future and, if so, how long? Since none of us knows the answer to this question, the simple recognition that "life goes on without you" is hard to comprehend. Having a serious illness, however, gets you started thinking about the future. In my case, although a positive surgical outcome was expected, there was no guarantee and, in addition, I had to prepare as best I could that more serious injury or death could result from having the surgery. Discussing these possibilities, while unpleasant, sometimes results in people reminding you that your chances of having a successful outcome far exceed that of less successful outcomes. Usually, if I would discuss any doubts about negative surgical outcomes, I would be reminded, "Look, you have a 95% chance that everything is going to work out fine." When I heard this attempt to calm my fears, I sometimes felt like responding, "Suppose I asked you to choose one of 20 playing cards and that one of the cards, if selected, would kill you. Do you still want to play?" When I first learned of my illness, I could not imagine anything more frightening and, like Woody Allen, my thoughts on the whole matter could be summed by saying, "It's not that I'm afraid to die, I just don't want to be there when it happens." Eventually, I came to recognize that while death or more serious injury (heart attack, stroke) was an unlikely outcome, I must be prepared (as best I could) to meet either outcome whether it occurred now or sometime later. Although this obvious realization sounds very rational, the process in getting to this point involved a great deal of emotional expression and spiritual effort.

Perhaps in our discussions regarding death and dying with students, there are academic exercises intended to bring into consciousness the realization of the seemingly short time that all of us share on this planet and intended life contributions each of us wants to make. We might ask our students to imagine what information would their tombstone epitaphs contain, what would be written in their obituaries, what families and friends would say about them publicly and privately after their deaths, and/or if they had one week to live—how would they spend their time? Such discussions provide insight as to how students perceive themselves, what they value, and what may be missing in their current lives. Although I did not complete any written narratives to address these questions, I often initiated internal dialogues when imagining these scenarios. By doing so, I found the experience provided me with a better appreciation of the ordinary. This realization is not cognitively profound but, on an emotional and spiritual level, it reminded me that basic, ordinary appreciation of life is a difficult concept to implement each day. As my medical condition improves with each month, I find that it is a lesson that needs constant reminding.

EVENTUAL APPRECIATION OF THE ORDINARY AND UNEXPECTED

There is a litany of metaphors and sayings that address the essential point of appreciating the everyday things in life including the unexpected occurrences that arise. The familiar phrase "Take time to smell the roses" comes to mind. Prior to my surgery, my approach to life could be described more in keeping with, "So, this is a rose. It sure is pretty. Hey, what about those daisies over there—could they use a little mulch?" It is hard to appreciate roses when you are more concerned about tending to the entire garden. During my recovery, I could think of many missed opportunities where I failed to slow down, observe what was around me and appreciate the ordinary but simple pleasures that life offers. As my recuperation progressed, the ordinary activities such as taking a hot shower, walking in the woods, playing checkers with my son, and talking with my wife were experiences that I appreciated more than ever before. In order to help me appreciate the mundane and miraculous, I take a few brief moments throughout each day to conduct a short and simple prayer of thanks. It allows me to be more present in the moment and gain a better appreciation of life. Taking this time accomplishes what singer/song writer Paul Simon referred to when he wrote, "Slow down. You move too fast. You've got to make the moments last." Making moments last—I guess if a film company could turn this phrase into a successful advertising campaign then it should be good enough for me.

Although I failed to recognize that having a serious illness could be a gift in disguise, like any adaptation process, time changes perspectives. When I first learned the extent of my illness, my prayers were directed at hoping that I would undergo "no more than an angioplasty with a stent or two." I thought if I could get by with this medical procedure then it would be sufficient in not only improving my physical health but also my spiritual well being. In essence, I was asking God that if you let me get out of this medical jam with limited complications and easy recovery; I would promise to become better spiritually. Anyone recognize some "bargaining" here? Although I had no clear idea of what becoming better spiritually meant, at the time, it seemed sincere if not misguided.

When learning that this procedure was not viable, and that more invasive surgery was in order, my reality went through another adjustment phase. The usual fears and resolution to having the surgery were quickly forgotten when I successfully emerged from the operation. A deep sense of gratitude of having a second chance at life was the central theme. Gradually, this feeling dissipated when I returned home. The physical pain, dependence on others, lack of energy, and, to my amazement, an internal debate about the merits of my surgical outcome contributed to depression. As my physical condition continued to improve, along with continued family support and prayer, I have gradually recognized the benefits of having bypass surgery. I firmly believe that I would not have devoted any serious efforts in making the kinds of life changes that I needed to make without having by-pass surgery. My attempts to develop a greater spiritual presence each day, to think more carefully about life choices I make, and to put forth effort to achieve a more satisfying life all occurred because of this experience. For now, the major task at hand is to retain this perspective as my recovery continues.

REMEMBERING REHABILITATION LESSONS

At this point of my rehabilitation, I have finished my cardiac outpatient program and I am completing the wellness program that follows. I am participating in Weight Watchers© and learning that the dietary changes

I need to make are lifelong. I also purposefully sought and I am working with a counselor who emphasizes spiritual growth (which, from his
perspective, includes everything). You would think with all of these support systems in place that it affords me the opportunity to institute some
healthier life changes. It does. Taking time to work on yourself sounds
like an opportunity of a lifetime. It is. Still, the greatest challenge for me
as I am now seven months post-surgery is to remember the life lessons
gained from this experience.

Holding on and building upon these gains is the current challenge at
hand. Already I realize that it is very easy to slip into some earlier practices
that contributed to coronary artery disease. One maladaptive practice is
a lack of patience that I have for myself. For example, several months
ago I engaged in physical activity that my cardiologist reprimanded me
for when I shared the fact that "I shoveled snow for several hours but
I took my time." When shoveling, I distinctly remember thinking how
wonderful it was to be able to perform this type of physical activity without experiencing profuse sweating, shortness of breath, and pain down
my left arm. I also thanked God for allowing me to engage in this activity. Despite my attempt to connect physical and spiritual well being, my
cardiac professionals saw things a bit differently. Apparently, my body
tended to agree with them as I paid for my physical/spiritual experience
over the next several days. As an additional reminder of not hurrying the
healing process, the next day's lead chapter in the local newspaper contained a story concerning several persons with cardiac problems who died
while shoveling snow. O.K., so I remain a little slow on the uptake, but
I think my recent indiscretion was because I wanted to reclaim an earlier
lifestyle. I am relearning that while this reclamation can be beneficial in
certain instances, in this case, it was not the best idea.

IMPLICATIONS FOR MY CAREER AS A REHABILITATION COUNSELOR EDUCATOR

When I return to work next academic year, I want to avoid making the
same mistakes that contributed to an unhealthy lifestyle. As it pertains to
work, it is my intention to remember past lessons that I have learned as a
result of illness and recovery. Those lessons have to do with feeling more
comfortable about asking for help, developing a greater connection with
a higher spiritual power, and placing less emphasis on my career in order
to have a more balanced life.

Most of the hassles associated with being an academic are related
to obtaining appropriate program resources, negotiating faculty issues
within the department, addressing student concerns, fulfilling professional

and administrative responsibilities, and balancing teaching, research, and professional service commitments. How well I met those challenges was often associated with how well I was able to effectively use the skills and talents of colleagues. Although I recognize this interdependence, it remains a concept that is sometimes difficult to practice especially as it concerns the issue of asking for help from colleagues. I find it interesting that asking for help as it related to my accomplishing individual rehabilitation goals was much easier than asking for help at work. Given conversations that I have with colleagues at other university settings, it seems that my predicament is not unique.

Part of the difficulty in asking for help is associated with the work climate that we perpetuate as academics—one that stresses individual achievement and independence (Herbert, 2001). In this type of setting, asking for help is viewed as a sign of weakness or incompetence and, by doing so, we are admitting that we are vulnerable (human)—an aspect that we try very hard to avoid. Being vulnerable necessitates sharing our thoughts and feelings with our colleagues. It requires us to get closer to one another even when there are obstacles that make it difficult. As I wrote in an earlier editorial (Herbert, 1984), this task would seem fairly easy given our academic training. Yet, how many times have we experienced faculty and student conflicts where we did not employ the same effective listening skills we taught in our counseling skills classes? Sometimes I ask myself, "How come I can demonstrate listening skills within a difficult client-counselor role-play exercise to my students but I cannot apply the same conditions with a work colleague who is stressed about a particular issue?"

Whether it is a fear of offending someone, an inability to see beyond my own perspective, or some other reason, my recent experience has reminded me that the only person I can change is me. Yes, I know that statement is an espoused mantra that we communicate to our students, but in trying to apply it to my future work I need to remind myself of the obvious. Further, in situations where I start to feel overwhelmed, I want to validate that it is OK to ask for and receive help. A simple declaration such as "I would like some help with _____. Can you help me?" is the first step. It took an illness to remind me that it is necessary to repeat it more often when I return to work.

Another outcome that resulted from this life-altering experience was the realization that there was great potential for me to have a stronger connection to God while I am working. Prior to my recent medical excursion, I cannot recall a single incident where I invoked prayer to help me in addressing a work problem. Certainly, there were plenty of opportunities to ask for help in being more patient with my students, more receptive to dissenting views, and more forgiving about personal shortcomings that manifest themselves at work. What seems so obvious now was completely missing in my daily work interactions. For me, God was an occasional afterthought who would only be considered in times of crises. Fortunately, while work can be trying, there was never any time during my academic life that represented a crisis or, at least, one that I would recognize as such. Besides, why would God care about my work problems? As a result, I did not ask for any spiritual help as I saw that aspect as totally disconnected to my work life. Sure, I could recite a prayer at the family dinner table or right before I went to sleep but asking for God's help at work?

Given my recent experience, however, I anticipate that there will be many occasions when I will ask or share some simple prayer at work. I anticipate that my prayers will ask God to help me listen better, forgive my own as well as others' shortcomings, and demonstrate patience in handling everyday work stress. I also anticipate giving prayers of thanks for the people I come in contact with each day that bring joy in my life. Through prayer, meditation, or reflection we have an untapped resource that is always available. As a rehabilitation counselor educator, it is my intention when I return next academic year to take a few moments each day to ask for that help. If nothing else, taking a few moments to collect your thoughts and declare honorable intentions to deal with the work conflicts and demands usually produces a calming effect. We all need a little more peace in our lives.

As I noted earlier, an important impact of my recent experience has resulted in rethinking the importance that work has played in my life. At this point, I need to reevaluate and question roles and responsibilities I have taken on at program, department, college, university, and professional levels. For starters, I made the decision to resign as Professor-in-Charge of the Rehabilitation Programs. This decision was both easy and difficult. Easy in the sense of acknowledging that it is time to tone down the importance that work has played in my life; difficult in the sense of letting go and having someone else assume a professional role that I have performed for nearly 13 years. "Passing the torch" signifies a time to let go that requires me to lead in a supportive rather than a proactive role. I expect that giving up perceived administrative control for a program will be difficult during those first several faculty meetings as I believe there will be a natural tendency for me to think, "How would I have handled that situation or that problem?" I imagine there is a natural tendency for most of us who assume administrative roles to believe that we are the best ones to perform these duties. With the successful transition from starting as a pre-tenured assistant professor to achieving subsequent tenure and promotion to associate and then full professor usually comes with increasing administrative responsibilities. Whether the same requirements to successfully negotiate this career path are the identical ones that make an outstanding administrator is questionable.

Working as an effective rehabilitation counselor educator does not guarantee that one also performs equally well as a program administrator. Certainly I made my share of mistakes in trying to do what I thought was best for the rehabilitation program. The current task for me, it seems, will be to have patience and show support for my colleague who most likely will experience a similar growth curve.

FINAL THOUGHT

I would like to finish this chapter with a brief story that reminds me of the work that lies ahead. Before my surgery, I was trying to tell my 6-year-old son what was about to happen. I did not want to worry him, yet I also wanted to explain in terms that he could understand why Dad needed surgery. I used a metaphor of how water from the kitchen faucet is decreased when debris gets clogged in the filter screen. I told him that the water pipes represented my heart arteries and that the water symbolized my blood. I also told him that my doctor was "kind of like a plumber who was going to clean and fix Dad's heart pipes." I thought I had reached him with this analogy and, after a few moments, I asked him if he understood. He understood in more ways than I anticipated. As he was sitting next to me, he placed his small hand on my heart and said, "Yes, Daddy's heart is blossoming. Just like a flower in a garden." Tears came to my eyes. He sure was right. Dad's heart continues to blossom.

REFERENCES

Herbert, J. T. (1984). From attitudes to academe: Can they change? [Editorial]. *Rehabilitation Education, 8,* 101–102.

Herbert, J. T. (2001). Thoughts on becoming a rehabilitation counselor educator. [Gray Matter]. *Rehabilitation Education, 15,* 307–315.

Perspective Exercise 4
Trauma Helicopter

PERSPECTIVE

All families are greatly relieved when a family member survives the initial stages of a trauma and is given the opportunity to continue life. This initial relief and joy often turns to distress and sadness when a family realizes that the person they knew left them when the injury occurred and now they are faced with the ongoing challenge of getting to know and accept a person who is a total or partial stranger. This often occurs when extraordinary and heroic efforts have less than ordinary or normal results. Although not disputing the motive and miraculous outcomes of most trauma rescue flights, some have resulted in complex situations for families.

EXPLORATION

1. Are there situations when medical care should be withheld at the scene of an accident?
2. How would you help a family who was enraged that their child was "saved" and must spend the rest of his/her life in a coma management unit?
3. Should a hospital or its personnel be responsible for the long-term care and financial costs if they resuscitate a person without the family's approval?

PART V

New Directions: Issues and Perspectives

Introduction to Part V

The selected articles included in Part I through Part IV of this fifth edition illustrate current theories, concepts, and approaches in the delivery of rehabilitation services. These articles identify issues and practices that represent another step from a rehabilitation past that has produced legislative policies and intervention styles directed toward providing a better quality of life for those with a disability. But this foundational past and the ever-evolving present, generating newer ideas and reformulating the meaning of disability itself, have provided markers to guide the growth of rehabilitation as it confronts significant, future issues. The articles of Part V were chosen to inform the reader about these important topics.

These articles highlight domains that invite new directions in rehabilitation. They also convey a sharp, bright color tone that hopefully will be imbued into the rehabilitation landscape for the next several decades. Included in the article titles are such positive words as "wellness, successful, promise, and recovery." All of these terms suggest the continuing development of newer, rehabilitation strategies, a focus on populations who have been underserved for vocational rehabilitation services, and attention to helping perspectives that may challenge the traditional mindset of professionals. Another article in Part V offers a necessary, timely overview to professionals of provocative issues related to euthanasia and physician-assisted suicide. Further, also included is a article by Dell Orto and Power, published in 2004 in *Families Living with Chronic Illness and Disability*, that places the rehabilitation past in a functional context, maximizes the opportunities of the present, and anticipates a rehabilitation future nurtured by optimism.

Yet, with the discussion of differing viewpoints on selected topics, these articles and the personal perspective do generate such themes as: (a) What are the psychosocial influences on recovery and life adaptation; (b) what are the challenges for the helping professional when attempting to implement new intervention approaches that emerge from reformulated rehabilitation concepts, policies, and paradigms; and (c) what actually can contribute effectively to a better quality of life for a person with a disability? Each is a question that invites the reader to consider how the future can bring help to those living with and often beyond the disability experience. The questions also provoke a reflection on what are the important, positive dimensions that must be confronted and perhaps resolved by the helping professional working in the 21st century.

This positive perspective is comprehensively discussed in Marini and Chacon's article: "The Implications of Positive Psychology and Wellness for Rehabilitation Counselor Education." The authors move away from the disease model of human functioning toward a focus on those unique qualities in healthy persons that lead to overall wellness. These qualities can consist of internal and external factors, each of which is elaborated on in their article. To be noted is that the authors' words are actually intended for professionals other than rehabilitation educators. This larger audience is implied by the authors' message: that for all those with a disability and for all the persons who are assisting them, wellness factors can be emphasized during the rehabilitation process. The article represents a challenge to helping professionals to explore and utilize these factors during helping efforts.

Minkler and Fadem's article, "Successful Aging: A Disability Perspective," presents a stimulating paradox that demands reflection for understanding this neglected topic. Successful aging, a positive achievement in itself, may, instead of reducing discrimination, only maintain the stigmatization and marginalization of those with substantial physical disabilities who are also aged. The three characteristics of successful aging are discussed, and the authors demonstrate that in spite of "aging well," by virtue of their disabilities this aging population still is discriminated against because the criteria for aging well are so narrowly defined. The authors, consequently, advocate for a broader ecological approach, moving beyond the successful aging paradigm. The older person with serious physical impairments can balance the losses with gains and seek to be perceived, not as someone who cannot function because of impairment but more importantly as one who needs an accommodation in order to function. This proposed new paradigm invites the attention of the reader because of its profound implications for rehabilitation practice.

An article by Smart on "The Promise of the International Classification of Functioning, Disability, and Health (ICF)," might appear as too theoretical as a useful tool in service delivery. But the author illustrates the benefits of a functional approach and indicates that disability should be understood more than as a medical diagnosis and really acknowledged as a subjective experience. This article challenges the total, exclusive acceptance of the medical model and presents a refreshing discussion on those issues related to more productive rehabilitation practice. This discussion is in harmony with existing vocational rehabilitation services that emphasize the individual and his or her work functions. This article also alerts the readers to the international classification of functioning that includes activities of daily living and recreation, in addition to work. Such a classification, according to the author, can serve as a catalyst for research which will become less medically and diagnostically driven, an opportunity for individuals with disabilities to be empowered to make more independent choices, and an incentive for collaboration among professionals. The classification arouses expectations for a future that promises more consumer satisfaction with rehabilitation services.

The word "recovery" is often understood, when applied to those with mental illness, in a restricted manner. It should not be limited to simply a successful rehabilitation outcome. Nemec and Gagne, in their article "Recovery From Psychiatric Disabilities," broaden the definition to include other quality-of-life factors, such as living in a comfortable home, having a conviction that life is worth living, and establishing close relationships. The authors also explain the distinctions among rehabilitation, adjustment, and recovery. They pinpoint the variables that can facilitate the broader process of recovery and include a section on the spiritual factors in recovery. Implications for practice are emphasized, with a focus on goal setting, responding to the service needs of the individual with mental illness, and developing a trusting relationship between the user and provider of rehabilitation services. This article affirms the belief that if this population is to have hope and higher expectations for a more fulfilling quality of life, then the helping professional should also possess not only the hope and positive expectations but also the knowledge of the recovery process and those facilities that can improve living with the mental disability.

Two articles discuss adaptation and recovery goals for those with either a mental or a physical disability. Livneh and Parker, in their article "Psychological Adaptation to Disability: Perspectives From Chaos and Complexity Theory," believe that the process of adaptation to an illness or disability condition is a process of self-organization that unfolds through the experiences of chaos and complexity. Though the literature is only beginning to emerge on chaos and complexity theories, the authors describe the usefulness of these theories in the context of illness and disability. The authors maintain that psychosocial adaptation can be perceived as a dynamic, nonlinear, and unpredictable process in which the individual undergoes four transitions, each of which is explained. Four models of adaptation are also reviewed, and Livneh and Parker advocate the consumer use of self-organization in psychosocial adaptation. For those who adopt this viewpoint, including the tenets of chaos and complexity theories, diverse intervention strategies are suggested. The theories offer a broad framework for interventions, which can be flexibly implemented according to individual needs. These articles should stimulate the reader to seriously consider the presented viewpoints, which when utilized could make a difference for psychosocial adaptation.

One of the more currently debated, controversial issues has rapidly evolved from the practice of eugenics, euthanasia, and physician-assisted suicide. Zanskas and Coduti provide a context for understanding both these practices and the intense debate in their article: "Eugenics, Euthanasia, and Physician-Assisted Suicide: An Overview for Rehabilitation Professions." The authors define eugenics, euthanasia, and physician-assisted suicide, in the historical milieu in which these current definitions developed. Conceptual models, international perspectives, social and ethical considerations, and economic aspects, as related to these debated terms, are further discussed. Implications for practice are suggested which accentuate the importance of educating individuals about options and resources that can make the decision to live with a disability more manageable. Unfortunately, according to Zanskas and Coduti, rehabilitation professionals have generally been absent from the discussion of the primary topics addressed in this article. But a careful reading of this article will bring an initial understanding of the important issues related to eugenics, euthanasia, and physician-assisted suicide. Knowledge can induce a greater awareness of their implications for consumer decision making and one's reasonable quality of life.

A chapter from an earlier publication by Power and Dell Orto was included in this Part V because it contains information that generates reflections on future coping and adaptation strategies for those with a disability. The variables of expectations, compassion, hope, and spirituality are particularly identified and discussed because they are dimensions that need to be considered when planning future disability policies and intervention paradigms. Though the population focus of the article is on families of those with mental or physical disabilities, the article reflections can be applied to all individuals with a disability. Importantly, myths that can be associated with the disability experience are also explained because they must be acknowledged when developing appropriate, helping approaches. The perspectives offered in the article for the delivery of rehabilitation services challenge the creative efforts of helping professionals. But the challenge is an invitation to the reader to understand those issues that can make a difference in how one can manage the living demands of illness and disability.

A "classic" article written by Irving Zola, and included in the third edition of the *Psychological and Social Impact of Disability"* in 1991, briefly addresses the questions: "How big a problem is disability?" and

"Is disability the same as it always was?" The author's reflections in the article "Aging and Disability: Toward a Unified Agenda" provide a predictive fact that the number of people with disabilities will only increase. Also, because of technological advances and the growing understanding of the fit between any impairment and the larger social environment, the meaning of disability is not the same today as it was 15 years ago. Awareness of this growth and environmental interaction offer a relevant incentive for the development of rehabilitation policies. Acceptance by the rehabilitation community of these policies and intervention strategies can bring a future of hope and promise to those with disabilities.

CHAPTER TWENTY-NINE

The Implications of Positive Psychology and Wellness for Rehabilitation Counselor Education

Irmo Marini and Mitka Chacon

The impact of a congenital or adventitious disability on an individual and his or her family poses many challenges regarding psychosocial adjustment, vocational options, and independent living functioning. In situations where a disability is relatively stable (e.g., spinal cord injury, amputation), planning for the future may not be as ambiguous or anxiety provoking as it may be for persons with unstable or uncertain diagnoses (e.g., multiple sclerosis, Alzheimer's disease). However, there are many instances where persons with stable disabilities succumb to secondary complications on a regular basis, whereas others with similar disabilities experience few, if any, further health-related problems throughout the remainder of their lives (Antonovsky, 1987).

Antonovsky (1987) distinguished between those individuals who regularly become ill (i.e., a pathological orientation) and those who remain basically healthy despite a severe disability (i.e., a salutogenic orientation). In treating persons with disabilities, a pathological orientation has

From "The implications of positive psychology and wellness for rehabilitation counselor education," by I. Marini and M. Chacon, 2002, *Rehabilitation Education, 16*(2), 149–164. Reprinted with permission of Rehabilitation Education.

traditionally been the focus for medical and mental health professionals (Trieschmann, 1981). Stereotypical beliefs and attitudes toward persons with disabilities as being sick, incapable, and dependent have likely facilitated this approach to treatment (Marini, 1994).

Rehabilitation counselor practice and education originated from the medical model, or a pathological orientation as well (Olkin, 1999; Trieschmann, 1981; Vash, 1981). The public vocational rehabilitation program's philosophy of assisting persons with disabilities to reach their maximum potential is a noble cause, but the program has never really been mandated to explore which factors are indicative of clients with disabilities who not only succeed but excel in all areas of their lives.

In exploring factors related to disability and wellness, many of the debilitating primary disabling conditions as well as their secondary complications found today can actually be minimized or even eliminated if individuals with disabilities were to adopt a wellness lifestyle (Pelletier, 1994; Schafer, 1996). Conditions such as high blood pressure, heart disease, coronary artery disease, rheumatoid arthritis, gastrointestinal disorders, alcohol and substance abuse, anxiety disorders, and stroke all carry self-induced aspects with them (Pelletier). Pelletier described the field of psychoneuroimmunology as the study of the mind–body connection and how what we think can directly and indirectly affect our physical health status.

This paper addresses some of the key research findings related to positive psychology and wellness by exploring significant factors of healthy individuals and their interaction with the environment. Specifically, what individual traits and practices appear to be related to mental and physical well-being, and what environmental conditions are necessary to nurture wellness in individuals? Research findings in these areas are then discussed with respect to potentially new and emerging areas of disability-related research for rehabilitation educators and areas of practice for rehabilitation counselors.

POSITIVE PSYCHOLOGY AND WELLNESS

The January 2000 issue of *American Psychologist* was devoted to the concept of happiness, excellence, and optimal human functioning. In that issue, American Psychological Association President Martin Seligman and Mihaly Csikszentmihalyi defined the field of positive psychology as being "about valued subjective experiences; well-being, contentment and satisfaction (in the past); hope and optimism (for the future); and flow and happiness (in the present)" (p. 5). At the individual level, positive personal traits such as subjective well-being, optimism, happiness, perseverance, and self-determination are contributing factors to wellness (Csikzentmi-halyi, 1990, 1999; Peterson, 1998; Peterson, Seligman, & Vaillant, 1988; Ryan & Deci, 2000; Seligman & Csikszentmihalyi, 2000; Weisse, 1992). On the environmental level, social support, a sense of belonging, faith in a higher power, having basic financial needs met, and perceived mastery or harmony with one's environment are main external factors contribut-ing to wellness (Argyle, 1986; Dohrenwend et al., 1982; Koenig, 1997; Mathews & Larson, 1997; Pavot, Diener, & Fujita, 1990).

Wellness is defined as "living well—mentally, spiritually and physi-cally—with illness, whether temporary or chronic" (Schafer, 1996, p. 37). Schafer further described a wellness lifestyle as one that includes taking care of the environment; effectively managing emotional problems; think-ing critically; maintaining a stable emotional state; spiritual wellness, as in having meaning or purpose; physical habits, including exercise and nu-trition; social habits, as in sharing intimacy and establishing good friend-ships; and time-management habits, such as maintaining a stable work pace and developing control over one's time and choices.

This section explores some of the major findings and concepts related to internal and external factors supportive of positive psychology and wellness. Where relevant, research findings regarding persons with dis-abilities is integrated with the concept being discussed. The central issue here pertains to how rehabilitation educators can begin to conceptualize researching/teaching about disability and adopt a salutogenic orientation.

INTERNAL FACTORS

Subjective Well-Being

The concept of subjective well-being (SWB) relates to individuals' cogni-tive and affective evaluations of their lives (Diener, 2000). It is not the nature of events themselves that elicit well-being, but rather our interpre-tation of these events. Three key concepts imbued in SWB, according to Diener, are adaptation, goals, and temperament. Regarding adaptation, Diener stated that we are on a hedonic treadmill where, once we have ob-tained a possession or accomplishment, we quickly habituate to this level and it no longer makes us happy. Conversely, when people experience misfortune, they also soon adapt emotionally (Brickman & Campbell, 1971). Silver (1982) found that persons with spinal cord injuries reported to be very unhappy immediately following their injuries, but then began to return to a baseline level of adaptation within 8 weeks.

Striving for realistic goals and movement toward obtaining one's goals is also important to SWB, as well as feelings of competence and self-esteem (Cantor & Sanderson, 1999; Diener, 2000). Bandura (1997) described self-efficacy in relation to how individuals feel about their ability or skills to achieve certain goals (efficacy expectations), in relation to the perceived rewards for putting forth the effort to obtain these goals (outcome expectations). If the perceived rewards are not worth the effort, an individual's motivation to pursue the goal is diminished. Marini and Stebnicki (1999) found support for this theory, noting that Social Security Disability Income beneficiaries often report that it is not financially worth the effort to leave disability rolls for minimum wage work and the risk of re-injury as well as the potential loss of health benefits.

One's temperament also appears to be related to SWB. Schafer (1996) cited a number of traits correlated with wellness, such as Type B behavior pattern (an absence of time urgency and hostility), trust in others, hardiness (liking a challenge, strong sense of commitment and a sense of control), a survivor personality (having grown stronger from some personal crisis), a sense of humor with the ability to laugh at oneself, and self-actualization.

Optimism

Optimism has been defined by Tiger (1979) as "a mood or attitude associated with an expectation about the social or material future—one which the evaluator regards as socially desirable, to his or her advantage, or for his or her pleasure" (p. 18). Peterson (2000) stated that optimism has been correlated with positive mood, effective problem solving, good health, longer life, and occupational and academic success (Peterson, 1988). Conversely, pessimism has been correlated with passivity, failure, morbidity and mortality, anxiety and depression.

Buchanan and Seligman (1995) described optimism in terms of an individual's characteristic explanatory style or how he or she attributes the causes of undesirable or poor outcome events. Optimists typically describe such undesirable events as having an external influence with specific causes, whereas pessimists describe undesirable events as being due to something internal and having a global cause. If an individual's response is unrelated to the outcome, this leads to learned helplessness. Seligman's (1991) research has led him to conclude that optimists respond to adversity by asserting internal control whenever feasible, become depressed less often, maintain better health habits, have a stronger immune system, and are healthier. Seligman further concluded that individuals can learn and unlearn to be optimistic or pessimistic.

Taylor (1983) formulated "cognitive adaptation theory," which evolved from interviewing women with breast cancer. Taylor found that those who had "unrealistic" positive beliefs about controlling their prognosis were not negatively affected when learning otherwise. Taylor and Brown (1988) noted that humans have three positive illusions—self-enhancement, unrealistic optimism, and an exaggerated perception of personal control—which have a positive psychological effect. Positive beliefs have additionally been associated with a stronger immune system whereby the type of belief (if positive) affects our emotional state and impacts our neuroendocrine system by eliminating bodily viruses or disease (Stone, Cox, Valdimarsdottir, Jandorf, & Neale, 1987).

The concept of unrealistic optimism is an interesting one because it fundamentally refutes past strategies of therapeutic treatment whereby clients are counseled to accept their disabilities. Freud (1928) believed that optimism was illusory and came with the cost of denying one's reality. According to Akhtar (1996), one of the defining features of a healthy individual is for him or her to be exposed to the reality of the situation no matter how painful. Current research regarding wellness, however, suggests otherwise (Peterson, 2000). Lazurus (1983) described positive denial as being a factor related to wellness in the presence of adversity. It appears that being overly optimistic about one's future (e.g., health, career) may contribute to a healthy immune system.

Conversely, some researchers believe that unrealistic optimism may have adverse effects on wellness (Oettingen, 1996). Oettingen stated that overly optimistic persons who believe they will not become ill may postpone or neglect visiting a doctor when they experience symptoms. Cigarette smokers, for example, may ignore or discount the harmful effects of smoking by adopting a bias or creating cognitive dissonance that they are not susceptible to the risks associated with smoking (Gibbons, Eggleston, & Benthin, 1997).

Self-Determination Theory

Self-determination theory is a widely researched and written-about approach to human motivation and personality (Ryan & Deci, 2000). It is the investigation of individuals' inherent growth tendencies and innate psychological needs that provide the basis for self-motivation and personality integration. Ryan and Deci defined three psychological needs: autonomy, competence and relatedness as concepts of self-determination. When these needs are met, an individual is self-motivated and mentally healthy. Environmental factors, however, can impede personal growth, well-being, and self-motivation (Ryan & Deci). For example, accessibility barriers and negative societal attitudes toward disability may thwart the growth and motivation of a person with a disability.

Autonomy in this context does not equate to independence but rather to the feeling of mastery one feels when completing a task without assistance. Competence refers to the feelings derived from performing something well, doing it with ease, and being recognized for the work (Harter, 1978). Relatedness refers to perceived support and security from significant others (Ryan & Grolnick, 1986). When we believe there is support available to assist if needed, we feel more secure in pursuing certain goals (Frodi, Bridges, & Grolnick, 1985).

Deci and Ryan (1985) postulated cognitive evaluation theory (CET) as a subtheory to self-determination theory. CET relates to social and environmental factors that facilitate or undermine an individual's intrinsic motivation. The conditions for well–being are more conducive when people are intrinsically motivated toward some goal as opposed to being extrinsically motivated. Intrinsic motivation is facilitated when autonomy, relatedness and competence are present. Ryan and Deci (2000) stated that positive feedback and rewards can enhance competence and intrinsic motivation. Kasser and Ryan (1993, 1996) found that individuals who placed great importance on intrinsic aspirations were more likely to exhibit indicators related to well-being, self-esteem, and self-actualization. The same study showed a negative relationship between a low importance rating of intrinsic aspirations and higher levels of anxiety and depression.

Ryan and Deci (2000) noted, however, that in many instances people are driven by extrinsic motivating factors such as threats, coercion, deadlines, and externally imposed goals. Individuals who are driven or externally motivated by environmental factors, will as a consequence, be inhibited in developing a sense of competence, autonomy, or well-being (deCharms, 1968).

Adaptive Mental Mechanisms

Vaillant (2000) described adaptive mental mechanisms as another internal factor related to positive psychology. Vaillant has identified five adaptive coping mechanisms found at the mature end of the Defensive Function Scale of the *Diagnostic and Statistical Manual of Mental Disorders-IV* (American Psychiatric Association, 1994). Lazurus and Folkman (1984) noted that individuals intentionally use conscious cognitive strategies to make the best of a bad situation. In addition, there are involuntary mental mechanisms that distort our perception of reality to reduce subjective distress.

The five adaptive defense mechanisms that Vaillant (2000) discussed are anticipation, altruism, humor, sublimation, and suppression. Vaillant indicated that adaptive defenses and healthy denial are synonymous. These defenses are independent of social class, education, and intelligence, and they become more salient as we move from adolescence into midlife

(Vaillant, 1977). Altruism refers to deriving pleasure from giving to or helping others. Sublimation is defined as a way of indirectly resolving a conflict without adverse consequences or loss of pleasure. Vaillant (2000) described how Beethoven, at the age of 31, contemplated suicide but instead turned this energy into his famous "Ode to Joy"—Ninth Symphony. Suppression involves a semiconscious decision to postpone paying attention to a conflict or emotional pain. Anticipation as a defense mechanism allows us to emotionally deal with some future conflict in small steps and involves both thinking and feeling about the future. Finally, humor can be an expression of emotion without individual discomfort. It can allow us to reframe and view some conflict from a different perspective.

Flow

Csikszentmihalyi (1975, 1978) described the concept of "flow" as optimal experiences characterized by high involvement, deep concentration, intrinsic motivation and perception, and difficult challenges matched by an individual's requisite skills. Somewhere between being overwhelmed or stressed and the apathy of being underwhelmed and bored lies the zone Csikszentmihalyi terms "flow." Optimal experience promotes individual development and growth as one successfully matches his or her skills to activities and challenges in the environment. Examples of activities that may create flow include sports, work, hobbies, and social interactions. These activities must be appropriately challenging and intrinsically motivating so that the individual perceives personal growth and derives a sense of competence and self-esteem from engaging in them. Activities that are contrary to flow include repetitive and simple tasks and being in an underemployed job. Massomini and Delle Fave (2000) argued that current social and work contexts do not always provide for growth opportunities. As such, more people are turning to leisure activities such as hiking, rock climbing, and high-risk sports for optimal experience. Delle Fave and Bassi (1998) stated that personal growth develops from a focused level of concentration, alertness, active participation and the perceived importance of the activity.

Research has suggested that persons with disabilities can experience flow (Delle Fave, 1996; Delle Fave & Maletto, 1992). Delle Fave (1996) found that persons who became blind or sustained a spinal cord injury later in life and developed a strategy called transformation of flow. Transformation relates to situations in which a person with an adventitious disability continues to cultivate former flow activities (e.g., returning to a challenging job). If this is not possible, some individuals seek new sources of concentration and challenge unrelated to their previous experiences.

Massomini and Delle Fave (2000) noted that behavioral flexibility is a crucial feature for adapting to a continually changing environment. Wright (1983) differentiated between coping or adapting to a disability and succumbing to it as well as the environmental barriers imposed by having a disability.

EXTERNAL FACTORS

External or environmental factors relate to dynamics outside of individual' experience that can either inhibit or enhance wellness. Myers (2000) discussed subjective well-being in terms of who is happy. Self-reports of happiness tend to be reasonably reliable over time despite changing life circumstances (Diener, 1994). Numerous studies provide inconsistent findings as to the current state of peoples' reported happiness. While some studies indicated people are happy overall, other studies showed that people are becoming increasingly more depressed (Diener & Diener, 1996; Lykken, 1999; Myers & Diener, 1996; Wholey, 1986). Pertinent to many of these studies is the impact that external factors appear to have (e.g., pollution, crime, poverty) on overall well-being.

Income Status

Research regarding wealth and well-being suggests that once people have their basic needs met (i.e., food and drink, safety and security of a home), there is relatively little difference in reported well-being between the poor and the wealthy (Diener, Horwitz, & Emmons, 1985; Inglehart, 1990; Lykken, 1999). Argyle (1986) noted that lottery winners gain only temporary joy from their winnings. Relatedly, persons whose incomes have doubled in the past decade are no happier than those whose incomes have not increased (Diener, Sandvik, Seidlitz, & Diener, 1993). Myers (2000) further noted that Americans' self-reports of being "very happy" over the last 40 years has slightly declined from 35% to 33%, citing the fact that we are twice as rich and no happier. In addition, teen suicide has tripled, divorce has doubled, and depression rates have soared among teens and young adults. These findings present an interesting argument against modern materialism.

Relationships

Along with modern materialism in America is the European American ideal of individualism and autonomy. Although individualism enhances one's identity and self-expression, it may come at a great price. Myers

(2000) noted how we spend billions of dollars on cosmetics, diets, and clothes in order to be accepted by others. We also fear loneliness and rejection so much that many people remain in abusive relationships for fear of being alone. In relation to well-being, Pennebaker (1990) found that close, intact relationships and friendships predict health. Studies show that people with leukemia or heart disease have higher survival rates if they have extensive social support (Case, Moss, Case, McDermott, & Eberly, 1992). When a spouse dies or people experience a job loss or divorce, researchers have found that immune defenses appear to weaken for varying periods of time and rates of death and disease increase (Dohrenwend et al., 1982; National Academy of Sciences, 1984).

In exploring findings regarding intimate relationships like marriage, Myers (2000) cited National Opinion Research Center statistics from 1972 and 1996 that indicated married people report being more satisfied with life than divorced or unmarried persons. They are also at less risk for depression. Persons in unhappy marriages, however, are less satisfied with life than unmarried or divorced persons. Further, Veenhoven (1988) found that happy people tend to be more appealing as marriage partners than unhappy persons.

Schafer (1996) described what happens to individuals who experience a loss of social attachments by citing five types of alienation that occur. People essentially may feel powerless (belief that one has little control over a situation), self-estrangement (sense of being separated from the fruit of one's labor), isolation (being detached from others), meaninglessness (life has little meaning or purpose), and normlessness (able to engage in socially unapproved behaviors—not working).

Faith

Gathering evidence suggests that an active religiousness is associated with mental health. Actively religious North Americans are much less likely to abuse drugs and alcohol, divorce, and commit suicide (Batson, Schoenrade, & Ventis, 1993). National Opinion Research Center surveys indicate that people who report being very happy also tend to report being very close to God (Myers, 2000). Seligman (1988) stated that the belief in something larger than ourselves diminishes feelings of loneliness and provides us comfort and feelings of security: The extensive review of the literature cited in Levin's (2001) book *God, Faith, and Health* correlated good health and longer life with factors such as the relationships of support from church gatherings, various religious doctrine principles about maintaining health (i.e., no drinking, drugs, smoking, or promiscuous sex), and the safety in believing God is a source of strength.

OTHER FACTORS RELATED TO WELLNESS

Goldberger (1982) discussed the concept of sensory deprivation regarding laboratory experiments concerning over- and understimulation; Too little stimulation or deprivational stress results when individuals are involved in boring, isolated jobs (e.g., assembly work); placed in institutions for prolonged periods, or isolated in their homes as is the case of many Medicare homebound patients (Blackwell, Marini, & Chacon, 2001). Goldberger (1982) stated that, after a time, sensory-deprived individuals begin to experience disorientation, anxiety, and depression. Schafer (1996) noted the positive impact of giving nursing home residents a plant to care for, which gives them a sense of control and purpose. For the approximate two thirds of Americans with disabilities who are chronically unemployed, having some other sense of purpose and stimulation becomes important to well-being (Olkin, 1999).

Pelletier (1994), in his book *Sound Mind, Sound Body*, outlined various emotions related to health and wellness versus illness. Wellness emotions include love, faith, will to live, determination, purpose, festivity, and laughter. Distress emotions include anxiety, depression, fear (of isolation and rejection), anger, shame, frustration, and guilt. Livneh (1991), in describing the stages of adjustment to disability, stated that although most persons with disabilities transition through stages of adjustment and subsequently experience many of these distress emotions for a short period, some persons may become "stuck" and never reach an adaptive state. In support of the stage model regarding the "getting stuck" concept, it is known that injured workers who have been off work for an extended period of time often report feelings of depression, anxiety, pessimism about their future, and worry about financially caring for their family (Power & Dell Orto, 1995). Arguing against the stage model, Kendall and Buys (1998) indicated that persons with disabilities go through lifelong periods of occasional sorrow related to their disabilities where many of these distress emotions are experienced on a periodic basis. This assertion is contrary to the findings of other research noted earlier, that persons with spinal cord injury return to an adaptive baseline state of subjective well-being typically within 8 weeks following their injuries (Brickman & Campbell, 1971; Silver, 1982). Seligman (1990) summarized his findings on learned pessimism by stating that it promotes depression and anxiety and that it can become a self-fulfilling prophecy.

Having outlined a number of concepts and research findings related to the psychology of wellness, what aspects of this knowledge is useful in studying disability issues and working with clients with disabilities? What areas of research are fruitful for rehabilitation educators to pursue related to wellness and disability? Finally, how can rehabilitation counselors improve their skills and approaches to counseling with this information?

SUGGESTED DIRECTIONS FOR FUTURE REHABILITATION RESEARCH

Perhaps the most significant research area derived from the wellness literature concerns not only how this information applies to persons with disabilities but which individual traits and environmental factors enhance the perceived success and wellness of a person with a disability. Vash (1981) cited a number of factors related to disability itself (e.g., time of onset, type of onset, severity, visibility) as well as cultural and environmental variables. However, Vash's factors are anecdotal and do not consider the wellness concepts discussed here. Wright (1983) also addressed concepts such as "as if" behavior (an individual with a disability behaves as if he or she doesn't have a disability) and a coping versus succumbing attitude (individuals either learn to cope and problem solve or give in and become dependent and learn to be helpless) as well as environmental stressors, such as requirement of mourning (an individual with a disability must feel badly and mourn his or her loss of function) and a "just world" phenomena (you deserve what you get), but again doesn't address factors related to those who excel. As such, specific research questions related to wellness and disability follow.

SUGGESTED RESEARCH QUESTIONS

How do persons with various types of disabilities perceive their situations And their futures? Do persons with various disabilities experience flow? Is there a longitudinal difference in self-perceptions and objective measures of health (including secondary complications) between unrealistic optimists and realists and/or pessimists? Are persons with disabilities who practice wellness behaviors (e.g., regular medical checkups, exercise, nutrition, no smoking or abusing substances, relaxation, positive thinking, adequate rest, social connectedness) less ill, less often, compared to those who do not practice wellness behaviors? Do those who practice wellness behaviors experience fewer secondary complications compared to those who do not practice wellness behaviors? What are the ethnic differences in wellness behavior, with specific focus on individualism versus collectivism ideologies? How do demographic variables such as marital status, socioeconomic status, number of close relationships, gender, employment, age, and ethnicity factor in? How do personality variables such as sense of humor, perseverance, locus of control, self-determination, extraversion, and self-concept impact overall wellness and perceived success? These are some intriguing questions for researchers that take us outside of the box regarding what typically, has been researched and instead deals with disability holistically.

IMPLICATIONS FOR REHABILITATION COUNSELORS

What can practitioners gain from understanding those individual and environmental elements that enhance a client's lifelong subjective well-being? The educational paradigm dictates that practitioners should teach or empower clients to do for themselves. Although employment and career aspirations have traditionally been a focus for rehabilitation counselors, the reality of secondary complications can often prohibit clients with disabilities from pursuing full-time or ongoing work. For example, persons with mental illness often have cyclical down periods, those with spinal cord injuries succumb to decubitus ulcers which requires bed rest and treatment for weeks or months at a time, and those with diabetes may experience a variety of complications, which could partially be controlled with regular exercise.

The wellness literature translates into a number of counseling strategies for practitioners. An initial technique in educating/encouraging wellness among clients would be to create a bibliography of readings and prescribe bibliotherapy homework for discussion in sessions. Topics on nutrition, exercise, faith, relaxation, positive thinking, and disability-specific complication prevention strategies would be beneficial. This education becomes particularly important due to managed care constraints and shorter lengths of stay for hospitalization as well as diagnostic-related group limitations. Patients are simply not receiving the education needed (i.e., diabetes education) to remain healthy once they leave the hospital.

Behavioral approaches are also relevant in facilitating a client's wellness lifestyle. A behavioral contract and assessment component could be established for a nutrition and exercise program as well as to control and monitor any substance use and abuse. Behavioral homework exercises could be used to build self-confidence by "doing" feared activities rather than simply talking about change. Making sure that clients follow through with stated goals is also possible in this way.

Finally, cognitive approaches could be employed to facilitate client wellness (Beck, 1995). Much of the positive psychology and wellness literature deals with cognitions or having a certain mindset. Subjective well-being, optimism, self-determination, self-efficacy, flow, and adaptive and defense mechanisms are some of the major concepts discussed to this point in the paper. Correcting irrational belief systems is a hallmark of Albert Ellis' (1977, as cited in Beck, 1995) rational emotive therapy. Cognitive reframing or restructuring is also an excellent technique in assisting clients to think and behave more positively. Seligman (1990) claimed it is possible to unlearn pessimistic ways of thinking in favor of a more optimistic outlook. Not to be overlooked, however, is the reality of environmental factors such as negative societal attitudes. Soliciting from clients what their perceptions are of the world around them becomes important in dispelling irrational beliefs or in acknowledging the accuracy of clients' beliefs.

CONCLUSION

Shorter lengths of hospital stays and reliance on the medical model approach of not dealing with the person "holistically" have rarely allowed acute medical personnel the time to educate patients on wellness or prevention of secondary complications of disability. Because rehabilitation counselors are often involved with clients post-recovery, it behooves researchers, educators, and counselors to not simply pay lip service to the concept of a holistic approach and begin exploring clients' all-around well-being. This involves exploring the wellness behaviors of persons with disabilities, informing students of these findings, and subsequently teaching students counseling skills that promote client wellness. With this truly holistic approach to counseling, clients may experience not only a longer work-life expectancy, but an enhanced state of subjective well-being and perceived quality of life.

REFERENCES

Akhtar, S. (1996). "Someday . . . " and "if only . . . " fantasies: Pathological optimism and inordinate nostalgia as related forms of idealization. *Journal of American Psycholoanalytic Association, 44*, 723–753.

American Psychiatric Association. (1994). *Diagnostic and statistical manual of mental disorders* (4th ed.). Washington, DC: Author.

Antonovsky, A. (1987). *Unraveling the mystery of health: How people manage stress and stay well.* San Francisco: Jossey-Bass.

Arglye, M. (1986). *The psychology of happiness.* London: Methuen.

Bandura, A. (1997). *Self-efficacy. The exercise of control.* New York: Freeman.

Batson, C. D., Schoenrade, P. A., & Ventis, W. L. (1993). *Religion and the individual: A social psychological perspective.* New York: Oxford University Press.

Beck, J. S. (1995). *Cognitive therapy: Basics and beyond.* New York: Guilford Press.

Blackwell, T. L., Marini, I., & Chacon, M. (2001). The impact of the Americans with Disabilities Act on independent living. *Rehabilitation Education, 15,* 395–408.

Brickman, P., & Campbell, D. T. (1971). Hedonic relativism and planning the good society. In M. H. Appley (Ed.), *Adaptation-level theory* (pp. 287–305). New York: Academic Press.

Buchanan, G. M., & Seligman, M. E. P. (1995). *Explanatory style.* Hillsdale, NJ: Erlbaum.

Cantor, N., & Sanderson, C. A. (1999). Life task participation and well-being: The importance of taking part in daily life. In D. Kahneman, E. Diener, & N. Schwarz (Eds.), *Well-being: The foundations of hedonic psychology* (pp. 230–243). New York: Russell Sage Foundation.

Case, R. B., Moss, A. J., Case, N., McDermott, M., & Eberly, S. (1992). Living alone after myocardial infarction: Impact on prognosis. *Journal of the American Medical Association, 267,* 515–519.

Csikszentmihalyi, M. (1975). *Beyond boredom and anxiety.* San Francisco: Jossey-Bass.

Csikszentmihalyi, M. (1978). Attention and the holistic approach to behavior. In K. S. Pope & J. L. Singer (Eds.), *The stream of consciousness* (pp. 335–358). New York: Plenum.

Csikszentmihalyi, M. (1990). *Flow: The psychology of optimal experience.* New York: Harper & Row.

Csikszentmihalyi, M. (1999). If we are so rich, why aren't we happy? *American Psychologist, 54,* 821–827.

deCharms, R. (1968). *Personal causation.* New York: Academic Press.

Delle Fave, A. (1996). Il processo di 'trasformazione di Flow' in un campione di soggetti medullolesi [The process of flow transformation in a sample of subjects with spinal cord injuries]. In F. Massimini, P. Inghilleri, & A. Delledr Fave (Eds.), *La selezione psicologica umana* (pp. 615–634). Milan: Cooperativa Libraria IULM.

Delle Fave, A., & Bassi, M. (1998, June). *Optimal experience and apathy: The meaning of experience fluctuation in adolescents.* Paper presented at the VI Biennial EARA Conference, Budapest, Hungary.

Delle Fave, A., & Maletto, C. (1992). Processi di attenzione e qualita dell'esperienza soggettiva [Attention processes and the quality of subjective experience]. In D. Galati (Ed), *La psicologia dei non vedenti* (pp. 321–353). Milan: Franco Angeli.

Diener; E. (1994). Assessing subjective well-being: Progress and opportunities. *Social Indicators Research, 31,* 103–157.

Diener, E. (2000). Subjective well-being: The science of happiness and a proposal for a national index. *American Psychologist, 55,* 34–43.

Diener, E., & Diener, C. (1996). Most people are happy. *Psychological Science, 7,* 181–185.

Diener, E., Horwitz, J., & Emmons, R. A. (1985). Happiness of the very wealthy. *Social Indicators, 16,* 262–274.

Diener, E., Sandvik, E., Seidlitz, L., & Diener, M. (1993). The relationship between income and subjective well-being: Relative or absolute? *Social Indicators Research, 28,* 195–223.

Dohrenwend, B., Pearlin, L., Clayton, P., Hamburg, B., Dohrenwend, B. P., Riley, M., & Rose, R. (1982). Report on stress and life events. In G. R. Elliott & C. Eisdorfer (Eds.), *Stress and human health: Analysis and implications of research* (pp. 19–37). New York: Springer.

Freud, S. (1928). *The future of an illusion.* London: Hogarth.

Frodi, A., Bridges, L., & Grolnick, W. S. (1985). Correlates of mastery-related behavior: A short-term longitudinal study of infants in their second year. *Child Development, 56,* 1291–1298.

Gibbons, F. X., Eggleston, T. J., & Benthin, A. C. (1997). Cognitive reactions to smoking relapse: The reciprocal relation between dissonance and self-esteem. *Journal of Personality and Social Psychology, 72,* 184–195.

Goldberger, L. (1982). Sensory deprivation and overload. In L. Goldberger & S. Breznitz (Eds.), *Handbook on stress: Theoretical and clinical aspects* (pp. 410–418). New York: Free Press.

Harter, S. (1978). Effectance motivation reconsidered: Toward a developmental model. *Human Development, 1,* 661–669.

Inglehart, R. (1990). *Modernization and postmodernization: Cultural, economic, and political change in societies.* Princeton, NJ: Princeton University Press.

Kasser, T., & Ryan, R. M. (1993). A dark side of the American dream: Correlates of financial success as a life aspiration. *Journal of Personality and Social Psychology, 65,* 410–422.

Kasser, T., & Ryan, R. (1996). Further examining the American dream: Differential correlates of intrinsic and extrinsic goals. *Personality and Social Psychology Bulletin, 22,* 280–287.

Kendall, E., & Buys, N. (1998). An integrated model of psychosocial adjustment following acquired disability. *Journal of Rehabilitation, 64*(3), 16–20.

Koenig, H. G. (1997). *Is religion good for your health? The effects of religion on physical and mental health.* Binghamton, NY: Haworth Press.

Lazarus, R. S. (1983). The costs and benefits of denial. In S. Benitz (Ed.), *Denial of stress* (pp. 1–30). New York: International Universities Press.

Lazarus, R., & Folkman, S. (1984). *Stress, appraisal and coping.* New York: Springer.

Levin, J. (2001). *God, faith, and health.* New York: Wiley.

Livneh, H. (1991). A unified approach to existing models of adaptation to disability: A model of adaptation. In R. P. Marinelli & A. E. Delldr Orto (Eds.), *The psychological and social impact of disability* (3rd ed., pp. 111–138). New York: Springer.

Lykken, D. (1999). *Happiness.* New York: Golden Books.

Marini, I. (1994a). Attitudes toward disability and the psychosocial implications for persons with SCI. *SCI: Psychosocial Process, 7*(4), 147–152.

Marini, I., & Stebnicki, M. (1999). Social security's alternative provider program: What can rehabilitation administrators expect. *Journal of Rehabilitation Administration, 23*(1), 31–41.

Massimini, F., & Delle Fave, A. (2000). Individual development in a bio-cultural perspective. *American Psychologist, 55*, 24–33.

Matthews, D. A., & Larson, D. B. (1997). *The faith factor: An annotated bibliography of clinical research on spiritual subjects* (Vols. I–IV). Rockville, MD: National Institute for Healthcare Research and Georgetown University Press.

Myers, D. G. (2000). The funds, friends, and faith of happy people. *American Psychologist, 55*, 56–67.

Myers, D. G., & Diener, E. (1996). The pursuit of happiness. *Scientific American, 274*, 54–56.

National Academy of Sciences. (1984). *Bereavement: Reactions, consequences, and care.* Washington, DC: National Academy Press.

Oettingen, G. (1996). Positive fantasy and motivation. In P. M. Gollwitzer & J. Bargh (Eds.), *The psychology of action: Linking cognition and motivation to behavior* (pp. 236–259). New York: Guilford Press.

Olkin, R. (1999). *What psychotherapists should know about disability.* New York: Guilford Press.

Pavot, W., Diener, E., & Fujita, F. (1990). Extraversion and happiness. *Personality and Individual Differences, 11*, 1299–1306.

Pelletier, K. R. (1994). *Sound mind, sound body.* New York: Simon & Schuster.

Pennebaker, J. (1990). *Opening up: The healing power of confiding in others.* New York: Morrow.

Peterson, C. (1988). Explanatory style as a risk factor for illness. *Cognitive Therapy Research, 12*, 119–132.

Peterson, C. (2000). The future of optimism. *American Psychologist, 55*, 44–55.

Peterson, C., Seligman, M. E. P., & Vaillant, G. E. (1988). Pessimistic explanatory style is a risk factor for physical illness: A thirty-five year longitudinal study. *Journal of Personality and Social Psychology, 55*, 23–37.

Power, P. W., & Dell Orto, A. E. (1995). Disability management: A family perspective. In D. E. Shrey & M. Lacerte (Eds.), *Principles and practices of disability management in industry* (pp. 411–432). Winter Park, FL: GR Press.

Ryan, R. M., & Deci, E. L. (2000). Self-determination theory and the facilitation of intrinsic motivation, social development, and well-being. *American Psychologist, 55*, 68–78.

Ryan, R. M., & Grolnick, W. S. (1986). Origins and pawns in the classroom: Self-report and projective assessments of individual differences in children's perceptions. *Journal of Personality and Social Psychology, 50*, 550–558.

Schafer, W. (1996). *Stress management for wellness.* Orlando, FL: Harcourt Brace.

Seligman, M. E. P. (1988). Boomer blues. *Psychology Today, October*, 50–55.

Seligman, M. E. P. (1990). *Learned optimism: The skills to overcome lift's obstacles.* New York: Pocket Books.

Seligman, M. E. P. (1991). *Learned optimism.* New York: Knopf.

Seligman, M. E. P., & Csikszentmihalyi, M. (2000). Positive psychology: An introduction. *American Psychologist, 55*, 5–14.

Silver, R. L. (1982). *Coping with an undesirable life event: A study of early reactions to physical disability.* Unpublished doctoral dissertation, Northwestern University, Evanston, IL.

Stone, A. A., Cox, D. X., Valdimarsdottir, H., Jandorf, L., & Neale, J. M. (1987). Evidence that secretory IgA antibody is associated with daily mood. *Journal of Personality and Social Psychology, 52,* 988–993.

Taylor, S. E. (1983). Adjustment to threatening events: A theory of cognitive adaptation. *American Psychologist, 38,* 1161–1173.

Taylor, S. E., & Brown, J. D. (1988). Illusion and well-being: A social psychological perspective on mental health. *Psychological Bulletin, 110,* 193–210.

Tiger, L. (1979). *Optimism: The biology of hope.* New York: Simon & Schuster.

Trieschmann, R. (1981). *Spinal cord injuries: Psychological, social and vocational adjustment.* New York: Pergamon.

Vaillant, G. E. (1977). *Adaptation to life.* Boston: Little, Brown.

Vaillant, G. E. (2000). Adaptive mental mechanisms: Their role in a positive psychology. *American Psychologist, 55,* 89–98.

Vash, C. (1981). *Psychology of disability.* New York: Springfield.

Veenhoven, R. (1988). The utility of happiness. *Social Indicators Research, 20,* 333–354.

Weisse, C. S. (1992). Depression and incompetence: A review of the literature. *Psychological Bulletin, 111,* 475–489.

Wholey, D. (1986). *Are you happy?* Boston: Houghton Mifflin.

Wright, B. A. (1983). *Physical disability: A psychological approach* (2nd ed.). New York: Harper & Row.

CHAPTER THIRTY

"Successful Aging"
A Disability Perspective[1,2,3]

Meredith Minkler and Pamela Fadem

For much of its short history, gerontology both reflected and reinforced a "decline and loss" paradigm. A heavy accent was placed on notions of aging as a series of decrements or losses in the individual, to which both elders and society needed to adapt or adjust (Phillipson, 1998).

The last 20 years have witnessed the emergence of several alternative perspectives that provide a sharp contrast to this negative view, key among them Rowe and Kahn's (1987, 1997, 1998) conceptualization of

From "Successful aging: A disability perspective" by M. Minkler and P. Fadem, 2002, *Journal of Disability Policy Studies, 12,* 229–235. Copyright 2002 PRO-ED, Inc. Reprinted with permission.

[1] Support for this project was provided by the University of California at Berkeley's Committee on Research.

[2] The authors also gratefully acknowledge the helpful comments received from Dr. Martha Holstein, Dr. Jae Kennedy, and members of UC Berkeley's Working Group of Aging. Thanks, finally, are also due to Lisa Butler and Laura Spautz for the research assistance and clerical support they provided.

[3] Due mainly to space limitations, we have intentionally focused this paper primarily on aging with physical disabilities. It should be noted, however, that many of the same arguments and issues discussed here can and should be raised with respect to successful aging and developmental and other mental disabilities. Although there is a relative paucity of work on aging and developmental disabilities in academia, this topic is well examined in the nonacademic literature, and the reader is referred to ARC's June 1999 *Newsletter* for excellent recent coverage of this topic (Brown & Murphy, 1999).

"successful aging." This popular perspective holds that many of the health and related problems associated with "normal aging" are in fact riot normal at all but, rather, are the result of lifestyle and other factors that put people at high risk for disease and disability in later life.

The concept of successful aging has been helpful in focusing renewed attention on health promotion, and disease and injury prevention, as means of adding life to years and not merely years to life. Multiple well-designed studies of successful aging similarly have made a real contribution to clarifying the many health-promotion and disease-prevention strategies that can help ensure a healthier old age (Rowe & Kahn, 1998; Seeman, 1994).

Yet, the new emphasis on successful aging is problematic, as well. The concept has been criticized for paying insufficient attention to (a) aging over the life course; (b) race, class, and gender inequities; and (c) the realities and importance of losses as well as gains in later life (M. Baltes & Carstensen, 1996; Riley, 1998; Scheidt, Humphreys, & Yorgason, 1999; Schulz & Heckhausen, 1996). Many of these criticisms are highly relevant to the issues and concerns of people with disabilities. To date, however, none of the extant critiques has focused specifically on the limitations of the successful-aging paradigm when applied to this population.

The present article attempts to address this gap. We begin with a brief overview of Rowe and Kahn's successful-aging paradigm and its three components—low probability of disease and disease-related disability; high cognitive and physical functioning; and active engagement with life. We then examine each of these characteristics specifically as they relate to the lives of older adults with substantial physical disabilities (see footnote 1). We suggest that although the concept of successful aging has moved the field forward in some important new ways, both the term itself and some of its specific dimensions and meanings may serve to further stigmatize and marginalize people who are aging with severe disabilities, and who may not meet the criteria for aging successfully. We conclude by making a case for the use of alternative conceptualizations that emphasize the environmental conditions needed to optimize the aging experience for both individuals with disabilities and those without.

SUCCESSFUL AGING: AN OVERVIEW

Although the term *successful aging* was coined more than half a century ago, its use in gerontology today is primarily in reference to Rowe and Kahn's (1987, 1997, 1998) paradigm. As suggested earlier, these investigators made a clear distinction between "successful aging" and "usual aging," with the latter referring to the large proportion of elders who function well but are at substantial risk for disease or disability.

Rowe and Kahn (1987) first described successful aging solely in reference to the avoidance of disease and disability. Aided by the MacArthur Study of Successful Aging, which they led—a $10 million, 10-year effort, by dozens of scientists, to develop a conceptual basis for a "new gerontology" based on an appreciation of the positive aspects of aging (Rowe & Kahn, 1998)—the model subsequently was broadened. Successful aging thus was seen as encompassing two additional components: maintenance of high physical and cognitive functional capacity, and active engagement in life. Briefly, the avoidance of disability involves increased, rather than decreased, attention to preventive health care and health promotion in the later years, in part to "compress" morbidity (Fries, 1980) so that illness and disability comprise a much smaller portion of the last years of life (Rowe & Kahn, 1998). Maintaining physical and mental function also involves an accent on both prevention and health promotion. This component of the successful-aging paradigm presupposes that (a) fears of loss of function are often greatly exaggerated, (b) much functional loss can indeed be prevented, and (c) many functional losses can be regained.

Finally, the third aspect of successful aging—active engagement with life—was put forward as a direct counter to the earlier (and now largely discredited) "disengagement theory" (Cumming & Henry, 1961). That theory had conceptualized late life as a time of mutual withdrawal and letting go, during which individuals gradually relinquished roles and responsibilities while society prepared to replace its older members. In contrast to disengagement theory, the third prong in Rowe and Kahn's (1998) conceptualization of successful aging suggests that "maintaining close relationships with others, and remaining involved in activities that are meaningful and purposeful, are important for well-being throughout the life course" (p. 46).

These three components were seen as hierarchically ordered such that

> the absence of disease and disability makes it easier to maintain mental and physical function. And maintenance of mental and physical function in turn enables (but does not guarantee) active engagement with life. It is the combination of all three—avoidance of disease and disability, maintenance of cognitive and physical function and sustained engagement with life—that represents the concept of successful aging most fully. (Rowe & Kahn, 1998, p. 39)

Each of these conceptual components has particular salience and meaning when viewed from a disability perspective.

LOW PROBABILITY OF DISEASE AND
DISEASE-RELATED DISABILITY

Proponents of the successful-aging paradigm are careful to acknowledge that "vulnerability to disease and disability is not wholly under our control, nor is it likely to become so" (Rowe & Kahn, 1998, p. 40). At the same time, they argue that many of the losses associated with usual aging are in fact caused primarily by extrinsic factors (e.g., diet and exercise) and therefore are subject to alteration. Rowe and Kahn indeed go further to suggest that "successful aging is dependent upon individual choices and behaviors. *It can be attained through individual choice and effort*" [italics added] (p. 37).

On the one hand, of course, few would argue that the high incidence of conditions such as diabetes and hypertension in the elderly reflect, to a considerable degree, earlier lifestyle and environmental factors, rather than normal, age-related changes. On the other hand, however, an overemphasis on the role of individual choices and behaviors in determining the probability of disease and disease-related disability is problematic. As Riley (1998) argued, such equations do not pay adequate attention to the fact that "changes in lives and changes in social structures are fundamentally interdependent" (p. 15). Such factors as the "structural opportunities in schools, offices, nursing homes, families, communities ... and society at large" (Riley, 1998, p. 151), in short, have a heavy impact on one's prospects for aging successfully.

The situation of people with disabilities represents a striking case in point. Data from the *Survey of Income and Program Participation* (SIPP) thus showed an employment rate of just 32.2% in 1994; and in 1995, men and women with disabilities earned, respectively, just 72.1% and 72.7% of the income earned by their counterparts without disabilities. For men, moreover, this income gap represents a substantial increase over recent years (Kaye, 1998). People with disabilities living in the community are also twice as likely as people without disabilities to live alone (19.6% vs. 8.4%; Kaye, 1998)—a factor that, like low income, is associated with poorer diet and exercise patterns and other risk factors (Seeman, 2000).

Although a 1994 Harris poll of Americans with disabilities had almost two thirds of the respondents reporting an improved quality of life over the preceding 4 years (Leitman, Cooner, & Risher, 1994), and although the 1990 Americans with Disabilities Act has substantially increased awareness of the need for environmental changes and accommodations, "statistical evidence for real improvements in the lives of those with disabilities—more opportunities for employment and improved economic status, greater freedom of movement and ease of access, and increased levels of social integration—has been slow to materialize" (Kaye,

1998, p. 1). Without concomitant action to substantially improve the "response-ability" of people with disabilities, including access to programs and policies that ensure a decent standard of living, and opportunities to build on strengths and participate fully in society, calls for greater personal responsibility for health are likely to have limited appeal (Minkler, 1996). Furthermore, an overemphasis on the resources and motivations of elders themselves also risks the implication of blame for elders who fail to meet the criteria for minimizing their risk of disease or disability (Cassell & Neugarten, 1991; Kennedy & Minkler, 1998; Minkler, 1990; Scheidt et al, 1999; Tornstam, 1992). Indeed, as Scheidt et al. pointed out, it is ironic that the successful-aging model's emphasis on the critical role of intrinsic factors, such as individual choice concerning smoking, diet, and exercise, is not supplemented by an equal emphasis on the role of extrinsic factors. The latter would include such factors as poverty and inaccessible and in other ways deleterious environments.

With regard to physical fitness and exercise, for example, which Rowe and Kahn (1998) identified as the crux of successful aging, recent analyses of Behavioral Risk Factor Surveillance System (http://www.cdc.gov/nccdphp/brfss) data, which were stratified by gender and controlled for education and race, are instructive. These analyses revealed that persons 65 and older who live in unsafe neighborhoods are significantly less likely to engage in regular exercise than those in safe neighborhoods (Weinstein et al., 1999). For elders with disabilities, the difficulties of engaging in regular exercise in high-crime neighborhoods are likely to be further compounded by heightened concerns about physical vulnerability and lack of environmental access.

MAINTENANCE OF HIGH PHYSICAL
AND COGNITIVE FUNCTION

Characterizations of successful aging as closely related to the maintenance of high physical and cognitive function also are problematic, particularly when used in relation to people who enter old age with significant (and often lifelong) disabilities. As Scheidt et al. (1999) noted, "The term *successful* as used to describe older individuals who age with no or minimal loss of function...connotes a fixed standard" (p. 279) and the achievement of static end points. As an example, they highlight Rowe and Kahn's (1997) argument that older persons can indeed move "*in and out* of success over time," with those who are most resilient being able to "return to meeting the criteria of success" (p. 439).

As Fadem (1999) has argued, people who have lived a substantial portion of their lives relying on others for assistance with activities of daily living long ago redefined for themselves what independence and effective functioning are about. Furthermore, they "are likely to repeat this process of redefinition many times as their level of physical functioning [changes] and slowly (or quickly) deteriorate[s]" (Fadem, 1999, p. 4). The difference here is subtle but important: People with progressive disabilities, and those for whom a "stable" disability becomes more limiting later in life, often continue to see themselves as functioning effectively and having a good quality of life, while acknowledging the need for increasing assistance and accommodations. Rather than viewing themselves as moving "out of success over time," they frequently view their functional ability as increasingly dependent on the success with which their *environments* can adapt and change to accommodate their changing bodies and personal needs.

This perspective is complemented by Fried et al.'s (1991) emphasis on "compensatory strategies," or manipulations of the environment that prevent an impairment from becoming disabling or restricting in terms of the individual's ability to perform particular tasks or functions. In the case of people who are already disabled, the level of financial and other resources available, which can determine the possibility of home modifications and other compensatory strategies, often is the key factor in determining whether effective adaptation (and successful aging) can be achieved.

As suggested below, the inclusion of "active engagement with life" as a component of successful aging in Rowe and Kahn's model was designed, in part, to make conceptual room for people such as physics great Stephen Hawking, who is highly successful and engaged with life despite being severely disabled by amyotropic lateral sclerosis (ALS), or Lou Gehrig's disease. Yet, when "high physical and cognitive function" is named as a necessary component of successful aging, a different and contradictory message may be sent. Indeed, in the forward to their book *Successful Aging*, which reports on the results of the MacArthur Study, Rowe and Kahn state that "in sum, we were trying to pinpoint the many factors that conspire to put one octogenarian on cross-county skis and another in a wheelchair" (p. xii).

Statements such as this one may serve to reinforce both handicappism and what Cohen (1988) called "the elderly mystique," which refers to the phenomenon of prejudice against the old in general being replaced with a more specific prejudice against elders who are or become disabled. This perspective frequently is internalized by elders themselves, who conclude that "when disability arrives, hope about continued growth, self realization and full participation in family and society must be abandoned so that all energy can he directed toward the ultimate defeat which is not death but institutionalization" (Cohen, 1988, p. 25). By substantially lowering the bar of dreams and expectations for and by elders with disabilities, this new variant of ageism ironically can mitigate against the very proactive health-promotion and health-maintenance activities advocated by proponents of successful aging (Minkler, 1996).

Taking a cue from Cohen (1998), we argue that considering "high mental and physical function" to be a necessary component of successful aging may serve to reinforce the fears and negative images that both elders themselves and society at large hold about aging with a substantial disability. The focus on personal responsibility, moreover, risks ignoring the environmental and policy contexts that can facilitate or severely limit an individual's ability to achieve and sustain high functioning in society.

ACTIVE ENGAGEMENT WITH LIFE

Rowe and Kahn's (1998) third and final component of successful aging—active engagement with life—was defined as having two dimensions: relating to and being connected with others through social relationships, and continuing productive activities. The first of these dimensions was used to underscore the plethora of evidence on the importance of social networks, and the social support given and received through those networks, for health and well-being in both earlier and later life (Cohen & Syme, 1985; Seeman, 2000). The second dimension stresses the importance of productive behavior, defined broadly as "all activities, paid or unpaid, that create goods or services of value" (Rowe & Kahn, 1997, p. 47). As noted earlier, the addition of this social dimension to a model that previously had focused solely on disease and disease-related disability has been hailed as an important step forward (Riley, 1998). And Rowe and Kahn (1998) did make a special effort to argue that even individuals with the most severe disabilities can remain actively engaged with others and make "heroic achievements" (p. 38) and contributions despite their functional limitations.

Fadem (1999) underscored this point, providing telling examples of individuals with severe disabilities who "effectively mobilized both consumer rights and political campaigns" (p. 5) and provided "seasoned peer mentorship" (p. 5) by telephone to scores of younger people with disabilities while never leaving home. Such constructive engagement is mirrored as well in the birth and evolution of one of the significant social movements of the latter part of the 20th century.

Traditional measures of social connection and productive engagement, however, may not fully capture the reality of the lives of older people with disabilities (Carstensen, 1991; Fadem, 1999; Holstein, 1998; Pennix et al., 1998). Pennix et al.'s (1998) study of emotional vitality among older women with disabilities, for example, revealed that with respect to social relations, the primary element valued was not "availability or frequency of contacts but perceiving enough warmth and understanding to meet an individual's needs" (p. 814). Similarly, as Carstensen has pointed out, selective *reduction* in the frequency of social interactions may help some individuals achieve a more satisfying and adaptive old age. Viewed from this perspective, efforts to either measure or enhance the social-relationships dimension of successful aging by simplistic, across-the-board approaches to what constitutes healthy social engagement may well miss the mark.

Furthermore, as Holstein (1998) has argued, although the concept of productive aging has been expanded to include voluntarism, informal caregiving, and other unpaid and often invisible activities, "productivity, understood culturally, is closely linked to paid work, a link that will be difficult to sever" (p. 363). She goes on to note, "A work-oriented definition of productivity can obscure diversity, establish new standards for an acceptable old age, and support someone else's vision of social and economic needs" (p. 366). For older people with disabilities, older women, older people of color, and low-income elders, whose relationship to the labor market often has been one of marginalization, viewing productive aging narrowly in terms of paid work is particularly dangerous.

Finally, beyond this very real concern lies the fact that a paid or unpaid "goods and services" approach to productive aging may leave little room for constructive engagement with questions of the meaning and significance of aging and old age. As Cole (1988) argued, the renewed emphasis on successful aging is part of an historical pattern based on dichotomizing old age into positive and negative poles and emphasizing one of those poles, rather than appreciating the essential unity and dialectic that aging ultimately represents. The latter, more complex perspective respects the diversity of aging and its place as part of a natural and unified lifetime (Cole, 1988). The vision of aging as a dialectic involving losses as well as gains holds particular relevance if we are to more fully value the lives and contributions of people who are aging with substantial disabilities. It also provides an important alternative to what Cole (1992) described as our culture's "relentless hostility to physical decline and its tendency to regard health"—and, we would add, the absence of disability—"as a form of secular salvation" (p. 239). He went on to note, "By transforming health as a means of living well into an end unto itself, 'successful aging' reveals its bankruptcy as an ideal" (p. 239), one that fails to make room for the realities of physical disability, decline, and death.

IMPLICATIONS

Successful aging has become a central theoretical paradigm within the fields of geriatrics and gerontology. Summarizing a large body of theoretical and empirical research on this paradigm, Seeman (1994) argued that

> the concept of successful aging provides for a critical refocusing of attention on the substantial heterogeneity in patterns of aging among older persons, particularly the existence of more positive trajectories of aging that avoid many, if not all, of the common age-related diseases and disabilities. (p. 61)

We agree with Seeman that a more positive view of aging can play a critical role in helping individuals achieve and maintain higher levels of function as they grow older. We would argue, however, that from a disability perspective, neither the semantics nor the theoretical conceptualization of successful aging constitutes the best approach to achieving this goal, for "disability, or more accurately the disablement process, is a dynamic social phenomenon that has as much to do with cultural norms and socioeconomic status as it does with individual physiological conditions" (Kennedy & Minkler, 1998, p. 92). Bearing this in mind, and building on the arguments presented in this article, we underscore the need for further research involving the development and testing of broader ecological approaches to successful aging with a disability. As defined by Brofenbrenner (1992), such approaches consider and attend to the individual, the immediate settings in which he or she lives, the larger contexts in which these settings are embedded, and the interactions among all of these levels.

An early and promising model in this regard was put forward by P. Baltes and Baltes (1990), who replaced the term *successful aging* with *optimal aging* in reference to "a kind of utopia, namely, aging under development-enhancing and age-friendly environmental conditions" (p. 8). As Marsiske, Lang, Baltes, and Baltes (1995) have suggested, the focus in such a model is on "how individuals and life environments can manage opportunities for, and limits on, resources at all ages" (p. 6). Such a perspective implicitly recognizes that social/physical environmental changes are critical if optimal aging—with or without a disability—is to be achieved (see also Kaplan et al., 1993; Satariano, 1997; and Verbrugge & Jette, 1994).

The continued development and refining of conceptual approaches to research that stress optimal aging is consistent with the "new paradigm of disability," which holds that a person with a disability "should no longer be viewed as someone who cannot function because of an impairment, but rather as someone who needs an accommodation in order to function" (Bleecker, 2000, p. 1). When this approach is taken, disability research and research-driven program and policy interventions stress changing the physical and social environments within which both aging and the disablement process take place.

Research also is needed into optimal aging for those who are growing older with developmental disabilities. Although organizations such as ARC have produced excellent material on aging with a developmental disability (Brown & Murphy, 1999), this topic has received scant attention in the academic literature (see LeBlanc & Matson, 1997; Walz, Harper, & Wilson, 1986). Many of the issues and concerns discussed in the present article with regard to successful aging and physical disability can and should also be raised with respect to aging and developmental disabilities. To better explore this area, further studies, including qualitative research into the lived experience of people aging with developmental disabilities, should be undertaken.

Finally, further research is needed into the development of theoretical approaches that move beyond dichotomous notions of successful/unsuccessful or healthy/unhealthy aging and old age. By acknowledging that losses as well as gains, and limits as well as potentials, are a critical part of the aging process (Baltes & Carstensen, 1996; Scheidt et al., 1999), these newer perspectives make room for questions about the meaning and significance of aging and old age. They help us move beyond what Moody (1988) described as the ever-more technical and "instrumental" orientation of academic gerontology, within which "the problems of later life are treated with scientific and managerial efficiency, but with no grasp of their larger political or existential significance. The last stage of life is progressively drained of meaning" (p. 82).

Continuing efforts to move beyond the confines of the successful-aging paradigm can build in part upon the foundations laid by feminist research. As Harper (1997) has pointed out, for example, feminist scholarship concerning new reproductive technologies and the control of women's bodies may hold special relevance for research into "the medicalization and control of the *ageing* body" (p. 167) and the associated development of successful-aging norms and ideals. Similarly, and building on Moody's (1988) concerns just noted, scholarship is needed that continues to question whether the narrow successful-aging paradigm is ultimately simply a logical extension of our continuing quest to fulfill scientific and biotechnological imperatives (Cassel & Neugarten, 1991).

From the perspective of practice, as Satariano (1997) has suggested, the conceptual framework provided by the "new paradigm of disability" suggests the importance of having public health professionals collaborate with architects, city planners, transportation experts, and engineers in the design of both indoor and outdoor environments that truly accommodate elders of diverse abilities and functional limitations. Taking a cue from the World Institute on Disability (WID), attending to the broader environments within which aging takes place also would have us explore the critical dimension of consumer control over personal assistance services (PAS) and other needed resources. WID's finding that publicly funded PAS programs around the nation often fail to provide services around the clock and/or 7 days a week is an example of the need for changing both current practices and policies that "represent a substantial barrier to full participation" (Bleecker, 2000, p. 3).

Finally, from a policy perspective, broader conceptualizations of optimal aging would have us work for legislation that supports, rather than hinders, the capacity of people aging with disabilities to participate fully in society, in part through the provision of adequate resources. Such policy-level change would include, for example, additional mandates and funding for responsive and affordable transportation services, and adequate personal assistance (including assistance outside the home) to enable people with disabilities to remain engaged in their communities.

In the conclusion to *Successful Aging*, Rowe and Kahn (1998) call for better allocation of paid employment, education, and training throughout the life course, as well as better integration of work, education, parenting, leisure, and other activities to "make successful aging more attainable for all of us" (p. 206). These recommendations are laudable and important; however, without far greater attention to the substantial and growing disparities among the old and the future old (Kaye, 1998), and similarly heightened attention to the ways in which a concept such as successful aging can inadvertently hurt those who are already devalued and marginalized in our society, such prescriptions are unlikely to be realized. As we attempt to design research, programs, and policies that can help maintain and promote health and well-being across the life course, therefore, we must ensure that those studies and interventions are in fact broadly inclusive. They should reflect the strengths, as well as the needs and concerns, of the "quiet revolution" represented by the greatest diversity of elders ever witnessed (Burton, Dilworth-Anderson, & Bengston, 1992, p. 129). Current and future elders with disabilities represent a critical part of this revolution, and one whose individual and collective voices concerning concepts such as successful aging must be sought out and heard.

REFERENCES

Baltes, M., & Carstensen, L. (1996). The process of successful aging. *Ageing and Society, 16,* 397–422.

Baltes, P. B., & Baltes, M. M. (1990). Psychological perspectives on successful aging: The model of selective optimization with compensation. In P. B. Baltes & M. M. Baltes (Eds.), *Successful aging: Perspectives from the behavioral sciences* (pp. 1–34). Cambridge, UK: Cambridge University Press.

Bleecker, T. (2000). The new paradigm of disability: Implications for research and policy. *Consumer Choice, 4,* 1, 3.

Bronfenbrenner, U. (1992). Ecological systems theory. In R. Vasta (Ed.), *Annals of child development. Six theories of child development: Revised formulations and current issues* (pp. 187–249). London: Jessica Kingsley.

Brown, A., & Murphy, L. (1999, June). Aging with developmental disabilities: Women's health issues. *ARC Newsletter.*

Burton, L., Dilworth-Anderson, P., & Bengston, V. (1992). Creating culturally relevant ways of thinking about aging and diversity: Theoretical challenges for the 21st century. In E. P. Stanford & F. M. Tores-Gil (Eds.), *Diversity: New approaches to ethnic minority aging* (pp. 129–140). New York: Baywood.

Carstensen, L. (1991). Selectivity theory: Social activity. In K. W. Schaie & M. P. Lawton (Eds.), *Annual review of gerontology and geriatrics* (pp. 195–217). New York: Springer.

Cassel, C. K., & Neugarten, B. (1991). The goals of medicine in an aging society. In R. Binstock & S. Post (Eds.), *Too old for health care?* (pp. 75–91). Baltimore: Johns Hopkins.

Cohen, E. (1988). The elderly mystique: Constraints on the autonomy of the elderly with disabilities. *The Gerontologist, 28* (Suppl.), 24–31.

Cohen, S., & Syme, S. L. (Eds.). (1985). *Social support and health.* New York: Academic Press.

Cole, T. (1988). The specter of old age: History, politics and culture in America. *Tikkun, 3,* 14–18, 93–95.

Cole, T. (1992). *The journey of life: A cultural history of aging in America.* Cambridge, UK: Cambridge University Press.

Cumming, E., & Henry, W. E. (1961). *Growing old: The process of disengagement.* New York: Basic Books.

Fadem, P. S. (1999, November). *Long-term disability and successful aging.* Paper presented at the annual meeting of the Gerontological Society of America, San Francisco, CA.

Fried, L. P., Herdman, S. J., Kuhn, K. E., Rubin, G., & Turano, K. (1990). Preclinical disability. *Journal of Aging and Health, 3,* 285–300.

Fries, J. F. (1980). Aging, natural death, and the compression of morbidity. *The New England Journal of Medicine. 303*(3), 130–135.

Harper, S. (1997). Constructing later life/constructing the body: Some thoughts from feminist theory. In A. Jamieson, S. Harper, & C. Victor (Eds.), *Critical approaches to ageing and later life* (pp. 160–172). Buckingham: Open University Press.

Holstein, M. (1998). Women and aging: Troubling implications. In M. Miner & C. L. Estes (Eds.), *Critical gerontology* (pp. 359–373). Amityville, NY: Haywood.

Kaplan, G. A., & Strawbridge, W. I. (1993). Behavioral and social factors in healthy aging. In R. A. Ables., H. C. Gift, & M. G. Ory (Eds.), *Aging and quality of life*. New York: Springer.

Kaye, H. S. (1998). Is the status of people with disabilities improving? *Disability Statistics Abstract, 21*, 1–4.

Kennedy, J., & Minkler, M. (1998). Disability theory and public policy: Implications for critical gerontology. In M. Minkler & C. L. Estes (Eds.), *Critical gerontology*. Amityville, NY: Baywood.

LeBlanc, L. A., & Matson, J. L. (1997). Aging in the developmentally disabled: Assessment and treatment. *Journal of Clinical Geropsychology, 3*(1), 37–55.

Leitman, R., Conner, E., & Risher, P. (1994). *N.O.D. Harris survey of Americans with disabilities*. New York: Louis Harris and Associates. Inc., N.O.D.

Marsiske, M., Lang, F. R., Baltes, P. B., & Baltes, M. M. (1995). Selective optimization and compensation: Life-span perspectives on successful human development. In R. A. Dixon & L. Blackman (Eds.), *Psychological compensation: Managing losses and promoting gains* (pp. 35–79). Hillsdale, NJ: Erlbaum.

Minkler, M. (1990). Aging and disability: Behind and beyond the stereotypes. *Journal of Aging Studies, 4*, 245–260.

Minkler, M. (1996). Critical perspectives on ageing: New challenges for gerontology. *Ageing and Society, 16*, 467–487.

Moody, H. (1988). *Abundance of life: Human development policies for an aging society*. New York: Columbia University Press.

Pennix, B., Guralinik, J. M., Simonsick, E. M., Kasper, J. D., Ferrucci, L., & Fried, L. P. (1998). Emotional vitality among disabled older women: The women's health and aging study. *Journal of the American Geriatrics Society, 46*, 807–815.

Phillipson, C. (1998). *Reconstructing old age: New agendas in social theory and practice*. London: Sage.

Riley, M. W. (1998). Letter to the editor. *The Gerontologist, 38*, 151.

Rowe, J., & Kahn, R. (1987). Human aging: Usual and successful. *Science, 137*, 143–149.

Rowe, J., & Kahn, R. (1997). Successful aging. *The Gerontologist, 37*, 433–440.

Rowe, J., & Kahn, R. (1998). *Successful aging*. New York: Random House.

Satariano, W. (1997). The disabilities of aging: Looking to the physical environment. *American Journal of Public Health, 87*, 331–332.

Scheidt, R. L., Humphreys, D. R., & Yorgason, 1. B. (1999). Successful aging: What's not to like? *The Journal of Applied Gerontology, 18*, 277–282.

Schulz, R., & Heckhausen, J. (1996). A life span model of successful aging. *The American Psychologist, 51*, 702–714.

Seeman, T. E. (1994). Successful aging: Reconceptualizing the aging process from a more positive perspective. In B. Vellas & J. Albarede (Eds.), *Facts and research in gerontology* (pp. 61–73). New York: Springer.

Seeman, T. E. (2000). Health promoting effects of friends and family on health outcomes in older adults. *American Journal of Health Promotion, 14,* 362–370.

Tornstam, L. (1992). The Quo Tad is of gerontology: On the scientific paradigm of gerontology. *The Gerontologist, 32,* 318–326.

Verbrugge, L., & Jette, A. (1994). The disablement process. *Social Science and Medicine, 38,* 1–14.

Wale, T., Harper, D., & Wilson, I. (1986). The aged developmentally disabled person: A. review. *Gerontologist, 26,* 622-629.

Weinstein, A., Feigley, P., & Pullen, P. (1999). Neighborhood safety and the prevalence of physical inactivity—selected states, 1996. *Morbidity and Mortality Weekly Report, 48,* 143–146.

CHAPTER THIRTY-ONE

The Promise of the International Classification of Functioning, Disability, and Health[1] (ICF)

Julie F. Smart

A disability scholar perceptively noted: "Although not posing any problem in principle, standardization of concepts and measures is no mere 'housekeeping' task. Definitional diversity is partly maintained because, even under the best of circumstances, extensive amounts of hard thought and labor are required to operationalize a concept. Moreover, even when all parties can agree that new concepts or measures are needed, disability definitions carry consequences for agencies, professionals, advocates, and politicians." (Walkup, 2000, p. 411).

Obviously, developing a comprehensive classification system such as the *International Classification of Functioning, Disability and Health* (ICF; WHO, 2001) is a massive undertaking, requiring years of preparation by task forces representing various professional and academic disciplines and necessitating substantial financial expenditure.

From "The Promise of the International Classification of Functioning, Disability and Health (ICF)," by J. Smart, 2005, *Rehabilitation Education*, 19(2&3), 191–199. Reprinted with permission of Rehabilitation Education.

[1] The author wishes to thank Debra Homa for editorial assistance with this article.

Walkup (2000) also understood the far-ranging impact of defining disability as a multifactorial experience. The definitional diversity of disability can be viewed as a progressive development that has tried to move away from viewing disability solely as a clinical diagnosis to the much broader conception of disability as an interactional experience that includes functional, psychological, and social forces in a developmental context. Walkup (2000) observed that a classification system based on defining, diagnosing, and describing disability as an interplay of factors has the potential to result in a better understanding among academic disciplines and the training these disciplines provide.

In addition, more consistent, standardized communication among professionals will lead to increased interdisciplinary collaboration which, in turn, will result in more flexible and comprehensive treatment and case management plans for people with disabilities. Describing the opportunity for working collectively to provide better services for people with disabilities, rather than being polarized into competing professional camps, Walkup (2000) also envisioned the definitional diversity of disability as an ascendant trajectory.

However, while Walkup includes agencies, professionals, policy-makers, and advocates as the stakeholders in these disability classification systems, he seems to have forgotten the most important group— people with disabilities; the people whose treatment plans, funding provisions, and, to some extent, their self-concept will result from classification systems.

In discussing the ways in which the ICF differs from its predecessor, the *International Classification of Impairments, Disabilities and Handicaps* (ICIDH; WHO, 1980), this article addresses the following topics: (1) a system that advocates both accommodation and rehabilitation; (2) a system that is individual-driven rather than diagnosis driven; (3) a system that will facilitate interdisciplinary collaboration; (4) a system in which physicians will no longer be the sole authority on disability; and (5) a system that will facilitate change in professional training and education. Finally, cautions for the use of the ICF are presented.

A COMPARISON OF THE ICIDH AND THE ICF

The ICF appears to have surmounted many of the conceptual problems that have plagued the ICIDH. Complementary narrative and standardized, structured information is provided in the ICF, thus allowing a change of emphasis "from a mechanistic, medically-driven process of physical medicine to a comprehensive, more socially driven form of rehabilitation" (Tate & Pledger, 2003, p. 292). Therefore, both rehabilitation (following the Biomedical Model's response to disability) and accommodation, (following ecological response to disability), can be recorded (Peterson, 2005; Peterson & Aguiar, 2004; Thomas, 2004; Wright, 1991).

As an individual's level of functioning or ability changes, the clinician, using the ICF, will be able to note whether the change is a result of the provision of accommodations or the result of some sort of change in the individual (Bickenbach, Somnath, Chatterli, Badley, & Üstün 1999). However, in the ICIDH, there was no way to record the effects of the individual's environment because the ICIDH did not consider the individual's environment, or his or her functions. The individual with a disability, according to the ICIDH, was a biological machine that was defective. People with disabilities were justifiably mistrustful of these classification systems, and often, were mistrustful of the clinicians who used these systems (Smart, 2005a, b). Diagnoses were considered to be objective and quantifiable facts that were wholly scientific (Davis, 1997; Dembo, 1974; Feinstein & Chapman, 2002). The ICIDH allowed users to view diagnoses as pathology. In the ICIDH, needs were defined as medical, so treatment plans, reimbursement systems, and research agendas were medically driven.

While the first priority of the ICIDH was to serve as a useful guide to treatment, individuals with the same diagnosis, regardless of resources, interests, or values, were provided similar treatment (Hahn, 1988; Kiesler, 1999; Longmore, 1995). The ICIDH did not allow the clinician to consider, understand, or authorize payment for the individual's non-medical needs. Furthermore, neither the developmental stage of the individual nor his or her cultural/ethnic/linguistic identification was included in the diagnosis or treatment plan. In short, the ICIDH was diagnosis-driven.

Diagnosis-driven, rather than individual-driven treatment plans, can result in categorization of people by their diagnosis; such as "the blind," "the mentally ill," or "the chronically ill" (Anspach, 1979; Bickenbach, 1993; Hahn, 1985, 1993; Hannah & Midlarsky, 1987; Smart, 2004). While not intentional, this categorization has effectively divided people with disabilities into competing groups and also robbed them of their collective history and memory. Perhaps most important, the self-concepts of these individuals have been powerfully shaped by medical diagnoses (Schur, 1971; Scott, 1969; Smart, 2001).

In the ICIDH, normality was viewed as synonymous with natural. Disability was not considered to be normal or natural, but rather abnormal, pathological, deviant, exotic, and alien (Goffman, 1963; Hahn, 1993, 1996). Based on this inaccurate view of disability, the popular media has been able to sell books, films, and television programs which have portrayed people with disabilities as deviant (Hahn, 1997). Zola (1993) observed that the question is not what is "normal," but rather the way in which normality is defined and sustained by political and social policy.

In contrast, the ICF employs an "ecological" view that considers the individual's functioning and environment as important factors in the determination of disability. This ecological framework, sometimes referred to as an interactional approach, can be thought of as a complex interplay between the individual's functioning and his or her environment. Nonetheless, elements of pathology/deviance/malfunctioning are present in interactional definitions of disability, such as those used in the ICF. Gill, Kewman, and Brannon (2003) explained: "However, although ecological frameworks indicate that the environment mediates the consequences of an individual's functional differences (through barriers or accommodations), those differences still are deemed aberrant or abnormal at the level of individual functioning" (2003, p. 306). Stated differently, it is better if the individual is able to perform his or her role demands.

In contrast, the Sociopolitical Model defines disability (and normality) as entirely socially constructed statuses (Smart & Smart, in press; Smart, 2005a, b). This is often termed the ontological definition of disability, which views disability not as a medical diagnosis but as a social and political status. However, to my knowledge, there is no classification based on these ontological definitions of disability.

Benefits of a Functional Approach

The functional definition of disability, in spite of its normative aspect, allows a greater understanding of the individual's experience of disability and has the potential to create individualized, cross-discipline treatment packages (Reno, Mashaw, & Gradison, 1997). Defining disability as more than a medical diagnosis will not only allow more flexibility in treatment and intervention, but may also result in cost savings. Certainly, one of the challenges is to fully capture and understand the individual and his or her subjective experiences (Dembo, 1982; Dembo, Leviton, & Wright, 1996; McCarthy, 1993, 2003; Smart, in press). It is possible to view individuals with disabilities as complete people rather than the "master" status of the disability (Schur, 1971).

The various "competing" definitions of disability have unnecessarily created barriers for individuals with disabilities. Obviously, while there are medical and biological aspects to disability, disability no longer need be defined only in medical terms (Scotch, 1988; Smart, 2001; Smart, in press; Tannebaum, 1986; Tate, 2001; Thomason, Burton, & Hyatt, 1998; Zola, 1989, 1993). As diagnoses shift emphasis, outcomes will be more focused on quality of life, wellness promotion, full independence and integration, avoiding secondary conditions and implications, and provision of assistive technology (Harper, 1991; Humes, Szymanski, & Hohenshil, 1989; Kerr & Myerson, 1987).

Challenging the Medical Paradigm

When the response to disability is no longer confined to medical fields, interdisciplinary collaboration will result (Linton, 2004; Myerson, 1988; Solarz, 1990). Financial resources will be allocated for psychosocial education, independent living, assistive technology, supportive counseling to assist the individual with confronting prejudice and discrimination, and the removal of barriers (Norcross, 2002; Parsons, Hernandez, & Jorgenson, 1988). Expanding the definition and conception of disability beyond the boundaries of medicine will result in less dependency, exclusion, and segregation for people with disabilities (Neath & Reed, 1998; Pledger, 2003). Rather than viewing the functional definition of disability as a challenge to the medical definition of disability, the ICF appears to consider the two definitions to be complementary.

Physicians will no longer be the only authorities on the experience of disability. This shift in authority will result in three major changes: 1) individuals with disabilities will be empowered to refuse the role of passive, compliant, subordinate, and dependent patients; 2) collaboration among professions will be facilitated and, accordingly, reimbursement systems will be expanded to include these other professionals, and 3) disability will become a topic for general discussion, dispelling many of the exaggerated and negative views of the disability experience.

The use of highly trained experts, such as physicians, has created a large power differential between the individual with the disability and the expert (Byrom, 2004; Eisenberg, Griggins, & Duval, 1982). In the past, most of the writing on disability was done by physicians, rather than by individuals with disabilities. Thus, physicians became the cultural translators of the disability experience (Ferguson, Ferguson, & Taylor, 1992). Like other American minority groups, people with disabilities are forging a group identity for themselves and wish to integrate their experiences and history into the multicultural and pluralistic society of the nation.

The use of medical experts has contributed to the public's lack of knowledge (or interest) of the disability experience (Eisenberg, Griggins, & Duval, 1982; Kleinfield, 1979). Conrad (2004) stated, "By defining a problem as medical it is removed from the public realm where there can be discussion by ordinary people and put on a plane where only medical people can discuss it" (p. 22).

It is society that has endowed the medical profession with such power (Engel, 1977; Fox, 1993). Understandably, the medical fields require high levels of training, expertise, and technology and because of this, it might appear appropriate that the experience of disability should be confined to medicine (Hahn, 1991; Higgins, 1992; Reynolds, 1973; Smart & Smart, in press). However, relinquishing some of the power to define and respond to disability will have profound effects. The noted disability scholar Harlan Hahn (1993) considered medicine's dominance in shaping the public's understanding of disability to have led to prejudice and discrimination because this dominance effectively relieved society of any need or responsibility to provide accommodations or to accord civil rights. Coupled with the strong normative basis of the Biomedical Model, the general public often thought that people with disabilities were biologically inferior and, therefore, the prejudice and discrimination did not appear to be prejudice and discrimination (Singer, 2000; Taylor & Bogden, 1992).

After all, the scientific credibility and rigor of the medical professional had effectively taught "society," (which includes people with disabilities), that people with disabilities were inferior, or somehow, "special" (Sobsey, 1994; Weisgerber, 1991; Wolfenberger, 1972).

Challenge to Entitlement Systems

The medical professions' dominance of the disability experience has a long history that has spanned centuries. Therefore, it is impossible to completely and thoroughly contemplate all the shifts that a new classification system, such as the ICF, will initiate. If the diagnosis/definition of disability changes, then the treatment/response also changes (Foote, 2000; Frank, Gluck, & Buckelew, 1990; Hulnick & Hulnick, 1989). If treatment changes, reimbursement systems also will be required to undergo extensive changes. In the past, under the dominance of the medical profession, the response to disability was a combination of medical treatment and financial indemnification, and physicians were the gatekeepers and supervisors of both of these responses (Berkowitz, 1987; Liachowski, 1988; Silbergard, 1997). Indeed, Stone (1984) characterized physicians as "agents of the state." Physicians documented the presence of a disability which allowed disability indemnification systems to provide financial maintenance (Berkowitz, 1987; Nagi, 1969; Liachowski, 1988; Stefan, 2001; Zola, 1989).

In these systems, functioning and the corresponding accommodations were rarely considered (Liachowitz, 1988; Stefan, 2001), and a massive system of financial work disincentives was constructed. The Social Security system and other insurance programs have experienced little change and thus reflect a view of disability and functioning that is obsolete. The Social Security Administration is a large system that affects millions of people and costs billions of dollars, all based on outmoded conceptualizations of disability. In contrast, the ICF implements a radically different approach which has the capability to incorporate the individual's strengths, resources, and assets, and the requirements of a changing labor market. Berkowitz and Hill (1986) viewed the incremental and disjointed disability policy to reach beyond the indemnification systems:

> Disability policy has not developed in the United States in a unified and coherent fashion. Unlike the attack on poverty in the 1970s or the current attention to the problems of aging, disability has not been the subject of concentrated concern (p. 26).

It is not an overstatement to observe that the ICF will lend credibility and support to a different view of disability and of the people who experience disability. Strongly entrenched systems will be subject to scrutiny and questioning, and the failure of the Social Security Administration to consider work accommodations will be challenged.

Challenge to Training Paradigms

Interagency and interprofessional collaboration are not the only factors that will change professional response to disability. These types of collaboration will require a transformation in training (Solarz, 1990). Professionals practice in the way in which they were trained (Bauman & Drake, 1997; Hogben & Waterman, 1997). Each profession and academic discipline can use its knowledge, skills, and expertise in serving people with disabilities, but only after these professions and disciplines obtain the requisite knowledge of disability (Allen-Meares & Gavin, 2000; Bluestone, Stokes, & Kuba, 1996; Kemp & Mallinkrodt, 1996). Since any consideration of an individual's level of functioning is closely tied to role demands, vocational adaptations, and assistive technology, physicians will require the assistance and collaboration of professionals who are knowledgeable in these areas (Akabas, 2000). Physicians will receive training and clinical experience on the day-to-day experience of living with a disability and the general counseling and psychology fields will provide their students with training and clinical experience with clients who have disabilities. Professional fields that previously have had little exposure to the disability experience will be expanded to include these topics. Architecture, engineering, and law students will become more aware of the needs of people with disabilities because clients with disabilities will use their services.

Rehabilitation Counseling: Paradigms of Practice

The use of the ICF will build upon the model and the foundation of rehabilitation counseling. Rather than a shift of focus, the information provided by the ICF will amplify and strengthen both the rationale and the practice of rehabilitation counseling, especially vocational rehabilitation (VR). Since its inception, vocational rehabilitation, both public and private, has been predicated on the functional model of disability in that the presence of a physical or mental disability is not the only eligibility criterion. In order to be declared eligible for services, it must be documented that the disability impedes the individual's work functioning. It is true that the only function considered in rehabilitation is work; while the ICF includes such functions as activities of daily living and recreation, in addition to work.

Nonetheless, the ICF is the classification/diagnostic system that most closely reflects the purposes, policy, and practice of the VR system. The successes of VR are even more remarkable when it is considered that disability diagnostic systems (until the ICF) have been confirmed to the biomedical model of disability.

The VR system is individual driven rather than diagnosis driven since the basis for all services is the individual and his or her work functions. VR counselors provide "employment supports," which are a type of functional supports. All VR services, including assessment, counseling, and vocational placement, are based on determining and providing functional supports. Modifying and adapting functions so the individual can succeed constitute a large part of VR services.

The ICF and Research

The ICF, and other classification systems, serve as catalysts for research and provide standardized, international definitions of variables. Wade and DeJong observed that classification systems "bring order and structure to research" (2000, p. 1386). Research and knowledge development will become less medically and diagnostic driven (Melia, Pledger, & Wilson, 2003; Perkins & Zimmeunan, 1995; Zimmerman & Warschausky, 1998). Independent variables that are not related to the disability or to the individual will be implemented, simply because the disability will no longer be viewed as the entire cause (or even the greatest source) of the individual's problems. Naturally, these independent variables will include social forces, and these will be more difficult to operationalize and standardize. Quality of life measures and wellness outcomes will serve as dependent variables.

While the first priority of the ICF is to act as a useful guide to treatment and intervention, it also will drive reimbursement and funding systems, shape the way in which services are provided, play an important role in professional education and training, and stimulate research and knowledge development. The ICF will be used in a larger array of professional settings than the ICIDH. In contrast to other classification systems, such as the *Diagnostic and Statistical Manual IV-TR* (*DSM-IV-TR*) (American Psychiatric Association, 2000), the ICF is the product of international collaboration and will be implemented throughout the world.

CAUTIONS IN THE USE OF THE ICF

The *International Classification of Functioning, Disability and Health* is strikingly different from its predecessor, *The International Classification of Impairments, Disabilities and Handicaps*. The development and publication of the ICF can be considered a landmark, major achievement. In this new classification, a shift in emphasis has occurred and disability is no longer viewed as simply a medical diagnosis. The ICF has taken many factors into consideration, and thus, it will be possible to more accurately describe the individual's experience with a disability.

It is difficult to state whether the ICF is simply a shift in emphasis or whether the ICF has redefined disability. Nonetheless, it is safe to say that the ICF will help shape the discussion of disability. Rather than viewing disabilities as conditions that objectively exist, the experience of a disability will be conceptualized as a phenomenon that is created though societal definitions and conditions. To the general public, the ICF will be seen as a technical manual used by professionals. However, its diagnostic classification system will serve to illuminate social problems and gaps in social policy.

No diagnostic or classification can completely satisfy every need (Smart & Smart, 1997). For example, using the ICF, it will be difficult to quantify or measure the extent of prejudice and discrimination against people with disabilities, in spite of the fact that many individuals say that such handicapism is their greatest obstacle. Furthermore, as has been discussed, there is still a normative element to the ICF.

The value of the ICF lies in its professional applications—the way in which clinicians accept and use it. In turn, its clinical use will depend upon the quality of training—both preservice and inservice.

REFERENCES

Akabas, S. H. (2000). Practice in the world of work. In P. Allen-Meares & C. Garvin (Eds.). *The Handbook of Social Work Direct Practice* (pp. 499–517). Thousand Oaks, CA: Sage.

Allen-Meares, P., & Gavin, C. (Eds.). (2000). *The handbook of social work direct practice*. Thousand Oaks, CA: Sage.

American Psychiatric Association. (2000). *Diagnostic and statistical manual of mental disorders* (Fourth edition—text revision; *DSM-IV-TR*). Washington, DC: Author.

Anspach, R.R. (1979). From stigma to identity politics: Political activism among the physically disabled and former mental patients. *Social Science and Medicine, 13A*, 765–773.

Bauman, H. D. L., & Drake, J. (1997). Silence is not without voice: Including deaf culture within the multicultural curricula. In L. J. Davis (Ed.), *Disability studies reader* (pp. 307–314). New York: Routledge.

Berkowitz, M. (1987). *Disabled policy: America's programs for the handicapped.* London, England: Cambridge University.

Berkowitz, M., & Hill, M. A. (Eds.). (1986). *Disability and the labor market: Economic problems, policies, and programs.* Ithaca, NY: Cornell University.

Bickenbach, J. E. (1993). *Physical disability and social policy.* Toronto: University of Toronto.

Bickenbach, J. E., Somnath, C., Badley, E. M., & Ustun, T. B. (1999). Models of disablement, universalism and the International Classification of Impairments, Disabilities, and Handicaps. *Social Science & Medicine, 48*, 1173–1187.

Bluestone, H. H., Stokes, A., & Kuba, S. A. (1996). Toward an integrated program design: Evaluating the status of diversity training in a graduate school curriculum. *Professional Psychology: Research and Practice, 27*, 394–400.

Byrom, B. (2004). A pupil and a patient: Hospital schools in progressive America. In S. Danforth & S. D. Taff (Eds.), *Crucial Readings in Special Education* (pp. 25–37). Upper Saddle River, NJ: Pearson-Merrill, Prentice-Hall.

Conrad, P. (2004). The discovery of hyperkinesis: Notes on the medicalization of deviant behavior. In S. Danforth & S. D. Taff (Eds.), *Crucial Readings in Special Education* (pp. 18–24). Upper Saddle River, NJ: Pearson-Merrill, Prentice-Hall.

Davis, L. J. (1997). Constructing normalcy: The bell curve, the novel, and the invention of the disabled body in the nineteenth century. In L. J. Davis (Ed.), *Disability studies reader* (pp. 307–314). New York: Routledge.

Dembo, T. (1982). Some problems in rehabilitation as seen by a Lewinian. *Journal of Social Issues, 38*, 131–139.

Dembo, T. (1974). The paths to useful knowledge. *Rehabilitation Psychology, 21*, 124–128.

Dembo, T., Leviton, G. L., & Wright, B. A. (1975). Adjustment to misfortune: A problem of social-psychological rehabilitation. *Rehabilitation Psychology, 2*, 1–100.

Eisenberg, M. G., Griggins, C., & Duval, R. J. (Eds.). (1982). *Disabled people as second class citizens.* New York: Springer.

Engel, G. L. (1977). The need for a new medical model: A challenge for biomedicine. *Science, 196*, 129–136.

Ferguson, P. M., Ferguson, D. L., & Taylor, S. J. (Eds.) (1992). *Interpreting disability: A qualitative reader.* New York: Teachers College, Columbia University.

Feinstein, A. R., & Chapman, H. (2002). *Principles of medical statistics.* Boca Raton, FL: CRC Press.

Foote, W. E. (2000). A model for psychological consultation in cases involving the Americans with Disabilities Act. *Professional Psychology, 31,* 190–196.

Fox, D. M. (1993). *Power and illness: The failure and future of America's health policy.* Berkeley: University of California Press.

Frank, R. G., Gluck, J. P., & Buckelew, S. P. (1990). Rehabilitation: Psychology's greatest opportunity? *American Psychologist, 45,* 757–761.

Goffman, E. (1963). *Stigma: Notes on the management of spoiled identity.* Englewood Cliffs, NJ: Prentice Hall.

Gill, C. J., Kewman, D. G., & Brannon, R. W. (2003). Transforming psychological practice and society: Policies that reflect the new paradigm. *American Psychologist, 58,* 305–312.

Hahn, H. (1985). Toward a politics of disability: Definitions, disciplines, and policies. *Social Science Journal, 22,* 87–105.

Hahn, H. (1988). The politics of physical differences: Disability and discrimination. *Journal of Social Issues, 44,* 39–47.

Hahn, H. (1991). Alternative views of empowerment: Social services and civil rights. *Journal of Rehabilitation, 57,* 17–19.

Hahn, H. (1993). The political implications of disability definitions and data. *Journal of Disability Policy Studies, 4,* 41–52.

Hahn, H. (1996). Antidiscrimination laws and social research on disability: The minority group perspectives. *Behavioral Sciences and the Law, 14,* 41–59.

Hahn, H. (1997). Advertising the acceptable employment image: Disability and capitalism. In L. J. Davis. (Ed.), *The Disability Studies Reader* (pp. 172–186). New York: Routledge.

Hannah, M. E., & Midlarsky, E. (1987). Differential impact of labels and behavioral descriptions on attitudes toward people with disabilities. *Rehabilitation Psychology, 32,* 227–238.

Harper, D. (1991). Paradigms for investigating rehabilitation and adaptation to childhood disability and chronic illness. *Journal of Pediatric Psychology, 16,* 533–542.

Higgins, P. C. (1992). *Making disability: Exploring the social transformation of human variation.* Springfield, IL: Charles C Thomas.

Hogben, M., & Waterman, C. K. (1997). Are all of your students represented in their textbooks? A content analysis of coverage of diversity issues in introductory psychology textbooks. *Teaching of Psychology, 24,* 95–100.

Hulnick, M. R., & Hulnick, H. R. (1989). Life's challenges: Curse or opportunity? Counseling families of persons with disabilities. *Journal of Counseling and Development, 68,* 166–170.

Humes, C. W., Szymanski, E. M., & Hohenshil, T. H. (1989). Roles of counseling in enabling persons with disabilities. *Journal of Counseling and Development, 68,* 145–150.

Kemp, N. T., & Mallinkrodt, B. (1996). Impact of professional training on case conceptualization of clients with a disability. *Professional Psychology: Research and Practice, 27,* 378–385.

Kerr, N., & Myerson, L. (1987). Independence as a goal and value of people with physical disabilities: Some caveats. *Rehabilitation Psychology, 32,* 173–180.

Kiesler, D. J. (1999). *Beyond the disease model of mental disorders.* Westport. CT: Praeger.

Kleinfield, S. (1979). *The hidden minority: A profile of handicapped Americans.* Boston: Atlantic Monthly Press.

Liachowitz, C. H. (1988). *Disability as a social construct: Legislative roots.* Philadelphia: University of Pennsylvania.

Linton, S. (2004). Divided society. In S. Danforth & S. D. Taff. (Eds.), *Crucial readings in special education* (pp. 138–147). Upper Saddle River, NJ: Merrill Prentice Hall.

Longmore, P. K. (1995). Medical decision making and people with disabilities: A clash of cultures. *Journal of Law, Medicine and Ethics, 23,* 82–87.

McCarthy, H. (1993). Learning with Beatrice A. Wright: A breath of fresh air that uncovers the unique virtues and human flaws in us all. *Rehabilitation Education, 10,* 149–166.

McCarthy, H. (2003). The disability rights movement: Experiences and perspectives of selected leaders in the disability community. *Rehabilitation Counseling Bulletin, 46,* 209–223.

Melia, R. P., Pledger, C., & Wilson, R. (2003). Disability and rehabilitation research. *American Psychologist, 58,* 289–295.

Meyerson, L. (1988). The social psychology of physical disability. *Journal of Social Issues, 44,* 173–188.

Nagi, S. Z. (1969). *Disability and rehabilitation: Legal, clinical, and self-concepts and measurements.* Columbus: Ohio State University.

Neath, J. F., & Reed, C. A. (1998). Power and empowerment in multicultural education: Using the radical democratic model for rehabilitation education, *Rehabilitation Counseling Bulletin, 42.*

Norcross, J. C. (Ed.). (2002). *Psychotherapy relationships that work: Therapist contributions and responsiveness to patient needs.* New York: Oxford University.

Parsons, R., Hernandez, S., & Jorgensen, J. (1988). Integrated problem solving. *Social Work, 33,* 417–421.

Perkins, D. D., & Zimmerman, M. A. (1995). Empowerment theory: Research and applications. *American Journal of Community Psychology, 23,* 569–579.

Peterson, D. B. (2005). International Classification of Functioning, Disability and Health (ICF): An introduction for rehabilitation psychologists. *Rehabilitation Psychology, 50,* 105–112.

Peterson, D. B., & Aguiar, L. J. (2004). History and systems: United States. In T. F. Riggar & D. R. Maki. (Eds.), *Handbook of Rehabilitation Counseling* (pp. 50–74). New York: Springer Series on Rehabilitation.

Pledger, C. (2003). Discourse on disability and rehabilitation issues. *American Psychologist, 58,* 279–284.

Reno, V. P., Mashaw, J. L., & Gradison, B. (Eds.). (1997). *Disability: Challenges for social insurance, health care financing, and labor market policy.* Washington, DC: National Academy of Social Insurance.

Reynolds, L. T. (1973). The medical institution. In L. T. Reynolds & J. M. Henslin. (Eds.), *American Society: A Critical Analysis* (pp. 198–324). New York: David McKay.

Schur, E. M. (1971). *Labeling deviant behavior: Its sociological implications.* New York: Harper and Row.

Scotch, R. K. (1988). Disability as a basis for a social movement: Advocacy and the politics of definition. *Journal of Social Issues, 44,* 159–172.

Scott, R. (1969). *The making of blind men: A study of adult socialization.* New York: Russell Sage Foundation.

Silbergard, C. (1997). A woman addresses her recurrent depression in psychotherapy: Private practice. In T. S. Kerson. (Ed.), *Social Work in Health Settings.*

Singer, P. (2000). *Writings on an ethical life.* New York: Ecco.

Smart, J. F. (2004). Models of disability: The juxtaposition of biology and social construction. In T. F. Riggar & D.R. Maki (Eds.), *Handbook of Rehabilitation Counseling* (pp. 25–49). Springer Series on Rehabilitation. New York: Springer.

Smart, D. W., & Smart, J. F. (1997). DSM-IV and culturally sensitive diagnosis: Some observations for counselors. *Journal of Counseling and Development, 75,* 392–398.

Smart, J. F. (2001). *Disability, society and the individual.* Austin, TX: Pro-Ed.

Smart, J. F. (2005a). Challenges to the biomedical model of disability: Changes to the practice of rehabilitation counseling. *Directions in Rehabilitation Counseling, 16,* 33–44.

Smart, J. F. (2005b). Tracing the ascendant trajectory of models of disability: Confounding competition or a cross model approach. Utah State University: unpublished manuscript.

Smart, J. F., & Smart, D. W. (In press). Models of disability: Implications for the counseling profession. *Journal of Counseling and Development.*

Smart, J. F. (in press). Challenges to the biomedical model of disability. *Advances in Medical Psychotherapy and Psychodiagnosis.* American Board of Medical Psychotherapists.

Sobsey, D. (1994). *Violence and abuse in the lives of people with disabilities: The end of silent acceptance.* Baltimore: Brookes.

Solarz, A.L. (1990). Rehabilitation psychologists: A place in the policy process? *American Psychologist, 45,* 766–770.

Stefan, S. (2001). *Unequal rights: Discrimination against people with mental disabilities and the Americans with Disabilities Act.* Washington, DC: American Psychiatric Association.

Stone, D. A. (1984). *The disabled state.* Philadelphia: Temple University.

Tannenbaum, S. J. (1986). *Engineering disability: Public policy and compensatory technology.* Philadelphia: Temple University.

Tate, D. G. (2001). Hospital to community: Changes in practice and outcomes. *Rehabilitation Psychology, 46,* 125–138.

Tate, D. G., & Pledger, D. C. (2003). An integrative conceptual framework of disability: New directions for research. *American Psychologist, 58,* 289–295.

Taylor, S. J., & Bogden, R. (1992). Defending illusions: The institution's struggle for survival. In P. M. Ferguson, D. L. Ferguson, & S. J. Taylor. (Eds.), *Interpreting disability: A qualitative reader* (pp. 78–98). New York: Teachers College, Columbia University.

Thomas, K. R. (2004). Old wine in a slightly cracked new bottle. *American Psychologist, 59*, 274–275.

Thomason, T., Burton, J. F., Jr., & Hyatt, D. R. (Eds.). (1998). *New approaches to disability in the work place*. Madison: University of Wisconsin.

Wade, D. T., & deJong, B. A. (2000). Recent advances in rehabilitation. *Behavioral Medicine Journal, 320*, 1385–1388.

Walkup, J. (2000). Disability, health care, and public policy. *Rehabilitation Psychology, 45*, 409–422.

Weisgerber, R. S. (1991). *Quality of life for persons with disabilities*. Gaithersburg, MD: Aspen.

Wolfensberger, W. (1972). *The principle of normalization in human services*. Toronto: National Institute on Mental Retardation.

World Health Organization. (1980). *International classification of impairments, disabilities and handicaps: A manual of classification relating to the consequences of disease*. Geneva, Switzerland: Author.

World Health Organization. (2001). *International Classification of Functioning, Disability, and Health*. Geneva, Switzerland: Author.

Wright, B. A. (1991). Labeling: The need for greater person-environment individuation. In C. R. Snyder & D. R. Forsythe (Eds.), *Handbook of social and clinical psychology* (pp. 469–487). Elmsford, NY: Pergamon.

Zimmerman, M.A., & Warschausky, S. (1998). Empowerment theory for rehabilitation research: Conceptual and methodological issues. *Rehabilitation Psychology, 43*, 3–16.

Zola, I. K. (1989). Toward the necessary universalizing of a disability policy. *Milbank Quarterly, 67*, 401–428.

Zola, I. K. (1993). Disability statistics, what we count and what it tells us. *Journal of Disability Policy Studies, 4*, 9–39.

CHAPTER THIRTY-TWO

Recovery From Psychiatric Disabilities

Patricia B. Nemec and Cheryl J. Gagne

"Recovery-oriented services" are explicitly valued in state mental health policies (Jacobson & Curtis, 2000), and increasingly prominent in national-level statements on mental health service needs and policies, such as reports from The President's New Freedom Commission on Mental Health (2003) and the Surgeon General's Office (US Department of Health and Human Services 1999), and a statement by Charles Curie (2005), administrator of the federal Substance Abuse and Mental Health Administration. "Recovery" means more than a successful rehabilitation outcome, such as keeping a job for a certain period of time. People who have psychiatric disabilities often see success for themselves in broader terms—not just obtaining a good job, but also living in a comfortable home, establishing close relationships with friends and family, and having a sense that life is worth living. People with psychiatric disabilities have come to describe this success as "recovery": the belief that life is purposeful and meaningful in spite of having a disability.

DEFINING RECOVERY

Patricia Deegan (1988), one of the earliest and most eloquent writers on the subject of recovery from a psychiatric disability, describes recovery

From "Recovery from psychiatric disabilities," by P. Nemec and C. Gagne, 2005, *Journal of Applied Rehabilitation Counseling, 36*(4), 4–10. Reprinted with permission of The National Rehabilitation Counseling Association.

as "the urge, the wrestle, and the resurrection" (p. 15). The choice of such poetic language is deliberate, as it captures the personal, emotional, and spiritual aspects of recovery. The word "resurrection" in particular implies a rising up from some depth of despair to an experience of light and hope. Clearly, this means more than just getting a job.

In more prosaic language, but still emphasizing more than work, Ruth Ralph (2000) describes recovery as "a process of learning to approach each day's challenges, overcome our disabilities, learn skills, live independently and contribute to society" (p. 27). Both Deegan and Ralph point out that the process of recovery, a "journey of the heart" (Deegan, 1996), is made possible through the support and shared hope of people who believe that such recovery is possible. Recovery, these experts emphasize, does not mean cure. A person can be "in recovery" or "recovered" even if symptoms or functional limitations remain.

The process of recovery is described more often and more consistently than the outcome of recovery, as the concept itself implies unfolding, developing, or changing in some way. Any static and measurable end point used to indicate that someone who had a psychiatric disorder is now "recovered" necessarily neglects the dynamic nature of the concept. If recovery is seen as a process more than as an outcome, the definition of "recovery-oriented services" has to include the service factors that facilitate that process. At a minimum, services and services systems must make a belief in recovery explicit through mission and policy statements, through implementing individualized procedures designed to help achieve personal goals, and through involving the people who use the services in service design, delivery, and evaluation (Anthony, 2000).

Rehabilitation vs. Recovery

Rehabilitation involves helping a person with a disability to achieve his or her life goals, most often through services that facilitate competitive employment and independent living. In psychiatric rehabilitation, those services typically include developing the skills and supports needed to be successful in a desired role and setting. Skills include both the things that a person needs to do well relative to the role, such as job-specific skills, and those needed to manage or compensate for the disabling condition. Similarly, supports include universal resource needs, such as transportation to work, the right work clothes, and so on, as well as disability-related supports and accommodations.

As is true of many theoretical constructs, the practical day-to-day distinction between rehabilitation and recovery may be difficult to make. Recovery-oriented services, like rehabilitation, may include developing skills and supports, but the focus is less on role achievement, and more on managing all that goes into life with a disability. In a global sense, success in rehabilitation, whether for a physical or a psychiatric disability, is measured by observable gains in such things as stamina, independence in activities of daily living, and income from competitive employment. In contrast, success or progress in recovery is more difficult to measure, as measures of recovery need to take into account such hard-to-quantify factors as self-esteem and quality of life.

Of course, success in rehabilitation can contribute to a sense of recovery. Consider, for example, a short-lived physical injury requiring rehabilitation: improvement in strength and mobility makes it easier to manage one's daily chores and to get back to work, yielding a sense of increased independence and accomplishment. In many instances, the severity of an injury and the degree of residual pain and dysfunction influence a person's perspective on whether the injury is/was just an inconvenience or represents a life-altering change. Any practicing rehabilitation counselor learns early on that some people weather illness, injury, and disability better than others, and that a positive rehabilitation outcome such as a return to work does not guarantee that the person will then believe that life is good. On the other hand, most rehabilitation counselors have met individuals who are content with life, who persevere through adversity, and are inspiring to others in spite of living with a significant and limiting disability or illness. It is the "life is good" part that is meant by "recovery."

Adjustment vs. Recovery

Many aspects of the recovery process are similar across disability groups (Anthony, 1993; Nemec & Taylor, 1990). The literature on adjustment to a physical disability provides parallels to the literature on recovery from a psychiatric disability. At least three important differences can be identified between "adjustment" and "recovery." First, the literature on adjustment to disability originated largely in the writings of service providers and researchers interested in producing a stage model, which often appears similar to the stage models of grief or bereavement. The literature on recovery grew out of personal descriptions of the experience written by people experiencing a psychiatric disability.

Second, the connotations of the term "adjustment" portray a passive individual learning to make do, even if that was never the intent of those writing about adjustment. In contrast, "recovery" suggests both the individual adaptation and the challenges imposed from outside, which often include troubles caused by the services and people who are supposed to be helping. Negative mental health service system experiences have led to the use of the term "survivor," or "consumer-survivor," to indicate that treatment itself can be a barrier to recovery.

Finally, the image of recovery includes a hopefulness that is, over and over, the driving theme in the literature. Adjustment, on the other hand, implies a sense of resignation rather than mastery. In addition to the importance of hope; recovery experts emphasize the importance of empowerment—recognizing both one's responsibility for and right to a better life.

Of course, any acquired disability is likely to require a period of adjustment while the person sorts out what she or he can and can not do, now that this disabling condition is a part of daily life. Changes in ability to conduct some activities can influence ability to fulfill a valued role, such as when a physical limitation makes it harder to be the kind of parent, or partner, or employee that someone wishes to be. Similarly, changes in abilities and role functioning can influence identity and self-image, such as when a disability prevents someone from continuing in a fulfilling job role or career. All of these changes involve adjustment, but these adjustments do not, by themselves, indicate recovery.

Physical Disabilities vs. Psychiatric Disabilities

Probably more significant than the difference in the broad categories of physical vs. psychiatric disability is the difference between disorders that are relatively stable and those that run a variable course. Most psychiatric disorders include some cyclical exacerbations and remissions, and these usually are unpredictable in timing and severity. In this sense; psychiatric disorders are more similar to physical disorders like multiple sclerosis or systemic lupus erythematosis (SLE) than to more stable disability categories like amputation, cerebral palsy, or spinal cord injury, or to conditions that, given today's limited intervention options, will likely deteriorate, such as Alzheimer's Disease or amyotrophic lateral sclerosis (ALS).

Dramatic variations in symptoms and functional limitations make generalizations about treatment and rehabilitation prognosis difficult for most of the severe psychiatric disorders. Variations in symptoms and in how a person is affected by those symptoms also occur in physical disorders, such as SLE, traumatic brain injury, and chronic back pain. Whatever the disability, these variations can complicate both rehabilitation and recovery, due to limited accuracy in assessment and an inability to predict the course of the disorder.

In addition, many psychiatric disorders can be considered "invisible" disabilities that, like SLE or chronic pain, can make other people doubt the severity of the disorder and consequently raise questions about the person's motivation to improve. The "invisibility" factor is compounded by negative public attitudes toward psychiatric disorders—attitudes that often are also held by the person diagnosed with a mental illness, causing both a negative self-image and a reluctance to seek help (Corrigan & Kleinlein, 2005). These attitudes may be related to the commonly held view that a psychiatric disorder is evidence of a personality flaw or character weakness—a misguided view that leads even some trained rehabilitation counselors to describe the disorganization of schizophrenia or the fatigue of depression as a "lack of motivation."

A final factor that seems to complicate rehabilitation and recovery, and that seems to differentiate most psychiatric disabilities from most physical disabilities, is that symptoms and functional limitations often affect interpersonal relationships. Schizophrenia may be the best example of a potentially disabling psychiatric condition that causes problems in social functioning, but affective disorders and anxiety disorders also may cause relationship problems. The relationship between a person using vocational rehabilitation (VR) services and his/her rehabilitation counselor is the medium through which positive outcomes occur, as evidence from the VR Longitudinal Study makes clear (Hayward & Schmidt-Davis, 2003). When that relationship is impaired, perhaps from a combination of poor social skills on the part of the person using services and lack of training or negative attitudes on the part of the person providing services, then rehabilitation outcomes will suffer.

Evidence of Recovery from Psychiatric Disabilities

Part of the negative attitudes of both the general public and of mental health and VR service providers comes from the erroneous belief that "once mentally ill, always mentally ill." In fact, research published over the past two decades indicates that most people diagnosed with a mental illness do recover in the sense that they go on to have productive lives that include work and positive relationships, and often do not require regular medication or other psychiatric treatment. Calabrese and Corrigan (2005) have concisely and clearly summarized this research, which provides a solid base of evidence that outcomes for people with schizophrenia and other severe psychiatric disorders is not always poor. In fact, rates of recovery range from 48% to 77% over multiple long-term studies, suggesting that most people with these serious disorders get better. In fact, with the right treatment at the earliest signs of psychosis, complete remission can occur in anywhere from 70% to 90% of people treated (Liberman & Kopelowicz, 2005).

While disability-related factors have some general relevance to prognosis for schizophrenia, such as age of onset and the presence of negative symptoms (e.g., avolition, flat affect), these factors cannot be used to accurately predict outcomes for any particular individual. Many factors are likely to contribute to positive outcomes, including access to treatment. Effective medications, treatments, and rehabilitation interventions have been developed, but are not used as widely as might be expected (Drake, Goldman, Leff et al., 2001), given the evidence of their effectiveness. However, access to "modern" medicine in countries categorized as "developed" is not necessarily the most important determinant of success. Contrary to expectation, people with schizophrenia in "developing" countries have tended to have higher success rates than people with schizophrenia in "developed" countries. Reasons for this difference are not clearly understood, but Calabrese and Corrigan (2005) suggest that the social and family environments, including attitudes toward mental illnesses, may play an important role. Treatment and rehabilitation, then, may contribute to recovery, but recovery can, and does, occur without these professional interventions (Anthony, 1993).

THE PROCESS OF RECOVERY

There is no standardized trajectory for recovery from a psychiatric disability. Although research suggests enough commonalities across individual experiences to suggest a framework, individual experiences should be expected to vary. There is no standardized course or process (Strauss, Hafez, Lieberman, & Harding, 1985), no predictable timeline, and no guarantee of continual "progress." Nonetheless, patterns can be found in individual descriptions elicited through research projects and published in first-person accounts. The tendency of experts in this area is to describe a discrete series of stages of recovery, but the reader is cautioned that real people in real time do not move along this type of linear track. The terms used here to describe these stages of recovery are based on a longitudinal study conducted at the Boston University Center for Psychiatric Rehabilitation (Gagne, 2005; Spaniol, Wewiorski, Gagne, & Anthony, 2002), and the terms used are not universal.

At the time of onset of a severe psychiatric disability, most people experience acute symptoms that can be frightening and disruptive. In the early days, months, and sometimes years of this experience, a person might be described as "overwhelmed by the disability." As with physical disorders that defy easy diagnosis and have an insidious onset, a person experiencing the first signs of a psychiatric disorder may be unsure what is happening. Some people are unwilling to acknowledge that difficulties could be due to a mental illness—not surprising given society's prejudice and fear toward "the mentally ill" (Corrigan, 2005). Negative public attitudes can affect a person's self-image, and even create a reluctance to seek treatment (Corrigan & Kleinlein, 2005).

As with any significant stressor, feeling overwhelmed may result from a whole host of burdens, rather than simply that one stressor. Clearly, the experience of having a psychiatric disorder is going to be difficult under any circumstances. But the added weight of poverty and a dangerous neighborhood, to name two common problems, will make it that much more likely that a person becomes overwhelmed. For some people, a psychiatric disorder has consequences that add to theft struggles, such as loss of work, loss of family and friends, and the weight gain from medications that then causes physical health problems.

With the right supports, including, for some people, treatment with medication and psychotherapy, acute symptoms wane and/or become more familiar and manageable. For many people, the variable course and unpredictable nature of the psychiatric disorder results in "struggling with the disability"—a time of searching for the right supports, learning to recognize warning signs of impending difficulties, and improving self-care to maintain health and prevent reoccurrences. The degree of "struggling," as with the degree of being overwhelmed, is likely to be affected by life circumstances, and by the degree to which treatments accessed provide benefit or harm.

As longitudinal research demonstrates, most people who experience a psychiatric disorder are able to overcome it in some way—either the disorder goes into remission, or is no longer present, or the person has found a way to manage in spite of some ongoing problems. The concept of psychiatric disability captures the idea that some people do have to live with a psychiatric disorder that lasts for a long time, and do have to alter their lives in some way to accommodate that fact. This is similar to experiencing a physical disability that remains present, such as the chronic pain of rheumatoid arthritis that limits functioning in some way, requires some form of medication, therapy, and good general health care, but that does not prevent a person from living a full life. The point where the person is able to go along in a fairly consistent manner, doing the things that she or he finds important, can be described as the stage of "living with the disability." Of course, a sudden change in life circumstances, or in the disorder itself, can cause some "recycling" of these stages, where someone may be "living with" for a while, then "struggling with" for a while, then able to "live with" again.

Longitudinal research and first-person accounts from people who have a psychiatric disability suggest that some individuals achieve a level of "living beyond the disability." This might be described as achieving a new meaning or purpose in life because of (not in spite of) the disability. This takes the form of a newly found appreciation for the preciousness of life, for the value of "living for today," for the gifts inherent in the many negative aspects of having to manage a disability. Some people find this meaning through advocating for systems change, through helping others directly, or through what might be described as a spiritual awakening.

Spiritual Factors in Recovery

If the essence of recovery is a sense of meaning and purpose in life, it is not surprising that the search for meaning often takes on a spiritual quality. For some, spirituality involves religious faith; for others, "spiritual" simply means exploring existential issues. Experiencing a disability that has long-term effects and creates ongoing problems in living often prompts questions like, "Why me?" and "Is living like this worth the effort?" and "Who am I now?" The depth of this sort of struggle is often best understood by someone who has experienced it, which may help explain the value of mutual help and peer support groups for people in recovery.

The search for faith or the struggle to find meaning in life may seem beyond the rehabilitation counseling relationship, particularly for a counselor focused primarily on job placement, support, or accommodation issues. It is important to remember, though, that a person's success at work may be intimately related to one's sense of worth, of social standing, of contribution to others, and of personal identity. Vocational rehabilitation offers more than just a job, and may raise questions beyond choice of occupation. For example, the decision to pursue a part-time hourly wage job as an unskilled worker is not a simple decision for someone who was studying pre-med at an Ivy League university before developing a psychiatric disorder.

While a rehabilitation counselor may be reluctant to tackle spiritual issues—whether due to a narrowly defined counselor role, lack of clinical training, or incompatible personal beliefs—the recognition that spiritual issues play a part in recovery may, at minimum, prompt a referral to a resource that can provide an opportunity to explore the use of spiritual beliefs and religious practices as an aid to coping with the experience and consequences of having a psychiatric disorder (Kehoe, 1999). Many people find their faith a source of comfort and strength. Faith does not necessarily refer to religion, as people also find renewal and solace through other "spiritual" avenues, such as creative endeavors or communing with nature.

Residual Limitations

Whether psychiatric or physical, achieving the point of being able to "live with" or "live beyond" a disability does not mean that all of the problems and burdens associated with the disability have vanished or that the person should be considered "cured." Many people who could be considered as having a psychiatric disability have some sort of ongoing difficulty, although the form and severity of that difficulty varies significantly from person to person, and often from time to time. Relapse or exacerbation of the disability is not evidence of failure to recover, but is part of living with a disability that runs a cyclical course. The experience of a relapse can be frightening, as it may trigger memories of earlier difficulties, and may raise the specter of failure and hopelessness. A person may temporarily lose sight of the strengths and coping strategies that worked in the past, and may need reminding.

In addition, many people who take psychotropic medication to help manage their disabilities find that the medications can create limitations as well. Sometimes it is impossible to accurately identify the cause of the limitation—for example, difficulty with concentration is a common problem that cuts across the psychiatric disability categories of schizophrenia, depression, and anxiety disorders. However, medications, environmental context (e.g., noise level), and co-occurring disorders (e.g., a learning disability) also can contribute to problems with concentration.

Rehabilitation counselors may find it more useful to focus on strengths and struggles with such work-related functions as attention, concentration, memory, and organization, rather than focus on symptoms or diagnosis (MacDonald-Wilson & Nemec, 2005). Once such functional limitations are identified, the individual can work with the rehabilitation counselor to identify needed skills, supports, and accommodations that will minimize the interference of these difficulties with job performance. Looking at a person's goals and abilities, rather than at his or her illness, is a defining characteristic of rehabilitation. Recovery-oriented services help further, by pointing out that who we are is not the same as what we can do or what illness or disability we might have. The process of recovery seems to include movement from identity with the illness ("I am a schizophrenic" or "I am a diabetic") to an identify separate from the illness ("I have schizophrenia" or "I have diabetes"), indicating "the capacity to recognize the presence of mental illness without being defined by it" (Davidson, Sells, Sangster, & O'Connell, 2005, p. 156).

Facilitators of Recovery

Given that recovery from a psychiatric disability can and does occur, the rehabilitation counselor will want to know whether there are potential predictive factors to gauge prognosis and/or potential interventions that can increase the likelihood of recovery. Epidemiological studies identify some factors that, across large numbers of people, help predict outcome (Liberman & Kopelowicz, 2005; Liberman, Kopelowicz, Ventura, & Gutkind, 2002). For example, age at onset, type of symptoms, and pre-morbid functioning are related to outcome. However, while research does suggest some prognostic factors, the evidence also suggests that prediction of individual success is virtually impossible. Therefore, it is best to assume that recovery is possible for anyone. The following descriptions of facilitators of recovery should not be considered an exhaustive list, but they do provide a broad overview of some factors that have been identified in the literature. Some have been initially studied as barriers—in fact, the absence of any of the facilitators listed could be considered a barrier. Some facilitators described may seem to fall far outside the purview of the rehabilitation counselor; others will have a more obvious relevance. Specific implications for rehabilitation counseling practice are included in the following section.

A person's life circumstances can influence the onset, severity, and course of a psychiatric disorder. People who have a favorable situation, including an adequate income, stable housing, loving friends and family, are likely to fare better than people living alone in poverty in a dangerous neighborhood. A person's internal resources also make a difference, and someone with a strong sense of self, good coping skills, assertiveness skills, and an optimistic outlook on life may be better able to face, accept, and manage a psychiatric disorder than someone without these resources. Related factors that can influence the course of recovery include cultural and personal beliefs about the cause, meaning, and proper treatment of a mental illness, and personal experiences, such as a history of child abuse or domestic violence.

Treatment often helps. People who have a psychiatric disability and get early access to effective treatment, including the right medication, seem to fare better in the long run. To some extent, this might be a matter of luck (e.g., living in a resource-rich area or finding the right psychiatrist), but research evidence is now suggesting that the design of mental health treatment systems and the approach of treatment personnel can make a significant difference. A good relationship and a sense of partnership with mental health services providers is beneficial, including helping the individual gain more of a sense of control or mastery over his or her disability.

Effective treatment and rehabilitation can be compromised by the presence of co-occurring psychiatric disorders and by poor physical health, which also can complicate recovery. Substance use and abuse can create barriers, while good self-care in symptom management, exercise, and diet can facilitate recovery. Integrated substance abuse and psychiatric treatment is important for maximizing success with these co-occurring disorders (Drake, Essock, Shaner, Carey, Minkoff et al., 2001), meaning that rehabilitation services are offered by one service provider or team, eliminating the necessity to coordinate services across programs and systems.

People with psychiatric disorders also need access to medical care and treatment that take into account their complex interaction with psychiatric treatment—perhaps through a similar integrated treatment model. Preventive care, such as smoking cessation, nutritional counseling, and guidance in designing an exercise program, are rarely made available to people who use public mental health services, but could be important factors for recovery.

Access to rehabilitation services gives people the opportunity to build both skills and supports. Rehabilitation programs that help a person gain meaning through work and education seem especially beneficial in promoting recovery, as does assistance in gaining stable and independent housing.

Social factors seem strongly related to the recovery process. Much of the recovery literature quotes individuals who say that the single greatest contributor to recovery was that "someone believed in me." A strong connection to others, involvement in social activities, and a good social support network contribute to recovery. Related literature emphasizes the role of social support in coping and resilience, and describes social support as a buffer against stress (Sarason & Duck, 2001). Given the common difficulties in social skills experienced by people with psychiatric disabilities, especially schizophrenia, the development of social skills and enhancement of social networks may be an important component of treatment, rehabilitation, and recovery-oriented services.

Some factors that facilitate recovery seem to transcend any of the categories mentioned so far. Research suggests the importance of hope (Russinova, 1999), of a commitment to making a change, and of a sense of empowerment, perhaps through involvement in a self-help community or advocacy effort. Hope is one example of a "transcendent" factor because it is influenced by an individual's natural optimism, personal experience with overcoming past difficulties, beliefs about mental illnesses, and the messages given by treatment and rehabilitation personnel—both intended and unintended messages.

IMPLICATIONS FOR PRACTICE

An understanding of the process of recovery from a psychiatric disability informs vocational rehabilitation practice in a number of ways, ranging from assessment, to goal-setting, to the types of services provided, and to the manner of interacting during an individual meeting.

When conducting an assessment, the person's current stage of recovery needs to be considered. Although no easy assessment measure exists, an experienced and knowledgeable rehabilitation counselor can explore whether the person's psychiatric disability is understood and effectively managed, and can gauge the degree to which that person is "struggling" or "living" with it. The presence of co-occurring psychiatric and physical disorders should be assessed, along with access to effective and integrated treatment—service gaps and conflicts are bound to interfere with a person's job-readiness and ability to deliver a consistent job performance. A focus on functioning is a more beneficial assessment approach than a focus on symptomatology. Both strengths and limitations need to be examined, especially in cognitive functions and social skills. When assessing cognitive functions, the person's own perspective on what is easy and what is difficult may yield more useful information than a formal psychological assessment.

Goal-setting is an essential part of the rehabilitation process. To promote recovery, goals must be set through an active partnership with the person receiving services. Interests, abilities, and options must be considered from the individual's point of view, and weighed against the person's preferences. Involvement in choosing goals and setting timelines creates a sense of ownership and commitment, and helps develop decision-making skills. In fact, recent research suggests that the experience of having an opportunity to change one's employment plan leads to better vocational outcomes (Hayward & Schmidt-Davis, 2003). Unfortunately, opportunities for choice are too rarely offered within the mental health and vocational rehabilitation services systems (Gagne, 2005).

The service needs of a person with a psychiatric disability are often more comprehensive than for people from other disability groups. Close coordination among service providers is essential, but, in order to promote recovery, the individual using all of those services needs to remain the center, and must be an active partner in determining what services and service providers are needed and desired. Referral to self-help and advocacy groups seems a valuable route to developing a sense of positive identity, of self-efficacy, and of empowerment.

In addition to any services that are directly related to achieving a particular employment goal, many people with psychiatric disabilities benefit from social skill development (Bellack, Mueser, Gingerich, & Agresta, 2003), especially those skills needed to get along with supervisors and coworkers. Assertiveness and self-advocacy skills may not directly translate to success on the job, but will improve an individual's self-efficacy and will likely improve his or her ability to manage multiple service providers arid the complexities of the psychiatric disability.

Perhaps the most important area for facilitating recovery is in developing a trusting relationship between the user and provider of rehabilitation services. Many rehabilitation counselors find it difficult to connect with someone who has a psychiatric disability, probably for many reasons.

As mentioned, many people with psychiatric disabilities have some difficulties with social skills, which can be a challenge for rehabilitation counselors who lack understanding of and experience with these disorders. Given common difficulties with concentration, organization, and fluctuating energy levels, people with psychiatric disabilities may be irregular in their attendance and their follow-up. The rehabilitation counselor must take some responsibility for minimizing attendance and follow-up difficulties, rather than giving up. Caseload pressures conspire against VR counselors in the public sector, as well as in other settings, making it difficult to take the time needed to work effectively with someone with a psychiatric disability, but also making it more critical to make the time for adequate exploration of an individual's situation.

Counseling skills become critical, as the rehabilitation counselor must learn to listen beyond the immediate job placement related issues. The atmosphere created within a counseling session needs to be accepting and calm—not critical, pressured, and demanding. Sensitive language use shows respect of the person, and cultural sensitivity communicates openness to understanding. Perhaps most important is to convey a sense of hope by clearly communicating the message that people with psychiatric disabilities can and do recover. This message needs to be explicit, but also conveyed through a willingness to persevere in the face of occasional failures, without resorting to blame, without attributing the failure to the mental illness itself, and without succumbing to the risk of frustration and burnout. Knowledge that recovery is a nonlinear process that often occurs over many years helps both the provider and user of rehabilitation services to mark progress, to tolerate "slips," and to remain open to revising plans and interventions to meet changing needs.

CONCLUSION

Rehabilitation and recovery are related, yet distinct, processes and outcomes. Good vocational rehabilitation practice will contribute to recovery, but is not sufficient. Knowledge of the possibility of recovery from psychiatric disabilities, of the recovery process, and of facilitators of recovery also can contribute to improving rehabilitation counseling practice, but often in intangible ways. Most important, perhaps, is the expectation of positive change and of hope for a better future. If a person is feeling overwhelmed by a psychiatric disability, or is struggling with it, the rehabilitation counselor may need to have enough hope for both. As the person gains a sense of control, stability, and eventually meaning and purpose in life, often through meaningful employment and education, that hope for the future is translated into present success.

REFERENCES

Anthony, W.A. (1993). Recovery from mental illness: The guiding vision of the mental health service system in the 1990s. *Psychosocial Rehabilitation Journal, 16*(4), 11–23.

Anthony, W.A. (2000). A recovery-oriented service system: Setting some system level standards. *Psychiatric Rehabilitation Journal, 24*(2), 159–168.

Bellack, A.S., Mueser, K.T., Gingerich, S., & Agresta, J. (2003). *Social skills training for schizophrenia.* NY: Guilford Press.

Calabrese, J., & Corrigan, P.W. (2005). Beyond dementia praecox: Findings from long-term follow-up studies of schizophrenia. In R.O. Ralph & P.W. Corrigan (Eds.), *Recovery in mental illness: Broadening our understanding of wellness* (pp. 63–84). Washington, DC: American Psychological Association.

Corrigan, P.W. (Ed.). (2005). *On the stigma of mental illness: Practical strategies for research and social change.* Washington, DC: American Psychological Association.

Corrigan, P.W., & Kleinlein, P. (2005). The impact of mental illness stigma. In P.W. Corrigan (Ed.), *On the stigma of mental illness: Practical strategies for research and social change* (pp. 11–44). Washington, DC: American Psychological Association.

Curie, C.G. (2005). Making a life in the community for everyone a reality for America: The Substance Abuse and Mental Health Services Administration (a special to the *Mental Health Weekly*), published in the *Mental Health E-News* from the New York Association of Psychiatric Rehabilitation Services, received January 5, 2005.

Davidson, L., Sells, D., Sangster, S., & O'Connell, M. (2005). Qualitative studies of recovery: What can we learn from the person? In R.O. Ralph & P.W. Corrigan (Eds.), *Recovery in mental illness: Broadening our understanding of wellness* (pp. 147–170). Washington, DC: American Psychological Association.

Deegan, P. (1988). Recovery: The lived experience of rehabilitation. *Psychosocial Rehabilitation Journal, 11*(4), 11–19.

Deegan, P. (1996). Recovery as a journey of the heart. *Psychiatric Rehabilitation Journal, 19,* 91–97.

Drake, R.E., Essock, S.M., Shaner, A., Carey, K.B., Minkoff, K., Kola, L., Lynde, D., et al. (2001). Implementing dual diagnosis services for clients with mental illness. *Psychiatric Services, 52,* 469–476.

Drake, R.E., Goldman, H.E., Leff, H., Lehman, A.F., Dixon, L., Mueser, K.T., et al. (2001). Implementing evidence-based practices in routine mental health service settings. *Psychiatric Services, 52,* 179–182.

Gagne, C.A. (2005). A qualitative study of consumer-survivors' perspectives about the effects of choice and coercion within the mental health system on recovery from psychiatric disability. Unpublished doctoral dissertation, Boston University.

Hayward, B., & Schmidt-Davis, H. (2003). *Longitudinal study of the Vocational Rehabilitation Services Program.* Retrieved February 2, 2004, from http://www.ed.gov/rschstat/eval/rehab/vr-final-report-2.pdf.

Jacobson, N., & Curtis, L. (2000). Recovery as policy in mental health services: Strategies emerging from the states. *Psychiatric Rehabilitation Journal, 23*(4), 333–341.

Kehoe, N.C. (1999). A therapy group on spiritual issues for patients with chronic mental illness. *Psychiatric Services, 50*(8), 1081–1083.

Liberman, R.P., & Kopelowicz, A. (2005). Recovery from schizophrenia: A criterion-based definition. In R.O. Ralph & P.W. Corrigan (Eds.), *Recovery in mental illness: Broadening our understanding of wellness* (pp. 101–129). Washington, DC: American Psychological Association.

Liberman, R.P., Kopelowicz, A., Ventura, J., & Gutkind, D. (2002). Operational criteria and factors related to recovery from schizophrenia. *International Review of Psychiatry, 14*(4), 256–272.

MacDonald-Wilson, K.L., & Nemec, P.B. (2005). The ICF in psychiatric rehabilitation. *Rehabilitation Education, 19*(2&3), 159–176.

Nemec, P.B., & Taylor, J. (1990). Adjustment to psychiatric disability. *Journal of Applied Rehabilitation Counseling, 21*(4), 49–51.

New Freedom Commission on Mental Health. (2003). *Achieving the promise: Transforming mental health care in America, Final Report.* DHHS Pub. No. SMA-0303832. Rockville, MD: 2003.

Ralph, R.O. (2000). *Review of recovery literature: A synthesis of a sample of recovery literature 2000.* Alexandria, VA: National Association of State Mental Health Program Directors (NASMHPD), National Technical Assistance Center for State Mental Health Planning (NTAC).

Russinova, Z. (1999). Providers' hope-inspiring competence as a factor optimizing psychiatric rehabilitation outcomes. *Journal of Rehabilitation, 65*(4), 50–57.

Sarason, B., & Duck, S. (Eds.). (2001). *Personal relationships: implications for clinical and community psychology.* NY: John Wiley.

Spaniol, L., Wewiorski, N.J., Gagne, C., & Anthony, W.A. (2002). The process of recovery from schizophrenia. *International Review of Psychiatry, 14,* 327–336.

Strauss, J.S., Hafez, H., Lieberman, P., & Harding, C.M. (1985). The course of psychiatric disorder, III: Longitudinal principles. *American Journal of Psychiatry, 142,* 289–296.

U.S. Department of Health and Human Services. (1999). *Mental health: A report of the Surgeon General.* Rockville, MD: Author.

CHAPTER THIRTY-THREE

Psychological Adaptation to Disability

Perspectives From Chaos and Complexity Theory

Hanoch Livneh and Randall M. Parker

The onset of a physically traumatic event and the diagnosis of a chronic, life-threatening illness set into motion a chain of psychosocial experiences, reactions, and responses. The study of the nature, formation, structure, and temporal sequencing of these experiences has occupied the clinical and research interests of disability studies and rehabilitation professionals for the past 50 years. A database search of the available literature that focuses on psychosocial adaptation and adjustment to chronic illness and disability (CID) reveals hundreds of "hits," strongly indicating the importance ascribed to understanding how individuals cope with the loss of body integrity and deteriorating health conditions.

In this paper, the authors will address the following areas: First, the various models of psychosocial adaptation to CID are briefly outlined. Second, the most salient elements of chaos and complexity theory (CCT) are described. Third, the convergent themes between CCT and psychosocial adaptation to CID are discussed. Finally theoretical and clinical applications of CCT to the understanding of the process and outcomes of adaptation to CID are suggested. The interested reader is referred to Barton (1994), Heiby (1995a, 1995b), and Parker, Schaller, and Hansmann (2003) for a succinct review of CCT's main components, and to Abraham and Gilgen (1995), Butz (1997), Chamberlain and Butz (1998), Masterpasqua and Perna (1997), and Robertson and Combs (1995), for a more detailed discussion of the theory with specific applications to the fields of psychology and psychotherapy.

MODELS OF PSYCHOSOCIAL ADAPTATION TO CHRONIC ILLNESS AND DISABILITY

Four models, or more accurately, theoretical frameworks, of psychosocial adaptation to CID are frequently cited in the literature. These models share certain common views, most notably that (a) the experience of psychosocial adaptation to CID is a dynamic, unfolding temporal process; (b) the process of psychosocial adaptation integrates both intrapersonal elements (e.g., coping mechanisms, past experiences, cognitive appraisals) and transpersonal elements (e.g., influence of social networks, encountered environmental barriers, availability of medical and rehabilitation resources); and (c) irrespective of the structural and dynamic components of the model (e.g., linear, cyclical, random), most individuals appear to move toward renewed personal growth and functional adaptation. Of the four outlined models, two are essentially linear in nature and two are nonlinear.

Stage—Phase Models

The earlier models of psychosocial adaptation to CID emphasized the linearity of the adaptation process (see Cohn-Kerr, 1961; Dunn, 1975; Falek & Britton, 1974; Fink, 1967; Shontz, 1965). These models posited a generally predictable progression of stages (temporally non-overlapping psychosocial experiences) and phases (partially overlapping experiences). Although the order of these mostly clinically postulated reactions or experiences differs slightly among the various models, they all argued for the existence of such psychosocial stages and phases as shock, denial, anxiety, anger, acceptance, and some form of reorganization or "final adjustment."

Common to all these models is the assumption that more distal reactions—those temporally removed from the onset of the traumatic event—are predicated upon experiencing more proximal reactions—those occurring earlier in the adaptation process. For example, reaching the stage of acceptance or reorganization is conditional upon successful navigation of earlier stages such as anxiety or depression. Seldom did these earlier models consider the interaction of interpersonal or transpersonal factors with the internal psychodynamics that may have influenced the nature, formation, progression, or valence of the psychosocial adaptation process to CID.

Linear-Like Models

Although still conceptualizing psychosocial adaptation to CID as essentially a linear process, these more structurally complex models have paid greater attention to other determining factors. Included among these factors are (a) CID-related characteristics, for example, type, severity, and duration of condition; (b) personality attributes, for instance, coping style and self-concept; and (c) environmental influences, such as architectural barriers and societal attitudes (Livneh, 2001; Livneh & Antonak, 1997; Moos & Schaefer, 1984; Trieschmann, 1988). The role of these additional factors was typically viewed as either interactive or mediating. With interactive processes, the psychosocial adaptation process follows different trajectories at different levels of the operating factor. For example, the use of problem-focused coping vs. emotional-regulation coping acts to moderate psychosocial adaptation to CID. With mediating processes, the implicated factor (for example, coping strategies) is seen as directly caused or influenced by an earlier variable (for instance, level of pain) and, in return, directly influences psychosocial adaptation to CID.

Pendular Models

Developed to account for the often-reported swings between predisability and postdisability identities or between illness and health, pendular models have sought to portray the process of psychosocial adaptation to permanent disability as a series of gradual changes in self-identity along a pendular trajectory (cf., Charmaz, 1991, 1995; Kendall & Buys, 1998; Yoshida, 1993). For example, Charmaz (1983, 1995) posited that these changes among people with CID reflect a recognition of a loss of their former self-image. The process of adaptation for most people with CID, according to Charmaz, consists of a gradual evolution of an altered self reconstructed to accommodate bodily and functional losses. It also unifies the altered body and the adjusting self. Hence, adaptation is not a single, linear event but rather a repeated series of experiences as new losses are encountered and assimilated.

In a similar vein, Yoshida (1993) conceptualized the reemergence of the self following CID as a pendular representation of identity reconstruction. Following CID, the individual is seen as moving back and forth between the nondisabled, former self and the present, disabled aspects of the self. Identity reconstruction is, therefore, viewed as a dual-directional, nonlinear process whose outcome is never fully certain. After reviewing the research of Charmaz (1983, 1995) and Yoshida (1993), Kendall and Buys (1998) concluded that the pendular model aptly describes the constantly shifting self-perceptions of people with disabilities from their predisability self to their postdisability identity and back again. Similar dual-directional paradigms are found in the literature on coping with the death of a loved one, in which the bereaved person is described as oscillating between loss and restoration-oriented coping (see Stroebe & Schut, 1999).

Interactive Models

Interactive models of psychosocial adaptation (PA) to CID typically maintain that there is a reciprocal, iterative process of adaptation that involves both the individual and the environment. Commonly traced to the earlier work of Kurt Lewin and his students in the field of somatopsychology, such as L. Meyerson, T. Dembo, R. Barker, and B. Wright, these models suggest that PA proceeds in a complex manner that incorporates two sets of interactive variables, namely, those internal and those external to the individual. First, the intra-individual variables are those associated with physical aspects (e.g., type and severity of CID) and psychological aspects (e.g., self-concept) of the person. These variables interact with existing environmental conditions that include the physical, social, and vocational environments. Using Lewin's formula, $B = f(I,E)$, behavior (level of adaptive functioning) is a function of the interaction between the individual and the environment. According to this perspective, the individual's overall degree of adaptation, following the onset of CID, may be mapped in a two-dimensional space, reflecting the joint "push and pull" of internal needs, motives and attributes, on the one hand, and external forces and barriers, on the other.

The foregoing four types of models, despite their time-honored contributions to the field of psychosocial adaptation to CID, are rather narrow in their focus. For example, all these models rely solely upon linear, homeostatic, or limited-cycle (disability as the center of mental gravity) notions that are often unfounded when applied to complex human systems (Butz, 1997; Cambel, 1993; Capra, 1996). In the following sections, therefore, a concerted effort is made to provide an overview of a relatively new framework for viewing psychosocial adaptation to CID that could greatly benefit our understanding of the process, dynamics, and complexity of life following the onset of disability.

CHAOS AND COMPLEXITY THEORY

Commensurate with the narrow aims of this paper, the authors provide a rather abbreviated review of the most essential concepts of CCT, followed by a discussion of their relevance to the field of psychosocial adaptation to CID. CCT has its origins in fields such as meteorology, mathematics, physics, biology, chemistry, geography, astronomy, and engineering. Because of its wide-ranging conceptual and empirical underpinnings, no unified theory of CCT exists. Many definitions have been undertaken, and most strive to highlight CCT's nonlinear, dynamic, interactive, turbulent, unpredictable, self-organizing, and fractal nature (Capra, 1996; Chamberlain, 1998; Gleick, 1987; Parker et al., 2003).

Unlike the earlier Newtonian notions espoused in the fields of physics and mathematics, which emphasized linear, deterministic, and mostly quantitative concepts, CCT seeks to demonstrate the existence of discontinuous, nonlinear forces in many life domains. Using both qualitative and quantitative approaches to studying unstable phenomena, CCT is a collection of mathematical, numerical, and geometrical techniques that allow us to venture into nonlinear problems to which there are no explicit, general solutions (Cambel, 1993; Kellert, 1993). Furthermore, by focusing on complex systems and behaviors, CCT has succeeded in showing that chaos, despite initial perceptions of it as purely random, ill-organized sets of processes, has in fact an inherently ordered and deterministic set of rules (Chamberlain, 1998; Freeman, 1991). As such, CCT is one of the most popular approaches to the study of complexity, which is typically viewed as occupying a position along a continuum that ranges from perfect order to total randomness (Pagels, 1988).

During the past two decades, preliminary work has been reported in the literature on possible applications of CCT to the behavioral and social sciences. Butz (1992) provided some general guidelines for applying CCT concepts to analytical (i.e., Jungian) psychotherapy. Viewing chaos as a state of overwhelming anxiety, Butz proceeded to suggest how psychologically experienced chaos could be transcended and harnessed into human growth. Heiby (1995a), suggested preliminary guidelines for applying CCT to intensive, single-subject, time-series research designs. Her approach placed particular emphasis on continuous assessment of self-reported depression in one's natural environment and on the search for nonlinearity as exemplified by unstable (e.g., bifurcated), irreversible transitional points. Goldstein (1995) explored the role of CCT in the context of psychoanalytical theory. He argued cogently that Freud's regulatory principles that include equilibrium-seeking systems (e.g., the pleasure principle) could be modified to include more complex, nonequilibrium, nonlinear, and self-organizing changes. In that context, the traditional clinical understating of equilibrium is viewed as only a phase within the more nonlinear dynamics of the human psyche. Moran (1998) further suggested that psychoanalytic interpretations and increased insight into unconscious material combine to create perturbations that "alter the trajectory of the patient's mental phenomena" (p. 35), thus paving the way to potentially improved emotional states.

Brabender (1997) drew attention to several similar lines between CCT and the life of psychotherapeutic groups. She identified parallels between the foregoing complex systems (CCT and group psychotherapy), such as irreversibility, constant exchange of information with the environment, and self-organization, and stressed the important role that chaos, as manifested in group members' unconscious-driven behaviors, plays in the life of the group. Warren, Franklin, and Streeter (1998) maintained that CCT is highly suitable to understanding system theory and related complex human systems. They went on to illustrate how a number of concepts advocated by CCT can be applied to the field of social work, with particular emphasis on brief therapies. These therapies initially trigger in the client small behavioral changes that later could mushroom into more fundamental and lasting changes in behavioral repertoires and personality structure. Finally, Duffy (2000) discussed the application of CCT to career plateau. She provided, albeit sketchily, a case study in which five CCT concepts, namely, trigger event, chaotic transition, order in chaos, order from chaos, and self-organization, are used to deal with stagnated careers. Further efforts to apply CCT to human behavior can be found in the literature and have included understanding of family dynamics (Butz, 1997; Hudgens, 1998), exploring religion and spirituality (Butz, 1997; Swinney, 1998), and analyzing the dynamics of substance abuse (Hawkins & Hawkins, 1998). CCT may be conveniently perceived as a broad effort to describe and understand systems that are nonlinear, dynamic, self-organizing, and self-similar. In the following paragraphs these concepts are briefly reviewed.

Nonlinearity

Nonlinear systems are those in which input does not equal output. Stated differently, cause and effect are not proportional, so that minor initial changes may result in large consequences (Cambel, 1993; Capra, 1996). This phenomenon is often referred to as "sensitive dependence on initial conditions." Even barely noticeable differences or changes in initial conditions might initiate a sequence of events that can culminate in a massively chaotic outcome (Butz, 1997; Lorenz, 1963). The behavior of nonlinear systems is, therefore, nonrepetitive, unpredictable, aperiodic, and unstable. Nonlinear systems typically contain as part of their operational space, referred to as *phase space*, critical junctions of instability that are termed *bifurcation points* (Abraham, 1995; Capra, 1996). A bifurcation point is located where the system encounters two separate choices (often portrayed as a fork in the road). When a system reaches a bifurcation point, its earlier stability has already been compromised because of internal or external forces. Immediately beyond this point, the system's properties undergo abrupt and seemingly unpredictable changes (Chamberlain, 1998; Coveney & Highfield, 1990). Following the bifurcation, or crisis point, the system increasingly adopts new behaviors and gradually becomes more stable as it reaches more adaptive levels of functioning, until the next bifurcation point (Chamberlain, 1998; Prigogine, 1980). A bifurcation is, therefore, that critical juncture where order and chaos are joined. It is also the point where order emerges from the shadows of chaos. Bifurcation has also been described as that point where, following a system's increasing unrest, *quantitative* changes transform into *qualitative* changes (Abraham, 1995). Finally, bifurcation is observed only in open systems operating far from equilibrium states (Prigogine, 1980).

A related concept frequently posited by CCT is that of attractors. An attractor is a pattern of behavior within a phase space toward which dynamic, nonlinear systems gravitate (Masterpasqua & Perna, 1997). Several types of attractors have been recognized.

Fixed-Point Attractors

These attractors portray predictable, stable, equilibrium-type points (in a phase space). When a fixed-point attractor operates (e.g., a pendulum at rest), the system gravitates to a single centering point and remains there (therefore the term fixed). The system's trajectory, then, spirals inwardly toward a central location (the reader may visualize waters approaching a drain or a whirlpool). In this homeostatic state, the system does not manifest any indications of change and is assigned a dimension of zero (a point in space has no dimensions) (Cambel, 1993; Capra, 1996).

Limited-Cycle (Periodic, Cyclic) Attractors

These attractors are represented by predictable loops, both closed and open. These periodic circle-, or ellipse-shaped trajectories are reflections of oscillatory behaviors (Butz, 1997; Cambel, 1993). Periodic attractors typically follow donut-shaped (at times referred to as *torus*) trajectories. The system, therefore, approaches two different points periodically but does not escape that cycle (Abraham, 1989). Examples include a pendulum in motion and the beating human heart (Cambel, 1993). Torus-shaped cyclic attractors represent first-order change and have a dimension of 2 (a surface). As a torus continues to move farther away from its periodic, ellipsoid cycle, it collapses into two or more tori, creating two outcome basins and taking the shape of a butterfly. This constitutes a second-order change.

Strange Attractors

These attractors indicate chaos, complexity, and unpredictability. Their trajectories are said to show "sensitive dependence on initial conditions." Put differently, the slightest initial difference between two systems will mushroom into an extremely large difference over time and space, demonstrating the so-called butterfly effect (Cambel, 1993; Capra, 1996). Strange attractors, because of their unfolding and stretching properties, display noninteger or fractal dimensions generally between two and three dimensions. As indicators of chaotic systems, they are said to exhibit third-level changes, since the periods of these systems have bifurcated for the third time (Cambel, 1993; Young, 1995).

DYNAMIC SYSTEMS

Real-life, complex systems are dynamic and are neither fully random nor fully deterministic. They exhibit properties of both qualities (Cambel, 1993). The components of the system are synergistically linked to one another. The degree of complexity inherent in a system depends on several factors, including the system itself, the context (or environment) that engulfs it, and the nature of the interaction between the two.

Complex systems, therefore, are open systems because they exchange energy, material, and information with their immediate environment; closed systems do not (Cambel, 1993: Prigogine, 1980). Furthermore, complex systems are dissipative because they experience energy losses over time; to survive, they must reduce internal disorder, referred to as *entropy*, and at the same time, receive energy and information from the environment (Cambel, 1993; Capra, 1996). This set of conditions is described by the second law of thermodynamics. The level of entropy in a system is, therefore, indicative of its degree of randomness, noise, and irreversibility; in other words, it is a measure of chaos (Cambel, 1993; Prigogine & Stengers, 1984). Unlike open systems, closed systems proceed from order to disorder. Hence, the entropy of closed systems continuously increases as this irreversible process results in dissipation of unrecoverable energy. Closed, environmentally isolated systems, then, are at equilibrium or a state of maximum entropy (Kossmann & Bullrich, 1997; Prigogine & Stengers, 1984).

Consistent with these views, dynamic systems typically proceed from a phase of stable, orderly functioning through, first, an unstable, bifurcation phase, and second, a chaotic period. The chaotic period culminates in a phase of new and more complex order (Butz, 1997; Kossmann & Bullrich, 1997). Hence, chaos is the necessary phase before reorganization of previously malfunctioning components within a system. Upon the dissipation of chaos a new and adaptive pattern (higher order) is likely to emerge as the system successfully, and creatively, reorganizes itself. From the dynamic perspective, therefore, chaos serves two primary purposes. First, it facilitates adaptive functioning. Chaotic activity propels the dissipation of disturbance (or disorder) in a system. Second, through its openness to environmental interactions and increased probability of change, chaos creates the system potential for creativity and evolution (Perna, 1997).

Self-Organization

Self-organizing, open systems possess certain unique characteristics, which include (a) nonlinear trajectories, (b) leap-like changes following a gradual aggregation of stresses, (c) spontaneous emergence of new structures and behavioral forms, and (d) internal feedback loops (Capra, 1996; Prigogine & Stengers, 1984). According to CCT, turbulent activity often appears random and irregular on a macroscopic level, but when viewed *microscopically*, it demonstrates a high degree of organization. Self-organization, then, is the process by which a chaotic system attains a new level of order, stability, and adaptation (Butz, 1997; Maturana & Varela, 1988).

The term *autopoiesis* (self-generating or "of the living") has been applied to describe the self-organizational proclivity of living systems (Maturana & Varela, 1980). Autopoiesis is a mode of autonomous organization within organic structures. It both creates and renews itself by virtue of its own processes and their interaction with the surrounding environment, referred to as "structural coupling with the environment" (Varela, 1989).

Self-Similarity

Chaotic systems frequently give rise to a peculiar phenomenon in which similar structures—including those in naturally occurring objects, such as snowflakes, coastlines, tree branches, and cloud formations—may be observed at consecutive levels of magnification. This phenomenon is called *self-similarity* (Butz, 1997; Mandelbrot, 1977). Certain self-similar patterns, termed *fractals* by Benoit Mandelbrot (1977), have been extensively studied because of their chaotic nature. Fractals are best explained as deterministic, self-similar formations that are defined by their similar shapes across a wide range of scales (Masterpasqua & Perna, 1997; Parker et al., 2003). Strange attractors (discussed earlier) are viewed as "trajectories in phase space that exhibit fractal geometry" (Capra, 1996, p. 139). Complex fractal structures can be generated mathematically by repeatedly solving certain iterative equations (Parker et al., 2003; Sabelli, Carlson-Sabelli, Patel, Levy, & Diez-Martin, 1995). Fractals exhibit noninteger dimensions (e.g., 1.84, 2.65), and they may be found in between traditional, integer-based Euclidian dimensions.

CCT AND PSYCHOSOCIAL ADAPTATION TO CHRONIC ILLNESS AND DISABILITY

Adaptation to Stress

Before considering the potential usefulness of CCT within the context of adaptation to CID, we briefly review its recent applications within psychology, focusing on coping with stress and crisis situations. During the past decade, concerted efforts have been made to elucidate the applicability of CCT-generated concepts to the psychodynamics of such diverse conditions as substance abuse, depression, anxiety, phobias, neurosis, disassociative identity disorder, and criminal behavior (Butz, 1997; Chamberlain, 1998; Masterpasqua & Perna, 1997; Robertson & Combs, 1995). Five themes, jointly linking CCT and psychology, are reviewed below.

Psychic System as a Nonlinear System

The psychic system is viewed by CCT proponents as operating at increasingly more complex levels (i.e., it is influenced by more intricate sets of attractors), as conditions of far-from-equilibrium present themselves (Goldstein, 1995). Under everyday conditions, human cognitions and behaviors can accommodate both linear (e.g., time) and nonlinear (e.g., space) themes. In contrast, under stressful conditions, they manifest more complex, unpredictable, and ultimately increased nonlinear dynamics.

Psychic System as Self-Organizing (Autopoietic)

Unlike noncomplex, closed systems, the psychic system structures itself through a dissipative exchange of energy and information with the external environment. The complex, dynamic psychic processes, with their inherent chaotic properties, serve an adaptive function in the long run (Perna, 1997). This adaptive function, it is argued, is manifested through activities that demonstrate creativity, spontaneity, and risk taking.

Human Behavior as Capable of Fractal Dimensionality

Human behavior, under stressful conditions, loses its integrative balance and attains fractional dimensionality. Examples of the self's fractional dimensionality include obsessions, compulsions, phobias, and, most likely, dissociative reactions (Marks-Tarlow, 1995). Pathological conditions, therefore, often function as attractors that reduce the system's dimensionality (or complexity) and propel it toward more stereotypical (or less adaptive) forms (Chamberlain, 1998). In a similar vein, Sabelli et al. (1995) have argued that the presence of chaotic (as opposed to rigidly structured) conditions may serve a role in increasing the dimensionality of homeostatic human functioning.

Defense Mechanisms and Coping Strategies as Special Types of Attractors

As unique attractors, defensive and coping strategies function to attain and maintain psychic stability (Butz, 1997; Torre, 1995). With repeated stressful encounters, individuals appear to regress to earlier forms of behavior. These more primitive (i.e., regressive) efforts to manage stress mirror what psychodynamic proponents refer to as *repetition compulsion*. Individuals also display self-similar forms in what is now a reduced dimensional space of human functioning (Marks-Tarlow, 1995). Indeed, the process of regression itself is capable of producing psychological and behavioral chaos in the self-system that is parallel to chaotic behavior in complex, nonlinear dynamic systems (Perna, 1995). Even more ostensibly adaptive and mature coping strategies, such as problem solving and cognitive restructuring, are not immune from gradually deteriorating into nonadaptive behavioral patterns (attractors). The reason for this is that over time they become more rigid and fail to transition or bifurcate into more situationally appropriate behaviors (Torre, 1995).

Chaos as an Indication of Overwhelming Anxiety

Psychic chaos, mostly equated with debilitating anxiety, is also capable of triggering a mixture of related emotions that include depression and anger (Butz, 1997; Chamberlain & Butz, 1998; Sabelli, 1989). The experience of profound heightened anxiety, as of other pathological psychic conditions, is likely to result in changes in the level of behavioral complexity (dimensionality). A psyche confronted with overwhelming anxiety transforms into a series of chaotic mental processes that serves both (a) the need to dissipate energy (i.e., decrease levels of anxiety) and (b) the pursuit of adaptive forms of behavior and reconstructed self-organization (Chamberlain, 1998; Conrad, 1986; Perna, 1997). The progression from the initial core anxiety state, through the chaotic turbulence, to a renewed stable and adaptive functioning constitutes a phase transition "as the original attractor becomes repellent and forces trajectories outward" (Lewis & Junyk, 1997, p. 60).

Adaptation to Chronic Illness and Disability

From the perspective of CCT, psychosocial adaptation to CID is nonlinear, unpredictable, and discontinuous. Similar opinions were voiced by Butz (1997) and Chamberlain and Butz (1998) regarding human adaptation to most stressful life events. The process of adaptation, then, is essentially a process of self-organization that unfolds through experiences of chaos (i.e., emotional turmoil) and complexity (i.e., cognitive and behavioral reorganization) to increased functional dimensionality and renewed stability, even if temporary.

Understanding the psychosocial self-organization that follows CID may benefit from adopting the applied models of chaotic dynamics posited by Lewis and Junyk (1997), Derrickson-Kossmann and Drinkard (1997), and Torre (1995). These models share the following elements with theories of self-organization, and their relevance to PA to CID is evident:

- Three components interact to play a dynamic role in the process of psychosocial self-organization following the onset of CID. These include cognitive appraisals, such as appraisals of loss; emotional experiences, such as experiences of anxiety and sadness; and behavioral responses, such as retreat from social encounters.
- Through the process of adaptation, these components interact with and activate each other recursively, proceeding from less harmonious to more harmonious coexistence.
- Experiences immediately following the onset of CID can be best understood within the context of sensitive dependence on initial conditions. Even minor, ostensibly insignificant, influences within the initial post-CID psychological, social, or environmental contexts could have powerful long-term implications (both salutary and detrimental) on psychosocial adaptation. Similar reasoning could be applied to rehabilitation interventions following the onset of CID. During this crisis-like period, minor changes in one's behavior or use of newly acquired coping strategies could quickly transform into long-term and more fundamental behavioral changes and life pursuits.
- Earlier in the process of adaptation (during the chaotic phase), substantial discrepancies, and even antagonistic trends, are likely to exist among the trajectories of these three components (cognitions, emotions, and behaviors) in both scope and valence. Put

differently, the normal and continuous convergence of feelings, thoughts, and behaviors that signifies the adaptive functioning under most life conditions becomes disrupted and disjointed.

- During the adaptation process, certain recurrent states, such as negative appraisals, hyperarousal, blaming others, and guilt, may be formed and may exert a powerful influence on the individual's thought processes and behaviors. These recurrent states are indicators of attractors in the self's phase space map.

- Throughout the adaptation process, as chaotic and complex conditions gradually give way to reorganization, self-correcting and self-stabilizing relations among the three sets of experiential components (cognitions, emotions, and behaviors) slowly converge to reestablish a unified functional front.

- Following a traumatic event, such as CID, the normal patterns of coping with manageable life stressors are no longer capable of containing the overwhelming anxiety and other distressing emotions. As a result, adaptation to CID leads to a series of bifurcations in the individual's customary life experiences. The impact of the CID, then, gives rise to newly formed attractors in the individual's perceptions, cognitions, level of affectivity, and daily activities. As some of these attractors transform into strange attractors, they draw into the CID-operating region (phase space) a wide range of behaviors (Francis, 1995). With time, chaotic perceptions and disorganized behaviors flood the psyche and gradually interfere with normal activities. Following a period of psychic decompensation, new patterns of self-organization gradually emerge, and these result in restoration of psychic balance and increased differentiation of mental processes.

- Psychosocial adaptation following CID may be perceived as a "dialectical interaction" (Perna, 1995) between the self-organization processes of the internal world made up of the postchaotic psyche-mending self and the prevailing social—physical context of the external world.

- Many natural phenomena and human experiences are cyclical. Natural phenomena are frequently gauged with references to seasons, period, and so on. A wide range of human activities and milestones are timed using cyclical-repetitious, albeit artificial, indicators (e.g., minutes, hours, days, months, years, anniversaries). Much of life, therefore, evolves around both fixed and limited-cycle attractors. These somewhat predictable continuous cycles are disrupted following the onset of life-altering, traumatic experiences such as CID. The trajectories of these mostly stable attractors (e.g., spending time at a work site, engaging in leisure time activities) are then transformed into those resembling unpredictable, turbulent strange attractors (life experiences that now follow highly irregular patterns).

Exploratory Suggestions for Rehabilitation Interventions

The CCT-based literature on psychotherapeutic interventions with clients who manifest clinical symptomatology (e.g., anxiety, depression, personality disorders, or disassociative reactions) or are confronted with stressful life events is only beginning to emerge (Butz, 1997; Chamberlain & Butz, 1998; Masterpasqua & Perna, 1997; Robertson & Combs, 1995). Moran (1998), adopting a psychodynamic perspective, argues that neurotic behaviors and the experiences of anxiety, depression, and stress act as attractors that reduce the psychic system's dimensionality. Neurotic behaviors, thus, result in a less complex and creative behavior, or alternatively, more rigid and stereotypical activities. With its emphasis on interpretations, gaining insights, and the therapeutic alliance, psychodynamic therapy introduces a series of perturbations that alter the trajectory of the client's cognitive schemata and gradually increase behavior complexity, leading to more adaptive levels of functioning. In a similar vein, Goldstein (1995) maintains that psychotherapy can be viewed as a "system transformation." From a linear-focused, rigid, and equilibrium-operated psychic system, the client is helped to attain a nonlinear, nonequilibrium, and more complex mode of functioning. Psychotherapy is, therefore, the transition work into more complex attractors and increased dimensionality.

The rehabilitation and disability studies literatures have yet to adopt the principles and insights of CCT to understanding psychosocial adaptation to CID. In the concluding section of this paper, possible applications of CCT to those fields are suggested. More specifically, we draw upon two interrelated concepts derived from CCT, namely, complexity/dimensionality and self-organization, to assist us in these efforts.

Complexity/Dimensionality

Immediately following the onset of CID, psychic disequilibrium ensues. Previously adhered-to emotional, cognitive, and behavioral processes are disrupted, and the generally stable pre-CID functional complexity is shattered and reduced to lower dimensionality. The reduction to lower dimensionality is evidenced as life's focus shifts into the "here and now," physiological survival, and deflection of impending psychosocial crises. Time and space are constrained to the present and the immediate surroundings (e.g., hospital and home). The role of the rehabilitation professional, under these circumstances, could be conceptualized as addressing the following broad goals:

- *Helping the client to regain the "lost" core of functional complexity.* This could be accomplished by shifting the focus from the present-oriented, space-restrained framework of the individual to future-oriented, goal-oriented, skill acquisition activities and to community-oriented participatory efforts. Moreover, as the external environment gradually assumes increased importance in the life of the individual with CID, rehabilitation efforts are directed not merely at environmental mastery but equally at modifying the person's home, work, and community environments. Since the impact of disability can best be understood as a continuous interaction among functional limitations and residual abilities (both stemming from the nature of the medical condition) and barriers imposed by both the physical and social–attitudinal environments, it is imperative that the rehabilitation professional incorporate the influences generated by these environments (i.e., dimensions) into a well-balanced rehabilitation plan.

- *Working with the client to extend functional dimensionality.* This could be pursued by gradually introducing into the client's life space additional domains (i.e., dimensions) that are likely to elevate functioning from its present health- and survival-oriented modes to include social, spiritual, vocational, and environmental mastery modes.

- *Working through and gaining insight into non-functional defenses.* Because of regressive tendencies that could follow the trauma of CID, the client may resort to adopting earlier (past-oriented) and no longer adaptive (rigid) defense mechanisms such as projection, splitting, and displacement (see, for example, Haan, 1977). Increased dimensionality, within the context of coping with stress, may take the form of increasing the individual's repertoire of future-oriented, flexible, and situationally adaptive coping strategies. These strategies could draw from both emotional- and cognitive-oriented approaches to regulate unremitting stress, and behavioral and problem-solving efforts to manage and directly address changeable circumstances (Devins & Binik, 1996; Zeidner & Saklofske, 1996). In addition, a wide range of environmental-based coping resources (e.g., financial, educational, vocational, social-supportive) should be made readily available to the individual.

- *Increasing the client's recognition of spontaneous, creative, and even risk-taking efforts.* Following sudden-onset CID, cognitive processes and daily activities are reduced to more rigid, risk-avoiding, and predictable patterns (lower dimensionality). Limited-cycle (periodic) attractors often emerge, and, as a result, many life experiences revolve around nonadaptive foci such as negative emotionality, resignation, succumbing to external barriers, social withdrawal, feelings of anger, and so on. It is incumbent upon the rehabilitation professional to arrange for or create perturbations that would open up additional life options, increase flexible and creative modes of problem solving, and expand the range of available experiences and behaviors for the client. These strategies seek to allow the client to reach higher dimensionality of cognition, emotion, and behavior, thus facilitating the process of psychosocial adaptation to CID.

Self-Organization

The seeds of self-organization may already be found in humanistic—existential theories, such as Rogers's person-centered therapy and Maslow's self-actualization approach. Rogers's concepts of the self-actualization tendency and organismic trusting and Maslow's concepts of self-actualization and growth motivation strongly indicate that these and other humanistic writers (e.g., Frankl and Perls) were well aware of the self-healing processes inherent in all human activities with the processes' innately self-organizing and self-regulating properties (Ford & Urban, 1998; Maddi, 1989). Relatedly, Mahoney and Moes (1997) argued that human patterns of personal–experiential development reflect lifelong self-organizing processes. Inherent in Mahoney and Moes's approach is the belief that life maintains its balance through dynamic and recurrent phases. Although periodic perturbations (e.g., stresses, crises, challenges) may occasionally disrupt this balance, these perturbations are usually accommodated in a successful manner. More severe perturbations (such as CID) may create turbulent cycles that result in disequilibrium, but, with time, life balance is typically restored.

Rehabilitation professionals who adopt this view may find the following broad strategies for promoting self-reorganization useful:

- Providing the client with the quintessential Rogerian conditions of change (e.g., empathic understanding, warmth, unconditional positive regard, genuineness) may be a necessary but certainly not a sufficient strategy required to induce change in the lives of people who have undergone the experience of CID. A derailment, albeit temporary, from the path of self-actualization and growth may necessitate an additional "jolt to the system" (such as a direct confrontation to or challenging of one's faulty cognitions and entrenched misperceptions). A temporary derailment may help the client resume the innate drive toward self-organization and self-constructing. Gestalt therapy and cognitive—behavioral strategies that seek to challenge the individual's psychological defensiveness, denial of affective involvement, and unrealistic cognitions regarding the CID and its impact may more effectively facilitate the client's movement toward a new order of adaptation.

- Self-organization entails efforts by the rehabilitation professional to move the person with CID past the chaos and complexity phases. This could be accomplished through facilitating realignment of the disrupted synchronicity among the cognitive, affective, and behavioral components of life experiences. Moreover, the pre-CID adaptive homeostasis between the self (internal world) and the environment (external reality) is also frequently disrupted following a traumatic physical or psychological event. To help the client reach a restored functionally adaptive state, the rehabilitation professional should consider garnering the combined facilitative influences of both experiential (e.g., Gestalt) and cognitive (e.g., cognitive—behavioral) interventions. In this search for restoration of functional adaptation, rehabilitation professionals should, likewise, pay particular attention to the immediate (proximal) and broad (distal) environments within which the person with CID functions. Examples of proximal selforganization-associated domains include, but are not limited to, family influences, financial resources, the local community (e.g., medical, rehabilitation, educational, transportation, vocational, and recreational resources), and attitudinal barriers and facilitators at each of these local settings. Distal self-organization—linked domains include, among others, prevailing sociocultural influences (including cultural beliefs, values, and perceptions), political climate, technological and medical advances, and the availability of federal and state funding for modifying environmental barriers and creating job opportunities for people with disabilities. Although beyond the scope of this paper, the rehabilitation professional should make every reasonable effort to consider these environmental influences as they may facilitate or hinder the process of self-organization and the attainment of person—environment congruence.

- If, indeed, after periods of chaos such as evidenced following the onset of CID, old patterns of cognitions and behaviors (e.g., earlier problem-solving and coping strategies) no longer succeed in their adaptive roles, the individual may be nearing a crucial psychic bifurcation point. This is the point of maximum potential that is required to undertake the necessary leap into adopting new behaviors (Chamberlain, 1998). This point also signifies what has been described as operating at the "edge of chaos" (Kauffman, 1995; Waldrop, 1992). This point reveals the complex Janus-faced phenomenon (or region) that retains residues of old and orderly patterns of behavior, but at the same time lays the ground for a system transformation, the emergence of a new order, openness to experience, alternative states of viewing the world, and the adoption of adaptive cognitive schemas and behaviors.

This is where the role of the rehabilitation professional becomes significant. The rehabilitation professional is in an excellent position to be a catalyst to guide the client's behavior toward new and adaptive patterns of cognition and behaviors, and ultimately to help in propelling the emergence of these patterns toward reorganization of the client's future hopes and goals.

SUMMARY

From the perspective of CCT, psychosocial adaptation to CID can be construed as a dynamic, nonlinear, and mostly unpredictable process in which the individual undergoes the following four transitions:

1. The initial poverty of the complexity/dimensionality of previously established behavioral, cognitive, and coping patterns following the impact of CID is followed by a gradual increase in dimensionality/complexity of behavior, as the process of identity reconstruction and self-reorganization unfolds.
2. The pre-CID life space, which typically included relatively stable period attractors (i.e., daily vocational, educational, familial, and avocational tasks and responsibilities), gradually shifts to include strange attractors or aperiodic, unpredictable experiences (emotional states, cognitive schemata) to which many life activities gravitate, leading to chaotic psychic experiences.
3. Following CID, the impact of physiological and biochemical elements (often triggered by the anatomical insult of the condition), new psychological and behavioral experiences, and environmental conditions (family reactions, social attitudes, architectural barriers) is filtered through the ingrained pre-CID personality attributes and demographic characteristics. As these many influences converge, the chaotic patterns evidenced in one's life space intensify

through a series of turbulent bifurcations, ultimately resulting in more intricately adaptive cognitive and behavioral patterns.

4. The adaptive behavioral patterns, as evidenced in a reconstructed self-identity, are manifested in several ways. These include increased spontaneity, creativity, cognitive flexibility, risk-taking behaviors (albeit within limits), pursuits that transcend rigid obligations and goals, appreciation of diverse activities and life goals, and a dynamic balance of vocational and avocational pursuits. These new and adaptive patterns recognize not only CID-influenced activities of daily living but also the many nonaffected spheres of life. In fact, some of the earlier propositions of Beatrice Wright and her coworkers on value transformation following CID demonstrate uncanny insight into this facet of CCT (Wright, 1983).

Finally, although CCT does not directly indicate which rehabilitation interventions are best suited for increasing psychosocial adaptation to CID, it does offer a general framework for interventions. Mostly, it suggests the supremacy of an eclectic approach that incorporates multifaceted, yet nonrigid, views of the human experience and its change following adverse physical and psychological conditions. Such an approach recognizes the complexity, uncertainty, transformation, and ever evolving dynamics of the human spirit, especially as it seeks to transcend the constraining barriers imposed by chronic illness and disability.

REFERENCES

Abraham, F. D. (1995). Dynamics, bifurcations, self-organization, chaos, mind, conflict, insensitivity to initial conditions, time, unification, diversity, free will, and social responsibility. In R. Robertson & A. Combs (Eds.), *Chaos theory in psychology and the life sciences* (pp. 155–173). Mahwah, NJ: Erlbaum.

Abraham, F., & Gilgen, A. (Eds.). (1995). *Chaos theory in psychology.* Westport, CT: Praeger.

Abraham, R. (1989). *On morphodynamics: Selected papers.* Santa Cruz, CA: Aerial Press.

Barton, S. (1994). Chaos, self-organization, and psychology. *The American Psychologist, 49,* 5–14.

Brabender, V. (1997). Chaos and order in the psychotherapy group. In F. Masterpasqua & P. A. Perna (Eds.), *The psychological meaning of chaos: Translating theory into practice* (pp. 225–252). Washington, DC: American Psychological Press.

Butz, M. (1992). Chaos: An omen of transcendence in the psychotherapy process. *Psychological Reports, 71,* 827–843.

Butz, M. (1997). *Chaos and complexity: Implications for psychological theory and practice*. Washington, DC: Taylor & Francis.

Cambel, A. B. (1993). *Applied chaos theory*. New York: Academic Press.

Capra, F. (1996). *The web of life*. New York: Anchor Books.

Chamberlain, L. (1998). An introduction to chaos and nonlinear dynamics. In L. L. Chamberlain & M. R. Butz (Eds.), *Clinical chaos: A therapeutic guide to nonlinear dynamics and therapeutic change* (pp. 3–14). Philadelphia: Brunner/Mazel.

Chamberlain, L., & Butz, M. (Eds.). (1998). *Clinical chaos: A therapist's guide to nonlinear dynamics and therapeutic change*. Philadelphia: Brunner/Mazel.

Charmaz, K. (1983). Loss of self: A fundamental form of suffering in the chronically ill. *Sociology of Health & Illness, 5*, 168–195.

Charmaz, K. (1991). *Good days, bad days*. New Brunswick, NJ: Rutgers University Press.

Charmaz, K. (1995). The body, identity, and self: Adapting to impairment. *The Sociological Quarterly, 36*, 657–680.

Cohn-Kerr, N. (1961). Understanding the process of adjustment to disability. *Journal of Rehabilitation, 27*, 16–18.

Conrad, M. (1986). What is the use of chaos? In A. V. Holden (Ed.), *Chaos* (pp. 3–14). Princeton, NJ: Princeton University Press.

Coveney, P., & Highfield, R. (1990). *The arrow of time: A voyage through science to solve time's greatest mystery*. New York: Fawcett Columbine.

Derrickson-Kossmann, D., & Drinkard, L. (1997). Dissociative disorders in chaos and complexity. In F. Masterpasqua & P. A. Perna (Eds.), *The psychological meaning of chaos: Translating theory into practice* (pp. 117–145). Washington, DC: American Psychological Association.

Devins, G. M., & Binik, Y. M. (1996). Facilitating coping with chronic physical illness. In M. Zeidner & N. S. Endler (Eds.), *Handbook of coping: Theory, research, applications* (pp. 640–696). New York: Wiley.

Duffy, J. A. (2000). The application of chaos theory to the career–plateaued worker. *Journal of Employment Counseling, 37*, 229–237.

Dunn, M. E. (1975). Psychological intervention in a spinal cord injury center: An introduction. *Rehabilitation Psychology, 22*, 165–178.

Falek, A., & Britton, S. (1974). Phases of coping: The hypothesis and its implications. *Social Biology, 21*, 1–7.

Fink, S. (1967). Crisis and motivation: A theoretical model. *Archives of Physical Medicine and Rehabilitation, 48*, 592–597.

Ford, D. H., & Urban, H. B. (1998). *Contemporary models of psychotherapy: A comparative analysis* (2nd ed.). New York: Wiley.

Francis, S. E. (1995). Chaotic phenomena in psychophysiological self–regulation. In R. Robertson & A. Combs (Eds.), *Chaos theory in psychology and the life sciences* (pp. 253–265). Mahwah, NJ: Erlbaum.

Freeman, W. (1991). The physiology of perception. *Scientific American, 264*, 78–85.

Gleick, J. (1987). *Chaos: Making a new science*. New York: Viking.

Goldstein, J. (1995). Unbalancing psychoanalytic theory: Moving beyond the equilibrium model of Freud's thought. In R. Robertson & A. Combs (Eds.),

Chaos theory in psychology and the life sciences (pp. 239–251). Mahwah, NJ: Erlbaum.

Haan, N. (1977). *Coping and defending*. New York: Academic Press.

Hawkins, R. C., & Hawkins, C. A. (1998). Dynamics of substance abuse: Implications of chaos theory for clinical research. In L. Chamberlain & M. R. Butz (Eds.), *Clinical chaos: A therapeutic guide to nonlinear dynamics and therapeutic change* (pp. 89–101). Philadelphia: Brunner/Mazel.

Heiby, E. M. (1995b). Chaos theory, nonlinear dynamic models, and psychological assessment. *Psychological Assessment, 7,* 5–9.

Heiby, E. M. (1995a). Assessment of behavioral chaos with a focus on transitions in depression. *Psychological Assessment, 7,* 10–16.

Hudgens, B. (1998). Dynamical family systems and therapeutic intervention. In L. Chamberlain & M. R. Butz (Eds.), *Clinical chaos: A therapeutic guide to nonlinear dynamics and therapeutic change* (pp. 115–126). Philadelphia: Brunner/Mazel.

Kauffman, S. (1995). *At home in the universe: The search for the laws of self-organization and complexity*. New York: Oxford University Press.

Kellert, S. H. (1993). *In the wake of chaos*. Chicago: University of Chicago Press.

Kendall, E., & Buys, N. (1998). An integrated model of psychosocial adjustment following acquired disability. *Journal of Rehabilitation, 64*(2), 16–20.

Kossmann, M. R., & Bullrich, S. (1997). Systematic chaos: Self-organizing systems and the process of change. In F. Masterpasqua & P. A. Perna (Eds.), *The psychological meaning of chaos: Translating theory into practice* (pp. 199–224). Washington, DC: American Psychological Association.

Lewis, M. D., & Junyk, N. (1997). The self-organzation of psychological defenses. In F. Masterpasqua & P. A. Perna (Eds.), *The psychological meaning of chaos: Translating theory into practice* (pp. 41–73). Washington, DC: American Psychological Association.

Livneh, H. (2001). Psychosocial adaptation to chronic illness and disability: A conceptual framework. *Rehabilitation Counseling Bulletin, 44,* 151–160.

Livneh, H., & Antonak, R. F. (1997). *Psychosocial adaptation to chronic illness and disability*. Gaithersburg, MD: Aspen.

Lorenz, E. N. (1963). Deterministic nonperiodic flow. *Journal of Atmospheric Sciences, 20,* 130–141.

Maddi, S. R. (1989). *Personality theories: A comparative analysis* (5th ed.). Chicago: Dorsey Press.

Mahoney, M. J., & Moes, A. J. (1997). Complexity and psychotherapy: Promising dialogues and practical issues. In F. Masterpasqua & P. A. Perna (Eds.), *The psychological meaning of chaos: Translating theory into practice* (pp. 177–198). Washington, DC: American Psychological Association.

Mandelbrot, B. (1977). *The fractal geometry of nature*. New York: Freeman.

Marks-Tarlow, T. (1995). The fractal geometry of human nature. In R. Robertson & A. Combs (Eds.), *Chaos theory in psychology and the life sciences* (pp. 275–283). Mahwah, NJ: Erlbaum.

Masterpasqua, F., & Perna, P. A. (Eds.). (1997). *The psychological meaning of chaos: Translating theory into practice*. Washington, DC: American Psychological Association.

Maturana, H., & Varela, F. (1980). *Autopoiesis and cognition.* Dordrecht, Holland: D. Reidel.

Maturana, H., & Varela, F. (1988). *The tree of knowledge: The biological roots of human understanding.* Boston: New Science Library.

Moos, R. H., & Schaefer, J. A. (1984). The crisis of physical illness. In R. H. Moos (Ed.), *Coping with physical illness. Vol. 2: New perspectives* (pp. 3–31). New York: Plenum Press.

Moran, M. G. (1998). Chaos theory and psychoanalysis. In L. Chamberlain & M. R. Butz (Eds.), *Clinical chaos: A therapeutic guide to non-linear dynamics and therapeutic change* (pp. 29–39). Philadelphia: Brunner/Mazel.

Pagels, H. (1988). *The dreams of reason.* New York: Simon and Schuster.

Parker, R. M., Schaller, J., & Hansmann, S. (2003). Catastrophe, chaos, and complexity models and psychosocial adjustment to disability. *Rehabilitation Counseling Bulletin, 46,* 234–241.

Perna, P. A. (1995). Regression as chaotic uncertainty and transformation. In R. Robertson & A. Combs (Eds.), *Chaos theory in psychology and the life sciences* (pp. 295–303). Mahwah, NJ: Erlbaum.

Perna, P. A. (1997). Regression as evolutionary process: A view from dialectics and chaos theory. In F. Masterpasqua & P. A. Perna (Eds.), *The psychological meaning of chaos: Translating theory into practice* (pp. 97–115). Washington, DC: American Psychological Association.

Prigogine, I. (1980). *From being to becoming—Time and complexity in the physical sciences.* San Francisco: W.H. Freeman.

Prigogine, I., & Stengers, I. (1984). *Order out of chaos: Man's new dialogue with nature.* New York: Bantam Books.

Robertson, R., & Combs, A. (Eds.). (1995). *Chaos theory in psychology and the life sciences.* Mahwah, NJ: Erlbaum.

Sabelli, H. C. (1989). *Union of opposites: A comprehensive theory of natural and human processes.* Lawrenceville, VA: Brunswick.

Sabelli, H. C., Carlson-Sabelli, L., Patel, M., Levy, A., & Diez-Martin, J. (1995). Anger, fear, depression and crime: Physiological and psychological studies using the process method. In R. Robertson & A. Combs (Eds.), *Chaos theory in psychology and the life sciences* (pp. 65–88). Mahwah, NJ: Erlbaum.

Shontz, F. C. (1965). Reactions to crisis. *The Volta Review, 67,* 364–370.

Stroebe, M., & Schut, H. (1999). The dual process model of coping with bereavement: Rationale and description. *Death Studies, 23,* 197–224.

Swinney, F. G. (1998). Creative consciousness process. In L. Chamberlain & M. R. Butz (Eds.), *Clinical chaos: A therapeutic guide to non-linear dynamics and therapeutic change* (pp. 135–146). Philadelphia: Brunner/Mazel.

Torre, C. A. (1995). Chaos, creativity, and innovation: Toward a dynamical model of problem solving. In R. Robertson & A. Combs (Eds.), *Chaos theory in psychology and the life sciences* (pp. 179–198). Mahwah, NJ: Erlbaum.

Trieschmann, R. B. (1988). *Spinal cord injuries: Psychological, social, and vocational rehabilitation* (2nd ed.). New York: Demos.

Varela, F. (1989). Reflections on the circulation of concept between a biology of cognition and systemic family therapy. *Family Process, 28,* 15–24.

Waldrop, M. (1992). *Complexity: The emergence of science at the edge of order and chaos*. New York: Simon & Schuster.

Warren, K., Franklin, C., & Streeter, C. L. (1998). New directions in system theory: Chaos and complexity. *Social Work, 43*, 357–372.

Wright, B. A. (1983). *Physical disability—A psychosocial approach*. New York: Harper & Row.

Yoshida, K. K. (1993). Reshaping of self: A pendular reconstruction of self and identity among adults with traumatic spinal cord injury. *Sociology of Health & Illness, 15*, 217–245.

Young, T. R. (1995). Chaos theory and social dynamics: Foundations of postmodern social science. In R. Robertson & A. Combs (Eds.), *Chaos theory in psychology and the life sciences* (pp. 217–233). Mahwah, NJ: Erlbaum.

Zeidner, M., & Saklofske, D. (1996). Adaptive and maladaptive coping. In M. Zeidner & N. S. Endler (Eds.), *Handbook of coping: Theory, research, applications* (pp. 505–531). New York: Wiley.

CHAPTER THIRTY-FOUR

Eugenics, Euthanasia, and Physician-Assisted Suicide

An Overview for Rehabilitation Professionals

Steve Zanskas and Wendy Coduti

EUGENICS

The concept of improving the human race through selective reproduction is reflected in Plato's *Republic* (Barnett, 2004; Larson, 2002). The Greek word eugenes means "well born" (Mahowold, 2003). Eugenics is defined as the study of hereditary improvements of the human race by controlled selective breeding (Smart, 2001). The word was conceived in England by Sir Francis Galton, a naturalist, statistician, and Charles Darwin's cousin. Sir Galton first used the word he coined in one of his publications in 1883 (Barnett, 2004).

The *eugenics* movement peaked in the United States between 1900 and 1935 (Lombardo, 2003). Eugenicists adopted two approaches, referred to as positive and negative eugenics, to prevent individuals considered to have disabilities from reproducing. Public education and voluntary abstinence were considered *positive eugenics*. Compulsory sterilization

From "Eugenics, euthanasia, and physician assisted suicide: An overview for rehabilitation professionals," by S. Zanskas and W. Coduti, 2006, *Journal of Rehabilitation*, 72(1), 27–34. Reprinted with permission of the National Rehabilitation Association.

was considered *negative eugenics* (Larson, 2002). Anyone the state considered socially undesirable appeared subject to involuntary sterilization, including individuals with hereditary deafness or blindness, those considered to have mental illness or developmental disabilities, individuals with epilepsy, criminals, prostitutes, or the poor (Larson, 2002; Lombardo, 2003). Social Darwinism, an outgrowth of Darwinism, proposed that social characteristics were inherited along with biological characteristics. Social Darwinism was used as a justification to eliminate socially undesirable characteristics through eugenic practices (Mostert, 2002). In the early 1900s, almost every state had at least one institution to segregate individuals with disabilities and 32 enacted compulsory sterilization laws. Between 1907 and 1945, 40,000 eugenic sterilization procedures were performed in the United States; half were conducted in the State of California (Bachraeh, 2004). More than 60,000 people were sterilized under these laws in the United States (Larson, 2002).

The most famous case of involuntary sterilization was that of Carrie Bell, a woman from Virginia who was alleged to have had mental retardation. Ms. Bell was the first woman in Virginia to undergo compulsory sterilization in the State of Virginia after the Supreme Court affirmed the State's compulsory sterilization law (Mostert, 2002; Larson, 2002; Lombardo, 2003; Palmer, 2003). The United States Supreme Court upheld Virginia's 1924 Involuntary Sterilization Act with its 1927 decision in *Buck v. Bell*. This Supreme Court decision has been repudiated but it has never been overruled (Palmer, 2003). The State of Virginia repealed its sterilization law in 1974.

Eugenics became associated with the concept of racial hygiene in Europe. In 1926, Denmark, Finland, Norway, and Sweden began institutionalized sterilization programs (Barnett, 2004). Influential social and economic forces in Germany, particularly after World War I, foreshadowed the genocide of people with disabilities (Mostert, 2002; Bachrach, 2004). In 1933, Germany's compulsory sterilization law was drafted (Mostert, 2002; Bachrach, 2004). Through a propaganda effort, individuals with disabilities became characterized as a separate group, perceived as different-criminals and of little or no economic value. Approximately 400,000 persons considered to have a hereditary sickness were sterilized under the Law for the Prevention for Genetically Diseased Offspring. Officially, another 70,273 adults with disabilities were euthanized through centers created by a program created in 1939 called Aktion T-4 (Mostert, 2002). Following World War II, public awareness of the Nazi Holocaust discredited the word eugenics and it essentially disappeared from use.

The genomic era of medicine began on April 14, 2003, approximately 50 years following the first description of the structure of DNA, when the

Human Genome Project completed the sequencing of the human genome (Guttmacher & Collins, 2003). Conservative estimates suggest at least 13 million people in the United States are affected by genetic conditions (Koch, 2001). Genetic researchers estimate that every individual carries 5 to 7 lethal recessive genes (Larson, 2002). Ethical debate about the Human Genome Project and genetic testing has fostered a resurgence of interest and debate regarding eugenics and genetic practices (Barnett, 2004).

EUTHANASIA

Euthanasia is derived from the Greek word eu, meaning "well," and thanatos meaning "death," and early on signified a "good" or "easy" death (Nadeau, 1995). Today euthanasia has come to mean "a deliberate intervention, by act or omission, in the life of a dying person with the intention of putting an end to that person's life and suffering" (Nadeau, 1995, p. 10). Euthanasia is performed by physicians and has been further defined as "active" or "passive." *Active euthanasia* refers to a physician deliberately acting in a way to end a patient's life. *Passive euthanasia* pertains to withholding or withdrawing treatment necessary to maintain life (Frileux, Lelievre, Munoz Sastre, Mullet, & Sorum, 2003). Sir Francis Bacon, an English philosopher and statesman, termed the phrase euthanasia early in the 17th century. At that time euthanasia was used as a way to describe a pain-free, peaceful, and natural death that individuals desired to have (Yount, 2000).

The historical societal perspectives of euthanasia often parallel those of suicide. During ancient times in Greece, individuals could request government assistance with suicide which was sometimes seen as a noble act (Yount, 2000). However, when Christianity became the dominant religion in the Western world, those beliefs changed. The condemnation of suicide became a part of Christian teachings, and there were even anti-suicide laws in place. It wasn't until the 20th century when these laws were reviewed. Society found that punishing the family of the person who committed suicide was not only unfair, but that those who did commit suicide usually were viewed as doing so because of a mental illness (Yount, 2000).

In the United States, the first bill to legalize voluntary euthanasia by a physician was introduced in the Ohio legislature in 1906, but failed (Yount, 2000). The idea of euthanasia was again brought to the social forefront during WWII and Nazi Germany, when adults and children considered mentally deficient involuntarily were put to death (McKhann, 1999). Currently in the United States the only state where physician-assisted dying, in the form of assisted suicide, is legal is in Oregon (Quill & Battin, 2004).

PHYSICIAN-ASSISTED SUICIDE

Physician-assisted suicide (PAS) differs from euthanasia as euthanasia embodies that the dying person may or may not be aware of what is happening to them, and may or may not have requested to die (Hawkins, 2002). With PAS, the terminal patient wants to die and seeks assistance from a doctor in doing so (Dworkin, Frey, & Bok, 1998). The U.S. Supreme Court ruled that individuals do not have a constitutional right to PAS on June 26, 1997 (Hawkins, 2002).

Euthanasia and PAS are often linked together and intertwined in discussions. Physician-assisted suicide is also associated with the right-to-die movement, which gained momentum in the 1970's as medical advances kept individuals living who previously would have died. Living wills were first developed during this time, as individuals wanted the right to refuse life-prolonging medical treatment and have some type of ownership over the quality of their life, especially during the very end stages (Yount, 2000).

During the 1980s the right-to-die movement gained even more momentum with the advent of durable power of attorney, which directed surrogates in making health care decisions for individuals if they were, or became, incompetent to do so for themselves (Yount, 2000). Physician-assisted suicide moved to the forefront in the 1990s, largely in part to Dr. Jack Kevorkian and his public crusade of practicing, and accepting, PAS (Yount, 2000). Dr. Kevorkian has been incarcerated for practicing PAS.

CONCEPTUAL MODELS

The polarization of opinion regarding eugenics, euthanasia, and physician-assisted suicide is represented by the differences between the medical and minority models of disability. One paradigm favors eugenics, euthanasia, and assisted suicide while the other opposes these practices and advocates social support for persons with disabilities (Koch, 2004). Historically, the field of genetic counseling has relied upon the medical model of health and disease (Patterson & Satz, 2002).

The medical model of disability conceptualizes disability as a negative variation of the physical or cognitive norm, disadvantaging a person's life and their quality of life (Koch, 2001). The traditional physical definition of disability used in the medical model portrays a person that cannot independently perform tasks or actions (Koch, 2001). Autonomy and self-sufficiency become the defining aspects of the normal human existence. The emphasis upon individual autonomy, self-determination, and independence is compatible with although not an endorsement, of the practices of eugenics, euthanasia or assisted suicide (Koch, 2001). Individual models of disability, particularly the medical model, have been criticized as inadequate for explaining the complex phenomena of disability (Reindal, 2000). Adhering to a causal understanding of the interaction between impairment and disability, the medical model of disability promotes value judgements by the professional community regarding the quality of life a person with a disability may lead (Reindal, 2000).

In contrast, the minority or social model of disability attributes the concept of disability to the lack of environmental accommodation and negative societal reaction to individuals with disabilities. The minority model suggests that rather than the limits a condition imposes, it is the lack of understanding about the effects of a disability, or a failure to accommodate a physical or cognitive difference, that is the source of disability (Olkin, 1999; Smart, 2001; Koch, 2004). Social difference theorists and disability rights advocates insist that a physically-dependent, or interdependent life is as full and viable as one that is autonomous and independent (Koch, 2004; Parens & Asch, 2003). Personhood is perceived as communal or relational rather than an individual experience. Individuals in this paradigm are defined not by their disease or limitations but their capacity for relationships with others. The value of a person is absolute, and cannot be decreased or withdrawn in this conceptualization. Many authors with disabilities argue the worst aspect of having a disability is not the disability itself, but the societal prejudice against any deviation from the norm (Chen & Schiffman, 2000). Eugenics, euthanasia, and assisted suicide are not supported by the minority or social perspective of disability (Koch, 2004).

INTERNATIONAL PERSPECTIVES

Eugenics

Internationally, China and the Netherlands continue eugenic practices. China passed the Maternal & Infant Health Care Law in 1994. In that year, China's population reached 1.2 billion people. A policy of one child per couple was established in order to achieve a population goal of less than 1.4 billion people in 2010 (Mao, 1998). A national survey in China conducted in 1987 revealed there were 51.64 million people with disabilities. Birth defects and genetic diseases accounted for 35.09% of the population of persons with a disability (Ming & Jixiang, 1993). A survey of Chinese geneticists suggested most Chinese perceived individuals with disabilities as a severe burden to families and society (Mao, 1998). Public education was considered an effective approach to reduce the number of genetic diseases. Social, cultural, and economic differences between China and the west were believed to be likely causes for differences regarding eugenics (Mao, 1998).

Galjaard's study of gene testing and social acceptance (as cited in Mao, 1998), revealed that the Netherlands operates seven regional genetics centers providing pre-and postnatal chromosomal analysis, biochemical and DNA diagnosis and genetic counseling services. The genetics centers are funded by national health insurance. As a result of the combined testing and counseling activities, it is estimated that the birth of 800–1600 children with severe disabilities are prevented annually. The annual cost of operating the genetic counseling centers is estimated at $50 million. However, the averted cost of care for the medical and psychosocial needs required by the 800–1600 children with disabilities prevented each year was calculated as ranging between $500 million and $1 billion during an average 10 year lifespan (Galjaard, 1997 as cited in Mao, 1998).

Euthanasia/PAS

Euthanasia, both active and passive, has been practiced in the Netherlands since the 1970s, and holds the largest source of data for physicians aiding in end-of-life decisions (Kaplan, Harrow, & Schneiderhan, 2002). In 1990 the Dutch government initiated the Remmelink Commission to survey the practice of PAS and euthanasia in the Netherlands. They found that at least 25,000 cases annually consisted of the withdrawal of life support (passive euthanasia), and of those, 27% were administered morphine in order to shorten life. About 9% of the deaths in the Netherlands in 1990 were attributed to PAS or euthanasia (Gentles, 1995).

The Remmelink Report, as it has now become known, found that between 6,000–12,000 cases annually were reported by Dutch hospitals in which PAS or euthanasia was practiced. In 90% of those cases, it was a question of involuntary euthanasia, even though active euthanasia remains illegal (Gentles, 1995). The Board of Royal Dutch Medicine Association endorses euthanasia for newborns and infants with extreme disabilities (Gentles, 1995).

In the Netherlands study, the reasons for choosing to die included a loss of dignity, intolerable pain, and not wanting to have an unworthy death. Wanting to avoid being, or becoming dependent on others, and feeling tired of life, were also cited as reasons in choosing to end one's life (Kaplan et al., 2002). Cases in Australia have been studied as well, regarding the choices people make for seeking PAS. In 1995, the Northern Territory of Australia legalized the option of euthanasia for the terminally ill, defined as those individuals having less than six months to live. In the first year under this policy seven individuals, all with cancer, sought to use this law to end their lives. Of those seven, pain did not appear to be a reason for their choosing to end their lives. Among the psychosocial factors listed as reasons for wanting to end one's life were social isolation, depression, anticipatory fear, sense of futility and a loss of dignity (Kaplan et al., 2002).

SOCIAL AND ETHICAL CONSIDERATIONS

Eugenics

The history of the eugenics movement has impacted the current practice of genetic counseling. Genetic counselors are guided by a nondirective standard of practice (Larson, 2003; Parens & Asch, 2003; Patterson & Satz, 2002). The goal of the therapist is to provide clear information in an unbiased manner (Saranji, 2002).

Knowledge and attitude of health care professionals is known to influence patient communication and medical decision making. In one study, medical students, residents, and genetic counseling students characterized as having minimal experience with disability or genetics completed a survey regarding their attitudes about disability and genetic screening (Ormond et al., 2003). The results of this study indicated the majority of the participants felt that disability caused significant suffering for the person with the disability and 64% felt that having a disability also caused significant suffering for family members. Perceptions about the quality of life for a person with a disability or their family were based upon cognitive functioning, pain experienced, and level of available social support. Sixty-two percent of those surveyed felt that research should be directed toward preventing genetic disability (Ormond et al., 2003).

Genetic testing can assist individuals with understanding the risk of having a child when a family history of a genetic disorder exists and how to manage personal health decisions when planning for a pregnancy (Bodenhorn & Lawson, 2003). Tests exist for genetic factors associated with more than 400 human conditions (Larson, 2002). Genetic tests fall within three broad categories; predictive gene testing, carrier testing, and prenatal testing (Glannon, 1998; Larson, 2002). However, identifying a genetic basis for a disability does not guarantee that a disabling condition exists or will develop (Larson, 2002).

Despite widespread prenatal testing, limited research has been conducted that addresses the decision making process during prenatal testing. Available studies are primarily qualitative and suggest that the perceived benefits and emotional factors influence the decision to undergo prenatal testing. Patient knowledge and actual risk factors have not been shown to be strong predictors of test use among those eligible for testing. Review of the literature reflects that deciding to undergo genetic testing is primarily related to subjective risk factors and emotions (Lerman et al., 2002). How a genetic test is offered also appears to influence whether or not a person will elect to undergo genetic testing. Individuals are more likely to undergo testing if it is offered in person and carried out immediately (Marteau & Croyle, 1998).

Research regarding the psychological impact of genetic testing is similarly limited. It does suggest, however, that adverse reactions to test results are uncommon when provided through a program that separates the offer of testing from the testing itself, and provides clear information and emotional support before and after testing (Lerman et al., 2002; Marteau & Croyle, 2001). The psychological impact of testing results appears to depend more on pretest expectations, mood, and social support than the test results themselves (Marteau & Croyle, 1998). As an example, pretest levels of depression and hopelessness were found to be the best predictors of levels of hopelessness following test result disclosure rather than the actual results (Meiser & Dunn, 2000).

The psychological impact of certain disease diagnoses does appear to be influenced by the nature of the diagnosis. Suicide occurs with an incidence 4 times greater than the general United States population following a diagnosis of Huntington's disease (Meiser & Dunn, 2000). Stress response syndrome has been predicted to develop in 20% of individuals receiving the results of a genetic risk for a "dire" illness (Horowitz et al., 2001). Knowledge about the phases of response, an individual's defensive style, and supportive counseling can assist recently-diagnosed individuals with understanding and integrating the implications of their diagnosis (Horowitz et al., 2001).

Family relationships may become strained by the results of genetic testing. Partners of the person undergoing testing may be more affected by the results of genetic testing than the person undergoing testing themselves (Marteau & Croyle, 2001). Compared with non-carrier's partners, the partners of carriers of Huntington's disease had substantially higher levels of distress at 1 week, 6 months, and three years after the disclosure of positive test results (Meiser & Dunn, 2000). A case study about a male spouse's experience during the decision to terminate a pregnancy reflects that he did not feel his grieving needs were met or recognized during genetic counseling (Robson, 2002). The increased need for family support is related to the sense of loss of control, feelings of guilt, and personal concerns that may affect others in the family who are not directly involved with the testing (Bodenhorn & Lawson, 2002).

Adults interviewed regarding their perception of genetic counseling appreciated the opportunity to receive direct education from experts in the field. Participants in this study indicated that they gained a thorough understanding of the risks and conditions, and appreciated having control of the decision making process. Positive genetic counseling experiences were associated with longer appointments than the traditional physician appointment times, provision of reading material, and the involvement of family members in the process (MacLeod et al., 2002).

Women at risk for carrying a fetus with Down's syndrome or spina bifida were surveyed regarding their experience with genetic counseling (Roberts et al., 2002). The survey reflected that 87% were referred for genetic counseling by their doctor with the primary concern being the woman's age. Sixty-five percent of those surveyed indicated they would terminate a pregnancy if a disorder was present in their fetus. Results indicated as knowledge of the resources available for individuals with disabilities increased, the choice to continue a pregnancy became more likely. However, the vast majority of the participants expressed they were not encouraged to meet with the parent of a disabled child by either their genetic counselor or other medical personnel, were not provided information regarding future quality of life issues for a child with a disability, and were not provided either the positive or negative aspects of giving birth to a child with a disability (Roberts et al., 2002).

Attitudes of people with physical disabilities toward genetic counseling and prenatal diagnosis have rarely been addressed in the literature. Anticipating that individuals with physical disabilities would parallel the literature and express skeptical or negative attitudes toward genetic counseling, 15 adults with physical disabilities were interviewed regarding their feelings about genetic counseling (Chen & Schiffman, 2000). Results in this study indicated that approximately 78% of the participants did not feel genetic counseling was eugenic. The majority of the participants did not correlate genetics with eugenics and expressed that they felt genetic advancements could improve the health of individuals. None of those interviewed recognized anti-disability perspectives about prenatal diagnosis (Chen & Schiffman, 2000).

Quality of life for persons with disabilities is central to the debate about eugenics, euthanasia, and assisted suicide. Semistructured interviews conducted with 153 persons described as having moderate to severe disabilities indicated that 54% reported experiencing an excellent or good quality of life (Albrecht & Devlieger, 1999). Analysis of the content of the interviews revealed the definition of quality of life was dependent upon finding a balance between body, mind, spirit, and maintaining relationships within the person's social context and environment (Albrecht & Devlieger, 1999). Interviews with persons having Huntington's disease or cystic fibrosis indicated that the participants felt that others perceived them as unworthy of life, and as unnecessary burdens upon society (Chapman, 2002).

Numerous fundamental ethical and value questions are raised throughout the present literature review. Examples of major value questions cited by Bodenhorn and Lawson (2002) include: What constitutes a life

worth living?; Who should make decisions?; and How should life be valued? Ensuring that the decision maker is provided with balanced and
current information to arrive at an informed decision and that each individual has the right to make decisions without external pressure presents
additional ethical concerns (Chapman, 2002).

Euthanasia/PAS

Kaplan et al. (2002) studied 93 of Dr. Jack Kevorkian's cases to understand
an individual's choice for PAS. Information was gathered through medical reports, death certificates and from medical examiners themselves. A
psychological autopsy was also administered to friends and relatives of
47 of Kevorkian's patients. The psychological autopsy has been widely
used to study individuals who have attempted suicide. It allows a reconstruction of the psychological profile of the decedent, garnered through
those closest to the person, and is parallel to physical autopsies (Kaplan
et al., 2002).

In the 97 cases studied, 87% of individuals chose PAS because of
a disability and another 36% were described as depressed. Fear of dependency occurred in 90% of the cases while 31.1% were terminally ill,
which was listed as having less than 6 months to live (Kaplan et al., 2002).
The gender ratio of general completed suicides in the United States was
18.9% women in 1995, but in the Kevorkian study 68% were women and
32% were men (Kaplan et al., 2002). Although 73.6% of the individuals
reported having pain, only 42.6% had an anatomical basis for that pain
(Kaplan et al., 2002). The average age of the decedents was 58.3 years
and the majority were white (Kaplan et al., 2002).

Additional studies have shown that "younger age, greater education,
affluence, and white race are all predictors of patient preference for less
aggressive treatment and in favor of physician aid in dying" (Steinberg &
Younger, 1998, p. 3). Treatment choices for patients, families and physicians, are influenced by age, religion, ethnicity, and socioeconomic status
(Steinberg & Younger, 1998).

What does the above information tell us about the social implications
of PAS? Perhaps most telling are the reasons an individual chooses PAS.
As the data from international studies show, the psychosocial aspects of
PAS are less related to physical burdens, and more towards personal.
Similar to the Kevorkian study, where Kaplan et al. (2002) correlated
women choosing PAS due to worries about their marriage breaking up
and a deterioration of their economic state, women in Oregon chose PAS
due to concerns about being a burden to their spouse.

Ethical considerations for physicians weigh heavily in the literature
regarding PAS and euthanasia. The ethical issues focus on patient choice
versus medical responsibility. Recently this debate was carried out in the

judicial arena, specifically with the Terri Schiavo case in Florida, which may ultimately change the face of the current movement (Campo-Flores, 2005).

ECONOMIC ASPECTS

Euthanasia/PAS

The argument regarding euthanasia and PAS becomes even more intense when economics are considered. Steinberg and Younger (1998) reported that the increased emphasis on cost savings and managed care will become the basis for decision making for the terminally ill, where as prior decisions were primarily clinically based. The business of healthcare generates the dilemma with which Americans are faced.

Estimates show that about 1/3 of all families with a terminally ill family member will end up in poverty (Bilchik, 1996). Bilchik (1996) also reported that care for the terminally ill accounts for 10% of the national healthcare costs and that 27% of all Medicare spending occurs during the last year of a person's life (40% of the total is for the last month alone). Drugs for assisted suicide cost between $35–$45 and could ultimately become considered the less expensive treatment for death (Marker & Hamlon, 2005).

In Oregon, 83% of doctors stated that financial pressures were a factor in a patient's request to die (Bilchik, 1996). Some fear that a right to die may soon become a duty to die, in order to eliminate families from financial ruin. A report from Harvard University stated that one-half of all bankruptcies in the U.S. are caused by medical bills. At the time of illness onset, more than three-quarters of those people had health insurance and most were middle class and educated (U.S. Newswire, 2005). Considering that 16.4% (46.2 million) of the individuals in the United States are uninsured, the idea of choosing death over bankruptcy of your family may become more appealing (Uninsured in America, 2000).

CONCLUSION

Implications for Practice

Rehabilitation professionals have been absent from the discussion about eugenics, euthanasia and assisted suicide. This absence reflects a large disservice to persons with disabilities. Many of the cases discussed in the available research involved individuals who would or could have participated in services provided by a rehabilitation professional. Counselors need to be aware of the social and economic implications for clients who feel like a burden to their family or lack the medical or economic resources to ensure a reasonable quality of life.

Educating individuals with disabilities about alternatives, options, and available resources may make the decision to live with a disability more manageable. Educating the general public about the resources available to enhance one's quality of life appears equally as important, as socially and environmentally-imposed handicaps appear to have a greater impact on the decision to undergo PAS or to terminate a pregnancy than the illness or disability itself.

Becoming aware of the psychosocial aspects of euthanasia and PAS also affect the field of rehabilitation. Factors leading to the decision to live, die, or terminate a pregnancy are entangled with race/ethnicity, age, spirituality, gender and the legal system. Knowing how all of these factors affect individuals with disabilities, and their decisions to live or die, should be a primary concern of the rehabilitation field.

FUTURE RESEARCH

Areas for future research related to the field of rehabilitation are numerous. Further the majority of the research regarding genetic counseling with persons who have a genetic condition or disability is qualitative, exploratory, or limited to opinion pieces. One of the most critical areas is the psychosocial aspects of patients choosing PAS, and the involvement of rehabilitation counselors. Additional studies regarding the attitudes of person's with disabilities toward genetic counseling and testing are needed. The role of rehabilitation professionals regarding how and when they could become involved in the decision-making process requires exploration. Issues regarding the economics of health care are another area ripe for research. Studying the relationship between health care costs, and decisions related to PAS and/or termination of pregnancy, could yield significant information for rehabilitation professionals.

Perhaps the starting point for research in the rehabilitation field should begin with the general knowledge, attitudes, and beliefs, rehabilitation professionals possess about the practices discussed in this paper. Developing a strong understanding of the attitudes and values rehabilitation professionals possess about quality of life decisions and the implications of eugenics, euthanasia, and PAS could lead to better training of rehabilitation counseling students. Expanded discussion of these topics appears appropriate for inclusion in courses about multicultural or psychosocial adjustment to disability issues. The research ideas mentioned above are starting points for developing a knowledge base specific to rehabilitation.

The time has come to align our knowledge and actions as rehabilitation professionals with the needs of persons with disabilities relative to eugenics, euthanasia and physician-assisted suicide.

REFERENCES

Albrecht, G.L., & Devlieger, P.J. (1999). The disability paradox: High quality of life against all odds. *Social Science & Medicine, 48*(8), 977–988.

Bachrach, S. (2004). In the name of public health-Nazi racial hygiene. *The New England Journal of Medicine, 351,* 417–420.

Barnett, R. (2004). Keywords in the history of medicine: Eugenics. *The Lancet, 363,* 1742.

Barr, O., & Millar, R. (2003). Parents of children with intellectual disabilities: Their expectations and experience of genetic counseling. *Journal of Applied Research in Intellectual Disabilities, 16,* 189–204.

Bilchik, G.S. (1996). Dollars & death. *Hospitals & Health Networks, 70,* 18–22.

Bodenhorn, N., & Lawson, G. (2002). Genetic counseling: Implications for community counselors. *Journal of Counseling and Development, 81,* 497–501.

Botkin, J.R. (2003). Prenatal diagnosis and the selection of children. *Florida State Law Review, 30*(2), 265–293.

Buck v. Bell, 274 U.S. 200 (1927).

Campo-Flores, Arian. (2005, April 4). The legacy of Terri Schiavo. *Newsweek,* 22–28.

Chapman, F. (2002). The social and ethical implications of changing medical technologies: The views of people living with genetic conditions. *Journal of Health Psychology, 7,* 195–206.

Chen, E.A., & Schiffman, J.F. (2000). Attitudes toward genetic counseling and prenatal diagnosis among a group of individuals with physical disabilities. *Journal of Genetic Counseling, 9*(2), 137–152.

Dworkin, G., Frey, R.G., & Bok, S. (1998). *Euthanasia and physician-assisted suicide.* Cambridge: United Kingdom: Cambridge University Press.

Frileux, S., Lelievre, C., Munoz Sastre, M.T., Mullet, E., & Sorum, P.C. (2003). When is physician assisted suicide or euthanasia acceptable? *Journal of Medical Ethics, 29,* 330–336.

Galjaard, H. (1997). Gene technology and social acceptance. *Pathologie Bioloogie, 45,* 250–255.

Glannon, W. (1998). Genes, embryos, and future people. *Bioethics, 12*(3), 187–211.

Guttemacher, A.E., & Collins, F.S. (2003). Welcome to the genomic era. *The New England Journal of Medicine, 349*(10), 996–998.

Hawkins, G. (2002). *Physician Assisted Suicide.* San Diego, CA: Greehnaven Press.

Himmelstein, D.U., Warren, E., Thorne, D., & Woolhandler, S. (2005, February 2). Illness and Injury as Contributors to Bankruptcy. Health Affairs, W5-63. Retrieved on April 24, 2005 from: http://content.healthaffairs.org/cgi/

content/full/hlthaff.w5.63/DC1?maxtoshow=&HITS=10&hits=
10&RESULTFORMAT=&fulltext=bankruptcy&andorexactfulltext=and
&searchid=1114371654575_1440&stored_search=&FIRSTINDEX=0
&resourcetype=1&journalcode=healthaff.

Holland, S. (2003). Selecting against difference: Assisted reproduction, disability
and Regulation. *Florida State Law Review, 30*(2), 401–410.

Horowitz, M., Sundin, E., Zanko, A., & Lauer, R. (2001). Coping with grim news
from genetic tests. *Psychosomatics, 42*(2), 100–105.

Kaplan, K.J., Harrow, M., & Schneiderhan, M. (2002). Suicide, physician-assisted
suicide and euthanasia in men versus women around the world: The degree
of physician control. *Ethics & Medicine, 18,* 33–50.

Kay, H., & Kingston, H. (2002). Feelings associated with being a carrier and characteristics of reproductive decision making in women known to be carriers
of x-linked conditions. *Journal of Health Psychology, 7,* 169–181.

Koch, Y. (2001). Disability and difference: Balancing social and physical constructions. *Journal of Medical Ethics, 27,* 370–376.

Koch, T. (2004). The difference that difference makes: Bioethics and the challenge
of "disability". Journal of Medicine and Philosophy, *29*(6), 697–716.

Lapham, E.V., Kozma, C., & Weiss, J. (1996). Genetic discrimination: Perspectives
of Consumers. *Science, 274,* 621–623.

Larson, E.F. (2002). The meaning of human gene testing for disability rights.
University Of Cincinnati *Law Review, 70,* 913–938.

Lerman, C. Croyle, R.T., Tercyak, K.P., & Hamman, H. (2002). Genetic testing:
Psychological aspects and implications. *Journal of Consulting and Clinical
Psychology, 70*(3), 784–797.

Lombardo, P. (2003). Eugenics bibliography. Retrieved January 22,
2005 from the University of Virginia Health System Website: www.
healthsystemvirginia.edu.

Lombardo, P.A. (2003). Taking eugenics seriously: Three generations of ??? are
enough? *Florida State Law review, 30*(2), 191–218.

MacLeod, R., Crawford, D., & Booth, K. (2002). Patient's perceptions of what
makes genetic counseling effective: An interpretive phenomenological analysis. *Journal of Health Psychology, 7,* 145–156.

Mahowald, M. B. (2003). Aren't we all eugenicists? Commentary on Paul Lombardo's "taking eugenics seriously." *Florida State Law Review, 30*(2), 219–
235.

Marker, R.L., & Hamlon, K. (2005). *Euthansia and Assisted Suicide:
Frequently Asked Questions.* International Task Force on Euthanasia and Assisted Suicide. Retrieved January 2, 2005 from http://www.
internationaltaskforce.org/faq.htm.

Mao, X. (1998). Chinese geneticists' views of ethical issues in genetic testing
and screening: Evidence for eugenics in China. *American Journal of Human
Genetics, 63,* 688–695.

Marteau, T.M., & Croyle, R.T. (1998). Psychological responses to genetic testing.
BMJ, 316, 693–696.

McKhann, C. (1999). *A Time to Die.* London. Yale University Press.

Meiser, B., & Dunn, S. (2000). Psychological impact of genetic testing for Huntington's Disease: An update of the literature. *Journal of Neurology, Neurosurgery, Psychiatry, 69,* 574–578.

Mostert, M. P. (2002). Useless eaters: Disability as genocidal marker in nazi germany. *The Journal of Special Education, 36,* 155–168.

Mortimer, D. P. (2003). The new eugenics and the newborn: The historical "cousinage" of eugenics and infanticide. *Ethics and Medicine, 19*(3), 155–169.

Nadeau, R. (1995). Charting the Legal Trends. In I. Gentles, *Euthanasia and Assisted Suicide: The Current Debate* (pp. 727). Toronto, Canada: Stoddart Publishing Co. Limited.

Olkin, R. (1999). *What psychotherapists should know about disability.* New York, NY: The Guilford Press.

Ormond, K.E., Gill, Semcik, P., & Kirschner, K.L. (2003). Attitudes of health care trainees about genetics and disability: Issues of access, health care communication, and decision making. *Journal of Genetic Counseling, 12*(4), 333–349.

Palmer, L.I. (2003). Genetic health and eugenic precedents: A voice of caution. *Florida State Law Review, 30*(2), 237–264.

Parens, E., & Asch, A. (2003). Disability rights critique of prenatal genetic testing: Reflections and recommendations. *Mental Retardation and Developmental Disabilities and Research Reviews, 9,* 40–47.

Patterson, A., & Satz, M. (2002). Genetic counseling and the disabled: Feminism examines the stance of those who stand at the gate. *Hypatia, 17*(3), 118–142.

Quill, T.E., & Battin, M.P. (2004). Physician assisted dying. Baltimore, MD: The John Hopkins University Press.

Reindal, S.M. (2000). Disability, gene therapy and eugenics—a challenge to John Harris. *Journal of Medical Ethics, 26,* 8994.

Rhoades, J.A., Vistnes, J.P., & Cohen, J.W. (2000, March). *Uninsured in America. Medical Expenditure Panel Survey.* Retrieved January 2, 2005 from http://www.meps.ahrq.gov/.

Roberts, C.D., Stough, L.M., & Parrish, L.H. (2002). The role of genetic counseling in the elective termination of pregnancies involving fetuses with disabilities. *The Journal of Special Education, 361*(1), 48–55.

Robson, F. (2002). "Yes!—a chance to tell my side of the story": A case study of a male partner of a woman undergoing termination of pregnancy for fetal abnormality. *Journal of Health Psychology, 7,* 183–193.

Saranji, S. (2002). The language of likelihood in genetic counseling discourse. *Journal of Language and Social Psychology, 21,* 7–31.

Smart, J. (2001). *Disabled, society, and the individual.* Austin, TX: Pro-Ed.

Smith, J.A., Michie, S., Stephenson, M., & Quarrell, O. (2002). Risk perception and decision-making processes in candidates for genetic testing for Huntington's disease. *Journal of Health Psychology, 7,* 131–144.

Steinberg, M.D., & Younger, S.J. (1998). *End of life decisions.* Washington, DC: American Psychiatric Press, Inc.

Yount, L. (2000). Physician-assisted suicide and euthanasia. New York, NY: Facts On File, Inc.

CHAPTER THIRTY-FIVE

Reflections and Considerations[1]

Arthur E. Dell Orto and Paul Power

Prior articles and chapters have presented the impact of illness and disability on the person and family from a life and living perspective. This perspective attempts to put the past in a functional context, maximizes the opportunities of present, and anticipates a future enhanced by optimism, tempered by reality, and enriched with hope. This chapter (a) reflects on some of the issues and complications related to the family's illness and disability experience; (b) discusses some possible myths that may be part of a person's or family's frame of reference; (c) explores selected research topics that may influence future coping and adaptation; and (d) identifies the specific issues of expectations, compassion, hope, and spirituality which are important dimensions when assisting families experiencing severe illness and disability.

REFLECTIONS

For those persons and families living the illness and disability experience, the past is unalterable, but the future can be somewhat controlled, even though it is very uncertain and unpredictable. When the impact and

---

[1] Some of the material in this chapter is updated and modified from Power and Dell Orto (2004); Dell Orto and Power (2000); and Power, Dell Orto, and Gibbons (1988). Reprinted with permission.

consequences of loss and change are most prominent in a family's life, there is always the temptation to replay the past and rethink the causal events, while hoping for a different or more palatable outcome (e.g., if I only I had made them wear a seatbelt they would not be disabled; if I had encouraged my wife to stop smoking she would not have lung cancer; if I had not told her that she must take the job in the World Trade Center, rather than going to school as she wanted to, she would be alive today). Decisions were made, and the consequences are permanent and have major implications for all involved.

When individuals and families experience and bear witness to the causes and consequences of many illnesses and disabilities, there is the drive and commitment to make sure that it does not happen again. In fact, having an illness or disability does not guarantee that a person will not have another that could be better or worse. For example, the possibility of another illness or disability is actually increased the longer we live and the more exposure we have, for example, being on the highway, on vacation, or at work includes risk for life-altering experiences.

Similarly, in some cases when successful rehabilitation interventions have increased independence and expanded life domains, there is an increased vulnerability to the very risks families are attempting to master and control. Consider the reaction of a family awarded $2 million in a personal injury case for their traumatically injured 17-year-old daughter. They bought her a sports car and, as a result, she was in a car accident because she was speeding and drinking. She became a quadriplegic and her brother was killed. At this point, her mother stated that their situation went from bad to worse—which she never could have imagined. The money promised a lot of hope, but delivered a great deal of pain. She added that they all would have been better off without it.

It is at this point that families are confused, angry, and vulnerable. The issue is not only who can be blamed or can pay but also what can be done to validate the person living with the consequences and make the life care process more reasonable. The problem is that no amount of money can regain what was lost, undo the pain and sorrow, and guarantee that life will be easier on all fronts. Although money can certainly relieve the financial burden and provide the resources needed to enhance quality of life, it can also cause additional unanticipated problems and difficulties.

Large cash settlements have distorted the issues and created a caste system. Some families must ask: "Why should someone else with a traumatic injury similar to my child's be awarded a multimillion dollar settlement and get the best of care while my child lives in squalor with a broken wheelchair and without personal care attendants just because he was injured by a person without insurance or even resources?" This is one of the many challenges facing health care and rehabilitation today. A system must be developed that is based on human value, respect for life, and family stabilization that includes more than is excluded. No cost is too great if it is helping those who have too little. Any cost is too great if it helps those who do not need it at the expense of those who do.

This is an ongoing complexity of life: There are no guarantees, only opportunities, choices, and consequences. We cannot prevent the inevitable, but we must try to provide meaningful intervention, nonjudgmental support, and consistent caring. However, it is critical that interventions be based on a realistic perspective of the human condition as it is and as it will become. People are in a constant state of growth and deterioration. We cannot be immunized from the human experience even if we or others are focused on this as a noble goal.

Callahan in his book, *False Hopes: Overcoming the Obstacles to a Sustainable, Affordable Medicine* (1999), makes some important points that have a direct bearing on how people and families respond to health and its deterioration:

> By its tacit implication that in the quest for health lies, perhaps, the secret of the meaning of life, modern medicine has misled people into thinking that the ills of the flesh, and mortality itself, are not to be understood and integrated into a balanced view of life but simply to be fought and resisted. It is as if the medical struggle against illness, aging and death is itself the source of (or at least a source of) human meaning. I refer not only to the almost religious devotion some have to improving their health and their bodies so that health itself becomes the goal of life, but also the idea that, in an other-wise meaningless world, the effort to relieve suffering becomes a source of meaning. (p. 31)

Many families find themselves in very complicated and demanding situations in which their medical condition cannot be improved or improvement could be made but the needed resources are not available or accessible. Loss and change are undeniable dimensions and forces of the human experience. Consequently, every effort should be made to help the person and family live their lives with human dignity and values that appreciate life, accept mortality, recognize vulnerability, promote hope, and demonstrate caring. Some of the most poignant statements a family can make are "we should have," "if only," "why us?" Rarely do people say, "why not?"

COMPLICATIONS

Families may also find themselves in situations where the solution to the presenting problem creates more problems than were expected or anticipated. The emotionality and complexity of the issues related to cardiopulmonary resuscitation, for example, and the burden placed on families who are hoping for full recoveries while faced with losses are discussed by Phipps (1998):

> Because families view rehabilitation, at least initially, with a hopefulness for the patient's full recovery, initiating discussions of this topic early on in the rehabilitation process may be experiences as too emotionally burdensome to yield informed decisions and may be viewed as counterproductive to establishing trust and rapport. Some families appear to welcome talk about their own concerns, while others do not want to or are unable to grapple with the topic. Families who ultimately choose against resuscitation for their family member may have shifted in their hopefulness about the patient's recovery; may have lived with a patient with a chronic debilitating illness and believe that should the patient arrest, resuscitation may not be in the patient's best interest or possibly not in theirs. (p. 97)

An alternative perspective on complications and unanticipated problems is the great appreciation families have for those heroic efforts which have kept their loved ones alive and have given them the chance to continue life but at a different level. As a wife stated:

> One day I have a husband who is the strength of the family, who makes everyone proud, and the next, I have this person who scares everyone with his temper and who thinks everything is fine when it's a sorry mess. But life is getting better. The two of us get along. Sometimes I even like the fact that my husband is around all the time. He can be good company . . . I guess we'll be a good old twosome until the day we die . . . Life is hard. I'm a survivor. (Dell Orto & Power, 2000)

In both of these examples, the common element is that the families are going to have to live with the consequences of their unique life experience. The challenge for society and health care is to provide the support, encouragement, and role models needed to keep illness and disability in perspective so that it does not become a ravaging force that destroys the family that is trying to survive against great odds.

Assisting families to cope with illness and disability is often a lifelong process. It demands creative efforts on the part of the health care and rehabilitation teams, as well as the commitment and investment of team members who are sensitive to and aware of the needs of the person and the family living an experience of ongoing change, loss, and perhaps even potential gains.

SELECTED MYTHS

A challenge is to approach health care, treatment, and rehabilitation from an optimistic as well as a realistic perspective. This is not an easy task because there are many myths that can influence individual and family expectations during the treatment and rehabilitation process. Some of these myths are described next.

Myth 1: All Illnesses and Disabilities Can Be Cured or Prevented

Although it is a noble goal to reduce all of the precipitating and causal factors related to the incidence of illness and disability, no amount of education or prevention will eradicate all the variables, conditions, and situations that cause illness and disability such as drunk driving, drug-related violence, war, crime, guns, alcohol, drugs, poor diet, genetics, poverty, accidents, terrorism, sports injuries, abuse, toxic environments, work injuries, cars, bicycles, or just the reality of the life and living process. And sometimes, even though there are helpful guidelines (e.g., seatbelt use, exercise, bicycle helmets, smoking cessation), there are many people who continue to engage in behaviors that place their health or that of their family a risk. An irony is that cars do hit some joggers in pursuit of wellness. Some have minor injuries, whereas others are severely injured or killed.

Myth 2: Restoration Is More Important Than Realistic Acceptance

Although significant gains have been made in illness and disability prevention, treatment, and rehabilitation, there are some voids which cannot be filled but which must be crossed, sometimes with the body, other times by the spirit. This may be an ultimate challenge for persons and families faced with the choice between retrieving who they were and accepting who they are now and who they are becoming.

Illness and disability will always be with us. So will hope, creativity, cure, restoration, and resilience. Approaching illness, disability, and aging in a holistic, caring, creative, and visionary way has the potential to enrich and enhance the quality of life of the person living with unique life circumstances as well as that of the family.

Myth 3: Someone Must Pay

For many families enduring the journey of treatment and rehabilitation, the idea that "someone must pay" can be a potential emotional and financial trap. Emotionally, a family may feel they have been wronged—and often justifiably so. For example, a family may feel a drunk driver, whose actions placed a child in a coma management program, has wronged them. But what if this person is uninsured, a repeat offender, or has no resources? Who becomes the object of attention? Is it the media who promote alcohol use and abuse or the manufacturers who portray reckless driving in their ads? Is it the employer who unjustly fires a person who then becomes angry and shoots a coworker resulting in a severe injury? What about the elderly driver whose poor skills and judgment cause a car accident and a subsequent injury or death of a child?

A great amount of emotional and physical of energy can be expended in focusing on the cause and circumstances related to the losses, illness, and disability. When all is said and done, the family may or may not be responsible for the problem, but they have the opportunity to be responsible for the solution.

Myth 4: The Family and the Individual Will Always Appreciate Medical Intervention

Another myth that creates stress for families is the expectation that all medical intervention is helpful and will be beneficial. When discussing catastrophic illness and disability, families and health care professionals must be able to discuss some very controversial, emotional, and difficult issues related to the cost, benefit, and effort related to intervention and outcome. For example, although some families are very happy that their family member's life was saved, even though there are severe limitations, other families may not be as pleased. This can occur as the long-term reality of the situation is comprehended and the future is more dismal than uplifting.

This point is well illustrated by the pain expressed by a mother who encouraged the heroic efforts made by the medical team that saved her son's life after an industrial accident, but a year after, when he was not making progress and his quality of life was deteriorating, she stated, "They just prevented him from dying." Now, from her perspective, both he and his family are relegated to an emotional and physical prison. Apart from the financial costs and physical and emotional toll, the outcome has been individual stress and familial chaos.

Myth 5: Unquestioning Faith in the Health Care Team and System

In some situations the needs of the family are secondary to the goals, interests, and resources of the people and systems involved in the care of a family member. Also, there are the inherent problems in the health care system that can make problems worse.

This is often an alien concept for families who have looked toward these resources and systems from an overly optimistic frame of reference. Families must often advocate for themselves if they cannot align themselves with people and systems that can provide relevant and meaningful support.

Although most health care professionals do their very best to provide the best of care for their patients, there are some situations, as reflected in the following comments, that are painful and do not have clear answers or easy resolutions:

- A veteran was asked, "Who took your leg off? A shoemaker?"
- A mother stated "I wish we had insisted on a mastectomy, rather than a lumpectomy. Then maybe she would still be alive."
- The doctor told us there would be no problems and never mentioned the possibility of death. We would never have had the corrective surgery.
- The nurses and doctors asked me why would I ever have another child after the birth of two severely disabled children.
- The doctor said to us, "If you had had the child in our hospital she would not have spina bifida."

Myth 6: Technology Will Provide All the Answers

Without doubt, technology has enhanced the lives of people with illness and disability and has increased the options and opportunities in the life, learning, and working domains. However, for some families existing technology may not be relevant to the needs of their family members or may not be accessible. This creates a unique set of stressors for the person and family faced with conditions and situations that are not resolved by technology.

Myth 7: My Family Will Always Be There for Me Because I Was There for Them

Some families have expended a great amount of energy on caregiving for other family members. A point of great stress occurs when they are in need and the family or its members are not there for them. As one person said, "I gave up a career and a family for you and now you do not have time for me? What a surprise and a major disappointment!" On the other hand there may be family members who have been outside of the family life and who emerge as positive forces in times of need. An example of this is a relative who was shunned by the family due to his lifestyle but who offered a kidney to a relative. This changed the family dynamic for the better.

Myth 8: If We Are Good to Others and Even Provide Financial Assistance, Caregiving, Aid Respite Care, They Will Be Good to Us or Respond in Kind

While this may occur, there are some situations where no matter what is done for others, family included, their response to the needs of those who have been responsive to them may be far less than ideal. Often this is the basis for many family conflicts and part of intergeneration issues and cutoffs. It is within this life and living perspective that many of the issues related to illness and disability, loss and change, treatment and rehabilitation, are cast in a different light.

RESEARCH

Although there is great value in ongoing family-relevant research, the emerging information must be assessed and considered in the context of how it impacts families and their abilities to process, integrate, and benefit from the data and policy generated. This point was emphasized in a report from the Agency for Health Care Policy and Research (1998):

> In addition to outcomes of changed patient functionality, there should be outcomes of changed family functionality. Since much of case management communication is directed toward helping family members learn what to expect and where to obtain services, relevant outcomes would include family use of community and rehabilitation services and indicators of family assertiveness about care expectations. (p. 8)

In the discussion of challenges in family health intervention research, Kazak (2002) stated:

> The argument has been made that the extraordinary stress associated with chronic illness heightens vulnerability to psychological difficulties and even psychiatric diagnosis. While there is increased vulnerability, the generally adaptive functioning of most patients translates into adaptive coping for many (if not most), episodic difficulties for some, and may provoke or coexist with more serious psychosocial or psychiatric problems for a minority. One of the major challenges to researchers in this field is to identify whether intervention will be directed towards the generally well-coping majority, the selected group of families with

distressing and probably episodic problems, or the subset that is likely to have multiple, ongoing, and potentially disabling psychological difficulties. (p. 54)

Consequently, family-focused research should address what families will need from different perspectives (Weihs, Fisher, & Baird, 2002). Kazak (2002) provides the following recommendations:

1. Use information of family risk and protective factors to design selective interventions that target the patients and families who lack resilience for disease management.
2. Emphasize family assessment prior to intervention to determine for which kinds of families the intervention worked and for which it did not.
3. Explore the use of noncategorical disease intervention programs.
4. Consider patient gender and family ethnicity as core concepts in designing family-focused interventions (p. 51).

These recommendations have a proactive dimension and sensitivity to the unique life and cultural experiences of families. Without these perspectives it is often presumptuous to decide what families are willing and capable of doing for themselves and for each other.

Given the demands faced by some families and individuals who may feel depersonalized and their quality of life diminished by today's health care system, Halstead (2001) stated:

In today's high-tech impersonal health care system the use of scientific methods to show that humanistic treatments are effective may represent a new frontier and an opportunity for rehabilitation research. (p. 149)

EXPECTATIONS

To expect the family to provide support to a member in need implies that the health care and rehabilitation team, as well as policy makers, are very aware of the rigors of treatment, rehabilitation, and recovery, and their impact on the family. They should appreciate, comprehend, and value the costs and rewards of adjusting to illness and disability, as well as the importance of assisting the family to stabilize, recover, and grow. To facilitate the process of learning, coping, and surviving, the family needs timely and relevant interventions, appropriate skills, and accessible support. When these needs are met, the family's reactions to and decisions about themselves and the person with an illness or disability can be made from a position of strength rather than from desperation and frustration.

Often the individual and family problems are related not only to the illness and/or disability concerns, but also consequent to the resources and supports. This does not mean that in all situations more resources and supports will result in more positive outcomes. It does imply that in many situations family problems can be addressed and responded to in an active and helpful way. Unfortunately, some of the basic needs of families are being considered as luxuries in the current health care environment when, in fact, they are essential and often critical. This is most alarming given the recent RAND report published in *The New England Journal of Medicine* in June 2003, and referenced in *The New York Times*, on July 2, 2003:

> A study published last week in the *New England Journal of Medicine* found that participants whose medical records were analyzed had failed to get the recommended treatment for their illnesses almost half the time. (p. A22)

Marginalization of patients and minimization of services by health care providers are often part of the driving force behind the family's outrage, disappointment, and distress. This energy may be redirected to focus on empowerment, advocacy, and other consumer movements that have set a course to meet the needs of families living with illness and disability experiences in spite of organizational obstacles, policy limitations, and competing interests for scarce and dwindling resources.

Occasionally, there is a rational framework that facilitates the acceptance of this reality, for example, that older persons have reached retirement age; have lived fulfilling lives; fulfilled their responsibilities; and had their physical, emotional, and cognitive abilities modified by the normal, or abnormal, conditions of aging. This point in life for some, however, also has its unique variations. Some elders are pleased with their lives, others are frustrated and or disappointed by what has, or has not, occurred. This is often intensified by the realization that options are confined and limited by the limited time individuals may have and the urgency to maximize what time and opportunities may be left for them.

The deterioration of an elderly person is a painful process, but it is more understandable than the randomness of illnesses and disabilities which assault children, adolescents, and adults at the most inopportune times of their lives. This is compounded by the fact that many illnesses and disabilities are a result of choices, actions, and behaviors which make accepting the irreversible consequences of accidents, lifestyle, trauma, and irrational violence difficult, at best, while raising a multitude of complex issues (Callahan, 1987; Phipps, 1998).

The situation becomes even more complicated when the solutions to the problems at hand do not meet, or even approximate, the hopes, aspirations, or expectations of the person or the family. It is at this point when families need the support and resources derived from compassion, hope, and spirituality.

Compassion

A powerful counterbalance to the stressors related to family illness and disability is active and responsive compassion. Blaylock (2000) reflected on compassion, the difficult situations families often face during treatment, and some of their needs:

> Patients and families are asked to endure debilitating treatments for the sake of a long-term goal, thrust into difficult caretaker roles, and called upon to cope with wrenching ethical dilemmas. In return they want compassion, respect, and information delivered in [a] sensitive manner. (p. 161)

During the health care and rehabilitation process it is important to note the importance and value of compassion as well as relationship-centered care by the health care team (Williams, Frankel, Campbell, & Deci, 2000).

In a discussion of compassion and caring, Halstead (2001) stated:

> Rehabilitation of persons with catastrophic illness or injuries is a complex, labor-intensive interaction between patients and caregivers. Experiences of overwhelming loss and suffering evoke strong emotions that shape the behavior of both patients and staff during the rehabilitation process. In response to each patient's unique experience, compassion, caring, and other humanistic qualities of the effective caregiver help create a healing environment. (p. 149)

Hope

Illness, disability, and other major life changes transform and challenge the entire family system. This process has the power to confuse the present, distort the past, and compromise the future. It also creates familial stress and disappointment, as well as the conditions for healing and hope. Hope has emerged as an important consideration in the life and living process that is affected by illness and disability (Gottschalk, 1985; Nunn, 1996; Magaletta & Oliver, 1999; Scheier & Carver, 1992, 1998: Snyder, Irving,

& Anderson, 1991). Hope is also a vital force in the families' journeys to move beyond what was and begin to understand and accept what is and what could be. The challenge can seem like transforming "millstones into stepping stones," which is not an easy task.

Many times families and individuals find themselves in situations where they are hopeless and/or hopeful and need responses that are relevant or useful at the present or in the future. A mother illustrated this point when she stated, "When my son was in the trauma unit it was not helpful to hear the long list of what he would never be able to do. We both needed some hope or something to move toward. I would never take that away from people even though what they would hope for may not happen."

The power and comfort of hope is reflected in a statement made by a friend of the author who was at the end of her life after a long experience with cancer. This very spirited 35-year-old woman, wife, and mother said, "I know I am dying, but as crazy as it sounds I still have hope. While I would like to live and hope for a miracle, at the same time I hope for the health, happiness, joy, and well-being of my family and friends. This gives me great comfort. While I am not that religious, I also hope that there will be another dimension where I can enjoy the future and be with my family. This is my hope." This woman died 2 hours after making this statement, and we can only hope her wishes were met.

It is important that families be helped to recognize the difference between hope based on desperation and hope based on reality. For some families hope is what keeps them going and denial may be a means to keeping hope alive. Rather than forcing the family to rush beyond where they are ready to be, there is a need to appreciate why they are where they are and facilitate the support that enables them to stabilize their situation, energize their resources, and maximize their potential. This is where self-help organizations and support groups can help develop functional perspectives for persons and families living in a twilight zone of confusion, pain, and overwhelming need. Although the "storm" of illness and disability may not be avoided, the accessibility to "safe harbors" can make surviving possible.

Spirituality

The relationship of spirituality to disability and illness is appearing with growing frequency in the research literature (Kay & Raghaven, 2000). Spirituality itself is the universal human desire for transcendence and connectedness (Carson, 1993). It spans the entire developmental life process, and includes participation in worship, prayer, and a sense of closeness to something greater than the self (Koestenbaum, 1977; Reed, 1991).

McColl et al. (2000) concluded:

> Individuals with recently acquired disabilities were able to speak with candor and eloquence about changes to the spiritual self that had occurred in the wake of the onset of disability. Approximately half of the sample identified an appreciable loss or gain in faith at the time of their injury. (p. 821)

For some, spirituality and religion are primary resources in understanding, comprehending, and negotiating the disability and illness experience. Kay and Raghavan (2002) stated that spirituality is a resource when dealing with critical and terminal illnesses, and that both patients and family members utilize it. In fact, "family members dealing with a critical illness report use of greater spiritual perspective" (Kay & Raghaven, p. 236). They need spiritual resources while caring for the sick person, and the individual with a disability or illness uses different spiritual activities to find purpose and meaning and a sense of hope for the future (Carroll, 1993; Young, 1993). Reflecting on his life threatening experience, Herbert (2003) also stated:

> One consequence of facing life-threatening or life-altering surgery is that it provides an opportunity to reflect on your life. For the first time, I began to think of my mortality and, in particular, my personal relationship with God. (p. 125)

In effect, major life changes related to illness and disability may create new dimensions for the spirituality of the family.

CONCLUSION

A common goal most people have is to attain or maintain a reasonable quality of life for themselves, their family, or significant others. Often this is within the context of their past, present, or future reality. A major step in the process of life goal attainment is the realization that illness and disability are dynamic forces that will influence this process.

An illness or disability experience has great variability for those who are living the process. For some it is the greatest loss; for some it is just bearable. For others it is an opportunity for personal as well familial growth and enhancement. This may occur when the family is able to embrace the potential of what remains and not be consumed by the sorrow of what has been lost.

Although more prominent for some more so than others, illness and disability are not the only challenges individuals and families must consider or respond to, but they are often the ones that will test many family's convictions, values, resources, and fortitude. The realities of change, loss, illness, disability, and aging can never be totally eliminated; but living with their consequences and implications certainly can be made more bearable.

REFERENCES

Agency for Health Care Policy and Research. (1998). Rehabilitation for Traumatic Brain Injury. Summary, Evidence Report/Technology Assessment, December 2, Portland, OR.

Blaylock, B. (2000). Patients' families as teachers: Inspiring an empathic connection. *Families, Systems, & Health, 18*(2), 161–175.

Callahan, D. (1987). *Setting limits: Medical goals in an aging society*. New York: Touchstone.

Callahan, D. (1999). *False hopes: Overcoming the obstacles to a sustainable, affordable medicine*. New Brunswick, NJ: Rutgers University Press.

Carroll, S. (1993). Spirituality and purpose in life in alcoholism recovery. *Journal of Studies on Alcohol, May*, 297–301.

Carson, V. B. (1993, Winter). Spirituality: Generic or christian? *Journal of Christian Nursing*, 24–27.

Dell Orto, A. E., & Power, P. W. (2000). *Brain injury and the family*. Boca Raton, FL: CRC Press.

Gottschalk, L. A. (1985). Hope and other deterrents to illness. *American Journal of Psychotherapy, 39*, 515–524.

Halstead, L. S. (2001, February 2001). The power of compassion and caring in rehabilitation healing. *Archives of Physical Medicine and Rehabilitation, 82*, 149–154.

Herbert, J. (2003). Recovery and the rehabilitation process: A personal journey. *Rehabilitation Education, 17*(2), 125–132.

Kazak, A. E. (2002). Challenges in family health intervention research. *Family Systems & Health, 20*(1), 51–59.

Kay, J., & Raghavan, S. K. (2002). Spirituality in disability and illness. *Journal of Religion and Health, 41*(3), 231–242.

Koestenbaum, R. J. (1977). Death and development through the life span. In H. Feifel (Ed.), *New meanings of death*. New York: McGraw-Hill.

Magaletta, P. R., & Oliver, J. M. (1999). The hope construct, wills and ways: Their relations with self-efficacy, optimism, and general well being. *Journal of Clinical Psychology, 55*(5), 539–551.

McColl, M. A., Bickenbach, J., Johnston, J., Nishihanma, S., Schumaker, M., Smith, K., et al. (2000). Changes in spiritual beliefs after traumatic disability. *Archives of Physical Medicine and Rehabilitation, 81*(6), 817–823.

Miller, W. R., & Thoresen, C. E. (2003). Spirituality, religion and health: An emerging research field. *American Psychologist, 58*(1), 24–35.

New York Times. (June 2003). *Improving the odds of good care*, p. A-22.

Nunn, K. (1996). Personal hopefulness: A conceptual review of the relevance of the perceived future to psychiatry. *British Journal of Medical Psychology, 69*, 227–245.

Phipps, E. J. (1998). Communication and ethics: Cardiopulmonary resuscitation in head trauma rehabilitation. *Journal of Head Trauma Rehabilitation, 13*(5), 95–98.

Powell, L., Shahabi, L., & Thoresen, C. (2003). Religion and spirituality. *American Psychologist, 58*(1), 36–52.

Power, P. W., Dell Orto, A. E., & Gibbons, M. (1988). *Family interventions throughout chronic illness and disability.* New York: Springer Publishing.

Reed, P. G. (1991). Toward a nursing theory of self-transcendence: Deductive reformulation using developmental theories. *Advances in Nursing Science, 13*(4), 64–77.

Seeman,T. E., Fagan-Dubin, L., & Seemen, M.(2003). Religiosity/spirituality and health. *American Psychologist, 58*(1), 53–63.

Scheier, M. F., & Carver, C. S. (1992). Effects of optimism or psychological and physical well being: Theoretical overview and empirical update. *Cognitive Therapy and Research, 16*, 201–228.

Snyder, C. R., Irving, L. M., & Anderson, J. (1991). Hope and health. In C. R. Snyder & D. R. Forsyth (Eds.), *Handbook of social and clinical psychology.* Elmsford, NY: Pergamon Press.

Weihs, K., Fisher, L., & Baird, M. (2002). Families, health, and behavior: A section of the commissioned report by the Committee on Health and Behavior: Research, practice, and policy. *Families, Systems & Health, 20*(1), 7–46.

Williams, G. C., Frankel, R. M., Campbell, T. L., & Deci, E. L. (2000). Research, on relationship-centered care and health outcomes from the Rochester biopsychosocial program: A self-determination theory integration. *Family, Systems & Health, 18*(1), 79–90.

Young, C. (1993). Spirituality and the chronically ill Christian elderly. *Geriatric Nursing, 14*(6), 298–303.

CHAPTER THIRTY-SIX

Aging and Disability

Toward a Unified Agenda

Irving Kenneth Zola

People who age and people with disabilities have traditionally been split into opposing camps in the eyes of both providers of service as well as their own self-perceptions.

An exclusively special needs approach to either group is inevitably a short-run approach. What we need are more universal policies that recognize that the entire population is "at risk" for the concomitants of chronic illness and disability. Without such a perspective we will further create and perpetuate a segregated, separate but unequal society—a society inappropriate to a larger and older "changing needs" population. It is, however, in the nature of this historical moment that such a change in perspective must take the form of a corrective—a reorientation of the general thinking about disability (Milio, 1981).

Two bases for such a reorientation underlie this article. The problems of disability are not confined to any small fixed number of the population. And the issues facing someone with a disability are not essentially medical (Hahn, 1984, 1985; Zola, 1982). They are not purely the result of some physical or mental impairment but rather of the fit of such impairments with the social, attitudinal, architectural, medical, economic, and political environment.

From "Aging and disability: Toward a unified agenda," by I. K. Zola, 19XX, *The Psychological and Social Impact of Illness and Disability*, 3rd Edition, NY: Springer.

NUMBERS: HOW BIG A PROBLEM IS DISABILITY?

Whether the unit of study be a city, a state, or a country, it is generally estimated that one out of eight people has a disability (National Center for Health Statistics, 1982; Office of Technology Assessment, 1982). Those numbers themselves would be of concern (e.g., 36–40 million people in the United States); but cast as a ratio, the numbers still convey the notion of a statistical minority. Thus a major concern is whether or not such figures are likely to increase (Colvez & Blanchet, 1981). Recent declines in various mortality statistics (e.g., the total death rate, infant and maternity mortality, condition-specific death rates), increases in life expectancy at birth, and remaining years of life at various later ages cause many to claim that our nation's health is improving. Time series studies of chronic illness and disability, however, provide a different and less optimistic picture.

When Wilson and Drury (1984) reviewed the twenty-year trends (1960–1981) in fifteen broad categories of chronic illness in the United States, they found that the prevalence of seven conditions had more than doubled; two had increased their prevalence from 50 to 99%; five had increased by up to 50 %; and only one condition had become less prevalent. The so-called "graying" of the population did not explain this as a similar pattern was observed for persons 45–64. For this latter group—the core of the workforce—chronic conditions translated into activity limitation with a more than doubling (from 4.4% to 10.8%) of the number of males who claimed they were unable to work because of illness or disability.

Looking at two subsets—the young and the old—is particularly instructive. While the absolute number of children (under 17) is not expected to increase, the proportion of those with a disability will. The United States National Health Interview Survey (Newacheck, Budetti, & Halfon, 1986) indicates that the prevalence of activity-limiting chronic conditions among children doubled between 1960 and 1981 from 1.8% to 3.8% with the greatest increase in the last decade. While much of this may be due to the survival of lower-weight newborns with various impairments, the major increase may well be due to shifting perceptions on the part of parents, educators, and physicians where changing educational concerns are making learning disabilities (e.g., dyslexia, etc.) the fastest growing disability in the country (Faigel, 1985). What new learning disabilities will be discovered when computer literacy becomes a sine qua non for success in contemporary society is anybody's guess.

All census data affirm that the fastest growing segment of the U.S. population is those over 65. In 1880 they numbered fewer than 2 million (3%) of the total population but by 1980 it was over 25 million (11.3%). By the year 2030 an estimated 20 to 25% of citizens is likely to be over 65 (Gilford, 1988). Put another way, throughout most of history only one in ten people lived past 65; now nearly 80% do. This traditional use of 65 as a benchmark, however, is deceptive, for the most phenomenal growth will occur in the even older age groups, those over 85. Individuals over 85 constituted 1% of the total population in 1980, but are projected to reach 3% in 2030 and over 5% in 2050. By then they could be nearly a quarter of all elderly people (Gilford, 1988). The service implications are worth noting. For while 3–5% of those 65–74 require assistance in basic activities of daily living, over one-third do so by age 85 (Feinstein, Gornick, & Greenberg, 1984; National Center for Health Statistics, 1983). Thus no matter how it is defined or measured the number of people in the United States with conditions that interfere with their full participation in society will inevitably increase.

NATURE: IS DISABILITY THE SAME AS IT ALWAYS WAS?

For years infant mortality has steadily decreased, in large part because of improvements in standards of living and prenatal care. Recently, these improvements have been supplemented by advances in the specialization of neonatology. Though the numbers are as yet small, it is clear that there are increasing numbers of low birth weight and other infants surviving into childhood and beyond with manifest chronic impairments. With advances in medical therapeutics, many children who would have died (from leukemia to spina bifida to cystic fibrosis) are now surviving into adulthood or longer. Diagnostic advances, as well as some life-extending technologies, allow many young people to survive with so-called "terminal" illnesses.

There is a similar trend evident in the young adult group. While trauma still continues to be a major cause of mortality in this group, there is a major turnaround in the survival rates of people with spinal cord injuries. As recently as the 1950s, death was likely in the very early stages or soon after because of respiratory and other complications: Thus in World War I only 400 men with wounds that paralyzed them from the waist down survived at all, and 90% of them died before they reached home. In World War II, 2000 paraplegics lived and 1,700—over 85% of them—were still alive in the late 1960s (President's Committee on the Employment of the Handicapped, 1967). Each decade since has seen a rapid decline in the death rate and thus of long-term survival—first of those with paraplegia, then with quadriplegia, and, now in the 1980s, those with head injuries.

At the moment, the situation with the older population may seem less predictable. At the very least, we can speculate that an aging population will be even more "at risk" for what were once thought "natural" occurrences (e.g., decreases in mobility, visual acuity, hearing) and with other musculoskeletal cardiovascular, and cerebrovascular changes whose implications are only beginning to be appreciated.

Still another unappreciated aspect of most chronic conditions is that although permanent, they are not necessarily static. While we do, of course, recognize at least in terminology that some diseases are "progressive," we are less inclined to see that there is no one-time, overall adaptation/adjustment to the condition. Even for a recognized progressive or episodic disorder, such as multiple sclerosis, attention only recently has been given to the continuing nature of adaptations (Brooks & Matson, 1987). The same is also true for those with end-stage renal disease (Gerhardt & Brieskorn-Zinke, 1986). With the survival into adulthood of people with diseases that once were fatal come new changes and complications. Problems of circulation and vision for people with diabetes, for example, may be due to the disease itself, the aging process, or even the original life-sustaining treatment (Turk & Speers, 1983). Ivan Illich (1976) in particular has drawn public attention to the iatrogenic costs of many medical interventions—costs that may show up only after many years, as one ages, or all too frequently in subsequent generations.

Perhaps the most telling example of a new manifestation of an old disease is the current concern over the so-called post-polio syndrome (Laurie & Raymond, 1984). To most of the public, to clinicians, and certainly to its bearers, polio has been considered a stable chronic illness. Following its acute onset and a period of rehabilitation, most people had reached a plateau and expected to stay there. For the majority, this may still be true, but for at least a quarter, it is not. Large numbers of people are experiencing new problems some 20–40 years after the original onset. The most common are fatigue, weakness in muscles previously affected and unaffected, muscle and joint pain, breathing difficulties, and intolerance to cold. Whether these new problems are the mere concomitant of aging, the reemergence of a still lingering virus, a long-term effect of the early damage or even of the early rehabilitation programs, or something else, is still at issue (Halstead & Wiechers, 1985). Whatever the etiology of this phenomenon, there will likely be many more new manifestations of old diseases and disabilities as people survive decades beyond the acute onset of their original diseases or disabilities (Funne, Gingher, & Olsen, 1989; Sato, 1989). Thus, the dichotomy between those people with a "progressive" condition versus those with a "static" one may well be, generally speaking, less distinct than once thought and indeed be more of a continuum.

Still another source of change is the fit between any impairment and the larger social environment. Simply put, some physical differences become important only in certain social situations (reading and writing difficulties where literacy or speed in literacy is deemed "essential" to success or mobility impairments in a sports-oriented society) or at certain times of life (sexual and reproductive issues are less important for the very young and the very old, and some for only one gender). The life-cycle theorists are quite aware of this and postulate different issues one must contend with and the resulting disablements if one does not. Yet, many of these theories and the resulting social policies are locked into a grid where the "final" stage of life begins around age 65. This might have been at least logical when the general lifespan was much shorter; then, each stage took about ten years (i.e., the seven stages of "man" covering three score plus ten). But what does it imply when the "last" stage is "occupied" primarily by women (Doress & Siegal, 1987) and continues far beyond a decade, with some (Gifford, 1988) estimating it could reach forty years or more. Surely neither society in general nor the individuals involved will tolerate one stage of life that covers nearly half of the lifespan. Later life is clearly an uncharted map that will inevitably bring new challenges requiring different capacities and evaluations (Katz et al., 1983) but also involving new diseases, problems, and disabilities.

CONCLUSION

While building bridges across constituencies is never an easy one, two final considerations, the empirical and the evaluative, make this coalition an overarching necessity. Empirically, we need to remember these facts: barring sudden death, those who are aging and those who have a disability can be only artificially separated at a particular moment in time. For except the possibility of sudden death, everyone with a disability will age, and everyone who is aging will acquire one or more disabilities. As for the evaluative component, the words of Erik Erikson (1964, p. 131) proclaim it: "Any span of the life cycle lived without vigorous meaning at the beginning, in the middle, or at the end endangers the sense of life and the meaning of death in all whose life stages are intertwined."

REFERENCES

Borgatta, Edgar F. and Montgomery, Rhonda J. (Eds.). *Critical Issues in Aging Policy—Linking Research and Values.* Newburg Park, CA: Sage Publishers, 1987.

Brooks, N. and R. Matson, 1987. Managing Multiple Sclerosis. In *Experience and Management of Chronic Illness.* ed. J. Roth and P. Conrad, 73–106. Greenwich: JAI Press.

Colvez, A. and M. Blanchet. 1981. Disability Trends in the United States Population 1966–76: Analysis of Reported Causes. *American Journal of Public Health* 71:464–471.

Doress, P. B. and Siegal, D. L. (1987). *Ourselves growing older: Women aging with knowledge and power.* New York: Simon & Schuster.

Erikson, Erik H. *Insight and Responsibility.* New York: W. W. Horton, 1964.

Faigel, Harris, "When the Learning Disabled Go to College," *Journal of American College Health, Vol. 43,* August 1985, pp. 18–22.

Feinstein, Patrice Hirsch, Gornick, Marian and Greenberg, Jay N. (Eds.), "The Need for New Approaches in Long-Term Care," in Feinstein, Patrice Hirsch, Gornick, Marian and Greenberg, Jay N. (Eds.). *Long-Term Care Financing and Delivery Systems: Exploring Some Alternatives,* Conference Proceedings, January 24, 1984, Washington, DC: Health Care Financing Administration, June 1984.

Funne, K. B., and N. Gingher, and L. M. Olsen. 1989. *A Survey of the Medical and Functional Status of Members of the Adult Network of the Spina Bifida Association of America.* Spina Bifida Association of America. Rockville, Maryland.

Gerhardt, U. and M. Brieskom-Zinke. 1986. Normalization of Hemodialysis at Home. In *The Adoption and Social Consequences of Medical Technologies.* ed. J. Roth and S. B. Ruzek, 4:271–317. Greenwich: JAI Press.

Gilford, D. M. ed. 1988. *The Aging Population in the Twenty-First Century: Statistics for Health Policy.* Washington, D.C.: National Academy Press.

Hahn, H. 1984. *The Issue of Equality: European Perceptions of Employment for Disabled Persons.* World Rehabilitation Fund monograph no. 24, New York.

Hahn, H. 1985. Disability Policy and the Problem of Discrimination. *American Behavioral Scientist* 28:293–318.

Halstead, L. S. and D. Wiechers. 1985. *Late Effects of Poliomyelitis.* New York: Symposia Foundation.

Illich, I. 1976. *Medical Nemesis.* New York: Pantheon.

Katz, J. 1984. *The Silent World of Doctors and Patients.* New York: The Free Press.

Katz, S., L. G. Branch, M. H. Branson, J. A. Papsidero, J. L. Beck, and D. S. Greer. 1983. Active Life Expectancy. *New England Journal of Medicine 309:* 1218–1224.

Laurie, G. and J. Raymond ed. 1984. *Proceedings of Rehabilitation Gazette's 2nd International Post–Polio Conference and Symposium on Living Independently with Severe Disability.* Gazette International Networking Institute, St. Louis, Missouri.

Milio, N. 1981. *Promoting Health Through Public Policy.* Philadelphia: F. A. Davis.

National Center for Health Statistics. 1983. *Americans Needing Help to Function at Home.* Public Health Service Advance Data No. 92, Department of Health and Human Services pub. no. 83-1250. Washington, D.C.

National Center of Health Services. 1982. *National Health Survey.* Department of Health and Human Services Series 10, no. 146. Washington, D.C.

Newacheck, P. W., P. P. Budetti, and N. Halfon. 1986. Trends in Activity-Limiting Chronic Conditions Among Children. *American Journal of Public Health* 76:178–183.

Office of Technology Assessment, Congress of the United States. 1982. *Technology and Handicapped People*. 11. Office of Technology Assessment. Washington, D.C.

President's Committee on Employment of the Handicapped. 1967. *Designs for All Americans*, 5. President's Committee on Employment of the Handicapped. Washington, D.C.

Sato, H. 1989. Secondary Disabilities of Adults with Cerebral Palsy in Japan. *Disability Studies Quarterly 9*:14.

Turk, D. C., and M. A. Speers. 1983. Diabetes: Mellitus: A Cognitive-Functional Analysis of Stress. In *Coping with Chronic Disease*. ed. T. G. Burish and L. A. Bradley, 191–217. New York: Academic Press.

Wilson, R. and T. Drury. 1984. Interpreting Trends in Illness and Disability. *Annual Review of Public Health 5*:83–106.

Zola, Irving Kenneth, "Medicine as an Institution of Social Control," *Sociological Review, vol. 20*, No. 4, November 1972, pp. 487–504.

Zola, Irving Kenneth. 1982. *Missing Pieces: A Chronicle of Living with a Disability*. Philadelphia: Temple University Press.

PART V

Discussion Questions

1. In your own life what are the characteristics that may contribute to the perception of your own wellness? Are the internal and external factors identified in Marini and Chacon's article applicable to your own wellness perception?
2. Can there be an objective standard for "successful aging," or is "successful aging" strictly a subjective belief?
3. How can the new classification of disability, discussed by Smart, make a difference in one's delivery of rehabilitation services?
4. After reading the article by Livneh and Parker on the psychological adaptation to disability, what interventions do you think are best suited for helping professionals who must work with those with a physical disability on a short-term basis?
5. Do you believe that "recovery" from a mental illness is a dynamic concept which is continually in process, or can recovery be perceived as a static concept, with a definite "end point" that indicates someone has "recovered"?
6. Why do you think rehabilitation professionals have been absent from the debate on euthanasia and physician-assisted suicide? Is it now possible to enter this conflictual discussion? Why?

PART V

Personal Statement

Alfred H. DeGraff

LIFE LESSONS TAUGHT ME BY MY DISABILITY

At the age of 18, I dove off a pier on Martha's Vineyard island and experienced a cervical spinal cord injury (SCI). I became, and remain, a quadriplegic dependent on motorized wheelchair mobility, daily physical help from personal assistants (PAs), and enough prescription medications to make several pharmaceutical companies financially dependent on *me*.

That was almost 40 years ago. I'm convinced from experience that my severe physical disability becomes more valuable to me and to society with each passing year. While it initially takes a burst of courage and coping skills to acknowledge and "accept" a fresh disability in its infancy, the real test of skills is their adequacy to support and maintain one's disability lifestyle over the long haul, decade after decade. Does the person have the staying power to survive daily health crises, hundreds of whining and immature PAs, and, for many, a chronic depression that makes addictions and suicide seem so attractive?

For some people, I'm convinced that the disability lifestyle is no longer viewed as a meaningless tragedy, but, instead, as a meaningful gift teaching life lessons. People with disabilities (PWD) encounter an endless stream of opportunities for unique experiences, learning, and growth.

My disability has gifted me with wisdom about humanity that I wouldn't have been able to realize, or realize in such detail and depth, had I been able bodied. This wisdom has given the disability a sense of worth. What follows is my "top ten" list of life lessons—my personal statement of what my disability has meant to me by way of personal experiences, learning, and growth. To many of my able-bodied peers without insightful experiences, these are nice clichés—the text of refrigerator magnets. Instead, for many of us with disabilities, these are lessons acquired from repeated experiences or crises. While coping with an active crisis, these lessons reveal themselves in response to our often-desperate plea to make sense of the situation, "Please show me what I'm to learn from *this* experience?"

I have learned that I have the choice of living this disability lifetime as a victor or a victim. While I attempt to live optimistically as a victor, I have found that no matter how deeply I might occasionally slip into the victim role, a return route is always made available to me.

Living with a life-long disability isn't easy. I have found that much of my success or failure has been dependent on how I view life. There is a big difference between whether I choose to be a victim or a victor. And I truly do always have a choice.

As a victim at various times, I have chosen to go through life in a semi-hopeless frame of mind. "Why me? I'll never get ahead, because I'm stuck in this wheelchair." Those who take up full-time residence as a victim erroneously believe they find comfort in wallowing in the anger, grief, sorrow, depression, and despair.

As a victor, I'm presented with the same rough times as the victim, however I work hard at staying in control of my disability and the quality of my life. As a victim, the nucleus of my daily life is my disability, and my lifestyle becomes a consequence of what my disability permits. As a victor, my soul or spirit is my nucleus, and the disability, like other personal characteristics, is one of many electrons orbiting around my soul or spirit.

I have learned the importance of taking the time to formally grieve a loss, instead of unemotionally trivializing or dismissing it with denial.

Life with a disability is one with many losses. We have lots of opportunity and need to practice grieving. We repeatedly have the choice of grieving now, or grieving later—of paying now, or paying later. There are many factors, outside the scope of this essay, that give us no choice but to grieve later or grieve over a long duration in bite-size pieces.

When we delay, we are sometimes sentenced to carry the weight of the loss's baggage. Grief baggage can manifest itself in many forms, including sorrow, frustration, anger, and depression.

When possible, I try to grieve my losses soon, to defuse grieving of its depressing power, and to move on. The relative absence of unaddressed grief is one of the elements that can reward us with that desirable state we call inner peace.

I have learned that life does not randomly expose me to coincidences, accidents, or seemingly meaningless tragedies in life. Instead, I am routinely meant to encounter learning and growth opportunities that are sent to me in a variety of disguises.

The Rolling Stones have sung, "You can't always get what you want, but you get what you need." The Dalai Lama was articulate in countering with, "Remember that not getting what you want is sometimes a wonderful stroke of luck." More recently, there has been yet another outlook that states, "Be careful of what you ask for, you might receive it."

My personal experience has shown me that if I am open to recognizing and learning from life's lessons, and flowing with life's rhythms instead of fighting or fleeing from them, then a whole world of benefits can open up to me.

I have learned that if I were given the opportunity either to shed my disability and return to the experiences, knowledge, and values that I had at the time of my disabling injury, or to keep my current disability with the wisdom it has taught me, I would usually choose to retain my disability.

What about those unique experiences—some joyful and some painful—that I would not have encountered without my paralysis? I usually take full advantage of them. Regardless of whether they were good or bad memories, I have usually succeeded in learning and growing because of them.

I have had first-hand experience in needing, receiving, and then returning human compassion. My disability has also given me first-person insights into prejudice, bigotry, discrimination, injustice, poverty, caring, love, support, integrity, and many other human qualities and inequalities.

I'm not saying I enjoy having my disability; however, it has enabled me to learn much more about humanity and life than I could have learned in an able-bodied lifetime. It's now been almost 40 years of these specialized experiences, learning, and growth. Were I actually presented with the chance of walking away from my wheelchair—but also the need to leave behind the insights I've acquired—I really doubt I'd accept walking back to the starting line of wisdom.

I have learned that it is never appropriate for me to try to shift my responsibilities, that are rightfully mine and for which I am capable of managing, to others, and then to blame them when my needs aren't accommodated.

I learned that I should never blame any provider for not doing what I should be doing for myself. In addition, I am always ultimately responsible for an aide failing to do a task, or doing it incompletely. Most of the assistance an aide gives me is the face-to-face kind. I am right there, and have a continual responsibility to do QC, or quality control. If an aide has helped me get dressed, and I arrive at my downtown office to find that I am wearing shoes but no socks, is my morning aide to blame? I don't think so.

Sure, I am annoyed that the aide totally spaced the socks this morning, after remembering them for the previous seven months. However, I have decided that my responsibility to watch my help providers is more realistic than attempt to hold anyone responsible for performing my help routine flawlessly with no mistakes. Indeed, I never hold a PA responsible for memorizing every detail of my routine. In the books I've written about PA management, I refer to working with an aide to be analogous to dancing. I expect each PA in each work shift to occasionally forget a detail—a dance step. As the PA and I dance through the routine's tasks, and I sense he/she has forgotten the next "step," it's my responsibility to subtly remind the PA of the next step so we can keep on dancing.

I have learned that I am the only valid source for my own joy, sorrow, and inner peace. My own inner peace most often occurs when my actions are in harmony and authentic with my perception of spiritual intentions.

Not only am I solely responsible for my own happiness, for answers to my own life questions, and for coordinating the help required to maintain my health, but no one else will care as much as I if I fail to reach my goals or permit my health to decline.

A rock star, who became addicted to drugs and then went through recovery, acknowledges that others can't be held responsible for his happiness or the consequences of not achieving happiness. Here is what Barry Manilow said—

> I believe that we are who we choose to be.
> Nobody is going to come and save you. You've got to save yourself.
> Nobody is going to give you anything. You've got to go out and fight
>   for it.
> Nobody knows what you want except you,
> and nobody will be as sorry as you if you don't get it.
> So don't give up your dreams!

I have learned that there is a difference between physical pain and emotional suffering. Physical pain is objective and physiological; emotional suffering is subjective and psychological. While I sometimes cannot control the physical pain, I usually do have the choice and ability to control the much more powerful suffering that is created in my mind.

There are psychological ways of alleviating many kinds of emotional suffering. What the mind has the power to create, it also has the power to take away. From many personal experiences, I have learned the difference between the different feelings of physical pain and emotional suffering. I can assure myself of my ability to control suffering, and this has saved my life several times.

I have learned about the powerful advantages and life-sustaining utility there are in making maximum use of mental discipline.

I've participated in many workshops and seminars that taught me skills of self hypnosis, healing mental imagery, and progressive relaxation. I had been routinely using these skills to consciously lower stress and relax, mindfully reduce constrictive asthma, and even attempt to image genital orgasms that I could no longer feel. My increasing skills at mind control had resulted in perhaps a 90 percent success rate for these varied objectives, while enabling me to occasionally reduce my need for prescription medications.

I have learned to live for today—in the present—because yesterday is gone and tomorrow might never happen. Today's events will never happen again, nor should they. Perhaps the predominate, daily challenge I have in living with my disability is in creating and maintaining a set of activities and goals that make life sufficiently interesting and important to merit my getting out of bed each morning.

When I first acquired my disability, I spent a lot of time living in the past. I would look at what I could no longer physically do, and think back to the good old days when I was able bodied and could do those things. This is, of course, a setup for depression—concentrating and aspiring to do what we cannot. If someone with diabetes lies in bed all day and thinks about hot fudge sundaes, he will get depressed. Crosby, Stills, and Nash, in the song "Judy Blue Eyes," sing "Don't let the past remind us of what we are not now."

People with disabilities should be cautious about reminiscing constantly about missing their able-bodied past or fantasizing about the shape of the future after their ship comes in (example, after they win the lottery) and how much better than their current lifestyle the future will be. Sometimes, when I repeatedly procrastinate about becoming involved in interesting events, I think of Stephen Levine. In his book "A Year to Live," he cites one quite effective way to identify one's current life purpose is to vividly imagine that you are going to die exactly one year from today. Ask yourself what priorities you consequently have during this final year of your life!

I have learned the difference between my accepting my own disability and society accepting it. For my own acceptance, I should formally acknowledge it, accept my limitations, and then concentrate instead on living within my abilities. If I concentrate on limitations and loss, I will become depressed. For the social acceptance of my disability, I should mostly ignore it. If I speak mostly about my disability instead of my true personal self and interests, it is unfortunately my disability that people will most remember.

During my undergraduate years, I lived purposely in a campus residence hall to facilitate my socialization. Disability-related discussions would crop up occasionally, but for a tiny minority of time. I didn't deny

I had a disability, or forbade my dorm mates "to talk about *it*"; instead, we had more important and interesting topics. One evening, a couple friends popped into my room and asked if I wanted to join them in casing out a new bar within walking distance from our living area. Out of curiosity, I asked if the entrance or interior had unavoidable steps. In response, they looked at each other and became very apologetic, "Oh, Al, we're so sorry, we forgot that was a concern." I grinned ear to ear and assured them they weren't guilty of anything. Indeed, they primarily invited me and my personal interests, and not the wheelchair. I felt quite honored that those were my friends' priorities!

So in conclusion to this essay, while I stay in continual communication with the physical and psychological aspects of my disability, it is essential that I concurrently transcend—rise above—this disability and its limitations. It is important that I be able to look beyond the limitations of the disability in order to see the benefits that it offers.

As my abilities decrease with progressing years and disability, it has become increasingly important for me to use my daily time, energy, and stamina as efficiently as possible. My daily aerobic workouts, my requirement for "smart food" quality nutrition, and other health measures are more important to me than to my able-bodied peers.

It has been said that freedom in life is not necessarily doing what one wishes, whenever one wishes to do so. Instead, true freedom is the ability to face, cope with, and successfully get through each of life's unpredictable crises. I believe that my disability and limitations have ironically taught me many lessons about freedom—wisdom that I would not have realized as an able-bodied person.

Personal Statement

Bernadette

ONE MORE BURDEN, A MOTHER'S PERSPECTIVE

I am a 51-year-old black woman who lives with my daughter in a small house in a quiet section of a southern city. My husband passed away many years ago. I worked as a kitchen helper for many years, but have been unemployed because of serious illnesses and disabilities. I suffer from asthma and a heart condition and receive Social Security Disability Insurance. I walk with great difficulty and I am not able to go up the stairs in my home. I have two other daughters who live nearby. One has completed the 11th grade and the other has completed 9th. Both are unemployed and receiving Aid to Families with Dependent Children because they have children of their own. Both daughters and their children were living with me until the serious accident of my third daughter.

My daughter, 25, was driving when she was hit from behind by a car that ran a stoplight, and she was thrown into the windshield. She was not wearing her seatbelt at the time of the accident, and she suffered a serious brain injury. She spent many months in the hospital. When they discharged her, she came to live with me, and my two daughters had to move out. Since she has been at home, she has been unemployed and has received medical certification that she is permanently disabled and unemployable. She tells me that she has a short-term memory impairment and she has frequent seizures, which really scares me. All of my family members are Baptists and we have strong religious beliefs, so I know God will get us through this. My daughter has tried to work for short periods of time, but has been unable to do so because of severe memory problems.

Before the accident, my daughter was a very good girl; she had a great job and her own apartment and she was dating. (The man eventually left her after the accident.) She was also involved in gospel singing at her church. Now all my daughter can do is help me around the house. My other daughters come over quite frequently to see us, and I think they are resentful of her because they had to move out when she left the hospital. Because of my sickness, I was unable to manage all of them under the same roof.

None of the family members believe that my daughter was at fault for the accident, though they all wonder why she was not wearing her seatbelt at the time. I remember telling her the morning of the accident that she should always wear her seatbelt, even if she were driving close to home. If she had done all of this, this accident might not have happened and she would not be limited as she is now, but I guess we all truly believe that the accident had just happened and not for any reason. Regardless, all of us know that she was such a good person before the accident. We were very impressed with her lifestyle—a nice apartment with fine furniture and plants everywhere. In our eyes, she was a successful, yet quiet person. Now after the accident she is thinner and even more energetic. Yet I don't say "energetic" in a positive sense. She really has changed for the worse. I still think my daughter is attractive, hopeful, caring, and friendly, but my other daughters think she is more irritable and even a troublemaker. They think that, though she is not the youngest, now she acts like she is the baby in the family. My injured daughter does not share in these beliefs; she feels that she has not changed that much, though she does realize that she is more dependent on all of us, and she has even said that she is less attractive now. After living with my daughter now for several months, I don't think she is going to change too much. We all hope that she will get much better, but I wonder about that.

The most stressful part of our family life now is living with the seizures. We just can't do anything about them, and I worry that they might be fatal and that I might have a heart attack because of the stress. When I get upset, I get chest pains. When we are all here and she has a seizure, we pray together that she will come out of it. Though we panic, we know enough to roll her over from side to side to keep her from swallowing her tongue. Because these seizures happen, and I have a hard time managing them, my daughters come over often just in case. I do get a "funny feeling" when a seizure happens, and I had that feeling the day of the accident. I expect the seizures will get worse, and I don't know what I can do about it. But my many friends and my church have been a support to me during this trial.

Deep down I think it is good for me to have my daughter at home. My friends also seem to visit often. I am happy if my children are all right, and right now I am not so happy because of this brain injury business. I believe that families should take care of each other. I took care of my mother when she was dying and I expect my children will take care of me just as I cared for them. I can manage if we have this togetherness. The doctors are necessary, but it is family that really counts. Though these seizures, are getting the best of us, we just group together and do the best we can. God will take care of us.

PART V

Perspective Exercise 5

Why Us?

PERSPECTIVE

Most families live life hoping and expecting they will avoid the losses, changes, traumas, and tragedies that are part of the total life experience. No one can find fault with this perspective, and hopefully most families will avoid the overwhelming traumas, tragedies, and losses that do occur. However, when a trauma does occur, it becomes an integral part of the family's life experience and collective memory. In many situations, in the throes of illness and disability, life does not seem fair, equitable, or even reasonable. In these situations, most families tend to focus their resources and make the necessary accommodations and often reach a level of life functioning that is balanced and manageable. The vulnerability of most families in this situation is that they believe that nothing could be worse. Unfortunately, the experience of one or more illnesses or disabilities does not make a person, or their loved ones, immune or insulated from additional loss sorrow, complications, and grief.

Loss, grief, and bereavement are part of the life and living process. Unfortunately, the losses and the subsequent grief are often sad, painful, overwhelming, and distressing. With an illness or disability, the losses may be major, minor, or somewhere in between. Often the loss associated with a disability is magnified by prior losses and the unresolved pain associated with the loss experience.

EXPLORATION

1. What was the most important thing you have lost in your life? Fear losing?

2. Who was the most important person you have lost?
3. What have you done or not done to help you resolve the loss and minimize the pain?
4. How has or how would a disability experience intensify prior losses?
5. What advice, help, or insights could you give a family member who cannot get beyond focusing on what they have lost as a result of a disability?
6. How would you and your family feel and act if you sustained a spinal cord injury, recovered, and were diagnosed with multiple sclerosis?
7. How would you feel if you had a disability and your spouse decided to place you in a nursing home so that better care could be given to your child who had a chronic illness?
8. Identify and discuss how relationships with others have changed during your life span.
9. Were any of these changes a result of unresolved issues among family members related to illness, sorrow, disability, or death?
10. What message has your family given to you regarding why people are injured?
11. What would be the first thing your family would say to you if you were disabled because you were driving while under the influence of alcohol?
12. How would your spouse respond if you refused to buy a bicycle helmet for your child, and as a result the child sustained a head injury? If he or she refused? How would you want and need to be treated?

APPENDIX A

Perspective Exercises

Introduction to Appendix A: Perspective Exercises

We have selected six additional perspective exercises to prompt the reader to explore further the meaning of illness and/or disability in one's life. These exercises enlarge the opportunity to personalize many of the disability-related issues explained in the text. The exercise, for example, "Who Needs This Kind of Help," brings one's attention to the kind of help family members actually need during their adjustment to living with an illness or disability. The Exercise "Is the Person with a Disability More Important Than the Family," urges the reader to reflect and even decide on family priorities when a family member sustains a severe disability. Each one of the exercises challenges us to confront our personal beliefs when these beliefs are impacted by the disability experience.

PERSPECTIVE EXERCISE 1

Common Pain, Mutual Support

Perspective

A harsh reality of illness and disability is that individuals within a family are often abandoned, isolated, and left on their own. Group counseling and peer support can provide a helpful alternative for those challenged by a variety of illnesses, losses, and changes by providing structure, role models, perspective, support, and resources at a time of ongoing crisis. When thinking about group counseling and self-help alternatives, it is important to recognize that many individuals are not accustomed to sharing feelings with strangers and may resist the group counseling experience.

Exploration

1. List five ways group counseling or peer support could help a person with a disability adjust to living with the effects of the disability or other major life events.
2. If you had a disability would you voluntarily enter a group? Why or why not?
3. What would be the most difficult aspect of group counseling for you as a group member?
4. Are there certain people with illnesses or disabilities you would not want to associate with?
5. List the characteristics of group members that make you uncomfortable.
6. If you could choose a group leader to lead a group for persons and families experiencing a major life changes, what would be many characteristics you would like this person to have?
7. What are the characteristics of a group leader or peer leader that would put you off?
8. Identify the most upsetting situation that could occur for you as a group member.
9. Should people with a disability and people without a disability be in the same group? Why or why not?
10. Should persons with a brain injury be in a group with individuals who are living with AIDS, spinal cord injury, or mental retardation?

PERSPECTIVE EXERCISE 2

Who Needs This Kind of Help?

Perspective

When families are in a state of crisis, they need to be listened to, responded to, and treated with sensitivity, caring, and respect. Often, the stress of health care and rehabilitation environments creates a situation in which professional and nonprofessional staff does not provide help but rather create pain by insensitive and non-helpful remarks.

Exploration

List examples of how health care and human service professionals could be helpful in dealing with the impact of an illness or disability.

Helpful responses:

(Example: It is not easy but we will be there to help.)

1.
2.

Not Helpful Responses:

(Example: After all, your daughter was an alcoholic who should not have been driving.)

1.
2.

PERSPECTIVE EXERCISE 3

Is the Person With a Disability More Important Than the Family?

Perspective

The occurrence of a severe disability often focuses all of the family's emotional resources on the person who has sustained the injury. Often this focusing is essential to contain the fallout from the injury as well as to stabilize the total family system. However, in order for families to realign their goals and to establish a different balance in their lives, they must make a transition. This transition should consider the individual needs of family members, the total needs of the family and the emerging, changing needs of the family and family member living with the opportunities and problems associated with an illness or disability.

Exploration

1. In coping with the demands of a disability in a family, how should the emotional resources be allocated? Financial resources?
2. Is it ever possible to regain balance in the family following an illness or disability? If so how?
3. How long is a long time?
4. Consider a severely disabled child with a grandparent with Alzheimer's disease and the other grandparent with a pre-existing psychiatric disorder. How should the emotional resources of a sibling be allocated?

PERSPECTIVE EXERCISE 4

Enough Is Enough

Perspective

An often overlooked factor in addressing the needs of the person with a disability and their family is the impact of additional illnesses on the patient, other family members and/or primary caregivers. This can be a major issue because the resources of the support system can be greatly stressed. An example of this would be the following case overview:

June

June was a 54-year-old wife and mother of four children when she had a stroke. She had lived a very active, vigorous life and was the central figure in her family system. Caring for and managing was facilitated by the commitment of her husband, John, who felt it was a privilege to care for his wife and best friend. Although their children were living in the same town, they were able to maintain their separate lives due to commitment and investment of their father. A major crisis occurred when their father suffered a severe heart attack and was in need of complete care himself. A temporary plan was to have an unmarried daughter move home to stabilize the situation. This worked for 3 weeks, until the daughter suffered a severe back injury while trying to lift her mother off of the floor.

Faced with a decision to either place the mother in a nursing home or have her move in with one of the children, the family was forced to realize that they had to become involved at a higher level of comitment and personal sacrifice. This decision never had to be made because both the mother and father died within one month. This case overview illustrates several points: (a) Viable care-giving arrangements can suddenly change, and (b) multiple illnesses can have a synergistic effect, overwhelming the resources of both caregiver and family.

Exploration

1. Having read the above case synopsis, list other additional factors, which could have further complicated this case.
2. Consider a specific family challenged by a stroke that had to deal with the impact of multiple illnesses? (a) What was the outcome? (b) Were there any intergenerational issues? (c) What would have been helpful?

3. What are some areas of competence that are important for family's care giving for a family member who has a stroke?
4. What are the assets and limitations of being involved with a self-help group?
5. Do you think that families can ever be normal again after a stroke?
6. Identify those extended family members who would not be helpful to you or your immediate family. State why.

PERSPECTIVE EXERCISE 5

Fragile: Handle With Care

Perspective

When families are forced by reality to address the complexity and permanence of a disability, there is an urgent need for them to be listened to, appreciated, valued, and understood.

By listening, caring, and responding, the family is validated and given the opportunity to establish a communication process that is based on real issues, mutual respect and hope, based on reality and not on desperation.

Exploration

1. Develop a list of what is needed to maintain a sense of well-being and a positive quality of family life.
   (a)
   (b)
   (c)
   (d)
   (e)
2. Develop a list of what is needed or would be needed to help negotiate the stress of a disability experience within the family.
   (a)
   (b)
   (c)
   (d)
   (e)

PERSPECTIVE EXERCISE 6

I Am in Love With a Stranger

Perspective

Most relationships are based on common goals, mutual respect, interpersonal concerns, and emotional security. For those and a variety of other reasons, people choose to be with each other and enter a long-term relationship. Unfortunately, illness in general and disability in particular can introduce elements into a relationship that are stressful, challenging, and sometimes overwhelming. Some relationships can negotiate their challenges, whereas others struggle and are eroded away.

1. Think of a couple you believe has an ideal relationship. How would this change if one of them acquired a disability? Who could cope the best as a caregiver? As a patient?
2. If you know a couple that has successfully experienced a major trauma, discuss what enabled them to survive.
3. If they did not do as well as they could have, what would they have needed?

APPENDIX B

Personal Perspectives

Introduction to Appendix B: Personal Perspectives

Available to the authors are the many dynamic stories of those who utilize different coping strategies to live and to grow despite a serious disability or illness. The personal perspectives provided earlier in his volume are a living illustration of how to be productive while experiencing significant life challenges. But we wish to include some additional personal perspectives that can broaden the reader's understanding of living with and beyond an illness or disability and also show that different perspectives of coping and living only enrich an understanding of the dimensions of the total human experience. These personal perspectives enlarge on Irving Kenneth Zola's conviction clearly stated in the forward of the third edition of *The Psychological and Social Impact of Disability*, "Disability was not merely a personal problem to be solved by individual effort...as much a social problem created and reinforced by social attitudes and prejudices whose solution would require governmental resources, protections, ad interventions."

These additional personal statements also further emphasize and extend the implications of the disability-related issues identified in Parts I–V of this book, The personal journeys of Robert Neumann and Tosca Appel illustrate both the material discussed by Livneh and Antonek on psychological adaptation to chronic illness and disability and the articles in Part III on Family Issues in Illness and Disability. These family issues are further highlighted by the narrative experiences of Judy Teplow, Karen's mother, and both Chris and his mother. Paul Egan's poignant account brings to life many of the concepts identified in the articles in Part II. With the

Reprinted from "Families Living with Chronic Illness and Disability," by P. W. Power and A. E. Dell Orto, pp. 271–277, 2004. NY: Springer.

description of David's experience, all of these Personal Statements provide the reader with an opportunity to understand the varied models of disability, discussed clearly in the article by Smart and Smart in Part I.

CHRIS AND HIS MOTHER: HOPE AND HOME RUNS, NOT STRIKEOUTS

The following personal perspective presents the often irrational life experience that can test and strengthen the human mind, body, and spirit. A son and his mother share their journey, as well as the hopes and dreams that had to be let go as well as aspired to.

CHRIS'S PERSPECTIVE

Prior to my injury in July 1991, my family had endured its share of trials and tribulations. I guess you could say we were a typical middle-class family. At least we considered ourselves middle class. Actually we were on the low-income end of middle class, but we were happy. We never felt deprived of anything; even though we didn't have a lot of money for clothes or extras, we never went without. My two older brothers and I shared many wonderful times with our parents. Everyone was always very close: church every Sunday, dinners together, and always discussions on how things were going. My parents, to my knowledge, never missed a sporting event or school function. Everyone was treated fairly, given the same opportunities, and encouraged to grow and learn by experiencing new things. We were always given the freedom to choose our activities, but we were expected not to quit halfway through. If we started something, we were always expected to give it a fair chance before deciding not to continue with it. I guess that's where I developed much of my determination.

My father and mother shared the responsibilities of keeping the household going. When my father lost his job, he took over all the household chores and my mother continued to work full time. Dad was always the athletic type and he instilled in us the belief that hard work, determination, and self-confidence would not only help us athletically, but later in our lives as we began to go out into the world. Our friends were always welcome in our house. I'll never forget how my Dad would fix lunch every day for me and my best friend during our senior year. There aren't too many guys who would want to go home every day for lunch, but I always felt very comfortable with it.

Mom has always been the matriarch of the family. Being an optimist, she is able to see the good in everything. Although she's a petite woman, she has a quiet, gentle strength about her. I never tried to "pull one over on her," since she always had a way of finding things out. When one of us boys would do something we shouldn't have, Mom always found out. This still amazes me.

My oldest brother was always quiet and kind of shy. Acting as a role model for me and my other brother, he worked hard in school and pursued extracurricular activities. At the time of my injury he was out of school and living on his own. As the middle child, my other brother was more aggressive and outgoing. Striving for independence, he couldn't wait to be out on his own. As the youngest of the three boys, I was always on the go. I was very popular in school and gifted athletically. I had just graduated from high school and had secured a baseball scholarship at a nearby university. It had always been my dream to play professional ball. It seemed I had been preparing my whole life to play in the "big show." Little did I know that I was really preparing for the challenge of my life.

After graduating from high school I was carefree and looked forward to a great future. I was planning on attending Walsh University, where I had been awarded a baseball scholarship, where I would major in business. I could not wait to start college, become independent, and meet new people. New challenges and new opportunities occupied my thoughts.

The summer after my graduation was a time I remember vividly. Playing 80-odd games in 6 weeks and enjoying my new freedom with friends, I thought I had it all. I figured as long as I had baseball, friends, and family, I had everything I would ever need. What I did not figure on was losing baseball, being separated from friends, and becoming almost completely dependent on my family.

On July 29, 1991, a friend and I went to the mall to do some school shopping. Afterwards we decided to hang out at the local strip and see what was going on. We ran into two of our friends, Valerie and Bobby Joe. The four of us talked and cruised around enjoying the cool summer night. Around 10:30 p.m. we decided to stop off at Taco Bell to go to the restroom and get some drinks. When we entered the Taco Bell I noticed nothing unusual so we proceeded to order. It was supposed to be a fun night out on the town, and it probably would have ended that way had the conclusion of the night not found me lying in a coma, fighting for my life.

As we were leaving the restaurant I still hadn't noticed anything unusual. As I proceeded out the door a couple of steps behind my friends, I was struck in the face by a fist. Swinging around to see who had struck me, I was disoriented. As soon as I swung around, I felt a glass bottle shatter over my right temporal lobe. I immediately fell to the ground where I was kicked and beaten for what felt like an eternity, but was actually only a few minutes. Afterward I slowly tried to regain consciousness. I was rushed to the hospital where I fell into a coma for a month.

Emerging from my coma was the greatest challenge of my life, a challenge I will never forget. It called for every resource I had if I were to breathe and walk again. It was like I was alone in a dense, thick fog groping for a familiar hand, yet unable to find anything concrete and strangely aware of a vast emptiness and solitude. This is a faint reflection of my coma. As I lay there, I experienced repeated flashes of light...my brain inevitably reacted. I wondered where the light came from! Had I really seen it or was it only a figment of my imagination? I convinced myself that the flash of light was real and, thus, my only hope of finding my way back home. From a great distance, I heard the distinct voices of my mother, father, and brothers, and Amy, the girl next door. Each time I heard their encouragement, I drew one step closer to the light. Although I felt like falling into despair, a word of love from God, my family, and my friends urged me forward. Without such love I would not have advanced even one step. Along with these words of love, I also heard the muffled voices of doctors and the high-pitched whispers of nurses as they wondered what they could do to help me. Eventually, they concluded that I would not make it. I was determined to prove them wrong.

Every day, I fought the coma with all of my might. Every day, I drew a little closer to the light. Finally, the day came when I opened my eyes and saw the heartbroken tears of the people I loved and longed to be with. Meanwhile, I could not move a single muscle in my body. I could not even talk. However, this did not bring my spirits down; somewhere deep within I knew that I had just answered the greatest challenge of all, the challenge of coming back from virtual death.

After awakening from my coma I slowly began to realize what had happened. I went from a fully functional young adult to practically a vegetable in a blink of an eye. I was left totally immobile, not able to talk, and my world had seemed to crumble to dust. My family and friends were there to support me; if not for them I think I would have died.

During the ensuing weeks, the doctors and nurses gave me little hope for recovery, but through persistent pleading, my mother convinced the doctors to give me time before decisions were made to institutionalize me. My family and I vowed to meet this brain injury head on and give it our best. I slowly regained mobility and could see gradual improvements. The doctors also saw my progress and decided to send me to a rehabilitation hospital to continue therapy.

It was at the rehabilitation hospital that my attitude and commitment to recovery preceded all other thoughts. My family, friends, therapist, nurses, and doctors were my team, and they were counting on me to bring them to victory. You see, it was the ninth inning, the game was tied, the bases were loaded, and I was at the plate facing a full count. It was the kind of situation I thrived on. It was do or die time. I could dig in, face the challenge, and try, or I could drop my bat, strike out, and die.

The choice was mine. What did I do? Well, I stepped up to the box, dug my feet in, and my mind focused on the pitcher, or in this case the injury. I saw the ball coming; it was like a balloon. I stepped toward the ball, made a smooth swing, and then I heard a crack. The ball ricocheted off my bat like a bullet from a gun. I just stood there and watched it soar high and long; I knew in an instant it was gone. As I touched each base, a part of my recovery passed, and before I knew it, I was home, starting school, and enjoying life again.

Although my recovery is not yet complete, I play a game every day in my head, and with every hit, catch, and stolen base, a part of my recovery passes. My next home run could be the one that brings me full circle. The pursuit of this dream is encompassed by the determination and hope that one day I will make it back to my ball field. All I can do is try and pray that everything will turn out right, and if it does not, I will still go on because I know I gave it my best.

The road to recovery has been long and wearisome, but I have already put many miles behind me and I know I will emerge completely triumphant. This experience has taught me many valuable lessons. Above all, it has convinced me that the human will can overcome obstacles that many consider insurmountable. I have walked through the valley of the shadow of death and have come out, not unscathed but undaunted. I am among the few people who can say that they have experienced near-death and were able to live and talk about it. I consider myself lucky and remain grateful to all who have helped me recover from this disaster. My experience has indisputably helped make me the person I am today.

Although many things helped my family overcome this catastrophe, the most helpful was first and foremost our faith in God and belief that He would make everything all right. Second, was the overwhelming support we received from family and friends. How could we not make it with such kindness and compassion? Third, was becoming knowledgeable about brain injury. This seemed to make us feel more in control of the situation, instead of relying on doctors and nurses for details of what was happening. Throughout the injury, we kept a positive outlook on life, knowing that we would pull through. The family, as a whole, had a kind of inner strength, which told each member things would work out in the end. Finally, we came to accept the situation and the consequences it has brought. The past cannot be changed, but the present and future can.

Intervention was never offered to my family. I often wonder why, but I guess no one ever thought to ask what the family needed. Intervention that would have been helpful to my family includes:

- A team of doctors that would offer in-depth knowledge on the subject of head injury, or offer literature or reading material in lay-person's terms.

- Counseling for family because just being able to talk to someone about what was happening would have helped. Information on support groups and meeting other families who have experienced such trauma would have been extremely soothing.
- Someone offering assistance with a list of attorneys, if needed, or other medical facilities better equipped and able to help patient progress.
- Someone who would have been able to structure a program that would have fit my family's needs, for example, phone numbers of groups or organizations that offer help, and if out of town, assistance with lodging, meals, churches, and so forth.

After reading and realizing the lack of professional help my family had, I have to wonder what really helped us get through this experience. It seemed that everything that was needed by the family, the family provided. I thank God for giving us the strength, courage, and wisdom to endure each day and for watching over us as we struggle through head injury.

HIS MOTHER'S PERSPECTIVE

I remember lying in bed the night we got the phone call. I was wondering why Chris was late. It was 10:30 p.m. He had gone school shopping at the mall with a friend. It wasn't like him not to call if he was going to stop somewhere else.

Just the weekend before, he had finished up a grueling summer baseball schedule, playing 80-odd games in 6 weeks. He had worked so hard on getting a scholarship, and we were very proud of him. I remember his last tournament game. When they lost, he quickly tossed his uniform, like only a ball player could, to get ready for the drive to Walsh University where he would be attending in the fall. It was orientation weekend, but he had come back to play his final game. His dad had said, "Well, Chris, that was your last game." A strange feeling passed through me, and I quickly added, "Until you get to college." As we later drove to the hospital that night, that conversation kept floating through my thoughts.

We really didn't know how bad things were until we arrived at the hospital. When they told us he was having seizures and would need immediate brain surgery, we were devastated. Some friends of ours had gone through a similar experience just the year before, so were all too aware of the seriousness of the situation. As friends and family gathered at the hospital to keep a constant vigil, the pain and devastation set in. So many questions kept going through our minds. Would he live? If he did, how would he be? Why was this happening to us? The nurses were very helpful and brought much-needed comfort during the long weeks while he was in a coma. My husband and I could not bear to leave the hospital. The doctors did not seem to be educated enough to deal with the situation, so we finally had to make the agonizing decision to have him moved. All along we prayed to God to give us the strength, courage, and wisdom to make the right decisions.

My husband was offered a job, and the decision was made for him to go to work as I stayed with Chris. My husband quickly took over all the responsibilities of working and running the household, plus handling all the stacks of paperwork. I, on the other hand, was learning, right along with Chris, about therapy. Together we struggled to help him get better. For him, it was a matter of working relentlessly to make his body do what he wanted it to do. For me, it was the anguish of watching and being there for my child, but not really being able make it all better. It was a feeling of helplessness. I was determined to learn everything I could about head injury. Somehow being more knowledgeable on the subject made me feel more in control. I always tried to keep a cheerful, encouraging face on for Chris even though my heart was breaking. My other two sons were great. The middle son remained at home with his father and did everything he could to help out. My oldest son visited Chris daily and opened his bachelor apartment, which he was sharing with two other guys, to me.

Although the outlook was bleak, we never gave up hope that Chris would return to normal. But as we've learned, nothing is ever normal. Our lives are constantly changing. As Chris begins to have more and more control over his body, he seems more content. When Chris started school again after his injury I never imagined he would do this well or go this far. Having him transferred so far from home has been hard on the whole family, but he seems so happy that it's hard not to be happy for him. From the beginning, he was always accepted for who he was, not for what his body had trapped him into. The son we had was taken from us, but the son we were given back is even better in so many ways. Chris is a constant inspiration to all who come in contact with him. There is not a doubt in my mind that he will succeed in life.

As I reflect back, the pain and hurt will never go away, but I developed a tolerance for it. Life for all of us in this world is a challenge. You draw strength to meet those challenges through those around you. Things are so unpredictable, but would we really want to know how things will turn out? All we can hope for is to be surrounded by love, and the courage to face what life has to offer. A Garth Brooks song better explains this point: "Yes my life is better left to chance. I could have missed the pain, but I'd had to miss the dance."

EPILOGUE

Today Chris is working, married, and has three children, and that has made it all worthwhile.

DISCUSSION QUESTIONS

1. If you were engaged and your fiancé had a traumatic brain injury, what would you do? What would your family suggest?
2. How would you respond if you or a family member were brain injured as a result of violence?
3. Discuss the athletic frame of reference that Chris had and how it was an asset in treatment, recovery, and rehabilitation.
4. Why was Chris's family able to rally in a time of crisis?
5. If your loved one were not expected to survive, what would you do if faced with the decision concerning the use of life supports?
6. After reading this personal perspective, would you consider rehabilitation at any cost?
7. What did Chris mean when he stated, "I know I gave it my best."
8. How can people learn to adapt to change as Chris and his family did?

PERSONAL PERSPECTIVE

Karen: My Daughter Forever

Medical History: Karen

Age	Medical Problem
4 weeks (4 1/2 pounds)	Open-heart surgery
10 months	Cerebral palsy diagnosed
2 1/2 years	Brace on leg to allow for walking
6 years	Heel cord surgery
7 years	Open-heart surgery
10 years	Muscle transplant—arm

I am the mother of this child. While it is she who must bear the trauma, the pain, and the limitations, it is I who suffers with her and sometimes, truthfully, because of her.

After writing the brief medical history, I thought I would try to compute the hours spent in and traveling to and from hospitals. I found it impossible—the hours are uncountable. Which is worse, I think, life-or-death surgery with comparatively little follow-up or routine orthopedic surgery, which requires trips to Boston (20 miles one way) three times a week for physical therapy. It has been almost a year since the last surgery and we are still making the trip twice a month. The exercises are never ending, the casts must be continually replaced, and trying to motivate acceptance of these responsibilities by Karen was, until recently, next to impossible.

She is mine forever, I sometimes think. I will never forget the doctor's response when I asked when all this would stop. His answer was to the point: "When her husband takes over." To him, she is not a person but an arm or a leg, depending on where the problems lay at the time.

I think back to her day of birth—thrilled with another girl. Karen was preemie weight but full term. Because she nursed well, she was allowed to come home with me. Symptoms began to appear within a few weeks, but nothing that didn't seem too unusual. A doctor who cared enough saw her once or twice a week to check and called me often when I didn't call him. Because he cared enough to keep a close watch, he was able to diagnose a congenital heart defect before it was too late—he saved her life. I had never dreamed of a problem of such magnitude.

The diagnosis was a septal defect in the heart. In other words, a hole in the heart that allowed oxygenated blood to mix with deoxygenated

Reprinted from "Role of the family in the rehabilitation of the physically disabled," by P. W. Power and A. E. Dell Orto, 1980. Baltimore: University Park Press.

blood. Emergency surgery was needed to repair the defect. The doctors would not give us any odds on Karen's survival of the surgery, but she had no chance at all if surgery was not performed. Karen was, at the time, one of the smallest (although not the youngest) infants to survive this surgery. We thought our problems were over until we discovered (when she was 10 1/2 months old) that Karen had cerebral palsy. It was years before I could say those last two words: cerebral palsy. I always said that she had damage to the motor area of the brain. Somehow that didn't seem so bad.

The cause will always remain unknown. It could be congenital, it could be due to a lack of oxygen before the corrective heart surgery, or it could have happened during the surgery at a time when techniques were not perfected for working on such a small child (she was hooked up to an adult size heart-lung machine, for example). The cause is unimportant. It is the effects that we must deal with.

At first, the attention a family gets in these circumstances is unbelievable. You're special, everyone wants to help, and there is a certain amount of glory or martyrdom involved. "How do you manage?" they ask. They could never do it. Well, the answer to that is, you do it because you have to. There is no one else to do it for you. You only wonder how you managed after the latest crisis has passed. Then it's on to the next crisis—always another one to look forward to. It's almost as if this child will be mine forever—in the sense that I will always be responsible for her. While this may sound selfish, I can't imagine any parent wanting to keep their children with them for the rest of their lives. Cop out? Maybe it is, but I can't help it.

How do we feel about Karen? It was a long time before I could say that sometimes I hate her for all the problems she presents. A parent cannot easily voice this emotion regarding a child, especially a handicapped child—it's almost inhuman. Karen's sisters could say "hate" much easier—children's feelings are much closer to the surface than those of adults.

On the other hand, these same sisters who sometimes hate her will rise to her defense when they see that she is treated badly. She is not, however, an easy child to get along with. Although Karen functions well in school with a great deal of supportive help (resource room, counseling, etc.), she is socially immature and has no real friendships to rely on. It is we at home who care for her who must bear the brunt of her frustrations—acting out and generally behaving abominably.

Of course we love Karen, but it is often difficult to show openly. A child of Karen's temperament can drain your emotions. The more affection and attention you give, the more she wants. I often feel as though I am bled dry. She is all-consuming.

Sometimes I feel pity. What will she be able to do? Because she appears almost normal, people expect normalcy from her. For that matter, so do we, for I am always afraid of selling her short. We demand that she perform tasks that are within her capabilities—even more. If I tie her shoes for her now, who will do it when I'm not here? She needs to know how to tie shoes with one hand. She must learn in spite of herself.

Often I feel compassion. How do you console a child who has no "real" friends? What playmates she does have are not above tormenting her in insidious ways. What do you say when she tells you that the kids at school call her "mental"? How does it feel knowing that if someone comes to call for you, it is only because no one else can come out to play? Telling her not to pay attention is almost ludicrous. These things hurt us both, but it is very difficult to build self-image in a child who is "different" and intelligent enough to know it.

I always feel guilty—not because I've somehow done this to her, but because she is so much better off than other victims of cerebral palsy. Cerebral palsy can be devastating to the point of total immobility and retardation. Karen is neither. Why then should I complain? I guess I can only say that this is our problem, and it is we who must deal with it.

At night I cry when I see her sleeping. She sleeps relaxed, the spasticity is gone, the cerebral palsy seems to have disappeared for 12 hours or so. But in the morning, Karen still limps, her hand is still misshapen and she still has trouble with school work and social adjustment. I cry now.

What will Karen be when she grows up? My head knows that there's a place for her somewhere—my heart wonders if she'll find it.

Update: 30 years later, Karen is married and is working.

Discussion Questions

1. What role do siblings play in the developmental process of a sibling who is disabled?
2. What role does birth order play in the area of sibling rivalry for an adolescent with a disability?
3. How can the family be a liability in the school-to-work transition for an adolescent with a disability?
4. How has the AIDS issue created additional concerns for families of adolescents with special needs?
5. How would you and your family feel if you had a child like Karen's child, and who was making great strides in managing the particular disability, but then was diagnosed with another debilitating disease?
6. What advice, help, or insight would you give a family member who may not stop focusing on what she or he has lost because of the caring demands associated with the severe disability of a child?

PERSONAL PERSPECTIVE: LIVING IN SPITE
OF MULTIPLE SCLEROSIS

Tosca Appel

Multiple sclerosis (MS) was something I knew nothing about or even considered being part of my life. Even if I did, it was more an illness for those who were young adults. However, I was one of those rare cases of MS that occur before age of 20—I was 11 years, 9 months old when my first symptom occurred.

My first attack of MS took the form of a lack of motor coordination of my right hand. I was unable to hold utensils and my hand was turned inward; my parents in their concern rushed me to the emergency room of the hospital. The intern who saw me at the emergency room told my parents without any exam that I had a brain tumor. Needless to say, this shocked my parents because, other than this attack, limited to my right hand, I was otherwise normal and healthy. I was admitted to the hospital, where I stayed for 12 days. Ten days after the initial attack the symptoms abated. Twelve days later I was discharged from the hospital and was totally back to normal. The doctors had put the blame of the attack on a bad case of nerves. Before the attack I was enrolled in Grove Lenton School of Boston. This was a very high-pressured school. From my A average in grammar school, my grades had dropped to roughly a B average. I was worried, and I spent many sleepless nights crying myself back to sleep. I could not handle the pressure of going to a private school. Consequently, I transferred to a public junior high school. Without the pressure, my grades went up to an A average. I was happier and everything was fine.

My second attack occurred when I was 16 years old and in the 11th grade. My mother and I were planning my sweet-16 birthday party. My mother rented a room in a nightclub. I was all excited, planning who I was going to invite, what it was going to be, and what the room was going to be like. One day before the party, my history teacher asked me a question. I stood up to answer and my speech came out all garbled. I was unable to string the words into a sentence. I was even unable to utter words. All that came out were sounds. I clutched my throat to help the words come out easier. At times they did, but at times it came out a garbled mess. I remembered the teacher's look. He looked at me in utter surprise and a little bit helplessly. In total utter shock, my attempts at speech sounded so ludicrous to me—so totally as if it did not belong to my head, and so totally foreign that I started laughing hysterically. I couldn't be serious about the

Reprinted from "Family interventions throughout chronic illness and disability," by P. W. Power, A. E. Dell Orto, and M. Blechar-Gibbons, 1988. NY: Springer.

sounds I was making. Again, my parents rushed me to the hospital where again another intern did his initial workup on me. However, the sounds that came out of me were so funny that I again started laughing almost hysterically, because I was well aware of what I wanted to say and I was also well aware that it was not coming out of my mouth right. The intern, in his wisdom, thought that this behavior was an attention-getter. He thought I was faking the whole thing.

After the first attack my mother had decided that she would not let me be admitted to the hospital. I was then not admitted, but I was instead seen on an outpatient basis. The inability to speak lasted roughly 2 weeks. I had the party and had a good time. But pictures were taken during this time, and I hated them. Why? My smile came out cockeyed. I smiled with the left half of my mouth, without moving the right side. To me it was quite ugly. After my speech returned, the doctors said that the right side of my mouth and tongue were numb, paralyzed, thus making it very hard for me to talk. Overall, I do not remember the attack. After 2 weeks of this attack, I again went into complete remission.

In 1967, at the age of 19, I applied to and was accepted at Northeastern University. However, during the fall term I started having trouble seeing. My father drove me to the train station so that I would be able to take the trolley to school. But after I got on the trolley, I took it beyond my stop, and went to the Massachusetts Eye and Ear Infirmary to have my eyes checked out. I did not tell my family about my concerns because I did not want to worry anybody. A doctor put me through a whole eye workup, and he said that he could not promise how much sight I would get back in my eye but that he would do all he could. Considering that I was an English major and I loved to read, this freaked me out. I asked him if glasses would help, and he said no, that he might be able to get all my sight back or none of it, but that he could not promise me anything. I had to call my mother after I left him. I first went into the restroom and cried. I controlled myself long enough to call my mother. I got off the phone with my mother as quickly as possible and left for school on the train.

During the ride, I was attempting to figure out if it would have been better to have been born blind and never have seen anything than to lose sight after having it and know what you are missing. As a result of this thinking process, I came to the conclusion that it would have been better for me to have been born blind, because I now knew the beauties of a sunset, of reading, of a flower, of all the things that people who have sight take totally for granted. I do not know how I would rationalize it now.

When I got to school I went into the cafeteria, sat with my friends, and began crying. Once I stopped crying, I got it all out of my system and my friends and I decided that crying would not solve anything, and the best thing I could do was to go home, take some medication, and see if my sight returned ... When I returned home, I did not initially tell my parents of what the doctor had said about the possibility that my sight might not return. I decided that my parents always got very nervous when something happened to me and that there was no need to worry them about me.

So, I did not say anything until my mother mentioned that she had spoken to my neurologist. At this time, unbeknownst to me, I was diagnosed as having MS. My neurologist had told my mother of the diagnosis and told her to tell me. My mother had refused. The doctor then told her that I would never forgive her if she did not tell me. She said that was something that she would have to deal with and did not want to tell me. Consequently, following my mother's wishes, the doctor naturally did not tell me.

The loss of sight in my left eye lasted 3 weeks, and then I went back to college and continued the daily routine of living. Still my mother had not told me about the MS. She bore it alone and did not tell anyone for 6 months after she knew. The only person she spoke to about my MS was my older sister, who is 6 years older than I am. When my mother would become depressed, she would call my sister and cry about the injustice of its having happened to me rather than to herself.

My mother's rationale for not telling me was basically twofold. First, she felt that she should not burden me with the knowledge of my chronic degenerative disease because the knowledge of MS could deter me from doing what I wished to do. Second, when my mother saw me running out of the house to go on a date or to a party, she would get scared and sad, thinking about the day that I would not be able to go out and enjoy myself. My mother felt that the knowledge would hang like a cloud over my head, so she made it her responsibility that I was not to know.

However, this conspiracy of silence put my doctors in a difficult position when I went to see them. I would beg the doctor to tell me what was wrong, but he could not because of a promise made to my mother. Because I remembered when a doctor had told me I might have had a brain tumor, which was incorrect, I asked my neurologist if I was going to die of a brain tumor—to which he said, "You can only die of a brain tumor if you have a brain." This may have been a joke to him; it was not for me! The worry about the brain tumor was a preoccupation of mine. My fingers would tingle, or I would feel something go wrong with my balance, and I would be worried that it might be caused by a brain tumor. I was really worried about dying. I found no comfort in the silly remark that I would need a brain to have a brain tumor. At the time, I told the doctor that I was not kidding and that I was very worried. To that, he replied that they did not know what was wrong with me, but when they discovered a pill for it they would rush it to me. I left his office feeling very depressed, very alone, and not understood.

Finally, when my mother told me I had MS I was sad and confused, but also very much relieved. Now there was a basis for my physical concerns. Because I had long periods of remission over the next 10 years, there were the low points of exacerbation but the long periods of life, living, and the pursuit of happiness. It was great to be a young adult who was living life and running ahead of the long-reaching shadow of MS.

At age 28, I reached a major crisis point in my life. I was faced with the reality of ongoing deterioration. My sight reached the point where I was not able to read the newspaper. In addition, I lost what functional use I had in my left hand. Although these losses may not seem to be catastrophic issues to the nondisabled, they were catastrophic to me. The reason was that they reaffirmed the reality that I had little control of my body and of what was happening to it.

The feeling intensified when I had to resign myself to the fact that I needed to use a wheelchair. To me, this was an admission of defeat and that my disease was getting the best of me. While I made the cognitive decision to continue to struggle, it was very difficult when the little physical control I had was slowly eroding away. As a result, I made the choice to live, rather than to deteriorate or die. Although this is easy to verbalize, it is often not easy to implement. I can choose to actualize myself, but I am limited by physical and emotional resources to follow through completely in that process.

My unique situation is that I was dependent upon my family, with whom I lived. I was also dependent upon my mother to provide me with the assistance I needed, such as cooking and partial dressing. Even though I wanted to live independently, I had to accept that I had a wonderful home life, caring parents, and a loyal brother.

The next major transition was when my father and mother died, both within the same year. While initially having to deal with the impact of the loss of people I care about, I also had to face the question of what would happen to me. Fortunately, when my parents became ill I made the choice to get an apartment and to develop the independent-living support systems I would need. Another possibility for me was to extend the relationship with my boyfriend, to whom I was once engaged and whom I had been dating for 15 years. However, this possibility is questionable, for there were reasons we did not get married and they are still real concerns.

This is my response to the disease that has plagued me for 24 years and has altered the course of my life. I will not let it beat me. What motivates me is the memory of my parents and the knowledge of my heritage. My mother and father spent years in a concentration camp, and many of my other family members perished there. I feel the obligation to make the best of my situation and draw on the strength of those persons who suffered far more than I am suffering. As I see it, the key to my ability to survive is the memory, support, and encouragement of others. They have made the difference, accepting me as I am and helping me to resolve my feelings about not being what I was or could have been.

Discussion Questions

1. What is your reaction to how Tosca was told about MS?
2. What are the family issues with Tosca that helping professionals should be aware of?
3. After reading her personal perspective, if you were in Tosca's situation, would you consider marriage or having a child?
4. How do societal roles and expectations for women create stress for women with disabilities?
5. Do you think that the mental health needs of women with disabilities are different from those of men with disabilities? If so, please explain in what way(s)?
6. How would you feel if your parents decided, at your age of 17 and with a crippling disability, to place you in another caring environment so that better care could be given to your sibling who also has a devastating illness?

PERSONAL PERSPECTIVE: SURVIVING ALS

A Daughter's Perspective: Judy Teplow

BETTY MILLER BELOVED WIFE, MOTHER, AND GRAND-MOTHER SEPTEMBER 4, 1986, AGE 70 YEARS

In the early spring, when the ground is soft, I will lay a marker on my mother's grave, a permanent marker to commemorate the life of a very special lady. The inscription will be short, impersonal, and incomplete—and somehow not befitting a woman who courageously struggled against a devastatingly cruel terminal illness.

I cannot inscribe her story in stone, but I can set it on paper as a lasting tribute. I hope it will be a comfort to those who are afflicted with a serious or terminal illness, and a help to the families and health professionals who are involved in their care and treatment.

It was going to be an unbearable, oppressive day, but my mother had no intention of sitting in her small, air-conditioned apartment. She set out early with her walking buddies on their 5-mile jaunt and, as usual, took the lead. She was amused that her companions, who towered over her 5-foot frame, could not keep up with her brisk pace.

Everything seemed to be going well for her and my dad. Retirement for them was not sedentary life, but rather one that was full and gratifying. In a few weeks, they would return to their apartment in Boston for 5 months of relief from Florida's intolerable heat.

But for now, Betty was enjoying her walk and thinking about how rich her life was. As she turned the bend, her thoughts were cut off abruptly by a stiffening in her left leg—perhaps a cramp—but she did not have the pain associated with a cramp. Her gait slowed down considerably, and in a minute she found herself lying on her side. She was stunned by this unexpected interruption. She did not stumble over a rock or a crack in the roadside. What should she attribute this weakness to?

It took 5 months for the doctors to make an accurate diagnosis. An electromyogram (EMG) was performed at the Brigham and Women's Hospital, and it was this test that ultimately determined that my mother had amyotrophic lateral sclerosis (ALS), Lou Gehrig's disease, a progressive, degenerative disease that is terminal. It is probably the most dreaded neurological disease, and is one with no known cause or cure .

Within 1 year of the first visible symptom, Betty would be a virtual paraplegic, confined to a wheelchair, unable to talk or to feed herself. Breathing and swallowing would become progressively more difficult. At no time would the disease affect her mental faculties, and she would always be aware of the creeping paralysis.

My initial reaction to the diagnosis was one of disbelief, devastation, and helplessness. How could such an active and health-conscious person be stricken with such a catastrophic illness? I felt a sadness for my parents, and I had real concerns about my dad's health also. It was conceivable to me that this tragedy could destroy him as well, and I prepared myself for the worst.

The family and doctors were in total agreement as to how much to tell my mother. She had always been petrified of doctors and hospitals, and was by nature very nervous and anxious. We knew that she could not cope with such outrageous news.

She was told that she had a chronic neuromuscular disease, and that she would need intensive therapy. We did not offer her hope of a cure, nor did we inform her that she was terminally ill. She asked very few questions, wanted to know as little as possible about her disease, and became adept at tuning out whatever she was not ready to hear.

Like my mother, my aunt, my father, and my brother went to great lengths to avoid the truth. Denial became a protective measure they were to use effectively throughout the course of the illness. As much as I tried to beat through this barrier, I was met with resistance. It was this resistance that was to become a great source of frustration and anger for me. My aunt held out the longest, talking about the research, cures, and the possibility of people living several years. My brother, who never coped with adversity too well, did not become an integral part of the team, and his visits to the nursing home were often sporadic and brief.

I had to know all the medical aspects of the disease, so I asked a lot of questions and read many books on ALS, and on death and dying. Someone had to take charge, to plan, and to carry the family through this crisis.

From the Brigham and Women's Hospital, my mother was transferred to the Braintree Rehabilitation Hospital. It was there that she was put on a daily regimen of physical, speech, and occupational therapies. She was extremely tense and frightened, but the staff was very professional and experienced, and knew how to respond to her emotional as well as physical needs. This was really not a time for rehabilitation as much as a time for enormous adjustment. It also allowed the family to make plans for home health care. I wished that my mother could stay at Braintree indefinitely, for I feared that the support systems at home would not be adequate.

My fears were well founded. She was not home 2 months when all systems began to break down. My mother required constant attention and the Visiting Nurse's Association and private-home health professionals were not able to keep up with her demands. Oftentimes, my father was left without help, and he had to assume the role as primary caregiver. Tensions mounted and tempers began to flare, and what was once a very happy marriage now appeared to be very strained. My dad's health was deteriorating as well as my mother's, and they looked to me for a quick solution.

I knew that my mother required round-the-clock care in a skilled nursing facility, but I did not want to be responsible for initiating the search. I could not find it in my heart to do this to her, especially when she threatened to commit suicide before she would enter a nursing home. My grandmother had taken her own life because she could not cope with a painful illness, so I was worried about my mother's intentions. I began to get pressure from her sister, also, in defiance of any plan to move my mom from her home. We were in a crisis and we needed help quickly.

I was fortunate to find a psychologist who would help me accept and confront problems that were difficult and painful. He helped me see issues more clearly when everything seemed overwhelming and confusing; and it was through him that I began to understand the complexities surrounding chronic and terminal illnesses. His continued support and genuine concern were to sustain me through some very difficult times, the first of which was my mother's move to a nursing home.

The transition from the apartment to the nursing home was traumatic for the family. Ostensibly, the home was attractive and meticulous, with spacious rooms and beautiful furnishings. In sharp contrast to this orderliness was a picture of deterioration—of very old people in their 80s and 90s ravaged by debilitating diseases, marked with permanent deformities, hooked up to life-supporting machines, impaired by mental illness—there was an aura of sadness and loneliness, and a sense that many of these people were deserted by their families.

I wished that I could put blinders on my mother's eyes—to shut out a world that was so unreal, but yet only too real and disheartening. My mother was only 69 years old and looked 10 years younger. How could we do this to her! I knew that there was no alternative, but I was stricken with guilt, a guilt that was to stay with me for a long time. It took a good 3 months before I could walk into the nursing home without feeling sick—without feeling very, very shaken.

I don't think my mother ever adjusted to nursing-home life. I think she resigned herself to her fate. I know she often felt very sad, lonely, and misunderstood, but I do not think she felt abandoned. She knew that the family was there for her, and it was this prevailing sense of security that kept her from slipping into a deep depression.

A schedule was worked out wherein one or two family members would visit daily. This was arranged, mostly out of love, partly out of guilt, and out of an acute awareness that strangers would not minister to her needs the way family would. We also knew that if we were going to survive this ordeal we would have to share the responsibilities, for each of us had a history of medical problems. Often, the burden of responsibility rested on my shoulders, and at times I felt overwhelmed. But I also felt that if my mother could cope with the effects of a very disabling disease, I could deal with any problems that arose.

I do not know how she endured all the suffering, and I do not understand what held her together. She certainly did not triumph over her disease—she did not write a book, or paint by mouth, or engage in anything that was extraordinary. She just tried to get through the day. There were many tears and many moments of anguish, but even in her despair she insisted on getting up, getting dressed, and—above all—having her hair done weekly. Thank God there was a hairdresser on the premises, and thank God she still cared about her appearance. Throughout her illness, she never lost her sense of humor or her ability to smile and laugh. But the laughing was done for the staff, and most of the crying was done with the family.

We tried to maintain a sense of equilibrium, but it was difficult to keep control when all systems were failing. The disease was progressing at an alarming rate, and we knew she would need the strong support of the family and the specialized services of many health care professionals. Some services were effective, but most fell short. Many professionals were not familiar with or could not cope with the demands of ALS. They were uneasy in treating a terminally ill patient, or clearly had an attitude problem toward the sick and the elderly. I must acknowledge, though, that most people did try to help, and I cannot fault them for their human limitations in dealing with a very difficult case.

I also believe that my mother's inability to speak had a lot to do with the quality of care she received. This was a great source of frustration for her as well as for the health professionals who worked with her. The family members were the only ones who had the patience to make use of the communication boards. We acted as liaison between my mother and the staff, so our involvement in her care was crucial.

We also acted as her advocates and protectors. There were aspects of nursing-home care that were unsettling, but because we had a very good working relation with the staff, most of our grievances were worked out. I can only think of one incident that was offensive and repulsive, and it was due to a personality conflict between my mother and an aide. An aide had lost control and, out of anger and impatience, threw a sheet over my mother's head. This was a gross violation of my mother's right to be treated as a living human being until the day she died.

The only other situation that disturbed me occurred outside the home. A week before my mother died, her doctor was called to check on her deteriorating condition. To our dismay we learned that the doctor was on vacation and had left instructions for the covering physician. Her doctor had promised to leave explicit directions regarding heroic measures. This was not an insignificant oversight. I had chosen this doctor because he had been highly recommended by another physician and was on staff at a hospital directly opposite the nursing home. Because of his close proximity, I thought that he would be accessible to my mother and the family, but unfortunately we found him to be very impersonal and distant.

Without the encouragement and concern of a handful of people the experience would have been unbearable. There were three exceptionally caring people who made a great impact on my mother.

Janet, a nurse's aide, became my mother's guardian angel, and she was to watch over her and attend to all her needs while she was in the nursing home. There was such a strong attachment between them that on the day my mom died Janet was unable to work.

Margaret, the Assistant Director of Nursing at the nursing home, had lost her mother to ALS, and she was familiar with the disease and its effects on the family. She was always available to us, and it was not unusual for her to interrupt a busy schedule to explain what comfort measures should be used. She was also instrumental in educating the staff about the nature of the disease. She was my inspiration and a great source of strength.

Bobby was a close friend of the family. He had experienced the loss of a loved one, so he was no stranger to personal tragedy. He attended many workshops with Elizabeth Kubler-Ross and was involved in hospice, and he knew how to relate to the terminally ill. Bobby showered my mother with gifts and flowers and made her feel very special. He was the only one who could talk to her about death and life after death, and ultimately helped her accept her mortality. He was a good friend to me, also, and I was able to talk with him about my greatest fear—the use of life-support systems.

The issue of support systems was always a source of great pain and anguish for me. My anxiety was heightened by my mother's refusal to discuss these matters and the inability of family members to agree on a specific course of action. I personally believed that the use of heroic measures, in my mother's case, would be cruel and inhumane—a prolongation of inexorable suffering pain—and an interference with the natural order of things.

But I had to know where my mother stood on these issues for, ultimately, it was her life and her decision. Three months before her death, she began to make her wishes known. She slowly spelled out the word die every day. She made it quite clear to me that she could no longer tolerate living. She finally came to terms with her death, knew it was imminent, and had an urgency to express her grief and fears about dying. Once she accepted her death, she became more tranquil.

I did not want my mother to die in the arms of strangers, nor did I want her to experience death alone. I was fortunate to be with her at the final moment of death. My aunt and I sat by her side and held her hands, and except for a brief interruption by staff this was a family affair. We exchanged a few words of support and comfort, but we were mostly caught up in remembering and recollecting. I wondered if my mother saw her life flashing before her, and if she were passing through the dark tunnel toward Omega, but I could not be sure....

Discussion Questions

1. What aspects of Judy's mother's transition from the apartment to the nursing home were most traumatic for the family?
2. How does the slow deterioration of an elderly parent emotionally affect immediate members of his/her family?
3. What is the meaning of the statement: "My mother's inability to speak had a lot to do with the quality of care she received."? What is the relationship between those two factors?
4. Are there additional roles, other than advocate and protector that an adult child of a chronically ill parent must play during the illness?
5. Of the three "exceptionally caring people who made a great impact on my mother," who would you choose if you could only select one to care for your own mother who may be chronically ill and needs care giving efforts?
6. What would be your reaction if you were in a similar situation with an elderly, chronically ill parent, to the statement: "She made it quite clear to me that she could no longer tolerate living"?

PERSONAL PERSPECTIVE: MY LIFE WITH A DISABILITY

Continued Opportunities: Paul Egan

For me life began very comfortably over 57 years ago, in a then affluent suburb of Greater Boston. I was the third son of a prominent up-and-coming general contractor. I also had an older sister. A month before I was born, tragedy befell the family when the firstborn son, then aged 6, died of diphtheria. So, when I arrived healthy and sound, I was a most welcome addition to a grieving mother and father. Just before I turned 2, another brother was born.

In September 1944, 1 entered the U.S. Navy and, after completing boot camp, I was initially assigned to motor-torpedo boats in the Philippines. I was then assigned to a yard minesweeper with a team of 22 officers and men. Our assignment consisted of sweeping (dragging) the shipping channels and ports of the Philippine Islands. During this time, my job performance was classified as outstanding, and I received many promotions. However, my life suddenly came apart. While I was moving a keg of concentrated ammonia across the deck, it blew up in my face. The ammonia burned my eyes, the linings of my nose and throat, and also the skin around my facial area. I was rendered unconscious, and upon regaining consciousness 3 days later, the doctor told me that my eyes were badly burned and that I would have to be patient and pray for a miracle to take place.

One year, seven hospitals, and several operations later, vision returned to my right eye to the degree of 20/70 with corneal scarring. Other complications emerged as my head and my right hand became involved in a constant tremor. This ailment was incorrectly diagnosed as a nervous anxiety reaction. So I became a psychiatric bouncing ball. In May of 1947 I was discharged with a 70% Veterans Administration (VA) compensation.

I immediately went to work for a friend, pumping gas in a gas station. But I had greater ambitions, and I enrolled at Boston Business Institute in a business administration curriculum for 2 years. Shortly after returning to school my mother developed cancer and passed away on December 15, 1947. This was a profound loss to all of us, as my mother was always on hand with her guidance and sense of fortitude. She was always there to listen, to encourage me to make the most of myself and to go back to school. In fact, in the initial stages of my readjustment to civilian life and to my own disability, it was Mom's positive attitude, including her

From "Family interventions throughout chronic illness and disability," by P. W. Power, A. E. Dell Orto, and M. Blechar-Gibbons, 1988. NY: Springer. Reprinted with permission.

expectations for me, that inspired me to move forward. Her philosophy of making one's residual assets work for the fulfillment of goals is one that I have adopted in my own life.

In June 1948, I married Marietta, a girl I had known before I entered the service. Around this time, my father went on a trip to Newfoundland, his place of birth, and came back a few months later, married. He had married his brother's housekeeper, a plain-appearing woman who was 25 years younger than he was. They immediately isolated themselves from all family and friends for years to come.

In June 1949, I graduated from business school and started experimenting with the real world. Although I was very fortunate in not being unemployed for more than a month during the next 24 years, my choice of expanding my horizons was limited greatly by an uninformed business environment. Time after time when applying for positions for which I was qualified, ignorance, fear, stigmatizations, and prejudices were barriers I found most difficult to overcome.

During the next 20 years, my wife gave birth to five daughters, we moved to a larger house, and I was employed in various jobs. Shortly after the birth of our first daughter, I began a series of operations on my left eye. These operations climaxed with an unsuccessful corneal transplant, which resulted in the surgical removal of my left eyeball. Soon after the birth of our second daughter, I had a laminotomy. I understood this operation as involving the transection of the thin layers of connective tissues around the optic nerve. The pain and suffering endured were the most excruciating of my life. But I was able to get through all of this because of the support of my wife. We didn't think about the past or about my other disabilities. We focused on the present, and together we often discussed our mutual concerns. This was a tremendous help to get through my own sufferings. But in 1968 my tremors got worse, and I went into a VA hospital for a brain operation. After doing an encephalogram, the doctor thought the risks were too high. Instead of the operation, a new experimental drug was tried, but that increased the body involvement and was quickly discontinued.

Moreover, a trauma occurred in our family, when on a night in January 1970 when the temperature was 25 degrees below zero, our oil-burning furnace exploded, destroying our home and all of our possessions. All of our neighbors came to our support, and they held a fund-raising party for us that resulted in not only a substantial amount of money but also in donations of services in our efforts to rebuild. Another factor in our rebuilding effort was that after an absence of over 20 years my father reappeared and lent us the remaining necessary funds to rebuild. After we had made a few repayments he said, "You've shown good faith," tore up the note, and then chose to go back into hibernation with his wife. I tried on numerous occasions to visit with him on his 90-acre farm, but he was always "out" or had to go someplace in a hurry.

After getting settled into our new home in June 1970, our life returned to a semblance of normalcy until late in 1973 when I lost my job. My employment was not the only loss, however, for I also lost my sense of dignity and self-respect, and I drifted aimlessly in a sea of self-pity and depression for nearly 4 years. Though my family was very supportive of me during this time, I knew this was my own struggle and they themselves had to survive. My daughters were married, had their own families, but seemed to be there when I needed someone to share my feelings.

In June 1977, I was classified as blind. That November I entered the VA Blind Rehabilitation Center at West Haven, Connecticut, and from that time on life took on a new perspective. After 14 weeks of intensive training and guidance, I was again doing things for and by myself. The educational-testing evaluations done at the center indicated a potential for higher education. So in September 1978, I returned to school with the goal of becoming a social worker. In May 1982, I received my B.S. from Suffolk University, and then in 1984 I earned an M.S. from Boston University. In April of that year, I began a new career as a field representative and outreach-employment specialist with the Blind Veteran's Association. Yet as I look back now on all of these years of family life, of living with my disabilities, and then finally becoming blind, I often think of my own family, with their patience and understanding. They made the difference so often during my many rehabilitation efforts. Even when I became depressed, they urged me to continue, for somehow they appreciated what I could still do. Probably I would never have gone back to school without their encouragement. Even my father, who died in 1978 and who really never got over the shock of seeing his first financial empire disintegrate, was there one time when we really needed some assistance. To all of my family, I say thank you.

Discussion Questions

1. After reading the personal perspective by Paul Egan, at what time during the progressive deterioration of his eyesight do you think that family intervention would have been most effective?

2. After reading the articles in Part IV related to intervention approaches, what do you consider the role of spirituality and could it be applicable to Paul Egan's family?

3. If disability or a severe illness occurred in your own family, and considering Brodwin, Star, & Cardoso's article of "The Use of Assistive Technology," how would you access the resources that could provide assistive technology?

4. Assuming that you have the opportunity for a meeting with Paul Egan and his wife at the time when he was discharged from the VA Blind Rehabilitation Center in 1977, design a family-assessment approach utilizing the discussion in Pederson and Revenson's article in Part IV.

5. Discuss the issues related to the following statement: "I really can't have any effective contact with a family that is living with a disability situation unless I have a degree in family counseling or family therapy."

PERSONAL PERSPECTIVE

For Better or for Worse: David by David Collins

Growing up in a family as the youngest of three boys, competition and survival were natural qualities. Athletics followed and played an important part of my life. During high school, my time was spent practicing for the upcoming game and "getting by" in the classroom to maintain eligibility. In college, my priorities changed and academics were goals I pursued to stay out of the draft more than anything else. At 23, Valerie, the girl I met in college, and I walked down the church aisle and professed our love to those in attendance. Nine months and 3 days later, we welcomed an addition to our union. As a coach and teacher, my skills were enhanced at classes or clinics; parenting, I hoped, would be a natural talent. As Kerry started to grow and reach her second birthday, we were good pals. If she misbehaved, this coach would make her sit on her plastic chair and not get up—probably a theory I had read about from one of my coaching journals. As Kerry grew, so did Valerie. She was expecting our second child in April. After some thinking, I chose to give up coaching and go into real estate sales and tax work. With a family it was important to look to the future and be prepared. I would make my mark and my family would enjoy the benefits. My planning was poor. After I played my last Christmas basketball game with fellow coaches, we convened at the local pub to review the game. After drinking beer and eating breakfast, I got in my car to drive home. Halfway home, I fell asleep and struck a utility pole while sitting atop my seatbelt. My life was instantaneously altered. As my pregnant wife entered the hospital emergency room at 4:00 a.m., the neurosurgeon blasted her about my high alcohol reading and poor prognosis. If I survived I'd need constant attention.

The accident occurred on December 27. My first recollection was in March. I called my wife by her maiden name, asked if we hadn't any children, and displayed not only confusion, but an indifference as well. I was not only brain injured, but I was a quadriplegic. At one point, I was convinced they had wheeled my bed up a floor to the obstetrics section, and I vividly remembered delivering a baby. My days were spent going to therapy and returning to bed and watching television. A young man started visiting and sharing his story. His name was Dave and he had fallen out of a tree and broken his back 7 years earlier when he was 16 years old. He was very muscular as he wheeled around the halls and explained things like driving a car with hand controls, bowel and bladder control, and sexual activities with his dates. Dave got me out of my room and wheeling outside; he explained his life in graduate school to me and it was appealing. In time I chose to attend graduate school at the University of Illinois, renowned for its accessible campus and wheelchair sports programs. After 6 months in the hospital, I was allowed to go home for weekends. My expectations upon returning home were that my relationship with my daughter and my wife would be as they were before. My foremost thought was to resume sexual activity with Valerie and provide for both our needs. At 27, I had serious doubts about being a person or a man and felt the only way to prove my virility was in the bedroom. Valerie was very patient and empathic to my needs. My hygiene was terrible, a tracheostomy was done on my throat, my bladder and bowel needed to be emptied prior to commencing intimacy, and there was always the chance of having an accident. To this day, I will always be indebted to her for allowing me to believe "I was a man." I told her she gave Oscar winning performances when I needed them.

When I made it home permanently and reentered the family unit, it had become apparent that Kerry, our precocious 3-year-old, had taken my place. She had to be moved out of the king-size bed and back to her room. My adjustment to returning home, I had told Valerie, would be unnoticeable—or so I thought. My first morning home, I had forgotten to put my clothes next to my bed on the wheelchair (dressing is done prone on the bed). After 15 minutes of yelling for Valerie, I finally got, "Yeah what?" to which I requested she get my pants for me, which were on the floor. "I'm changing the baby and can't get back to you for 45 minutes," she said. I was livid. "Bullshit," I mumbled as I got in my chair, retrieved my trousers, and, getting back in bed, got dressed. Upon coming out to the kitchen and observing Valerie drinking coffee and reading a magazine, I let loose. "What in the hell is going on?!" I screamed. After 5 minutes of ranting, I stormed off. Today, Valerie and I use this story at workshops and seminars on coping to health care professionals and families. We refer to this as the "Pants Story," and the lesson we convey is that never again did I forget my pants. I'm sure it was hard for Valerie to hear my pleas and not give in, but the lesson we learned is it is a disservice to perform a task for an individual without his or her attempting the feat first.

As time progressed, I entered graduate school and due to the insight of my counselor, who suggested that only two courses be taken to start out, I succeeded. As I wheeled across the street on a campus of 45,000 students, my name was yelled out and I stopped. A fellow approached and asked, "Didn't you play basketball for Brother Rice in Chicago?" "Yeah," I said, and as we continued our discussion, I recognized him as a wide receiver for a rival high school in Chicago. He went on to tell me he was pursuing his Ph.D. in therapeutic recreation/administration. He then asked if I would be interested in going out for the track team. The bewilderment on my face led him to explain therapeutic recreation and how the University of Illinois had wheelchair track, basketball, football, and a variety of other sports for those who are physically challenged. Practices were to start in 2 weeks. At my first practice, I was amazed to see the number of participants and their varying levels of function. I started to bring my daughter to practices and all of us seemed to enjoy ourselves. At various meets, my family would join me when ribbons were awarded and have their pictures taken—each of us was proud. The practices and the meets turned into family outings. Valerie coordinated things well by loading the car with the kids, a wheelchair, and me. I could sense my becoming less competitive with the girls.

As they became older, they became interested in playing sports. As a former coach, I had to use restraint as I cheered on from the sidelines at their t-ball games. One parent asked me if I would assist him in coaching the girls' basketball team which both our daughters were on. Reluctantly, I agreed, but again my daughters were proud of their dad sitting on the courtside bench. We truly began to communicate better and spoke about events that occurred in the practices or games.

I followed both girls as they progressed through the years. When they were younger, they didn't know that fathers on wheelchairs weren't cool. As they grew older, their parents knew less than they did, but I could tell that had nothing to do with my being in a wheelchair—just a normal reaction to parents. One time, as I pulled into a mall, Kerry asked, "Why do you park in wheelchair parking?" "Why not?" I replied. "You compete in 10K races and can wheel better than some of these older people can walk," she said. I thought for a few minutes and felt somewhat flattered and responded, "Yeah, I suppose you're right." "It sounds like a special favor you're taking advantage of," she said. "I'll remember that in the future" was my response.

It was August when both girls asked if I would drive them and their friends to an amusement park. Our group had about eight people waiting in a long line to ride the attraction. As we sweltered in 90° temperature, a woman who took tickets came up to me and asked, "Are you familiar with our wheelchair policy?" I said no, and she explained that any wheelchair patrons and their guests do not have to wait in line. They may go to the front and stay on the ride for a second time if they chose. I looked at my oldest daughter and said, "I don't know. It kind of sounds like a special favor to me. What do you think?" "Oh no, dad. This is okay this time." Later in the month, my wife offered to take the girls to the same amusement park to which they quickly responded, "Can Dad come?"

In my relationships with my spouse and daughters, I live by showing them that we all have choices—sometimes because of our behavior we must accept the consequences. We all have special qualities and are unique. When we speak to others, communication is stressed as very important. Times are difficult for a lot of people, and the key to my living is accepting and liking myself and taking it one day at a time.

During graduate school, I went to see the psychologist who worked at the rehabilitation center to inquire about what personal changes might I expect. His response stayed with me and makes a lot of sense: "If you were an S.O.B. before using a wheelchair, the chances are, post-trauma, you will be an S.O.B. in a wheelchair." The point is we usually don't plan bad things to happen to us: trauma, divorce, death, and so forth, but we still have the opportunity to change. Some are given a second chance, but that alone does not mean success. We are all individuals who need to work on our relationships within families as well as outside families. If we take one day at a time and keep a positive attitude, good things can result. In dealing with others, I clarify that my point is not to downplay or minimize trauma and its consequences. However, when one feels good about himself or herself, regardless of the circumstances, he or she can share routine feelings with others. Each of us has a choice—choice can never be taken away.

Allied health providers and all members in society must recognize each individual as unique and possessing skills others don't have. No two people are alike—uniqueness in abilities is our gift to one another.

Discussion Questions

1. What is lost/gained when a young athlete is faced with changes subsequent to a disability? Are there any inherent or positive traits an athlete may possess to aid the process of rehabilitation?
2. How can long-term goals be a source of stress for a person whose life is altered by a brain injury? How does this compare with the immediate stress related to hygiene, dressing, eating, and so forth?
3. Is a single person with a brain injury better off than a married person with young children?
4. Was the response of the neurosurgeon helpful to David's wife?
5. How would you respond if your spouse did not remember who you were and whether or not you had children?
6. How can exposure to role models be a positive or stressful experience (e.g., having David meet with an active person who has mastered a disability)?
7. How can the need or intimacy become a major priority for a person returning home from the hospital? How did Valerie facilitate the adjustment? What if the roles were reversed and Valerie had the injury? What issues could emerge?

8. How could re-entry into the family have been facilitated by creative discharge planning?
9. How would your spouse respond if he or she had to choose between your needs and those of a child?
10. Why were sports a critical element in David's adjustment to his family?
11. What does David mean when he states, "Each of us has a choice?"

PERSONAL PERSPECTIVE: EXPERIENCING SEXUALITY AS AN ADOLESCENT WITH RHEUMATOID ARTHRITIS

Robert J. Neumann

It was a walk I'd taken many times before, down to the train station of our town in suburban Chicago to watch the sleek yellow Milwaukee Road streamliners pass through. Usually it was nothing for the healthy 12-year-old kid that I was. Just seven or eight shady, tree-lined blocks—but today it felt like miles. With every step my right knee was aching more, feeling more stiff.

My friend Terry was walking along with me. I gritted my teeth against the rising pain and struggled to maintain a steady gait. I didn't want Terry to know. I sensed that this was no ordinary ache, and I feared he would not understand. I was right on both counts.

Finally, I could stand it no longer. "You know, Terry, my right knee's feeling awfully stiff and sore," I said.

Without missing a beat, my horror-film-aficionado friend shot back, "Must be *rigor mortis*!"

Happily, *rigor mortis* it wasn't, just rheumatoid arthritis. Yet it would be 5 painful months before I and my family had even the small comfort of that diagnosis. But, in a way, Terry was right: It was the demise of the lifestyle I had known for my entire previous 12 years.

By my 12th birthday, I was just beginning to feel that things were going really well. I enjoyed getting out of the house by taking long rides on my bicycle; the guys were actually beginning to seek me out to play baseball with them; and I was positively ecstatic when my parents allowed me to take my first long-distance train trip all alone to visit an aunt in Pittsburgh.

The arthritis changed all that. Literally within days my right knee became so stiff, swollen, and sore that it was all I could do to hobble from bedroom to bathroom to kitchen. I began seeing a bewildering succession of doctors who could not even arrive at a diagnosis, much less an effective treatment. They hypothesized tuberculosis or cancer of the bone. Their treatments were progressively more drastic-aspiration of the knee, a leg brace, exploratory surgery. None accomplished much more than aggravating the condition physically, and sending me emotionally even deeper into fear and depression. This was the late 1950s, and apparently in those days even the medical profession was less aware that rheumatoid arthritis can and does affect people of all ages, young as well as old.

From "Family interventions throughout chronic illness and disability," by P. W. Power, A. E. Dell Oreto, and M. Blechar-Gibbons, 1988. NY: Springer. Reprinted with permission.

Early in 1960, I went to the Mayo Clinic, where my arthritis was diagnosed at last, and where more appropriate treatment was prescribed. Nonetheless, even this was not able to halt the progression of the disease to my other joints. First it was my other knee, then my ankles, then my fingers, then my elbows, then my neck, then my hips, then.... With a sort of gallows humor, I'd say I had joined the Joint-of-the-Month Club. But behind this facade, I was terrified at how my body was progressively deteriorating before my eyes. Actually, I would avoid seeing it—or letting others see me—as much as possible. I would refuse all invitations to go to the beach or park for fear I would have to wear shorts that would expose my spindly, scarred legs. I would wear hot, long-sleeved shirts on even the most blistering summer days to avoid anyone's seeing my puny arms.

One day, almost by chance, I could avoid it no longer. I caught a good look at myself in a full-length mirror and was appalled at what I saw. I had remembered myself as having an able body. The person I saw looking back at me had a face swollen from high doses of cortisone, hands with unnaturally bent fingers, and legs that could barely support his weight.

I felt devastated. But as I look back on it now, I believe that experience of seeing myself as I really was, was the first step in becoming comfortable with the person I am. Of course, what I did not realize then was that I was a victim, not just of a disease, but of that even more insidious social phenomenon that Beatrice Wright (1983) has identified as the idolization of the normal physique. As a society, we celebrate the body beautiful, the body whole. As Dion, Berscheid, and Walster's (1972) research has demonstrated, we believe that what is beautiful in conventional terms is good, and we equate physical attractiveness with greater intelligence, financial success, and romantic opportunities. Media images of all types reinforce the notion that being young, active, and attractive is the ticket to the good life. Lose that attractiveness, lose that physical perfection, the images imply, and gone as well are the chances for success in love and life. This is definitely not the type of foundation on which an adolescent's fragile self-concept is likely to develop a solid, confident base.

But, painful as it was, looking at myself in the mirror and seeing myself as I really was, was the prerequisite for self-acceptance. It was acknowledging the physical facts, if not liking them. It was not until years later when I was in graduate school that I attended a seminar given by a marvelous person named Jesse Potter, and came to understand our culture's body-beautiful emphasis is only one way—one narrow, constricting way—of viewing reality. She helped me redefine my experience and understand that a person's attractiveness, a person's value, depends on who one is, not on how one appears. Simple as it sounds, for me that was a revelation and a liberation, to realize that in the words of the Velveteen

Rabbit (Williams, 1975), "once you are real, you can't be ugly—except to those who don't understand."

If my rheumatoid arthritis was a trauma for me, its effects also extended to stress other members of the family. My mother was a quiet source of support, and preferred to keep her feelings about the disease to herself. Often she would cry alone in her room; she told me this only years later. But nowhere were the effects of the disease more evident than on my father. A traveling salesman with stubborn ways and volatile temperament, my father would frequently return from business trips edgy, angry, and generally out of sorts. This in turn caused me to dread these homecomings, because as an adolescent I had no way of predicting what mood he might be in or what might set him off. It was only after I had moved from home and was employed as a hospital-based psychologist that he felt free enough to tell me how he could do nothing but think of me at home while he was spending those long hours driving the expressways and lonely country roads, worried by how sick I was and frustrated by his own powerlessness to do anything about it. If only he had been able to express those feelings openly and directly 20 years earlier.

One subject my father was able to express himself directly on was the topic of education and my future. He put it in his customary unvarnished manner: "Bob, you don't have much of a body. But you got a good mind. If you're going to succeed, you've got to use it." And, as I was growing up, there never was any question I would succeed. It was simply assumed I would do well in school, go on to college, and get well-paid employment. Clearly I internalized these expectations for academic success even more than my father intended. But there is no doubt his high expectations functioned as a self-fulfilling prophecy. In large measure, I owe the Ph.D. behind my name, the jobs I have had, and many of the wonderful people I have met to my father's simple belief that I could and would. And today, when I work with clients, it is a particular frustration to see how many parents needlessly limit their disabled children's life possibilities through well-intentioned but misguided protectionism or realism that lowers expectations for success by focusing on all the problems rather than on the potentials.

During my high school days, my social life was virtually nonexistent. Because I received physical therapy at home in the afternoon and because my stamina was poor in any event, I only attended school until about 1 p.m. This eliminated any possibility of interacting with peers in extracurricular activities. To complicate the situation further, because my life revolved around classes and studying, I routinely received unusually good grades and routinely broke the class curve-much to the animosity of those peers I did interact with. But perhaps most significantly, the school I attended was a Catholic, all-boy high school. This removed me from any contact whatsoever with the female part of the population at a time when my interest was anything but dormant. I literally had only one date, with the daughter of family friends, during my entire 4 years of high school. This situation bothered me enough that I eventually discussed it with my biology teacher. A layman, he suggested that things would be better when I got to college, a response that was only partially more reassuring and accurate than that of the priests who counseled cold showers when issues like these arose.

These less than satisfying experiences have led me to be a strong advocate of mainstreaming. From one perspective I was fortunate to have experienced a limited form of mainstreaming in an era before the advent of Public Law 94-142. At least the interactions I had with male peers gave me a basic idea of how able-bodied adolescent males view the world. Unfortunately, neither the school authorities nor my parents understood how important it was to ensure that deficits in social skills would not develop through lack of informal, out-of-classroom socialization with male peers and the total lack of contact with any female ones. Meanwhile, I unsuspectingly continued to study and dream of the day I would start college and the active love life I had fantasized about for so long.

Finally, the big day arrived. Armed with a body of knowledge about women derived solely from TV, James Bond movies, and the Playboy magazines my younger brother smuggled in, I arrived at a small Midwestern college never dreaming I was, in reality, as green as the lovely pines that graced the campus.

It took only a short while before I noticed my actual accomplishments with women were falling far short, not only of my expectations, but also of the experiences of my friends and acquaintances. Within a few months most of the people I knew—both men and women—had developed ongoing intimate relationships. Everywhere the couples were obvious: sitting together in classes, dining together in the cafeteria, partying together at dances, studying together, walking together, sleeping together. I, on the other hand, became frustratingly adept at performing all these activities alone.

Actually, I was quite good at developing nonsexual friendships with women, especially those who had other boyfriends. I could relate well to them because there was no need for me to do the mating dance, no need for me to call on sociosexual skills I had never learned. These friendships were a mixed blessing. They provided emotional support and the beginning of much-needed learning about the opposite sex. But inevitably there were many poignant moments when my friend would go off to her lover, and I would go off alone. As unpracticed as I was in picking up social cues, I continually confused friendship and romantic messages when meeting apparently available new women. A poem I wrote at that time unintentionally reflected the confusion:

LOST
I like you
when we joked and laughed 'bout people that we knew. I wanted
    you
when you softly said
that you must have love too. I love you
then you took his hand, and oh, I knew, I knew.

It was a depressing pattern. A woman would express an incipient interest; I would misread the cues and respond inappropriately, then feel crushed when the relationship died. Rejection and depression became themes that were only too familiar. I became convinced I was unlovable.

Finally, my roommate Michael decided to do something about the situation. A self-styled ladies' man with the body and bravado of a Greek god, Michael appointed himself my teacher. My first assignment was to read a book he provided me with called Scoremanship. Once I had finished the book, Michael proclaimed me ready for field experience. It was late on Friday afternoon, and Michael and I were having an early supper in the cafeteria.

"Bob," he nudged me. "Isn't that that Jane over there you've been wanting to go out with?"

"Yeah," I responded dubiously, looking at a woman several tables from us. "Well, remember the book. Just go up and ask her to go to a movie tonight." "Tonight?" I nearly choked. "But it's too late. She's probably got ten dozen things to do."

"Self-defeating talk is unknown to the Scoreman," Michael smiled serenely. "Just go and do it!"

Michael would not let me back out, so I figured I had no alternative but go forward and experience my next rejection. Slowly I walked over to her table. "Oh, hi, Jane!" I said, as if I'd just noticed her. "You know, uh, seeing you here reminds me. I was thinking of going to a movie tonight. Would you like to come?" Listening to myself, I was sure she'd never buy this one. "Why I'd love to!" she enthused. "Pick me up at my dorm in a half hour!"

I could hardly believe it. I rushed back to our table. "My God! She actually said yes. She actually said yes! What do I do now?"

Michael gazed at me with a smile of patient superiority. "You take her to the movie. Then you bring her back to our room. I'll fix everything up. Don't you worry about a thing."

The date itself was fine. The movie was enjoyable, the conversation relaxed and friendly. She even agreed to come back to the room for a drink.

I put the key in the door. As I opened it, I discovered just how much fixing Michael had done. Out billowed clouds of incense. Inside the room, candles everywhere cast their flickering light on Playboy magazines that had been artfully strewn about and opened to the most suggestive pages. Clothes and books were piled high on all the furniture except my bed. (So she would have to sit right beside me, Michael later explained.) But the crowning touch came when I noticed that on the night table beside my bed, Michael had arranged a little altar, complete with candles, a small Playboy calendar, and an opened package of condoms. I could have died.

Needless to say, seeing all this, Jane instantly developed a headache that required her immediate return to her dorm. After she had set out for her dorm, and though Michael had been trying to be a friend, I was embarrassed and set out to find him and relate my feelings.

Obviously, my role models were not always the most appropriate. And being the only disabled person on that small campus meant I did not have the benefit of interacting with and learning from other disabled peers. Nonetheless, I was learning, observing which things I did worked and which did not. Over time, even I could see that I was gradually improving my relationships.

My senior year eventually arrived, and I celebrated my 21st birthday—still without ever having experienced a physical relationship. Chronologically, I had come of age, but emotionally I still felt insecure, lacking the physical experience that symbolized manhood. I assumed my disability was largely to blame, since by then I knew I could develop non-sexual friendships with ease. Increasingly I came to view my virginity as a barrier in need of being surmounted. But this was not just a matter of desire, a stirring of hormones. To me it was also a matter of self-worth and self-esteem. For as long as I was valued by others only for my companionship and intelligence, I still was not being related to as a whole person, a person with sexual dimensions as well as emotional, intellectual, and spiritual ones—and I feared for whether I ever would be a whole person.

As it happened, that doubt was soon to be laid to rest in a manner I could never have foreseen. It was a Saturday night and my friend Justin and I had just finished viewing an on-campus theatrical production by the Garrick Players when we encountered Sarah in the foyer. Justin had been friends with her for some time, but I knew her only peripherally from having shared a class or two and an occasional meal in the cafeteria. Generally, Sarah traveled in a different circle than mine. But tonight she was alone, so after some discussion we three agreed it would be fun to drive to town to get a drink.

We stopped at the Nite-N-Gale, a popular campus hangout, and had a couple of glasses of wine. But mostly we just talked. The conversation was good: comfortable and convivial, a pleasant mix of the light-hearted and the more serious. After a while, we headed back to Sarah's room on campus and continued in the same vein. Midnight arrived, and Justin declared himself tired and left for his room, leaving Sarah and me alone.

The conversation turned more serious. She asked me what it was like to live with arthritis. I told her about the Joint-of-the-Month Club and looking in the mirror. She in turn shared some of the hurts she felt in growing up in poverty with parents in ill health. Finally, I noticed it was approaching 2 a.m. "Well, I guess it's time to go," I said.

"You don't sound too wild about it, Bob."

I was surprised she had picked up on a reluctance I thought I was not showing. "Yeah, you're right," I sighed. "It's just that when I get back to the room I'll find Michael there with his girlfriend. It's damn depressing. Hell, I met her before he did! I liked her too!"

For a long second, Sarah just stared at me. Then a smile, warm and tender like I had never before seen, began to cross her face. "Bob, you know you don't have to," she said.

I will never forget Sarah, perhaps more than most people will never forget their first. What we shared was physical, but also far more. With her, I did not have to worry about how to handle the issue of my disability because to my astonishment, she did not view my disability as an issue: The mere fact that our relationship was physical confirmed as nothing else could that this, too, was possible. The effect on my self-esteem was tremendous. As a disabled colleague once remarked, "When most of your problems have been on a physical level, it's on the physical level that you're most strongly reassured." That statement has always stayed with me, even though I would amend the thought somewhat. Self-esteem is most enhanced when one's positive expectations converge with the reality of one's experience. Lack one or the other, and the individual suffers. At any rate, I still recall how brilliantly the sun was shining the next day as Sarah and I walked across the campus.

REFERENCES

Dion, K., Berscheid, E., & Walster, E. (1972). What is beautiful is good. *Journal of Personality and Social Psychology, 24,* 285–290.

Williams, M. (1975). The velveteen rabbit. New York: Avon.

Wright, B. (1983). Physical disability: A psychosocial approach (2nd ed). New York: Harper & Row.

Discussion Questions

1. What was your reaction to the statement by Neumann: "Self-esteem is most enhanced when one's positive expectations converge with the reality of one's experiences"?
2. Who should be responsible for sex education programs for adolescents coping with disabilities?
3. What role has society played in the formulation of attitudes toward the sexuality of persons with disabilities?
4. Would there be a significant difference in the critical issues with a young woman who has had an experience similar to that of Neumann as related in his personal perspective?
5. How is an adolescent's search for self-identity complicated by a serious, chronic disability?
6. What is the role of the health professional in working with parents concerned about the sexuality of their children?

Index